Magazine Markets for Children's Writers

Writer's Institute Publications

Acknowledgments

The editors of this directory appreciate the generous contributions of our instructors and students, and the cooperation of the magazine editors who made clear their policies and practices.

Marni McNiff, Editor

Susan Tierney, Articles Editor

Barbara Cole, Associate Editor

Sherri Keefe, Assistant Editor

Connor Lofink, Research Assistant

Amanda Norelli, Research Assistant

Contributing Writers: Susan Anderson, Kristen Bishop, Jennifer Ponte Canning, Susan Tarrant

Cover Design: Joanna Horvath
Cover illustrations supplied by Getty Images

International Standard Book Number 978-1-889715-50-6

1-800-443-6078. www.writersbookstore.com
email: services@writersbookstore.com

Contents

Step-by-Step through the Submissions Process

This section offers tips and step-by-step instructions for researching the market; writing query letters; preparing manuscript packages and bibliographies; initiating follow-up; and understanding copyrights, permissions, and other common publishing terms.

Gateway to the Markets

Contents (cont.)

Step-by-Step through the Submissions Process

Selling Your Big Idea

Do you have a big idea? The editors of every one of the 20,000 magazines in North America are in search of big ideas on a daily basis—and yours could be one of them. The right idea can be your entrée into magazine publishing, but only if you know how to sell it.

Contrary to what you might think, your first job as a freelance writer is to sell your idea, not your article. (In fact, most professional writers don't write the article until they've already sold their idea.) Whether you've written the article already, or if you've just done the necessary research to be sure you can deliver on your idea, the first step on the road to publication is marketing.

Marketing Smart

Just as market research is an essential part of any successful business, it plays an equally significant role in selling your writing. Even if you've come up with an article idea that takes a fresh perspective on a particular subject, your idea won't sell unless you market it correctly. Magazine editors are always looking for the perfect match between a writer's idea and their magazine; if you can make that connection, your chances for making a sale will dramatically increase.

But making the perfect match often involves more than just finding a magazine that publishes articles like yours. It also means making smart submissions that are well researched and maximize your sales potential.

For example, you may know a young volunteer in your community who would make a great subject for a profile article. Without doing any market research you might conclude that *American Girl* is a good fit, based on your familiarity with the magazine and its articles. It probably is a good fit for this idea, but take a close look at the listing: 4% of the magazine is written by nonstaff writers, and it publishes only 5 freelance submissions yearly, 2% of which are written by unpublished writers.

Further research might reveal other, more promising markets, particularly for unpublished writers. *Girls' Life*, written for a similar age group, has a continuously running department that features profiles of real girls. It is 25% written by nonstaff writers, and publishes 40 freelance submissions yearly, 10% of which are by unpublished writers. And depending on the slant and subject of your article, deeper research may yield some additional, unexpected potential markets. *Hopscotch*, a magazine designed to be both "entertaining and educational," is aimed at 5- to 14-year-old girls. *Hopscotch* is 80% written by nonstaff writers, and publishes 100–120 freelance submissions yearly. Check its upcoming themes and read a few recent issues. If your idea fits with this magazine's style and editorial mission, then you may have found your perfect match at last.

With this directory in hand, you already have one of the best tools available to help market your work. The rest of your marketing strategy depends on crafting the right idea to begin with, starting with its very foundation: the topic.

Choosing a Topic

Whether your topic is fiction or nonfiction, you'll increase your publication odds if you know what topics interest children. For example, an article about the basic principles of electricity would be more interesting for kids if presented through the eyes of the famous magician, Jean Eugéne Robert-Houdin. This approach also connects the past to the present, a learning concept that appeals to classroom magazine editors. When you're thinking about ideas, consider how a young person views the world. What is their typical day like? What kinds of things are they interested in? Questions like these can produce a number of interesting subject leads.

Another way to find an appropriate subject is to review current publications. Start by surveying the categories of magazines in *Magazine Markets for Children's Writers*. The category index on pages 325–368 is an excellent guide to finding magazines that publish the types of articles or stories you write on the subjects that interest you. You'll find everything from general interest publications, like *Boys' Quest* or *Highlights for Children*, to special interest periodicals on topics such as sports, careers, crafts, current events, parenting, geography, health and fitness, and more.

> **To build your credibility, consider specializing in a particular subject area. Think about what subjects you have specialized knowledge or interest in, and develop a portfolio of articles within that field.**

Continue your research online or at libraries. What magazines are out there, for what ages, and what subjects do they cover? Along with magazines targeted specifically to children, be sure to check parenting, educational, and regional magazines.

You'll find that each magazine covers numerous subjects from month to month or year to year, even special interest publications that cover a niche more deeply than widely. Read several issues of each magazine to find out which subjects a potential target magazine has covered recently and how it has approached particular subjects in the past. Begin to make a list of the magazines that cover subjects of interest to you.

Targeting Your Readers

Subject and audience often go hand in hand, though many subjects can be geared toward a variety of audiences, with the right treatment. Select a subject slant that is age-appropriate for your intended audience and your potential market. For example, if you'd like to take on the subject of architecture you might write a story on the basics of building design for younger readers, or cover the more complex slant of conservationist/green design for high-school readers. Both articles vary in the amount and complexity of information offered, and in tone. Determine each magazine's target age and how the publication speaks to that age, through voice and purpose.

To learn more about the developmental level of your intended age range, go to the Internet and other media, as well as to schools and children's activities. For example, at the Google Directory (www.google.com/dirhp) click on Kids and Teens. Look at the topics under preschool, school time, teen life, and other categories. The arts section in particular has many interesting sites that relate to every age group.

Understanding the Magazine

Once you have a good handle on your subject and your audience, start doing in-depth research for those magazines you intend to target. Create a magazine market file for publications that seem to match your interests. Use index cards, a notebook, or your computer to develop a file for each magazine for your initial list of publications.

Sample Guidelines Request

Name
Address
City, State ZIP

Date

Dear (Name of Current Editor):

I would like to request a copy of your writers' guidelines and editorial calendar. I have provided a self-addressed, stamped envelope for your convenience.

Sincerely,

Your name

Review the Writers' Guidelines

If the listing for a particular magazine indicates that it offers writers' guidelines, either send a letter to the publication along with an SASE (see the sample on page 7) to request the guidelines, or check the magazine's website. (The listing will specify where to look for this information.) Writers' guidelines, editorial calendars, and theme lists may give you specific topics to write about, or they may be more general.

Either way, follow the guidelines carefully, or your submission could be rejected by the editor. Guidelines are key to the needs of publications and often new writers give them too little weight.

Some guidelines are more detailed and helpful than others, but virtually all will tell you something about the readership, philosophy, and voice, as well as word length requirements, submission format, and payment. More than that, some guidelines give writers specific insight into the immediate needs of a magazine. For example, *Adoptive Families* magazine has thorough guidelines that include a listing of its departments, instructions on how to submit your work, subject areas editors are looking to cover, and suggestions for writers, such as "have a clear sense of your central theme," and "focus on choices made and strategies used to deal with a particular situation." *Pack-O-Fun*'s guidelines offer a detailed list of the kinds of crafts its editors are looking for year-round.

Depending on their level of detail, some guidelines may also indicate the rights a publication purchases, payment policies, and many more specifics—factors you'll consider as you get closer to submission. Many experienced writers do not sell all rights, unless the fee is high enough to be worth it; reselling articles or stories for reprint rights can be an

---

Magazine Description Form

Name of Magazine: *The Science Teacher*   **Editor:** Meghan Sullivan
Address: 1840 Wilson Blvd., Arlington, VA 22010-3000

Freelance Percentage: 100%

**Percentage of Authors Who
Are New to the Magazine:** 50%

**Description
What subjects does this magazine cover?** Science education, biology, Earth science, computers, social issues, space, technology, and sports medicine

**Readership
Who are the magazine's typical readers?** Science educators of grades 7–12

**Articles and Stories
What particular slants or distinctive characteristics do its articles or stories emphasize?** New and creative ideas for the secondary science classroom that provide practical help for teachers. Classroom activities, teaching techniques, and scientific research are all areas of interest.

**Potential Market
Is this magazine a potential market?** Yes. My article fits with an upcoming theme, and *Science Teacher* welcomes freelance writers and new writers.

**Ideas for Articles or Stories
What article, story, or department idea could be submitted?** My article focuses on the use of Earthcaching in the classroom. In addition to teaching students how to use a GPS receiver, Earthcaching requires them to take that knowledge outside the classroom to visit a local Earthcache site, which could include anything from fossil sites and canyons to caves and hot springs.

additional source of income. (See the discussion of rights on page 27.)

Review Sample Issues

Get sample issues of the magazines and read them, either by requesting them from the publisher; finding copies at the library, the bookstore, or through friends; or by reviewing articles on the magazine's website. The listings in *Magazine Markets for Children's Writers* will tell you if writers' guidelines, an editorial calendar, or a theme list are available, as well as the cost of a sample copy requested directly from the publisher.

Review each of the magazines in more detail for subjects similar to yours. You should also check the *Readers' Guide to Periodical Literature* in your library to see if a target magazine has covered your topic within the past two years. If so, you may want to find another magazine or, depending on the publication, develop a new slant if you find that your subject is already well covered.

Use the Magazine Description Form (see page 8) to continue your detailed analysis of the publications, especially those you're beginning to hone in on as good matches. Evaluate how you could shape or present your manuscript to improve your chances of getting it published. If you're new to a particular magazine, a good way to get your foot in the door may be to pitch a short article for the front pages or a particular department, rather than a full-length feature article. If a particular idea or target magazine doesn't work out now, it may in the future—or it may lead to other ideas, angles, or possible markets. Review your market files periodically to generate ideas.

Your review of sample magazines and guidelines should include:

- **Editorial objective.** In some cases, the magazine's editorial objective is stated inside the publication, on the same page as the masthead, where the names of the editors are listed; it is also usually stated on the website. For example, the editorial objective of *Highlights for Children* is summarized in its simple subhead, "Fun with a Purpose." Does your story or article fit your targeted magazine's purpose?

New Angles, New Audiences

A substantial amount of research goes into writing magazine articles, and it's to your advantage to make the most of this time. In many cases, the research for one article can be used for other articles, as long as they reach different audiences and have fresh angles. To find additional sales opportunities, consider other markets that might be interested in the information—religious publications, arts and crafts magazines, science magazines, etc. Then investigate angles that would be of most interest to them. Make a list of the possibilities, like the ideas below, and keep it handy for future reference.

Subject: Shadow Drawings

Magazine	Audience	Slant
Pack-O-Fun	6- to 12-year-olds	How to make shadow drawings
Chicago Parent	Parents	"Short Stuff" column about a local teacher who used shadow drawings as part of a summer enrichment program; include directions on how to make the drawings
Science and Children	Science teachers	How to teach concepts of light and shadow through the classroom activity of making shadow drawings

- **Audience.** What is the age range of the readers and the characters? For fiction, is your main character at the upper end of that range? Kids want to read about characters their own age or older. For nonfiction, take a look at the advertisements, which have been expertly tailored to the target audience. They can offer valuable clues about the magazine's readers and their interests.

- **Article and story types.** Examine the types of articles in the issue, paying special attention to article construction. Are the articles informal, or are they filled with facts and statistics? Are they interactive? Do they use anecdotes or personal experience stories to illustrate a point? Has your topic already been covered by this magazine recently? For fiction, what genres does it cover? What is the average story or article length?

- **Layout and formatting.** Examine the overall look of an article. Are sidebars, subheads, and/or other elements included? Is the magazine highly visual or does it rely primarily on text? Will photographs or illustrations be a consideration for you? Will your article work using the magazine's preferred format?

- **Style.** Become familiar with the magazine's editorial style, and how it is impacted by the age of the audience. Does it strive for a conversational, energetic style, or a straightforward, educational one? Are the sentences simple or complex, or a mixture of both? Are there numerous three-syllable words, or mostly simple words? Do the writers speak directly to the readers or is the voice appropriately authoritative?

- **Editor's comments.** Very often the writers' guidelines include insight from the editor about the feel of a magazine. For example, *Instructor* magazine's guidelines state, "Write in your natural voice, as if you were talking to a colleague. We shy away from wordy, academic prose." *Breakaway* magazine's guidelines describe it as "fast-paced," "compelling," and "out of the ordinary."

Magazine Markets for Children's Writers includes a section called Editor's Comments in each listing. Study this section carefully for similar remarks about what editors want to see, or don't need.

> When you're ready to query, use the information from your sample issue review to show the editor that you're familiar with the publication. Pitch your article to a specific section of the magazine, or mention a recent article in your query.

Refine Your Magazine List

After you analyze your selected magazines, rank them by how well they match your idea, subject, style, and target age. Then return to the listings to examine other factors, such as the magazine's freelance potential, its receptivity to new or unpublished writers, rights purchased, and payment.

Not only should your decision to submit be based on how well your idea matches a particular publication, you should also consider which publications match you as a writer. An examination of magazine business policies—not just current editorial needs—can reveal significant details about the magazine that you can use to your advantage as a freelance writer. For example, many published writers prefer magazines that:

- respond in one month as opposed to three or more;
- pay on acceptance rather than on publication;
- do not purchase all rights (see the rights discussion on p. 27);
- publish a high percentage of authors who are new to the magazine.

If you're not yet published, however, writing for a nonpaying market or taking risks in other areas (such as signing a work-for-hire contract or agreeing to payment on publication rather than on acceptance) may be worth the effort to earn the clips needed for future submissions. Once you've acquired credentials in these markets, you can list these published pieces in your queries to other markets.

Submitting Your Work to an Editor

Submission policies vary across the board; some magazines accept queries only, others accept complete manuscripts or queries, while others want queries accompanied by writing samples, a synopsis, an outline, or other information. A query may be sufficient for some editors; others prefer to get a more complete sense of you and your work before making a determination. To know for sure what to send, check the writers' guidelines for the publication you're interested in. Expect that the editor who accepts a complete, unsolicited manuscript may require even more revisions or rewrites than if you had queried first.

The Right Stuff

So you've looked it up, and the guidelines of your target magazine say to "query with outline, bibliography, and clips or writing samples." In this case, you should send the following:

- One-page query letter
- Brief outline of article topics
- Bibliography of research sources
- Selected clips (published writing) or writing samples (unpublished writing, such as blog entries, Web content, letters to editors, etc.)
- SASE

For nonfiction submissions, it's always a good idea to include a bibliography of your research sources, whether you're sending a query letter or a complete manuscript. A well-rounded bibliography with a variety of sources demonstrates a professional approach. For complete manuscript submissions of both fiction and nonfiction, include a cover letter that briefly introduces the work (see p. 19). And unless you're submitting via email (see below), an SASE is a necessary part of any submission package.

Email Submissions

Email is an efficient means of communication in business today, but publications still vary widely in their policies regarding email submissions: Some publishers prefer to receive submissions via email, others accept both print and email submissions, and still others avoid email submissions altogether. The only way to know for sure is to check each publisher's guidelines.

Before you submit via email, be sure that your electronic query is as carefully crafted as a print one. Email queries by nature are slightly less formal, but not sloppy, and the content of your query should be as informative and engaging as a traditional one. Beware, however, the conversational, too-familiar tone of many emails, which is inappropriate for queries and submissions. Your query is your first contact with an editor, so write in a professional manner. Pay close attention to grammar and punctuation and avoid using cutesy email addresses and emoticons. And remember—email does not always mean faster response times, so be patient with the editor and respect his or her time.

Before you hit the send button, check that you've complied with any guidelines specific to email submissions, such as:

- *File formats:* Should the submission be included in the body of the email or as an attachment? Should files be sent in Microsoft Word or Rich text format?
- *Subject line:* Should your subject line say "Query" or "Submission," and include your name or the title of the work?
- *Contact information:* Your name, address, email address, and telephone number should be included below your "signature."

Crafting a Query Letter

The query letter is a writer's most important marketing tool: In the same way the back cover blurb of a book draws in potential readers, your query must intrigue an editor enough to make him or her want to see your work. While writing a query can be challenging, it's an art worth practicing—good query letters are few and far between, and a standout will make an editor take notice.

There are several advantages to using a query letter. First, it is the preferred submission method of many publications. Editors are deluged with pitches, and queries offer a quick, easy way to identify those with potential. Also, many query letters are written before the manuscript. Whether or not this is the case, phrase your letter as if the article is in the planning stage. Editors prefer pieces written specifically for their publication; early involvement also allows them to mold the piece to their specifications. Some writers even find that crafting a query pitch helps keep them focused while writing.

Essential Elements of a Query

Editors always appreciate a well-written query that catches their interest and gets to the point quickly. The following elements are part of every good query letter, though some elements may be emphasized more than others.

Article/story summary. The purpose of a query is to pique the interest of an editor, not to provide a detailed outline of your nonfiction article or in-depth coverage of your story's plot. More important at this stage is getting across the basic idea of your piece—what it is about and who are the key players—in a lively, professional manner. Start your letter with a lead-in that hooks the editor, and state your article or story's unique point of view upfront. Remember to include the approximate word count of the article, as well as any sidebars or other elements, in your letter.

Your qualifications. Pitching yourself—not just your article—is another key component. List your publishing credits if you have them; if not, don't mention it at all. Even if you haven't been published, you may have experience in some other area that proves relevant to the topic you're writing about. For example, if you're pitching an article to a children's

---

Query Checklist

❑ Direct your query to a specific editor. Verify the spelling of the name and address.

❑ Begin with a lead paragraph that "hooks" the editor and conveys your slant.

❑ Include a brief description of your article that conveys your central idea.

❑ Show how your idea meets the editorial goals of the targeted magazine.

❑ Indicate approximate word length of main article, along with any sidebars.

❑ Provide specific details about the content—compelling anecdotes, case histories, relevant personal experience stories, etc.

❑ Cite sources and planned interviews to show that you have access to sources.

❑ Include a unique, attention-grabbing title.

❑ If applicable, indicate number and type of photographs or illustrations available.

❑ List your publishing credits, or emphasize your relevant or unique experience.

❑ Close by asking if the magazine is interested; mention whether your query is a simultaneous submission.

❑ Include other information if requested, such as an outline, bibliography, or resume.

science magazine on how bees make honey and you once worked as a researcher in this area, you are particularly qualified to write such a piece even if you've never been published before. Note any background or experience you have that gives you credibility in writing this piece for this particular audience.

Knowledge of the market. Know your audience, and know the magazine you're pitching to inside and out. Tailor your idea to work specifically for that publication. Know the word limit the magazine prefers and whether or not it requires a bibliography of sources. Know its tone and style, and mold your article to match. For example, if the magazine only publishes how-to articles and interviews, pitch a unique article in one of those categories. Or, if the magazine often includes information from an expert's perspective, find an expert who's willing to participate in an interview for your article and include his or her name in the letter. Understanding a magazine's "personality" will help you make a convincing argument as to why your article will benefit that publication.

Professional presentation. Some editors stop reading a query altogether after finding a mistake, so take a few extra minutes to make sure your letter is ready to send. Proofread for grammar, spelling, and typos throughout. Double-check the spelling of the publication, the address, and the editor's name. Use a letter-quality printout, with crisp, dark type, single-spaced, and a font close to Times Roman 12-point. Make sure your contact information is included, along with a self-addressed, stamped envelope or postcard for the editor's reply.

Use this list of essentials to determine if your query is getting the point across in the most effective and professional manner possible. A good query letter is short and to the point. If you can't get your idea across in one page or less, your article may not be as tightly focused as it should be. Similarly, if you've sent out the same query many times with no response, it may be that your article or story's basic concept is the problem, not the query.

Article Appeal

If you're pitching a nonfiction article, one of the ideas below might be just what your manuscript needs to get noticed.

- **Photographs.** While most publications don't require photos with a submission, most welcome them. To add visuals to your article, you can either take pictures yourself and send them with your query, or search online for images. Government sources, PR departments, museums, and historical associations are all good places to search. Let the editor know that you've located good-quality, accessible photos and where. A submission with a visual component is more likely to get an editor's attention.

- **Sidebars.** Magazines specialize in serving up small bits of information, and one way to "chunk" your manuscript is through the use of sidebars. The contents of a sidebar may include fast facts, checklists, instructions, definitions, quizzes, quotes, or crafts to support the article. Sidebars offer readers an additional point of entry to the larger article, and serve as a visual element. Sidebar titles, concepts, and word counts should be mentioned in your query as an optional addition to the main article.

- **Unusual formatting.** There are many ways to present facts, and the traditional narrative format is just one of them. Some magazines are very visual, and prefer art-driven pieces, relying heavily on charts, photos, games, captions, etc. Other innovative formats include Q & A's, profiles, interviews, quizzes, lists, and crossword puzzles. Use your imagination to think of alternative formats that might be appropriate for your subject.

Sample Query Letter

Address
Phone Number
Email
Date

Cobblestone Publishing
30 Grove Street, Suite C
Peterborough, NH 03458

Dear Editor,

Imagine yourself being up to bat. Fans are screaming your name, up on their feet cheering and chanting. You're in the zone. You can't hear any of it. You've got your head in the game. You think you're tuned out to the sound because you're focused? Not in this case. You can't hear it because you're deaf.

I am proposing a profile on William "Dummy" Hoy, a major influence in baseball history who doesn't seem to get a lot of attention. This 712-word profile aimed at ages 7-12 provides interesting history on William Hoy's silent but strong influence on major league baseball. This Cincinnati native has affected several aspects of the sport, including the uniforms and why they don't have pockets! I believe this article would fit very well with your focus on history as stated on your website.

I've also included a 55-word sidebar that highlights other deaf professional athletes including Lance Allred of the Cleveland Cavaliers basketball team.

I have been published in *Highlights* and *Stories for Children.com*. I have submitted this article to other publishers as well.

Thank you for your time. I look forward to hearing from you.

Sincerely,

Katherine Ruskey

Sample Query Letter

Address
Phone Number
Email
Date

Ms. Christine French Clark
Highlights for Children
803 Church Street
Honesdale, PA 18431-1895

Dear Ms. Clark:

Consider the drinking straw: a simple, functional, benign object.

But the history of the drinking straw shows us that while it may always have been simple and functional, it has not always been benign. In ancient times, a drinking straw was, well, made from a piece of straw (or reed), and imparted its own flavor to drinks. After a few sips, it became a soggy mess, like the paper straws of the 1900s.

I am an archaeologist who works with teachers, and my colleagues and I recovered many plastic drinking straws from an excavation we carried out on the grounds of an elementary school. Thus, I was spurred to research this most mundane of artifacts: What could we tell the students about drinking straws? My research led me to the Middle East, then to a tavern in our nation's capital, and even to a chemical laboratory in England.

If you think your young readers would be interested in an 800-word nonfiction article about the history of the drinking straw, entitled "Sippin History," I would be pleased to send it to you for your review.

Sincerely,

A. Gwynn Henderson
Archaeologist/Education Coordinator
Kentucky Archaeological Survey

Sample Query Letter

Sample Query

Address
Phone Number
Email
Date

Boy Scouts of America
Paula Murphey, Senior Editor
1325 West Walnut Hill Lane
P.O. Box 152079
Irving, TX 75015-2079

Dear Ms. Murphey,

Divers weave through a forest of marine life after a long day of studying coral and fish. They're heading home. However, they're not heading to the surface. Their home is underwater.

My article entitled, "Getting Their Feet Wet" (793 words), showcases Aquarius, an underwater ocean laboratory that recently took on its 100th mission. Aquarius is not only dedicated to protecting one of Florida's most valuable marine resources, but it will continue to expand our knowledge of coral reefs, our oceans, and our planet. I think young readers will be as fascinated as I was to learn that Aquarius lies 60 feet deep in the ocean, and is the size of a large mobile home; and that aquanauts are underwater for days and must endure 17 hours of decompression to return to the surface.

I consulted with Dr. Ellen Prager, the chief scientist at Aquarius. Dr. Prager can provide high resolution digital photos and there is no fee for photo use.

I've had numerous articles published in *Stories for Children Magazine*, and have forthcoming articles in *AppleSeeds*, *Focus on the Family Clubhouse Jr.*, and the Institute of Children's Literature's Web resource, *Rx for Writers*. I'm also a member of SCBWI.

Thank you for your time and consideration.

Sincerely,

Lori Calabrese

Enc.: Article outline, Bibliography, SASE

Sample Query Letter

Address
Phone Number
Email
Date

Elizabeth Crooker Carpentiere, Editor
FACES
Cobblestone Publishing
30 Grove Street, Suite C
Peterborough, NH 03458

Dear Ms. Carpentiere:

Ever write a story about your family? Draw pictures of someplace special you visited on a family vacation? Taken a picture of a favorite aunt you haven't seen in a while? The native people of Southern Alaska did the same thing hundreds of years ago, but in a very different way. Instead of using paper and markers or snapping a digital photo, they carved images into the wood of ancient red cedar trees.

I am proposing a 650- to 700-word article, tentatively titled "Totem Poles: An Ancient Alaskan Art." I'd like to incorporate a craft activity into the piece for making a mini 3-D totem pole. A photo of the completed project is available upon request. An optional sidebar could include a key to the meanings behind the traditional symbols used by the Inuit people.

I am enclosing a detailed outline of the proposed piece as well as a bibliography.

Previously my short stories and articles have appeared in publications both in print and online.

If you are interested in seeing the finished article, I would be happy to submit it for your consideration. I have enclosed an SASE and I look forward to your reply.

Sincerely,

Ruth Schiffmann

Sample Query Letter

Address
Phone Number
Email
Date

Elizabeth Lindstrom, Editor
Odyssey
Carus Publishing
30 Grove Street, Suite C
Peterborough, NH 03458

Dear Ms. Lindstrom:

In math classrooms, students seem to understand the concepts in class only to turn around and fail a test given the next day. What's the deal? The majority of students don't know how or what to study for math tests because studying for math is totally different than studying for other school subjects.

I've prepared a 966-word article tentatively titled "Passing with Flying Colors: How to Ace a Mathematics Test" that outlines specific tips to help students receive an excellent grade on any math test. The article begins with a brief conversation between study partners to grab attention. Following this, I cite math test-taking tips such as active daily learning, using flash cards, studying over time, and taking a practice test.

As a middle-school math teacher, I witness the common studying mistakes that students make. By using the tips mentioned in the article, teenagers can learn how to prepare and study for a math test and wow their teachers and parents with their grades.

If you are interested in seeing the finished article, I would be happy to submit it for your consideration. I have enclosed a self-addressed, stamped envelope and I look forward to your reply.

Best regards,

Janae Rosendale

Enc.: SASE

Preparing a Manuscript Package

The following guide shows how to prepare and mail a professional-looking manuscript package. However, you should always adhere to an individual magazine's submission requirements as detailed in its writers' guidelines and its listing in this directory.

Cover Letter Tips

Always keep your cover letter concise and to the point. Provide essential information only.

If the letter accompanies an unsolicited manuscript submission (see below), indicate that your manuscript is enclosed and mention its title and word length. If you're sending the manuscript after the editor responded favorably to your query letter, indicate that the editor requested to see the enclosed manuscript.

Provide a brief description of the piece and a short explanation of how it fits the editor's needs. List any publishing credits or other pertinent qualifications. If requested in the guidelines or listing, note any material or sources you can provide. Indicate if the manuscript is being sent to other magazines as well (a simultaneous submission). Mention that you have enclosed a self-addressed, stamped envelope for return of the manuscript.

Sample Cover Letter

Address
Phone Number
Email
Date

Boys' Quest
P.O. Box 227
Bluffton, OH   45817-0227

Dear Editor:

Twenty-five percent of the population has a sense of taste that is three times stronger than most. These people are commonly referred to as 'supertasters.' This is the topic of an article I have enclosed for consideration in an upcoming issue of *Boys' Quest*.

The piece titled "Do My Taste Buds Have Super Powers?" is 483 words, not including a crossword puzzle and an activity on how to determine if you're a supertaster. The focus of the article is to explore what it's like to be a supertaster and to better understand why they don't enjoy certain foods.

The article is intended for intermediate readers, suitable for your target audience. It received an honorable mention in the December 2007 Short Article Contest for *ByLine Magazine*. Note: *ByLine* does not routinely print winning entries, allowing the author to sell first rights later.

Thank you for your consideration, and I hope you enjoy the article. I have enclosed a bibliography, copies of the sources cited in the bibliography, photographs, and an SASE for your convenience.

Sincerely,

Julie M. Smith

Encl.: Manuscript, Bibliography, Source copies, Photographs, SASE

Subject/ Specifications:
A brief description of the topic and its potential interest to the magazine's readers. Word lengths, age range, availability of photos, and other submission details.

Closing:
Be formal and direct.

Standard Manuscript Format

The format for preparing manuscripts is fairly standard—an example is shown below. Double-space manuscript text, leaving 1- to 1½-inch margins on the top, bottom, and sides. Indent 5 spaces for paragraphs.

In the upper left corner of the first page (also known as the title page), single space your name, address, phone number, and email address. In the upper right corner of that page, place your word count.

Center the title with your byline below it halfway down the page, approximately 5 inches. Then begin the manuscript text 4 lines below your byline.

In the upper left corner of the following pages, type your last name, the page number, and a word or two of your title. Then, space down 4 lines and continue the text of the manuscript.

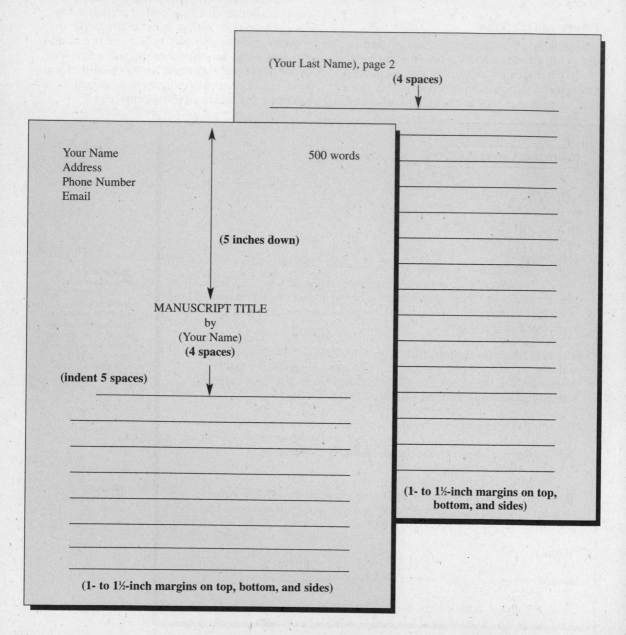

(Your Last Name), page 2

(4 spaces)

Your Name
Address
Phone Number
Email

500 words

(5 inches down)

MANUSCRIPT TITLE
by
(Your Name)
(4 spaces)

(indent 5 spaces)

(1- to 1½-inch margins on top, bottom, and sides)

(1- to 1½-inch margins on top, bottom, and sides)

Sample Cover Letter

Address
Phone Number
Email
Date

Submissions Editor, *Cricket*
Carus Publishing
70 East Lake Street, Suite 300
Chicago, IL 60601

Dear Editor,

Eleven-year-old Aden returns to his favorite fishing spot early one spring afternoon only to find all the fish lying dead upon the shore. What caused this horrible tragedy? How did the fish die? Will Aden's favorite spot ever be the same again? As one clue leads to another, Aden and his friend Sammy scramble to solve this science-based mystery and save the fish.

Touching on the potential loss of the fish and of one child's special place, this 1,130-word story is sure to capture the interest of young readers ages 8 to 10. In addition, this story is based on a true ecologic crisis, the invasion of the zebra mussel that has recently occurred in many parts of the United States. A sidebar with factual information about nonnative zebra mussels and how they are affecting local ecosystems like the one in this story can easily be included for even greater interest.

As a high school science teacher, former park ranger, and environmental educator, ecological mysteries and animal adaptations are a favorite teaching topic of mine. Enclosed you will find a copy of "The Mystery of the Dead Fish" for your consideration.

I look forward to hearing from you and I have included an SASE for your convenience. This manuscript has been sent exclusively to you at this time.

Sincerely,

Eliza Bicknell

Sample Cover Letter

Address
Phone Number
Email
Date

Suzanne Hadley
Focus on the Family Clubhouse Jr.
8605 Explorer Drive
Colorado Springs, CO 80920

Dear Ms. Hadley:

Max has made a mess and blamed it on his brother Seth. Seth is only two and can't tell Mom that Max lied. Seth wouldn't get in any real trouble. So what's the harm? Will Max's conscience catch up to him?

I have enclosed a lively story entitled "Max's Mistake" for 4- to 8-year-old children. Along with my manuscript, I have enclosed an SASE for your reply.

Thank you for your time and I look forward to hearing from you.

Sincerely,

Casey Brown

Enc: Manuscript, SASE

Sample Cover Letter

Address
Phone Number
Email
Date

Editor
Boys' Quest
P.O. Box 227
Bluffton, OH 45817-0227

Dear Editor,

Don't think you can enjoy your favorite pastime of fishing in the dead of winter? Well, think again. Unbelieveably, fishing on a frozen lake is possible and fish can be plentiful. Not only is it exciting to learn a new way to fish, you will also enjoy the great outdoors in a very different way.

For many years my father took me on ice fishing trips. I always found it amazing that you could drill holes in the ice and catch live fish out of the frozen lake.

Enclosed for your consideration is a 500-word article on ice fishing entitled, "Fishing Through a Frozen Lake." The article includes information on safety tips, equipment, clothing, and tips for ice fishing. As per your writers' guidelines, I have included two black-and-white photos, which I have the JPEG files for if you are interested. I have also included a bibliography for your review.

I am a graduate of the Institute of Children's Literature and a member of SCBWI. My writing has been published in *Stories for Children Magazine, A Long Story Short, Kid Magazine Writers,* and *The National Writing for Children Center.*

Thank you for your time and consideration. I look forward to your response. An SASE is enclosed for your reply.

Sincerely,

Donna M. McDine

Enc: Ms, bibliography, B&W photos & SASE

Sample Outline

ARTICLE OUTLINE FOR "GETTING THEIR FEET WET"

I. Underwater home
   A. In Key Largo, Florida, scientists wake up, brush their teeth, and eat breakfast underwater.
   B. Dr. Ellen Prager has been studying coral reefs and marine science for years and is now chief scientist at Aquarius.
   C. Aquarius is an underwater ocean laboratory based at Conch Reef in the Florida Keys National Marine Sanctuary.
   D. Recently, Aquarius took on its 100th mission called Teacher Under the Sea.

II. Why study these habitats?
   A. Coral is an animal, but it creates a rock called limestone.
   B. Most corals are colonies of tiny animals called polyps. Over time, polyps grow and build up into underwater structures called reefs.
   C. Coral reefs provide food and shelter for a whole community of marine animals.
   D. The reefs protect beaches from waves that would wash the sand away, and the fish around reefs provide food to many countries.

III. How are the scientists able to live underwater?
   A. Aquanaut trainees undergo five days of training before each mission.
   B. Divers must know their depth at all times.
   C. Since they're underwater for days, their bodies fill with gas due to the higher pressure at the surface.
   D. Aquanauts must go through 17 hours of decompression before returning to the surface.

IV. Just like home
   A. The pressure inside Aquarius is the same pressure as the water outside.
   B. Air is piped in from the surface, so the aquanauts can breathe.
   C. The entryway, called the moon pool, remains open as the air pressure inside prevents the water from flowing in.
   D. Aquarius provides living and working space for a six-person crew.
   E. Amenities include air conditioning, a hot water shower, toilet, cooler, and microwave.

V. Conclusion
   A. Aquarius is not only dedicated to protecting one of Florida's most valuable marine resources, but it will continue to expand our knowledge of coral reefs, our oceans, and our planet.
   B. Perhaps Aquarius shows what life might be like in the future.

Bibliography

A thorough bibliography is particularly valuable to editors, who use these source lists as a way to determine how extensively a manuscript has been researched. In fact, many nonfiction editors review the bibliography even before the manuscript. A well-rounded, diverse bibliography not only shows that you've properly acknowledged and credited your sources of information, but that the finished piece is likely to present an original point of view that is supported by credible sources.

Some magazines require a bibliography as part of a submission package for nonfiction articles. (Bibliographies are rarely required for fiction, with the possible exception of historical fiction.) Unique research methods are required for every project but, in general, the bibliography should be made up of resources that are both historical and current, target adults and children, and cover primary and secondary sources. Search museums, libraries, and other organizations for primary documents such as naval reports, maps, bills of lading, court documents, song lyrics, and more. Your bibliography should also show that you plan on culling information from other sources, such as interviews with experts or other relevant individuals (a profile subject and those who know him or her, for example). It's also a good idea to mention your research in your cover letter, to explain your main sources and any other research-related issues.

Citation styles vary greatly, but several references are available and generally accepted for bibliographic format. Among these are: *The Chicago Manual of Style*; *Modern Language Association (MLA) Handbook*; or handbooks by news organizations such as the *New York Times*.

To find expert sources to interview, read newspapers, magazines, and journals with articles about your topic. Current articles may include the names of specialists who are doing work in your area of interest, some of whom may be available for interviews.

Sample Bibliography

Bibliography for "Doctor Dog" by Jennifer Mattox

"Animal-Assisted Therapy Brings Patients One Step Closer to Healing," *Columbus Parent Magazine*, March 2007.

"Canine Companions for Independence," www.caninecompanions.org.

"Columbus Children's Hospital Staffs Full-Time 'Medical Dog' In New Animal-Assisted Therapy Program," March 2007, www.columbuschildrens.com.

Lundine, Jennifer. Telephone Interview. March 31, 2007. Speech pathologist at Children's Hospital, Columbus, Ohio.

Mehus-Roe, Kristen. *Working Dogs: True Stories of Dogs and Their Handlers.* Irvine, California: BowTie Press, 2003.

Writing Your Résumé

Many publications request a resume along with queries or sample clips. You may have a resume you use for job-hunting, but it isn't likely to address the needs of an editor, who is only interested in your writing experience. By reviewing a resume, an editor can determine if a prospective writer has the necessary experience to research and write material for his or her publication.

If you have few writing credits, format your resume so that your writing-related skills and experience appear first, such as writing a company newsletter or reports, or creating volunteer materials. Then briefly list your work history and educational information, followed by awards and professional memberships such as SCBWI. Pertinent job experience should always be highlighted, both on your resume and in your cover or query letter.

Many writers tailor their resume to be most relevant to the particular job or opportunity they are seeking. For example, if you're querying an educational publication, emphasize your experience as a writing instructor or a teacher; for a nonfiction editor, highlight any nonfiction writing credits first.

No one style or format is preferred, but make sure your name and email address appear at the top of the page. Keep your resume concise—it should not be more than one page.

Sample Résumé

Joanna Coates
Address
Phone
Email

EDUCATION:

University of Missouri, Columbia, MO
1980   M.Ed. Reading
1975   B.A. English Education

Missouri Certified Teacher of English and Reading Specialist

TEACHING EXPERIENCE:
1997–present   Instructor
Adult Continuing Education ESL Classes
Springfield College, Springfield, MO

1981-1995   Classroom Teacher
Middle School English and Reading
John Jay Middle School, Thornfield, MO

EDUCATIONAL MATERIAL PUBLISHED:
Educational Insights
1995   FUN WITH READING II
Story/activity kit
1993   FUN WITH READING I
Story/activity kit

MEMBERSHIP:
Society of Children's Book Writers and Illustrators

Copyright and Contracts

Just like the movie you watched last night and the CD you listened to on the way to work this morning, your magazine article is one of many creative works that is afforded the protection of copyright. As one of the nation's "copyright-based industries," publishing relies heavily on the concept of obtaining legal ownership of written works. When you write an article, you own the legal rights to the manuscript, as well as the right to decide how it is reproduced and, for certain works, how it is performed or displayed.

As of 1998, your heirs can also enjoy the fruits of your labor: That's when Congress passed the Copyright Term Extension Act, which offers you copyright protection for your work created during or after 1978 for your lifetime plus 70 years, until you choose to sell all or part of the copyright for this work.

Do You Need to Register Your Work?

Thanks to copyright law, your work is protected from the moment it is recorded in a tangible medium, such as a computer file or on paper, without any need for legal action or counsel. You don't even need to register your work with the United States Copyright Office; in fact, most editors view an author's copyright notice on manuscripts as the sign of an amateur. A copy of the manuscript and a dated record of your submission will provide proof of creation, should the need arise.

If you do decide to register your work, obtain an application form and directions on the correct way to file your copyright application. Write to the Library of Congress, Copyright Office, 101 Independence Ave. S. E., Washington, DC 20559-6000. These forms and directions are also available online at: www.copyright.gov/forms. Copyright registration fees range from $35 (online) to $65 (paper).

If you have registered your unpublished manuscript with the Library of Congress, notify your editor of that fact once it is accepted for publication.

Rights Purchased by Magazines

As a writer and copyright holder, you have the right to decide how your work should be shared with the world. By agreeing to publication in a magazine, you also agree to transfer some of your rights over to the magazine so that your article can be printed and distributed as part of that publication. A publisher is restricted, however, on when, how, and where he or she may publish your manuscript—terms that are set down in a publishing contract. Below is a list of common rights that are purchased by magazines:

All World Rights: The publisher purchases all rights to publish your work anywhere in the world any number of times. This includes all forms of media (both current and those which may be developed later). The publisher also has the right to all future use of the work, including reprints, syndication, creation of derivative works, and use in databases. You no longer have the right to sell or reproduce the work, unless you can negotiate for the return of certain rights (for example, book rights).

All World Serial Rights: The publisher purchases all rights to publish your work in newspapers, magazines, and other serial publications throughout the world any number of times. You retain all other rights, such as the right to use it as a chapter in a book.

First Rights: A publisher acquires the right to publish your work for the first time in any specified media. Electronic and nontraditional markets often seek these rights. All other rights, including reprint rights, belong to you.

Electronic Rights: Publishers use this as a catch-all for inclusion in any type of electronic publication, such as CD-ROM, websites, ezines, or in an electronic database.

First North American Serial Rights: The publisher can publish your work for the first time in a U.S. or Canadian periodical. You retain the book and North American reprint rights, as well as first rights to a foreign market.

Second or Reprint Rights: This allows a publication non-exclusive rights to print the material for the second time. You may not authorize second publication to occur until after the work has appeared in print by the publisher who bought first rights. **One-time Rights:** Often bought by regional publications, this means the publication has bought the right to use the material once. You may continue to sell the material elsewhere; however, you should inform the publisher if this work is being simultaneously considered for publication in a competing magazine.

You should be aware that an agreement may limit a publisher to the right to publish your work in certain media (e.g., magazines and other periodicals only) or the agreement may include wider-ranging rights (e.g., the right to publish the manuscript in a book or an audiocassette). The right may be limited to publishing within a specific geographic region or in a specific language. Any rights you retain allow you to resell the manuscript within the parameters of your agreement.

It is becoming increasingly common for magazines to purchase all rights, especially those that host Internet sites and make archives of previously published articles available to readers. Unless you have extensive publishing credentials, you may not want to jeopardize the opportunity to be published by insisting on selling limited rights.

Contracts and Agreements

Typically, when a publisher indicates an interest in your manuscript, he or she specifies what rights the publication will acquire. Then usually a publisher will send you a letter of agreement or a standard written contract spelling out the terms of the agreement.

If a publisher does not send you a written contract or agreement, you need to consider your options. While an oral agreement may be legally binding, it is not as easy to enforce as a written one. To protect your interests, draft a letter outlining the terms as you understand them (e.g., a 500-word article without photos, first North American serial rights, paying on acceptance at $.05 a word). Send two copies of the letter to the editor (with a self-addressed, stamped envelope), asking him or her to sign one and return it to you if the terms are correct.

Every writer has the right to negotiate

contract terms, so take a close look at yours before you sign. For example, payment may be an issue, but before you start negotiating you should know exactly what the job is worth to you. Put a monetary value on your time: How long will it take you to produce the work? Calculations like these can help determine an appropriate rate of pay, and help justify your request for additional money.

If you do need to negotiate, always be professional, and act as a partner with the editor, working toward terms that will benefit both parties. If you don't understand something, ask. Most editors work with freelance writers on a daily basis and are willing to make changes. If an agreement can't be reached, you always have the option of not signing—and selling your work somewhere else.

Work Made for Hire

Another term that is appearing more frequently in contracts is *work made for hire*. As a freelance writer, most editors treat you as an independent contractor (not an employee) who writes articles for their publication.

Get It in Writing

If you've been offered a publishing contract, it's smart to make sure that all the details are down in writing. The following is a partial list of items that may seem obvious to both parties, but that should be clearly noted in your agreement:

- Are any expenses, i.e. telephone, gas, etc., covered for research purposes?

- Will you be able to see the article before publication?

- If the article will be accompanied by artwork, who is responsible for finding the art and/or paying for it?

- In what form does the magazine expect the manuscript to be delivered? On paper? Disk? Via e-mail?

- What is the due date?

- What is the length of the work?

- Are payment terms according to word length, time spent, or another measure?

Magazine editors can assign or commission articles to freelancers as works made for hire, making the finished article property of the publisher.

Under current copyright laws, only certain types of commissioned works are considered works made for hire, and only when both the publisher and the commissioned writer agree in writing. These works typically include items such as contributions to "collective works" such as magazines. A contract or agreement clearly stating that the material is a work made for hire must be signed by both parties and be in place before the material is written. Once a writer agrees to these terms, he or she no longer has any rights to the work.

Most writer organizations recommend not signing a work-for-hire agreement in any situation, but there are some instances in which work-for-hire contracts may be appropriate. The ideal is to sell as few rights as possible, leaving the magazine to re-negotiate with you if it wants to purchase additional rights. This scenario ensures that you won't lose out on any compensation related to future use of your work. Before you refuse a work-for-hire arrangement, however, consider the market, the article topic, and the pay. If the initial pay is very good, or if chances are slim that you'll be able to sell the article elsewhere, signing might be your best option.

Note that a pre-existing piece, such as an unsolicited manuscript that is accepted for publication, is not considered a commissioned work.

Guidelines for Permission to Quote

When you want to quote another writer's words in a manuscript you're preparing, you must get that writer's permission. If you don't, you could be sued for copyright infringement. Here are some guidelines:

- Any writing published in the U.S. prior to 1923 is in the public domain, as are works created by the U.S. government. Such material may be quoted without permission, but the source should be cited.
- No specific limits are set as to the length of permitted quotations in your articles: different publishers have various requirements. Generally, if you quote more than a handful of words, you should seek permission.

Always remember to credit your sources.
- The doctrine of "fair use" allows quoting portions of a copyrighted work for certain purposes, as in a review, news reporting, nonprofit educational uses, or research. Contrary to popular belief, there is no absolute word limit on fair use. But as a general rule, never quote more than a few successive paragraphs from a book or article and credit the source.
- If you're submitting a manuscript that contains quoted material, you'll need to obtain permission from the source to quote the material before it is published. If you're uncertain about what to do, your editor should be able to advise you.

Resources

Interested in finding out more about writers and their rights under the law? Check these sources for further information:

The Publishing Law Center
www.publaw.com/legal.html

The Copyright Handbook: What Every Writer Needs to Know, 10th Edition by Attorney Stephen Fishman. Nolo, 2008.

Copyright Companion for Writers by Tonya Evans-Walls. Legal Write Publications, 2007.

Last Steps and Follow Up

Before mailing your manuscript, check the pages for neatness, readability, and proper page order. Proofread for typographical errors. Redo pages if necessary. Keep a copy of the manuscript for your records.

Mailing Requirements

Assemble the pages (unstapled) and place your cover letter on top of the first page.

Send manuscripts over 5 pages in length in a 9x12 or 10x13 manila envelope. Include a same-size SASE marked "First Class." If submitting to a foreign magazine, enclose the proper amount of International Reply Coupons (IRC) for return postage. Mail manuscripts under 5 pages in a large business-size envelope with a same-size SASE folded inside.

Package your material carefully and address the outer envelope to the magazine editor. Send your submission via first-class or priority mail. Don't use certified or registered mail. (See Postage Information, page 34.)

Follow Up with the Editor

Some writers contend that waiting for an editor to respond is the hardest part of writing. But wait you must. Editors usually respond within the time period specified in the listings.

If you don't receive a response by the stated response time, allow at least three weeks to pass before you contact the editor. At that time, send a letter with a self-addressed, stamped envelope requesting to know the status of your submission.

The exception to this general rule is when you send a return postcard with a manuscript. In that case, look for your postcard about three weeks after mailing the manuscript. If you don't receive it by then, write to the editor requesting confirmation that it was received.

If more than two months pass after the stated response time and you don't receive any response, send a letter withdrawing your work from consideration. At that point, you can send your query or manuscript to the next publication on your list.

What You Can Expect

The most common responses to a submission are an impersonal rejection letter, a personalized rejection letter, an offer to look at your material "on speculation," or an assignment.

If you receive an impersonal rejection note, revise your manuscript if necessary, and send your work to the next editor on your list. If you receive a personal note, send a thank-you note. If you receive either of the last two responses, you know what to do!

Set Up a Tracking System

To help you keep track of the status of your submissions, you may want to establish a system in a notebook, in a computer file, or on file cards (see below).

This will keep you organized and up-to-date on the status of your queries and manuscripts and on the need to follow up with certain editors.

SENT QUERIES TO THE FOLLOWING PUBLICATIONS						
Editor	Publication	Topic	Date Sent	Postage	Accepted/ Rejected	Rights Offered

SENT MANUSCRIPTS TO THE FOLLOWING PUBLICATIONS						
Editor	Publication	Title	Date Sent	Postage	Accepted/ Rejected	Rights Offered

Frequently Asked Questions

How do I request a sample copy and writers' guidelines?

Write a brief note to the magazine: "Please send me a recent sample copy and writers' guidelines. If there is any charge, please enclose an invoice and I will pay upon receipt." The magazine's website, if it has one, offers a faster and less expensive alternative. Many companies put a part of the magazine, writers' guidelines, and sometimes a theme list or editorial calendar on the Internet.

How do I calculate the amount of postage for a sample copy?

Check the listing in this directory. In some cases the amount of postage will be listed. If the number of pages is given, use that to estimate the amount of postage by using the postage chart at the end of this section. For more information on postage and how to obtain stamps, see page 34.

Should my email submission 'package' be different than a submission via snail mail?

In general, an email submission should contain the same elements as a mailed one—i.e. a solid article description, sources, etc. In all cases, writers' guidelines should be followed to the letter when it comes to sending writing samples, bibliographies, and other requirements, either as separate file attachments or embedded in the email text.

What do I put in a cover letter if I have no publishing credits or relevant personal experience?

In this case, you may want to forego a formal cover letter and send your manuscript with a brief letter stating: "Enclosed is my manuscript, (Insert Title), for your review." For more information on cover letters, see pages 19–22.

How long should I wait before contacting an editor after I have submitted my manuscript?

The response time given in the listings can vary, and it's a good idea to wait three to four weeks after the stated response time before sending a brief note to the editor asking about the status of your manuscript. You might use this opportunity to add a new sales pitch or include additional material to show that the topic is continuing to generate interest. If you do not get a satisfactory response or you want to send your manuscript elsewhere, send a certified letter to the editor withdrawing the work from consideration and requesting its return. You are then free to submit the work to another magazine.

I don't need my manuscript returned. How do I indicate that to an editor?

With the capability to store manuscripts electronically and print out additional copies easily, some writers keep postage costs down by enclosing a self-addressed, stamped postcard (SASP) saying, "No need to return my manuscript. Please use this postcard to advise me of the status of my manuscript. Thank you."

Common Publishing Terms

All rights: Contractual agreement by which a publisher acquires the copyright and all use of author's material (see page 27).

Anthology: A collection of selected literary pieces.

Anthropomorphization: Attributing human form or personality to things not human (i.e., animals).

Assignment: Manuscript commissioned by an editor for a stated fee.

Bimonthly: A publication that appears every two months.

Biweekly: A publication issued every two weeks.

Byline: Author's name credited at the heading of an article.

Caption: Description or text accompanying an illustration or photograph.

CD-ROM (compact disc read-only-memory)**:** Non-erasable compact disc containing data that can be read by a computer.

Clip: Sample of a published work.

Contributor's copies: Copies of the publication issue in which the writer's work appears.

Copyedit: To edit with close attention to style and mechanics.

Copyright: Legal rights that protect an author's work (see page 27).

Cover letter: Brief letter sent with a manuscript introducing the writer and presenting the materials enclosed (see page 19).

Disk submission: Manuscript that is submitted on a computer disk.

Early readers: Children 4 to 7 years.

Editorial calendar: List of topics, themes, or special sections that are planned for upcoming issues for a specific time period.

Electronic submission: Manuscript transmitted to an editor from one computer to another through a modem.

Email (electronic mail)**:** Messages sent from one computer to another via computer network or modem.

English-language rights: The right to publish a manuscript in any English-speaking country.

Filler: Short item that fills out a page (e.g., joke, light verse, or fun fact).

First serial rights: The right to publish a work for the first time in a periodical; often limited to a specific geographical region (e.g., North America or Canada) (see page 27).

Genre: Category of fiction characterized by a particular style, form, or content, such as mystery or fantasy.

Glossy: Photo printed on shiny rather than matte-finish paper.

Guidelines: See **Writers' guidelines.**

In-house: See **Staff written.**

International Reply Coupon (IRC): Coupon exchangeable in any foreign country for postage on a single-rate, surface-mailed letter.

Kill fee: Percentage of the agreed-upon fee paid to a writer if an editor decides not to use a purchased manuscript.

Layout: Plan for the arrangement of text and artwork on a printed page.

Lead: Beginning of an article.

Lead time: Length of time between assembling and printing an issue.

Libel: Any false published statement intended to expose another to public ridicule or personal loss.

Manuscript: A typewritten or computer-printed version of a document (as opposed to a published version).

Masthead: The printed matter in a newspaper or periodical that gives the title and pertinent details of ownership, advertising rates, and subscription rates.

Middle-grade readers: Children 8 to 12 years.

Modem: An internal device or a small electrical box that plugs into a computer; used to transmit data between computers, often via telephone lines.

Ms/mss: Manuscript/manuscripts.

One-time rights: The right to publish a piece once, often not the first time (see page 28).

On spec: Refers to writing "on speculation," without an editor's commitment to purchase the manuscript.

Outline: Summary of a manuscript's contents, usually nonfiction, organized under subheadings with descriptive sentences under each.

Payment on acceptance: Author is paid following an editor's decision to accept a manuscript.

Payment on publication: Author is paid following the publication of the manuscript.

Pen name/pseudonym: Fictitious name used by an author.

Pre-K: Children under 5 years of age; also known as *preschool*.

Proofread: To read and mark errors, usually in printed text.

Query: Letter to an editor to promote interest in a manuscript or an idea.

Rebus story: A "see and say" story form, using pictures followed by the written words; often written for pre-readers.

Refereed journal: Publication that requires all manuscripts be reviewed by an editorial or advisory board.

Reprint: Another printing of an article or story; can be in a different magazine format, such as an anthology.

Reprint rights: See **Second serial rights.**

Response time: Average length of time for an editor to accept or reject a submission and contact the writer with his or her decision.

Résumé: Account of one's qualifications, including educational and professional background, as well as publishing credits.

SAE: Self-addressed envelope (no postage).

SASE: Self-addressed, stamped envelope.

SASP: Self-addressed stamped postcard.

Second serial rights: The right to publish a manuscript that has appeared in another publication; also known as *Reprint rights* (see page 27).

Semiannual: Occurring every six months or twice a year.

Semimonthly: Occurring twice a month.

Semiweekly: Occurring twice a week.

Serial: A publication issued as one of a consecutively numbered and indefinitely continued series.

Serial rights: See **First serial rights.**

Sidebar: A short article that accompanies a feature article and highlights one aspect of the feature's subject.

Simultaneous submission: Manuscript submitted to more than one publisher at the same time; also known as multiple submission.

Slant: Specific approach to a subject to appeal to a certain readership.

Slush pile: Term used within the publishing industry to describe unsolicited manuscripts.

Solicited manuscript: Manuscript that an editor has requested or agreed to consider.

Staff written: Prepared by members of the magazine's staff; also known as *in-house*.

Syndication rights: The right to distribute serial rights to a given work through a syndicate of periodicals.

Synopsis: Condensed description or summary of a manuscript.

Tabloid: Publication printed on an ordinary newspaper page, turned sideways and folded in half.

Tearsheet: A page from a newspaper or magazine (periodical) containing a printed story or article.

Theme list: See **Editorial calendar.**

Transparencies: Color slides, not color prints.

Unsolicited manuscript: Any manuscript not specifically requested by an editor.

Work made for hire: Work specifically ordered, commissioned, and owned by a publisher for its exclusive use (see page 28).

World rights: Contractual agreement whereby the publisher acquires the right to reproduce the work throughout the world (see page 27); also known as *all rights*.

Writers' guidelines: Publisher's editorial objectives or specifications, which usually include word lengths, readership level, and subject matter.

Writing sample: Example of your writing style, tone, and skills; may be a published or unpublished piece.

Young adult: Readers 12 to 18 years.

Postage Information

How Much Postage?

When you're sending a manuscript to a magazine, enclose a self-addressed, stamped envelope with sufficient postage; this way, if the editor does not want to use your manuscript, it can be returned to you. To help you calculate the proper amount of postage for your SASE, here are the U.S. postal rates for first-class mailings in the U.S. and from the U.S. to Canada based on the latest increase (2009). Rates are expected to increase again, so please check with your local Post Office, or check the U.S. Postal Service website at usps.com.

Ounces	9x12 Envelope (Approx. no. of pages)	U.S. First-Class Postage Rate	Rate from U.S. to Canada
1	1–5	$0.88	$1.03
2	6–10	1.05	1.29
3	11–15	1.22	1.55
4	16–20	1.39	1.81
5	21–25	1.56	2.07
6	26–30	1.73	2.33
7	31–35	1.90	2.59
8	36–40	2.07	2.85

The amount of postage and size of envelope necessary to receive a sample copy and writers' guidelines are usually stated in the magazine listing. If this information is not provided, use the chart above to help gauge the proper amount of postage.

How to Obtain Stamps

People living in the U.S., Canada, or overseas can acquire U.S. stamps through the mail from the Philately Fulfillment Service Center. Call 800-STAMP-24 (800-782-6724) to request a catalogue or place an order. For overseas, the telephone number is 816-545-1100. You pay the cost of the stamps plus a postage and handling fee based on the value of the stamps ordered, and the stamps are shipped to you. Credit card information (MasterCard, Visa, and Discover cards only) is required for fax orders. The fax number is 816-545-1212. If you order through the catalogue, you can pay with a U.S. check or an American Money Order. Allow 3–4 weeks for delivery.

Gateway to
the Markets

Making Sense of Fiction Genres

By Pamela Holtz Beres

Submission details in *Magazine Markets for Children's Writers* provide vital clues about the fiction editors prefer: "Genres include adventure, mystery, sports stories, multicultural fiction, and retellings of traditional stories" (*Highlights for Children*) or "humor; fantasy; fairy tales; folktales; and realistic, historical, and science fiction" (*Spider*).

Yet writers need to take such specific information another step. If a talking dog and cat romp through the woods looking for their missing friend, Mr. Chirp, is the story an animal story? Adventure? Mystery? If the dog is a wise-cracking canine, is the story humor? Will it work for *Nature Friend? Jack and Jill? Fun for Kidz?* If Wise-Cracking Dog is reading a newspaper dated 1829, have you written historical fiction? Understanding genres and their different styles and content results in better-targeted submissions.

Genre Defined

Fiction genres can take complex forms, consisting of subgenres within a genre: Think time travel/fantasy/historical fiction novel. But for children's magazine

writers, *genre* basically means *category* or *story type.* While a children's story may have elements of several genres, it will be defined by its most prominent feature, the element that drives the story. Since it is hard to look past the unreality of a wise-cracking dog with a feline sidekick, "Wise-Cracking Dog" would be defined as fantasy. The funny doggie detective may be solving a mystery in the year 1829, but the story will be categorized as fantasy by an editor. If the magazine does not accept fantasy, the editor will reject the piece.

Associate Editor Joelle Dujardin explains that while *Highlights for Children* accepts fiction on its merits rather than on category, the editors respect that certain genres need to meet expectations to satisfy fans. "A story that sets itself up as an adventure ought to have a good amount of physical action and risk," she says. "The conflict of a sports story ought to center on the issues that arise in playing a sport (or on the effect of some other issue on playing a sport). A mystery should present a question that the protagonist can realistically solve using available clues—and the story's climax should be the moment when the mystery is solved. In fantasy, magic should play a role in furthering the protagonist's journey, which often involves a quest to conquer evil."

Writer and *Stories for Children* founder and Editor in Chief VS Grenier says, "A mystery not only has a problem for the main character to solve, but clues, false leads, and cliffhangers. Fantasy usually has some sort of magic or unknown force at work, science fiction has scientific facts in the story, and humor has events in which the main character feels awkward or where out-of-the-normal things happen, causing the reader to laugh."

Science fiction is premised on scientific fact and adds the *what if* factor. Imagination takes over to explore what could be, but the created world must be possible or at least plausible. Today's kids are savvy; scientific accuracy is necessary for readers to suspend disbelief and allow the impossible to be possible.

Similarly, historical fiction requires research to help create a basis in real events, a believable core. Stephanie Lile, Managing Editor of *COLUMBIAKids*, believes, "Historical fiction, when accurate to a place and time, not only gives kids a sense of what it was like from a practical standpoint to live in another time, it can help them build empathy for and under-

standing of cultural exchanges, both positive and negative." When kids see a situation through a character's eyes, they can relate to complex events in human history, Lile says. *COLUMBIAKids* is an online magazine about the Pacific Northwest, for children from 4 to 14.

"Research is critical, but the type of research needed for historical fiction is often unexpected," Lile continues. It includes not only the big picture historical context but also the details of every-

---

Genre fans may have specific story expectations that editors want to meet: risk in adventure, conflict in sports, magic in fantasy.

---

day life. "You can't have a character in the 1880s spreading jam with a plastic knife because plastic for that type of use wasn't invented until after the 1930s."

Nature stories are a genre often misunderstood. Setting fiction outdoors does not make for a nature story. Having a protagonist whose goal it is to protect an abandoned nest of baby rabbits does. An animal or other living creature may be in the spotlight, but it cannot be anthropomorphized. Nature fiction, like historical fiction, has a foundation in the real world.

Age Matters

Audience age enters into how a genre story fits together. In fantasy for middle-grade readers, the main character may be on a journey where magic is used. But younger readers may not have developed the skills and knowledge to know what is real and what is magic. How do they know that rabbits don't grow from or live in hats?

A magazine like *Crow Toes Quarterly,* which targets middle-graders, looks for "playfully dark" stories, with tongue-in-cheek humor. *The Magazine of Fantasy & Science Fiction,* which targets young adults and adults, looks for speculative science fiction, and upbeat visions of the future, but as its guidelines say, it has "no formula for fiction."

Jacquitta McManus founded a fantasy and adventure magazine called *Labyrinth's Door.* As an admirer of the genre, McManus prefers "fresh adventures in worlds we haven't seen, in places that are new to the readers but still feel familiar, and if they are not familiar, they are places that engage the mind." (*Labyrinth's Door* is not currently publishing, but McManus hopes to relaunch the magazine.)

Indeed, the middle-grade reader expects to be transported to new lands, often where good battles evil. Princes, princesses, knights, and dragons are common characters as are fairies, wizards, and sea creatures. A vivid imagination is vital both in creating a believable, magical world, as well as a plot with fresh twists and turns.

For younger children, fantasy stories may feature talking animals. But in this subgenre, writers need to beware of blurring the lines between reality and fantasy: Some editors hate talking animal stories, and all are reluctant to confuse readers. Animals should only talk to other animals, with no humans present, and they should also stay true to their animal nature.

Whatever the genre, Grenier says,

"The biggest thing to keep in mind when writing for younger kids is how they see the world around them." Without enough life experience, they do not yet have the how and why behind what they know. The example Grenier gives is that a young child only knows that a pot is hot because Mom or Dad has told them; he or she does not understand that the stove has heated the pot.

A realistic contemporary story in *Highlights* plays to this level of understanding in a delightful way. In "The Crooked Pumpkin," by Patti Werner Hillenius (October 2008), Nicolas grows attached to the misshapen pumpkin he found on a trip to the pumpkin patch. He keeps the pumpkin safe in his room, not wanting the pumpkin carved and put on display. When it is time to dispose of the pumpkins, Nicolas hides his pumpkin in the backyard. In spring, he is disappointed to find that the pumpkin is gone, but is surprised later when he finds a small patch of new pumpkins.

Humor is another category where reader age is definitively connected to what works to make a story funny. Editor Lonnie Plecha says, "*Cricket* loves humor that speaks to the experiences of middle-grade kids, and many *Cricket* stories have wonderful touches of humor in them."

Plecha cites two recently accepted stories, "Boarding School" and "First Impressions," both by Timothy Tocher. "In 'Boarding School,' a boy crawls into the attic of his school, where he ends up spending the night. (His mother thinks he is on a sleepover.) In the morning, he overhears teachers discussing him in the lounge, and accidentally crashes through the ceiling in the middle of their meeting," he says. "'First Impressions' is a boy-tries-to-impress-girl story in which the boy stumbles all over the place, gets locked out of the house, has the police called on him, and so on, but of course, gets together with the girl in the end." These stories have exaggerated slapstick elements but still focus on experiences with which the middle-grade reader identifies.

Humor is often about taking the expected in a particular situation and twisting it into something unexpected. The middle-grader is firmly planted in the world of school and community, and humor is often found in those settings. A preschooler and early reader's world consists mostly of family, with just the beginnings of exploration beyond those boundaries. Exaggeration, surprise, and very basic wordplay are common tools in writing humor for this age group.

Pamela Dell's Doodlebug and Dandelion series in *Spider* features all three elements. In "Tomiko's House," (May/June 2008), brothers Doodlebug and Dandelion are riding the Burpmobile (school bus) when they meet Tomiko, who invites them to her house. Doodlebug has been plagued by hiccups for a half-hour. He hiccups exactly 43 times in the short walk from the bus to her house. The boys gawk at the gadgets and gizmos filling Tomiko's yard, including a mini-Ferris wheel birdfeeder spewing seed across the lawn. Inside, the brothers explore the "gizmo-and-gadget museum" home and Doodlebug (hiccupping more than ever) eventually settles into a comfy-looking chair. The chair comes alive, scaring the hiccups out of Doodlebug.

Editors are quick to point out that some stories cannot be forced into one particular category, however, and should not be. Dujardin says, "*Highlights* publishes a good number of stories that don't fit in any one genre and many that cross over genres." Crossing over is one thing; jumbled is another. Writers need to take care that a story works, and that the genres are not merely jumbled.

Grenier believes that writers achieve stronger stories when they have a specific category in mind. That working platform "gives the writer a better focus on what they are trying to say." But again, category goes hand in hand with the kind of audience. "Know your reader or have a clear idea who you think the reader would be for your story," Grenier says.

Niches and Beyond

Beyond incorporating identifying characteristics and age appeal, genre fiction may need to address the needs of special niches.

Laura Matanah, Publisher and Executive Director of *Rainbow Rumpus*, a magazine for children with parents in the gay and lesbian community, says, "We are working to create both children's and young adult fiction of all genres in which the protagonist has one or more lesbian, gay, bisexual, or transgender (LGBT) parents. You'll find everything from realistic fiction to mysteries to sci-fi in our archives."

She was recently impressed with "Private Detective Ryan Patterson and the Ping in the Night," by Eva Apelqvist. "The first thing we look for is strong writing, and the story came in well-written." Matanah says that the story had three other things going for it: "a male protagonist, a farm setting, and being in the mystery genre." She would love to see more humor and adventure stories, male protagonists, and stories about families of color. She is also looking for fiction that takes place in rural settings.

While *Cricket* publishes literary fiction in many genres, Plecha says, "We consider mostly the quality of the story, whatever the genre, when deciding whether or not to publish it in *Cricket*." Open to all kinds of good stories, the editors "would like to see more stories about contemporary kids, but these need to have well-drawn characters, a solid story arc, and aim at the preteen or early teen reader. We are interested in seeing more fantasy, but stories need to be character-driven and not primarily about battles."

Plecha would also like to see more science fiction and humor but warns writers, "Genre fiction doesn't mean formulaic fiction in *Cricket*. It means quality literature for children in the style of some great traditions."

Lile advises historical fiction writers, "Find the pivotal moment in an event and concentrate on bringing that day to life. Be true to the time, place, people, and historical subject." She concludes by saying, "Most of all, tell us a story complete with conflict, action, and emotional arc."

Grenier sees many stories for all ages and genres, but adds, "The one category we would like to see more is true stories, which are only found if one really looks for them." While *Stories for Children* is not a paying market, Grenier notes the benefits of writing for her magazine: "We are committed to giving authors and illustrators new to children's writing a chance to get their works published in *Stories for Children*." She says she and her staff work tirelessly to help promote their authors and illustrators by featuring a Good News column, listing books published by contributors in the website's bookstore, and offering a chance to be published in a *Best of* anthology. Grenier hopes to pay writers in the future. "We are working toward that goal each and every day."

Strong characters, engaging plots, and satisfying resolutions are critical elements in publishable stories. Writers who take the extra step and also consider and embrace genre will be steps ahead in finding their work in the pages of a children's magazine.

Action! Writing about Sports, Games, and Activities

By Elizabeth Carpentiere

Play ball! Or checkers. Or hide-and-go-seek. Whatever the game, kids love to play. When writing about sports and activities for kids, the article, like the games themselves, should be fun, lively, and full of action.

When writing a sports or activity-related article, magazines such as *Sports Illustrated for Kids* and *Baseball Youth* are certainly ideal markets. But you should also consider other magazines that do not necessarily have a sports or activities focus. Doing so will dramatically increase your chances at publication.

Play the Angle

Cobblestone, an award-winning history magazine for readers ages 9 to 14, may not be the first magazine that comes to mind when considering a market for your sports-related piece, but it should not be ruled out solely due to its history focus. If you can connect your piece to the magazine's theme, *Cobblestone* Editor Meg Chorlian wants to hear from you. (Article author Elizabeth Carpentiere is Editor of Cobblestone Publishing's *Faces*.)

"In a recent issue we devoted to George Washington, we included a sidebar on his athleticism as a boy—his love of horseback riding and his general athletic ability," says Chorlian. "When we did an issue on Native Americans of the Northeast, we included an article on the history of lacrosse. And we did an issue on the Roaring 20s, which was a period when sports personalities first became hugely popular. We included short biographical sketches of some of the more famous sports figures from that era. That was a fun article because it introduced different personalities and their respective sports and then we found fun art to help make it visually appealing for our readers."

Odyssey Editor Beth Lindstrom has a similar perspective. Although *Odyssey* is a science-focused magazine, she publishes six to ten sports or activity-related articles each year, including Science Scoops, a news column consisting of short takes (up to 250 words) on new developments in science. As for *Cobblestone*, writers must submit queries that relate to an upcoming theme. Themes are posted on the website months in advance.

"All full-length features have a science slant, like 'What's the Real Science Behind Skating' or 'Make It Snow!'—the science behind making snow for skiing," says Lindstrom. "We have done complete issues with sports themes, including the Science of Extreme Sports. That issue included an article on Lance Armstrong and the Tour de France with sidebars called 'The Math of Muscle,' an interview, and 'Building Mental Muscle.' It also included articles on sports injuries and performance-enhancing drugs, as well as articles dealing with the physics involved in kiteboarding, stunt bicycling, and karate. I think the most out-of-the-box article in that issue was called 'Extreme Napping,' on the sleep science behind how multiple short naps help solo long-distance sailors break records."

Inside Scoops

Whatever magazine you hope to sell your work to, a sports piece should include information presented from an angle that will be new to the audience. It is important to go beyond what readers will find in encyclopedias or other general sources.

Linda K. Rose, Assistant Editor at *Highlights for Children,* says that when she is looking at a sports or activity article she considers many factors about the content and presentation. "Regarding the

information itself, is it something that kids can easily find elsewhere or are already likely to know, or will it give our readers the sense of being on the inside, knowing privileged information of some sort? Is it rich in quotes and anecdotes, or does it have too much exposition and sound encyclopedic? How reliable are the sources? Is backup material included? Has the author had this reviewed by an expert in the field or, in the case of a biography, by the person being profiled? Has he or she included a copy of that

---

A surefire way to bring sports alive for the reader is to include quotes from participants.

---

correspondence and response? How current is the information?" Rose says.

So how does a writer give readers the inside scoop? A surefire way to bring sports and activities alive for the reader is to include quotes from participants.

"There is no question that kids like to read interviews with real people," says Chorlian. "It could be somebody famous, such as a professional player, but average people have interesting or inspirational stories to tell, too. Decide what the angle of your interview is going to be and help the readers get to know and care about the person. Also, for a publication like *Cobblestone*, good visuals are essential, particularly for an interview. If there is a description of a great or famous play made by the interviewee, it would be great to have a photograph of that to help bring the event to life. In some ways, it's almost helpful to know what images exist before the text of an article or interview is considered."

Rose says *Highlights* publishes about five sports or activity articles annually and most are in the form of profiles of famous and not-so-famous athletes. *Highlights* recently profiled world champion skateboarder Andy Macdonald and an inspirational blind skier. But don't assume just because an athlete is a household name that *Highlights* will be interested in an article on them. The person being profiled must be someone *Highlights* would want to hold up to its readers as a spokesperson and role model. It's important that readers feel a connection to the individual.

"Kids want to feel that they've gotten to know that person, that they have been privileged to hear or even to be in conversation with him or her. They want to see beyond the public persona to the actual person. Kids often want to know something about how that person felt as a child or what influenced him or her," Rose says.

Backstage Pass

Rose encourages writers to give readers a "backstage pass" by including information about a person that readers won't find anywhere else. "Don't waste an opportunity by serving up just overused quotes and basic stats. Use it to tell them what the sports icon eats for breakfast, what she or he still goofs up at or has to work hard to overcome, how he or she laughs with family over inside jokes, how a close connection with mom and dad keep him or her grounded, or what his or her teammates tease him or her about, for example," she says.

Just as writers should consider alternative markets for their sports and activity articles, they should consider lesser known sports and activities.

Mary Dalheim, Editorial Director of children's magazines for the National Wildlife Federation (NWF), looks for articles that feature family-oriented activities. For example, they recently published a *Ranger Rick* article titled "Let's Go Tubing" that followed a dozen kids (and a couple adults) as they tubed down a river in Texas. The NWF also publishes *Animal Baby* and *Your Big Backyard*.

Sure to catch the eye of many children's magazine editors are articles about kids themselves as athletes or participants in games or activities. Kids love reading about what their peers are doing —the kinds of sports they play and what activities they participate in.

Dalheim encourages writers to include lots of kid quotes. The funnier the better. "Have fun with the story. It's okay to be a little silly," she says. Also of high interest to editors at the National Wildlife Federation are minority kids participating in a sport or activity.

Note that the NWF publications use freelance writers, but in a limited way. Dalheim explains, "For the last five years or so, we have rarely bought an unsolicited manuscript. We have been assigning stories to freelancers (mostly to members of a small stable that we cultivate), but only about six or seven a year. We'll assign fewer freelance stories this year— but hope to get back to our previous routine after 2010."

Energized

No matter what sport, game, or activity you choose to write about, it is important to get your facts straight and to convey the right feel. The more you know, the more natural the language in your article will be. Writing about an exciting game of chess is not the same as writing about hurling. Keep the audience in mind when you select terms to use. Your readers may not be familiar with your subject, so keep things simple when describing a sport and don't assume that the reader knows the lingo.

When an article's aim is to describe a sport, some editors suggest a sidebar glossary. Trying to define numerous technical or sport-specific terms within an article can bog it down. This is especially true when writing about sports and activities from other countries, and foreign words are likely. Pronunciation guides for unfamiliar words are a plus.

It is also important to choose your words carefully when writing about sports and other activities. The more action-packed words you use, the livelier your article will be. Instead of "The boy hit the ball," try "The lanky batter smashed the ball to deep right field."

Like all good writing, the opening line should pull readers in and have them wanting more. "If I had to choose some adjectives to describe sports, they would be *active, exciting,* and *suspenseful,* so a manuscript needs to reflect that. An opening sentence or paragraph that conveys energy and activity will draw the reader right in," says Chorlian.

"Many of the common mistakes we see are not specific to these topics alone," says Rose, in discussing the submissions she sees. "Relying on Internet or substandard sources for information, not having a profile reviewed for accuracy, neglecting quotes and anecdotes, not digging below the surface in research and therefore proffering only commonly known material, trying to cover too much ground instead of narrowing one's focus, writing in a lackluster tone, writing above or below the skill level of the target audience: These mistakes can be seen in many of the nonfiction articles we receive, as well as in some fiction stories that rely on factual information."

Good sports and activity writing makes the topic come alive to readers. If you keep it lively, fun, and full of rich details, readers will not only want to read your article, they may also want to try the sport or activity out for themselves. Let your own enthusiasm animate your work. If you are excited about writing the article, kids will be excited to read it.

How to Write How-to and How-Things-Work Articles

By Katherine Swarts

Teaching children the way to do or understand something you know well is an excellent way to break into a magazine market. Not only are how-to and how-things-work articles fairly easy to put together if you are well-versed in a subject, but your personal enthusiasm will fuel reader interest.

Follow the how-to's of a how-to: (1) Select an appealing and well-targeted topic. (2) Know the subject well. (3) Supplement personal knowledge with good research. (4) Write clearly and with a laser focus on the age of your reader. (5) Bring your own passions to the forefront with exciting writing.

Tell All

An important proviso in this category: Do not forget that readers know your topic less well than you do. It is easy to assume that everyone knows the basics, but young readers may not. They may not know relevant terms. They may find that a project does not work because you left out a fundamental step—one that is simple and obvious to you but not to them.

"It's always better to err on the side of telling more rather than less," says Susan Buckley, Editor of Carus Publishing's social studies magazine *AppleSeeds*, which targets readers in third and fourth grade.

"Make sure every step is clear and in order," says Nancy Gruver, founder and CEO of New Moon Girl Media, which publishes *New Moon Girls* magazine for ages 8 to 12. "A skilled writer knows how to read through her text as if she's someone with no knowledge of the subject. If you can do that, you'll quickly uncover flaws."

Never rely on editors to uncover errors or gaps in a how-to. If they cannot visualize from a quick read of your article how a project will work, your chances for a sale evaporate. Worse, if the omissions are not obvious, someone may actually publish the article—and be bombarded with complaints from readers who tried the project and found that it doesn't work.

Note that just because an adult might figure out instructions does not mean a 7- or 10-year-old can. Few children's magazines want projects that require much, if any, adult assistance. "We want readers to experience success" on their own, says Linda K. Rose, Assistant Editor of *Highlights for Children*.

In the Know

Age-appropriate, thorough writing will not sell unless editors think your basic idea will catch their readers' attention. "A writer needs to keep an ear to the ground to recognize topics of current interest," says Tim Grant, Co-Editor of *Green Teacher,* a quarterly on environmental issues for educators. "The next step is to find a publication that would welcome articles on those topics."

Even if you know your topic like a college professor, it is best not to rely on your brain alone. "A number of how-does-it-work websites offer excellent, simple information," says Buckley. But Web research alone is rarely adequate. Consult books and articles, and it is a good idea to have at least one flesh-and-blood resource.

"At *Highlights* we prefer research based on firsthand experience, consultation with experts, or primary sources. We also encourage authors to have their articles reviewed by an expert before submission and ask that they include a copy of the expert's response with their submission," says Rose. "I would suggest that an author avoid submitting a how-to about something he or she has not tried! Even if you're quoting an expert, it can really help to try the activity yourself. If you're writing a piece on how to improve

Sample How-to Articles

AppleSeeds:
- "How Do You Tell a Robot What to Do?"
- "How to Tell a Really Scary Story"
- "It's a Candy World After All,". making a miniature roller coaster from candy
- "How Green Can You Be?" conserving energy at home
- "Keep Your Own Food Journal"
- "Make a Greek Vase"
- "S'More Energy, Please," making a solar oven
- "Star in Your Own Myth," writing a mythic story
- "Want to Travel the World? Try a Penpal!"
- "A Rainbow of Dirt," making a *dirt rainbow* in a jar

Green Teacher:
- "Creating Earth Adventures," self-guided programs to connect children with nature
- "Field Backpacks," how to make and use them
- "From Seals to Snails: Helping Students Understand Eelgrass"
- "Harnessing the Power of Poetry for Environmental Education"
- "How to Teach About the Sun's Movement," from Western science and Native American science viewpoints
- "Making a Refuge for Slugs, Bugs, and Other Invertebrates"
- "Teaching Carbon Regulation in the High School Classroom"
- "Using Acting to Learn about Forms of Energy"

Highlights for Children:
- "'Changing-Up' Your Pitching"
- "It's Showtime!" puppetry
- "Laundry-Basket Theater," filling baskets with props for creative plays
- "Making a Lay-Up"
- "Sidewalk Games"
- "Try This! One Penny's Time to Shine," how to clean a penny thoroughly

your free throws in basketball, for example, try out the expert's advice. You may develop follow-up questions for your expert this way—questions that a reader would also have."

Rose adds that *Highlights* seeks sports pieces, for which "suggestions or tips from a well-known figure, someone worthy of imitation, are always welcome."

Conversely, people who know little about a topic can be invaluable for reviewing a how-to, to spot oversights or obfuscations. "We recommend that before writers send their submissions," says Grant, "they ask colleagues who have no familiarity with the topic to critique their articles. That review should illuminate what is missing or too briefly described."

Buckley agrees: "If possible, ask a child of the relevant age to review the article, explanations, and diagrams" before sending the article to a publisher.

With how-to articles, just reading often isn't test enough. "Have at least one person within your target audience try out the project," says Rose, "someone who isn't already familiar with it. Don't coach him through. That is oh-so-tempting when you're standing right there watching and you know just how he ought to be folding the paper or looping the *magic* string. But if the tester isn't doing it right, perhaps something in the instructions isn't clear enough. Or you may be surprised to find that something you assumed chil-

dren would know is not within their repertoire."

Hands-on is a good idea for you, too, especially if it is a task you have not done in precisely the way you are writing about. "Try the project out yourself!" says Gruver. "Learning a skill or topic helps capture its energy and excitement —so you can convey some of that into the ultimate story."

Diagrammatic

When it comes to how-to and how-it-works articles, even the best verbal description is improved with visuals. In this genre, literal *showing* is virtually mandatory, but it can be accomplished in a variety of ways. "I favor bulleted paragraphs with diagrams," says Buckley, "rather than what usually turn out to be very wordy paragraphs. In *AppleSeeds*, we often use a quasi-cartoon format for how-to articles."

Few magazine editors want writers to draw the pictures themselves. "*Apple-Seeds* assigns all of its own illustration, so we do not want author-illustrated articles," says Buckley. Grant says, "Many magazines, such as *Green Teacher*, commission an illustrator after accepting an article."

Better an unillustrated manuscript than one cheapened by second-rate sketches, but always check writers' guidelines for editorial preferences. Some procedures, hard to describe in words, make it difficult for an editor to judge the value of a manuscript without some visual assistance. "Supplying rough diagrams with the manuscript can show where you think the instructions need supplementation," says Rose.

If you think a rough diagram would be helpful to the editor, but do not know anyone who can draw even a brick wall in a form the average person would recognize, Grant has a suggestion: "There are lots of freelance illustrators who are just starting their careers and might be willing to donate their services in exchange for the exposure." If you do not know anyone who fits this description, art programs at local colleges and trade schools can probably recommend somebody. Again, though, do this only if you are certain it would be helpful for a specific article; often, it isn't worth the trouble.

Photographs are another possibility. While relatively few book publishers want amateur photographs, magazines are sometimes more accepting. At the same time, they must be good photos, and a publication such as *Highlights* wants to see the best.

"If the author submits photos of a quality we can use," says Rose, "we may purchase them along with the manuscript. When appropriate, submitting quality photos or identifying where such photos are available can make the difference between a piece that will work for us and a piece that would be too costly in the long run to be worth purchasing."

If you want to submit photographs of yourself (or, preferably a child in the appropriate age group) carrying out the steps of a project, make them clear, well-composed, in-depth images of the truly important steps. For some subjects, you can offer to obtain pictures from other sources. "There are countless ways to acquire images," says Gruver, "including stock photo houses, Web-based sources, and professional illustrators or photographers. How-to articles in *New Moon Girls* often focus on simple science experiments, so we often obtain images from

professional associations, or from the girl authors, who photograph themselves doing the experiment or activity."

Don't Forget

Your primary responsibility is still to the text, and following a magazine's editorial instructions is vital. A perennial pet peeve of editors is writers who ignore clearly stated policies. If a magazine says "personal experience articles only," it means personal experience articles only—and not one converted into or from what is essentially a how-to. Pay attention to all other specifications: Some magazines buy only from authors who live in a certain region, have experience in a certain industry, or are in another specific demographic group. *New Moon Girls*, for instance, buys most material from girls, and "accepts very few adult submissions," says Gruver, written by females only. Adult women may submit queries or manuscripts for the Herstory, Women's Work, and fiction sections.

Authors who read only the guidelines also can fall short. Guidelines rarely say whether a specific magazine prefers, for example, a bulleted list or traditional paragraph format for how-to articles. Review issues and articles closely. "A magazine's style will always determine format," says Gruver. "For *New Moon Girls,* most how-to articles are hybrids: paragraphs to explain the overall purpose, context, or theory, followed by lists of steps and materials. The most important first step is to read the magazine you're considering—to see the publication's style, flavor, and philosophy."

"Writers hoping to submit to *Highlights* are strongly encouraged to examine both our guidelines and several recent issues," says Rose, "to familiarize themselves with the kinds of material we publish. Writers may also find helpful insights about our philosophies in the Highlights.com About Us area, under In Detail/Guiding Practices."

Following instructions is important in any kind of writing (how much more so in a how-to). So is being accurate and interesting. And so are certain other points:

Get off to a good start. Notes Rose: "If your lead says 'This craft is really fun!' then it's already sounding forced." Instead, give some specific examples of why it's fun, without saying so.

Never talk down to your audience. Sounding like a finger-wagging parent is among the surest ways to send readers straight to the next article—and is a particularly insidious temptation when writing for those a generation younger than you. "Don't over- or underestimate the comprehension level of your audience," says Buckley. Be thorough, but never condescending.

Cut out all padding. "Don't include throwaway words that only detract from your manuscript," says Rose. "Keep your writing tight."

Edit, edit, edit. Don't expect your article to be finished in one draft, or even two. "Read and reread your copy to be sure that your explanations are clear," says Buckley.

Enjoy your work. Genuine enthusiasm on your part is a major aspect of good writing—and good reading for a young audience eager to learn hands-on.

Listings

How to Use the Listings

The pages that follow feature profiles of 616 magazines that publish articles and stories for, about, or of interest to children and young adults. Throughout the year, we stay on top of the latest happenings in children's magazines to bring you new and different publishing outlets. This year, our research yielded over 55 additional markets for your writing. They are easy to find; look for the listings with an exclamation point in the upper right corner.

A Variety of Freelance Opportunities

This year's new listings reflect the interests of today's magazine audience. You'll find magazines targeted to readers interested in nature, the environment, computers, mysteries, child care, careers, different cultures, family activities, and many other topics.

Along with many entertaining and educational magazines aimed at young readers, we list related publications such as national and regional magazines for parents and teachers. Hobby and special interest magazines generally thought of as adult fare but read by many teenagers are listed too.

In the market listings, the Freelance Potential section helps you judge each magazine's receptivity to freelance writers. This section offers information about the number of freelance submissions published each year.

Further opportunities for selling your writing appear in the Additional Listings section on page 254. This section profiles a range of magazines that publish a limited amount of material targeted to children, young adults, parents, or teachers. Other outlets for your writing can be found in the Selected Contests and Awards section, beginning on page 310.

Using Other Sections of the Directory

If you are planning to write for a specific publication, turn to the Magazine and Contest Index beginning on page 369 to locate the listing page. The Category Index, beginning on page 325, will guide you to magazines that publish in your areas of interest. This year, the Category Index also gives the age range of each publication's readership. To find the magazines most open to freelance submissions, turn to the Fifty+ Freelance index on page 324, which lists magazines that rely on freelance writers for over 50% of the material they publish.

Check the Market News, beginning on page 322, to find out what's newly listed, what's not listed and why, and to identify changes in the market that have occurred during the past year.

About the Listings

We revisited last year's listings and, through a series of mailed surveys and phone interviews, verified editors' names, mailing addresses, submissions and payment policies, and current editorial needs. All entries are accurate and up-to-date when we send this market directory to press. Magazine publishing is a fast-moving industry, though, and it is not unusual for facts to change before or shortly after this guide reaches your hands. Magazines close, are sold to new owners, or move; they hire new editors or change their editorial focus. Keep up to date by requesting sample copies and writers' guidelines.

Note that we do *not* list:

- Magazines that did not respond to our questionnaires or phone queries. Know that we make every effort to contact each editor before press date.

- Magazines that *never* accept freelance submissions or work with freelance writers.

To get a real sense of a magazine and its editorial slant, we recommend that you read several recent sample issues cover to cover. This is the best way to be certain a magazine is right for you.

Babybug

Cricket Magazine Group
70 East Lake Street, Suite 300
Chicago, IL 60601

Who to contact —— Assistant Editor: Jenny Gillespie

DESCRIPTION AND INTERESTS

Profiles the publication, its interests, and readers

Babybug is a "listening and looking magazine" in the form of a board book for babies and toddlers. It features simple stories, Mother Goose rhymes, short poems, and parent-child activities. Circ: 50,000.

Audience: 6 months–2 years
Frequency: 9 times each year
Website: www.babybugmagkids.com

FREELANCE POTENTIAL

100% written by nonstaff writers. Publishes 30–40 freelance submissions yearly; 50% by authors who are new to the magazine. Receives 2,400 unsolicited mss yearly.

Designates the amount and type of freelance submissions published each year; highlights the publication's receptivity to unpublished writers

SUBMISSIONS

Provides guidelines for submitting material; lists word lengths and types of material accepted from freelance writers

Send complete ms. Accepts hard copy and simultaneous submissions if identified. SASE. Responds in 6 months.

- Articles: 10 words. Features material that conveys simple concepts and ideas.
- Fiction: 4–6 short sentences. Simple stories.
- Artwork: By assignment only. Send sample tearsheets, photoprints, or photocopies to be kept on file.
- Other: Parent-child activities, to 8 lines. Rhyming and rhythmic poetry, to 8 lines. Action rhymes, 4–8 lines.

SAMPLE ISSUE

24 pages (no advertising): 2 stories; 5 poems; 1 activity. Sample copy, $5. Guidelines available at website.

- "Kim and Carrots." Recurring story describes a little girl's tea party with her mom and favorite stuffed toys.
- "Flying Lesson." Story tells of a father penguin who takes his fledgling to the playground to experience the thrill of "flying."
- "Zoom, Zoom, Zoom." Action rhyme about flying to the moon is accompanied by simple hand motions.

Analyzes a recent sample copy of the publication; briefly describes selected articles, stories, departments, etc.

RIGHTS AND PAYMENT

Lists types of rights acquired, payment rate, and number of copies provided to freelance writers

All or second North American serial rights. Written material, $25+. Artwork, $500 per spread, $250 per page. Pays on publication. Provides 6 contributor's copies.

❖ EDITOR'S COMMENTS

Please do not query first. We will consider manuscripts or art samples sent on speculation and accompanied by an SASE.

Offers advice from the editor about the publication's writing style, freelance needs, audience, etc.

Icon Key

 New Listing   E-publisher   Overseas Publisher

 Accepts agented submissions only   Not currently accepting submissions

Abilities

401-340 College Street
Toronto, Ontario M5T 3A9
Canada

Managing Editor: Jaclyn Law

DESCRIPTION AND INTERESTS
Abilities, Canada's lifestyle magazine for people with disabilities, features articles on a multitude of lifestyle topics. It seeks to provide information, inspiration, and opportunity to learn about Canadian resources that facilitate independence and self-empowerment. Circ: 20,000.

Audience: People with disabilities
Frequency: Quarterly
Website: www.abilities.ca

FREELANCE POTENTIAL
50% written by nonstaff writers. Publishes 25 freelance submissions yearly; 15% by unpublished writers, 25% by new authors. Receives 180 queries, 120 unsolicited mss yearly.

SUBMISSIONS
Prefers query with writing samples; will accept complete ms. Prefers email submissions to jaclyn@abilities.ca; will accept hard copy. No simultaneous submissions. SAE/IRC. Responds in 2–3 months.

- Articles: 800–2,000 words. Informational, self-help, and how-to articles; profiles; and interviews. Topics include health, technology, careers, relationships, parenting, travel, and social issues.
- Depts/columns: 500–1,500 words. News, media and product reviews, profiles, family life, parenting, education, sports, travel, health, relationships, employment, housing, sexuality, and humor.

SAMPLE ISSUE
54 pages (50% advertising): 2 articles; 13 depts/columns. Sample copy available at website. Guidelines available.

- "The Ultimate High: Sarah Doherty Reaches for the Sky." Article recounts the mountain climbing adventure of a young woman with one leg.
- Sample dept/column: "Parenting" profiles multi-sensory Snoezelen rooms.

RIGHTS AND PAYMENT
First-time serial and non-exclusive electronic rights. Written material, $25–$300. Kill fee, 50%. Pays 2 months after publication. Provides 2 contributor's copies.

⟶EDITOR'S COMMENTS
All articles must provide our readers with information as well as inspiration.

Ad Astra

1155 15th Street NW, Suite 500
Washington, DC 20005

Assignment Editor: Katherine Brick

DESCRIPTION AND INTERESTS
Its name means "to the stars," and that's just where this publication of the National Space Society takes its readership. Its editorial content chronicles the most important developments in space exploration and aerospace science. Circ: 20,000.

Audience: YA–Adult
Frequency: Quarterly
Website: www.nss.org

FREELANCE POTENTIAL
95% written by nonstaff writers. Publishes 50 freelance submissions yearly. Receives 65 queries and unsolicited mss yearly.

SUBMISSIONS
Query or send complete ms with resume. Accepts disk submissions and email to adastra@nss.org. SASE. Response time varies.

- Articles: Word lengths vary. Informational and factual articles; profiles; and interviews. Topics include science and technology related to space exploration; and issues related to the aerospace industry.
- Depts/columns: 600–750 words. Reviews and opinion pieces.
- Artwork: 8x10 color digital images at 300 dpi.

SAMPLE ISSUE
64 pages (14% advertising): 8 articles; 4 depts/columns. Sample copy, $11.25 with 9x12 SASE ($4 postage). Guidelines and editorial calendar available.

- "Space Solar Power." Article posits that gathering sunlight in space and sending it to Earth is an important long-term solution for meeting energy needs.
- Sample dept/column: "The Space Movement" examines how space settlement and space tourism make an ideal marriage.

RIGHTS AND PAYMENT
First North American serial rights. Written material, payment rates vary. Artwork, payment rates negotiable. Payment policy varies.

⟶EDITOR'S COMMENTS
If you have expertise in the field, we welcome your submissions. With the exception of "Spotlight" and "Community," all sections of the magazine are open to new writers.

ADDitude

39 West 37th Street, 15th Floor
New York, NY 10018

Editorial Assistant: Caitlin Ford

DESCRIPTION AND INTERESTS
Families touched by attention deficit disorder turn to *ADDitude* for medical, behavioral, and educational information. Its articles address issues faced by both children and adults with ADD. Circ: 40,000.
Audience: Parents/Adults
Frequency: 5 times each year
Website: www.additudemag.com

FREELANCE POTENTIAL
80% written by nonstaff writers. Publishes 15–20 freelance submissions yearly; 30% by unpublished writers, 30% by authors who are new to the magazine. Receives 96 queries each year.

SUBMISSIONS
Query. Prefers email queries to submissions@additudemag.com; will accept hard copy. SASE. Responds in 6–8 weeks.

- Articles: To 2,000 words. Informational articles and personal experience pieces. Topics include ADD and ADHD, education, medication, recreation, organization, parenting, and child development.
- Depts/columns: Word lengths vary. Profiles of students, teachers, and schools; first-person essays; healthy living; organization; product reviews; and ADD/ADHD news.

SAMPLE ISSUE
62 pages (33% advertising): 2 articles; 22 depts/columns. Sample copy, $6.95. Guidelines available at website.

- "Smart Foods for the ADD Brain." Article provides healthy snack ideas that satisfy the stomach and nourish the brain.
- "I Can't Stop Doing It." Article delves into the difference between ADD and obsessive-compulsive disorders.

RIGHTS AND PAYMENT
First rights. Written material, payment rates vary. Kill fee, $75. Pays on publication. Provides a 1-year subscription.

➡ EDITOR'S COMMENTS
While we do accept first-person articles by parents, teachers, and those who have experience with ADD and learning disabilities, most of our articles are written but journalists and mental health professionals.

Administrator

Scholastic Inc.
557 Broadway
New York, NY 10012

Editorial Director: Dana Truby

DESCRIPTION AND INTERESTS
This professional magazine targets school administrators. Its articles offer strategies and solutions for more effective leadership, and cover trends, legislation affecting school administration, management challenges, and professional development. Circ: 240,000.
Audience: School administrators, K–12
Frequency: 8 times each year
Website: www.scholastic.com/administrator

FREELANCE POTENTIAL
80% written by nonstaff writers. Publishes 25 freelance submissions yearly; 10% by unpublished writers.

SUBMISSIONS
Query with résumé. Accepts hard copy and email queries to dtruby@scholastic.com. SASE. Responds in 3–4 months.

- Articles: 1,200 words. Informational and how-to articles; profiles; and interviews. Topics include teacher recruitment and retention, salary negotiation, intervention programs, working with school boards, gifted education, school menus, grants and spending, crisis management, social issues, education trends and legislation, and technology.
- Depts/columns: Word lengths vary. News, opinions, technology, and book reviews.

SAMPLE ISSUE
64 pages: 4 articles; 7 depts/columns. Sample copy available at website. Guidelines available.

- "Wired Up: Tuned Out." Article examines how technology has changed not only how students learn, but how teachers must teach.
- "One Laptop, One Child." Article addresses the issues associated with having each student use their own laptop in class, and the issue of sharing the school's network.

RIGHTS AND PAYMENT
All rights. All material, payment rates vary. Pays on publication.

➡ EDITOR'S COMMENTS
We prefer to accept material from professional administrators, teachers, and other school professionals rather than general freelance writers. Our magazine provides for an exchange of professional ideas, experiences, and strategies. If you can add something to that discussion, please submit your article.

Adoptalk

North American Council on Adoptable Children
970 Raymond Street, Suite 106
St. Paul, MN 55114-1149

Editor: Diane Riggs

DESCRIPTION AND INTERESTS
Issues affecting adoption and foster care are covered in this newsletter, published by the NACAC. Circ: 3,700.

Audience: Adults
Frequency: Quarterly
Website: www.nacac.org

FREELANCE POTENTIAL
25% written by nonstaff writers. Publishes 8 freelance submissions yearly; 5% by unpublished writers, 10% by authors who are new to the magazine. Receives 6 queries, 2 unsolicited mss yearly.

SUBMISSIONS
Query or send complete ms with brief author biography. Accepts hard copy and email submissions to dianeriggs@nacac.org. SASE. Responds in 2–3 weeks.

- Articles: To 2,200 words. Informational articles; personal experience pieces; profiles; and interviews. Topics include adoptive and foster care, parenting, recruitment, adoption news, conference updates, and NACAC membership news and updates.
- Depts/columns: Word lengths vary. Book reviews and first-person essays.

SAMPLE ISSUE
16 pages (no advertising): 8 articles; 3 depts/columns. Sample copy, free with 9x12 SASE ($1.14 postage).

- "Creative Respite Programs Help Parents Take a Break." Article explains how respite programs can be a valuable tool for parents and children.
- "The Story of a Wonderful Girl." Article depicts the ups and downs of a relationship between an adoptive mother and daughter.
- Sample dept/column: "In the News" provides domestic and international information updates that affect adoption.

RIGHTS AND PAYMENT
Rights vary. No payment. Provides 5 contributor's copies.

☛EDITOR'S COMMENTS
While most of our articles are written by our staff, we do welcome submissions from those who have personal or professional child welfare experience and/or expertise.

Adoptive Families

39 West 37th Street, 15th Floor
New York, NY 10018

Editorial Assistant: Caitlin Ford

DESCRIPTION AND INTERESTS
Families before, during, and after the adoption process turn to this magazine that provides independent and authoritative information in a reader-friendly format. Circ: 40,000.

Audience: Adoptive parents
Frequency: 6 times each year
Website: www.adoptivefamilies.com

FREELANCE POTENTIAL
75% written by nonstaff writers. Publishes 100 freelance submissions yearly; 20% by unpublished writers, 50% by authors who are new to the magazine. Receives 500–600 queries and unsolicited mss yearly.

SUBMISSIONS
Query with clips for articles. Send complete ms for personal essays. Prefers email to submissions@adoptivefamilies.com (Microsoft Word attachments); will accept hard copy. SASE. Responds in 6–8 weeks.

- Articles: 500–1,800 words. Informational, self-help, and how-to articles; and personal experience pieces. Topics include preparing for adoption; health; education; birth families; and parenting tips.
- Depts/columns: To 1,200 words. Pre-adoption issues, birthparents, advice, opinion pieces, personal essays, single parenting, cultural diversity, child development, legal issues, and book reviews.

SAMPLE ISSUE
66 pages (40% advertising): 4 articles; 10 depts/columns. Sample copy, $6.95. Guidelines available at website.

- "Bringing Up Adoption at School." Article discusses the pros and cons of speaking with your child's teacher about their adoption.
- "A Gowing Awareness." Article examines the complex emotions preteens have as they begin to understand adoption.

RIGHTS AND PAYMENT
All rights. Written material, payment rates vary. Payment policy varies. Provides 2 copies.

☛EDITOR'S COMMENTS
We are looking for articles that address the preteen and teen years. We are open to working with new writers who are familiar with our style and content.

Alateen Talk

Al-Anon Family Group Headquarters
1600 Corporate Landing Parkway
Virginia Beach, VA 23454-5617

Associate Editor: Mary Lou Mahlman

DESCRIPTION AND INTERESTS
This newsletter is written specifically for Alateen members—children and teens whose lives are affected by someone else's alcoholism. Each issue includes first-person pieces from young people that enable them to share experiences, discuss difficulties, and find strength, hope, and encouragement from other members. Circ: 4,000.
Audience: 6–18 years
Frequency: Quarterly
Website: www.al-anon.alateen.org

FREELANCE POTENTIAL
90% written by nonstaff writers. Publishes 85–120 freelance submissions yearly; 80% by unpublished writers, 75% by authors who are new to the magazine. Receives 100–150 unsolicited mss yearly.

SUBMISSIONS
Accepts submissions from Alateen members only. Send complete ms. Accepts hard copy. SASE. Responds to mss in 2 weeks.

- Articles: Word lengths vary. Self-help and personal experience pieces. Topics include alcoholism and its effects on relationships; social issues; and family life.
- Depts/columns: Staff written.
- Artwork: B/W line art.
- Other: Poetry.

SAMPLE ISSUE
8 pages (no advertising): 2 articles; 4 letters. Sample copy, free with 9x12 SASE ($.87 postage). Guidelines available to Alateen members only.

- "Why We Keep Coming Back." Article shares members' experiences on how Alateen has changed their lives for the better.
- "Sponsor Corner." Article profiles an Alateen Group Sponsor in the United Kingdom who tells why she became involved in the program.

RIGHTS AND PAYMENT
All rights. No payment.

➻EDITOR'S COMMENTS
The purpose of our newsletter is to allow young people to learn effective ways to cope with their problems, to find strength from others, and to help them understand the principles of our program. Note that we accept submissions from Alateen members only.

Alfred Hitchcock Mystery Magazine

475 Park Avenue South
New York, NY 10016

Editor: Linda Landrigan

DESCRIPTION AND INTERESTS
This digest-sized magazine is all about mystery and suspense in its truest sense. It accepts short stories of any type in the mystery genre. Though written for adults, many of its stories appeal to young adults. Circ: 75,000.
Audience: Adults
Frequency: 10 times each year
Website: www.themysteryplace.com

FREELANCE POTENTIAL
97% written by nonstaff writers. Publishes 90–100 freelance submissions yearly; 5% by unpublished writers, 5–10% by authors who are new to the magazine. Receives 2,400 unsolicited mss yearly.

SUBMISSIONS
Send complete ms. Accepts hard copy. No simultaneous submissions. SASE. Responds in 3–5 months.

- Fiction: To 12,000 words. Genres include classic crime mysteries, detective stories, suspense, private investigator tales, courtroom drama, and espionage.
- Depts/columns: Word lengths vary. Reviews, puzzles, and profiles of bookstores.

SAMPLE ISSUE
112 pages (2% advertising): 6 stories; 5 depts/columns. Sample copy, $5. Guidelines available at website.

- "Oil Slick." Story tells of an oft-repeated oil con gone terribly wrong.
- "Blind Eye." Story features two police detectives dealing with their own problems as they try to solve the case of a missing man, a cheating wife, and a blood-stained floor.
- Sample dept/column: "Booked & Printed" offers a review of *The Green Revolution*, a book that blends humor and mystery around a very bad college football season.

RIGHTS AND PAYMENT
First serial, anthology, and foreign rights. Written material, payment rates vary. Pays on acceptance. Provides 2 contributor's copies.

➻EDITOR'S COMMENTS
Finding new authors is a great pleasure for us, so rest assured all submissions are read carefully. All stories must have a mystery element. We sometimes accept ghost stories, but they must involve a crime.

American Baby

375 Lexington Avenue, 10th Floor
New York, NY 10017

Editorial Assistant: Jessica Wohlgemuth

DESCRIPTION AND INTERESTS
Newborns may not come with a manual, but if they did, it might look something like *American Baby*. This popular parenting magazine covers everything from pregnancy to childbirth to toddlerhood. Circ: 2.1 million.

Audience: Parents
Frequency: Monthly
Website: www.americanbaby.com

FREELANCE POTENTIAL
55% written by nonstaff writers. Publishes 24 freelance submissions yearly; 20% by unpublished writers. Receives 996 queries and unsolicited mss yearly.

SUBMISSIONS
Query with clips and writing samples; or send complete ms. Accepts hard copy and simultaneous submissions if identified. SASE. Responds in 2 months.

- Articles: 1,000–2,000 words. Informational and how-to articles; profiles; interviews; humor; and personal experience pieces. Topics include pregnancy, childbirth, parenting, child care and development, health, fitness, nutrition, religion, and family travel.
- Depts/columns: 1,000 words. Health briefs, fitness tips, new products, and fashion.
- Other: Submit seasonal material 3 months in advance.

SAMPLE ISSUE
80 pages (50% advertising): 5 articles; 13 depts/columns. Sample copy available at newsstands. Guidelines available.

- "Required Reading." Article provides advice to help new mothers get through the first crazy days after giving birth.
- Sample dept/column: "10 Things to Know About . . ." gives an overview of when, why, and how babies start walking.

RIGHTS AND PAYMENT
First serial rights. Articles, to $2,000. Depts/columns, to $1,000. Pays on acceptance. Provides 5 contributor's copies.

⏩EDITOR'S COMMENTS
While we prefer to work with established writers, we do use a small number of unpublished writers each year. We are especially interested in articles written for those having their first child.

American Careers

6701 West 64th Street
Overland Park, KS 66202

Editor: Mary Pitchford

DESCRIPTION AND INTERESTS
This annual career-development magazine is published in high school and middle school editions each fall. Offering articles related to a variety of career and industry clusters, it is distributed to students directly through the school market. Circ: 400,000.

Audience: 12–18 years
Frequency: Annually
Website: www.carcom.com

FREELANCE POTENTIAL
10% written by nonstaff writers. Publishes 2 freelance submissions yearly; 50–100% by authors who are new to the magazine. Receives 100+ queries yearly.

SUBMISSIONS
Query with résumé and clips. Accepts hard copy. Responds in 2 months.

- Articles: 300–750 words. Informational and how-to articles; profiles; and personal experience pieces. Topics include types of careers, career planning, and education.
- Artwork: Color prints; high-resolution digital images.
- Other: Quizzes and self-assessments.

SAMPLE ISSUE
64 pages (no advertising): 21 articles; 3 self-assessments. Sample copy, $4 with 9x12 SASE (5 first-class stamps). Guidelines available.

- "Ensuring a Safe Environment." Article profiles an environmental engineer who specializes in hazardous materials abatement.
- "Orchestrating Government." Article describes the role of Delaware's Director of the Office of Management and Budget.
- "Does a Health Career Await You?" Article spotlights the respective duties of a dental hygienist and a nurse.

RIGHTS AND PAYMENT
All rights. All material, payment rates vary. Pays on acceptance. Provides 2 contributor's copies.

⏩EDITOR'S COMMENTS
We make work-for-hire assignments, yet often stories are assigned based on ideas proposed by writers. Most assignments are for short career profiles; other topics may require additional space for impact and clarity. Stories should exhibit a balanced national focus. Use the *Associated Press Stylebook* as a guide.

American Cheerleader

110 William Street, 23rd Floor
New York, NY 10038

Editor-in-Chief: Marisa Walker

DESCRIPTION AND INTERESTS
This magazine is full of "cheer." With a bright layout and upbeat text, it profiles cheerleaders and squads, and keeps readers abreast of cheerleading news and trends. Circ: 150,000.

Audience: 13–18 years
Frequency: 6 times each year
Website: www.americancheerleader.com

FREELANCE POTENTIAL
40% written by nonstaff writers. Publishes 30 freelance submissions yearly; 20% by unpublished writers, 10% by authors who are new to the magazine. Receives hundreds of queries, few unsolicited mss yearly.

SUBMISSIONS
Query with clips; or send complete ms. Prefers email to mwalker@americancheerleader.com; will accept hard copy. SASE. Responds in 3 months.

- Articles: To 1,000 words. Informational and how-to articles; profiles; interviews; personal experience pieces; and photo-essays. Topics include cheerleading, cheerleaders and teams, workouts, competitions, scholarships, college, careers, and popular culture.
- Depts/columns: Word lengths vary. Safety issues, health, nutrition, beauty, fashion, fundraising, and new product information.
- Artwork: High-resolution digital images; 35mm color slides.

SAMPLE ISSUE
94 pages (40% advertising): 6 articles; 16 depts/columns. Sample copy, $3.99 with 9x12 SASE ($1.70 postage). Editorial calendar available.

- "Daring Dakota." Article features a Q&A interview with actress Dakota Fanning about becoming a cheerleader at her high school.
- "Camp Idols." Article describes the role of a cheerleading-camp staffer.
- Sample dept/column: "Squad of the Month" profiles the Brother Martin High School Crusaders from New Orleans.

RIGHTS AND PAYMENT
All rights. All material, payment rates vary. Pays on publication. Provides 1 contributor's copy.

➥EDITOR'S COMMENTS
Our magazine is considered the unofficial bible for the nearly 4 million cheerleaders in the U.S.

American Educator

555 New Jersey Avenue NW
Washington, DC 20001

Assistant Editor: Jennifer Dubin

DESCRIPTION AND INTERESTS
Educators and administrators read this professional magazine to stay abreast of current research, issues, trends, and policies regarding education. It also features thought-provoking opinions and essays exploring current issues in education. It is published by the American Federation of Teachers. Circ: 900,000.

Audience: Teachers, professors, policymakers
Frequency: Quarterly
Website: www.aft.org/pubs-reports/
  american-educator/index.htm

FREELANCE POTENTIAL
25% written by nonstaff writers. Publishes 5–6 freelance submissions yearly; 10% by unpublished writers, 20% by authors who are new to the magazine. Receives 360 queries each year.

SUBMISSIONS
Query with contact information. Accepts hard copy and email submissions to amered@aft.org. SASE. Responds in 2 months.

- Articles: 1,500–3,000 words. Informational articles; profiles; and opinion pieces. Topics include trends in education, politics, education law, professional ethics, social and labor issues, and international affairs.

SAMPLE ISSUE
44 pages (9% advertising): 8 articles; 1 dept/column. Guidelines available.

- "There's a Hole in State Standards: And New Teachers Like Me Are Falling Through." Opinion piece argues that new teachers get frustrated when states offer no clear, grade-by-grade standards.
- "Common Ground." Article posits that teachers would be able to better prepare students for tests if the standards were written with more specifics.

RIGHTS AND PAYMENT
All rights. Written material, payment rates vary. Pays on publication. Provides 10 contributor's copies.

➥EDITOR'S COMMENTS
Freelancers should note that while we encourage educators and administrators to write and share their knowledge and opinions, we do not publish many personal narratives of classroom experience. Those that are chosen are short, concise, and timely.

American Girl

American Girl Publishing
8400 Fairway Place
Middleton, WI 53562

Editorial Assistant

DESCRIPTION AND INTERESTS
American Girl is about self-confidence, curiosity, and big dreams. Its pages are filled with articles and activities that help girls grow up in a wholesome way while encouraging fun and enchanting play. Circ: 700,000.

Audience: 8–12 years
Frequency: 6 times each year
Website: www.americangirl.com

FREELANCE POTENTIAL
4% written by nonstaff writers. Publishes 5 freelance submissions yearly; 2% by unpublished writers, 2% by authors who are new to the magazine. Receives 780 queries yearly.

SUBMISSIONS
Query. Accepts hard copy and simultaneous submissions if identified. SASE. Responds in 4 months.

- Articles: 500–1,000 words. Informational articles; profiles; and interviews. Topics include history, nature, food, hobbies, crafts, sports, and culture.
- Depts/columns: 175 words. Profiles, how-to pieces, and craft ideas.

SAMPLE ISSUE
72 pages (no advertising): 4 articles; 1 story; 8 depts/columns. Sample copy, $4.50 at newsstands. Guidelines available.

- "Girls at Work." Article profiles five girls who have interesting jobs, including a theatre usher, junior zookeeper, and bag designer.
- "Island Party." Article describes step-by-step instructions for planning the perfect island party at home.
- Sample dept/column: "Cooking" offers ideas for homemade ice cream sandwiches.

RIGHTS AND PAYMENT
Rights vary. All material purchased under work-for-hire agreement. Written material, payment rates vary. Pays on acceptance. Provides 3 contributor's copies.

➤EDITOR'S COMMENTS
We celebrate girls and all that they can be. We're looking for material that affirms self-esteem, celebrates achievement, and fosters creativity. Unsolicited fiction submissions are not accepted at this time.

American Libraries

American Library Association
50 East Huron Street
Chicago, IL 60611

Acquisitions Editor: Pamela Goodes

DESCRIPTION AND INTERESTS
Written for and by librarians, this publication offers comprehensive coverage of the issues, concerns, and developments of libraries today. It also features news on the American Library Association. Circ: 56,000.

Audience: Librarians
Frequency: 10 times each year
Website: www.ala.org/alonline

FREELANCE POTENTIAL
60% written by nonstaff writers. Publishes 10 freelance submissions yearly; 50% by authors who are new to the magazine. Receives 492 unsolicited mss yearly.

SUBMISSIONS
Send complete ms. Accepts hard copy and email submissions to americanlibraries@ ala.org. No simultaneous submissions. SASE. Responds in 8–10 weeks.

- Articles: 600–2,000 words. Informational articles; profiles; interviews; and personal experience pieces. Topics include modern libraries, library and ALA history, technology, leadership, advocacy, funding, and privacy.
- Depts/columns: Word lengths vary. News, opinions, profiles, media reviews, information technology, ALA events, career leads, and professional development.

SAMPLE ISSUE
72 pages (27% advertising): 5 articles; 15 depts/columns. Sample copy, $6. Writers' guidelines available.

- "Building Science 101." Article suggests several steps to take in order to save money, energy, and resources.
- Sample dept/column: "Internet Librarian" discusses a recent study that outlines the way students use library technology.

RIGHTS AND PAYMENT
First North American serial rights. Written material, $50–$400. Pays on acceptance. Provides 1+ contributor's copies.

➤EDITOR'S COMMENTS
We will review your article only if you are a professional librarian. We look for informative, experienced-based articles written in an informal and readable style. All statements must be backed by responsible research and interviews.

American School & University

9800 Metcalf Avenue
Overland Park, KS 66212

Executive Editor: Susan Lustig

DESCRIPTION AND INTERESTS
This magazine serves those responsible for
the planning, design, construction, retrofit,
operations, maintenance, and management
of educational facilities. Circ: 65,000.
Audience: School facilities managers
Frequency: Monthly
Website: www.asumag.com

FREELANCE POTENTIAL
35% written by nonstaff writers. Publishes 40
freelance submissions yearly; 30% by authors
who are new to the magazine. Receives 180
queries yearly.

SUBMISSIONS
Query with outline. Prefers email queries to
slustig@asumag.com; will accept hard copy.
SASE. Responds in 2 weeks.

- Articles: 1,200 words. Informational and
  how-to articles. Topics Include educational
  facilities management, maintenance, security,
  planning, design, construction, operations,
  and furnishings.
- Depts/columns: 250–350 words. Opinions,
  environmental practices, technology, planning issues, and new products.

SAMPLE ISSUE
58 pages (55% advertising): 5 articles; 7
depts/columns. Sample copy, $10. Guidelines
and editorial calendar available.

- "Mind Shifts." Article posits that schools and
  universities need to do a better job of identifying and providing treatment for students
  with mental health problems.
- "Simple Strategies." Article tells how an
  investment in green construction practices
  can reap rewards.
- Sample dept/column: "Know-How" stresses
  the importance of safety considerations in
  the planning of playgrounds.

RIGHTS AND PAYMENT
All rights. Written material, payment rates vary.
Payment policy varies. Provides 2 copies.

⟶EDITOR'S COMMENTS
Please be aware of our audience. Our readers
are not teachers or students; we do not talk
about school curricula. Feature articles should
inform the reader about a process, trend, or
general category of product or service of interest to educational facilities administrators.

American Secondary Education

Ashland University
Dwight Schar COE, Room 231
401 College Avenue
Ashland, OH 44805

Editorial Assistant: Becky Hannan

DESCRIPTION AND INTERESTS
This journal features research-based articles
on current theories and practices in secondary
education. Read by teachers, administrators,
and researchers, it also includes book reviews.
Circ: 450.
Audience: Secondary school educators
Frequency: 3 times each year
Website: www3.ashland.edu/ase

FREELANCE POTENTIAL
99% written by nonstaff writers. Publishes 20
freelance submissions yearly; 75% by authors
who are new to the magazine. Receives 40–50
unsolicited mss yearly.

SUBMISSIONS
Send complete ms with 100-word abstract and
credentials. Prefers email to rhannan@
ashland.edu; will accept hard copy. No simultaneous submissions. SASE. Response time
varies.

- Articles: 10–25 double-spaced ms pages.
  Informational articles. Topics include secondary and middle school education
  research and practice.
- Depts/columns: Word lengths vary. Book
  reviews.

SAMPLE ISSUE
96 pages (no advertising): 6 articles; 1 book
review. Sample copy, free. Guidelines available
in each issue.

- "Excluding Ethical Issues from U.S. History
  Textbooks: 911 and the War on Terror." Article
  discusses the moral and ethical issues that are
  omitted from American history textbooks, and
  their implications for learning.
- "New Roles for the Principal of the Future."
  Article describes emerging trends that school
  principals should follow to meet the challenges of the future.
- Sample dept/column: "Book Review" takes a
  look at a book about a school reform model
  meant to prepare all students for success
  after graduation.

RIGHTS AND PAYMENT
All rights. No payment. Provides 1 copy.

⟶EDITOR'S COMMENTS
We want to hear about innovative school and
district programs, effective classroom practices, and issues affecting adolescents.

American String Teacher

4153 Chain Bridge Road
Fairfax, VA 22030

Editor: Mary Jane Dye

DESCRIPTION AND INTERESTS
This magazine is written for and by members of the American String Teacher Association, providing information and tips to further professional growth. It is read by elementary, secondary, and collegiate string educators, as well as students, conductors, and performers. Circ: 11,500.

Audience: String instrument teachers
Frequency: Quarterly
Website: www.astaweb.com

FREELANCE POTENTIAL
100% written by nonstaff writers. Publishes 30 freelance submissions yearly; 5% by unpublished writers, 50% by authors who are new to the magazine. Receives 50 queries yearly.

SUBMISSIONS
Prefers query; will accept 5 copies of complete ms. Prefers email to maryjane@astaweb.com; will accept hard copy. No simultaneous submissions. SASE. Responds in 3 months.

- Articles: 1,000–3,000 words. Informational and factual articles; profiles; and association news. Topics include teaching, methodology, techniques, competitions, and auditions.
- Depts/columns: Word lengths vary. Teaching tips, opinion pieces, and industry news.

SAMPLE ISSUE
80 pages (45% advertising): 5 articles; 9 depts/columns. Sample copy, free with 9x12 SASE ($3.25 postage). Guidelines available at website.

- "A Totally New Concept: Big Band Music for Strings?" Article provides information on how orchestral educators can meet certain instructional standards.
- "Is That in Tune, Mr. Mozart?" Article discusses pitch and tuning problems that arise and how to overcome them.
- Sample dept/column: "Showcase" includes updates on new strings and other products.

RIGHTS AND PAYMENT
All rights. No payment. Provides 5 copies.

☛EDITOR'S COMMENTS
Articles should be precise, accurate, and thoroughly documented, with a well-defined purpose. We especially like to see material that offers new information or insight and that challenges a reader's thinking.

Analog Science Fiction and Fact

Dell Magazine Fiction Group
475 Park Avenue South
New York, NY 10016

Editor: Stanley Schmidt

DESCRIPTION AND INTERESTS
This digest-sized magazine publishes science fiction tales in which future science or technology is integral to the plot. In addition, it features articles on science, research, and the technology of the present and near future. Circ: 40,000.

Audience: YA–Adult
Frequency: 10 times each year
Website: www.analogsf.com

FREELANCE POTENTIAL
100% written by nonstaff writers. Publishes 80–90 freelance submissions yearly; 10% by unpublished writers, 10% by authors who are new to the magazine. Receives 6,000 unsolicited mss yearly.

SUBMISSIONS
Query for serials. Send complete ms for shorter works. Accepts hard copy. SASE. Responds in 6 weeks.

- Articles: To 6,000 words. Informational articles. Topics include science and technology.
- Fiction: Serials, 40,000–80,000 words. Novellas and novelettes, 10,000–20,000 words. Short stories, 2,000–7,000 words. Physical, sociological, psychological, and technological science fiction.
- Depts/columns: Staff written.

SAMPLE ISSUE
240 pages (7% advertising): 2 articles; 1 serial; 1 novella; 3 novelettes; 5 short stories; 6 depts/columns. Sample copy, $5 with 9x12 SASE. Guidelines available at website.

- "A Plethora of Truth." Story finds two competing televangelists wrangling for public support and hawking their wares, including a telephone that reaches God, and vitamin supplements that wash away past sins.
- "The Challenge of the Anthropic Universe." Article makes the case for intelligent design in physics.

RIGHTS AND PAYMENT
First North American serial and non-exclusive rights. Serials, $.04 per word; other written material, $.05–$.08 per word. Pays on acceptance. Provides 2 contributor's copies.

☛EDITOR'S COMMENTS
We have no strict requirements for stories, as science fiction is such a broad field.

AppleSeeds

Cobblestone Publishing Company
30 Grove Street
Peterborough, NH 03458

Editor: Susan Buckley

DESCRIPTION AND INTERESTS
This multidisciplinary social studies magazine for children in grades three and four features historically accurate and interesting stories, articles, and activities. Each issue is centered around a different theme. Circ: 10,000.
Audience: 8–10 years
Frequency: 9 times each year
Website: www.cobblestonepub.com

FREELANCE POTENTIAL
80% written by nonstaff writers. Publishes 90–100 freelance submissions yearly; 33% by authors who are new to the magazine. Receives 600+ queries yearly.

SUBMISSIONS
Query with clips, source list, and proposed word count. Accepts email queries to susanbuckleynyc@gmail.com (no attachments). Responds in 2–3 months only if interested.

- Articles: 150–600 words. Informational and how-to articles; profiles; and interviews. Topics include history, biography, biology, geology, technology, geography, literature, and the environment.
- Depts/columns: "Reading Corner," 300–600 words. "By the Numbers," "Your Turn," and "Experts in Action," 150 words. "From the Source," 150–300 words.
- Artwork: B/W and color prints.
- Other: Theme-related games and activities.

SAMPLE ISSUE
34 pages (no advertising): 9 articles; 5 depts/columns. Sample copy available. Guidelines and theme list available at website.

- "Civil War President." Article describes Abraham Lincoln's challenges during the early days of his presidency.
- "The Lincoln Memorial." Article discusses the importance of the Lincoln Memorial and why it was built.

RIGHTS AND PAYMENT
All rights. Written material, $50–$200. Artwork, $15–$100. Pays on publication. Provides 2 contributor's copies.

➥EDITOR'S COMMENTS
We look for articles that will stimulate the curiosity of the child. Please be sure your article idea closely relates to the theme of the issue.

Arizona Parenting

2535 West Plata Avenue
Mesa, AZ 85202

Editor: Lyn Wolford

DESCRIPTION AND INTERESTS
Arizona Parenting serves families throughout the state with authoritative articles on parenting, family life, education, and child development. It also presents regional information on events, camps, family recreation, and schools. Circ: 70,000.
Audience: Parents
Frequency: Monthly
Website: www.azparenting.com

FREELANCE POTENTIAL
50% written by nonstaff writers. Publishes 20 freelance submissions yearly; 5% by unpublished writers, 25% by new authors. Receives 520 queries, 300 unsolicited mss yearly.

SUBMISSIONS
Query or send complete ms. Prefers email to lyn.wolford@azparenting.com; will accept hard copy. SASE. Responds in 2–3 months.

- Articles: 850–2,400 words. Informational articles; profiles; interviews; and humorous pieces. Topics include parenting and family issues, education, personal finances, health, fitness, recreation, travel, computers, electronics, and sports.
- Depts/columns: 400–850 words. Child development, cooking and nutrition, new product reviews, and short news items.
- Artwork: B/W prints and transparencies.

SAMPLE ISSUE
66 pages (50% advertising): 6 articles; 5 depts/columns. Sample copy and editorial calendar, free with 9x12 SASE ($2 postage). Guidelines available at website.

- "Money Matters." Article provides tips for teaching kids how to save money and budget effectively.
- Sample dept/column: "Parents Ask" offers answers to parents' questions regarding discipline issues.

RIGHTS AND PAYMENT
First North American serial and electronic rights. All material, payment rates vary. Pays on publication. Provides 2–3 author's copies.

➥EDITOR'S COMMENTS
Please write for Arizona parents. Articles need to address timely, regionally relevant issues. Most articles also require localized sidebars as well.

Art Education

University of Cincinnati
Department of Art Education
Aronoff 6431C, P.O. Box 210016
Cincinnati, OH 45221-0016

Editor: Dr. Flavia Bastos

DESCRIPTION AND INTERESTS
Published by the National Art Education Association, this professional journal deals with issues of interest to art educators of all levels. Circ: 20,000.
Audience: Art educators
Frequency: 6 times each year
Website: www.arteducators.org/
   publications.html

FREELANCE POTENTIAL
88% written by nonstaff writers. Publishes 36 freelance submissions yearly; 40% by unpublished writers, 40% by authors who are new to the magazine. Receives 120 unsolicited mss each year.

SUBMISSIONS
Send 3 copies of complete ms. Accepts hard copy with disk and simultaneous submissions if identified. SASE. Responds in 8–10 weeks.

- Articles: To 3,000 words. Research-based informational articles; profiles; interviews; and personal experience pieces. Topics include the visual arts, curriculum planning, art history, and art criticism.
- Depts/columns: To 2,750 words. "Instructional Resources" features lesson plan ideas.
- Artwork: 8x10 or 5x7 B/W prints or slides; digital images.

SAMPLE ISSUE
54 pages (7% advertising): 6 articles; 1 dept/column. Sample copy, $3 with 9x12 SASE ($1.85 postage). Writers' guidelines available at website.

- "Radical Puppets and the Language of Art." Article discusses the use of "radical puppets" as a means to generate dialogue about social and political issues through art.
- Sample dept/column: "Instructional Resources" uses the history of a female pharaoh in ancient Egypt as a way to study art, sculpture, and the power of an image.

RIGHTS AND PAYMENT
All rights. No payment. Provides 2 copies.

➟ EDITOR'S COMMENTS
Each submission is first read by an editor, then by members of our review panel for further consideration. Please be patient as your work goes through this review process.

Arts & Activities

12345 World Trade Drive
San Diego, CA 92128

Editor: Maryellen Bridge

DESCRIPTION AND INTERESTS
Art teachers of all grade levels turn to this magazine for its fresh ideas and successful teaching strategies used in art classrooms. Most of its freelance articles are written by art educators. Circ: 20,000.
Audience: Art educators, grades K–12
Frequency: 10 times each year
Website: www.artsandactivities.com

FREELANCE POTENTIAL
95% written by nonstaff writers. Publishes 100 freelance submissions yearly; 50% by unpublished writers, 50% by authors who are new to the magazine. Receives 240 unsolicited mss each year.

SUBMISSIONS
Send complete ms. Accepts disk submissions with hard copy. Availability of artwork improves chance of acceptance. No simultaneous submissions. SASE. Responds in 4–8 months.

- Articles: Word lengths vary. Informational, how-to, and practical application articles; and personal experience pieces. Topics include art education, program development, collage, printmaking, art appreciation, and composition.
- Depts/columns: Word lengths vary. New product information, news items, and media reviews.
- Artwork: High-resolution digital images.
- Other: Lesson plans for classroom projects.

SAMPLE ISSUE
60 pages (29% advertising): 15 articles; 3 depts/columns. Sample copy, $3 with 9x12 SASE ($2 postage). Writers' guidelines and theme list available.

- "Jurassic Park Insects." Article discusses a lesson in which students design and create a prehistoric insect.
- Sample dept/column: "Shop Talk" reviews new art products and books.

RIGHTS AND PAYMENT
First North American serial rights. All material, payment rates vary. Pays on publication. Provides 2 contributor's copies.

➟ EDITOR'S COMMENTS
We prefer articles written in a narrative style as opposed to step-by-step. Illustrations must accompany all submissions.

Asimov's Science Fiction

Dell Magazine Group
267 Broadway, 4th Floor
New York, NY 10007

Editor: Sheila Williams

DESCRIPTION AND INTERESTS
Short stories and novelettes in the genres of science fiction and fantasy are published in this award-winning and well-known journal. Poetry and book reviews are also featured in each issue. Circ: 60,000.
Audience: YA–Adult
Frequency: 10 times each year
Website: www.asimovs.com

FREELANCE POTENTIAL
97% written by nonstaff writers. Publishes 85 freelance submissions yearly; 10% by unpublished writers, 30% by authors who are new to the magazine. Receives 8,400 unsolicited mss each year.

SUBMISSIONS
Send complete ms. Accepts hard copy. No simultaneous submissions. SASE. Responds in 6–8 weeks.

- Fiction: To 20,000 words. Genres include science fiction and "borderline" fantasy.
- Depts/columns: Word lengths vary. Book and website reviews.
- Other: Poetry, to 40 lines.

SAMPLE ISSUE
112 pages (10% advertising): 2 novelettes; 5 stories; 5 poems; 6 depts/columns. Sample copy, $5 with 9x12 SASE ($.77 postage). Guidelines available.

- "Blue." Short story tells of two laboratory students creating less-than-appetizing experiments with leftover food.
- "California Burning." Novelette tells of a man looking to uncover secrets about his deceased father's life when two strange men come to visit.
- Sample dept/column: "On the Net" examines several writing awards.

RIGHTS AND PAYMENT
First worldwide English-language serial rights. Fiction, $.06–$.08 per word. Poetry, $1 per line. Depts/columns, payment rates vary. Pays on acceptance. Provides 2 author's copies.

✎ EDITOR'S COMMENTS
Many of our contributors are well known in the science fiction field; however, we are always happy to read submissions from new writers. Borderline fantasy stories are fine, but no sword and sorcery or sex and violence.

ASK

Carus Publishing
70 East Lake Street, Suite 300
Chicago, IL 60601

Submissions Editor

DESCRIPTION AND INTERESTS
ASK is written for kids who want to know how the world works and how discoveries are made. It challenges children to explore new ideas, and answers such questions as: How did dogs become domesticated? How are robots designed? and Why do we sleep? Circ: 42,000.
Audience: 7–10 years
Frequency: 9 times each year
Website: www.cricketmag.com

FREELANCE POTENTIAL
80% written by nonstaff writers.

SUBMISSIONS
Send résumé and clips. All material is commissioned from experienced authors.

- Articles: To 1,500 words. Informational articles; interviews; and photo-essays. Topics include science, nature, technology, math, history, and the arts.
- Depts/columns: Word lengths vary. Science news and Q&As.
- Other: Activities, cartoons, and contests.

SAMPLE ISSUE
34 pages (no advertising): 4 articles; 2 depts/columns; 1 activity; 2 cartoons; 1 contest. Sample copy available at website.

- "Dino-mite." Article shares amazing, unusual, and unexpected dinosaur discoveries.
- "To Fly Without Wings." Article explains the history of horses and their relationship with humans; a sidebar describes the horse's physical evolution.
- Sample dept/column: "Scoops" describes a recent study of leaf-cutter ants.

RIGHTS AND PAYMENT
Rights vary. Written material, payment rates vary. Payment policy varies.

✎ EDITOR'S COMMENTS
ASK goes beyond simple facts: It's funny, even poetic. Its articles are dramatic; its pictures are beautiful. It's written by award-winning children's authors and filled with cartoon characters, activities, and contests. If you are a published author who can write engaging nonfiction for children, we will be happy to review your past work. Please note that we do not accept queries on specific topics or unsolicited manuscripts, however.

Atlanta Parent

2346 Perimeter Park Drive
Atlanta, GA 30341

Managing Editor: Kate Parrott

DESCRIPTION AND INTERESTS
Local information for parents living in the greater Atlanta region is offered by this magazine. It features articles on parenting, education, and child development issues, along with local listings of events and recreational opportunities. Circ: 120,000.

Audience: Parents
Frequency: Monthly
Website: www.atlantaparent.com

FREELANCE POTENTIAL
40% written by nonstaff writers.

SUBMISSIONS
Send complete ms. Prefers email to editor@atlantaparent.com (Microsoft Word attachments); will accept hard copy and disk submissions. SASE. Response time varies.

- Articles: 800–1,200 words. Informational and how-to articles; and humor. Topics include education, child care, child development, health, and parenting.
- Depts/columns: Word lengths vary. Health, trends, medical advice, parenting tips, and humorous pieces.
- Other: Submit secular holiday material 6 months in advance.

SAMPLE ISSUE
82 pages (55% advertising): 5 articles; 12 depts/columns; 1 special section; 2 calendars. Sample copy, $3 with 9x12 SASE. Writers' guidelines available.

- "30 Ways to Beat the Heat in Your Own Back Yard." Article suggests water-centered backyard toys and games to keep children cool and entertained in the summer.
- Sample dept/column: "Hip Mom" explains how common foods in one's refrigerator can be used to rejuvenate and protect the face.

RIGHTS AND PAYMENT
One-time and Internet rights. Written material, $35–$50. Pays on publication. Provides 1 contributor's tearsheet.

❧ EDITOR'S COMMENTS
All material must have relevance for parents in the Atlanta region. The ones that rise to the top of the pile will be those that use local subject matter and sources, and provide our readers with practical parenting or family information they can use.

Autism Asperger's Digest

P.O. Box 1519
Waynesville, NC 28786

Managing Editor: Veronica Zysk

DESCRIPTION AND INTERESTS
Parents and educators of children with autism and Asperger's syndrome are the audience for this award-winning magazine. Its content combines personal experience pieces with educational and strategies-based articles. All of its articles are written in a friendly, conversational tone. Circ: 12,000.

Audience: Parents and professionals
Frequency: 6 times each year
Website: www.autismdigest.com

FREELANCE POTENTIAL
90% written by nonstaff writers. Publishes 45 freelance submissions yearly; 60% by unpublished writers, 60% by authors who are new to the magazine. Receives 300 queries yearly.

SUBMISSIONS
Query with 25- to 30-word author bio. Accepts hard copy and email queries to editor@autismdigest.com. SASE. Responds in 2–4 weeks.

- Articles: Personal experience pieces, 1,000–1,200 words. Informational and how-to articles, 1,200–2,000 words. Topics include living with autism, strategies for parents and educators, and current research.
- Depts/columns: Newsbites, 100–300 words.
- Artwork: Color prints; JPEGs at 300 dpi.

SAMPLE ISSUE
58 pages: 8 articles; 7 depts/columns. Guidelines available.

- "Sensible Supplement Use." Article explains the ins and outs of supplements and how best to introduce them.
- "Let's Make Faces." Article discusses the benefit of drawing faces to help children express themselves.
- Sample dept/column: "Postcards from the Road Less Traveled" discusses the importance of knowing when to ask for help.

RIGHTS AND PAYMENT
First rights. No payment. Provides contributor's copies and a 1-year subscription.

❧ EDITOR'S COMMENTS
If your article is educational, instructional, motivational, or shares strategies or how-to tips, it's probably a good fit for our magazine. All submissions must be ASD focused and ASD specific.

Babybug

Cricket Magazine Group
70 East Lake Street, Suite 300
Chicago, IL 60601

Assistant Editor: Jenny Gillespie

DESCRIPTION AND INTERESTS
Babybug is a "listening and looking magazine" in the form of a board book for babies and toddlers. It features simple stories, Mother Goose rhymes, short poems, and parent-child activities. Circ: 50,000.

Audience: 6 months–2 years
Frequency: 9 times each year
Website: www.babybugmagkids.com

FREELANCE POTENTIAL
100% written by nonstaff writers. Publishes 30–40 freelance submissions yearly; 50% by authors who are new to the magazine. Receives 2,400 unsolicited mss yearly.

SUBMISSIONS
Send complete ms. Accepts hard copy and simultaneous submissions if identified. SASE. Responds in 6 months.

- Articles: 10 words. Features material that conveys simple concepts and ideas.
- Fiction: 4–6 short sentences. Simple stories.
- Artwork: By assignment only. Send sample tearsheets, photoprints, or photocopies to be kept on file.
- Other: Parent-child activities, to 8 lines. Rhyming and rhythmic poetry, to 8 lines. Action rhymes, 4–8 lines.

SAMPLE ISSUE
24 pages (no advertising): 2 stories; 5 poems; 1 activity. Sample copy, $5. Guidelines available at website.

- "Kim and Carrots." Recurring story describes a little girl's tea party with her mom and favorite stuffed toys.
- "Flying Lesson." Story tells of a father penguin who takes his fledgling to the playground to experience the thrill of "flying."
- "Zoom, Zoom, Zoom." Action rhyme about flying to the moon is accompanied by simple hand motions.

RIGHTS AND PAYMENT
All or second North American serial rights. Written material, $25+. Artwork, $500 per spread, $250 per page. Pays on publication. Provides 6 contributor's copies.

◆ EDITOR'S COMMENTS
Please do not query first. We will consider manuscripts or art samples sent on speculation and accompanied by an SASE.

BabyTalk

460 North Orlando Avenue, Suite 200
Winter Park, FL 32789

Editor-in-Chief: Ana Connery

DESCRIPTION AND INTERESTS
With the goal of helping women navigate the realities of being a new mom, *BabyTalk* provides a mix of news, solutions, and expert advice from doctors and moms who "tell it like it is." Circ: 2 million.

Audience: Parents
Frequency: 10 times each year
Website: www.babytalk.com

FREELANCE POTENTIAL
50% written by nonstaff writers. Publishes 40 freelance submissions yearly; 20% by authors who are new to the magazine. Receives 500 queries yearly.

SUBMISSIONS
Query with clips or writing samples. Accepts hard copy. No simultaneous submissions. SASE. Responds in 2 months.

- Articles: 1,500–2,000 words. Informational, how-to, and self-help articles; and personal experience pieces. Topics include fertility, pregnancy, childbirth, new motherhood, breastfeeding, infant health and development, baby care, juvenile equipment and toys, day care, nutrition, and marital issues.
- Depts/columns: 500–1,200 words. Baby health, milestones, product information, postpartum issues, Q&As, home economics, and humor.

SAMPLE ISSUE
64 pages (50% advertising): 5 articles; 11 depts/columns. Sample copy, free with 9x12 SASE. Guidelines available. Editorial calendar available at website.

- "Boy Crazy!" Personal experience piece tells how a mom of two boys adjusted to life with a new daughter.
- Sample dept/column: "Baby Yourself" includes advice on beating the winter blues.

RIGHTS AND PAYMENT
First rights. Articles, $1,000–$2,000. Depts/columns, $300–$1,200. Pays on acceptance. Provides 2–4 contributor's copies.

◆ EDITOR'S COMMENTS
More than 75 years after its launch, our magazine continues to offer advice and support to millions of new moms, having evolved into the essential source for "straight talk" about the challenges of new motherhood.

Baltimore's Child

11 Dutton Court
Baltimore, MD 21228

Editor: Dianne R. McCann

DESCRIPTION AND INTERESTS
Parenting information and articles on a host of family- and child-related topics fill this magazine. It targets parents of several counties around Baltimore and offers them information localized to their region. Circ: 60,000.

Audience: Parents
Frequency: Monthly
Website: www.baltimoreschild.com

FREELANCE POTENTIAL
90% written by nonstaff writers. Publishes 250 freelance submissions yearly; 5% by unpublished writers, 10% by authors who are new to the magazine.

SUBMISSIONS
Prefers query; will accept complete ms. Accepts email submissions to dianne@baltimoreschild.com. Response time varies.

- Articles: 1,000–1,500 words. Informational articles. Topics include parenting, education, health, fitness, child care, social issues, and regional news.
- Depts/columns: Word lengths vary. Music, family cooking, pet care, baby and toddler issues, parenting children with special needs, parenting teens, and family finances.

SAMPLE ISSUE
92 pages: 4 articles; 14 depts/columns; 4 calendars; 1 party directory. Sample copy and guidelines available at website.

- "Learning Foreign Languages: The Earlier, the Better, N'est-ce Pas?" Article argues that foreign language instruction at an early age can have a positive effect on a child's intellectual growth.
- "Are Your Kids Ready to Rumble?" Article discusses the importance of getting children a complete physical exam before playing a school sport.
- Sample dept/column: "Focus on Fathers" discusses a documentary film about stay-at-home fathers.

RIGHTS AND PAYMENT
One-time rights. Written material, payment rates vary. Pays on publication.

➡EDITOR'S COMMENTS
We care more about what you have to say (and how you say it) than whether you have been published before.

Baseball Youth

Dugout Media
P.O. Box 983
Morehead, KY 40351

Managing Editor: Nathan Clinkenbeard

DESCRIPTION AND INTERESTS
"The nation's baseball magazine for kids" profiles Major League players, offers tips from legends such as Cal Ripken, and spotlights young players from around the country. Circ: 100,000.

Audience: Boys, 7–14 years
Frequency: 6 times each year
Website: www.baseballyouth.com

FREELANCE POTENTIAL
50% written by nonstaff writers. Publishes 10–20 freelance submissions yearly.

SUBMISSIONS
Query with word length and availability of artwork. Prefers email queries to nathanc@dugoutmedia.com (Microsoft Word attachments); will accept hard copy. Availability of artwork improves chance of acceptance. SASE. Response time varies.

- Articles: Word lengths vary. Informational and how-to articles; profiles; interviews; photo-essays; and personal experience pieces. Topics include youth baseball, major and minor league baseball, players, coaches, training, ballparks, baseball equipment, and baseball cards.
- Depts/columns: Word lengths vary. Baseball news, card collections, mascot interviews, fan club information, first-person essays, and video game reviews.
- Artwork: Color digital images or prints.
- Other: Puzzles, quizzes, and comics.

SAMPLE ISSUE
46 pages: 4 articles; 10 depts/columns. Sample copy available at website. Guidelines available.

- "On Top of the World." Article features an interview with Boston pitcher Josh Beckett, conducted by a 15-year-old writer.
- Sample dept/column: "Baseball and Beyond" features the journal of a former Little League champion who is heading to high school.

RIGHTS AND PAYMENT
All rights. Written material, payment rates vary. Payment policy varies.

➡EDITOR'S COMMENTS
We're looking for future sports writers. If you would like to get in the business and interview professional players, give us a shout. Who knows—we might be able to send you to a Major League or Minor League baseball game.

Bay State Parent

117 Elm Street
Millbury, MA 01527

Editor: Carrie Wattu

DESCRIPTION AND INTERESTS
Parents living in eastern and central Massachusetts read this magazine for its useful information on a variety of topics, including child development, relationships, health, travel, and local entertainment. Circ: 42,000.

Audience: Parents
Frequency: Monthly
Website: www.baystateparent.com

FREELANCE POTENTIAL
95% written by nonstaff writers. Publishes 72–144 freelance submissions yearly; 5% by unpublished writers, 30% by new authors. Receives 120 queries yearly.

SUBMISSIONS
Query. Accepts email queries to editor@baystateparent.com (Microsoft Word attachments). Availability of artwork improves chance of acceptance. Responds in 1 month.

- Articles: To 2,000 words. Informational and how-to articles; and humor. Topics include parenting and family issues, regional and local events, health, travel, books, arts and crafts, family finance, and computers.
- Depts/columns: To 1,500 words. Family health, working mothers, adoption, entertainment, relationships.
- Artwork: B/W or color prints; JPEG images at 200 dpi.
- Other: Submit seasonal material 4 months in advance.

SAMPLE ISSUE
60 pages (15% advertising): 7 articles; 6 depts/columns. Sample copy, free. Writers' guidelines available.

- "Meet the Animals of Central Mass." Article profiles different animal-focused organizations, from shelters to an organic farm.
- Sample dept/column: "Under My Roof" describes the author's feelings about losing his father.

RIGHTS AND PAYMENT
First Massachusetts exclusive and electronic rights. Articles, $50–$85. Depts/columns, no payment. Kill fee varies. Pays on publication.

➼ EDITOR'S COMMENTS
If you live in this region and have an interesting—and local—perspective to share, please send us a query.

BC Parent News Magazine

Sasamat RPO 72086
Vancouver, British Columbia V6R 4P2
Canada

Editor: Elizabeth Shaffer

DESCRIPTION AND INTERESTS
Vancouver, British Columbia, has been ranked the best place in the world to live by *The Economist*, so it's no surprise that families choose to make their homes there. *BC Parent News Magazine* serves these families with coverage of the issues—regional, national, and international—that most affect them. Circ: 45,000.

Audience: Parents
Frequency: 9 times each year
Website: www.bcparent.ca

FREELANCE POTENTIAL
80% written by nonstaff writers. Publishes 25 freelance submissions yearly; 10–30% by authors who are new to the magazine.

SUBMISSIONS
Send complete ms. Prefers email submissions to eshaffer@telus.net (RTF attachments); will accept disk submissions. No simultaneous submissions. SAE/IRC. Responds in 2 months.

- Articles: 500–1,000 words. Informational articles. Topics include pregnancy, childbirth, adoption, baby and child care, teen issues, family issues, health care, education, computers, sports, money matters, the arts, and community events.
- Depts/columns: Word lengths vary. Parent health, family news, and media reviews.

SAMPLE ISSUE
30 pages: 4 articles; 3 depts/columns. Guidelines and editorial calendar available.

- "Celebrating Grandparents." Article emphasizes the importance of children spending quality time with their grandparents.
- "Home Is Where the Heart Is." Article looks at the benefits of co-op and condo living for families in Vancouver.
- Sample dept/column: "BC Parent Event Planner" describes upcoming happenings in British Columbia.

RIGHTS AND PAYMENT
First rights. Articles, $85. Reprints, $50. Depts/columns, payment rates vary. Pays on acceptance.

➼ EDITOR'S COMMENTS
We're looking for cutting-edge articles about today's parenting issues. We will consider reprints of articles that have previously appeared outside of our market.

Better Homes and Gardens

1716 Locust Street
Des Moines, IA 50309-3023

Department Editor

DESCRIPTION AND INTERESTS

This magazine is loaded with information and ideas about home decor, gardening, food, and home improvements. It also provides parents with a host of articles on topics of special interest to them, including child development, parenting, crafts, and family health. Circ: 7.6 million.

Audience: Adults
Frequency: Monthly
Website: www.bhg.com

FREELANCE POTENTIAL

10% written by nonstaff writers. Publishes 25–30 freelance submissions yearly; 25% by authors who are new to the magazine. Receives 240 queries yearly.

SUBMISSIONS

Query with résumé and clips or writing samples. Accepts hard copy. SASE. Responds in 1 month.

- Articles: Word lengths vary. Informational and how-to articles; profiles; and personal experience pieces. Topics include food and nutrition, home design, gardening, outdoor living, travel, the environment, health and fitness, holidays, education, parenting, and child development.
- Depts/columns: Staff written.

SAMPLE ISSUE

236 pages (48% advertising): 37 articles; 5 depts/columns. Sample copy, $3.49 at newsstands. Guidelines available.

- "It Pays to Go Green." Article outlines the ways a Texas family saved time, energy, and money while making environmentally friendly changes to their house.
- "On the Same Page." Article offers information for keeping children safe as they surf the Internet.

RIGHTS AND PAYMENT

All rights. Written material, payment rates vary. Kill fee, 25%. Pays on acceptance. Provides 1 contributor's copy.

►►EDITOR'S COMMENTS

We prefer writers who have professional expertise in the area in which they are writing. For family issues or parenting advice, we loosen that rule if you have something to say that will help other parents.

Beyond Centauri

P.O. Box 782
Cedar Rapids, IA 52406

Managing Editor: Tyree Campbell

DESCRIPTION AND INTERESTS

Publishing "science fiction and fantasy for the next generation," *Beyond Centauri* features stories of outer space and other adventures. Much of its content is written by youngsters themselves. Circ: 150.

Audience: 9–18 years
Frequency: Quarterly
Website: www.samsdotpublishing.com

FREELANCE POTENTIAL

95% written by nonstaff writers. Publishes 100 freelance submissions yearly; 20% by unpublished writers, 20% by authors who are new to the magazine. Receives 120 queries, 480 unsolicited mss yearly.

SUBMISSIONS

Query or send complete ms. Accepts hard copy and email to beyondcentauri@yahoo.com (RTF attachments). SASE. Responds to queries in 2 weeks, to mss in 2–3 months.

- Articles: To 500 words. Informational articles; opinion pieces; and media reviews. Topics include space exploration, science, and technology.
- Fiction: To 2,500 words. Genres include science fiction, fantasy, and adventure.
- Artwork: B/W illustrations.
- Other: Poetry, to 50 lines. Science fiction, fantasy, and insect themes.

SAMPLE ISSUE

52 pages (no advertising): 1 essay; 12 stories; 1 book excerpt; 17 poems. Sample copy, $7 with 9x12 SASE. Guidelines available.

- "For Want of a Butler." Story tells of a girl who learns from an eccentric and estranged aunt that she has supernatural powers.
- "Just Imagine." Humorous essay illustrates how the author uses his imagination to get out of sticky situations.

RIGHTS AND PAYMENT

First North American serial rights. Articles, $3. Fiction, $5. Poetry, $2. Artwork, $5. Pays on publication. Provides 1 contributor's copy.

►►EDITOR'S COMMENTS

We still need science fiction adventures set in outer space for children and young adults. Tell us about space settlements, new geographies, plants, and animals, and how people relate to them in other worlds.

Big Apple Parent

1040 Avenue of the Americas, 4th Floor
New York, NY 10018

Editor-in-Chief: Danielle Sullivan

DESCRIPTION AND INTERESTS

They say that New York is the city that never sleeps. This Manhattan-based magazine aims to help New York parents, at least, to sleep a bit better, through helpful articles on raising happy, healthy children in the Big Apple. Circ: 285,000.

Audience: Parents
Frequency: Monthly
Website: www.nymetroparents.com

FREELANCE POTENTIAL

50% written by nonstaff writers. Publishes 300 freelance submissions yearly; 20% by unpublished writers, 10% by authors who are new to the magazine. Receives 12 queries, 72 unsolicited mss yearly.

SUBMISSIONS

Query or send complete ms. Prefers email submissions to dsullivan@davlermedia.com; will accept hard copy. SASE. Responds in 1 week.

- Articles: 800–1,000 words. Informational articles; profiles; interviews; and personal experience pieces. Topics include family issues, education, camp, health, nutrition, fitness, current events, and regional news.
- Depts/columns: Staff written.
- Other: Submit seasonal material 4 months in advance.

SAMPLE ISSUE

66 pages: 11 articles; 10 depts/columns. Sample copy, free with 10x13 SASE.

- "After-School Classes & Programs: What Kids and Parents Want Now." Article identifies the newest trends and hottest programs to help parents choose the right after-school activity for their child.
- "The Gluten-Free Diet for Children with Autism." Article provides an in-depth look at an alternative treatment for autism spectrum disorders in children.

RIGHTS AND PAYMENT

First New York area rights. No payment.

➥EDITOR'S COMMENTS

As we are no longer paying for articles, we are happy to read and consider all submissions. Note that email submissions are preferred. Please do not send fiction, poetry, or memoirs. We will be happy to send a free sample issue on request.

Birmingham Christian Family

P.O. Box 383203
Birmingham, AL 35238

Editor: Julie Moore

DESCRIPTION AND INTERESTS

This magazine serves Christian families in the Birmingham region of Alabama with articles on family life, education issues, living a Christian life, and regional resources. Circ: 35,000.

Audience: Families
Frequency: Monthly
Website:
    www.christianfamilypublications.com

FREELANCE POTENTIAL

72% written by nonstaff writers. Publishes 15 freelance submissions yearly; 5% by unpublished writers, 3% by authors who are new to the magazine. Receives 240 queries yearly.

SUBMISSIONS

Query with artwork, if applicable. Accepts email to julie@christianfamilypublications.com. Availability of artwork improves chance of acceptance. Responds in 1 month.

- Articles: To 500 words. Informational, self-help, and how-to articles; profiles; and personal experience pieces. Topics include love, family life, parenting, Christianity, churches, philanthropy, education, recreation, the arts, travel, and sports.
- Fiction: To 500 words. Inspirational and humorous stories.
- Depts/columns: To 500 words. Media and restaurant reviews; faith in the workplace; financial, health, home improvement, and business tips; recipes; and family travel.
- Artwork: B/W or color prints.

SAMPLE ISSUE

30 pages (25% advertising): 2 articles; 21 depts/columns. Sample copy, free with 9x12 SASE ($3 postage). Editorial calendar available.

- "The Strong Shoulder." Personal experience piece relates how the author's relationship with God helped him through his deployment to Iraq.
- Sample dept/column: "Family Flicks" offers a review of the Passion Conference DVD series that targets young adult Christians.

RIGHTS AND PAYMENT

Rights vary. No payment.

➥EDITOR'S COMMENTS

We welcome all articles, as long as they are on a family- or home-related topic, have a Christian viewpoint, and have local information.

The Black Collegian

140 Carondelet Street
New Orleans, LA 70130

Chief Executive Officer: Preston J. Edwards, Sr.

DESCRIPTION AND INTERESTS
African American students turn to this magazine for its comprehensive information and motivating articles on careers and professional development. It also regularly covers graduate school programs, internships, and job trends. Circ: 121,000.

Audience: African Americans, 18–30 years
Frequency: Twice each year
Website: www.blackcollegian.com

FREELANCE POTENTIAL
95% written by nonstaff writers. Publishes 20 freelance submissions yearly; 33% by authors who are new to the magazine. Receives 24 queries yearly.

SUBMISSIONS
Query. Prefers email queries to preston@ imdiversity.com; will accept hard copy. SASE. Responds in 3 months.

- Articles: 1,500–2,000 words. Informational, self-help, and how-to articles; profiles; and personal experience pieces. Topics include careers, job opportunities, graduate and professional school, internships, study-abroad programs, personal development, financial aid, history, technology, and multicultural and ethnic issues.
- Depts/columns: Word lengths vary. Health issues and media reviews.
- Artwork: 5x7 and 11x14 B/W and color transparencies. B/W and color line art.

SAMPLE ISSUE
72 pages: 10 articles; 1 dept/column. Sample copy and guidelines available at website.

- "Barack Obama: The Making of a President." Article follows Mr. Obama's life from his political beginnings to his induction as the first black president.
- "How to Find Your Dream Job in a Nightmare Economy." Article offers tips for finding a good, stable job.

RIGHTS AND PAYMENT
One-time rights. All material, payment rates vary. Pays after publication. Provides 1 contributor's copy.

⏵EDITOR'S COMMENTS
Your submission should be timely and offer practical information that our readers can use to help them launch their careers.

Blaze Magazine

P.O. Box 2660
Niagara Falls, NY 14302

Editor: Brenda McCarthy

DESCRIPTION AND INTERESTS
Blaze Magazine targets "horse-crazy kids" and delivers articles on all sorts of horsey things—including equine health, breed information, and riding techniques—and profiles of other horse-crazy kids. Circ: 4,000.

Audience: 8–14 years
Frequency: Quarterly
Website: www.blazekids.com

FREELANCE POTENTIAL
50% written by nonstaff writers. Publishes 25–30 freelance submissions yearly.

SUBMISSIONS
Query. Accepts email queries to brenda@ blazekids.com. Availability of artwork improves chance of acceptance. Response time varies.

- Articles: 200–500 words. Informational and how-to articles; and profiles. Topics include horseback riding, training, and breeds.
- Fiction: Word lengths vary. Stories featuring horses.
- Depts/columns: Word lengths vary. Short news items, arts and crafts.
- Artwork: B/W and color prints and transparencies.
- Other: Puzzles and games.

SAMPLE ISSUE
40 pages (15% advertising): 4 articles; 1 story; 5 depts/columns; 5 puzzles and games. Sample copy, $3.75

- "Kentucky Horse Park Is a Dream Come True." Article relates the author's fantastic vacation at Kentucky Horse Park.
- "There Once Was a Horse Named Zipper." Story lauds a horse who worked at the fictional Bar RB ranch in Dallas.
- Sample dept/column: "Craft Stall" provides instructions for making a horse-themed savings jar.

RIGHTS AND PAYMENT
Rights vary. Written material, $.25 per word. Payment policy varies.

⏵EDITOR'S COMMENTS
There are two important things to remember before you send us your query: We cater to a young, horse enthusiasts who may or may not actually own horses, and all articles must be factually correct yet still capture the imagination of our readers.

bNetS@vvy

1201 16th Street NW, Suite 216
Washington, DC 20036

Editor: Mary Esselman

DESCRIPTION AND INTERESTS
bNetS@vvy is a comprehensive Internet safety e-zine from the National Education Association Health Information Network. It publishes practical articles designed to help parents and teachers teach kids to be safe when using the Internet, particularly its social networking sites. Hits per month: Unavailable.

Audience: Parents and teachers
Frequency: 6 times each year
Website: www.bnetsavvy.org

FREELANCE POTENTIAL
90% written by nonstaff writers. Publishes 20 freelance submissions yearly; 80% by unpublished writers, 90% by authors who are new to the magazine.

SUBMISSIONS
Query. Accepts email queries with clips (or links to published work) to internetsafety@nea.org. Responds in 2 weeks.

- Articles: 600–950 words. Informational and how-to articles; and reviews. Topics include the Internet and Internet safety, and social networking sites.
- Depts/columns: 600–950 words. Expert advice and ideas from parents and teens.

SAMPLE ISSUE
1 article; 3 depts/columns. Sample copy and guidelines available at website.

- "How Typical Kids—One 11, One 15—Use Social Technology." Article provides an interview with two typical children on the technology they use and how they use it.
- Sample dept/column: "The Experts" offers strategies for helping kids make safe choices as they explore cyberspace in the summer.
- Sample dept/column: "The Teacher's Desk" interviews teacher Paula White about how she uses the Internet for education, and asks her to give parents tips for guiding their own children safely through cyberspace.

RIGHTS AND PAYMENT
All rights. Written material, payment rates vary. Payment policy varies.

➪EDITOR'S COMMENTS
Our goal is to guide parents and educators as they teach children to use the Internet responsibly. If you have the expertise to help us in that mission, send us your ideas.

Bonbon

2123 Preston Square Court, Suite 300
Falls Church, VA 22043

Publisher: Sitki Kazanci

DESCRIPTION AND INTERESTS
The nation's only Turkish-English bilingual magazine for children, *Bonbon* has an editorial mission to serve the educational needs of Turkish-American children and build a strong sense of community. It features articles on Turkey's history and culture, general education topics, and fiction—many in both languages. Circ: 6,000.

Audience: 6–14 years
Frequency: 6 times each year
Website: www.bonbonkids.com

FREELANCE POTENTIAL
60% written by nonstaff writers. Publishes 30 freelance submissions yearly; 25% by unpublished writers, 10% by authors who are new to the magazine.

SUBMISSIONS
Query with brief author biography. Accepts email queries to info@bonbonkids.com (include "Bonbon queries" in subject field). Responds in 2 weeks.

- Articles: 250 words. Informational articles; profiles; and interviews. Topics include the Turkish language, culture, and traditions; news; animals; nature; and history.
- Fiction: 500 words. Stories that feature Turkish traditions, culture, and values.
- Other: Comics, puzzles, games, jokes, and activities. Poetry.

SAMPLE ISSUE
26 pages: 4 articles; 2 stories; 5 depts/columns; 5 comics; 2 games and activities.

- "Mount Nemrut." Article describes the archeological site Mount Nemrut in Turkey, which has been declared a World Cultural Heritage site by UNESCO.
- "The Little Match-Seller." Story is a retelling of the famous folktale.

RIGHTS AND PAYMENT
One-time rights. No payment.

➪EDITOR'S COMMENTS
Our goal is to reflect Turkish culture, traditions, and values while teaching our children tolerance and understanding. By printing several articles in each issue in both Turkish and English, we hope to help Turkish children learn English and help Turkish-American children learn Turkish.

Book Links

American Library Association
50 East Huron Street
Chicago, IL 60611

Editor: Laura Tillotson

DESCRIPTION AND INTERESTS
Book Links features comprehensive information on using books in the classroom, including thematic bibliographies, author interviews, and essays. Each issue is centered around a curriculum theme such as science, fine arts, history, multicultural literature, or social studies. Circ: 20,577.
Audience: Teachers and librarians
Frequency: Quarterly
Website: www.ala.org/booklinks

FREELANCE POTENTIAL
90% written by nonstaff writers. Publishes 60 freelance submissions yearly; 20% by unpublished writers, 30% by authors who are new to the magazine. Receives 96 queries and unsolicited mss yearly.

SUBMISSIONS
Query or send complete ms. Accepts email to ltillotson@ala.org. Response time varies.

- Articles: Word lengths vary. Informational and how-to articles; profiles; interviews; and annotated bibliographies. Topics include multicultural literature, literacy, language arts, core curriculum subjects, education, the arts, authors, illustrators, and teaching techniques.
- Depts/columns: Word lengths vary. Curriculum ideas, personal essays, and themed book lists.

SAMPLE ISSUE
64 pages (28% advertising): 12 articles; 10 depts/columns. Sample copy, $6. Guidelines and editorial calendar available at website.

- "A Poetry Book of Their Own." Article discusses how to create a bookmaking center in the classroom for budding writers.
- Sample dept/column: "Thinking Outside the Book" explains an interactive online tool that allows students to create and share writing products.

RIGHTS AND PAYMENT
All rights. Articles, $100. Pays on publication. Provides 2 contributor's copies.

➥EDITOR'S COMMENTS
Our audience includes teachers, librarians, library media specialists, booksellers, parents, and others interested in connecting children with high-quality books.

The Boston Parents' Paper

51 Morgan Drive, Suite 11
Norwood, MA 02062

Associate Editor: Georgia Orcutt

DESCRIPTION AND INTERESTS
Parents living in and around Boston turn to this magazine for all sorts of information pertaining to family life. It features articles on parenting, child development, family fun, education, fitness, and family events—all localized to the Boston area. Circ: 75,000.
Audience: Parents
Frequency: Monthly
Website: http://boston.parenthood.com

FREELANCE POTENTIAL
50% written by nonstaff writers. Publishes 36 freelance submissions yearly; 10% by unpublished writers, 50% by authors who are new to the magazine. Receives hundreds of queries each year.

SUBMISSIONS
Boston-area authors only. Query with clips or writing samples. Accepts email queries to georgia.orcutt@parenthood.com. Availability of artwork improves chance of acceptance. Response time varies.

- Articles: Word lengths vary. Informational articles; profiles; and interviews. Topics include child development, education, parenting, family issues, and health.
- Depts/columns: To 1,800 words. Short news items, parenting tips, and profiles.
- Artwork: B/W prints. Line art.
- Other: Submit seasonal material 6 months in advance.

SAMPLE ISSUE
70 pages (45% advertising): 3 articles; 5 depts/columns; 1 calendar. Guidelines and theme list available.

- "Back to School." Article provides practical tips parents can use to get the school year off to a good start.
- "End of Summer Adventures." Article provides several ideas for local family fun in the great outdoors.

RIGHTS AND PAYMENT
All rights. All material, payment rates vary. Pays within 30 days of publication. Provides 5 contributor's copies.

➥EDITOR'S COMMENTS
We're interested in queries from local writers who can address the needs of families residing in eastern Massachusetts.

Boys' Life

Boy Scouts of America
1325 West Walnut Hill Lane
P.O. Box 152079
Irving, TX 75015-2079

Senior Writer: Aaron Derr

DESCRIPTION AND INTERESTS
This magazine from the Boy Scouts of America publishes articles of interest to all boys, on topics ranging from outdoor activities to pop culture. Circ: 1.3 million.

Audience: 6–18 years
Frequency: Monthly
Website: www.boyslife.org

FREELANCE POTENTIAL
80% written by nonstaff writers. Publishes 50 freelance submissions yearly; 1% by unpublished writers, 2% by authors who are new to the magazine.

SUBMISSIONS
Query for articles and depts/columns. Query or send complete ms for fiction. Accepts hard copy. SASE. Responds to queries in 4–6 weeks, to mss in 6–8 weeks.

- Articles: 500–1,500 words. Informational and how-to articles; profiles; and humor. Topics include sports, science, American history, geography, animals, nature, and the environment.
- Fiction: 1,000–1,500 words. Genres include adventure, mystery, and science fiction.
- Depts/columns: 300–750 words. News and entertainment notes, collecting, hobbies, history, cars, gear, gaming, Scout stories, advice, humor, computers, pets, and program information.
- Other: Puzzles, jokes, and cartoons.

SAMPLE ISSUE
52 pages (18% advertising): 5 articles; 7 depts/columns; 6 comics. Sample copy, $3.60 with 9x12 SASE. Guidelines available.

- "The Long Goodbye." Article describes the last outing of a group of Eagle Scouts who explored Missouri's Current River via canoe and cave.
- Sample dept/column: "BL Headliners" includes a profile of three teens who shared the starring role in Broadway's *Billy Elliott*.

RIGHTS AND PAYMENT
First rights. Articles, $400–$1,500. Fiction, $750+. Depts/columns, $150–$400. Pays on acceptance. Provides 2 contributor's copies.

➪EDITOR'S COMMENTS
We cover everything from professional sports to American history to how to pack a canoe.

Boys' Quest

P.O. Box 227
Bluffton, OH 45817-0227

Editor: Marilyn Edwards

DESCRIPTION AND INTERESTS
Boys' Quest publishes articles, fiction, nonfiction, and poetry dealing with timeless topics of interest to boys—pets, nature, hobbies, science, carpentry projects, and more. Each issue centers on a theme. Circ: 12,000.

Audience: 6–13 years
Frequency: 6 times each year
Website: www.boysquest.com

FREELANCE POTENTIAL
70% written by nonstaff writers. Publishes 100–150 freelance submissions yearly; 30% by unpublished writers, 40% by authors who are new to the magazine. Receives 120 queries, 2,400 unsolicited mss yearly.

SUBMISSIONS
Prefers complete ms; will accept query. Accepts hard copy and simultaneous submissions if identified. Availability of artwork improves chance of acceptance. SASE. Responds to queries in 1–2 weeks, to mss in 2–3 months.

- Articles: 500 words. Informational and how-to articles; profiles; personal experience pieces; and humor. Topics include nature, pets, hobbies, sports, family, and careers.
- Fiction: 500 words. Genres include adventure, mystery, and multicultural fiction.
- Depts/columns: 300–500 words. Science experiments and carpentry projects.
- Artwork: B/W and color prints.
- Other: Puzzles and games. Poetry.

SAMPLE ISSUE
48 pages (no advertising): 12 articles; 8 depts/columns; 8 puzzles. Sample copy, $6. Guidelines and theme list available at website.

- "Tips for Taking Great Photos." Article tells how to get action, night, and nature shots.
- Sample dept/column: "Workshop" provides instructions for making a camera magnifier.

RIGHTS AND PAYMENT
First North American serial rights. Articles and fiction, $.05+ per word. Depts/columns, $35. Poetry and puzzles, $10+. Artwork, $5 per photo. Pays on publication. Provides 1 copy.

➪EDITOR'S COMMENTS
If you don't receive a quick response to your submission, it means we're holding it and giving it serious consideration.

Brass

P.O. Box 1220
Corvallis, OR 97339

Editorial Content Manager: Jennie Bartlemay

DESCRIPTION AND INTERESTS
Brass is a lifestyle and finance magazine written for young adults by young adults about the "money side of life." Its editorial focus is to convey the importance of understanding money and how it works, and to help readers make money. Circ: Unavailable.

Audience: 16–25 years
Frequency: Monthly
Website: www.brassmagazine.com

FREELANCE POTENTIAL
50% written by nonstaff writers. Publishes 20–30 freelance submissions yearly; 40% by unpublished writers, 40% by authors who are new to the magazine. Receives 24 queries and unsolicited manuscripts yearly.

SUBMISSIONS
Prefers query; will accept complete ms. Accepts email to editor@brassmagazine.com. Response time varies.

- Articles: 500–700 words. Informational, self-help, and how-to articles; and profiles. Topics include personal improvement, professional advancement, education, fashion, sports, entertainment, health, travel, investments, saving strategies, banking, and portfolio management.
- Depts/columns: Word lengths vary. Starting a business, finance fundamentals, and trends.
- Other: Crossword puzzles.

SAMPLE ISSUE
28 pages: 3 articles; 6 depts/columns; 1 puzzle. Guidelines available at website.

- "Marc Davis: High Octane Success." Article profiles a teenage NASCAR driver who has also started a motorsports business.
- Sample dept/column: "Fundamentals" provides an introduction to savings accounts.

RIGHTS AND PAYMENT
All rights. Written material, payment rates vary. Pays on publication. Provides up to 5 contributor's copies.

➨ EDITOR'S COMMENTS
We're looking for articles on different varieties of financial products and services, as well as those concerning economics. Interested writers should sign up at our website (click on "contribute") for updates on current article assignments.

Bread for God's Children

P.O. Box 1017
Arcadia, FL 34265-1017

Editorial Secretary: Donna Wade

DESCRIPTION AND INTERESTS
Each issue of this Christian magazine contains one story written for young children and one story written for tweens and teens, along with regular columns that "teach how to live and walk in the Spirit-filled life." Articles for parents are often published as well. Circ: 5,000.

Audience: Families
Frequency: 6 times each year
Website: www.breadministries.org

FREELANCE POTENTIAL
10% written by nonstaff writers. Publishes 15–20 freelance submissions yearly; 70% by unpublished writers, 80% by authors who are new to the magazine. Receives 1,200 unsolicited mss yearly.

SUBMISSIONS
Send complete ms. Accepts hard copy and simultaneous submissions if identified. SASE. Responds in 2–3 months.

- Articles: To 800 words. Informational and self-help articles; and personal experience pieces. Topics include religion, spirituality, and morality.
- Fiction: Stories for young children, to 800 words. Stories for middle-grade readers and young adults, to 1,800 words. Themes include biblical principles.
- Depts/columns: To 800 words. "Let's Chat," "Teen Page," Bible studies, ministry highlights, family activities, and book reviews.
- Other: Filler.

SAMPLE ISSUE
28 pages (no advertising): 3 stories; 7 depts/columns. Sample copy, free with 9x12 SASE (5 first-class stamps). Guidelines available.

- "The Bells That Drew Me." Story tells of a Korean girl who convinces her mother to forsake Buddhism for Christianity.
- Sample dept/column: "Bible Study" describes the four faces of Jesus.

RIGHTS AND PAYMENT
First rights. Fiction, $40–$50. Articles and depts/columns, $25. Filler, $10. Pays on publication. Provides 3 contributor's copies.

➨ EDITOR'S COMMENTS
Stories must be written from a child's viewpoint and convey a message without preaching or moralizing.

Brilliant Star

1233 Central Street
Evanston, IL 60201

Associate Editor: Susan Engle

DESCRIPTION AND INTERESTS
Published by the National Spiritual Assembly of the Bahá'ís of the United States, *Brilliant Star* features editorial material that promotes good character and service to community. Circ: 7,000.

Audience: 8–12 years
Frequency: 6 times each year
Website: www.brilliantstarmagazine.org

FREELANCE POTENTIAL
35% written by nonstaff writers. Publishes 5 freelance submissions yearly; 5% by unpublished writers, 80% by new authors. Receives 24 queries, 120 unsolicited mss yearly.

SUBMISSIONS
Query with clips for nonfiction. Send complete ms for fiction. Accepts hard copy, email queries to brilliant@usbnc.org, and simultaneous submissions. SASE. Responds in 6–8 months.

- Articles: To 350 words. Informational and how-to articles; personal experience pieces; profiles; and biographies. Topics include historical Bahá'i figures, religion, history, ethnic and social issues, travel, music, and nature.
- Fiction: To 700 words. Early reader fiction. Genres include ethnic, historical, contemporary, and problem-solving fiction.
- Depts/columns: To 600 words. Profiles of kids; religion; ethics.
- Other: Puzzles, activities, and games.

SAMPLE ISSUE
30 pages: 3 articles; 1 story; 6 depts/columns; 4 activities/games; 1 comic; 1 song. Sample copy, $3 with 9x12 SASE (5 first-class stamps). Writers' guidelines and theme list/editorial calendar available.

- "High-Flying Teamwork." Article uses geese and their V-shaped flight pattern to illustrate the importance of teamwork.
- Sample dept/column: "Stargazer" provides an interview with a yo-yo champ about the importance of setting goals.

RIGHTS AND PAYMENT
All or one-time rights. No payment. Provides 2 contributor's copies.

➥ EDITOR'S COMMENTS
We welcome submissions from contributors of all ages. Material should promote appreciation for diversity, peace, and equality.

Brooklyn Parent

1440 Broadway, 5th Floor
New York, NY 10018

Editorial Director: Phyllis Singer

DESCRIPTION AND INTERESTS
Brooklyn Parent is the magazine parents in Brooklyn, New York, turn to for up-to-date articles on parenting, education trends, and child development issues. It also carries a host of localized articles on family resources, entertainment, and recreation. Circ: 400,000.

Audience: Parents
Frequency: Monthly
Website: www.nymetroparents.com

FREELANCE POTENTIAL
50% written by nonstaff writers. Publishes 300 freelance submissions yearly. Receives 12 queries, 72 unsolicited mss yearly.

SUBMISSIONS
Query or send complete ms. Accepts hard copy. SASE. Responds in 1 week.

- Articles: 800–1,000 words. Informational articles; profiles; interviews; and personal experience pieces. Topics include family issues, education, health, nutrition, fitness, current events, and regional news.
- Depts/columns: Staff written.
- Other: Submit seasonal material 4 months in advance.

SAMPLE ISSUE
52 pages: 3 articles; 8 depts/columns. Sample copy, free with 10x13 SASE.

- "Prospect Playmates." Article profiles several members of the Prospect Park Alliance Playground Committee who are committed to saving playgrounds.
- "Happy Birthday, Baby!" Article offers ideas for throwing age-appropriate parties with sense and sensibility.
- "Summer Travel." Article provides ideas for family vacation activities and destinations, from "staycations" to adventurous road trips.

RIGHTS AND PAYMENT
First New York area rights. No payment.

➥ EDITOR'S COMMENTS
We look for articles that pack a lot of information into a tiny space—that is, articles that offer practical ideas and strategies that parents can replicate on their own. All articles must be related to the Brooklyn area, with local sources and resources. We do not require that you be a published writer; just that you know what you're writing about.

Broomstix for Kids

BYU Magazine

P.O. Box 8139
Bridgewater, NJ 08807

Editor: Natalie Zaman

DESCRIPTION AND INTERESTS
An online magazine written "from and for a pagan perspective," *Broomstix for Kids* features themed and seasonal stories, poetry, and artwork. Hits per month: 6,000.

Audience: Children
Frequency: 8 times each year
Website: www.broomstix.com

FREELANCE POTENTIAL
15% written by nonstaff writers. Publishes 15 freelance submissions yearly; 75% by unpublished writers, 50% by authors who are new to the magazine. Receives 24–60 unsolicited mss each year.

SUBMISSIONS
Send complete ms. Accepts hard copy. SASE for artwork only; does not return mss. Responds in 2 weeks.

- Articles: To 750 words. Informational articles. Topics include nature-based spirituality, pagan rituals and Sabbats, the environment, social and multicultural issues, and the arts.
- Fiction: To 750 words. "Pagan Parables," including folktales and myths.
- Depts/columns: 500 words. "Hearth and Home," "Pruitt the Druid," "Wicc'ed Ways," and craft projects.
- Artwork: B/W and color prints. Line art.
- Other: Theme-related and seasonal poetry.

SAMPLE ISSUE
Sample copy, guidelines, and theme list available at website.

- "Honor Your Mother—Lights Out!" Article looks at the annual Earth Hour observance.
- Sample dept/column: "Wicc'ed Ways" tells how chimney sweeps came to represent luck.

RIGHTS AND PAYMENT
One-time electronic rights. Written material, $.01 per word; $10 maximum. Artwork, payment rates vary. Pays 1 month after publication.

➥EDITOR'S COMMENTS
We're always looking for people to write stories and poems for "Pagan Parables." We are also looking for regular writers for "Hearth and Home" and a new column, "Pruitt the Druid," which focuses on gods and goddesses of different cultures. We would also like people to submit for "Wicc'ed Ways," telling us about their traditions and Sabbat practices.

218 UPB
Provo, UT 84602

Editor: Jeff McClellan

DESCRIPTION AND INTERESTS
This magazine is written for students, alumni, and faculty of Brigham Young University. It covers anything and everything related to the university's people and programs, including the Church of Jesus Christ of Latter-day Saints. Circ: 200,000.

Audience: YA–Adult
Frequency: Quarterly
Website: http://magazine.byu.edu

FREELANCE POTENTIAL
45% written by nonstaff writers. Publishes 10–15 freelance submissions yearly; 5% by authors who are new to the magazine. Receives 120 queries yearly.

SUBMISSIONS
Query with writing samples. Accepts email queries to magazine@byu.edu. Responds in 6–12 months.

- Articles: 1,000–3,000 words. Informational, factual, inspirational, self-help, and how-to articles; profiles; and personal experience pieces. Topics include BYU faculty, students, alumni, programs, and services; and the Mormon faith.
- Depts/columns: To 1,500 words. Commentary, campus news, book reviews, alumni updates, and family issues.
- Artwork: Digital images.

SAMPLE ISSUE
80 pages (15% advertising): 5 articles; 10 depts/columns. Sample copy, free. Writers' guidelines available.

- "The Many Names of Danny Ainge." Article profiles the BYU alumnus, a former basketball player, coach, and sportscaster who is now general manager of the Boston Celtics.
- Sample dept/column: "Alumni Report" describes the experiences of several alumni who took an extensive tour of Latter-day Saints historical sites.

RIGHTS AND PAYMENT
First serial and electronic rights. Articles, $.50+ per word. Pays on acceptance. Provides contributor's copies on request.

➥EDITOR'S COMMENTS
We seek engaging features and lively news stories by, for, and about members of the BYU community.

Cadet Quest

Calvinist Cadet Corps
1333 Alger Street SE
P.O. Box 7259
Grand Rapids, MI 49510

Editor: G. Richard Broene

DESCRIPTION AND INTERESTS

Filled with stories and nonfiction that appeal to pre-adolescent boys, *Cadet Quest* chooses material that fits its goal of helping boys to grow in their Christian faith. Circ: 8,000.

Audience: Boys, 9–14 years
Frequency: 7 times each year
Website: www.calvinistcadets.org

FREELANCE POTENTIAL

58% written by nonstaff writers. Publishes 25 freelance submissions yearly; 3% by unpublished writers, 5% by authors who are new to the magazine. Receives 360 unsolicited mss each year.

SUBMISSIONS

Send complete ms. Accepts hard copy, email to submissions@calvinistcadets.org (no attachments), and simultaneous submissions if identified. SASE. Responds in 1 month.

- Articles: 400–1,000 words. Informational and factual articles; profiles; and interviews. Topics include religion, spirituality, stewardship, camping, crafts and hobbies, sports, the environment, and serving God.
- Fiction: 1,000–1,300 words. Stories that appeal to boys' sense of adventure and humor; must fit one of the planned themes.
- Depts/columns: Word lengths vary. Cadet Corps news items, Bible lessons.
- Other: Puzzles and cartoons.

SAMPLE ISSUE

24 pages (2% advertising): 2 articles; 2 stories; 4 depts/columns. Sample copy, free with 9x12 SASE ($1.17 postage). Guidelines and theme list available at website.

- "Left Alone." Story tells of a boy all alone in a deserted wilderness lodge who finds a Psalm that gives him courage.
- Sample dept/column: "News" reviews the annual Snow Derby held in Michigan.

RIGHTS AND PAYMENT

First and second serial rights. Written material, $.04–$.05 per word. Other material, payment rates vary. Pays on acceptance. Provides 1 contributor's copy.

➽EDITOR'S COMMENTS

Stories and nonfiction articles should have general appeal to boys, and offer a wholesome message and a Christian perspective.

Calliope

Cobblestone Publishing
30 Grove Street, Suite C
Peterborough, NH 03458

Editor: Rosalie Baker

DESCRIPTION AND INTERESTS

Calliope seeks to bring world history alive for its young readers with dramatic tales, action-packed plays, and articles illustrated with art from leading museums. Circ: 13,000.

Audience: 8–14 years
Frequency: 9 times each year
Website: www.cobblestonepub.com

FREELANCE POTENTIAL

85% written by nonstaff writers. Publishes 75 freelance submissions yearly; 15–20% by unpublished writers, 60–70% by authors who are new to the magazine. Receives 240 queries each year.

SUBMISSIONS

Query with outline, bibliography, and writing sample. All material must relate to upcoming themes. Accepts hard copy. SASE. Responds 5 months prior to theme issue publication.

- Articles: Features, 700–800 words. Sidebars, 300–600 words. Informational articles and profiles. Topics include world history.
- Fiction: To 800 words. Genres include historical and multicultural fiction, adventure, and historical plays.
- Depts/columns: 300–600 words. Current events, archaeology, languages, book reviews.
- Artwork: B/W and color prints. Line art.
- Other: To 700 words. Activities, word puzzles, games, crafts, and recipes.

SAMPLE ISSUE

48 pages (no advertising): 16 articles; 7 depts/columns; 3 activities. Sample copy, $6.95 with 9x12 SASE ($2 postage). Guidelines and theme list available at website.

- "Early Baghdad." Article tells of the founding and development of this key Islamic city.
- Sample dept/column: "Off the Shelf" suggests three books about ancient history.

RIGHTS AND PAYMENT

All rights. Articles and fiction, $.20–$.25 per word. Artwork, $15–$100. Other material, payment rates vary. Pays on publication. Provides 2 contributor's copies.

➽EDITOR'S COMMENTS

Authors are urged to use primary sources and up-to-date scholarly resources in their bibliography, and to submit available photographs with their queries.

Camping Magazine

American Camp Association
5000 State Road 67 North
Martinsville, IN 46151-7902

Editor-in-Chief: Harriet Lowe

DESCRIPTION AND INTERESTS
This publication of the American Camp Association serves owners and directors of youth, educational, and recreational camp programs. It publishes articles on industry trends, cutting-edge programming, and youth development. Circ: 7,500.

Audience: Camp managers and educators
Frequency: 6 times each year
Website: www.ACAcamps.org/campmag

FREELANCE POTENTIAL
98% written by nonstaff writers. Publishes 20 freelance submissions yearly; 50% by unpublished writers, 30% by authors who are new to the magazine. Receives 96 unsolicited mss each year.

SUBMISSIONS
Send complete ms. Accepts disk submissions with hard copy and email submissions to magazine@acacamps.org (Microsoft Word attachments). Response time varies.

- Articles: 1,500–3,000 words. Informational and how-to articles. Topics include camp management, special education, social issues, careers, health, recreation, crafts, and hobbies.
- Depts/columns: 800–1,000 words. News, opinion pieces, risk management, and building and construction information.
- Artwork: Color prints; high-resolution JPEGs or TIFFs at 300 dpi.

SAMPLE ISSUE
52 pages (20% advertising): 5 articles; 10 depts/columns. Sample copy, $4.50 with 9x12 SASE. Guidelines and editorial calendar available at website.

- "Camp Yofi." Article profiles a camp for children with autism.
- Sample dept/column: "Risk Management" offers advice for camps for adapting to the tight economy without increasing risk.

RIGHTS AND PAYMENT
All rights. No payment. Provides 3 copies.

⟶EDITOR'S COMMENTS
We accept articles on topics related to the camp profession. The focus may be theory or practice. Academic research articles must be sent using the online submission form; other articles may be sent as described above.

Canadian Guider

Girl Guides of Canada
50 Merton Street
Toronto, Ontario M4S 1A3
Canada

Submissions: Veveen Gregory

DESCRIPTION AND INTERESTS
Girl Guide leaders—or "Guiders," as they're known in Canada—read this official magazine for ways to empower and inspire the girls in their groups. Its departments also keep leaders apprised of Girl Guide business, such as fundraising, membership development, and conferences. Circ: 40,000.

Audience: Girl Guide leaders
Frequency: 3 times each year
Website: www.girlguides.ca

FREELANCE POTENTIAL
75% written by nonstaff writers. Receives 12 queries yearly.

SUBMISSIONS
Accepts submissions from Girl Guide leaders only. Query with résumé for articles; send complete ms for depts/columns. Accepts hard copy. Availability of artwork improves chance of acceptance. SASE. Responds in 1 month.

- Articles: To 200 words. Informational and how-to articles; profiles; interviews; and personal experience pieces. Topics include leadership, life skills, crafts, activities, community service, camping, outdoor adventure, nature, the arts, social issues, and international travel.
- Depts/columns: 50–100 words. Leadership profiles, program ideas, personal experience pieces, contests, and organization business.
- Artwork: B/W and color prints. Digital images at 300 dpi.

SAMPLE ISSUE
48 pages (12% advertising): 6 articles; 15 depts/columns. Sample copy, $3 with 9x12 SASE. Guidelines available.

- "Stepping 'Outside the Box.'" Article tells how to foster creativity in girls.
- Sample dept/column: "Challenges" recounts how a Pathfinders group in Ontario wrote, designed, and produced a play.

RIGHTS AND PAYMENT
All rights. No payment. Provides 2 copies.

⟶EDITOR'S COMMENTS
Each of our articles helps readers deliver the best possible information and programming to Canadian girls and young women, offering ideas that they can put into action. Please note: you must be a Girl Guider to submit.

Capper's

1503 SW 42nd Street
Topeka, KS 66609

Editor-in-Chief: Katherine Compton

DESCRIPTION AND INTERESTS
Articles, fiction, poetry, and nostalgia fill the pages of this tabloid, which embraces and reflects the values of family and good country living. Circ: 15,000.

Audience: Families
Frequency: Monthly
Website: www.cappers.com

FREELANCE POTENTIAL
90% written by nonstaff writers. Publishes 40–50 freelance submissions yearly; 50% by unpublished writers, 70% by authors who are new to the magazine. Receives 480 unsolicited mss yearly.

SUBMISSIONS
Send complete ms with artwork for articles. Query for fiction. Accepts hard copy. SASE. Responds to queries in 1 month, to mss in 3–4 months.

- Articles: 700 words. Informational, general interest, historical, inspirational, and nostalgic articles. Topics include family life, travel, hobbies, and occupations.
- Fiction: To 25,000 words. Serialized novels.
- Depts/columns: 300 words. Personal experience pieces, humor, and essays.
- Artwork: 35mm color slides, transparencies, or prints.
- Other: Jokes, 5–6 per submission.

SAMPLE ISSUE
48 pages (3% advertising): 26 articles; 1 serialized novel; 8 depts/columns. Sample copy, $1.95. Guidelines available.

- "City Dogs Discovering Joys of Herding." Article profiles a ranch that takes in city dogs and lets them do some herding.
- Sample dept/column: "Heart of the Home" offers personal experience and nostalgia pieces from contributors.

RIGHTS AND PAYMENT
Standard rights. Articles, $2.50 per column inch. Serialized novels, $75–$300. Pays on publication for nonfiction; on acceptance for fiction. Provides up to 5 contributor's copies.

➻EDITOR'S COMMENTS
A good portion of our editorial makeup is our reader experiences and remembrances, called Heart of the Home. We are open to articles on a variety of topics.

Careers and Colleges

2 LAN Drive, Suite 100
Westford, MA 01886

Editor: Anne Kandra

DESCRIPTION AND INTERESTS
This "guide toward a successful future" helps high school students make the right college and career choices. While it is open to free-lance submissions, such opportunities are limited because much of its editorial consists of updates of prior material. Circ: 752,000.

Audience: 15–18 years
Frequency: 3 times each year
Website: www.careersandcolleges.com

FREELANCE POTENTIAL
80% written by nonstaff writers. Publishes 6 freelance submissions yearly; 10% by authors who are new to the magazine. Receives 50 queries yearly.

SUBMISSIONS
Query with clips; or send complete ms. Accepts email to editor@careersandcolleges.com. Responds in 2 months.

- Articles: 800–2,400 words. Informational and how-to articles; profiles; interviews; and personal experience pieces. Topics include post-secondary education, independent living, campus life, career choices, social issues, and personal growth.
- Depts/columns: Staff written.

SAMPLE ISSUE
32 pages (29% advertising): 8 articles; 2 depts/columns. Sample copy available at website. Guidelines available.

- "Who Ya Gonna Call?" Article tells students where to find the answers to their questions about the college admissions process.
- "Test Prep Made Easy." Article provides tips for earning good SAT and ACT scores.
- "Find a College You'll Love." Article guides students toward identifying schools where they will thrive academically and socially.

RIGHTS AND PAYMENT
First North American serial and electronic rights. Written material, payment rates vary. Pays 2 months after acceptance. Provides 2 contributor's copies.

➻EDITOR'S COMMENTS
Our mission is to help students achieve their goals. Each issue focuses on a single theme and is intended to serve as a complete reference guide that students will keep and use for months to come.

Carolina Parent

5716 Fayetteville Road, Suite 201
Durham, NC 27713

Editor: Crickett Gibbons

DESCRIPTION AND INTERESTS
Parents and child caregivers read this regional magazine for comprehensive information on everything from child development and education to family finances. Circ: 54,000.

Audience: Parents
Frequency: Monthly
Website: www.carolinaparent.com

FREELANCE POTENTIAL
60% written by nonstaff writers. Publishes 156 freelance submissions yearly; 2% by unpublished writers, 5% by new authors. Receives 600 queries, 480 unsolicited mss yearly.

SUBMISSIONS
Query with outline and writing samples. New writers, send complete ms. Accepts hard copy and email submissions to editorial@ carolinaparent.com (Microsoft Word attachments). SASE. Response time varies.

- Articles: 500–1,600 words. Informational, self-help, and how-to articles; and profiles. Topics include college planning, technology, crafts, hobbies, education, health, fitness, humor, music, nature, the environment, parenting, children's issues, recreation, regional news, sports, and travel.
- Depts/columns: Word lengths vary. "Ages and Stages," family finances, family issues, home and garden, child development, pregnancy, health, news, and events.

SAMPLE ISSUE
96 pages: 10 articles; 17 depts/columns. Guidelines and editorial calendar available.

- "Everyone Needs a Good Night's Rest." Article discusses the link between bad behavior and lack of sleep and includes tips for helping everyone in the family sleep well.
- Sample dept/column: "Family Finance" explains the difference between good and bad debt.

RIGHTS AND PAYMENT
First and electronic rights. Written material, payment rates vary. Pays on publication.

➺EDITOR'S COMMENTS
Articles with a local relevancy from writers living within our region are always welcome. Feature articles require thorough research, knowledge, and concise interviewing and writing skills.

Catholic Digest

1 Montauk Avenue, Suite 200
P.O. Box 6015
New London, CT 06320

Articles Editor: Kerry Weber

DESCRIPTION AND INTERESTS
Newly acquired by the international publisher Bayard, *Catholic Digest* continues to publish articles and true stories of faith that are designed to serve modern families seeking to deepen their spirituality. Circ: 285,000.

Audience: Families
Frequency: 11 times each year
Website: www.catholicdigest.com

FREELANCE POTENTIAL
44% written by nonstaff writers. Publishes 100–200 freelance submissions yearly; 12% by authors who are new to the magazine. Receives 4,800 unsolicited mss yearly.

SUBMISSIONS
Send complete ms. Accepts hard copy and email submissions to cdsubmissions@ bayard-us.com. No simultaneous submissions. SASE. Responds in 6–8 weeks.

- Articles: 1,000–2,000 words. Informational articles; profiles; and personal experience pieces. Topics include religion, prayer, spirituality, relationships, family issues, history, and nostalgia.
- Depts/columns: 50–500 words. True stories about faith, and profiles of volunteers.
- Other: Filler, to 1,000 words.

SAMPLE ISSUE
128 pages (13% advertising): 9 articles; 18 depts/columns. Sample copy, free with 6x9 SASE ($1 postage). Guidelines available.

- "Volunteering on Vacation." Article profiles a number of individuals and families who are changing their recreational travel into "voluntourism."
- "Help! This Economy is Stressing Me Out." Article offers six tips for coping with trying economic times.

RIGHTS AND PAYMENT
One-time rights. Articles, $100–$400. Depts/columns, $2 per published line. Pays on publication. Provides 2 contributor's copies.

➺EDITOR'S COMMENTS
We strongly favor the anecdotal approach to articles. All articles must be tightly focused on a definitive topic, and hold a national appeal. Due to the number of articles we receive, we are unable to provide individual feedback, or respond personally to every submission.

Catholic Forester

P.O. Box 3012
335 Shuman Boulevard
Naperville, IL 60566-7012

Editorial Assistant: Margaret Rice

DESCRIPTION AND INTERESTS
This publication of the Catholic Order of Foresters, a fraternal life benefits insurance society, combines industry and association news with general interest articles. It accepts some parenting and children's issues-related articles. Circ: 100,000.
Audience: Catholic Forester members
Frequency: Quarterly
Website: www.catholicforester.org

FREELANCE POTENTIAL
20% written by nonstaff writers. Publishes 4–8 freelance submissions yearly; 20% by new authors. Receives 240 unsolicited mss yearly.

SUBMISSIONS
Send complete ms. Accepts hard copy and email to mrice@catholicforester.com. SASE. Responds in 3–4 months.

- Articles: 1,000 words. Informational and inspirational articles; and profiles. Topics include money management, fitness, health, family life, investing, senior issues, careers, parenting, and nostalgia.
- Fiction: 500–1,000 words. Genres include inspirational, humorous, and light fiction.
- Depts/columns: Staff written.

SAMPLE ISSUE
40 pages (no advertising): 5 articles; 1 story; 2 activities; 5 depts/columns. Sample copy, free with 9x12 SASE (3 first-class stamps). Guidelines available at website.

- "The Comeback." Inspirational story tells of a young boy who finds support from his baseball team after being treated for leukemia.
- "Men's Guide to the Delivery Room." Article delivers a humorous take on a man's experiences during the birth of his child.
- "Supporting Religious Vocations." Article reports on various groups' efforts to prepare members for religious vocations.

RIGHTS AND PAYMENT
First North American serial rights. Written material, $.50 per word. Reprints, $50. Pays on acceptance. Provides 3 contributor's copies.

➬EDITOR'S COMMENTS
Although we are more interested in nonfiction articles, we also like to entertain our readers with humor and light fiction or a good children's story.

Catholic Library World

Catholic Library Association
100 North Street, Suite 224
Pittsfield, MA 01201-5178

Editor: Mary E. Gallagher, SSJ

DESCRIPTION AND INTERESTS
As the official publication of the Catholic Library Association (CLA), *Catholic Library World* provides professional librarians with reviews of books, DVDs, and other media. It also publishes feature articles relevant to the field. Though its readers are primarily members of the CLA, it does not limit reviews to religious materials. Circ: 1,100.
Audience: Library professionals
Frequency: Quarterly
Website: www.cathla.org

FREELANCE POTENTIAL
90% written by nonstaff writers. Publishes 12–16 freelance submissions yearly. Receives 20 queries, 16–20 unsolicited mss yearly.

SUBMISSIONS
Query or send complete ms. Accepts hard copy and email submissions to cla@cathla.org (Microsoft Word attachments). SASE. Response time varies.

- Articles: Word lengths vary. Informational articles and reviews. Topics include books, reading, library science, and Catholic Library Association news.
- Depts/columns: 150–300 words. Media and book reviews. Topics include biography, fiction, multicultural issues, picture books, reference materials, science, social studies, and Catholic values.
- Artwork: B/W or color prints or transparencies. Line art.

SAMPLE ISSUE
80 pages (2% advertising): 4 articles; 3 depts/columns; 109 reviews. Sample copy, $15. Guidelines available.

- "What I've Learned From 30 Years of Managing Libraries." Article shares what the author wishes he had known when he began his library career.
- Sample dept/column: "Children/Young Adults" includes a review of *The Child Cruncher* by Mathilde Stein.

RIGHTS AND PAYMENT
All rights. No payment. Provides 1 copy.

➬EDITOR'S COMMENTS
Manuscripts will be sent out for review according to our journal's established referee procedures.

Celebrate

2923 Troost Avenue
Kansas City, MO 64109

Senior Editor: Melissa K. Hammer

DESCRIPTION AND INTERESTS
This Sunday school publication, targeted to kids in preschool and kindergarten, presents a Bible-based curriculum that is relevant to everyday life. Its pages are filled with easy-to-follow Bible stories, fun activities, songs, and poems. Circ: 40,000.

Audience: 3–6 years
Frequency: Weekly
Website: www.wordaction.com

FREELANCE POTENTIAL
90% written by nonstaff writers. Publishes 100 freelance submissions yearly; 30% by unpublished writers, 35% by authors who are new to the magazine. Receives 200 queries yearly.

SUBMISSIONS
Query. Accepts hard copy. SASE. Responds in 2–4 weeks.

- Fiction: Word lengths vary. Stories that show children dealing with the issues related to a Bible story or lesson.
- Other: Bible stories, songs, finger plays, action rhymes, crafts, activities. Poetry, 4–8 lines.

SAMPLE ISSUE
4 pages (no advertising): 1 story; 1 dept/column; 4 activities. Sample copy, free with #10 SASE (1 first-class stamp). Guidelines and theme list available.

- "Jesus Speaks to Saul." Bible story tells how Jesus turns Saul from a naysayer into one of his believers.
- "A Riverside Service." Bible story tells how one woman became a Christian after hearing Jesus speak.
- Sample activity: "Chalk Shadows" describes an activity using sidewalk chalk that teaches children about shadows.

RIGHTS AND PAYMENT
Rights vary. Written material, payment rates vary. Payment policy varies.

➻EDITOR'S COMMENTS
We're committed to providing ministry tools that will bring about a lifetime of holy living and share the good news of Jesus Christ with even our youngest readers. Each week, our publication follows a theme. We'd like to hear from writers who have fresh, creative ideas that will inspire our audience.

Central Penn Parent

1500 Paxton Street
Harrisburg, PA 17104

Editor: Nikki M. Murry

DESCRIPTION AND INTERESTS
Central Penn Parent offers informative and reader-friendly articles on parenting issues, as well as in-depth coverage of regional events and resources. It targets parents living in Pennsylvania's Dauphin, Lancaster, Cumberland, and York counties. Circ: 35,000.

Audience: Parents
Frequency: Monthly
Website: www.centralpennparent.com

FREELANCE POTENTIAL
75% written by nonstaff writers. Publishes 60 freelance submissions yearly; 20% by unpublished writers, 10% by authors who are new to the magazine. Receives 1,300 queries yearly.

SUBMISSIONS
All articles are assigned to local writers. Query for reprints only. Accepts email queries to nikkim@journalpub.com. Availability of artwork improves chance of acceptance. SASE. Responds in 2 weeks.

- Articles: 1,200–1,500 words. Informational articles and reviews. Topics include local family events and activities, health, nutrition, discipline, education, home life, technology, literature, parenting, and travel.
- Depts/columns: 700 words. Family finances, health, infant issues, news, and education.
- Artwork: Color prints and transparencies. Line art.
- Other: Submit seasonal material at least 2 months in advance.

SAMPLE ISSUE
46 pages (50% advertising): 2 articles; 13 depts/columns; 1 calendar. Sample copy, free. Guidelines available.

- "10 Tips to Keep Your Picnic Safe." Article explains how to prepare and store picnic foods to avoid food poisoning.
- Sample dept/column: "Dear Teacher" suggests tips for keeping children's math skills sharp over the summer.

RIGHTS AND PAYMENT
All rights. Reprints, $35–$50. Pays on publication. Provides author's copies upon request.

➻EDITOR'S COMMENTS
Preference is given to writers living in one of the counties we serve. Articles should target parents of newborns through teens.

Charlotte Parent

2125 Southend Drive, Suite 253
Charlotte, NC 28230

Editor: Eve White

DESCRIPTION AND INTERESTS
A variety of parenting topics are offered in this magazine, targeting families living in and around Charlotte, N.C. Informative articles, tips, and advice are part of its mix. Circ: 127,000.

Audience: Parents
Frequency: Monthly
Website: www.charlotteparent.com

FREELANCE POTENTIAL
50% written by nonstaff writers. Publishes 45 freelance submissions yearly; 15% by unpublished writers, 25% by new authors. Receives 1,000 queries, 800 unsolicited mss yearly.

SUBMISSIONS
Query or send complete ms with résumé and bibliography. Prefers email to editor@ charlotteparent.com; will accept hard copy, Macintosh disk submissions, and simultaneous submissions. SASE. Responds if interested.

- Articles: 500–1,000 words. Informational and how-to articles; profiles; and personal experience pieces. Topics include parenting, family life, finances, education, health, fitness, vacations, entertainment, regional activities, and the environment.
- Depts/columns: Word lengths vary. Child development, restaurant and media reviews, and children's health.
- Artwork: High-density Macintosh images.
- Other: Activities. Submit seasonal material 2–3 months in advance.

SAMPLE ISSUE
72 pages (50% advertising): 7 articles; 11 depts/columns; 1 calendar. Sample copy, free with 9x12 SASE (5 first-class stamps). Guidelines and editorial calendar available.

- "Putting a Stop to Childhood Obesity." Article explains the risk factors of childhood obesity, and how to keep children healthy.
- "Creating a Successful Study Space." Article offers tips on setting a child up for a successful and productive homework routine.

RIGHTS AND PAYMENT
First and Internet rights. Written material, payment rates vary. Pays on publication. Provides 1 contributor's copy.

➥EDITOR'S COMMENTS
Localized articles will get our attention better than ones that are for a general audience.

ChemMatters

American Chemical Society
1155 16th Street NW
Washington, DC 20036

Editor: Patrice Pages

DESCRIPTION AND INTERESTS
Targeting introductory chemistry students and their teachers around the world, *ChemMatters* sets its sights on providing interesting, informative, and accurate articles about everyday chemistry. Circ: 40,000.

Audience: YA–Adult
Frequency: Quarterly
Website: www.acs.org/chemmatters

FREELANCE POTENTIAL
90% written by nonstaff writers. Publishes 24 freelance submissions yearly; 70% by unpublished writers. Receives 30–40 queries yearly.

SUBMISSIONS
Query with abstract, outline, source list, possible artwork, estimated word count, writing samples, and résumé. Prefers email queries to chemmatters@acs.org; will accept hard copy. Availability of artwork improves chance of acceptance. SASE. Responds in 2 weeks.

- Articles: 1,400–2,100 words. Informational articles. Topics include the chemical aspects of things we take for granted, such as food, beverages, and biological functions, as well as hot topics such as forensic science.
- Depts/columns: 100 words. News; chemistry of everyday products used by teens.
- Artwork: JPEG and GIF images.

SAMPLE ISSUE
20 pages (no advertising): 6 articles; 2 depts/ columns. Sample copy available at website. Guidelines and theme list available via email request to chemmatters@acs.org.

- "Chocolate: The New Health Food. Or Is It?" Article examines the research behind the claim that chocolate can be healthy.
- "Using Chemistry to Protect the Environment." Article interviews an environmental chemist at the Woods Hole Oceanographic Institution in Massachusetts.

RIGHTS AND PAYMENT
All rights. Articles, $500–$1,000. Depts/ columns, $.50 per word. Pays on acceptance. Provides 5 contributor's copies.

➥EDITOR'S COMMENTS
A typical article deals with something that young people are interested in and reveals an underlying chemical story.

Chesapeake Family

929 West Street, Suite 210
Annapolis, MD 21401

Editor: Kristen Page-Kirby

DESCRIPTION AND INTERESTS
This regional magazine covers "home, health, and living for today's parent." It focuses on universal parenting topics as well as information specific to the Chesapeake Bay area of Maryland. Circ: 40,000.

Audience: Parents
Frequency: Monthly
Website: www.chesapeakefamily.com

FREELANCE POTENTIAL
80% written by nonstaff writers. Publishes 40 freelance submissions yearly; 10% by unpublished writers, 40% by authors who are new to the magazine. Receives 1,200 queries, 480 unsolicited mss yearly.

SUBMISSIONS
Prefers query; will accept complete ms. Accepts email to editor@chesapeakefamily.com. Response time varies.

- Articles: 1,000–1,200 words. Informational and how-to articles. Topics include parenting, education, the environment, entertainment, regional news and events, family health, and family travel.
- Fiction: Word lengths vary. Stories by local children ages 4–12.
- Depts/columns: Staff written.
- Other: Poetry by children ages 4–12. Submit seasonal material 6 months in advance.

SAMPLE ISSUE
64 pages (45% advertising): 5 articles; 7 depts/columns. Sample copy, guidelines, and editorial calendar available.

- "More Than Lanyards: The Benefits of Camp." Article details what parents should look for in a camp and what children can learn from attending one.
- "Making Dental Visits Easy on Kids." Article tells how dentists and parents can ensure a smooth dental visit for children.

RIGHTS AND PAYMENT
One-time print and electronic rights. Articles, $75–$150. Depts/columns, $50. Reprints, $35. Kill fee, $25. Payment policy varies.

➹EDITOR'S COMMENTS
We would like to receive more articles on topics of local interest, including education. Please remember that we're not a magazine for kids—we're a magazine for *parents*.

Chess Life

P.O. Box 3967
Crossville, TN 38557-3967

Editor: Daniel Lucas

DESCRIPTION AND INTERESTS
Chess players of all ages and skill levels read this magazine for articles about the game and profiles of prominent players. It covers strategies, beginner to expert play, and tournaments throughout the world. Circ: 80,000.

Audience: YA–Adult
Frequency: Monthly
Website: www.uschess.org

FREELANCE POTENTIAL
75% written by nonstaff writers. Publishes 30 freelance submissions yearly; 30% by unpublished writers. Receives 180–420 queries yearly.

SUBMISSIONS
Query with clips or writing samples. Accepts hard copy and email queries to dlucas@ uschess.org. SASE. Responds in 1–3 months.

- Articles: 800–3,000 words. Informational, how-to, and historical articles; profiles; humor; and personal experience and opinion pieces. Topics include chess games and strategies, tournaments and events, and personalities in the game.
- Depts/columns: To 1,000 words. Book and product reviews, short how-to's, and brief player profiles.
- Artwork: B/W and color prints.
- Other: Chess-oriented cartoons, contests, and games.

SAMPLE ISSUE
72 pages (16% advertising): 4 articles; 11 depts/columns. Sample copy, free with 9x12 SASE. Guidelines available at website.

- "Blueprint for Success: Eight Ways to Grow Your Local Chess Club." Article provides tips for promoting chess in one's community and increasing involvement in chess clubs.
- Sample dept/column: "Chess to Enjoy" discusses the "luck" element in chess, both good and bad.

RIGHTS AND PAYMENT
All rights. Written material, $100 per page. Artwork, $15–$100. Kill fee, 30%. Pays on publication. Provides 2 contributor's copies.

➹EDITOR'S COMMENTS
Freelancers stand the best chance of acceptance with profiles of relatively unknown chess personalities, stories about chess in everyday life, or chess news.

Chess Life for Kids

P.O. Box 3967
Crossville, TN 38577

Editor: Glenn Petersen

DESCRIPTION AND INTERESTS
The United States Chess Federation publishes this magazine for members of its scholastic chess program. With articles on chess instruction, tips from grandmasters, and profiles of young champions, *Chess Life for Kids* hopes to inspire readers to master the game and acquire skills that will translate to academic success as well. Circ: 22,700.
Audience: Up to 12 years
Frequency: 6 times each year
Website: www.uschess.org

FREELANCE POTENTIAL
30% written by nonstaff writers. Publishes 12–18 freelance submissions yearly; 10% by unpublished writers. Receives 36 queries, 12 unsolicited mss yearly.

SUBMISSIONS
Query or send complete ms. Accepts email submissions to gpetersen@uschess.org and simultaneous submissions if identified. Responds in 2 weeks.

- Articles: To 1,000 words. Informational and instructional articles; and profiles. Topics include chess strategies, tournaments, masters, camps, and lessons.
- Depts/columns: Staff written.

SAMPLE ISSUE
24 pages: 10 articles; 4 depts/columns.

- "Attack and Defense in the Colle System." Article describes one of the best opening systems for scholastic chess players.
- "It'Snow Joke!" Article profiles 11-year-old Joel Pena, leader of the 2008 World Chess Live Junior Grand Prix.
- "A Few More 'Must-Know' Endings." Article details two great rook and pawn endings.

RIGHTS AND PAYMENT
First North American serial rights. Written material, $75 per page. Pays on publication.

➥EDITOR'S COMMENTS
Our editorial emphasis is on chess instruction and tournament participation, but there is often room for articles concerning chess camps and other related activities. Writing should reflect the energy and enthusiasm of our young readership while maintaining a respect for the game. Obviously, contributors must possess significant knowledge of chess.

Chicago Parent

141 South Oak Park Avenue
Chicago, IL 60302

Editor: Tamara O'Shaughnessy

DESCRIPTION AND INTERESTS
Targeting Chicago-area families, this magazine features child-oriented articles on parenting issues, education, recreation, and health. All information is localized. Circ: 138,000.
Audience: Parents
Frequency: Monthly
Website: www.chicagoparent.com

FREELANCE POTENTIAL
85% written by nonstaff writers. Publishes 50+ freelance submissions yearly; 30% by unpublished writers, 45% by authors who are new to the magazine. Receives 1,560 queries yearly.

SUBMISSIONS
Query with résumé and clips. Accepts email queries to chiparent@chicagoparent.com. Responds in 6 weeks.

- Articles: 1,500–2,500 words. Informational articles; profiles; personal experience pieces; and humor. Topics include pregnancy, childbirth, parenting, grandparenting, foster care, adoption, day care, child development, health, education, recreation, and family issues.
- Depts/columns: 850 words. Crafts, activities, media reviews, health, travel, family finances, and regional events.
- Other: Cartoons for parents. Submit seasonal material at least 2 months in advance.

SAMPLE ISSUE
100 pages (60% advertising): 5 articles; 13 depts/columns. Sample copy, $3.95. Guidelines and editorial calendar available.

- "The Pros of Procrastination." Article makes the argument that it can be healthy to give oneself time before acting on something.
- Sample dept/column: "Parenting Isn't for Sissies" offers advice and resources for families struggling through divorce.

RIGHTS AND PAYMENT
One-time and northwest Indiana and Illinois exclusive rights. Articles, $125–$350. Depts/columns, $25–$100. Kill fee, 10%. Pays on publication. Provides contributor's copies upon request.

➥EDITOR'S COMMENTS
We absolutely prefer to work with local writers, and that's mostly due to our restriction that articles have a Chicago-area slant.

Child Care Information Exchange

P.O. Box 3249
Redmond, WA 98073-3249

Associate Editor: Donna Rafanello

DESCRIPTION AND INTERESTS
Previously listed as *Exchange*, this magazine for early childhood program leaders has been "exchanging" useful information on child care and development for two decades. Circ: 30,000.

Audience: Child-care professionals
Frequency: 6 times each year
Website: **www.childcareexchange.com**

FREELANCE POTENTIAL
75% written by nonstaff writers. Publishes 60 freelance submissions yearly; 50% by unpublished writers, 60% by new authors. Receives 75 unsolicited mss yearly.

SUBMISSIONS
Send complete ms with brief author bio and list of article references. Accepts email submissions to donna@childcareexchange.com (Microsoft Word attachments) plus hard copy. Availability of artwork improves chance of acceptance. SASE. Response time varies.

- Articles: 1,800 words. Informational, how-to, and self-help articles. Topics include child development; education; and social, multicultural, and ethnic issues.
- Depts/columns: Word lengths vary. Staff development and training, parent perspectives, child nutrition, program profiles, and product reviews.
- Artwork: Color prints. Line art.

SAMPLE ISSUE
104 pages: 14 articles; 15 depts/columns. Sample copy, $8. Guidelines and theme list available at website.

- "Keeping Children Active." Article describes ways in which early childhood teachers can help their charges fight childhood obesity.
- Sample dept/column: "A Program Showcase" profiles St. Mary's Kindergarten in Kyoto, Japan.

RIGHTS AND PAYMENT
All rights. Articles, $300. Pays on publication. Provides 2 contributor's copies.

➦EDITOR'S COMMENTS
We are committed to supporting early childhood professionals worldwide in their efforts to craft early childhood environments where adults and children thrive—environments that foster friendship, curiosity, self-esteem, joy, and respect.

Childhood Education

Association for Childhood Education International
17904 Georgia Avenue, Suite 215
Olney, MA 20832

Editor: Anne W. Bauer

DESCRIPTION AND INTERESTS
This magazine serves as the voice of the Association for Childhood Education International. It provides professional resources and articles for those concerned with the education and well-being of children from infancy through early adolescence. Circ: 10,000.

Audience: Educators; child-care professionals
Frequency: 6 times each year
Website: **www.acei.org**

FREELANCE POTENTIAL
98% written by nonstaff writers. Publishes 40 freelance submissions yearly; 75% by authors who are new to the magazine. Receives 120 unsolicited mss yearly.

SUBMISSIONS
Send 4 copies of complete ms. Accepts hard copy, Macintosh disk submissions, and email submissions to abauer@acei.org. SASE. Responds in 3 months.

- Articles: 1,400–3,500 words. Informational articles. Topics include innovative teaching strategies, the teaching profession, research findings, parenting and family issues, communities, drug education, and safe environments for children.
- Depts/columns: 1,000 words. Research news, education issues, parenting, and book and media reviews.

SAMPLE ISSUE
194 pages: 5 articles; 8 depts/columns. Sample copy, free with 9x12 SASE (3 first-class stamps). Writers' guidelines and editorial calendar available.

- "Understanding Children with Asthma: Trouble and Triggers." Article examines all aspects of this common childhood ailment and describes ways teachers can work around it.
- "Childhood Obesity in the Testing Era: What Teachers and Schools Can Do." Article offers strategies for dealing with students who fall behind in the fitness test.

RIGHTS AND PAYMENT
All rights. No payment. Provides 5 copies.

➦EDITOR'S COMMENTS
Because this is a professional journal, all articles submitted are anonymously reviewed by at least three professional peers.

Children and Families

102 Bramley Drive
Camillus, NY 13031

Editor: Julie Antoniou

DESCRIPTION AND INTERESTS
The National Head Start Association publishes this magazine to aid early childhood education professionals in their quest for excellence. It features articles on early childhood development, administrative issues, curriculum-related topics, and fundraising. Circ: 10,000.
Audience: Early childhood professionals
Frequency: Quarterly
Website: www.nhsa.org

FREELANCE POTENTIAL
90% written by nonstaff writers. Publishes 25 freelance submissions yearly; 30% by unpublished writers, 70% by authors who are new to the magazine. Receives 24 queries yearly.

SUBMISSIONS
Query with biography, outline, and possible sidebar information. Accepts email queries to julie@nhsa.org. Responds in 1–3 months.

- Articles: 1,800–3,800 words. Informational and how-to articles. Topics include teaching skills, advocacy strategies, problem-solving, administrative issues, school readiness, professional development, special needs and inclusion, parental involvement and partnerships, and child development research.
- Depts/columns: Word lengths vary. News, tips for home visits, teaching tactics, leadership advice, lesson plans, literacy projects, and baby-care issues.

SAMPLE ISSUE
62 pages (20% advertising): 2 articles; 7 depts/columns. Sample copy and guidelines available at website.

- "Health and Safety Training for Head Start Staff." Article outlines strategies for implementing successful health and safety training for staff of Head Start programs.
- Sample dept/column: "Leading the Way" explains the benefits of having a mentor program within a Head Start program.

RIGHTS AND PAYMENT
First rights. No payment. Provides 2+ contributor's copies.

➥EDITOR'S COMMENTS
We ask for your biographical information for two reasons: to illustrate you have a legitimate background in early childhood education, and to print it at the end of your article.

Children's Ministry

1515 Cascade Avenue
Loveland, CO 80539

Associate Editor: Carmen Kamrath

DESCRIPTION AND INTERESTS
Written for Christian leaders and volunteers who minister to children in preschool through sixth grade, this magazine features practical and inspirational articles to help children grow spiritually. Circ: 65,000.
Audience: Children's ministry leaders
Frequency: 6 times each year
Website: www.childrensministry.com

FREELANCE POTENTIAL
60–80% written by nonstaff writers. Publishes 25–35 freelance submissions yearly; 60% by unpublished writers, 60% by authors who are new to the magazine. Receives 2,400 unsolicited mss yearly.

SUBMISSIONS
Send complete ms. Prefers email submissions to ckamrath@cmmag.com; will accept hard copy. SASE. Responds in 2–3 months.

- Articles: 500–1,700 words. Informational and how-to articles; and personal experience pieces. Topics include Christian education, family issues, child development, and faith.
- Depts/columns: 50–300 words. Educational issues, activities, devotionals, family ministry, parenting, crafts, and resources.
- Other: Activities, games, and tips. Submit seasonal material 6–8 months in advance.

SAMPLE ISSUE
106 pages (50% advertising): 10 articles; 12 depts/columns. Sample copy, $2 with 9x12 SASE. Guidelines available.

- "The 10/13 Window." Article explains why all pre-teens have the capabilities to be tomorrow's leaders.
- "The Best Intentions." Article offers ideas for instilling confidence and God's love with carefully chosen words.
- Sample dept/column: "Family Ministry" discusses guidelines for keeping family the top ministry priority.

RIGHTS AND PAYMENT
All rights. Articles, $40–$400. Depts/columns, $40–$75. Pays on acceptance. Provides 1 contributor's copy.

➥EDITOR'S COMMENTS
We seek articles that communicate with children on faith, morals, friends, and choices. We do not accept fiction, prose, or poetry.

Children's Voice

Child Welfare League of America
2345 Crystal Drive, Suite 250
Arlington, VA 22202

Managing Editor: Emily Shenk

DESCRIPTION AND INTERESTS
Children's Voice is published by the Child Welfare League of America (CWLA) to keep child advocates apprised of national, state, and local news affecting youth and families. Circ: 25,000.

Audience: Child welfare advocates
Frequency: 6 times each year
Website: www.cwla.org/voice

FREELANCE POTENTIAL
20% written by nonstaff writers. Publishes 12 freelance submissions yearly; 50% by unpublished writers, 50% by authors who are new to the magazine. Receives 60 queries yearly.

SUBMISSIONS
Query. Accepts email queries to voice@cwla.org (text only). Responds in 1 month.

- Articles: 2,000–2,500 words. Informational and how-to articles; profiles; interviews; and personal experience pieces. Topics include child welfare issues, nonprofit management and leadership, legal issues, and agency programs and practices.
- Depts/columns: 200–500 words. Agency news, public policy alerts, state-level child welfare news, staff Q&As, and reports on special education.

SAMPLE ISSUE
40 pages (20% advertising): 4 articles; 8 depts/columns. Sample copy, $10. Guidelines available at website.

- "Changing a Critical Practice." Article explores how policy and practice can improve visits between parents and their children in foster care.
- "Improving Response to Critical Situations." Article offers lessons learned from CWLA members' firsthand experiences.
- Sample dept/column: "The Down to Earth Dad" examines a father's role in his daughter's body image.

RIGHTS AND PAYMENT
All rights. No payment. Provides contributor's copies and a 1-year subscription.

➥EDITOR'S COMMENTS
We encourage suggestions for guest columns, interviews, and new departments, as well as submissions of success stories to our existing "Spotlight On" column. Innovative programs with positive results are especially of interest.

Children's Writer

Institute of Children's Literature
95 Long Ridge Road
West Redding, CT 06896-1124

Editor: Susan Tierney

DESCRIPTION AND INTERESTS
Children's Writer is a monthly newsletter covering trends in children's publishing. It offers tips on writing everything from picture books to young adult novels to magazine articles, while its Marketplace section highlights specific publishers' needs. Circ: 14,000.

Audience: Adults
Frequency: Monthly
Website: www.childrenswriter.com

FREELANCE POTENTIAL
100% written by nonstaff writers. Publishes 75 freelance submissions yearly; 10% by unpublished writers, 15% by authors who are new to the magazine. Receives 60+ queries yearly.

SUBMISSIONS
Query with outline and brief résumé. Prefers submissions via website; will accept hard copy. SASE. Responds in 2 months.

- Articles: 1,700 words. Informational and how-to articles; publisher profiles; and interviews with editors and writers. Topics include children's book and magazine publishing trends, new markets, genres, writing techniques, research, motivation, and business issues.
- Depts/columns: To 750 words, plus 125-word sidebar. Writing and career tips, commentary, technology, and practical motivational pieces.

SAMPLE ISSUE
12 pages (no advertising): 3 articles; 7 depts/columns. Sample copy, free with #10 SASE (1 first-class stamp). Guidelines available at website or with SASE.

- "Create Depth in the Picture Book Pool." Article provides guidance for writing a successful picture book.
- Sample dept/column: "Craft" discusses the importance of word choice.

RIGHTS AND PAYMENT
First North American serial rights. Written material, $135–$300. Pays on publication.

➥EDITOR'S COMMENTS
Our aim is to report and analyze current markets; to help writers of all levels to strengthen their writing with markets in mind; and to inspire, motivate, and encourage the children's writing community.

Christian Home and School

3350 East Paris Avenue SE
Grand Rapids, MI 48512-3054

Managing Editor: Amy Bross

DESCRIPTION AND INTERESTS
This publication of Christian Schools International features articles that promote Christian education while encouraging readers to practice Christian parenting skills. Circ: 66,000.
Audience: Parents
Frequency: 3 times each year
Website: www.csionline.org

FREELANCE POTENTIAL
95% written by nonstaff writers. Publishes 20–25 freelance submissions yearly; 10% by unpublished writers, 30% by authors who are new to the magazine. Receives 60 queries, 150 unsolicited mss yearly.

SUBMISSIONS
Query or send complete ms. Accepts hard copy, email to mleon@csionline.org, and simultaneous submissions if identified. SASE. Responds in 7–10 days.

- Articles: 1,000–2,000 words. Informational, how-to, and self-help articles; and personal experience pieces. Topics include education, parenting, life skills, decision-making, self-control, discipline, family travel, faith, marriage, and social issues.
- Fiction: Word lengths vary. Stories with Christian themes and stories about Christmas.
- Depts/columns: "Parentstuff," 100–250 words. Reviews and parenting tips, word lengths vary.

SAMPLE ISSUE
34 pages (15% advertising): 5 articles; 10 depts/columns. Sample copy, free with 9x12 SASE ($1.11 postage). Guidelines available.

- "Help! The Kids Won't Clean Up!" Article provides guidelines for helping parents teach their children organizational skills.
- Sample dept/column: "Parentstuff" explains the stages at which children obtain traffic awareness while biking.

RIGHTS AND PAYMENT
First rights. Written material, $50–$250. Pays on publication. Provides 5 contributor's copies.

➥EDITOR'S COMMENTS
Want to really grab our attention with your article? Make sure it has a topic that parents can relate to, and offers practical advice or guidance for dealing with the topic. A Christian message on top of it is a great plus!

The Christian Science Monitor

1 Norway Street
Boston, MA 02115

Home Forum Editors:
Susan Leach & Marjorie Kehe

DESCRIPTION AND INTERESTS
The "Home Forum" section of this international daily newspaper covers parenting topics and other family issues. It is especially interested in humorous personal essays describing the joys and challenges of family life. Circ: 80,000.
Audience: Adults
Frequency: Daily
Website: www.csmonitor.com

FREELANCE POTENTIAL
99% written by nonstaff writers. Publishes 1,000 freelance submissions yearly; 10% by unpublished writers, 40% by authors who are new to the magazine. Receives 6,600 unsolicited mss yearly.

SUBMISSIONS
Send complete ms. Accepts email submissions to homeforum@csmonitor.com. Responds in 3 weeks.

- Articles: 300–1,000 words. Personal experience pieces and humor. Topics include home, family, and parenting.
- Other: Short informational bits, 150–400 words. Poetry, to 20 lines. Submit seasonal material 1 month in advance.

SAMPLE ISSUE
20 pages (15% advertising): 14 articles; 8 depts/columns. Guidelines available.

- "Two Worlds, One Classroom." Article reports on an American school in India that opens its doors to impoverished local children.
- "Over the Hedge." Essay recounts the novel discipline technique used by a widowed mother of four.
- "A Natural Foods Junkie at McDonald's." Essay expresses a newfound appreciation for the kid-friendly amenities of fast-food joints.

RIGHTS AND PAYMENT
Exclusive rights. Essays, $75–$160. Poetry, $20–$40 per poem. Short bits, $70. Pays on publication. Provides 1 contributor's copy.

➥EDITOR'S COMMENTS
Unfortunately, we have discontinued our "Kidspace" section. However, we will continue to cover parenting and family topics in "Home Forum." Please note that we cannot consider any essay longer than 1,200 words, and works of that length will have to be trimmed if they are published.

Christian Work at Home Moms

P.O. Box 974
Bellevue, NE 68005

Editor: Jill Hart

DESCRIPTION AND INTERESTS
This website, newsletter, and blogging center features resources mothers can use to find work-at-home careers, as well as tips for establishing an effective work-at-home lifestyle. It also accepts devotions and other information to help work-at-homers grow in their faith. Hits per month: 1.5 million.
Audience: Parents
Frequency: Weekly
Website: www.cwahm.com

FREELANCE POTENTIAL
50% written by nonstaff writers. Publishes 50–100 freelance submissions yearly; 20% by unpublished writers, 20% by authors who are new to the magazine. Receives 120 unsolicited mss yearly.

SUBMISSIONS
Send complete ms. Accepts submissions through website only. Response time varies.

- Articles: 600–800 words. Informational and how-to articles; profiles; interviews; and personal experience pieces. Topics include telecommuting, home businesses, website management and design, search engine optimization, copywriting, money management, blogging, marriage, parenting, spiritual growth, and homeschooling.
- Depts/columns: Word lengths vary. Book and media reviews, information on careers, blogs, devotionals.

SAMPLE ISSUE
Sample copy and writers' guidelines available at website.

- "Why You Should Start a Day Care in a Recession." Article explains why, in harsh economic times, an at-home day care center can be a big success.
- Sample dept/column: "Book Review" examines the book *Devotions for Families That Can't Sit Still.*

RIGHTS AND PAYMENT
Electronic rights. No payment.

❖EDITOR'S COMMENTS
We would like to receive more articles on homeschooling and telecommuting, as well as profiles of successful work-at-home moms. While we do not offer payment, authors get a bio/business plug at the end of each piece.

Cicada

70 East Lake Street, Suite 300
Chicago, IL 60601

Executive Editor: Deborah Vetter

DESCRIPTION AND INTERESTS
Part of Carus Publishing's Cricket Magazine Group, *Cicada* is a literary magazine for teen and young adult readers. It publishes fiction, poetry, and first-person creative nonfiction by both adult and teen writers. Circ: 10,000.
Audience: 14–21 years
Frequency: 6 times each year
Website: www.cicadamag.com

FREELANCE POTENTIAL
95% written by nonstaff writers. Publishes 100 freelance submissions yearly; 40% by unpublished writers, 50% by authors who are new to the magazine. Receives 1,000 unsolicited mss each year.

SUBMISSIONS
Authors previously published in *Cicada* only. Send complete ms with word count; line count for poetry. Accepts hard copy. SASE. Responds in 4 months.

- Articles: To 5,000 words. Creative nonfiction and personal experience pieces.
- Fiction: To 5,000 words. Genres include adventure; fantasy; humor; romance; and historical, contemporary, and science fiction. Also considers plays and stories presented in sophisticated cartoon format. Novellas, to 15,000 words.
- Depts/columns: "Expressions," 350–2,000 words.
- Other: Poetry, to 25 lines. Creative endeavors.

SAMPLE ISSUE
48 pages (no advertising): 4 stories; 1 dept/column; 19 poems. Sample copy, $8.50. Guidelines available at www.cricketmag.com.

- "The Fairy's Challenge." Story is a humorous fantasy tale about fairy sprites who present each other with difficult challenges, mostly involving stealing from humans for sport.
- "On Wednesday." Story is a touching tale of the usual Wednesday night activities when a father gets to see his daughter.

RIGHTS AND PAYMENT
Rights vary. Written material, payment rates vary. Pays on publication.

❖EDITOR'S COMMENTS
Our submission policy changes frequently, depending on what we need. Please check www.cricketmag.com for updates.

City Parent

447 Speers Road, Suite 4
Oakville, Ontario L6K 3S7
Canada

Editor: Diane Tierney

DESCRIPTION AND INTERESTS
Parents throughout the greater Toronto area
read *City Parent* to stay apprised of family-
oriented events, activities, issues, and news.
Circ: 70,000.
Audience: Parents
Frequency: Monthly
Website: www.cityparent.com

FREELANCE POTENTIAL
60% written by nonstaff writers. Publishes
24–30 freelance submissions yearly; 10% by
authors who are new to the magazine.
Receives 300+ unsolicited mss yearly.

SUBMISSIONS
Send complete ms. Accepts email submissions
to cityparent@haltonsearch.com. Availability of
artwork improves chance of acceptance.
Responds immediately if interested.

- Articles: 500–1,000 words. Informational
  articles. Topics include arts and entertainment, health, fitness, multicultural and
  ethnic issues, recreation, self-help, social
  issues, travel, and crafts for children.
- Depts/columns: Word lengths vary. Child-
  development stages, education tips, environmental issues, teen issues, and reviews of
  parenting and children's books.
- Artwork: Color prints or transparencies.

SAMPLE ISSUE
48 pages (65% advertising): 8 articles; 7 depts/
columns. Sample copy available at website.
Guidelines and editorial calendar available.

- "Recession Proof Your Family." Article offers
  practical strategies to help families deal with
  adversity, financial and otherwise.
- "Camp Prep 101." Article tells how to effectively pack for summer camp.
- Sample dept/column: "Snapshots: Baby"
  summarizes new research into infants'
  understanding of failure.

RIGHTS AND PAYMENT
First rights. Written material, $50–$100. Pays
on publication. Provides 1 contributor's copy.

➵EDITOR'S COMMENTS
Topics for features stories are quite varied—
we look for anything of interest to Metro-area
parents. We always have a need for articles
on such perennial subjects as summer camp,
birthday parties, and day care.

CKI Magazine

Circle K International
3636 Woodview Trace
Indianapolis, IN 46268-3196

Executive Editor: Amberly Peterson

DESCRIPTION AND INTERESTS
Replacing the more frequent *Circle K* magazine, this annual publication is distributed
to Circle K International members. Its articles
promote the service initiative of the organization and address topics of general interest to
college students. Circ: 10,000.
Audience: YA–Adult
Frequency: Annually
Website: www.circlek.org

FREELANCE POTENTIAL
20% written by nonstaff writers. Publishes 2–4
freelance submissions yearly; 5% by authors
who are new to the magazine. Receives 24–48
queries yearly.

SUBMISSIONS
Query. Accepts hard copy, email queries to
ckimagazine@kiwanis.org, and faxes to 317-
879-0204. SASE. Responds in 2 weeks.

- Articles: 1,500–2,000 words. Informational
  and self-help articles. Topics include social
  issues, collegiate trends, community service,
  leadership, fundraising, and career planning
  and development.
- Depts/columns: Word lengths vary. News and
  information about Circle K activities.
- Artwork: 5x7 or 8x10 glossy prints. TIFF or
  JPEG images at 300 dpi or higher.

SAMPLE ISSUE
24 pages (no advertising): 4 articles; 7 depts/
columns. Sample copy available at website.
Guidelines available.

- "It Pays to Plan." Article offers tips for effective fundraising.
- "State of Convention." Article comments on
  the low attendance rate at CKI conventions.
- Sample dept/column: "Spotlight" tells about
  CKI members at Purdue University making
  chemotherapy caps for children.

RIGHTS AND PAYMENT
First North American serial rights. Written mate-
rial, $150–$400. Artwork, payment rates vary.
Pays on acceptance. Provides 3 author's copies.

➵EDITOR'S COMMENTS
While we publish only one print issue per
year—available each April—we do update our
website with articles periodically. Authors
must base their stories on interviews and
research rather than on personal insights.

The Claremont Review

4980 Wesley Road
Victoria, British Columbia V8Y 1Y9
Canada

The Editors

DESCRIPTION AND INTERESTS
This "international magazine for young writers" showcases the work of both established and up-and-coming writers ages 13 through 19. Short stories, poetry, and plays are featured. Circ: 500.

Audience: 13–19 years
Frequency: Twice each year
Website: www.theclaremontreview.ca

FREELANCE POTENTIAL
100% written by nonstaff writers. Publishes 100 freelance submissions yearly; 95% by unpublished writers, 95% by authors who are new to the magazine. Receives 240–360 unsolicited mss yearly.

SUBMISSIONS
Send complete ms with biography. Accepts hard copy. SAE/IRC. Responds in 4–6 weeks.

- Articles: Word lengths vary. Interviews with contemporary authors and editors.
- Fiction: To 5,000 words. Genres include traditional, literary, experimental, and contemporary fiction.
- Artwork: B/W or color prints or transparencies.
- Other: Poetry, no line limit. Plays.

SAMPLE ISSUE
120 pages (2% advertising): 10 stories; 49 poems; 5 visual art submissions. Sample copy, $10 with 9x12 SAE/IRC. Guidelines available at website.

- "Natural History." Story tells of a woman who takes her grandchildren to a natural history museum and finds constant reminders that she is aging.
- "Pile of Straw." Story is narrated by a young boy whose mother tells him he is mentally handicapped.
- "Missing: Runaway." Story follows a parent's thoughts when her daughter is discovered missing.

RIGHTS AND PAYMENT
Rights vary. No payment. Provides 1 contributor's copy.

➥EDITOR'S COMMENTS
We strongly urge contributors to read back issues of our magazine to learn what we are looking for. Many of our writers are from Canada, but we accept work from anywhere in the English-speaking world.

The Clearing House

Heldref Publications
1319 18th Street NW
Washington, DC 20036

Managing Editor: Sarah Vogelsong

DESCRIPTION AND INTERESTS
The peer-reviewed articles appearing in this educational journal report on useful practices, research findings, trends, issues, and teaching strategies. Circ: 1,500.

Audience: Educators
Frequency: 6 times each year
Website: www.heldref.org/tch.php

FREELANCE POTENTIAL
95% written by nonstaff writers. Publishes 65 freelance submissions yearly; 60% by authors who are new to the magazine. Receives 121 unsolicited mss yearly.

SUBMISSIONS
Send complete ms. Accepts online submissions at http://mc.manuscriptcentral.com/tch. Responds in 3–4 months.

- Articles: To 3,500 words. Informational and how-to articles. Topics include educational trends and philosophy, pre-service and in-service education, curricula, learning styles, discipline, guidance and counseling, gifted and special education, teaching techniques, educational testing and measurement, and technology.
- Depts/columns: Word lengths vary. Education news, opinion pieces, and book reviews.

SAMPLE ISSUE
42 pages (no advertising): 9 articles; 1 dept/column. Sample copy, $19. Guidelines available at website and in each issue.

- "The Role and Function of High School Department Chairs." Article examines the leadership capacity and roles of high school department chairs.
- "Identifying and Using a Teacher-Friendly Learning-Styles Instrument." Article assesses the validity and reliability of the author's new learning tool.
- "Reading Educational Philosophies in *Freedom Writers*." Article reviews this movie about a real-life inner-city teacher and identifies her successful methods.

RIGHTS AND PAYMENT
All rights. No payment. Provides free online access for life and discounted author's copies.

➥EDITOR'S COMMENTS
We seek material that will be useful to our readers, including personal opinion pieces.

Cleveland Family

11630 Chillicothe Road
Chesterland, OH 44026

Editor: Terri Nighswonger

DESCRIPTION AND INTERESTS
Parents in Ohio's Cuyahoga and Lorain counties find articles on parenting, child development information, educational resources, and calendars of local events and recreation in this regional publication. Circ: 7,500.
Audience: Parents
Frequency: Monthly
Website: www.neohiofamily.com

FREELANCE POTENTIAL
50% written by nonstaff writers. Publishes 40–50 freelance submissions yearly; 33% by authors who are new to the magazine. Receives 9,000+ queries yearly.

SUBMISSIONS
Query. Accepts email queries to editor@tntpublications.com. Responds if interested.

- Articles: 500+ words. Informational, self-help, and how-to articles; profiles; and reviews. Topics include the arts, animals, computers, crafts, health, fitness, education, popular culture, sports, the environment, religion, family travel, and regional issues.
- Depts/columns: Word lengths vary. News, advice, education, teen issues, humor, and stepfamilies.
- Artwork: High-resolution JPEG and TIFF files.

SAMPLE ISSUE
42 pages (50% advertising): 5 articles; 8 depts/columns. Editorial calendar available.

- "Ten Fun Things to Do." Article provides ideas for inexpensive and easy summer fun for the whole family.
- Sample dept/column: "Special-Needs Kids" explains when ADHD is a true disorder and when it is not.

RIGHTS AND PAYMENT
Exclusive rights. Written material, payment rates vary. Pays on publication. Provides 1 contributor's copy.

➦ EDITOR'S COMMENTS
When it comes to topics we are interested in, the field is fairly open. To catch our attention, an article should be of interest to parents, provide practical information, be well written, and relate in some way to the northeastern Ohio region. We happily accept queries from unpublished authors, as long as the four requirements above are met.

Click

Carus Publishing
70 East Lake Street, Suite 300
Chicago, IL 60601

Editor: Amy Tao

DESCRIPTION AND INTERESTS
With the editorial mission of "opening windows for young minds," *Click* gives young children age-appropriate information about their world. Each themed issue contains a mix of nonfiction and fiction, in addition to cartoons and activities. Circ: 62,000.
Audience: 3–7 years
Frequency: 9 times each year
Website: www.cricketmag.com

FREELANCE POTENTIAL
70% written by nonstaff writers. Of the freelance submissions published yearly, 10% are by authors who are new to the magazine. Receives 48–60 queries yearly.

SUBMISSIONS
All material is commissioned from experienced writers. Send résumé and clips. Accepts hard copy. SASE. Response time varies.

- Articles: To 1,000 words. Informational articles; interviews; and photo-essays. Topics include the natural, physical, and social sciences; the arts; technology and science; math; and history.
- Fiction: Word lengths vary. Stories that relate to the issue's theme.
- Other: Poetry, cartoons, and activities.

SAMPLE ISSUE
36 pages (no advertising): 3 articles; 2 stories; 2 cartoons; 2 activities. Sample copy available through website.

- "If You Go to Antarctica." Article explains the living situation of the scientists who work at McMurdo Station in Antarctica.
- "Life on the Ice." Article details living conditions at the North and South Poles, and how people must dress in order to survive there.
- "Yo Wants to Know." Story features a father explaining to his young son why it is so cold at the North Pole.

RIGHTS AND PAYMENT
Rights vary. Written material, payment rates vary. Payment policy varies.

➦ EDITOR'S COMMENTS
We are open to ideas that will stimulate a young child's thirst for knowledge. All material must be presented in an age-appropriate manner and offer facts or other information related to an issue's theme.

Cobblestone

Cobblestone Publishing
30 Grove Street, Suite C
Peterborough, NH 03458

Editor: Meg Chorlian

DESCRIPTION AND INTERESTS
Each issue of this magazine tackles a person, place, or event from American history. The articles, stories, poetry, and activities featured all relate to a particular theme. Circ: 27,000.

Audience: 8–14 years
Frequency: 9 times each year
Website: www.cobblestonepub.com

FREELANCE POTENTIAL
85% written by nonstaff writers. Publishes 180 freelance submissions yearly; 20% by unpublished writers, 25% by authors who are new to the magazine. Receives 600 queries yearly.

SUBMISSIONS
Query with outline, bibliography, and clips or writing samples. All queries must relate to upcoming themes. No unsolicited mss. Accepts hard copy. SASE. Responds 5 months prior to theme issue publication.

- Articles: Features, 700–800 words. Sidebars, 300–600 words. Informational articles; profiles; and interviews. Topics include American history and historical figures.
- Fiction: To 800 words. Genres include historical, multicultural, and biographical fiction; adventure; and retold legends.
- Artwork: Color prints and slides. Line art.
- Other: Activities, to 700 words. Puzzles and games. Poetry, to 100 lines.

SAMPLE ISSUE
52 pages (no advertising): 15 articles; 2 activities; 1 cartoon; 7 depts/columns. Sample copy, $6.95 with 10x13 SASE ($2 postage). Guidelines and theme list available at website.

- "An Unjust War." Article discusses the strong opposition by some Americans to the U.S.-Mexican War.
- Sample dept/column: "Going Global" tells how different global groups work toward fostering peace.

RIGHTS AND PAYMENT
All rights. Written material, $.20–$.25 per word. Artwork, $15–$100. Pays on publication. Provides 2 contributor's copies.

❖EDITOR'S COMMENTS
We're currently seeking to publish more activities and games. Articles should have historical accuracy and a lively, original approach to their subjects.

College Outlook

20 East Gregory Boulevard
Kansas City, MO 64114-1145

Editor: Kellie Houx

DESCRIPTION AND INTERESTS
College-bound students turn to this magazine for information on everything they need to know, from college applications to career planning, and everything in between. Its editorial content is a mix of practical and how-to articles, and personal experience pieces. Circ: 440,000 (spring); 710,000 (fall).

Audience: College-bound students
Frequency: Twice each year
Website: www.collegeoutlook.net

FREELANCE POTENTIAL
20% written by nonstaff writers. Publishes 4–5 freelance submissions yearly; 10% by unpublished writers, 20% by authors who are new to the magazine. Receives 5 queries yearly.

SUBMISSIONS
Query with clips or writing samples. Accepts hard copy. Availability of artwork improves chance of acceptance. SASE. Responds in 1 month.

- Articles: To 1,500 words. Informational and how-to articles; personal experience pieces; and humor. Topics include school selection, financial aid, scholarships, student life, extracurricular activities, money management, and college admissions procedures.
- Artwork: 5x7 B/W and color transparencies.
- Other: Gazette items on campus subjects, including fads, politics, classroom news, current events, leisure activities, and careers.

SAMPLE ISSUE
40 pages (15% advertising): 11 articles. Sample copy, free. Guidelines available.

- "Financial Aid Takes on Many Forms." Article describes how to best tackle the intimidating financial aid application process and its mountain of paperwork.
- "Help That College-Bound Student Find a Major." Article guides parents in helping their kids find a suitable major by determining what type of student they are.

RIGHTS AND PAYMENT
All rights. All material, payment rates vary. Provides contributor's copies.

❖EDITOR'S COMMENTS
Our goal is to be the must-have resource for high school juniors and seniors as they ready themselves for the college experience.

Columbus Parent

7801 North Central Drive
Lewis Center, OH 43035

Editor: Staci Perkins

DESCRIPTION AND INTERESTS
Columbus Parent delivers local news and in-depth features on important health, education, and child development issues, and spotlights local events and entertainment venues for families. Circ: 125,000.
Audience: Parents
Frequency: Monthly
Website: www.columbusparent.com

FREELANCE POTENTIAL
100% written by nonstaff writers. Publishes 48 freelance submissions yearly; 25% by authors who are new to the magazine. Receives 100 queries yearly.

SUBMISSIONS
Query. Accepts email to columbusparent@thisweeknews.com. Response time varies.

- Articles: 700 words. Informational, self-help, and how-to articles; profiles; interviews; and reviews. Topics include current events, family health, child development, education, humor, music, recreation, and travel.
- Depts/columns: 300 words. Recipes, travel, health, nutrition, education, news, events, sports, family humor, behavioral development, and media and product reviews.
- Artwork: Color prints and transparencies.
- Other: Submit seasonal material 2 months in advance.

SAMPLE ISSUE
56 pages (50% advertising): 5 articles; 16 depts/columns. Sample copy, free. Guidelines and editorial calendar available.

- "Don't Be Left 404." Article helps adults to decode contemporary kids' slang.
- Sample dept/column: "Education Edge" introduces Ohio's new Family Score Reports to accompany standardized test results.

RIGHTS AND PAYMENT
Rights vary. Written material, $.10–$.20 per word. Pays on publication.

➡️EDITOR'S COMMENTS
All story submissions should appeal specifically to Columbus parents and should have a local tie and/or local sources. We will consider pieces that are well-researched, offer practical advice, reveal previously unreported topics, or take a unique approach to a familiar topic. Articles should follow AP Style.

Community Education Journal

3929 Old Lee Highway, Suite 91A
Fairfax, VA 22030

Executive Director: Beth Robertson

DESCRIPTION AND INTERESTS
Community Education Journal is a forum for the exchange of ideas and practices in adult continuing education and after-school programs for youngsters. It seeks articles of interest to the academic community as well as to practitioners, including descriptions of successful programs and research projects. Circ: Unavailable.
Audience: Community educators
Frequency: Quarterly
Website: www.ncea.com

FREELANCE POTENTIAL
85% written by nonstaff writers. Publishes 24 freelance submissions yearly; 20% by unpublished writers, 45% by authors who are new to the magazine. Receives 12–24 unsolicited mss each year.

SUBMISSIONS
Send complete ms. Accepts email submissions to ncea@ncea.com (Microsoft Word or PDF attachments). Responds in 2 months.

- Articles: 1,500–2,000 words. Informational articles and opinion pieces. Topics include community education programs, research projects, and trends.

SAMPLE ISSUE
36 pages (no advertising): 6 articles. Sample copy, guidelines, and theme list, $5.

- "Professionalizing the Field of Youth Work." Article discusses the importance of aligning training, certificates, and degrees in community education.
- "How Higher Education Is Working with Volunteers to Help Alleviate Poverty and Revitalize Rural Communities." Article describes one such program in North Dakota.

RIGHTS AND PAYMENT
All rights. No payment. Provides up to 5 contributor's copies.

➡️EDITOR'S COMMENTS
We are particularly interested in articles that are visionary and creative. Please keep all writing as jargon-free as possible, write in the active voice, and use AP style. Place all references at the end of the article. Articles of any length will be considered, but the preferred length is 1,500 to 2,000 words. Longer articles may be edited at our discretion.

Complete Woman

875 North Michigan Avenue, Suite 3434
Chicago, IL 60611-1901

Executive Editor: Lora Wintz

DESCRIPTION AND INTERESTS
Women turn to this magazine for its honest and friendly approach to covering topics of importance to them. The latest information on fashion, health and fitness, careers, relationships, and celebrities is featured in each issue. Circ: 875,000.

Audience: Women
Frequency: Quarterly
Web: www.thecompletewomanmagazine.com

FREELANCE POTENTIAL
90% written by nonstaff writers. Publishes 75 freelance submissions yearly; 20% by unpublished writers, 30% by authors who are new to the magazine. Receives 720 queries yearly.

SUBMISSIONS
Query with clips; or send ms. Accepts hard copy and simultaneous submissions if identified. SASE. Responds in 3 months.

- Articles: 800–1,200 words. Self-help articles; confession and personal experience pieces; humor; profiles; and interviews. Topics include health, fitness, beauty, skin care, fashion, dining, relationships, romance, sex, business, self-improvement, and celebrities.
- Depts/columns: Word lengths vary. Careers, new products, beauty tips, and news briefs.

SAMPLE ISSUE
106 pages (15% advertising): 15 articles; 28 depts/columns. Sample copy, $4.50 at newsstands.

- "Hot Shots: Confessions of a Female Bartender." Article features an interview with a Chicago bartender.
- "Ten Things to Buy Before You Die." Article lists a woman's must-have items, including a little black dress, a handbag, and a red lipstick.
- Sample dept/column: "Living Right" offers tidbits of information about exercise, food, and overall health.

RIGHTS AND PAYMENT
Rights vary. Written material, payment rates vary. Pays on publication. Provides 1 contributor's copy.

❖EDITOR'S COMMENTS
Subject matter is limited only by your imagination and understanding of what it means to be a complete woman in today's society.

Conceive Magazine

622 East Washington Street, Suite 440
Orlando, FL 32801

Editorial Director: Beth Weinhouse

DESCRIPTION AND INTERESTS
Conceive Magazine provides information and support to help women prepare for a happy and healthy pregnancy. It focuses on general reproductive health, fertility, conception, adoption, and early pregnancy. Circ: 200,000.

Audience: Women
Frequency: 5 times each year
Website: www.conceiveonline.com

FREELANCE POTENTIAL
75% written by nonstaff writers. Publishes 60 freelance submissions yearly; 5% by unpublished writers, 10% by authors who are new to the magazine. Receives 1,200 queries yearly.

SUBMISSIONS
Query with résumé and clips. Accepts hard copy and email to beth@conceivemagazine.com. SASE. Response time varies.

- Articles: Word lengths vary. Informational articles; profiles; and interviews. Topics include family planning, infertility issues, adoption, and baby products.
- Depts/columns: Word lengths vary. News, reproductive health notes, fitness tips, medical updates, relationship issues, expert advice, and personal experience pieces.

SAMPLE ISSUE
96 pages: 4 articles; 13 depts/columns. Sample copy, $4.99 at newsstands. Guidelines available at website.

- "Small Changes, Big Gains." Article details simple steps women can take to increase their fertility.
- "The Uncommon Uterus." Article describes rare uterine abnormalities and how they affect pregnancy.
- Sample dept/column: "Conceptual News" includes an item about actress Nicole Kidman's belief in Aboriginal "fertility waters."

RIGHTS AND PAYMENT
All or first rights. Written material, $.50–$1 per word. Kill fee varies. Pays on publication.

❖EDITOR'S COMMENTS
Our readers aren't pregnant yet, but hope to be soon. We look for articles that celebrate the creation of families. If you have a compelling story to tell about your own journey to parenthood, please submit it to our "A Family Is Born" column.

Connect for Kids

Forum for Youth Investment
The Cady-Lee House
7064 Eastern Avenue NW
Washington, DC 20012

Editor: Caitlin Johnson

DESCRIPTION AND INTERESTS
Published by the child-advocacy organization
Forum for Youth Investment, *Connect for Kids*
keeps parents and professionals apprised of
developments in education, health, legislation,
and other areas concerning children. Hits per
month: 50,000+.
Audience: Parents & child welfare professionals
Frequency: 26 times each year
Website: www.connectforkids.org

FREELANCE POTENTIAL
40% written by nonstaff writers. Publishes 24
freelance submissions yearly; 25% by authors
who are new to the magazine. Receives 150
queries yearly.

SUBMISSIONS
Query. Accepts email queries to caitlin@
connectforkids.org. Response time varies.

- Articles: 900–1,500 words. Informational
  articles; profiles; reviews; and photo-essays.
  Topics include adoption, foster care, the
  arts, child abuse and neglect, health, education, child care and development, politics,
  juvenile justice, community building, learning disabilities, crime and violence prevention, parent involvement in education,
  out-of-school time, diversity and awareness,
  education, family income, volunteering, and
  mentoring programs.

SAMPLE ISSUE
Sample copy and guidelines available at website.

- "A Toolkit for Funding." Article provides
  resources to help those doing community
  work to obtain grants and other sources of
  program funding.
- "Health Care Reform: What's In It for Kids &
  Families." Article explains how ongoing
  efforts to reform our health care system may
  ultimately affect children.

RIGHTS AND PAYMENT
First rights. No payment.

➡EDITOR'S COMMENTS
Reprints and adaptations are our main focus
at this point. However, we will consider pro-
posals for original articles on child welfare,
juvenile justice, and current news and policy
developments that have an impact on children and youth.

Connecticut Parent

420 East Main Street, Suite 18
Branford, CT 06405

Editor & Publisher: Joel MacClaren

DESCRIPTION AND INTERESTS
With a tight focus on regional topics, events,
and activities, this magazine is filled with arti-
cles about family and parenting, as well as
local directories. Circ: 60,000.
Audience: Parents
Frequency: Monthly
Website: www.ctparent.com

FREELANCE POTENTIAL
20% written by nonstaff writers. Publishes 50
freelance submissions yearly; 10% by authors
who are new to the magazine. Receives 1,000+
unsolicited mss yearly.

SUBMISSIONS
Send complete ms. Prefers email submissions
to ctparent@aol.com; will accept hard copy.
SASE. Response time varies.

- Articles: 500–1,000 words. Informational,
  self-help, and how-to articles; profiles; and
  interviews. Topics include maternity and
  childbirth issues, parenting, regional news,
  family relationships, social issues, education,
  special education, health, fitness, nutrition,
  safety, entertainment, and travel.
- Depts/columns: 600 words. Family news,
  new product information, and reviews.

SAMPLE ISSUE
84 pages (60% advertising): 6 articles; 3
depts/columns. Sample copy, $5 with 9x12
SASE. Guidelines available.

- "Red Cross Celebrates True Heroes." Article
  previews a Red Cross awards breakfast by
  profiling the nominees.
- "Feeling the Luck of the Irish." Article presents several kid-friendly activities that
  parents can organize at home to celebrate
  St. Patrick's Day.
- Sample dept/column: "Small Talk" contains
  news of a Dr. Seuss musical.

RIGHTS AND PAYMENT
One-time rights. Written material, payment
rates vary. Pays on publication. Provides 1 contributor's tearsheet.

➡EDITOR'S COMMENTS
All topics of interest to Connecticut parents
and families are of interest to us. Articles
must be well written, of course, but our first
priority is that they be informative. All articles must have a Connecticut connection.

Countdown for Kids

Juvenile Diabetes Research Foundation
120 Wall Street, 19th Floor
New York, NY 10005

Submissions Editor: Marieke Gartner

DESCRIPTION AND INTERESTS
This magazine is for children with Type 1 diabetes and their parents. It offers educational and uplifting articles on the various social and emotional issues of dealing with the disease. Profiles and personal experience pieces are also included. Circ: Unavailable.

Audience: 10+ years
Frequency: Twice each year
Website: www.jdrf.org

FREELANCE POTENTIAL
50% written by nonstaff writers. Publishes 6–8 freelance submissions yearly; 10% by unpublished writers. Receives 120 queries and unsolicited mss yearly.

SUBMISSIONS
Query or send complete ms. Accepts hard copy. SASE. Response time varies.

- Articles: Word lengths vary. Informational, factual, and self-help articles; personal experience pieces; profiles; and interviews. Topics include coping with Type 1 diabetes, health, fitness, careers, college, popular culture, social issues, and diabetes research.
- Depts/columns: Word lengths vary. Diabetes news and information; career profiles; and advice.

SAMPLE ISSUE
16 pages (1% advertising): 3 articles; 2 depts/columns. Sample copy available.

- "Success at Sports." Article stresses that kids with diabetes can excel at sports and includes tips for managing the disease.
- "What Is Diabetes?" Article explains the difference between the two types of diabetes and how research is searching for a cure.
- Sample dept/column: "Role Model" profiles a successful 21-year-old race car driver who has diabetes.

RIGHTS AND PAYMENT
First North American serial rights. Written material, payment rates vary. Pays on publication. Provides 1 contributor's copy.

➥EDITOR'S COMMENTS
We are always in need of age-appropriate articles that speak to the day-to-day issues that our readers are facing. Information on current diabetes research and stories that provide hope are also encouraged.

Creative Connections

P.O. Box 98037
135 Davie Street
Vancouver, British Columbia V6Z 2Y0
Canada

Editor: Kalen Marquis

DESCRIPTION AND INTERESTS
"Weaving words of wisdom, wonder, and wellness," *Creative Connections* publishes short essays, articles, poems, and reviews that promote creativity, connection, and human growth and development. Circ: 150.

Audience: 2–21 years
Frequency: Quarterly
Website: http://kalenmarquis. shawwebspace.ca

FREELANCE POTENTIAL
90% written by nonstaff writers. Publishes 360 freelance submissions yearly; 50% by unpublished writers, 75% by authors who are new to the magazine. Receives 120 queries, 360 unsolicited mss yearly.

SUBMISSIONS
Query with writing samples; or send complete ms. Accepts hard copy and simultaneous submissions if identified. SAE/IRC. Responds in 4 months.

- Articles: 300 words. Informational articles; opinion and personal experience pieces; profiles; interviews; and book reviews. Topics include nature, the arts, current events, history, multicultural and ethnic issues, music, health and nutrition, and popular culture. Also publishes biographies of painters, writers, and inventors.
- Fiction: 300 words. Genres include contemporary, historical, multicultural, and inspirational fiction; and adventure.
- Artwork: Line art.
- Other: Poetry, 4–16 lines. Accepts seasonal material 6 months in advance.

SAMPLE ISSUE
10 pages (no advertising): 6 stories; 6 poems. Sample copy, $2 with #10 SAE/IRC. Writers' guidelines available.

- "This Feeling." Essay describes a snowboarder's exhilaration as she once again navigates her favorite trail.
- "Shop Cat." Essay tells of a lonely cat living in a woodcarver's shop.

RIGHTS AND PAYMENT
One-time rights. No payment. Provides 1 copy.

➥EDITOR'S COMMENTS
We happily publish as many original pieces and as many new writers as space allows.

Creative Kids

Prufrock Press
P.O. Box 8813
Waco, TX 76714-8813

Editor: Lacy Compton

DESCRIPTION AND INTERESTS
This magazine publishes stories, essays, poems, and other works created by children to entertain and inspire their peers. Circ: 3,600.

Audience: 8–16 years
Frequency: Quarterly
Website: www.prufrock.com

FREELANCE POTENTIAL
95% written by nonstaff writers. Publishes 150 freelance submissions yearly; 75% by unpublished writers, 75% by authors who are new to the magazine. Receives 1,800 unsolicited mss each year.

SUBMISSIONS
Child authors only. Send complete ms. Accepts hard copy with author's birthday, grade, and school. SASE. Responds in 4–6 weeks.

- Articles: 500–1,200 words. Informational, self-help, and how-to articles; profiles; essays; photo-essays; humor; and personal experience pieces. Topics include pets, sports, social issues, travel, and gifted education.
- Fiction: 500–1,200 words. Genres include realistic, inspirational, historical, and multicultural fiction; mystery; suspense; folktales; humor; and problem-solving stories. Also publishes plays.
- Depts/columns: Word lengths vary. Short opinion pieces.
- Artwork: B/W and color photos; color copies of paintings; colored-pencil sketches; collages. Line art.
- Other: Poetry and songs. Puzzles, games, and cartoons. Submit seasonal material 1 year in advance.

SAMPLE ISSUE
34 pages (no advertising): 4 articles; 6 stories; 1 dept/column; 11 poems; 2 cartoons; 7 activities. Sample copy and writers' guidelines available at website.

- "The Disappearing Rainforest." Article explains the dire situation facing rainforests.
- "Spelling Mistakes." Story is a humorous tale of miscommunication through misspelling.

RIGHTS AND PAYMENT
Rights vary. No payment. Provides 1 copy.

❖EDITOR'S COMMENTS
We will not accept any submission that does not include the author's age.

Cricket

Carus Publishing
70 East Lake Street, Suite 300
Chicago, IL 60601

Submissions Editor

DESCRIPTION AND INTERESTS
Cricket operates on the belief that kids love a good story. It publishes a variety of writing, including fiction, poetry, nonfiction, history, folktales, biographies, and activities—each featuring informative comments in the margins from a cast of bug characters. Circ: 55,000.

Audience: 9–14 years
Frequency: 9 times each year
Website: www.cricketmag.com

FREELANCE POTENTIAL
100% written by nonstaff writers. Publishes 100 freelance submissions yearly; 30% by unpublished writers, 50% by authors who are new to the magazine. Receives 12,000 unsolicited mss yearly.

SUBMISSIONS
Send complete ms; include bibliography for nonfiction. Accepts hard copy and simultaneous submissions if identified. SASE. Responds in 4–6 months.

- Articles: 200–1,500 words. Informational and how-to articles; biographies; and profiles. Topics include science, art, technology, history, architecture, geography, foreign culture, adventure, and sports.
- Fiction: 200–2,000 words. Genres include humor, mystery, fantasy, science fiction, folktales, fairy tales, mythology, and historical and contemporary fiction.
- Depts/columns: Staff written.
- Other: Poetry, to 50 lines. Puzzles, games, crafts, recipes, and science experiments; word lengths vary.

SAMPLE ISSUE
48 pages (no advertising): 2 articles; 4 stories; 1 poem; 5 depts/columns. Sample copy, $5 with 9x12 SASE. Guidelines available at website.

- "The Herd Boys of Lesotho." Article provides information about young livestock herders.
- "Communication." Story tells of a young boy who finds a way to "talk" to his soldier father.

RIGHTS AND PAYMENT
Rights vary. Articles and fiction, to $.25 per word. Poetry, to $3 per line. Pays on publication. Provides 6 contributor's copies.

❖EDITOR'S COMMENTS
We would like to see more fantasy and science fiction submissions.

Crinkles

3520 South 35th Street
Lincoln, NE 68506

Editor: Deborah D. Levitov

DESCRIPTION AND INTERESTS
Geared toward elementary school children, *Crinkles* is designed to stimulate children's curiosity about people, places, and things. Its articles are meant to develop critical thinking skills, and promote independent research and good study habits. Each issue features hands-on activities and puzzles. Circ: 6,000.

Audience: 7–12 years
Frequency: 6 times each year
Website: www.crinkles.com

FREELANCE POTENTIAL
70% written by nonstaff writers. Publishes 2–3 freelance submissions yearly; 10% by unpublished writers, 50% by authors who are new to the magazine. Receives 36 queries yearly.

SUBMISSIONS
Query with résumé. Accepts email queries to deborah.levitov@abc-clio.com. Responds in 1 month.

- Articles: Word lengths vary. Informational, factual, and how-to articles. Topics include history, geography, multicultural and ethnic subjects, social issues, science, animals, nature, the arts, and sports.
- Other: Puzzles, mazes, games, and crafts.

SAMPLE ISSUE
50 pages (no advertising): 11 articles; 7 activities. Sample copy and writers' guidelines available at website.

- "Notable Nigerian Women." Article profiles the international achievements of Dr. Ndi Okereke-Onyiuke and Dr. Ngozi Okonjo-Iweala of Nigeria.
- "Slave Trade Centered in Nigeria." Article explains the African slave trade that was centered in Nigeria.

RIGHTS AND PAYMENT
All rights. Written material, $150. Payment policy varies. Provides contributor's copies upon request.

⇢EDITOR'S COMMENTS
Each of our issues focuses on a central theme, and all articles in that issue deal with the people, places, events, and things that relate to that topic. We prefer to assign most articles according to our upcoming themes, so query us with your credentials in order to get on our list of possible freelancers.

Curious Parents

2345 Bethel Avenue
Merchantville, NJ 08109

Editor: Karli Morello

DESCRIPTION AND INTERESTS
A full range of family-oriented articles appear in this magazine, which serves families in the Pennsylvania, New Jersey, and Delaware triangle. Each of its articles provides practical information on parenting strategies, and each is localized to the region. Circ: 265,000.

Audience: Parents
Frequency: Monthly
Website: www.curiousparents.com

FREELANCE POTENTIAL
99% written by nonstaff writers. Publishes 40 freelance submissions yearly; many by unpublished writers and authors who are new to the magazine.

SUBMISSIONS
Send complete ms with brief description and brief author biography. Accepts email submissions to editor@curiousparents.com. Response time varies.

- Articles: Word lengths vary. Informational, how-to, and self-help articles. Topics include crafts, hobbies, current events, recreation, education, safety, health, family entertainment, networking, parenting, and travel.
- Depts/columns: Word lengths vary. Health issues and automobile safety; book reviews.

SAMPLE ISSUE
40 pages: 12 articles; 3 depts/columns. Sample copy, free with 9x12 SASE. Guidelines available at website.

- "Kids Going to Sleepaway Camp? How to Not Worry and Rest Tight." Article provides insight to giving one's child a good foundation for a successful camp experience.
- "Preventing Summer Amnesia." Article provides tips for keeping kids' minds active during the lazy days of summer.

RIGHTS AND PAYMENT
All rights. No payment.

⇢EDITOR'S COMMENTS
We welcome submissions from readers, professionals in the child development or family relationship arenas, and parents who have successful parenting strategies to share. A main goal of ours is to share parenting resources with our readers; therefore, all articles must have a regional connection to our tri-state circulation area.

Current Health 1

Weekly Reader Publishing
1 Reader's Digest Road
Pleasantville, NY 10570-7000

Editor: Erin R. King

DESCRIPTION AND INTERESTS

As part of the Weekly Reader magazine group, *Current Health 1* provides its middle-grade readers with current information on health, fitness, social issues, and emotional development topics. It is distributed through schools and contains a teacher's guide. Circ: 163,973.

Audience: Grades 4–7
Frequency: 8 times each year
Website: www.weeklyreader.com/ch1

FREELANCE POTENTIAL

75% written by nonstaff writers. Publishes 40 freelance submissions yearly; 25% by authors who are new to the magazine. Receives 60 queries yearly.

SUBMISSIONS

All articles are assigned. Query with letter of introduction, areas of expertise, publishing credits, and clips. No unsolicited mss. Accepts email queries to currenthealth@weeklyreader.com. Responds in 1–4 months.

- Articles: 850–1,000 words. Informational articles. Topics include nutrition, fitness, disease prevention, drugs, alcohol, emotional well-being, and first aid.
- Depts/columns: Word lengths vary. Physical activities, health news and advice, safety tips, and summaries of medical research.

SAMPLE ISSUE

32 pages (no advertising): 6 articles; 6 depts/columns. Sample copy available. Guidelines provided upon assignment.

- "Decision Time." Article explains how to make wise choices, and how to handle it when a decision turns out to be a bad one.
- "Cancer Answers." Article provides an explanation of cancer and answers some very common questions kids may have about the disease.
- Sample dept/column: "Get Up and Go!" offers exercise ideas that are fun as well as good for you.

RIGHTS AND PAYMENT

All rights. Articles, $150+. Payment policy varies. Provides 2 contributor's copies.

➡️EDITOR'S COMMENTS

While we handle the assignments in-house, we are always looking to take on writers who can deal authoritatively with our subject matter.

Current Health 2

Weekly Reader Publishing
1 Reader's Digest Road
Pleasantville, NY 10570-7000

Senior Editor: Meredith Matthews

DESCRIPTION AND INTERESTS

Distributed through the classroom, *Current Health 2* covers general health topics as they relate to teens. Each issue comes with a teacher's guide and a human sexuality newsletter; however, the editors seek submissions of magazine articles only. Circ: 195,000.

Audience: Grades 7–12
Frequency: 8 times each year
Website: www.weeklyreader.com/ch2

FREELANCE POTENTIAL

67% written by nonstaff writers. Publishes 36 freelance submissions yearly; 15% by unpublished writers, 30% by authors who are new to the magazine. Receives 12–24 queries yearly.

SUBMISSIONS

Query with outline and sources. Accepts email queries to currenthealth@weeklyreader.com (Microsoft Word attachments). Responds in 1–4 months.

- Articles: 800–1,000 words. Informational articles. Topics include personal and public health, fitness, nutrition, sexuality, disease, psychology, first aid, safety, drug education, risky behavior, and relationships.
- Depts/columns: Word lengths vary. Health news, safety issues, Q&As, fitness tips, and careers in the healthcare field.

SAMPLE ISSUE

32 pages (1% advertising): 5 articles; 6 depts/columns. Sample copy, guidelines, and editorial calendar available.

- "Don't Delay, Act Now!" Article emphasizes how students' future health is being shaped today, and suggests proactive strategies.
- "What's In Your Medical Future?" Article previews several cutting-edge advancements in medical technology.
- Sample dept/column: "Get Up and Go!" offers ideas for a fitness plan.

RIGHTS AND PAYMENT

All rights. Articles, $.50 per word. Depts/columns, payment rates vary. Pays on publication. Provides 2 contributor's copies.

➡️EDITOR'S COMMENTS

Please note that we do not accept pitches of articles unrelated to our theme list. Writers must consult our editorial calendar and specify which issue they wish to write for.

The Dabbling Mum

508 West Main Street
Beresford, SD 57004

Editor: Alyice Edrich

DESCRIPTION AND INTERESTS
The Dabbling Mum is a free, online magazine for busy parents—especially those who own small businesses and/or work from home. It covers such topics as balancing work and family, Christian parenting and home life, running a small business, writing for websites or for print, and finding family-friendly entertainment. Hits per month: 40,000.

Audience: Parents
Frequency: Weekly
Website: www.thedabblingmum.com

FREELANCE POTENTIAL
90% written by nonstaff writers. Publishes 100 freelance submissions yearly; 20% by unpublished writers, 60% by authors who are new to the magazine. Receives 240 queries yearly.

SUBMISSIONS
Query with writing samples. Accepts queries via website only. Responds in 2–4 months.

- Articles: 500–1,500 words. Informational and how-to articles; and personal experience pieces. Topics include family life, parenting, women's issues, home businesses, sales and marketing, Christian living, marriage, entertainment, education, child development, teen issues, and contemporary social concerns.

SAMPLE ISSUE
Sample copy and writers' guidelines available at website.

- "Monitoring Television Time." Article looks at the dilemma of a child who is overly engrossed in watching TV.
- "12 Ways to Successfully Use LinkedIn." Article offers tips for using the networking site.
- Sample dept/column: "Advice on Christianity" talks of finding peace during tough times.

RIGHTS AND PAYMENT
One-month exclusive online rights; indefinite archival rights. Written material, $20–$40; reprints, $5. Pays on acceptance.

●◆EDITOR'S COMMENTS
Right now we're focusing on our small business section. If you can help us expand this section by donating an article or querying us regarding a paying article, we'd be much obliged! We are especially interested in donated articles from experts in fields that can help small businesses grow.

Dallas Child

Lauren Publications
4275 Kellway Circle, Suite 146
Addison, TX 75001

Editorial Content: Joylyn Niebes

DESCRIPTION AND INTERESTS
A regional Texan publication, *Dallas Child* claims to be "the magazine parents live by in Dallas and Collin counties." It features profiles of local mothers and fathers, parenting advice, and articles on family issues written from a local perspective. Circ: 80,000.

Audience: Parents
Frequency: Monthly
Website: www.dallaschild.com

FREELANCE POTENTIAL
30% written by nonstaff writers. Publishes 25 freelance submissions yearly; 5–10% by authors who are new to the magazine. Receives 396 queries yearly.

SUBMISSIONS
Query with résumé. Accepts hard copy, email queries to editorial@dallaschild.com, faxed queries to 972-447-0633, and simultaneous submissions if identified. SASE. Responds in 2–3 months.

- Articles: 1,000–2,000 words. Informational self-help, and how-to articles; profiles; interviews; humor; and personal experience pieces. Topics include parenting, education, child development, family travel, regional news, recreation, entertainment, current events, social issues, multicultural and ethnic subjects, health, fitness, and crafts.
- Depts/columns: 800 words. Local events, travel tips, and health news.

SAMPLE ISSUE
78 pages (14% advertising): 2 articles; 20 depts/columns. Sample copy and guidelines available at website.

- "Don't Just Lounge . . . Learn!" Article suggests specialty camps and other brain-boosting activities to keep kids busy over the summer.
- Sample dept/column: "Dallas County Parenting" includes an interview with a local father who started Dads Club DFW.

RIGHTS AND PAYMENT
First rights. Written material, payment rates vary. Pays on publication. Provides contributor's copies upon request.

●◆EDITOR'S COMMENTS
We strive to include fresh voices, ideas, and perspectives. We emphasize stories with a local focus and prefer to work with area writers.

Dance International

667 Davie Street
Vancouver, British Columbia V6B 2G6
Canada

Managing Editor: Maureen Riches

DESCRIPTION AND INTERESTS
Published by the Vancouver Ballet Society,
Dance International focuses on dance in Canada
and beyond. It provides profiles and reviews
of dancers, programs, and performances.
Circ: 4,000.
Audience: YA–Adult
Frequency: Quarterly
Website: www.danceinternational.org

FREELANCE POTENTIAL
85% written by nonstaff writers. Publishes 95
freelance submissions yearly; 9% by authors
who are new to the magazine.

SUBMISSIONS
Send complete ms. Accepts email submissions
to danceint@direct.ca (attach file) and disk
submissions (RTF files). SASE. Responds in
2 months.

- Articles: 1,500 words. Informational articles;
  profiles; interviews; opinion pieces; and
  media reviews—all related to dance.
- Depts/columns: 1,000 words.
  Commentaries, and book and performance
  reviews.

SAMPLE ISSUE
62 pages (10% advertising): 7 articles; 23
depts/columns. Guidelines available at website.

- "Unlimited Possibilities." Article profiles cho-
  reographer Alonzo King, founder of LINES
  Ballet company in San Francisco.
- "Grand Dame of Design." Article profiles
  Canadian artist Kandis Cook, who designs
  the costumes for dance companies around
  the world.
- Sample dept/column: "Prairie Report" offers
  news from several dance companies in
  Alberta, Winnipeg, and Calgary.

RIGHTS AND PAYMENT
First rights. Articles, $100–$150. Depts/
columns, $100. Kill fee, 50%. Pays on publica-
tion. Provides 2 contributor's copies.

⚫EDITOR'S COMMENTS
We cover dance both nationally and interna-
tionally, and are always pleased to hear from
writers who can report from dance venues
around the globe. We focus on contemporary
dance and ballet. Freelancers should not
bother to submit material if they are not well-
versed in the subject of dance.

Dance Magazine

110 William Street, 23rd Floor
New York, NY 10038

Editor-in-Chief: Wendy Perron

DESCRIPTION AND INTERESTS
This is a magazine that keeps its readers on
their toes with articles about all aspects of
dance, including profiles of dancers and companies. It is read by students, teachers, and
professional dancers. Circ: 50,000.
Audience: YA–Adult
Frequency: Monthly
Website: www.dancemagazine.com

FREELANCE POTENTIAL
80% written by nonstaff writers. Publishes 200
freelance submissions yearly; 5% by unpublished writers, 25% by authors who are new to
the magazine. Receives many queries yearly.

SUBMISSIONS
Query. Accepts hard copy and email queries to
wperron@dancemedia.com. SASE. Response
time varies.

- Articles: To 1,500 words. Informational articles; profiles; and interviews. Topics include
  dance, dance instruction, choreography, the
  arts, family, and health concerns.
- Depts/columns: Word lengths vary. New
  product information, reviews, dance news,
  and instruction.

SAMPLE ISSUE
138 pages (33% advertising): 5 articles; 15
depts/columns.

- "Ballerina, Interrupted." Article profiles Janie
  Taylor, who has returned to dance after an
  illness and injury.
- "A Clean Sweep." Article discusses the
  importance of keeping stage and studio
  floors in good condition to avoid injuries
  to dancers.
- Sample dept/column: "Do's and Don'ts"
  offers tips for getting beautiful body lines
  and long extension.

RIGHTS AND PAYMENT
Rights vary. Written material, payment rates
vary. Pays on publication.

⚫EDITOR'S COMMENTS
We expect all of our writers to be dancers
themselves, or at least to be knowledgeable
about the art of dance. We favor articles that
provide information and instruction for young
dancers, as well as reviews and updates of
performances and dance companies throughout the country.

Dance Teacher

110 William Street, Floor 23
New York, NY 10038

Managing Editor: Jeni Tu

DESCRIPTION AND INTERESTS

Focusing less on the art of dance than on the art (and business) of teaching dance, this magazine publishes articles on the ins and outs of teaching dance or running a dance studio. It features information on management, finances, insurance, attracting students, instructional programs, and creativity. Circ: 25,000.

Audience: Dance teachers and students
Frequency: Monthly
Website: www.dance-teacher.com

FREELANCE POTENTIAL

67% written by nonstaff writers. Publishes 100–120 freelance submissions yearly; 10% by unpublished writers, 10–15% by authors who are new to the magazine. Receives 100 queries each year.

SUBMISSIONS

Query. Accepts hard copy and email to jtu@ dancemedia.com. SASE. Responds in 2 months.

- Articles: 1,000–2,000 words. Informational and how-to articles; and personal experience pieces. Topics include dance education, business, nutrition, health, injuries, performance production, competitions, and dance personalities.
- Depts/columns: 700–1,200 words. Fashion, teaching, competition, dance history, media and product reviews, and industry news.

SAMPLE ISSUE

80 pages (50% advertising): 5 articles; 10 depts/columns. Sample copy, free with 9x12 SASE ($1.37 postage). Guidelines and theme list available.

- "Growth Chart." Article reports on the careers of three professional dance teachers, what they have learned about the profession, and how they grew their businesses.
- "Three Graces." Article profiles three dancers who now serve as role models for the next generation of dancers.

RIGHTS AND PAYMENT

All rights. Articles, $200–$300. Depts/columns, $150–$250. Pays on publication. Provides 1 contributor's copy.

↔EDITOR'S COMMENTS

We are interested in articles on the business of dance, as well as pieces meant to inspire up-and-coming dancers and teachers.

Davey and Goliath's Devotions

Augsburg Fortress Publishers
P.O. Box 1209
Minneapolis, MN 55440-1209

Lead Editor: Becky Weaver Carlson

DESCRIPTION AND INTERESTS

Each issue of this devotional publication is divided into weekly sections, which in turn are divided into four pages of content: the first two pages focus on a Bible story and related activities, while the last two pages are filled with content designed to bring the story alive for kids. Circ: 50,000.

Audience: 3–9 years
Frequency: Quarterly
Website: www.augsburgfortress.org/dg/ devotions

FREELANCE POTENTIAL

100% written by nonstaff writers. Publishes 40 freelance submissions yearly; 25% by unpublished writers, 50% by authors who are new to the magazine. Receives 40 queries yearly.

SUBMISSIONS

Query with sample content per guidelines. Accepts email submissions to cllsub@ augsburgfortress.org (with "Family Devotions" in subject line). All work is assigned. Response time varies.

- Articles: Bible stories, 100–170 words.
- Depts/columns: Questions and prayers, 15–20 words. Bible facts and parenting tips, 30–50 words. Family discussion topics, 100–125 words.
- Other: Puzzles, mazes, activities, and games.

SAMPLE ISSUE

64 pages (no advertising): 44 depts/columns. Sample copy available at website. Guidelines available at www.augsburgfortress.org/company/ submitcongregational.jsp.

- "Precious Promise." Article tells the story of God's covenant with Noah after the flood.
- Sample dept/column: "Bible Activity" recommends that families make cardboard rainbows on which they write about God.
- Sample dept/column: "Caring for Kids" tells parents to remind their children that God uses rain to make rainbows.

RIGHTS AND PAYMENT

All rights. Written material, payment rates vary. Pays on acceptance. Provides 2 copies.

↔EDITOR'S COMMENTS

Our content is designed to help families with young children explore and share faith together at home and on the go.

Delmarva Youth Magazine

1226 North Division Street
Salisbury, MD 21801

Editor: Maria Cook

DESCRIPTION AND INTERESTS
Parenting issues, family relationships, education, child development, and family fun—all related to the Delmarva Peninsula region of Maryland—are covered at length in this family magazine. It also includes listings of local events. Circ: 15,000.

Audience: Parents
Frequency: 10 times each year
Website: www.delmarvayouth.com

FREELANCE POTENTIAL
80% written by nonstaff writers. Publishes 60 freelance submissions yearly; 15% by unpublished writers, 20% by authors who are new to the magazine.

SUBMISSIONS
Query or send complete ms. Accepts email to delmarvayouth@hotmail.com (Microsoft Word attachments). Response time varies.

- Articles: 500–3,000 words. Informational and how-to articles; and interviews. Topics include parenting, family life, family events and activities, travel, education, health, music, sports, and family finance.
- Depts/columns: Word lengths vary. School and camp news, family health and fitness, and the arts.

SAMPLE ISSUE
54 pages (15% advertising): 12 articles; 5 depts/columns; 1 calendar. Sample copy, $2.50. Guidelines available at website.

- "Solving a Bully of a Problem." Article examines the growing issue of bullying in schools, and provides some solutions.
- "Building Bridges to Our Gen Y Kids." Article provides tips for communicating with teens in their own technology-themed "language."
- Sample dept/column: "Sports Talk" puts a positive spin on playing the outfield.

RIGHTS AND PAYMENT
First print and electronic rights. Articles, $25–$150. Pays on publication. Provides 1 contributor's copy.

➥EDITOR'S COMMENTS
We look for articles that will "hit home" with parents, and give them the information they are looking for, support and encouragement, or a good laugh. Local writers get preference, but all pieces must be localized.

Devozine

1908 Grand Avenue
P.O. Box 340004
Nashville, TN 37203-0004

Editor: Sandy Miller

DESCRIPTION AND INTERESTS
Devozine is written by teens and the adults who love them. It publishes articles that help readers grow in their faith, aid their prayer life, and encourage them in the life of discipleship. Stories of faith are also included. Circ: 90,000.

Audience: 15–19 years
Frequency: 6 times each year
Website: www.devozine.org

FREELANCE POTENTIAL
100% written by nonstaff writers. Publishes 400 freelance submissions yearly; 50% by authors who are new to the magazine. Receives 150+ queries, 1,000+ unsolicited mss yearly.

SUBMISSIONS
Query for feature articles. Send complete ms for daily meditations. Accepts hard copy and email submissions to devozine@ upperroom.org. SASE. Responds in 4 months.

- Articles: 150–500 words. Informational articles; profiles; personal experience pieces; and reviews. Topics include faith, mentoring, independence, courage, teen parenting, creativity, social issues, and relationships.
- Fiction: 150–250 words. Genres include adventure, and historical and multicultural fiction.
- Depts/columns: 75–100 words. Reviews, new product information.
- Other: Daily meditations, 150–250 words. Prayers and poetry, 10–20 lines. Submit seasonal material 6–8 months in advance.

SAMPLE ISSUE
80 pages (no advertising): 4 articles; 31 devotionals; 2 depts/columns. Guidelines and theme list available at website.

- "Brooke Barrettsmith: Trusting God." Article profiles the singer-songwriter-musician about what her faith means to her.
- "Father Knows Best." Meditation based on a verse from Proverbs encourages teens to respect the guidance of their parents.

RIGHTS AND PAYMENT
First and second rights. Features, $100. Meditations, $25. Pays on acceptance.

➥EDITOR'S COMMENTS
Meditations should be first-person stories of faith and devotion.

Dig

Cobblestone Publishing
30 Grove Street, Suite C
Peterborough, NH 03458

Editor: Rosalie Baker

DESCRIPTION AND INTERESTS
Published in partnership with *Archaeology* magazine, *Dig* introduces students to the wonders of the ancient world through technological and scientific discoveries. Circ: 18,000.

Audience: 8–14 years
Frequency: 9 times each year
Website: www.digonsite.com

FREELANCE POTENTIAL
85% written by nonstaff writers. Publishes 40–45 freelance submissions yearly; 10% by unpublished writers, 70% by authors who are new to the magazine. Receives 240 queries each year.

SUBMISSIONS
Query with outline, bibliography, and writing sample. All material must relate to upcoming themes. Accepts hard copy. SASE. Responds 5 months prior to theme publication date.

- Articles: Features, 700–800 words. Sidebars, 300–600 words. Informational articles and photo-essays. Topics include archaeology, history, nature, science, and technology.
- Fiction: To 800 words. Genres include historical fiction, adventure, and folklore.
- Depts/columns: 300–600 words. Art, archaeological facts and discoveries, and projects.
- Artwork: B/W and color prints. Line art.
- Other: To 700 words. Activities, word puzzles, mazes, games, crafts, woodworking projects, and recipes.

SAMPLE ISSUE
32 pages (no advertising): 9 articles; 8 depts/columns; 1 word puzzle. Sample copy, $6.95 with 9x12 SASE ($2 postage). Guidelines and theme list available at website.

- "In the Beginning." Article separates fact from fiction regarding the origins of Rome.
- Sample dept/column: "Art-i-facts" features a digital reproduction of the hypogeum, the lower level of the Colosseum.

RIGHTS AND PAYMENT
All rights. Articles and fiction, $.20–$.25 per word. Artwork, $15–$100. Other material, payment rates vary. Pays on publication. Provides 2 contributor's copies.

➡EDITOR'S COMMENTS
If you would like to know if your query has been received, include a stamped postcard.

Dimensions

DECA, Inc.
1908 Association Drive
Reston, VA 20191-1594

Editor: Christopher Young

DESCRIPTION AND INTERESTS
Published by DECA, an international association of marketing students, *Dimensions* covers topics of interest to its members and augments the information they discuss at meetings. It features articles on business, marketing trends, presentation skills, and leadership, as well as association news. Circ: 176,000.

Audience: 14–18 years
Frequency: Quarterly
Website: www.deca.org

FREELANCE POTENTIAL
25% written by nonstaff writers. Publishes 6–8 freelance submissions yearly; 50–75% by authors who are new to the magazine.

SUBMISSIONS
Query or send complete ms with author bio. Accepts hard copy, email submissions to deca_dimensions@deca.org, Macintosh disk submissions (RTF files), and simultaneous submissions if identified. SASE. Response time varies.

- Articles: 800–1,200 words. Informational and how-to articles; profiles; interviews; and personal experience pieces. Topics include general business, management, marketing, sales, leadership development, entrepreneurship, franchising, personal finance, advertising, e-commerce, business technology, and career opportunities.
- Depts/columns: 400–600 words. DECA chapter news briefs and opinions.

SAMPLE ISSUE
24 pages (45% advertising): 10 articles; 5 depts/columns. Sample copy, free with 9x12 SASE. Guidelines available.

- "Apple Barrel Store Achieves Success." Article profiles a successful school store that is built on student dedication and superior customer service.
- Sample dept/column: "My Turn" offers tips for public speaking.

RIGHTS AND PAYMENT
First serial rights. Written material, payment rates vary. Pays on publication. Provides 2 copies.

➡EDITOR'S COMMENTS
Our readers' interests are diverse, and we like articles that speak plainly to our members rather than sling industry jargon around.

Dimensions of Early Childhood

Southern Early Childhood Association
P.O. Box 55930
Little Rock, AR 72215-5930

Editor: Janet B. Stivers

DESCRIPTION AND INTERESTS
This refereed journal serves the interests of early childhood educators concerned with child development, including university researchers and teacher educators; early childhood, kindergarten, and primary-grade teachers; and early childhood program administrators and proprietors. Members of the Southern Early Childhood Association receive a subscription to the magazine. Circ: 19,000.

Audience: Early childhood professionals
Frequency: 3 times each year
Website: www.southernearlychildhood.org

FREELANCE POTENTIAL
99% written by nonstaff writers. Publishes 40 freelance submissions yearly; 10% by unpublished writers, 80% by authors who are new to the magazine. Receives 50 unsolicited mss each year.

SUBMISSIONS
Send complete ms. Accepts email submissions to editor@southernearlychildhood.org. Responds in 3–4 months.

- Articles: Word lengths vary. Informational articles. Topics include emergent curriculum for children, effective classroom practices, theory, research, program administration, family relationships, and resource systems.
- Depts/columns: Word lengths vary. Reviews.

SAMPLE ISSUE
40 pages (5% advertising): 5 articles; 2 book reviews. Sample copy, $5. Writers' guidelines available.

- "Block Play: Practical Suggestions for Common Dilemmas." Article identifies common problems teachers face with block play and tells how to remedy them.
- "Environmental Print: Real-World Early Reading." Article posits that drawing young children's attention to signs around them can result in early literacy.
- Sample dept/column: "Book Reviews" includes a look at *Sharing Books Together*.

RIGHTS AND PAYMENT
All rights. No payment. Provides 2 copies.

⇢EDITOR'S COMMENTS
Please submit manuscripts (via email) that are typed and double-spaced, with references in APA style.

Discovery Girls

4300 Stevens Creek Boulevard, Suite 190
San Jose, CA 95129

Editorial Director: Sarah Verney

DESCRIPTION AND INTERESTS
Started by a mother who remembered all too clearly her middle-school years, *Discovery Girls* celebrates each girl's uniqueness and inspires them to believe in themselves. Most of its regular content is contributed by readers via the website. Circ: 220,000.

Audience: Girls, 7–13 years
Frequency: 6 times each year
Website: www.discoverygirls.com

FREELANCE POTENTIAL
25% written by nonstaff writers. Publishes 10–18 freelance submissions yearly; 50% by authors who are new to the magazine.

SUBMISSIONS
Query with sample paragraph; or send complete ms. Accepts hard copy, email submissions to sarah@discoverygirls.com, and submissions from girls via website. SASE. Response time varies.

- Articles: Word lengths vary. Informational and how-to articles; and personal experience pieces. Topics include friendship, family relationships, self-esteem, peer pressure, fitness, health and beauty, entertainment, recreation, crafts, and social issues.
- Depts/columns: Word lengths vary. Celebrity news, relationship advice, embarrassing moments, opinions, health and beauty, and book reviews.
- Other: Quizzes and contests.

SAMPLE ISSUE
58 pages: 7 articles; 14 depts/columns; 5 quizzes/contests. Sample copy, $4.50. Editorial calendar available at website.

- "I Wish My Parents Knew . . ." Article examines the pressures faced by today's pre-teens and suggests ways to convey them to parents.
- "Telling Lies . . . How Does It Affect You?" Article tells where to draw the line when it comes to telling the truth.
- Sample dept/column: "Embarrassing Moments" shares readers' anecdotes.

RIGHTS AND PAYMENT
All rights. Written material, payment rates vary.

⇢EDITOR'S COMMENTS
"Real" girls model, write for, and help create the magazine. Please see our website for details on how to contribute.

Dramatics

Educational Theatre Association
2343 Auburn Avenue
Cincinnati, OH 45219

Editor: Donald Corathers

DESCRIPTION AND INTERESTS
This magazine for theater students and teachers publishes articles on the various aspects of acting, stagecraft, and playwriting. It accepts profiles, news from the theater, and factual or instructional articles. Circ: 37,000.
Audience: High school students and teachers
Frequency: 9 times each year
Website: www.edta.org

FREELANCE POTENTIAL
80% written by nonstaff writers. Publishes 41 freelance submissions yearly; 25% by unpublished writers, 50% by authors who are new to the magazine. Receives 480 unsolicited mss each year.

SUBMISSIONS
Send complete ms. Accepts hard copy and email submissions to dcorathers@edta.org. SASE. Responds in 2–4 months.

- Articles: 750–4,000 words. Informational articles; interviews; and book reviews. Topics include playwriting, musical theater, acting, auditions, stage makeup, set design, and theater production.
- Fiction: Word lengths vary. Full-length and one-act plays for high school audiences.
- Depts/columns: Word lengths vary. Industry news, acting techniques.
- Artwork: 5x7 or larger B/W prints; 35mm or larger color transparencies; high-resolution JPEGs or TIFs. Line art.

SAMPLE ISSUE
60 pages (40% advertising): 1 article; 4 depts/columns; 1 play. Sample copy, $3 with 9x12 SASE. Guidelines available.

- "One Song, Glory." Article outlines the various song types musical theater actors must have in their repertoire for auditions.
- Sample dept/column: "Strut and Fret" discusses the growing problem of frequency interference in wireless stage microphones.

RIGHTS AND PAYMENT
First rights. Written material, $100–$500. Pays on publication. Provides 5 author's copies.

✦EDITOR'S COMMENTS
We always welcome fresh ideas, as the theater industry is always evolving. Articles should be aimed at actors, singers, or writers working to break in to professional theater.

Earlychildhood News

2 Lower Ragsdale, Suite 200
Monterey, CA 93940

Assistant Editor: Susan Swanson

DESCRIPTION AND INTERESTS
Earlychildhood News is an online magazine and resource center for parents and teachers of children up to age eight. It publishes articles on childhood development, teaching strategies, homeschooling, and assessment. Hits per month: 50,000.
Audience: Early childhood professionals, teachers, and parents
Frequency: Monthly
Website: www.earlychildhoodnews.com

FREELANCE POTENTIAL
99% written by nonstaff writers. Publishes 10+ freelance submissions yearly; 5% by unpublished writers, 15% by authors who are new to the magazine. Receives 96 queries yearly.

SUBMISSIONS
Query with author biography. Accepts email to sswanson@excelligence.com. No simultaneous submissions. Responds in 2 months.

- Articles: 800–1,200 words. Informational, how-to, and research-based articles; and personal experience pieces. Topics include child development, curricula, family relationships, health and safety, nutrition, behavior management, and professional development.
- Other: Activities and crafts.

SAMPLE ISSUE
Sample copy, guidelines, and editorial calendar available at website.

- "Summer Getaways and Activities for Families." Article explores the many different ways families can share fun time together without breaking the bank—or, in some cases, without even leaving home.
- "Read Me a Story!" Article suggests ways to incorporate reading into a parent and child's daily activities.

RIGHTS AND PAYMENT
All rights. Written material, $75–$300. Pays on acceptance.

✦EDITOR'S COMMENTS
We look for articles that offer practical strategies for educators and parents of young children, as well as curriculum and program ideas. We expect all of our writers to be early childhood development professionals, or at the very least a parent with some good ideas to share!

Early Childhood Today

Scholastic Inc.
557 Broadway
New York, NY 10012-3999

Editor: Tia Kaul Disick

DESCRIPTION AND INTERESTS
This online magazine from Scholastic equips preschool teachers with the latest research and resources in the area of early childhood development, including curriculum ideas. Most of its content is contributed by professionals in the field. Hits per month: 55,000.

Audience: Early childhood professionals
Frequency: 8 times each year
Website: www.earlychildhoodtoday.com

FREELANCE POTENTIAL
100% written by nonstaff writers. Publishes 10 freelance submissions yearly; 50% by authors who are new to the magazine. Receives 10–15 queries yearly.

SUBMISSIONS
Query. Accepts queries via website and email to ect@scholastic.com. Responds in 1 month.

- Articles: Word lengths vary. Informational, educational, and how-to articles. Topics include child advocacy, child development, special needs, communication, learning, family issues, health, technology, and cultural issues.
- Depts/columns: Word lengths vary. News, teacher tips, health information, and ideas for age-appropriate activities.

SAMPLE ISSUE
Sample copy and writers' guidelines available at website.

- "What Should a Preschooler Know About Technology?" Article offers guidance for choosing and using technology in the preschool classroom.
- "The Beat Goes On!" Article explains how the use of music and musical activities in the classroom can promote early mathematical thinking in children.

RIGHTS AND PAYMENT
All rights. Written material, payment rates vary. Pays on acceptance.

➽EDITOR'S COMMENTS
As we are a trusted resource for early childhood professionals, we insist upon publishing only sound, research-supported articles that cite—or, better yet, are written by—those well established in the field. Please note that we no longer publish a print edition. Visit our website before querying.

Educational Horizons

Pi Lambda Theta
4101 East Third Street
P.O. Box 6626
Bloomington, IN 47407-6626

Managing Editor

DESCRIPTION AND INTERESTS
The official publication of Pi Lambda Theta, *Educational Horizons* offers scholarly essays and research articles on a multitude of educational issues. Circ: 17,000.

Audience: Pi Lambda Theta members
Frequency: Quarterly
Website: www.pilambda.org

FREELANCE POTENTIAL
95% written by nonstaff writers. Publishes 10–15 freelance submissions yearly; 75% by authors who are new to the magazine. Receives 60 queries, 12 unsolicited mss yearly.

SUBMISSIONS
Prefers query with proposed word count; will accept complete ms. Accepts hard copy, disk submissions (.txt files), email to publications@ pilambda.org, and simultaneous submissions if identified. SASE. Responds to queries in 1 month, to mss in 3–4 months.

- Articles: Research articles, 2,500–4,000 words. Scholarly essays, 1,000–2,000 words. Topics include educational, social, and cultural topics of significance.
- Depts/columns: 500–750 words. Education topics in the news, multicultural education, legal issues, and book reviews.
- Artwork: Graphs and charts set in Microsoft Excel and saved as separate files.

SAMPLE ISSUE
68 pages (4% advertising): 4 articles; 5 depts/ columns; 3 book reviews. Sample copy, $5 with 9x12 SASE. Writers' guidelines available at website.

- "Dropping the Ball on Dropouts." Article compares various studies on dropout rates and finds plenty of room for interpretation.
- Sample dept/column: "Legal Update" addresses the law concerning public school employees' rights to political expression.

RIGHTS AND PAYMENT
First rights. No payment. Provides 5 contributor's copies.

➽EDITOR'S COMMENTS
Our goal is to publish essays, articles, and research that interest the reflective and inquiring educator. All material must relate to the educational or cultural issues involving schools and administration.

Educational Leadership

ASCD
1703 North Beauregard Street
Alexandria, VA 22311-1714

Editor-in-Chief: Marge Scherer

DESCRIPTION AND INTERESTS
Published by the Association for Supervision and Curriculum Development (ASCD), *Educational Leadership* features research-based articles of interest to teachers, principals, and school superintendents. Circ: 170,000.
Audience: Educators
Frequency: 8 times each year
Website: www.ascd.org

FREELANCE POTENTIAL
95% written by nonstaff writers. Publishes 130 freelance submissions yearly; 50% by unpublished writers, 50% by authors who are new to the magazine. Receives 900 unsolicited mss each year.

SUBMISSIONS
Send 2 copies of complete ms. Accepts hard copy. SASE. Responds in 2 months.

- Articles: 1,500–2,500 words. Informational, how-to, and research-based articles; program descriptions; and personal experience and opinion pieces. Topics include reading, assessment, instructional strategies, student achievement, gifted and special education, science, technology, multicultural issues.
- Depts/columns: Word lengths vary. Opinions, accountability issues, research findings, leadership challenges, principals' perspectives, ASCD news, and policy reviews.
- Artwork: B/W or color prints or slides; digital images at 300 dpi. Line art. Send only upon request.

SAMPLE ISSUE
96 pages (25% advertising): 15 articles; 9 depts/columns. Sample copy, $7. Guidelines and theme list available at website.

- "Creating Excellent and Equitable Schools." Article profiles five urban schools that made organizational changes to help improve student achievement.
- Sample dept/column: "The Principal Connection" explains how principals formally assess the preceding year each spring.

RIGHTS AND PAYMENT
All or first rights. No payment. Provides 5 copies.

••EDITOR'S COMMENTS
Articles should have fresh information and offer practical guidance. Classroom examples are appreciated.

Education Forum

60 Mobile Drive
Toronto, Ontario M4A 2P3
Canada

Managing Editor: Rhonda Allan

DESCRIPTION AND INTERESTS
This professional journal covers topics of interest to teachers and administrators in Ontario. It publishes articles and essays related to classroom management, best practices, and industry trends. Circ: 50,000.
Audience: Educators
Frequency: 3 times each year
Website: www.osstf.on.ca

FREELANCE POTENTIAL
90% written by nonstaff writers. Publishes 35 freelance submissions yearly; 20% by unpublished writers, 80% by authors who are new to the magazine. Receives 48 queries and unsolicited mss yearly.

SUBMISSIONS
Query with clips or writing samples; or send ms. Accepts hard copy. No simultaneous submissions. SAE/IRC. Responds in 1–2 months.

- Articles: To 2,500 words. How-to and practical application articles; essays; and opinion pieces. Topics include education trends, teaching techniques, and controversial issues relating to education.
- Depts/columns: "Openers," to 300 words; news and opinion pieces. "Forum Picks," word lengths vary; media and software reviews.
- Artwork: B/W and color prints and color transparencies. Line art.
- Other: Classroom activities, puzzles, and games. Submit seasonal material 8 months in advance.

SAMPLE ISSUE
46 pages (18% advertising): 4 articles; 8 depts/columns. Sample copy, free with 9x12 SAE/IRC. Guidelines available.

- "Commitment to Accessibility." Article reports on the speech of Ontario's lieutenant governor regarding a mandate to make learning accessible to all abilities.
- Sample dept/column: "Openers" discusses the challenges of diversity and accessibility.

RIGHTS AND PAYMENT
First North American serial rights. No payment. Provides 5 contributor's copies.

••EDITOR'S COMMENTS
We are open to articles that explore the contemporary issues that are shaping education.

Education Week

6935 Arlington Road, Suite 100
Bethesda, MD 20814-5233

Executive Editor: Greg Chronister

DESCRIPTION AND INTERESTS

For more than two decades, this tabloid journal has been providing education professionals with news and alerting them to trends in the field. Its articles cover emerging technologies, teaching techniques, and legislation affecting the education of children in kindergarten through grade 12. Circ: 50,000.

Audience: Educators
Frequency: 45 times each year
Website: www.edweek.org

FREELANCE POTENTIAL

8% written by nonstaff writers. Publishes 125 freelance submissions yearly; 80% by unpublished writers, 75% by authors who are new to the magazine. Receives 600 unsolicited mss each year.

SUBMISSIONS

Send complete ms. Accepts disk submissions. SASE. Responds in 6–8 weeks.

- Articles: 1,200–1,500 words. Essays about child development and education related to grades K–12 for use in "Commentary." News articles, staff written.
- Depts/columns: Staff written.

SAMPLE ISSUE

40 pages (25% advertising): 10 articles; 3 commentaries; 12 depts/columns. Sample copy, $3 with 9x12 SASE ($1 postage). Writers' guidelines available.

- "Get Performance Pay Right." Essay argues that misconceptions about performance-based pay have derailed early efforts to achieve it.
- "When the Swine Flu Strikes Your School." Personal essay written by a high school principal describes the complicated chain of events that ensued when a student was diagnosed with a "probable" case of swine flu.

RIGHTS AND PAYMENT

First rights. "Commentary" essays, $200. Pays on publication. Provides 2 contributor's copies.

➡EDITOR'S COMMENTS

We have a staff of reporters to handle our news coverage, but we rely on education professionals to supply us with thought-provoking opinion pieces on topics of interest to their peers.

EduGuide

Partnership for Learning
321 North Pine
Lansing, MI 48933

Editor: Mary Kat Parks-Workinger

DESCRIPTION AND INTERESTS

With separate editions serving the specific needs of its elementary, middle school, high school, and college audiences, *EduGuide* speaks to students and their parents about what they need to succeed. Circ: 600,000.

Audience: Parents and students
Frequency: Annually
Website: www.eduguide.org

FREELANCE POTENTIAL

40% written by nonstaff writers. Publishes 25–30 freelance submissions yearly; 10% by unpublished writers, 40% by authors who are new to the magazine.

SUBMISSIONS

Query. Accepts hard copy. SASE. Responds in 4–6 weeks.

- Articles: 500–1,000 words. Informational and how-to articles; profiles; interviews; and personal experience pieces. Topics include the arts, college, careers, computers, gifted education, health, fitness, history, humor, mathematics, music, science, technology, special education, and issues related to elementary and secondary education.
- Depts/columns: Staff written.
- Artwork: Color prints and transparencies. Line art.
- Other: Submit seasonal material 3 months in advance.

SAMPLE ISSUE

16 pages: 5 articles; 3 depts/columns. Sample copy, $3 with 9x12 SASE ($1 postage). Guidelines and editorial calendar available.

- "Helping Your Child Stay Ahead of the Curve." Article reports on the program priorities of the Michigan Department of Education and how parents can help their children at home.
- "There's a Smarter Way to Save." Article offers information about ways to save on college costs.

RIGHTS AND PAYMENT

First or second rights. All material, payment rates vary. Pays on acceptance. Provides 5 contributor's copies.

➡EDITOR'S COMMENTS

We welcome queries from professionals in all areas of education.

Edutopia

The George Lucas Educational Foundation
P.O. Box 3494
San Rafael, CA 94912

Executive Editor: Jennifer Sweeney

DESCRIPTION AND INTERESTS
Star Wars creator George Lucas founded *Edutopia* to promote positive change in education through the sharing of fresh ideas and inspiring success stories. The journal's name is derived from the vision of "a new world of learning," where innovation is the rule rather than the exception. Circ: 100,000.

Audience: Teachers, parents, policy-makers
Frequency: 8 times each year
Website: www.edutopia.org

FREELANCE POTENTIAL
70% written by nonstaff writers. Publishes 20 freelance submissions yearly; 30% by authors who are new to the magazine. Receives 36–60 queries yearly.

SUBMISSIONS
Query with résumé and clips. Accepts email to edit@edutopia.org. Response time varies.

- Articles: 300–2,500 words. Informational and how-to articles; and personal experience pieces. Topics include education, computers, science, technology, social issues, current events, health and fitness, nature and the environment, popular culture, recreation, and travel.
- Depts/columns: 700 words. Health, education, and ethnic and multicultural issues.

SAMPLE ISSUE
56 pages (35% advertising): 10 articles; 10 depts/columns. Sample copy, $4.95. Guidelines available.

- "Federal Education Funding Prompts New Hopes." Article examines how $100 billion in economic-stimulus funds earmarked for education can be used to bring authentic and lasting change to public schools.
- Sample dept/column: "Head of Class" includes a piece on how video cameras worn by students are helping teachers evaluate their own habits.

RIGHTS AND PAYMENT
First North American serial rights. Written material, payment rates vary. Pays on acceptance. Provides 2 contributor's copies.

◆▸EDITOR'S COMMENTS
Our mission relies on input and participation from a dedicated audience that actively contributes success stories from the field.

Elementary School Writer

Writer Publications
P.O. Box 718
Grand Rapids, MI 55744-0718

Editor: Emily Benes

DESCRIPTION AND INTERESTS
Founded in 1984 by an English teacher, this tabloid publishes the articles, essays, fiction, and poems of elementary school children. Its purpose is to encourage creativity, and to help students learn from reading each other's works. Circ: Unavailable.

Audience: Elementary and middle school students and teachers
Frequency: 6 times each year
Website: www.writerpublications.com

FREELANCE POTENTIAL
100% written by nonstaff writers. Publishes 300 freelance submissions yearly; 95% by unpublished writers, 75% by authors who are new to the magazine. Receives 100 unsolicited mss yearly.

SUBMISSIONS
Accepts complete ms from subscribing teachers only. Accepts hard copy, email submissions to writer@mx3.com (ASCII text only), and simultaneous submissions if identified. SASE. Response time varies.

- Articles: To 1,000 words. Informational and how-to articles; profiles; humor; opinions; and personal experience pieces. Topics include current events, multicultural and ethnic issues, nature, the environment, popular culture, sports, and travel.
- Fiction: To 1,000 words. Genres include humor, science fiction, and stories about nature and sports.
- Other: Poetry, no line limit. Seasonal material.

SAMPLE ISSUE
8 pages (no advertising): 15 articles; 3 stories; 9 poems. Guidelines available in each issue and at website.

- "Hail." Article explains how to make hail in a classroom lab or at home.
- "Beach Storm." Article relates the author's scary experience of being caught in a sudden storm on a Florida beach.

RIGHTS AND PAYMENT
One-time rights. No payment.

◆▸EDITOR'S COMMENTS
We accept submissions only from teachers who subscribe to our publication and use it as a classroom tool. All submissions should be respectful in tone.

Ellery Queen's Mystery Magazine

475 Park Avenue South, 11th Floor
New York, NY 10016

Editor: Janet Hutchings

DESCRIPTION AND INTERESTS
This journal accepts original stories of mystery, suspense, and private eye fiction. Though intended for an adult audience, some material may have crossover appeal to mature young adults. Circ: 120,000.
Audience: Adult
Frequency: 10 times each year
Website: www.themysteryplace.com/eqmm

FREELANCE POTENTIAL
100% written by nonstaff writers. Publishes 125 freelance submissions yearly; 7% by unpublished writers, 25% by authors who are new to the magazine. Receives 2,600 unsolicited mss yearly.

SUBMISSIONS
Send complete ms. Accepts hard copy and simultaneous submissions if identified. SASE. Responds in 3 months.

- Fiction: Feature stories, 2,000–12,000 words. Minute Mysteries, 250 words. Novellas by established authors, to 20,000 words. Genres include contemporary and historical crime fiction, psychological thrillers, mystery, suspense, and detective/private eye stories.
- Depts/columns: Book reviews.
- Other: Poetry.

SAMPLE ISSUE
112 pages (6% advertising): 11 stories; 2 book reviews. Sample copy, $5.50. Writers' guidelines available.

- "Telegraphing." Story includes a planned Indian casino, stolen lands, a murder mystery, and a private investigator who works the "moccasin telegraph," a gossipy network of Native Americans, to solve the crime.
- "Suitcase and Slow Time." Story slows down the time between the moment the bomb in a man's suitcase explodes and the moment he dies a millisecond later, so that all of his thoughts are revealed.

RIGHTS AND PAYMENT
First and anthology rights. Written material, $.05–$.08 per word. Pays on acceptance. Provides 3 contributor's copies.

◆ EDITOR'S COMMENTS
We are happy to review first stories by unpublished authors. Those submissions should be addressed to the Department of First Stories.

Equine Journal

103 Roxbury Street
Keene, NH 03431

Editor: Kelly Ballou

DESCRIPTION AND INTERESTS
The Equine Journal covers all breeds and all riding disciplines for horse enthusiasts at all levels. It is published in several regional editions. Circ: 30,000.
Audience: 14 years–Adult
Frequency: Monthly
Website: www.equinejournal.com

FREELANCE POTENTIAL
95% written by nonstaff writers. Publishes 100 freelance submissions yearly; 3% by authors who are new to the magazine. Receives 36–60 queries yearly.

SUBMISSIONS
Query with résumé. Accepts email queries to editorial@equinejournal.com. Responds in 2 weeks.

- Articles: 1,800 words. Informational and how-to articles. Topics include horse breeds; horseback riding; carriage driving; horse training, housing, transportation, and care; ranch management; and equine insurance.
- Depts/columns: 600 words. "Horse Health" and "Last Laugh."

SAMPLE ISSUE
138 pages (66% advertising): 11 articles; 10 depts/columns. Sample copy, $4. Guidelines and editorial calendar available.

- "Introduction to Carriage Driving." Part one of a three-part series of articles offers guidelines for harness selection and fit.
- "Barn Design." Article describes what owners like and dislike about three distinct horse barns in different areas of the country.
- Sample dept/column: "Horse Health" stresses the importance of good barn ventilation.

RIGHTS AND PAYMENT
First North American serial rights. Written material, $150–$175. Pays on acceptance. Provides 1 contributor's copy.

◆ EDITOR'S COMMENTS
The purpose of our editorial is to educate, entertain, and enable amateurs and professionals alike to stay on top of new developments in the field. Our articles and columns span the length and breadth of horse-related activities and interests from all corners of the country. We do not accept poetry, fiction, or stories told from a first-person perspective.

Exceptional Parent

416 Main Street
Johnstown, PA 15901

Managing Editor: Jan Hollingsworth

DESCRIPTION AND INTERESTS
While this magazine originally focused on children with disabilities, as medical advances and better care have increased their life expectancy, *Exceptional Parent* has broadened its editorial mission to address issues across the life-span, from infants to seniors. Circ: 70,000.

Audience: Parents and professionals
Frequency: Monthly
Website: www.eparent.com

FREELANCE POTENTIAL
90% written by nonstaff writers. Publishes 250 freelance submissions yearly; 30% by unpublished writers, 30% by authors who are new to the magazine. Receives 840 queries yearly.

SUBMISSIONS
Query. Accepts email queries to jhollingsworth@eparent.com. Responds in 3–4 weeks.

- Articles: To 2,500 words. Informational articles; profiles; interviews; and personal experience pieces. Topics include the social, psychological, legal, political, technological, financial, and educational concerns of individuals with disabilities and their caregivers.
- Depts/columns: Word lengths vary. Opinions, personal essays, news, new product information, and media reviews.

SAMPLE ISSUE
98 pages (50% advertising): 19 articles; 13 depts/columns. Sample copy, $4.99 with 9x12 SASE ($2 postage). Guidelines and editorial calendar available at website.

- "Richter-Scale Tantrums: New Hope for Exhausted Parents." Article describes research into the complementary use of medication and behavioral training to curb the extreme tantrums of autistic children.
- Sample dept/column: "Living with a Disability" provides ways to manage stress.

RIGHTS AND PAYMENT
All rights. No payment. Provides 6 copies.

➥EDITOR'S COMMENTS
We strive to maintain respect and consideration for both the professional and the caregiver; therefore, our tone is "how to work together." As journalists, we examine *all* sides of controversial issues. We are currently seeking articles about mental health issues faced by adults and children.

Faces

Cobblestone Publishing
30 Grove Street, Suite C
Peterborough, NH 03458

Editor: Elizabeth Carpentiere

DESCRIPTION AND INTERESTS
Faces shows young readers how people live in other countries, regions, and places. It publishes articles and fiction designed to encourage readers to think from a new, global perspective. Each issue focuses on a single country or region. Circ: 15,000.

Audience: 9–14 years
Frequency: 9 times each year
Website: www.cobblestonepub.com

FREELANCE POTENTIAL
60% written by nonstaff writers. Publishes 50–60 freelance submissions yearly; 20% by unpublished writers, 20% by authors who are new to the magazine. Receives 480–600 queries yearly.

SUBMISSIONS
Query with outline, bibliography, and clips or writing samples. Accepts email queries to facesmag@yahoo.com. Responds in 5 months.

- Articles: 800 words. Sidebars, 300–600 words. Informational articles and personal experience pieces. Topics include culture, geography, the environment, cuisine, special events, travel, history, and social issues.
- Fiction: To 800 words. Stories, legends, and folktales from around the world.
- Depts/columns: Staff written.
- Artwork: Color prints or transparencies.
- Other: Games, crafts, puzzles, and activities, to 700 words. Poetry, to 100 lines.

SAMPLE ISSUE
50 pages (no advertising): 12 articles; 1 story; 8 depts/columns. Sample copy, $6.95 with 9x12 SASE ($2 postage). Guidelines and theme list available at website.

- "Nature's Majesty." Article introduces readers to the incredible national parks of Alaska and Hawaii.
- "Village Voices." Article provides a tour of the Alaska Native Heritage Center, which brings Alaska's history to life.

RIGHTS AND PAYMENT
All rights. Articles and fiction, $.20–$.25 per word. Activities and puzzles, payment rates vary. Pays on publication. Provides 2 copies.

➥EDITOR'S COMMENTS
We look for writing that brings its subjects alive for our readers.

Face Up

Faith & Family

Redemptorist Communications
75 Orwell Road
Rathgar, Dublin 6
Ireland

Editor: Gerard Moloney

432 Washington Avenue
North Haven, CT 06473

Assistant Editor: Robyn Lee

DESCRIPTION AND INTERESTS

Face Up is billed as a magazine for young people who want something deeper. Although published by a Catholic organization, it is filled with lifestyle features, celebrity interviews, personality profiles, and articles that tackle today's tough social issues and topics that relate to a teen's life. Circ: 12,000.

Audience: 14–18 years
Frequency: 10 times each year
Website: www.faceup.ie

DESCRIPTION AND INTERESTS

This magazine seeks to inspire Catholic families "who are trying to achieve holiness, but who aren't perfect and need healing." It takes a contemporary, savvy approach to current issues and events of specific interest to Catholic mothers. Circ: 35,000.

Audience: Catholic mothers
Frequency: 6 times each year
Website: www.faithandfamilylive.com

FREELANCE POTENTIAL

50% written by nonstaff writers. Publishes 60 freelance submissions yearly; 25% by unpublished writers, 25% by authors who are new to the magazine. Receives 300 unsolicited mss each year.

FREELANCE POTENTIAL

75% written by nonstaff writers. Publishes 35 freelance submissions yearly; 15% by unpublished writers, 10% by authors who are new to the magazine. Receives 300 queries yearly.

SUBMISSIONS

Send complete ms. Accepts email submissions to info@faceup.ie. Responds in 1 month.

- Articles: 900 words. Informational and how-to articles; profiles; and personal experience pieces. Topics include college; careers; current events; relationships; health; fitness; music; popular culture; celebrities; sports; and multicultural, ethnic, and social issues.
- Depts/columns: 500 words. Opinions, essays, reviews, advice, self-help, profiles, interviews, and "Words of Wisdom."
- Other: Quizzes and crossword puzzles.

SUBMISSIONS

Query. Accepts email queries to editor@ faithandfamilylive.com. Responds in 2–3 months.

- Articles: 600–2,000 words. Informational, inspirational, how-to, and self-help articles; profiles; interviews; and personal experience pieces. Topics include home, family, parenting, marriage, relationships, spirituality, personal development, virtues, children's books, and current events and issues—all from a broad Catholic perspective.
- Depts/columns: Word lengths vary. Home, self-improvement, finance, health, fitness, marriage, Catholic holidays, food, entertainment, spiritual guidance, crafts, activities, and personal experience pieces.
- Artwork: Color prints or slides.

SAMPLE ISSUE

48 pages (5% advertising): 6 articles; 13 depts/columns; 1 quiz; 1 puzzle. Sample copy available at website. Guidelines and editorial calendar available.

- "When Suicide Seems the Only Option." Article examines the issue of teen suicide by interviewing survivors and the bereaved.
- Sample dept/column: "Our Sporting Life" profiles some Irish synchronized swimmers, and explains that it's more than just pointing your toes and looking graceful.

SAMPLE ISSUE

96 pages (30% advertising): 5 articles; 15 depts/columns. Sample copy, $6. Guidelines available.

- "A Mother's Easter Triumph." Personal essay describes how a certain picture book helped the author as both a child and a mother.
- Sample dept/column: "Marriage Matters" tells how a couple dealt with the husband's shoplifting addiction.

RIGHTS AND PAYMENT

Rights vary. Written material, payment rates vary. Pays on publication. Provides 2 copies.

✏️ EDITOR'S COMMENTS

We like articles that treat our readers like they are mature people who are interested in serious issues.

RIGHTS AND PAYMENT

First North American serial rights. Written material, $.33 per word. Pays on publication.

✏️ EDITOR'S COMMENTS

We look for high-quality writing that is accessible, creative, and concise. Write for the glory of God and the service of your reader!

Faith Today

M.I.P. Box 3745
Markham, Ontario L3R 0Y4
Canada

Senior Editor: Bill Fledderus

DESCRIPTION AND INTERESTS
This magazine of the Evangelical Fellowship of Canada seeks to "connect, equip, and inform" church members. Circ: 20,000.
Audience: Evangelical Christians
Frequency: 6 times each year
Website: www.evangelicalfellowship.ca

FREELANCE POTENTIAL
60% written by nonstaff writers. Publishes 120 freelance submissions yearly; 1% by unpublished writers, 10% by authors who are new to the magazine. Receives 120 queries yearly.

SUBMISSIONS
Query. Prefers email to editor@faithtoday.ca (Microsoft Word attachments); will accept hard copy. SAE/IRC. Responds in 3 weeks.

- Articles: 800–1,800 words. Cover stories, 2,000 words. Essays, 650–1,200 words. Informational and how-to articles; profiles; interviews; and opinion pieces. Topics include Christianity in Canada, ministry initiatives, prayer, the Bible, and issues of concern to Evangelical Christians.
- Depts/columns: "Kingdom Matters," 50–350 words. News, 300–700 words. Media reviews, to 300 words.

SAMPLE ISSUE
47 pages (20% advertising): 5 articles; 13 depts/columns. Sample copy, free. Guidelines available at website.

- "How to Rise Above the Economic Crisis." Article provides biblical wisdom on personal money management.
- Sample dept/column: "Christ & Culture in Canada" examines whether Canadian morality has declined in recent years.

RIGHTS AND PAYMENT
First North American serial and perpetual electronic rights. Articles, $.25 Canadian per word. Essays, $.15 per word. Depts/columns, $.20 per word. Kill fee, 30–50%. Pays within 6 weeks of acceptance. Provides 2 copies.

☛EDITOR'S COMMENTS
Each issue of our magazine includes a mix of four to six feature stories. A typical feature is written in the third person and has a point of view that is supported by clear arguments based on sound research and interviews with Canadian sources.

Families on the Go

Life Media
P.O. Box 55445
St. Petersburg, FL 33732

Editor: Barbara Doyle

DESCRIPTION AND INTERESTS
Appearing online and in print, *Families on the Go* provides parents with information on health and wellness, education, child-rearing, and family activities that empower them to nurture positive relationships. It has four editions, each serving a different region of Florida. Circ: 120,000.
Audience: Parents
Frequency: 6 times each year
Website: www.familiesonthego.org

FREELANCE POTENTIAL
80% written by nonstaff writers. Publishes 50 freelance submissions yearly; 25% by unpublished writers, 20% by authors who are new to the magazine.

SUBMISSIONS
Query or send complete ms. Accepts hard copy and email submissions to editor@ familiesonthego.org (Microsoft Word attachments). SASE. Responds if interested.

- Articles: 350–750 words. Informational articles. Topics include health, wellness, fitness, parenting issues, education, family relationships, home and garden, the arts, travel, and entertainment.
- Depts/columns: Word lengths vary. Community news.

SAMPLE ISSUE
48 pages: 3 articles; 13 depts/columns. Sample copy, free with 9x12 SASE (4 first-class stamps); also available at website. Guidelines available at website.

- "Staycations: Vacations Close to Home." Article profiles several family-friendly destinations within a close distance.
- Sample dept/column: "Sun and Safety" explains the SPF ratings on sunscreen, and provides tips for protecting children's skin from the sun.

RIGHTS AND PAYMENT
Exclusive regional rights. Written material, payment rates vary. Pays on publication. Provides 2 contributor's copies.

☛EDITOR'S COMMENTS
Any article that will inform, support, or guide parents will be of interest to us. All articles should relate to one of our publishing areas. Practical tips are always a plus.

Family Circle

Meredith Corporation
375 Lexington Avenue, 9th Floor
New York, NY 10017

Executive Editor: Darcy Jacobs

DESCRIPTION AND INTERESTS
Food, health and fitness, home decor, and, of course, family life . . . this popular women's magazine covers it all. Its pages include a mix of practical and how-to articles, slice-of-life stories, and profiles. Circ: 3.8 million.

Audience: Families
Frequency: 15 times each year
Website: www.familycircle.com

FREELANCE POTENTIAL
80% written by nonstaff writers. Publishes many freelance submissions yearly. Receives hundreds of queries yearly.

SUBMISSIONS
Query with clips (including 1 from a national magazine) and author bio. Accepts hard copy. No simultaneous submissions. SASE. Responds in 6–8 weeks if interested.

- Articles: 1,000–2,000 words. Informational and how-to articles; profiles; and personal experience pieces. Topics include parenting, relationships, health, safety, fitness, home decor, travel, fashion, and cooking.
- Depts/columns: 750 words. "My Hometown," "My Family Life," "Good Works," recipes, beauty tips, shopping tips, fitness routines, and advice.

SAMPLE ISSUE
210 pages (48% advertising): 18 articles; 1 story; 20 depts/columns. Sample copy, $1.99 at newsstands. Guidelines available.

- "Single Mom Seeks Date." Article shares the author's experiences dating again, this time as a single mom.
- "Lose Weight Faster." Article details an eating plan that allows one to eat more often and lose weight.
- Sample dept/column: "Food News" looks at in-season vegetables and discusses how to choose and use them.

RIGHTS AND PAYMENT
All rights. Written material, payment rates vary. Kill fee, 25%. Pays on acceptance. Provides 1 contributor's copy.

➠EDITOR'S COMMENTS
Look at past issues to gain an understanding of the kinds of subjects we tackle. Remember that we are a general interest women's magazine with a focus on family.

The Family Digest

P.O. Box 40137
Fort Wayne, IN 46804

Manuscript Editor: Corine B. Erlandson

DESCRIPTION AND INTERESTS
This Catholic magazine celebrates the everyday joys of family and faith, and encourages active participation in parish life. Circ: 150,000.

Audience: Families
Frequency: Quarterly

FREELANCE POTENTIAL
95% written by nonstaff writers. Publishes 44 freelance submissions yearly; 30% by authors who are new to the magazine. Receives 500 unsolicited mss yearly.

SUBMISSIONS
Send complete ms. Accepts hard copy. No simultaneous submissions. Previously published material will be considered. SASE. Responds in 1–2 months.

- Articles: 700–1,200 words. Informational, self-help, how-to, and inspirational articles; and personal experience pieces. Topics include parish and family life, spirituality, Catholic traditions, the saints, prayer life, and seasonal material.
- Depts/columns: Staff written.
- Other: Humorous anecdotes, 15–100 words. Cartoons. Submit seasonal material 7 months in advance.

SAMPLE ISSUE
48 pages (no advertising): 11 articles; 5 depts/columns. Sample copy, free with 6x9 SASE (2 first-class stamps). Guidelines and theme list available.

- "Heavy Housework on Sunday?" Personal essay shares the writer's view on keeping the Sabbath holy.
- "St. Thomas Aquinas, Patron Saint of Students." Article profiles the thirteenth-century scholar nicknamed "Dumb Ox."

RIGHTS AND PAYMENT
First North American serial rights. Articles, $40–$60. Anecdotes, $25. Cartoons, $40. Pays 1–2 months after acceptance. Provides 2 contributor's copies.

➠EDITOR'S COMMENTS
We prefer to purchase and publish previously unpublished articles, but will sometimes consider previously published material. Please include the publication history with your article submissions. Note that we do not publish poetry or fiction.

Family Fun

47 Pleasant Street
Northampton, MA 01060

Department Editor: John Adolph

DESCRIPTION AND INTERESTS
This popular family magazine presents ideas and information on ways families can have fun together. It publishes articles on travel, food, crafts, parties, games, holidays, and toys. Circ: 2 million.
Audience: Parents
Frequency: 10 times each year
Website: www.familyfun.com

FREELANCE POTENTIAL
80% written by nonstaff writers. Publishes 100+ freelance submissions yearly; 1% by unpublished writers, 2% by authors who are new to the magazine. Receives thousands of queries and unsolicited mss yearly.

SUBMISSIONS
Query for features. Send complete ms for depts/columns. Accepts hard copy and email to queries.familyfun@disney.com. SASE. Responds in 4–6 weeks.

- Articles: 850–3,000 words. Informational and how-to articles. Topics include food, crafts, parties, holidays, sports, and games.
- Depts/columns: 50–1,200 words. See guidelines for details. Crafts, nature activities, recipes, family getaways and traditions, household hints, healthy fun, home decorating and gardening tips, and product reviews.
- Other: Submit seasonal material 6 months in advance.

SAMPLE ISSUE
120 pages (47% advertising): 6 articles; 8 depts/columns. Sample copy, $3.95 at newsstands. Guidelines available.

- "Jungle Party." Article explains how to throw a wild and fun jungle-themed birthday party, and includes instructions for games, food, and decorations.
- Sample dept/column: "Family Ties" offers a touching essay about a father's attempts to stay connected to and needed by his growing daughter.

RIGHTS AND PAYMENT
First serial rights. Written material, payment rates vary. Pays on acceptance.

➥EDITOR'S COMMENTS
Our needs and payment rates are spelled out in our guidelines. We look for projects that are fun, easy, and original.

Family Works Magazine

4 Joseph Court
San Rafael, CA 94903

Editor: Lew Tremaine

DESCRIPTION AND INTERESTS
Family Works Magazine seeks to reach people of all ages and stages of family development in California's Marin and Sonoma counties. It offers parenting advice as well as coverage of regional events and activities. Circ: 20,000.
Audience: Parents
Frequency: 6 times each year
Website: www.familyworks.org

FREELANCE POTENTIAL
80% written by nonstaff writers. Publishes 75 freelance submissions yearly; 25% by authors who are new to the magazine. Receives 100+ unsolicited mss yearly.

SUBMISSIONS
Send complete ms. Accepts hard copy, disk submissions, and email submissions to familynews@familyworks.org. Availability of artwork improves chance of acceptance. SASE. Responds in 1 month.

- Articles: 1,000 words. Informational articles; profiles; and interviews. Topics include parenting, family issues, recreation, education, finance, crafts, hobbies, sports, health, fitness, nature, and the environment.
- Depts/columns: Word lengths vary. Community news, reviews, and recipes.
- Artwork: B/W or color prints.

SAMPLE ISSUE
24 pages (46% advertising): 10 articles. Sample copy available at website. Guidelines available.

- "Three Tricks to Bouncing Back Aboard the Weight-Loss Wagon." Article provides strategies for getting on—and staying on—the fitness track.
- "The Prince/Princess Syndrome." Article tells how to deal with children who must always get their way . . . or else.
- "From a Z Student to an A Student." Personal essay tells how the author drastically changed his academic performance.

RIGHTS AND PAYMENT
One-time rights. No payment. Provides 3 contributor's copies.

➥EDITOR'S COMMENTS
We look for insightful articles on raising children, improving family communication, and building compassion. Both established and first-time writers are welcome to contribute.

Faze

4936 Yonge Street, Suite 2400
North York, Ontario M2N 6S3
Canada

Editor-in-Chief: Dana Marie Krook

DESCRIPTION AND INTERESTS
This magazine for young women promotes a positive, educational, and empowering message. Embracing a fun, energetic, and exciting tone, it publishes articles on celebrities, pop culture, world issues, sports, beauty, fashion, and technology. Circ: 120,000.
Audience: Girls, 13–24
Frequency: 5 times each year
Website: www.faze.ca

FREELANCE POTENTIAL
35–40% written by nonstaff writers. Publishes 50–60 freelance submissions yearly; 10% by unpublished writers, 10% by authors who are new to the magazine. Receives 150 queries each year.

SUBMISSIONS
Query with résumé and writing samples. Accepts email queries to editor@fazeteen.com. Responds if interested.

- Articles: Word lengths vary. Informational and factual articles; profiles; interviews; and personal experience pieces. Topics include current affairs, real-life and social issues, celebrities, entertainment, sports, science, travel, business, technology, and health.
- Depts/columns: Word lengths vary. Short profiles, career descriptions, new products.

SAMPLE ISSUE
66 pages (30% advertising): 9 articles; 8 depts/columns. Sample copy, $3.50 Canadian. Guidelines available at website.

- "Kreesha Turner: Taking the Lead." Article profiles the persistence and passion of the Canadian pop sensation.
- "Rock Star." Article interviews Amy Lee of Evanescence about becoming a success in a predominantly male profession.

RIGHTS AND PAYMENT
All rights. Written material, $50–$250. Payment policy varies. Provides 1 contributor's copy.

➙EDITOR'S COMMENTS
The best advice we can give writers hoping to be published in our magazine is "share your vision." Each of our writers brings something to the table that is his or her own. We want pieces that speak to our readers on their level, and that give young women positive reinforcement about their own awesomeness.

Fertility Today

P.O. Box 117
Laurel, MD 20725

Editor: Diana Broomfield, M.D.

DESCRIPTION AND INTERESTS
Fertility Today is a comprehensive, multidisciplinary magazine that provides reproductive-age couples and individuals with information on fertility and infertility. It addresses the biological, scientific, and emotional issues of the topic. Circ: 175,000.
Audience: Adults
Frequency: Quarterly
Website: www.fertilitytoday.org

FREELANCE POTENTIAL
75% written by nonstaff writers. Publishes 150 freelance submissions yearly; 15% by authors who are new to the magazine. Receives 144 queries yearly.

SUBMISSIONS
Query with author biography; physicians should also include address of practice. Accepts email queries to articles@ fertilitytoday.org. Responds in 2 months.

- Articles: 800–1,800 words. Informational articles; profiles; interviews; and opinion and personal experience pieces. Topics include fertility issues and treatments, and male and female reproductive health.
- Depts/columns: 1,800 words. "Exercise and Nutrition," "Adoption/Child-Free Living," "Mind, Body & Soul," "My Story." Reviews of books on fertility topics. "Health Forum," written by physicians.

SAMPLE ISSUE
96 pages (25% advertising): 2 articles; 11 depts/columns. Sample copy, $6.95. Guidelines and editorial calendar available at website.

- "Ovarian Function." Article discusses the normal function of the ovaries, and includes information on irregularities that may exist, decreasing fertility or making reproduction more difficult.
- Sample dept/column: "Child-Free Living" looks at the pros and cons of choosing to remain childless.

RIGHTS AND PAYMENT
All rights. Written material, $.50 per word. Kill fee, $100. Pays on acceptance. Provides 3 contributor's copies.

➙EDITOR'S COMMENTS
All articles must be scientifically valid, but free of medical jargon.

FitPregnancy

21100 Erwin Street
Woodland Hills, CA 91367

Executive Editor: Sharon Cohen

DESCRIPTION AND INTERESTS
Keeping fit during pregnancy to help ensure a good delivery and healthy baby is what this publication is about. But it goes even further than fitness, publishing articles on all topics related to pregnancy and childbirth, fashion, and wellness. Circ: 500,000.

Audience: Women
Frequency: 6 times each year
Website: www.fitpregnancy.com

FREELANCE POTENTIAL
40% written by nonstaff writers. Publishes 50 freelance submissions yearly; 30% by authors who are new to the magazine. Receives 360 queries yearly.

SUBMISSIONS
Query with clips. Accepts email to scohen@ fitpregnancy.com. Responds in 1 month.

- Articles: 1,000–1,800 words. Informational articles; profiles; and personal experience pieces. Topics include prenatal fitness and nutrition, postpartum issues, breastfeeding, baby care, psychology, and health.
- Depts/columns: 550–1,000 words. Essays by fathers, family issues, prenatal health, new-born health, psychology, childbirth, prenatal nutrition, and relevant news briefs. "Time Out," 550 words.
- Other: Recipes and meal plans.

SAMPLE ISSUE
128 pages (42% advertising): 5 articles; 12 depts/columns. Sample copy, $4.95 at news-stands. Guidelines available at website.

- "All About the First Trimester." Article offers a primer on the first three months of pregnancy, from cravings to morning sickness to calculating due dates.
- "Watermelon Wonders." Article reports on the many prenatal benefits of eating watermelon, and provides some delicious summer recipes featuring the fruit.

RIGHTS AND PAYMENT
Rights vary. Written material, payment rates vary. Pays on publication. Provides 2 contributor's copies.

➝ EDITOR'S COMMENTS
We get a lot of the "usual" topics pitched to us. Get our attention by teaching us something we didn't know.

FLW Outdoors

30 Gamble Lane
Benton, KY 42054

Editor: Jason Sealock

DESCRIPTION AND INTERESTS
Fishing enthusiasts read this magazine to satisfy their need for fishing information, tales, and news of tournaments. It has several editions dedicated to various types of fishing, and each one features something—including photo spreads—for very young anglers. Circ: 100,000.

Audience: 5–12 years; Adults
Frequency: 8 times each year
Website: www.flwoutdoors.com

FREELANCE POTENTIAL
50% written by nonstaff writers. Of the free-lance submissions published yearly, 10% are by authors who are new to the magazine. Receives 300 queries yearly.

SUBMISSIONS
Query with writing sample. Accepts email queries to info@flwoutdoors.com. Responds in 1 week.

- Articles: 200 words. Informational and how-to articles; profiles; and humor. Topics include fish, fishing techniques, fishing gear, nature, and the environment.
- Fiction: To 500 words. Genres include adventure. Also publishes nature stories.
- Depts/columns: Word lengths vary. Boat technology, tournaments, fishing destinations, product reviews, and environmental issues.
- Other: Puzzles.

SAMPLE ISSUE
88 pages: 5 articles; 13 depts/columns. Sample copy, $3.95 at newsstands. Writers' guidelines available.

- "Pad Bass." Article explains the ins and outs of finding—and catching—bass among the lily pads.
- Sample dept/column: "Boat Tech" offers suggestions for aftermarket customization of a boat without a big price tag.

RIGHTS AND PAYMENT
First North American serial rights. Written material, $200–$500. Payment policy varies.

➝ EDITOR'S COMMENTS
A large portion of our readers are tournament anglers, but many are fairly new to the sport; therefore, we are open to articles that target either demographic. We're always looking for information about fishing with kids and getting youngsters interested in the sport.

Focus on the Family Clubhouse

Focus on the Family
8605 Explorer Drive
Colorado Springs, CO 80920

Editor: Jesse Florea

DESCRIPTION AND INTERESTS
With articles, stories, puzzles, and games rooted in Christian values, *Focus on the Family Clubhouse* targets middle-grade readers. Circ: 85,000.
Audience: 8–14 years
Frequency: Monthly
Website: www.clubhousemagazine.com

FREELANCE POTENTIAL
75% written by nonstaff writers. Publishes 70 freelance submissions yearly; 5% by unpublished writers, 15% by authors who are new to the magazine. Receives 900 unsolicited mss each year.

SUBMISSIONS
Send complete ms. Accepts hard copy. SASE. Responds in 6–8 weeks.

- Articles: 800–1,000 words. Informational, how-to, and factual articles; interviews; personal experience pieces; and humor. Topics include sports, nature, travel, history, religion, current events, multicultural issues, and noteworthy Christians.
- Fiction: Humor, 500 words. Historical Christian fiction, 900–1,600 words. Choose-your-own adventure stories, 1,600–1,800 words. Mysteries and contemporary, multicultural, fantasy, and science fiction, 1,600 words.
- Depts/columns: 300 words. Short, humorous news articles emphasizing biblical lessons.
- Other: Activities, quizzes, jokes, and recipes.

SAMPLE ISSUE
24 pages (5% advertising): 4 articles; 1 story; 9 depts/columns; 4 puzzles; 1 cartoon. Sample copy, $1.50 with 9x12 SASE (2 first-class stamps). Guidelines available.

- "Jumping the Wake." Article profiles world champion wakeboarder Emily Copeland Durham, who "rides for God."
- Sample dept/column: "High Voltage" answers readers' questions about the media.

RIGHTS AND PAYMENT
First rights. Written material, to $150. Pays on acceptance. Provides 5 contributor's copies.

➥EDITOR'S COMMENTS
Approximately 10 percent of our content is written by our readers and members. We are always looking for articles and fiction geared toward a tween audience.

Focus on the Family Clubhouse Jr.

Focus on the Family
8605 Explorer Drive
Colorado Springs, CO 80920

Editor: Suzanne Hadley

DESCRIPTION AND INTERESTS
This younger sibling of *Focus on the Family Clubhouse* sends the same Christian message to little kids through fun stories and activities. Circ: 65,000.
Audience: 4–8 years
Frequency: Monthly
Website: www.clubhousejr.com

FREELANCE POTENTIAL
45% written by nonstaff writers. Publishes 10–15 freelance submissions yearly; 5% by unpublished writers, 10% by authors who are new to the magazine. Receives 720 unsolicited mss yearly.

SUBMISSIONS
Send complete ms. Accepts hard copy. No simultaneous submissions. SASE. Responds in 4–6 weeks.

- Articles: To 600 words. Informational articles. Topics include entertainment, sports, recreation, fitness, health, nature, the environment, hobbies, and multicultural issues.
- Fiction: 250–1,000 words. Genres include Bible stories; humor; folktales; and religious, contemporary, and historical fiction. Also publishes rebuses.
- Depts/columns: Word lengths vary. Personal anecdotes, humor, recipes, and crafts.
- Other: Games, jokes, and comic strips.

SAMPLE ISSUE
24 pages (no advertising): 2 articles; 1 rebus; 6 depts/columns; 2 comic strips; 1 poem; 1 game. Sample copy, $1.50 with 9x12 SASE (2 first-class stamps). Guidelines available.

- "Made for a Purpose." Article by Christian singer Jason Barton of 33Miles makes an analogy between riding bikes and knowing one's God-given purpose.
- Sample dept/column: "You Make It" provides recipes for insect-themed snacks.

RIGHTS AND PAYMENT
First North American serial rights. Written material, to $150. Pays on acceptance. Provides 2 contributor's copies.

➥EDITOR'S COMMENTS
Our readers love projects such as crafts, cooking, and science experiments. Our editors love such projects that impart a Christian message while teaching about the world.

The Forensic Teacher

P.O. Box 5263
Wilmington, DE 19808

Editor: Mark Feil

DESCRIPTION AND INTERESTS
Teachers in middle school, high school, and college read this professional journal for better, easier, and more engaging ways to teach forensics. Articles are practice-based and filled with tips and techniques. Circ: 30,000.

Audience: Teachers, middle school–college
Frequency: Quarterly
Website: www.theforensicteacher.com

FREELANCE POTENTIAL
50% written by nonstaff writers. Publishes 18 freelance submissions yearly. Receives 24–60 queries, 24–36 unsolicited mss yearly.

SUBMISSIONS
Query with clips or writing samples; or send complete ms. Accepts email submissions to admin@theforensicteacher.com (attach photos separately). Availability of artwork improves chance of acceptance. Responds to queries in 2 weeks, to mss in 2 months.

- Articles: 400–2,000 words. Informational and how-to articles; lesson plans; photo-essays; and personal experience pieces. Topics include forensics, industry news, science, technology, and forensic law.
- Depts/columns: Word lengths vary. Classroom mystery projects, forensic history and trivia, book reviews.
- Other: Submit seasonal information 6 months in advance.
- Artwork: Color prints.

SAMPLE ISSUE
32 pages: 8 articles; 6 depts/columns. Sample copy, $5. Guidelines available at website.

- "Practical Dental Exercises for Teachers." Article provides several resources for teaching how to use dental charts in forensics.
- Sample dept/column: "Mini-Mystery" offers the details of a mystery that a forensics class can solve.

RIGHTS AND PAYMENT
First, second, and electronic rights. Articles and depts/columns, $.02 per word. News items, $10 each. Pays 60 days after publication.

➥EDITOR'S COMMENTS
Our advice to new writers would be to write for the forensic teacher who is looking to learn a better, more streamlined way of teaching the topic.

For Every Woman

General Council of the Assemblies of God
1445 North Boonville Avenue
Springfield, MO 65802

Administrative Coordinator: Deborah Hampton

DESCRIPTION AND INTERESTS
This e-zine is written for Christian women in all stages of life. Its content is primarily made up of articles on motherhood and family life. Hits per month: 83,000.

Audience: Women
Frequency: Ongoing
Website: www.women.ag.org

FREELANCE POTENTIAL
50% written by nonstaff writers. Of the freelance submissions published yearly, 80% are by unpublished writers and 10% are by authors who are new to the magazine. Receives 240–360 unsolicited mss yearly.

SUBMISSIONS
Send complete ms. Accepts email submissions to dhampton@ag.org (Microsoft Word attachments). Response time varies.

- Articles: 500–800 words. Informational, inspirational, and self-help articles; and personal experience pieces. Topics include blended families, marriage, family life, special education, health, crafts, hobbies, multicultural and ethnic issues, music, popular culture, religion, faith, and social issues.
- Other: Submit seasonal material 4–6 months in advance.

SAMPLE ISSUE
Sample copy, guidelines, and theme list available at website.

- "Help! I'm Wrecking My Kids!" Article reassures readers that they don't need to be perfect parents.
- "I'm Not That Kind of Mother." Personal essay tells how a woman realized there were no boundaries to her motherhood.
- "Connecting with Your Son." Article suggests several fun activities for mothers and sons to do together.

RIGHTS AND PAYMENT
One-time and electronic rights. No payment.

➥EDITOR'S COMMENTS
We are actively seeking submissions on being the mother of a special child, coping with the death of a child, or motherhood in general. We are particularly interested in inspirational stories containing scriptural support. Please refrain from sending us articles on health topics—we're currently overstocked.

Fort Myers & Southwest Florida

15880 Summerlin Road, Suite 189
Fort Myers, FL 33908

Publisher: Andrew Elias

DESCRIPTION AND INTERESTS
The arts, education, lifestyle, and events of southwestern Florida are covered in detail in this regional magazine. It also features articles on health and fitness, travel, and parenting issues. Circ: 20,000.

Audience: Adults
Frequency: 6 times each year
Website: www.ftmyersmagazine.com

FREELANCE POTENTIAL
75–90% written by nonstaff writers. Publishes 20–30 freelance submissions yearly; 80% by unpublished writers, 75% by authors who are new to the magazine. Receives 50–75 queries each year.

SUBMISSIONS
Send complete ms. Accepts email submissions to ftmyers@optonline.net (Microsoft Word attachments or pasted in body of email). Responds in 1–6 weeks.

- Articles: 500–2,000 words. Informational articles; profiles; interviews; reviews; and local news. Topics include the arts, media, entertainment, travel, computers, crafts, current events, health and fitness, history, popular culture, recreation, social and environmental issues, and parenting.
- Depts/columns: Word lengths vary. Sports, recreation, and book reviews.
- Artwork: JPEG, TIFF, or PDF images.

SAMPLE ISSUE
28 pages (40% advertising): 1 article; 6 depts/columns; 1 calendar. Sample copy, $3 with 9x12 SASE ($.77 postage). Guidelines and editorial calendar available at website.

- "Sinclair's Sexy Sci-Fi Saga." Article examines the life and career of local science fiction author Linnea Sinclair.
- "Finding Beauty in Destruction." Article profiles a sculptor who specializes in turning fallen trees into works of art.

RIGHTS AND PAYMENT
One-time rights. Written material, $.10 per word. Artwork, $20–$50. Pays 30 days from publication. Provides 2 contributor's copies.

➥EDITOR'S COMMENTS
All of our articles have a local flair or angle and appeal to our affluent and educated readers. Good photography is also important.

Fort Worth Child

Lauren Publications
4275 Kellway Circle, Suite 146
Addison, TX 75001

Editorial Director: Gretchen Sparling

DESCRIPTION AND INTERESTS
This "magazine parents live by in Tarrant County" keeps on top of current issues related to child-rearing, while also providing fresh takes on perennial topics. Circ: 45,000.

Audience: Parents
Frequency: Monthly
Website: www.fortworthchild.com

FREELANCE POTENTIAL
25% written by nonstaff writers. Publishes 12–15 freelance submissions yearly; 20% by authors who are new to the magazine. Receives 240 queries yearly.

SUBMISSIONS
Query with résumé. Accepts hard copy, email queries to editorial@dallaschild.com, faxes to 972-447-0633, and simultaneous submissions if identified. SASE. Response time varies.

- Articles: 1,000–2,500 words. Informational self-help, and how-to articles; humor; profiles; and personal experience pieces. Topics include parenting, education, child development, family travel, regional news, recreation, entertainment, current events, social issues, multicultural and ethnic subjects, health, fitness, and crafts.
- Depts/columns: 800 words. Family activities, health, safety, news briefs, education, child development, humor, fathers' perspectives, and reviews.

SAMPLE ISSUE
66 pages (14% advertising): 2 articles; 12 depts/columns. Sample copy, free with 9x12 SASE. Guidelines available at website.

- "Why Texans Should Care About Children's Health Insurance." Article discusses efforts to expand the state's CHIP coverage to middle-class families.
- Sample dept/column: "Take Note" offers solutions to children's bedwetting.

RIGHTS AND PAYMENT
First rights. Written material, payment rates vary. Pays on publication. Provides contributor's copies upon request.

➥EDITOR'S COMMENTS
While many parenting issues are universal, we seek articles that are written specifically for our readers in greater Forth Worth. Please research local sources if you plan to query us.

Fostering Families Today

541 East Garden Drive, Unit N
Windsor, CO 80550

Editor: Richard Fischer

DESCRIPTION AND INTERESTS
This is a magazine written about the parents, children, and professionals involved with the child welfare system. It features articles about foster care, domestic adoption, the legal and emotional issues involved, and personal stories of success. Circ: 26,000.

Audience: Adoptive and foster parents
Frequency: 6 times each year
Website: www.fosteringfamiliestoday.com

FREELANCE POTENTIAL
85% written by nonstaff writers. Publishes 40–45 freelance submissions yearly; 30% by unpublished writers, 30% by authors who are new to the magazine. Receives 72–120 unsolicited mss yearly.

SUBMISSIONS
Send complete ms with permission agreement form (available at website). Accepts hard copy and email submissions to louis@adoptinfo.net (attach file). SASE. Response time varies.

- Articles: 500–1,200 words. Informational and how-to articles; profiles; and personal experience pieces. Topics include adoption, foster parenting, child development, relevant research, health, education, and legal issues.
- Depts/columns: Word lengths vary. News, opinions, advice, profiles, legislation, book reviews, and child advocacy.
- Other: Poetry.

SAMPLE ISSUE
62 pages (no advertising): 14 articles; 8 depts/columns. Sample copy and guidelines available at website.

- "Choosing Schools—Know Your Child." Article examines the many factors that go into choosing a school—public or private—for an adopted child.
- Sample dept/column: "A+ Teacher" offers ideas for sharing one's adoptive status with teachers and classmates.

RIGHTS AND PAYMENT
Non-exclusive print and electronic rights. No payment. Provides 3 contributor's copies and a 1-year subscription.

➡️ EDITOR'S COMMENTS
We are open to hearing your personal story of foster care and/or adoption, especially if other parents can benefit from it.

Fox Valley Kids

2920 South Webster Avenue
Green Bay, WI 54301

Editor: Jen Hogeland

DESCRIPTION AND INTERESTS
Fox Valley Kids offers family-centered articles as well as activities. It focuses on parenting and family issues of interest to Wisconsin readers. Circ: 40,000.

Audience: Families
Frequency: Monthly
Website: www.newandfoxvalleykids.com

FREELANCE POTENTIAL
30% written by nonstaff writers. Publishes 10–12 freelance submissions yearly; 10% by unpublished writers, 10% by authors who are new to the magazine. Receives 120–240 queries yearly.

SUBMISSIONS
Query or send complete ms. Accepts email to jlhogeland@yahoo.com. Response time varies.

- Articles: To 750 words. Informational, how-to, and humorous articles. Topics include parenting, education, recreation, crafts, hobbies, music, the arts, health, fitness, sports, pets, family travel, and home improvement.
- Depts/columns: To 750 words. Reader stories, news briefs, and crafts.
- Other: Submit seasonal material at least 4 months in advance.

SAMPLE ISSUE
12 pages (50% advertising): 5 articles; 4 depts/columns; 1 calendar. Sample copy available at website. Guidelines and editorial calendar available.

- "Bacteria: The Good Guys." Article explains that while some bacteria are indeed harmful, many are beneficial, and killing all of them through over-sanitizing can be detrimental to children's health in the long run.
- Sample dept/column: "Decorating Eggs" offers step-by-step instructions for decorating eggs (or other items) in the bathtub using finger paints.

RIGHTS AND PAYMENT
Rights negotiable. All material, payment rates vary. Pays on publication. Provides 1 contributor's copy upon request.

➡️ EDITOR'S COMMENTS
We'd like to see more articles on family activities; building morals; positive discipline techniques; and teaching ethics, honesty, and integrity to children.

The Friend

The Church of Jesus Christ
of Latter-day Saints
50 East North Temple, 24th Floor
Salt Lake City, UT 84150

Managing Editor: Julie Wardell

DESCRIPTION AND INTERESTS
Written for children up to 12 years old, this
magazine is filled with true-life stories that
show the Gospel of Jesus Christ at work in
kids' lives. It also publishes poetry and activi-
ties, as well as true stories written by children.
Circ: 285,000.
Audience: 3–12 years
Frequency: Monthly
Website: www.lds.org

FREELANCE POTENTIAL
60% written by nonstaff writers.

SUBMISSIONS
Send complete ms. Accepts hard copy and
email submissions to friend@ldschurch.org. No
simultaneous submissions. SASE. Responds in
2 months.

- Articles: To 900 words. Informational and
  factual articles; profiles; true stories; photo-
  essays; and personal experience pieces.
  True stories for young readers and preschool
  children, 250 words. Topics include spirituality, the Mormon church, personal faith,
  and conflict resolution.
- Depts/columns: Word lengths vary. Profiles
  of children from different countries.
- Artwork: B/W and color prints.
- Other: Poetry, line limits vary. Puzzles, activities, crafts, and cartoons. Submit seasonal
  material 8 months in advance.

SAMPLE ISSUE
48 pages (no advertising): 12 articles; 2 depts/
columns; 1 poem; 9 activities and puzzles.
Sample copy, $1.50 with 9x12 SASE (4 first-
class stamps). Guidelines available at website.

- "Standing Up for Caleb." True story relates
  how a young girl had the courage to stick up
  for a new boy in class.
- Sample dept/column: "Making Friends" profiles a boy in Brazil who is a budding gymnast and a Mormon.

RIGHTS AND PAYMENT
First rights. Written material, $100–$250. Poetry,
$25. Activities, $20. Pays on acceptance.
Provides 2 contributor's copies.

➼EDITOR'S COMMENTS
All stories should be about real children
discovering or applying Gospel truths in overcoming temptations or conflicts.

Fun For Kidz

P.O. Box 227
Bluffton, OH 45817-0227

Editor: Marilyn Edwards

DESCRIPTION AND INTERESTS
Published in alternate months from its compan-
ions *Boys' Quest* and *Hopscotch*, this activity-
filled magazine makes learning fun. Circ: 7,000.
Audience: 6–13 years
Frequency: 6 times each year
Website: www.funforkidz.com

FREELANCE POTENTIAL
70% written by nonstaff writers. Publishes
100–150 freelance submissions yearly; 40% by
unpublished writers, 40% by authors who are
new to the magazine. Receives 120 queries,
1,200 unsolicited mss yearly.

SUBMISSIONS
Prefers complete ms; will accept query.
Accepts hard copy and simultaneous submis-
sions if identified. Availability of artwork
improves chance of acceptance. SASE.
Responds in 4–6 months.

- Articles: 500 words. Informational and how-
  to articles. Topics include nature, science,
  pets, hobbies, cooking, sports, and careers.
- Fiction: 500 words. Genres include adventure, mystery, and humor.
- Depts/columns: Word lengths vary. Activities
  and science experiments.
- Artwork: B/W and color prints. Line art.
- Other: Puzzles, games, and cartoons. Poetry.
  Submit seasonal info 6–12 months in
  advance.

SAMPLE ISSUE
48 pages (no advertising): 8 articles; 6 depts/
columns; 7 puzzles; 3 poems; 4 cartoons.
Sample copy, $6. Guidelines and theme list
available at website.

- "What Causes Wind?" Article explains how
  airflow between high-pressure areas and low-
  pressure areas creates wind.
- Sample dept/column: "Computer Quest"
  explains how to write a program that forecasts the weather.

RIGHTS AND PAYMENT
First North American serial rights. Articles and
fiction, $.05+ per word. Poetry and puzzles,
$10+. Artwork, $5–$35. Pays on publication.
Provides 1 contributor's copy.

➼EDITOR'S COMMENTS
We're looking for lively writing that involves a
wholesome and unusual activity.

Games

6198 Butler Pike, Suite 200
Blue Bell, PA 19422-2600

Editor-in-Chief: R. Wayne Schmittberger

DESCRIPTION AND INTERESTS
This "magazine for creative minds at play" features puzzles and challenges for young adult and adult brains. It also publishes articles about the history of puzzles and games and the art of creating them, as well as contests and reviews. Circ: 75,000.

Audience: YA–Adult
Frequency: 10 times each year
Website: www.gamesmagazine-online.com

FREELANCE POTENTIAL
86% written by nonstaff writers. Publishes 200+ freelance submissions yearly; 10% by unpublished writers, 20% by authors who are new to the magazine. Receives 960 queries and unsolicited mss yearly.

SUBMISSIONS
Query with outline; or send complete ms. Accepts hard copy and email to games@ kappapublishing.com. SASE. Responds in 6–8 weeks.

- Articles: 1,500–3,000 words. Informational articles; profiles; and humor. Topics include game-related events and people, wordplay, and human ingenuity. Game reviews by assignment only.
- Depts/columns: Staff written, except for "Gamebits."
- Other: Visual and verbal puzzles, quizzes, contests, two-play games, and adventures.

SAMPLE ISSUE
80 pages (8% advertising): 6 articles; 2 depts/columns; 20 puzzles and activities. Sample copy, $4.50 with 9x12 SASE ($1.24 postage). Guidelines available.

- "The $100,000 Rebus Contest and the Search for Amelia Earhart." Article provides a historical look at a 1937 puzzle craze and how it connects to the search for the aviator.
- "The Puzzle Sculptor." Article dissects the games and puzzles of George Hart.

RIGHTS AND PAYMENT
All North American serial rights. Articles, $500–$1,200. "Gamebits," $100–$250. Pays on publication. Provides 1 contributor's copy.

➬EDITOR'S COMMENTS
We, and our readers, take games and puzzles very seriously. All puzzles should include an answer key.

Genesee Valley Parent

1 Grove Street, Suite 204
Pittsford, NY 14534

Managing Editor: Jillian Melnyk

DESCRIPTION AND INTERESTS
Filled with parent-friendly articles on children's health, education, and development, as well as a multitude of family topics, *Genesee Valley Parent* targets parents in the greater Rochester, New York, region. Circ: 30,000.

Audience: Parents
Frequency: Monthly
Website: www.gvparent.com

FREELANCE POTENTIAL
75% written by nonstaff writers. Publishes 50 freelance submissions yearly; 5% by authors who are new to the magazine. Receives 240 queries yearly.

SUBMISSIONS
Query with clips or writing samples. Accepts hard copy and simultaneous submissions if identified. SASE. Responds in 1–3 months.

- Articles: 700–1,200 words. Informational and how-to articles; profiles; reviews; humor; and personal experience pieces. Topics include regional family events, local goods and services, special and gifted education, social issues, family problems, health and fitness, and parenting.
- Depts/columns: 500–600 words. Family health, teen issues, toddler issues, and short news items.
- Other: Submit seasonal material 4 months in advance.

SAMPLE ISSUE
68 pages (50% advertising): 5 articles; 9 depts/columns; 1 calendar. Guidelines and editorial calendar available.

- "25 Must-Read Books." Article surveys local librarians for their suggestions of books, all at varying reading levels, that should be on children's summer reading lists.
- Sample dept/column: "Family Time" offers ideas for making outdoor fitness fun for everyone in the family.

RIGHTS AND PAYMENT
Second rights. Articles, $30–$45. Depts/columns, $25–$30. Pays on publication. Provides 1 tearsheet.

➬EDITOR'S COMMENTS
All articles must have relevance to the Rochester-area parent, either through local subject matter or local sources.

GeoParent

16101 North 82nd Street, Suite A-9
Scottsdale, AZ 85260

Editors: Betsy Bailey & Nancy Price

DESCRIPTION AND INTERESTS
This online magazine is filled with articles and resources to help parents raise happy and healthy children in a supportive environment. It offers informative articles on parenting and child development issues, family matters, and health. Hits per month: Unavailable.
Audience: Parents
Frequency: Weekly
Website: www.geoparent.com

FREELANCE POTENTIAL
90% written by nonstaff writers. Publishes 50 freelance submissions yearly. Receives 50 queries and unsolicited mss yearly.

SUBMISSIONS
Prefers query; will accept complete ms. Accepts hard copy, email submissions to content@coincide.com, and submissions via the website. SASE. Response time varies.

- Articles: 500–2,500 words. Informational articles; and advice. Topics include parenting, child development, family issues, pregnancy and childbirth, infancy, child care, nutrition, health, education, and gifted and special education.
- Depts/columns: Word lengths vary. Parenting tips and advice.

SAMPLE ISSUE
Sample issue and writers' guidelines available at website.

- "B Is for Burnout: Are Your Kids Overscheduled?" Article examines the fact that the packed schedules many students keep may be burning them out.
- "Cooking with Kids: How to Make Strawberry Freezer Jam." Article offers a way to share a a bonding moment with your children while making strawberry jam.

RIGHTS AND PAYMENT
Rights vary. Written material, $25–$50; $10 for reprints. Pays on publication.

➥EDITOR'S COMMENTS
Because we are an e-zine, and therefore readily accessible by parents across the country, we are not bound by regional stories. Your article should have a broad appeal to parents, provide them with information or support, and perhaps give them a laugh. Pieces must be accurate and researched.

Georgia Family Magazine

523 Sioux Drive
Macon, GA 31210

Publisher: Olya Fessard

DESCRIPTION AND INTERESTS
Parents residing in central Georgia rely on this magazine for its insightful and timely articles on helping children live up to their potential. It covers education issues, health, finance, and lifestyles. A calendar of family events and activities is also featured. Circ: 20,000.
Audience: Families
Frequency: Monthly
Website: www.georgiafamily.com

FREELANCE POTENTIAL
60% written by nonstaff writers. Publishes 100–125 freelance submissions yearly.

SUBMISSIONS
Send complete ms. Accepts email submissions to publisher@georgiafamily.com. Response time varies.

- Articles: Word lengths vary. Informational articles. Topics include parenting, family issues, education, gifted and special education, health, and fitness.
- Depts/columns: Word lengths vary. Financial and money matters, science and technology, travel, the arts, etiquette, home and garden, and media and new product reviews.

SAMPLE ISSUE
64 pages; 4 articles; 14 depts/columns. Guidelines available at website.

- "How to Choose the Right School." Article explains how to determine the type of school that is best for one's children.
- "Thunderstorm Safety." Article reviews tips for keeping everyone in the family safe during summer storms.
- "Your Daughter's First Gynecological Exam." Article discusses the importance of such an exam and what to expect.

RIGHTS AND PAYMENT
One-time, reprint, and electronic rights. Articles, $20–$90. Reprints, $10–$30. Pays on publication. Provides 1 tearsheet.

➥EDITOR'S COMMENTS
A large percentage of our articles are purchased from freelance writers. We are looking for carefully researched articles that demonstrate independent reporting, and that feature well-developed story lines. Let us know if you have a fresh slant, particularly with a local angle, on a topic of interest to parents.

Gifted Education Press Quarterly

10201 Yuma Court
P.O. Box 1586
Manassas, VA 20109

Editor & Publisher: Maurice D. Fisher

DESCRIPTION AND INTERESTS
Each online and print edition of this scholarly newsletter addresses the how's and why's of teaching gifted children. It seeks to publish articles that are useful to parents as well as educators. Circ: 15,000.

Audience: Educators and parents
Frequency: Quarterly
Website: www.giftededpress.com

FREELANCE POTENTIAL
75% written by nonstaff writers. Publishes 14 freelance submissions yearly; 67% by authors new to the magazine. Receives 30 queries each year.

SUBMISSIONS
Query with writing sample. Accepts email queries to mfisher345@comcast.net. Responds in 1 week.

- Articles: 2,500–4,000 words. Informational, how-to, and research articles; personal experience pieces; profiles; interviews; and scholarly essays. Topics include gifted education; multicultural, ethnic, and social issues; homeschooling; multiple intelligence; parent advocates; academic subjects; the environment; and popular culture.

SAMPLE ISSUE
18 pages (no advertising): 5 articles. Sample copy available at website.

- "Gifted Education in China: A Transition Toward Student-Centered Instruction." Article describes how Illinois' Knox College has been working with a Chinese university on instituting literature-based teaching methods in the classroom.
- "Parent/School Communication in Gifted Education." Article explains the importance of educating parents about raising a gifted child, and looks at the method and degree of such communication in Ohio schools.

RIGHTS AND PAYMENT
All rights. No payment. Provides a 1-year subscription.

⇒ EDITOR'S COMMENTS
Our only specific guidelines are that we prefer well-written, jargon-free articles that run on the shorter end of our word-length spectrum, from 2,500 to 3,000 words. Be prepared to include about five to ten references.

Girls' Life

4529 Harford Road
Baltimore, MD 21214

Editor: Katie Abbondanza

DESCRIPTION AND INTERESTS
Girls' Life is packed with the stuff girls crave— useful information and advice on such topics as academic success, peer pressure, time management, stress relief, growing up, and boosting self-esteem. Circ: 400,000.

Audience: Girls, 10–15 years
Frequency: 6 times each year
Website: www.girlslife.com

FREELANCE POTENTIAL
25% written by nonstaff writers. Publishes 40 freelance submissions yearly; 10% by unpublished writers, 20% by authors who are new to the magazine. Receives 1,200 queries yearly.

SUBMISSIONS
Query with outline. Accepts hard copy and email queries to katie@girlslife.com. SASE. Responds in 3 months.

- Articles: 1,200–2,500 words. Informational, service-oriented articles. Topics include self-esteem, health, friendship, relationships, sibling rivalry, school issues, facing challenges, and setting goals.
- Fiction: 2,000–2,500 words. Stories featuring girls.
- Depts/columns: 300–800 words. Celebrity spotlights; profiles of real girls; advice about friendship, beauty, and dating; fashion trends; decorating tips; cooking; crafts; and media reviews.
- Other: Quizzes; fashion spreads.

SAMPLE ISSUE
96 pages (30% advertising): 5 articles; 23 depts/columns; 2 quizzes. Sample copy, $5. Guidelines and editorial calendar available at website.

- "When Love Hurts." Article tells the stories of teen girls who were abused by their boyfriends, and provides warning signs to look for.
- Sample dept/column: "*GL* What's Hot" includes an interview with actress Bonnie Wright of the *Harry Potter* films.

RIGHTS AND PAYMENT
All or first rights. Written material, payment rates vary. Pays on publication. Provides 1 copy.

⇒ EDITOR'S COMMENTS
Our profiles of real girls facing real challenges have amazed and inspired readers for almost 15 years.

Green Teacher

95 Robert Street
Toronto, Ontario M5S 2KS
Canada

Co-Editor: Tim Grant

DESCRIPTION AND INTERESTS
Green Teacher provides youth educators with practical articles, ready-to-use activities, and lesson plans for enhancing environmental education in schools. Circ: 7,500.
Audience: Teachers, grades K–12
Frequency: Quarterly
Website: www.greenteacher.com

FREELANCE POTENTIAL
100% written by nonstaff writers. Publishes 120 freelance submissions yearly; 80% by unpublished writers. Receives 500 queries and unsolicited mss yearly.

SUBMISSIONS
Prefers query with outline; will accept complete ms with 8–10 photos. Prefers email submissions to tim@greenteacher.com (Microsoft Word, RTF, or TXT attachments); will accept disk submissions with hard copy. Availability of artwork improves chance of acceptance. SAE/IRC. Responds in 2 months.

- Articles: 1,500–3,000 words. Informational and how-to articles; opinion pieces; and lesson plans. Topics include environmental and global education.
- Depts/columns: Word lengths vary. Resources, reviews, and announcements.
- Artwork: JPEG and TIFF images at 300 dpi; B/W and color prints or slides. Line art.
- Other: Submit Earth Day material 6 months in advance.

SAMPLE ISSUE
48 pages (12% advertising): 12 articles; 2 depts/columns. Sample copy and guidelines available at website.

- "Creating Earth Adventures: Self-Guided Programs to Connect Children with Nature." Article suggests outdoor lessons that teach environmental appreciation.
- "Greening the Elementary Education Curriculum One Course at a Time." Article offers tips for incorporating environmental education into teachers' college courses.

RIGHTS AND PAYMENT
Rights negotiable. No payment. Provides 5 contributor's copies and a free subscription.

➡ EDITOR'S COMMENTS
Most articles are written by educators, but we welcome submissions from others.

Grit

1503 SW 42nd Street
Topeka, KS 66609-1265

Editor-in-Chief: K. C. Compton

DESCRIPTION AND INTERESTS
Having "grit" aptly describes many families who live off the land they sow. *Grit* provides families such as these with practical information on how to best live a contented—and successful—rural life. Circ: 150,000.
Audience: Families
Frequency: 6 times each year
Website: www.grit.com

FREELANCE POTENTIAL
90% written by nonstaff writers. Publishes 80–90 freelance submissions yearly; 50% by unpublished writers, 50% by new authors. Receives 2,400 queries yearly.

SUBMISSIONS
Query. Prefers email queries to grit@grit.com (include "Query" in subject line); will accept hard copy. SASE. Response time varies.

- Articles: 800–1,500 words. Informational and how-to articles; profiles; and personal experience pieces. Topics include American history, rural family lifestyles, parenting, pets, crafts, community involvement, farming, gardening, and antiques.
- Depts/columns: 500–1,500 words. Farm economics, comfort food, technology, equipment, and medical advice. "Grit Gazette" items, 350–700 words; news items.
- Artwork: 35mm color slides and prints; digital images. B/W prints for nostalgia pieces.

SAMPLE ISSUE
96 pages (50% advertising): 7 articles; 11 depts/columns. Sample copy and editorial calendar, $4 with 9x12 SASE. Guidelines available at website.

- "Country Women Rock!" Article discusses the tough multitasking that farm women—many of them mothers—must do each day.
- Sample dept/column: "Sow Hoe" explains how families can produce their own antioxidants by growing blueberries.

RIGHTS AND PAYMENT
Shared rights. Articles and depts/columns, $.35 per word. Grit Gazette items, $50–$75 each. Artwork, $35–$175 per photo. Pays on publication. Provides 3 contributor's copies.

➡ EDITOR'S COMMENTS
Please do not attempt to write for us if you know nothing about rural life.

Group

Group Publishing, Inc.
P.O. Box 481
Loveland, CO 80539-0481

Associate Editor: Scott Firestone

DESCRIPTION AND INTERESTS
Targeting youth ministry leaders, this interdenominational magazine puts a premium on ideas. Its articles are designed to spark ideas, commitment, passion, and purpose in its readers, all for the cause of helping them help their members strengthen their faith and relationship with Christ. Circ: 40,000.

Audience: Youth ministry leaders
Frequency: 6 times each year
Website: www.youthministry.com

FREELANCE POTENTIAL
60% written by nonstaff writers. Publishes 200 freelance submissions yearly; 50% by unpublished writers, 80% by authors who are new to the magazine. Receives 300 queries yearly.

SUBMISSIONS
Query with outline and clips or writing samples; state availability of artwork. Accepts hard copy. SASE. Responds in 2–3 months.

- Articles: 500–1,700 words. Informational and how-to articles. Topics include youth ministry strategies, recruiting and training adult leaders, understanding youth culture, professionalism, time management, leadership skills, and the professional and spiritual growth of youth ministers.
- Depts/columns: "Try This One," to 300 words. "Hands-On Help," to 175 words.
- Artwork: B/W or color illustration samples. No prints.

SAMPLE ISSUE
82 pages (30% advertising): 3 articles; 23 depts/columns. Sample copy, $2 with 9x12 SASE. Guidelines available.

- "Dang It . . . It's Almost Fall!" Article proclaims fall as a great time to recruit new leaders for a ministry.
- "The Only Audience That Matters." Article discusses the fact that untimely death happens, that we may suddenly have an audience with God, and what we can do to ready ourselves for that day.

RIGHTS AND PAYMENT
All rights. Articles, $125–$225. Depts/columns, $50. Pays on acceptance.

➤ EDITOR'S COMMENTS
We are always looking for writers who can help our readers grow their youth ministries.

Guide

Review and Herald Publishing Association
55 West Oak Ridge Drive
Hagerstown, MD 21740

Editor: Randy Fishell

DESCRIPTION AND INTERESTS
Through its "true stories pointing to Jesus," *Guide* seeks to show readers how to walk with God now and forever. Circ: 26,000.

Audience: 10–14 years
Frequency: Weekly
Website: www.guidemagazine.org

FREELANCE POTENTIAL
95% written by nonstaff writers. Publishes 250 freelance submissions yearly; 15% by unpublished writers, 20% by authors who are new to the magazine. Receives 840 unsolicited mss each year.

SUBMISSIONS
Send complete ms. Prefers email submissions to guide@rhpa.org; will accept hard copy and simultaneous submissions if identified. SASE. Responds in 4–6 weeks.

- Articles: 450–1,200 words. Inspirational articles; personal experience pieces; Christian humor; and biography. Topics include adventure, angels, Bible doctrine, compassion, integrity, faith, family, health, media choices, personal growth, social issues, and Seventh-day Adventist history.
- Other: Puzzles, activities, and games. Submit seasonal material about Thanksgiving, Christmas, Mother's Day, and Father's Day 8 months in advance.

SAMPLE ISSUE
32 pages: 6 articles, 2 activities. Sample copy, free with 9x12 SASE (2 first-class stamps). Guidelines available.

- "Too-Early Goodbye." Personal experience piece shares a girl's grief upon learning of her father's death.
- "The Night Uncle Jess Disappeared." Personal experience piece relates the author's fear of losing her great-uncle, and her gratitude toward God when he is found alive.

RIGHTS AND PAYMENT
First serial rights. Articles, $.07–$.10 per word. Games and puzzles, $30–$40. Pays on acceptance. Provides 3 contributor's copies.

➤ EDITOR'S COMMENTS
We seek Christian humor that appeals to junior high school students. Use a light-hearted story line that goes beyond one-liners to expose a character-building principle.

Gwinnett Parents Magazine

3651 Peachtree Parkway, Suite 325
Suwanee, GA 30024

Editor: Terrie Carter

DESCRIPTION AND INTERESTS
The articles in this magazine are designed to educate, assist, and empower parents in their everyday decision-making, whether it be about childcare, education, healthcare, personal finance, shopping, or entertainment. It targets families living in Georgia's Gwinnett County. Circ: Unavailable.

Audience: Parents
Frequency: Monthly
Website: www.gwinnettparents.com

FREELANCE POTENTIAL
75% written by nonstaff writers. Publishes several freelance submissions yearly; 5% by unpublished writers, 14% by new authors.

SUBMISSIONS
Query or send complete ms. Accepts email submissions to editor@gwinnettparents.com (include "Editorial Submission" in subject line). Responds in 3–4 weeks.

- Articles: 500–1,000 words. Profiles, 350–450 words. Informational and self-help articles; profiles; and personal experience pieces. Topics include education, recreation, sports, health, working parents, and family finances.
- Depts/columns: Word lengths vary. Parenting advice, health, education, community news, recipes, home improvement, and reviews.

SAMPLE ISSUE
60 pages (50% advertising): 5 articles; 15 depts/columns. Sample copy, $4 with 9x12 SASE ($.77 postage). Guidelines available.

- "Five Ways to Raise Globally Conscious Kids." Article suggests ways to make children think about "we" instead of "me."
- "Baby Swimming Classes and Your Infant." Article examines the growing popularity of swimming lessons for babies.
- Sample dept/column: "Teen Talk" offers tips parents can use to help their kids deal with the transition to high school.

RIGHTS AND PAYMENT
First and non-exclusive online archival rights. Written material, $25–$75. Profiles, $25–$50. Pays on publication.

➡ EDITOR'S COMMENTS
We're interested in articles that emphasize the pleasures of parenting, especially those with a local angle.

Happiness

P.O. Box 2379
Midland, MI 48641

Editor: Diane Lynn Nolan

DESCRIPTION AND INTERESTS
This family-centered magazine strives to finish the sentence, "Happiness is . . ." with articles, poems, and advice that focus on the positive things that can make life happier for its readers. It also includes a weekly television viewing guide. Circ: 150,000.

Audience: Families
Frequency: Weekly
Website: www.happiness.com

FREELANCE POTENTIAL
75% written by nonstaff writers. Of the freelance submissions published yearly, 25% are by unpublished writers, 25% are by authors who are new to the magazine.

SUBMISSIONS
Send complete ms. Accepts hard copy. Availability of artwork improves chance of acceptance. SASE. Responds in 3 months.

- Articles: 500 words. Informational, self-help, and how-to articles; humor; and personal experience pieces. Topics include careers, education, health, fitness, hobbies, animals, pets, nature, the environment, recreation, and travel.
- Depts/columns: 25–75 words. Cooking, health, humor, and tips from readers.
- Artwork: Color prints.
- Other: Puzzles and games. Poetry. Submit seasonal material 4 months in advance.

SAMPLE ISSUE
16 pages (no advertising): 2 articles; 8 depts/columns; 10 activities. Writers' guidelines available.

- "Words that Heal." Article discusses ways to enrich the lives of those around you by using words that heal.
- Sample dept/column: "Happiness Tip" offers 26 ways (one for each letter of the alphabet) to be an active and involved parent.

RIGHTS AND PAYMENT
First rights. All material, payment rates vary. Pays on publication.

➡ EDITOR'S COMMENTS
We want our readers to be inspired and, well, happy after reading each issue. We accept material that is positive, encouraging, and uplifting. Subjects should focus on love, parenting, family, and good health.

Higher Things

Dare To Be Lutheran

Good Shepherd Lutheran Church
5009 Cassia Street
Boise, ID 83705

Managing Editor: Adriane Dorr

DESCRIPTION AND INTERESTS

Aimed at enriching the faith of Lutheran youth, *Higher Things* focuses on Christ and His work for humankind. More specifically, it publishes articles that help readers apply the Gospel to their daily lives. Circ: Unavailable.

Audience: 13–19 years
Frequency: Quarterly
Website: www.higherthings.org

FREELANCE POTENTIAL

60% written by nonstaff writers. Publishes 36 freelance submissions yearly; 40% by unpublished writers, 30% by authors who are new to the magazine. Receives 12 queries, 24 unsolicited mss yearly.

SUBMISSIONS

Query or send complete ms. Accepts hard copy and email submissions to submissions@higherthings.org. SASE. Response time varies.

- Articles: 500–800 words. Informational and how-to articles; profiles; interviews; and personal experience pieces. Topics include religion, current events, recreation, social issues, and travel.
- Depts/columns: Staff written.

SAMPLE ISSUE

32 pages (10% advertising): 10 articles; 2 depts/columns. Sample copy, $3. Guidelines and theme list available.

- "No More Stressing." Essay encourages teens to be themselves and stop obsessing about how popular they are.
- "The Enemy: Death." Essay posits that original sin created death, and disputes evolutionary theory.
- "Jan Hus: Champion of Christian Freedom." Article describes the first Reformation, led by a Czech pastor in the early 1400s.

RIGHTS AND PAYMENT

Rights vary. No payment. Provides several contributor's copies.

⟋EDITOR'S COMMENTS

Consider your audience. This magazine is geared toward youth in general and teens specifically. Write to the quiet 14-year-old computer nerd, to the outgoing 17-year-old football player, or to the troubled 19-year-old ready to leave for college. Keep your writing exciting and fresh, and avoid using big words.

Highlights for Children

803 Church Street
Honesdale, PA 18431

Manuscript Coordinator

DESCRIPTION AND INTERESTS

Dedicated to helping children grow in basic skills, knowledge, and creativeness, *Highlights for Children* offers fun stories, articles, crafts, and activities. Circ: Unavailable.

Audience: Up to 12 years
Frequency: Monthly
Website: www.highlights.com

FREELANCE POTENTIAL

99% written by nonstaff writers. Publishes 200 freelance submissions yearly; 40% by unpublished writers, 60% by authors who are new to the magazine. Receives 6,500 unsolicited mss each year.

SUBMISSIONS

Send complete ms for fiction. Query or send complete ms for nonfiction. Accepts hard copy. SASE. Responds to queries in 2–4 weeks, to mss in 4–6 weeks.

- Articles: To 500 words for 3–7 years; to 800 words for 8–12 years. Informational articles; interviews; profiles; and personal experience pieces. Topics include nature, animals, science, crafts, hobbies, world cultures, history, arts, and sports.
- Fiction: To 500 words for 3–7 years; to 800 words for 8–12 years. Genres include adventure, mystery, sports stories, multicultural fiction, and retellings of traditional stories.
- Depts/columns: Word lengths vary. Science experiments and crafts.
- Other: Puzzles, games. Poetry, to 10 lines.

SAMPLE ISSUE

44 pages (no advertising): 4 articles; 5 stories; 12 poems; 1 rebus; 6 activities; 7 depts/columns. Sample copy, free with 9x12 SASE (4 first-class stamps). Guidelines available.

- "The Stowaway Fox." Article tells of a blue-gray Arctic fox that survived two weeks in a shipping container and was later nursed back to health by zookeepers.
- "Macaroni and Fleas." Story revolves around a young girl and a missing box of macaroni.

RIGHTS AND PAYMENT

All rights. Written material, payment rates vary. Pays on acceptance. Provides 2 copies.

⟋EDITOR'S COMMENTS

We encourage authors to have their nonfiction articles reviewed by an expert first.

Home Education Magazine

P.O. Box 1083
Tonasket, WA 98855

Articles Editor: Jeanne Faulconer

DESCRIPTION AND INTERESTS
This magazine covers homeschooling and the issues of importance and concern to homeschooling families, advocates, and supporters. Circ: 110,000.

Audience: Parents
Frequency: 6 times each year
Website: www.homeedmag.com

FREELANCE POTENTIAL
90% written by nonstaff writers. Publishes 35–40 freelance submissions yearly; 25% by unpublished writers, 40% by authors who are new to the magazine. Receives 240 queries, 240 unsolicited mss yearly.

SUBMISSIONS
Prefers complete ms; will accept query. Prefers email to articles@homeedmag.com (Microsoft Word attachments); will accept hard copy. SASE. Responds in 1–2 months.

- Articles: 900–1,700 words. Informational and how-to articles; profiles; interviews; and personal experience pieces. Topics include homeschooling, activism, lessons, and parenting issues.
- Depts/columns: Staff written.
- Artwork: B/W and color prints; digital images at 200 dpi (300 dpi for cover images).

SAMPLE ISSUE
44 pages (13% advertising): 7 articles; 9 depts/columns. Sample copy, $6.50. Guidelines available at website.

- "Old Games, New Tricks." Article explains how to put a new spin on old board games to increase learning, creativity, and fun.
- "Interview with Kathleen McCurdy." Article interviews a homeschool advocate and founder of the Family Learning Organization.

RIGHTS AND PAYMENT
First North American serial and electronic rights. Articles, $50–$100. Artwork, $12.50; $100 for cover art. Pays on acceptance. Provides 1+ contributor's copies.

➽EDITOR'S COMMENTS
We continue to be interested in personal accounts of homeschool successes and challenges faced by parents and older homeschoolers. You don't need to be an education professional to write for us—just a parent with homeschooling experience.

Home Educator's Family Times

P.O. Box 6442
Brunswick, ME 04011

Editor: Jane R. Boswell

DESCRIPTION AND INTERESTS
This newspaper and e-zine features relevant and timely articles on homeschooling issues, as well as resources intended to support and encourage homeschooling parents and families. Circ: 25,000. Hits per month: 400,000.

Audience: Parents
Frequency: 6 times each year
Website: www.homeeducator.com/familytimes

FREELANCE POTENTIAL
90% written by nonstaff writers. Publishes 50 freelance submissions yearly; 25% by authors who are new to the magazine.

SUBMISSIONS
Send complete ms with author biography and permission statement from website. Accepts CD submissions and email to famtimes@blazenetme.net (Microsoft Word or text attachments). SASE. Response time varies.

- Articles: 1,000–1,500 words. Informational and how-to articles; opinion pieces; and personal experience pieces. Topics include homeschooling methods and lessons, family life, parenting, pets, reading, art, science, and creative writing.
- Depts/columns: Staff written.

SAMPLE ISSUE
24 pages (41% advertising): 11 articles; 2 depts/columns. Sample copy and guidelines available at website.

- "The Magic of 'Thank You!'" Article states the author's opinion of the value and importance of saying "thank you"—not just for the person who is being thanked, but also for the person who is doing the thanking.
- "Wildlife Class at Magic Sky." Essay reveals lessons the author's family learned about wildlife from being outside in nature, rather than in a classroom.

RIGHTS AND PAYMENT
One-time and electronic reprint rights. No payment.

➽EDITOR'S COMMENTS
We welcome submissions from writers who have an interesting perspective on educating today's children. Each article we publish includes the author's website and contact information, as well as a short biography.

Homeschooling Today

P.O. Box 244
Abingdon, VA 24212

Editor-in-Chief: Jim Bob Howard

DESCRIPTION AND INTERESTS
The goal of this magazine is to encourage, challenge, and support homeschooling families. The articles in each of its themed issues have a special focus on Christian living as well as literature and fine arts. Circ: 11,500.

Audience: Parents
Frequency: 6 times each year
Website: www.homeschooltoday.com

FREELANCE POTENTIAL
85% written by nonstaff writers. Publishes 60–70 freelance submissions yearly; 6% by unpublished writers, 14% by authors who are new to the magazine. Receives 60–120 unsolicited mss yearly.

SUBMISSIONS
Send complete ms. Accepts email submissions to management@homeschooltoday.com with "Article Submission" in subject line (Microsoft Word attachment). Responds in 3–6 months.

- Articles: 1,400–2,000 words. Informational, self-help, and how-to articles; profiles; and personal experience pieces. Topics include education, religion, music, technology, special education, the arts, history, mathematics, and science.
- Columns: Staff written.
- Departments: 875 words. Time management, history, music, religion, the arts, and homeschooling tips. Book and media reviews, 250–500 words.

SAMPLE ISSUE
68 pages: 4 articles; 18 depts/columns. Sample copy, $5.95. Guidelines and theme list available at website.

- "Finding 'Normal' Again." Article discusses ways to return to a normal routine after unexpected turns in life.
- Sample dept/column: "For Instructions in Righteousness" offers ideas for including religious hymns in everyday life.

RIGHTS AND PAYMENT
All rights. Written material, $.08 per word. Pays on publication. Provides 1 contributor's copy.

☛ EDITOR'S COMMENTS
We do not send notification if we decide not to publish your article. If you do not hear from us within six months, assume that we will not use your article.

Hopscotch

P.O. Box 164
Bluffton, OH 45817-0164

Editor: Marilyn Edwards

DESCRIPTION AND INTERESTS
This magazine for girls leaves romance, cosmetics, and fashion to other publications, focusing instead on wholesome activities and creative fiction. Circ: 16,000.

Audience: Girls, 6–13 years
Frequency: 6 times each year
Website: www.hopscotchmagazine.com

FREELANCE POTENTIAL
80% written by nonstaff writers. Publishes 80–100 freelance submissions yearly; 30% by unpublished writers, 40% by authors who are new to the magazine. Receives 240 queries, 2,400 unsolicited mss yearly.

SUBMISSIONS
Prefers complete ms; will accept query. Accepts hard copy and simultaneous submissions if identified. Availability of artwork improves chance of acceptance. SASE. Responds to queries in 1–2 weeks, to mss in 2–3 months.

- Articles: 500 words. Informational and how-to articles; profiles; personal experience pieces; and humor. Topics include nature, pets, hobbies, sports, cooking, and careers.
- Fiction: To 1,000 words. Genres include adventure, mystery, and historical and multicultural fiction.
- Depts/columns: 500 words. Crafts, cooking.
- Artwork: B/W and color prints. Line art.
- Other: Puzzles and games. Poetry.

SAMPLE ISSUE
48 pages (no advertising): 10 articles; 2 stories; 5 depts/columns; 5 puzzles; 1 poem; 1 cartoon. Sample copy, $6 with 9x12 SASE. Guidelines and theme list available at website.

- "Rocks in My Pocket." Story set in 1913 tells how a skinny 14-year-old girl finds a job to help her family.
- Sample dept/column: "Cooking" offers a recipe for chocolate cake.

RIGHTS AND PAYMENT
First North American serial rights. Articles and fiction, $.05+ per word. Poetry and puzzles, $10+. Artwork, $5 per photo. Pays on publication. Provides 1 copy.

☛ EDITOR'S COMMENTS
As we use three times as much nonfiction as fiction, we are always seeking articles with high-quality photo support.

The Horn Book Magazine

56 Roland Street, Suite 200
Boston, MA 02129

Editor-in-Chief: Roger Sutton

DESCRIPTION AND INTERESTS
Targeting teachers, librarians, and parents, this magazine focuses on children's literature. But rather than publishing literary works, it instead features articles, essays, and reviews *about* children's literature. Circ: 16,000.
Audience: Parents, teachers, librarians
Frequency: 6 times each year
Website: www.hbook.com

FREELANCE POTENTIAL
70% written by nonstaff writers. Publishes 12–15 freelance submissions yearly; 10% by unpublished writers, 30% by authors who are new to the magazine. Receives 240 queries, 120 unsolicited mss yearly.

SUBMISSIONS
Query or send complete ms. Prefers email to info@hbook.com; will accept hard copy. SASE. Responds in 4 months.

- Articles: To 2,800 words. Informational articles; interviews; essays; criticism; and book reviews. Topics include children's and young adult literature, authors, illustrators, and editors.
- Depts/columns: Word lengths vary. Perspectives from illustrators, children's publishing updates, and special columns.

SAMPLE ISSUE
112 pages (20% advertising): 3 articles; 72 reviews; 4 depts/columns. Sample copy, free with 9x12 SASE. Guidelines and editorial calendar available at website.

- "Still Hot: Great Food Moments in Children's Literature." Article argues that children relate food with love, and explains how that relationship has been used in children's stories.
- Sample dept/column: "Book & Bar Man" presents an essay that points out the pros (and some cons) of reading a book while eating or drinking.

RIGHTS AND PAYMENT
All rights. Written material, payment rates vary. Pays on publication. Provides 1 author's copy.

➡ EDITOR'S COMMENTS
We like our articles lively, our reviews insightful, and our columns sharp. All articles submitted must be of a critical nature on some aspect of children's literature. Please note that we do not publish fiction, nor do we publish work by children.

Horsemen's Yankee Pedlar

83 Leicester Street
North Oxford, MA 01537

Editor: Molly Johns

DESCRIPTION AND INTERESTS
If it has to do with horses, it's in here. *Horsemen's Yankee Pedlar* is filled with information on all breeds of horses and all disciplines of riding. It covers equine health, training, breeding, and riding, as well as riding tournaments and horse shows. Circ: 50,000.
Audience: YA–Adult
Frequency: Monthly
Website: www.pedlar.com

FREELANCE POTENTIAL
50% written by nonstaff writers. Publishes 40 freelance submissions yearly; 5% by authors who are new to the magazine. Receives 360 queries, 240 unsolicited mss yearly.

SUBMISSIONS
Query or send complete ms. Accepts hard copy and simultaneous submissions if identified. SASE. Responds to queries in 1–2 weeks, to mss in 2–3 months.

- Articles: 500–800 words. Informational and how-to articles; interviews; reviews; and personal experience pieces. Topics include horse breeds, disciplines, training, health care, and equestrian management.
- Depts/columns: Word lengths vary. News, book reviews, business issues, nutrition, and legal issues.
- Artwork: B/W and color prints.

SAMPLE ISSUE
226 pages (75% advertising): 39 articles; 15 depts/columns. Sample copy, $3.99 with 9x12 SASE (7 first-class stamps). Guidelines available.

- "Newport Coaching Weekend: Revival of a Great American Pastime." Article covers this horse enthusiast event, in which horse-pulled coaches parade through historic Newport, Rhode Island.
- Sample dept/column: "Trail Talk" discusses the do's and don'ts of being a responsible trail rider.

RIGHTS AND PAYMENT
First North American serial rights. Written material, $2 per published column inch. Show coverage, $75 per day. Pays 30 days after publication. Provides 1 tearsheet.

➡ EDITOR'S COMMENTS
Covering a smaller show is a great way for us to get to know you.

Horsepower

P.O. Box 670
Aurora, Ontario L4G 4J9
Canada

Managing Editor: Susan Stafford

DESCRIPTION AND INTERESTS
This magazine "for young horse lovers" is published as a supplement to *Horse Canada*. Its content primarily consists of educational articles on horseback riding, equine care, and horse training, though it does occasionally print short fiction and humor. Circ: 10,000.

Audience: 8–16 years
Frequency: 6 times each year
Website: www.horse-canada.com

FREELANCE POTENTIAL
90% written by nonstaff writers. Publishes 15–18 freelance submissions yearly; 5% by unpublished writers, 10% by authors who are new to the magazine. Receives 60 queries, 48 unsolicited mss yearly.

SUBMISSIONS
Query or send complete ms with résumé. Accepts hard copy, disk submissions, and email to info@horse-canada.com. SAE/IRC. Responds to queries in 1–2 weeks, to mss in 2–3 months.

- Articles: 500–1,000 words. Informational and how-to articles; profiles; and humor. Topics include riding and stable skills, equine health, horse breeds, training issues, equine celebrities, and equestrian careers.
- Fiction: 500 words. Horse–related stories.
- Depts/columns: Staff written.
- Artwork: B/W and color prints.
- Other: Activities, games, and puzzles.

SAMPLE ISSUE
16 pages (20% advertising): 3 articles; 6 depts/columns; 3 puzzles; 2 contests. Sample copy, $3.95 Canadian. Guidelines and editorial calendar available.

- "Smile! Healthy Teeth = Happy Horses." Article stresses the importance of equine dental care, and explores it as a career.
- "Hip Hip Hooray for Hippotherapy!" Article tells how horses are used to help people with disabilities.

RIGHTS AND PAYMENT
First North American serial rights. Written material, $50–$90 Canadian. Artwork, $15–$75 Canadian. Pays on publication. Provides 1 copy.

➥EDITOR'S COMMENTS
We rarely accept "non-Canadian" contributions due to Canadian content laws. Please note we're not currently accepting fiction.

Hudson Valley Parent

174 South Street
Newburgh, NY 12550

Editor: Terrie Goldstein

DESCRIPTION AND INTERESTS
Parenting issues and resources are covered in detail in this magazine for families living in New York's Hudson Valley area. It regularly spotlights regional family activities and events as well. Circ: 50,000.

Audience: Parents
Frequency: Monthly
Website: www.hvparent.com

FREELANCE POTENTIAL
60% written by nonstaff writers. Publishes 52 freelance submissions yearly; 5% by unpublished writers, 20% by authors who are new to the magazine. Receives 240 queries, 120 unsolicited mss yearly.

SUBMISSIONS
Query with writing samples; or send complete ms with sidebar and author bio. Accepts email submissions to editor@excitingread.com. Responds in 3–6 weeks.

- Articles: 700–1,200 words. Informational and how-to articles. Topics include child care and development, discipline, education, learning disabilities, family health, recreation, travel, and entertainment.
- Depts/columns: 700 words. Health, education, behavior, and kid-friendly recipes.
- Artwork: 8x10 B/W and color prints.
- Other: Submit seasonal material 6 months in advance.

SAMPLE ISSUE
58 pages (50% advertising): 5 articles; 1 special section; 7 depts/columns. Sample copy, free with 9x12 SASE. Guidelines and editorial calendar available.

- "Quirky Dutchess County Destinations." Article suggests day trips that can be fun for the entire family.
- "Preventing the Summer Brain Drain." Article explores ways to keep children's minds active during the summer break.

RIGHTS AND PAYMENT
One-time rights. Articles, $50–$120. Reprints, $25–$35. Pays on publication. Provides 2 contributor's copies.

➥EDITOR'S COMMENTS
We seek carefully researched articles by writers with well-developed interviewing styles and a clear knowledge of our audience.

Humpty Dumpty's Magazine

Children's Better Health Institute
1100 Waterway Boulevard
P.O. Box 567
Indianapolis, IN 46206-0567

Editor: Terry Harshman

DESCRIPTION AND INTERESTS

Targeting emergent and new readers, *Humpty Dumpty's Magazine* promotes healthy living through stories, articles, poems, and activities that are both educational and entertaining. Circ: 236,000.

Audience: 4–6 years
Frequency: 6 times each year
Website: www.humptydumptymag.org

FREELANCE POTENTIAL

50% written by nonstaff writers. Publishes 45 freelance submissions yearly; 5% by unpublished writers, 12% by authors who are new to the magazine.

SUBMISSIONS

Send complete ms. Accepts hard copy. SASE. Responds in 2–3 months.

- Articles: To 350 words. Informational and how-to articles. Topics include health, fitness, sports, science, nature, animals, crafts, and hobbies.
- Fiction: To 350 words. Genres include early reader contemporary and multicultural fiction; stories about sports; fantasy; folktales; mystery; drama; and humor.
- Depts/columns: Word lengths vary. Recipes, health advice, and book excerpts.
- Other: Puzzles, activities, and games. Poetry, line lengths vary. Submit seasonal material 8 months in advance.

SAMPLE ISSUE

36 pages (2% advertising): 1 article; 2 stories; 3 depts/columns; 9 activities; 1 poem. Sample copy, $1.25. Writers' guidelines available at website.

- "I See the Moon!" Article celebrates the 40th anniversary of the first moon landing with fun facts and figures.
- "Bully and Peep." Story tells of a frog who learns to love his name after befriending another frog with a silly name too.

RIGHTS AND PAYMENT

All rights. Written material, $.22 per word. Pays on publication. Provides 10 author's copies.

❧EDITOR'S COMMENTS

We are accepting well-written, age-appropriate submissions in all categories. We do not accept items from children except for our children's columns.

Illuminata

5486 Fairway Drive
Zachary, LA 70791

Editor-in-Chief: Bret Funk

DESCRIPTION AND INTERESTS

Intelligent writing and clever critique drives this online magazine, which is read by writers and readers of the science fiction and fantasy fiction genres. In addition to short and speculative fiction, it publishes articles on the art of writing and book reviews. Hits per month: 600.

Audience: YA–Adult
Frequency: Quarterly
Website: www.tyrannosauruspress.com

FREELANCE POTENTIAL

25% written by nonstaff writers. Publishes 5–10 freelance submissions yearly; 95% by unpublished writers, 50% by authors who are new to the magazine. Receives 10 queries each year.

SUBMISSIONS

Query. Accepts email queries to info@tyrannosauruspress.com (no attachments). Responds in 1–3 months.

- Articles: 1–2 pages. Informational articles. Topics include writing science fiction, fantasy, and horror.
- Fiction: Word lengths vary. Genres include science fiction, fantasy, and horror.
- Depts/columns: "Reviews," 500–1,000 words. Reviews of science fiction and fantasy books and stories.

SAMPLE ISSUE

26 pages (no advertising): 5 articles; 1 story; 5 depts/columns. Sample copy and guidelines available at website.

- "Game-Based Booty." Article explains that Dungeons and Dragons was the genesis for most contemporary gaming, and how smart companies have capitalized on the popularity of role-playing games to create books, games, and interactive video games.
- "Reading Books on Writing." Article discusses the many books available to help fledgling writers of all types.

RIGHTS AND PAYMENT

Rights vary. No payment.

❧EDITOR'S COMMENTS

We want writers who really know what they're writing about when it comes to science fiction and fantasy (and we'll be able to tell). Please make your query brief.

Imagination-Café

P.O. Box 1536
Valparaiso, IN 46384

Editor: Rosanne Tolin

DESCRIPTION AND INTERESTS
A mix of kid-relevant articles, interviews, puzzles, and games make up the content of this e-zine. Topics cover everything from sports, history, and science, to careers and cooking. Hits per month: Unavailable.

Audience: 7–12 years
Frequency: Updated daily
Website: www.imagination-café.com

FREELANCE POTENTIAL
75% written by nonstaff writers. Publishes 40–50 freelance submissions yearly; 10% by experts. Receives 1,800 queries, 1,560 unsolicited mss yearly.

SUBMISSIONS
Prefers complete ms; will accept query. Accepts email to editor@imagination-café.com (no attachments). Response time varies.

- Articles: Word lengths vary. Informational and how-to articles; profiles; interviews; and reviews. Topics include animals, careers, crafts, hobbies, history, science, technology, sports, and celebrities.
- Depts/columns: Word lengths vary. "Cool Careers," "Before They Were Famous," "Celebrity Screw-Ups," and "School Strategies."
- Other: Puzzles, mazes, word games, quizzes, and recipes.

SAMPLE ISSUE
Sample articles and writers' guidelines available at website.

- "That'll Do, Rabbit." Article profiles a special rabbit that takes the place of a working dog on a Montana sheep farm.
- Sample dept/column: "Cool Careers" interviews the associate art museum curator at the Huntington Museum of Art located in West Virginia.

RIGHTS AND PAYMENT
Non-exclusive print and electronic rights. Written material, $20–$100. Pays on acceptance.

➤ EDITOR'S COMMENTS
Our readership includes kids 12 and under who are interested in general interest games, puzzles, and articles that inspire them to think about the future. Your best bet is to check our website before submitting, to be sure you won't be duplicating material that has already appeared.

Indy's Child

1901 Broad Ripple Avenue
Indianapolis, IN 46220

Executive Editor: Lynette Rowland

DESCRIPTION AND INTERESTS
Indy's Child addresses current parenting issues from an Indianapolis perspective. It places a particular emphasis on how and where to find family-oriented events, goods, and services in the region. Circ: 120,000.

Audience: Parents
Frequency: Monthly
Website: www.indyschild.com

FREELANCE POTENTIAL
95% written by nonstaff writers. Publishes 240+ freelance submissions yearly; 35% by unpublished writers, 60% by authors who are new to the magazine. Receives 600 unsolicited mss yearly.

SUBMISSIONS
Query with writing sample; state areas of interest. Accepts email to editor@indyschild.com. Responds if interested.

- Articles: 1,500–2,000 words. Informational and how-to articles; profiles; and humor. Topics include parenting, child development, family-oriented events, sports, travel, health, balancing work and family, and fatherhood.
- Depts/columns: 800–1,000 words. "Ages & Stages," "One Chic Mama," "My Parent, My Mentor," "Growing Up Online," and "Tweens and Teens." News, education issues, pediatric health, special needs, local profiles, and media reviews.
- Artwork: Color digital images.
- Other: Submit seasonal material 2 months in advance.

SAMPLE ISSUE
54 pages (50% advertising): 3 articles; 18 depts/columns. Sample copy, guidelines, and editorial calendar available at website.

- "Hidden Treasures in Central Indiana." Article showcases local venues for a budget-friendly spring break.
- Sample dept/column: "Ages & Stages (8–12)" discusses adolescent responses to divorce.

RIGHTS AND PAYMENT
First rights. Written material, $.10–$.15 per word. Reprints, $40–$75. Pays 30 days after publication. Provides 1 contributor's copy.

➤ EDITOR'S COMMENTS
We're looking for freelance writers who are comfortable working on assignment.

Inland Empire Family

11731 Stearling, Suite H
Riverside, CA 92503

Editor: Lynn Armitage

DESCRIPTION AND INTERESTS
Inland Empire Family is a parenting magazine serving families in California's Riverside and San Bernadino counties. It publishes articles on parenting and family issues, child health and development, education issues, and family events and recreational opportunities in the region. Circ: 55,000.
Audience: Parents
Frequency: Monthly
Website: www.inlandempirefamily.com

FREELANCE POTENTIAL
95% written by nonstaff writers. Publishes several freelance submissions yearly.

SUBMISSIONS
Query. Accepts hard copy. SASE. Response time varies.

- Articles: Word lengths vary. Informational and how-to articles. Topics include parenting, child care and development, education, entertainment, sports, recreation, health, nutrition, travel, summer camp, and pets.
- Depts/columns: Word lengths vary. Parenting advice by age group; self-help for mothers and couples; children's health, fashion, and essays; food and dining; media reviews; and education issues.

SAMPLE ISSUE
106 pages: 1 article; 15 depts/columns. Sample copy and guidelines available.

- "Happy, Happy Birthdays: The 10 Best Kids' Parties Ever!" Article breaks down kids' party ideas by age and interest level, and includes ideas for games, decorations, and food.
- Sample dept/column: "Education" offers ideas for keeping summer minds stimulated.
- Sample dept/column: "Time for Two" presents nine ways to show your love.

RIGHTS AND PAYMENT
All rights. Articles, $100–$500. Depts/columns, payment rates vary. Kill fee, $50. Pays within 45 days of publication.

➥EDITOR'S COMMENTS
Yes, we want articles on parenting, family, and child development issues, but we want them localized to our demographic region. That means local sources and local quotes. We always welcome articles with ideas for family fun and events in our region.

Insight

55 West Oak Ridge Drive
Hagerstown, MD 21740

Editor: Dwain Neilson Esmond

DESCRIPTION AND INTERESTS
Insight, a Christian magazine for teens, features relationship advice, answers to Bible questions, teen testimonials, Bible stories, articles on teen issues, and profiles of people with inspirational experiences. Circ: 12,000.
Audience: 13–19 years
Frequency: Weekly
Website: www.insightmagazine.org

FREELANCE POTENTIAL
50% written by nonstaff writers. Publishes 200–300 freelance submissions yearly; 50% by unpublished writers, 70% by authors who are new to the magazine. Receives 700 unsolicited mss yearly.

SUBMISSIONS
Send complete ms. Accepts hard copy and email submissions to insight@rhpa.org (Microsoft Word attachments). SASE. Responds in 1–3 months.

- Articles: 500–1,500 words. Informational articles; profiles; biographies; and humor. Topics include religion, social issues, and careers.
- Depts/columns: Word lengths vary. Bible lessons, relationship advice, true stories, and personal experience pieces.
- Other: Submit seasonal material 6 months in advance.

SAMPLE ISSUE
16 pages (2% advertising): 3 articles; 3 depts/columns. Sample copy, $2 with 9x12 SASE (2 first-class stamps). Writers' guidelines available at website.

- "The $685 Paper Clip." Article tells how a young man traded one paper clip for loot that included a digital camera and an Xbox.
- "I Don't Believe in this Book." Essay attempts to convey the validity of the Bible.
- Sample dept/column: "Cornerstone Connections" examines the Bible story of Jesus having dinner with tax collectors.

RIGHTS AND PAYMENT
First rights. Written material, $50–$125. Pays on acceptance. Provides 3 author's copies.

➥EDITOR'S COMMENTS
Through our magazine, we intend to offer teens practical information on how to grow in a relationship with Jesus.

InSite

P.O. Box 62189
Colorado Springs, CO 80962-2189

Editor: Martha Krienke

DESCRIPTION AND INTERESTS

As the flagship publication of the Christian
Camp and Conference Association (CCCA),
InSite covers critical aspects of Christian camp-
ing ministries—from practical management
guides to inspirational tales of God's work.
Circ: 8,500.

Audience: Adults
Frequency: 6 times each year
Website: www.ccca.org.com

FREELANCE POTENTIAL

95% written by nonstaff writers. Publishes 40
freelance submissions yearly; 15% by unpublished writers, 22% by authors who are new to
the magazine. Receives 20 queries yearly.

SUBMISSIONS

Query with résumé and writing samples.
Accepts email queries to editor@ccca.org.
Availability of artwork improves chance of
acceptance. Responds in 1 month.

- Articles: 800–1,500 words. Informational and
  how-to articles; profiles; and interviews.
  Topics include Christian camp and conference operations, programs, fundraising, leadership, personnel, recreation, religion, social
  issues, crafts, hobbies, health, fitness, multicultural and ethnic issues, nature, popular
  culture, and sports.
- Depts/columns: Staff-written.
- Artwork: Color prints and digital images.
- Other: Submit seasonal material 6 months
  in advance.

SAMPLE ISSUE

50 pages (25% advertising): 8 articles; 10
depts/columns. Sample copy, $4.95 with 9x12
SASE ($1.40 postage). Guidelines and editorial
calendar available at website.

- "Nursing Needs." Article provides tips for setting up and maintaining a health center.
- "Legends of the Night." Article tells how to
  create captivating after-dark activities.

RIGHTS AND PAYMENT

First rights. Articles, $.20 per word. Artwork,
$25–$250. Pays on publication. Provides 1
contributor's copy.

➥EDITOR'S COMMENTS

Profiles and interviews are the best bet for
newcomers and freelancers. We will generally
arrange for photographs of individuals profiled in the magazine.

Instructor

Scholastic Inc.
557 Broadway
New York, NY 10012

Editorial Assistant: Megan Kaesshaefer

DESCRIPTION AND INTERESTS

This magazine from Scholastic serves an audience of busy elementary and middle-school
educators with articles of support in every area
of teaching: from lesson planning and classroom management to career development and
work-life advice. Circ: 200,000+.

Audience: Teachers, grades K–8
Frequency: 6 times each year
Website: www.scholastic.com/instructor

FREELANCE POTENTIAL

90% written by nonstaff writers. Publishes 55
freelance submissions yearly; 10% by unpublished writers. Receives 100 queries yearly.

SUBMISSIONS

Query. Accepts email queries to instructor@
scholastic.com. Availability of artwork
improves chance of acceptance. SASE.
Responds in 3–4 months.

- Articles: 1,200 words. Informational and
  how-to articles; and personal experience
  pieces. Topics include lesson planning,
  classroom management, career development, workplace issues, learning and literacy
  issues, and technology.
- Depts/columns: News, Q&As, technology
  briefs, book reviews, and "Teachers' Picks,"
  word lengths vary. Classroom activities, to
  250 words. Humorous or poignant personal
  essays, to 400 words.
- Artwork: Color prints or transparencies.

SAMPLE ISSUE

64 pages (40% advertising): 4 articles; 11
depts/columns. Sample copy, $3 with 9x12
SASE. Guidelines available.

- "8 Great Teacher Habits Parents Love." Article
  lists communication techniques to help
  teachers connect with students' families.
- "Too Cool for School?" Article provides
  strategies for motivating negative students.
- Sample dept/column: "Idea Swap" includes
  ways to celebrate Earth Day.

RIGHTS AND PAYMENT

All rights. Written material, $.80 per word. Pays
on publication. Provides 2 contributor's copies.

➥EDITOR'S COMMENTS

Our readers are the engaging teachers who
are making an impact in their classrooms,
their schools, and their communities.

InTeen

1551 Regency Court
Calumet City, IL 60409

Editor: LaTonya Taylor

DESCRIPTION AND INTERESTS
This Christian magazine for urban teens uses Bible lessons and inspirational articles to help connect Christian principles to the reader's everyday life. It is published by the African American Christian Publishing and Communications Company. Circ: 75,000.

Audience: 15–17 years
Frequency: Quarterly
Website: www.urbanministries.com

FREELANCE POTENTIAL
90% written by nonstaff writers. Publishes 52 freelance submissions yearly.

SUBMISSIONS
All material is written on assignment. Send résumé with writing samples. SASE. Responds in 3–6 months.

- Articles: Word lengths vary. Bible study guides and lessons; how-to articles; profiles; interviews; and reviews. Topics include religion, college and careers, black history, music, social issues, and multicultural and ethnic issues. Also publishes biographies.
- Fiction: Word lengths vary. Stories may be included in Bible lessons. Genres include inspirational, multicultural, and ethnic fiction; and real-life and problem-solving stories.
- Other: Puzzles, activities, and poetry. Submit seasonal material 1 year in advance.

SAMPLE ISSUE
48 pages (no advertising): 7 articles; 2 poems; 14 Bible studies. Guidelines available.

- "Finding Identity in Christ." Article includes an interview with Israel Houghton, worship leader and member of the band New Breed.
- "Showing Real Mercy." Bible study explains the importance of helping those who can't help themselves.

RIGHTS AND PAYMENT
All rights. All material, payment rates vary. Pays 2 months after acceptance. Provides 2 contributor's copies.

◆EDITOR'S COMMENTS
Our mission is to empower God's young people, especially within the black community, to evangelize, disciple, and equip others for serving Christ and their church. We want writers who can effectively speak to the needs of urban teens.

InTeen Teacher

1551 Regency Court
Calumet City, IL 60409

Editor: LaTonya Taylor

DESCRIPTION AND INTERESTS
Christian educators who work with urban teens use this magazine, which offers easy-to-use teaching plans and Bible study guides that stimulate as they educate. Circ: 75,000.

Audience: Religious educators
Frequency: Quarterly
Website: www.urbanministries.com

FREELANCE POTENTIAL
90% written by nonstaff writers. Publishes 52 freelance submissions yearly.

SUBMISSIONS
All material is written on assignment. Send résumé with writing samples. SASE. Responds in 3–6 months.

- Articles: Word lengths vary. Bible study plans and guides for teaching Christian values to African American teens; and how-to articles.
- Fiction: Word lengths vary. Stories may be included as part of study plans. Genres include inspirational, multicultural, and ethnic fiction; and real-life and problem-solving stories.
- Other: Puzzles, activities, and poetry. Submit seasonal material 1 year in advance.

SAMPLE ISSUE
96 pages (no advertising): 2 articles; 14 teaching plans; 14 Bible study guides. Writers' guidelines available.

- "The Fine Is Paid." Teaching plan includes a story, activities, and discussion ideas for a lesson on asking Jesus for forgiveness.
- "The Best Way to Lead." Teaching plan outlines ways to show that following Jesus means a life of service and humility.
- "Christ as Messiah." Bible study guide uses Scriptures from Matthew to help students accept Jesus as the Messiah and share this news with others.

RIGHTS AND PAYMENT
All rights. Written material, payment rates vary. Pays 2 months after acceptance. Provides 2 contributor's copies.

◆EDITOR'S COMMENTS
We are always interested in hearing from new writers who are experienced Christian teachers. Material should be age-appropriate, culturally relevant, and offer theologically sound explanations of Bible passages.

International Gymnast

P.O. Box 721020
Norman, OK 73070

Editor: Dwight Normile

DESCRIPTION AND INTERESTS
Profiles of gymnasts, competition reports, and training tips and techniques are all presented in this magazine dedicated to the sport. Its focus is on gymnasts in their pre-teen and teen years. Circ: 14,000.

Audience: Gymnasts, 10–16 years
Frequency: 10 times each year
Website: www.intlgymnast.com

FREELANCE POTENTIAL
10% written by nonstaff writers. Publishes 5 freelance submissions yearly; 50% by authors who are new to the magazine. Receives 12 unsolicited mss yearly.

SUBMISSIONS
Send complete ms. Accepts hard copy and simultaneous submissions if identified. SASE. Responds in 1 month.

- Articles: 1,000–2,250 words. Informational articles; profiles; and interviews. Topics include gymnastics competitions, coaching, and personalities involved in the sport around the world.
- Fiction: To 1,500 words. Gymnastics stories.
- Depts/columns: 700–1,000 words. News, training tips, and opinion pieces.
- Artwork: B/W prints. 35mm color slides for cover art.

SAMPLE ISSUE
46 pages (14% advertising): 4 articles; 12 depts/columns. Sample copy, $5 with 9x12 SASE. Guidelines available.

- "Dynamic Duel." Article describes how Shawn Johnson defeated another top-ranked U.S. gymnast to win her second consecutive senior title.
- "Quiet Confidence." Article spotlights a gymnast from Stanford University.
- Sample dept/column: "IG Kids Klub!" profiles an up-and-coming gymnast who has set her sights on the 2012 Olympics.

RIGHTS AND PAYMENT
All rights. Written material, $15–$25. Artwork, $5–$50. Pays on publication. Provides 1 contributor's copy.

➡️EDITOR'S COMMENTS
We like to see articles with new information or little-known facts from writers who are experts in the sport.

Jack And Jill

Children's Better Health Institute
1100 Waterway Boulevard
P.O. Box 567
Indianapolis, IN 46206-0567

Editor: Terry Harshman

DESCRIPTION AND INTERESTS
This magazine is designed to educate and entertain young readers and to promote good health and fitness. Circ: 200,000.

Audience: 7–10 years
Frequency: 6 times each year
Website: www.jackandjillmag.org

FREELANCE POTENTIAL
50% written by nonstaff writers. Publishes 24 freelance submissions yearly; 70% by authors who are new to the magazine. Receives 1,200 unsolicited mss yearly.

SUBMISSIONS
Send complete ms. Accepts hard copy. SASE. Responds in 3 months.

- Articles: 500–600 words. Informational and how-to articles; humor; profiles; and biographies. Topics include sports, health, exercise, safety, nutrition, and hygiene.
- Fiction: 500–900 words. Genres include mystery, fantasy, folktales, humor, science fiction, and stories about sports and animals.
- Artwork: Submit sketches to Jennifer Saulovic, art director; submit photos to Terry Harshman, editor.
- Other: Poetry. Games, puzzles, activities, and cartoons. Submit seasonal material 8 months in advance.

SAMPLE ISSUE
36 pages (4% advertising): 2 articles; 2 stories; 3 depts/columns; 3 activities; 1 cartoon; 3 poems. Sample copy, $3.95 ($2 postage). Guidelines available.

- "Bear-ly Spring." Article discusses how bears stay in shape during hibernation and how kids can do similar exercises to get ready for warmer weather.
- "The Case of the Runaway Telephone." Story tells of a young boy who plays detective to help find his grandmother's phone.

RIGHTS AND PAYMENT
All rights. Written material, $.17 per word. Artwork, payment rates vary. Pays on publication. Provides 10 contributor's copies.

➡️EDITOR'S COMMENTS
At this time, we're particularly seeking material that will introduce kids to fun and interesting topics, as well as profiles of regular kids engaged in interesting pursuits.

JAKES Magazine

P.O. Box 530
Edgefield, SC 29824

Editor: Matt Lindler

DESCRIPTION AND INTERESTS
JAKES Magazine is designed to inform, educate, and involve youth in wildlife conservation and the wise stewardship of the earth's natural resources. Published by the National Wildlife Turkey Federation, it is read by members of the organization. Circ: 170,000.
Audience: 10–17 years
Frequency: Quarterly
Website: www.nwtf.org/jakes

FREELANCE POTENTIAL
50% written by nonstaff writers. Publishes 30 freelance submissions yearly; 10% by unpublished writers, 30% by authors who are new to the magazine. Receives 150–200 queries and unsolicited mss yearly.

SUBMISSIONS
Query or send complete ms. Accepts material between May and December only. Accepts hard copy, email to mlindler@nwtf.org, and simultaneous submissions if identified. SASE. Response time varies.

- Articles: 600–1,200 words. Informational articles; profiles; and personal experience pieces. Topics include nature, the environment, animals, pets, hunting, fishing, and other outdoor and extreme sports.
- Fiction: 800–1,200 words. Historical fiction.
- Depts/columns: Association news, new products and gear, essays.

SAMPLE ISSUE
18 pages: 2 articles; 8 depts/columns. Guidelines available at website.

- "How a Fish Is Like a Tree." Article explains that you can determine the age of a fish as you would that of a tree—by counting rings.
- "The Beaver: Nature's Busy Engineer." Article describes how beavers build dams and looks at their benefits and hindrances.
- Sample dept/column: "Super Jakes" is an essay from a young member about killing his first turkey.

RIGHTS AND PAYMENT
Rights vary. Written material, $100–$300. Pays on publication. Provides 2 author's copies.

➔ EDITOR'S COMMENTS
We like our feature stories to be supplemented by sidebars, bulleted lists, subheads, and other kid-friendly graphic elements.

Jeunesse
Young People, Texts, Cultures

Dept. of English, University of Winnipeg
515 Portage Avenue
Winnipeg, Manitoba R3B 2E9
Canada

Editor: Mavis Reimer

DESCRIPTION AND INTERESTS
This bilingual academic journal, formerly called *Canadian Children's Literature*, provides a forum for discussion about children's literature in all media. It includes interviews with children's authors, book reviews, and articles examining the digital culture and historical and contemporary functions of today's children. Circ: 400.
Audience: Educators, scholars, and librarians
Frequency: Twice each year
Website: www.jeunessejournal.ca

FREELANCE POTENTIAL
95% written by nonstaff writers. Publishes 25 freelance submissions yearly; 10% by unpublished writers, 40% by authors who are new to the magazine. Receives 40 mss yearly.

SUBMISSIONS
Send complete ms. Prefers email submissions to jeunesse@uwinnipeg.ca (Microsoft Word or RTF attachments); will accept 3 hard copies. SAE/IRC. Responds in 3 months.

- Articles: 2,000–6,000 words. Informational articles; reviews; profiles; and interviews. Topics include children's literature; film, video, and drama for children; and children's authors.

SAMPLE ISSUE
200 pages (2% advertising): 11 articles. Sample copy, $10. Guidelines and theme list available at website.

- "Anne of Green Gables, Elijah of Buxton, and Margaret of Newfoundland." Article examines *Anne of Green Gables* against some contemporary reworkings, as well as a new novel set in the same period.
- "Same Old Stories? A Feminist Critique of Juvenile Biographies." Article reviews a diverse group of 12 biographies that, according to the author, have glossed over the realities of sexism and racism in Canadian society.

RIGHTS AND PAYMENT
First serial rights. No payment. Provides 1 contributor's copy.

➔ EDITOR'S COMMENTS
Our scope is international. While we have a special interest in Canada, we welcome submissions concerning all areas and cultures. Check our website for our editorial themes.

Journal of Adolescent & Adult Literacy

International Reading Association
800 Barksdale Road
P.O. Box 8139
Newark, DE 19714-8139

Managing Editor: James Henderson

DESCRIPTION AND INTERESTS
Described as the only professional literacy journal exclusively for teachers of older learners, *Journal of Adolescent & Adult Literacy* provides practical classroom-tested ideas that are solidly based on research and theory. It includes reviews of student resources, teaching tips, and information on current trends and research. Circ: 16,000.

Audience: Reading education professionals
Frequency: 8 times each year
Website: www.reading.org

FREELANCE POTENTIAL
95% written by nonstaff writers. Publishes 50 freelance submissions yearly; 30% by unpublished writers, 50% by authors who are new to the magazine. Receives 300 unsolicited mss each year.

SUBMISSIONS
Send complete ms. Accepts electronic submissions via http://mc.manuscriptcentral.com/jaal. Responds in 2–3 months.

- Articles: 5,000–6,000 words. Informational and how-to articles; and personal experience pieces. Topics include reading theory, research, and practice; and trends in teaching literacy.
- Depts/columns: Word lengths vary. Opinion pieces, reviews, and technology information.

SAMPLE ISSUE
88 pages (7% advertising): 6 articles; 4 depts/columns. Sample copy, $10. Guidelines available at website.

- "Lana's Story: Re-Storying Literacy Education." Article recommends using adult students' interests and experiences to build an effective curriculum.
- Sample dept/column: "Research Connections" examines a project used in the San Diego school system that introduced literacy instruction using content area texts.

RIGHTS AND PAYMENT
All rights. No payment. Provides 5 contributor's copies for articles, 2 for depts/columns.

⟶EDITOR'S COMMENTS
Please familiarize yourself with the types of articles we publish to gain insight about the voice, tone, and format that is appropriate for our audience.

Journal of Adventist Education

12501 Old Columbia Pike
Silver Spring, MD 20904-6600

Editor: Beverly J. Rumble

DESCRIPTION AND INTERESTS
This professional journal reaches Seventh-day Adventist teachers and educational administrators. It publishes practical and theoretical articles on a variety of topics related to education. All articles must incorporate Seventh-day Adventist beliefs and values. Circ: 15,000.

Audience: Teachers and administrators
Frequency: 5 times each year
Website: http://JAE.adventist.org

FREELANCE POTENTIAL
90% written by nonstaff writers. Publishes 30 freelance submissions yearly. Receives 24–48 queries yearly.

SUBMISSIONS
Query. Accepts email queries to rumbleb@gc.adventist.org (Microsoft Word attachments). Availability of artwork improves chance of acceptance. Responds in 3–6 weeks.

- Articles: To 2,000 words. Informational and how-to articles. Topics include parochial, gifted, and special education; new teaching methods and educational approaches; school administration and supervision; classroom management; religion; mathematics; science; and technology.
- Depts/columns: Staff written.
- Artwork: Color prints or slides; JPEG or TIFF images at 300 dpi. Charts and graphs.

SAMPLE ISSUE
48 pages (5% advertising): 9 articles; 1 dept/column. Sample copy, $3.50 with 9x12 SASE ($.68 postage). Guidelines available.

- "Creating Successful Strategies for ESL Instruction." Article offers teachers practical ideas and strategies for their English as a Second Language classes.
- "Student Missionaries and English Language Learners." Article interviews several college-age students about their experiences in teaching the English language as part of their missionary work.

RIGHTS AND PAYMENT
First North American serial rights. Articles, to $100. Artwork, payment rates vary. Pays on publication. Provides 2 contributor's copies.

⟶EDITOR'S COMMENTS
We always prefer articles that provide practical information for use in the classroom.

Journal of School Health

American School Health Association
7263 State Route 43
P.O. Box 708
Kent, OH 44240-0708

Editor: James H. Price

DESCRIPTION AND INTERESTS

All topics relating to maintaining a healthy school environment are covered in this professional publication. It targets school administrators and school health professionals and keeps them abreast of research and trends in the field. Circ: 5,000.

Audience: School health professionals
Frequency: 10 times each year
Website: www.ashaweb.org

FREELANCE POTENTIAL

95% written by nonstaff writers. Publishes 60 freelance submissions yearly; 90% by authors who are new to the magazine. Receives 120 queries and unsolicited mss yearly.

SUBMISSIONS

Query or send ms. Accepts electronic submissions via http://mc.manuscriptcentral.com/josh. Responds to queries in 2 weeks, to mss in 3–4 months.

- Articles: 2,500 words. Informational articles; research papers; commentaries; and practical application pieces. Topics include teaching techniques, health services in the school system, nursing, medicine, substance abuse, nutrition, counseling, and ADD/AHD.

SAMPLE ISSUE

58 pages (no advertising): 3 articles; 4 research papers; 1 commentary. Sample copy, $8.50 with 9x12 SASE. Writers' guidelines available at website.

- "Examining the Consulting Physician Model to Enhance the School Nurse Role for Children with Asthma." Research paper examines the effectiveness of using a consulting physician to mitigate the number of children sent home from school or absent due to asthma-related reasons.
- "Body Mass Index Measurement in Schools." Article discusses the implementation of school-based BMI measurements to identify students at risk for childhood obesity.

RIGHTS AND PAYMENT

All rights. No payment. Provides 2 copies.

➥EDITOR'S COMMENTS

All articles must be research-based, accurate, and have all sources noted. Articles should give school health professionals information to do their jobs more effectively.

Junior Baseball

14 Woodway Lane
Wilton, CT 06897

Editor/Publisher: Jim Beecher

DESCRIPTION AND INTERESTS

Parents, coaches, players, and others involved in youth baseball organizations read this magazine for its coverage of age-appropriate aspects of the sport, including playing tips and coaching strategies. Circ: 50,000.

Audience: 7–17 years; parents; coaches
Frequency: 6 times each year
Website: www.juniorbaseball.com

FREELANCE POTENTIAL

50% written by nonstaff writers. Publishes 20 freelance submissions yearly; 10% by unpublished writers, 20% by authors who are new to the magazine. Receives 50 queries and unsolicited mss yearly.

SUBMISSIONS

Query with writing samples; or send complete ms with artwork. Accepts email submissions to jim@juniorbaseball.com (Microsoft Word attachments or text files). Availability of artwork improves chance of acceptance. SASE. Responds in 1–2 weeks.

- Articles: 750–1,500 words. Informational and how-to articles; profiles; and interviews. Topics include playing tips, teams and leagues, and player safety.
- Depts/columns: "Player's Story," 500 words. "In the Spotlight," news and reviews, 50–100 words. "Hot Prospects," 500–1,000 words. "Coaches Clinic," 100–1,000 words.
- Artwork: 4x5, 5x7, and 8x10 color prints; color digital images at 300 dpi.

SAMPLE ISSUE

40 pages (30% advertising): 11 articles; 9 depts/columns. Sample copy, $3.95 with 9x12 SASE ($1.35 postage). Guidelines available.

- "Shhh! Don't Tell the Hitters!" Article outlines five secrets that pitchers don't want hitters to know.
- Sample dept/column: "Coaches' Clinic" argues that coaches cannot overstate the importance of the fundamentals.

RIGHTS AND PAYMENT

All rights. Articles, $.20 per word. Depts/columns, $25–$100. Artwork, $50–$100. Pays on publication. Provides 1 contributor's copy.

➥EDITOR'S COMMENTS

To even be considered, writers should demonstrate a knowledge of youth baseball.

Junior Shooters

7154 West State Street, #377
Boise, ID 83714

Editor: Andrew Fink

DESCRIPTION AND INTERESTS
Junior Shooters is dedicated to advancing children's involvement in all disciplines of shooting sports. It covers techniques, training, gear, and events. Circ: 30,000.

Audience: 8–21 years
Frequency: Twice each year
Website: www.juniorshooters.net

FREELANCE POTENTIAL
60% written by nonstaff writers. Publishes several freelance submissions yearly; 60% by unpublished writers, 40% by authors who are new to the magazine.

SUBMISSIONS
Send complete ms. Accepts email submissions to articles@juniorshooters.net and CD submissions (PC format) in Microsoft Word; all submissions should be accompanied by form found at website. Materials are not returned. Response time varies.

- Articles: Word lengths vary. Informational articles; profiles; and personal experience pieces. Topics include all disciplines of shooting sports, techniques, training, coaching, products, and gear.
- Depts/columns: Word lengths vary. Shooting tips, gun safety, new products and gear.
- Artwork: High-resolution digital images.

SAMPLE ISSUE
Sample copy available. Guidelines and editorial calendar available at website.

- "Benjamin Discovery Air Rifle from Crosman." Article offers a review and description of this new air gun.
- "Opportunity of a Lifetime for Junior Shooters." Article discusses the five-day shooting camp that allowed up-and-comers to learn from the U.S. Army's International Rifle Team.
- Sample dept/column: "Tips and Hints of the Week" explains how shooting sports help children focus in school.

RIGHTS AND PAYMENT
Non-exclusive rights. No payment.

➔EDITOR'S COMMENTS
Many of our writers are juniors themselves. We are also interested in articles by coaches, shooting organizations, parents, manufacturers, and others who have information about supporting juniors in shooting sports.

JuniorWay

P.O. Box 436987
Chicago, IL 60643

Editor: Katherine Steward

DESCRIPTION AND INTERESTS
JuniorWay is written for Christian children in African American churches. Its Bible lessons and activities are designed to educate and empower readers to serve Jesus, the church, and the world. Circ: 75,000.

Audience: 9–11 years
Frequency: Quarterly
Website: www.urbanministries.com

FREELANCE POTENTIAL
95% written by nonstaff writers. Publishes 52 freelance submissions yearly. Receives 240 queries yearly.

SUBMISSIONS
Query with résumé and writing samples. All material is written on assignment. Response time varies.

- Articles: Word lengths vary. Bible lessons; personal experience pieces; and humor. Topics include religion, relationships, social issues, hobbies, crafts, sports, recreation, and multicultural subjects.
- Fiction: Word lengths vary. Inspirational stories with multicultural or ethnic themes, adventure stories, humor, and folktales.
- Artwork: B/W or color prints or transparencies.
- Other: Puzzles, activities, games, and jokes. Poetry. Seasonal material about Vacation Bible School.

SAMPLE ISSUE
32 pages (no advertising): 13 Bible lessons; 6 activities; 1 poem; 1 comic. Sample copy, free. Guidelines and theme list available.

- "I Agree?" Bible lesson uses the Ten Commandments as an example of established rules that people are expected to follow.
- "Please Don't Pick Me." Bible lesson tells how a girl made excuses when she didn't want to do something, similar to how Moses made excuses to God.

RIGHTS AND PAYMENT
All rights. All material, payment rates vary. Pays on publication.

➔EDITOR'S COMMENTS
In order to write for us, you must be a practicing Christian who is familiar with Sunday school curricula. You should also be knowledgeable about the Bible. Fresh ideas will get our attention.

Justine

6263 Poplar Avenue, Suite 1154
Memphis, TN 38119

Publisher/Editorial Director: Jana Petty

DESCRIPTION AND INTERESTS

This magazine for "just teens" aims to be classy but cool with the latest on affordable style, fashion, and beauty. Each issue captures the world of teen girls while encouraging them to live a healthy lifestyle. Circ: 250,000.

Audience: Girls, 13–18 years
Frequency: 6 times each year
Website: www.justinemagazine.com

FREELANCE POTENTIAL

20% written by nonstaff writers. Publishes 25 freelance submissions yearly; 25% by unpublished writers, 90% by authors who are new to the magazine. Receives 100 queries yearly.

SUBMISSIONS

Query with résumé and clips. Accepts hard copy. SASE. Response time varies.

- Articles: Word lengths vary. Informational articles; profiles; interviews; and personal experience pieces. Topics include popular culture, celebrities, style, fashion, nutrition, health, fitness, recreation, travel, family, and relationships.
- Depts/columns: Word lengths vary. Beauty, decorating, and fashion tips; nutrition; relationship advice; and social issues.
- Other: Quizzes and contests.

SAMPLE ISSUE

96 pages: 5 articles; 32 depts/columns; 1 quiz. Sample copy, $2.99 at newsstands.

- "Evan Taubenfeld." Article profiles this musician, who has released a solo album after working with Avril Lavigne for three years.
- "Shawn Johnson . . . Golden Girl!" Article features an interview with the Olympic gymnast as she embarks on *Dancing with the Stars*.
- Sample dept/column: "Just Life" suggests healthy snacks for school.

RIGHTS AND PAYMENT

Rights vary. Written material, payment rates vary. Pays 30 days after publication.

⌖EDITOR'S COMMENTS

Our readers care about more than celebrity gossip and fashion that doesn't fit their budgets. That's why we keep things real, from getting glamorous to giving back. If you have insight into what's on the minds of teen girls these days, we'd like to hear from you.

JVibe

90 Oak Street, 4th Floor
P.O. Box 9129
Upper Falls, MA 02464

Editor-in-Chief: Lindsey Silken

DESCRIPTION AND INTERESTS

Targeting Jewish teens, this magazine is filled with celebrity interviews, pop culture updates, articles about social issues, and information on other topics of interest to teens in general, and Jewish teens in particular. Circ: 15,000.

Audience: 9–18 years
Frequency: 6 times each year
Website: www.jvibe.com

FREELANCE POTENTIAL

90% written by nonstaff writers. Publishes 90 freelance submissions yearly; 10% by unpublished writers, 20% by authors who are new to the magazine. Receives 120 queries yearly.

SUBMISSIONS

Query. Accepts email queries to editor@ jvibe.com. Responds in 1 week.

- Articles: 1,400 words. Informational articles; profiles; interviews; reviews; and personal experience pieces. Topics include religion, Israel, popular culture, music, sports, current events, humor, college, careers, and the arts.
- Depts/columns: Staff written.
- Other: Submit seasonal material at least 3 months in advance.

SAMPLE ISSUE

38 pages (10% advertising): 4 articles; 6 depts/columns. Sample copy, guidelines, and editorial calendar available.

- "Are We Becoming Too Diverse?" Article presents a roundtable discussion among American Hebrew Academy students about the evolving Jewish community.
- "Schmoozin' with . . . Matisyahu." Article offers a profile of the reggae-rapper and explains why he should be on teens' musical radar screens.

RIGHTS AND PAYMENT

All rights. Written material, payment rates vary. Pays on publication. Provides 2 contributor's copies.

⌖EDITOR'S COMMENTS

We are always in search of excellent writers with flair. Here's a tip for hitting just the right note with your article: Think back to when you were a teen and what interested you; then keep the word count down and the enthusiasm up.

Kaboose.com

Disney Online Mom and Family Portfolio
5161 Lankershin Boulevard, 4th Floor
North Hollywood, CA 91601

Vice President: Emily Smith

DESCRIPTION AND INTERESTS
Recently acquired by Disney, *Kaboose.com* is now part of the Disney Online Mom and Family Portfolio of websites, which also includes *FamilyFun.com, Wondertime.com, iParenting.com,* and *BabyZone.com,* among others. As always, its goal is to provide ideas and inspiration for mothers on a variety of topics important to today's families. Hits per month: 3.6 million.

Audience: Mothers
Frequency: Unavailable
Website: www.kaboose.com

FREELANCE POTENTIAL
95% written by nonstaff writers. Publishes 30 freelance submissions yearly; 10% by unpublished writers, 30% by authors who are new to the magazine. Receives 150 queries yearly.

SUBMISSIONS
Query with outline. Accepts hard copy. Response time varies.

- Articles: 2,000 words. Informational and how-to articles. Topics include parenting, pregnancy, child care, health, fitness, food, kids' activities, celebrity updates, style, home and garden, crafts, hobbies, and pets.
- Depts/columns: 500 words. Advice, travel, recipes, and entertaining.
- Other: Submit seasonal material 6 months in advance.

SAMPLE ISSUE
Sample copy available at website.

- "And the Winner Is . . ." Article spotlights the editors' picks for the 10 best lip glosses.
- "The Toddler Tantrum Survival Guide." Article details when and why children have tantrums, how to avoid triggering them, and how to handle them when they do happen.

RIGHTS AND PAYMENT
Rights vary. Written material, $.85 per word. Pays on acceptance.

➦EDITOR'S COMMENTS
Our new portfolio of sites will reach nearly one in five moms online, which is more than the reach of any other family and parenting online destination today. While we will retain our distinct voice and editorial focus, we will also be developing new content and promotions to incorporate our other sites.

Kaleidoscope
*Exploring the Experience of Disability
Through Literature & Fine Arts*

701 South Main Street
Akron, OH 44311-1019

Editorial Coordinator: Mickey Shiplett

DESCRIPTION AND INTERESTS
This is a publication that celebrates, supports, and understands disabilities. Its articles, short stories, poetry, reviews, and visual art express the experiences of disability. It accepts material from the disabled, their family members and caregivers, and professionals. Circ: 1,000.

Audience: YA–Adult
Frequency: Twice each year
Website: www.udsakron.org

FREELANCE POTENTIAL
90% written by nonstaff writers. Publishes 40 freelance submissions yearly; 10% by unpublished writers, 50% by authors who are new to the magazine. Receives 240 queries, 420–540 unsolicited mss yearly.

SUBMISSIONS
Query or send complete ms with author bio. Accepts hard copy and email submissions to mshiplett@udsakron.org (Microsoft Word attachments). SASE. Responds to queries in 2 weeks, to mss in 6 months.

- Articles: To 5,000 words. Informational articles; profiles; interviews; reviews; humor; and personal experience pieces. Topics include art, literature, biography, multicultural and social issues, and disabilities.
- Fiction: 5,000 words. Genres include folktales, humor, and multicultural and problem-solving fiction.
- Other: Poetry.

SAMPLE ISSUE
64 pages (no advertising): 6 articles; 4 stories; 10 poems. Sample copy, $6 with 9x12 SASE. Guidelines and editorial calendar available.

- "No Say in the Matter of Me." Personal essay reflects on the author's fears and feelings of vulnerability while living in hospitals as a child with polio.
- "The Dependable Density of Water." Article provides insight into the lives of a couple who strain to deal with their son's psychosis.

RIGHTS AND PAYMENT
First rights. Written material, $25–$100. Poetry, $10. Pays on publication. Provides 2 contributor's copies.

➦EDITOR'S COMMENTS
Each of our issues is themed. A list of upcoming themes can be found at our website.

Key Club

Key Club International
3636 Woodview Trace
Indianapolis, IN 46268-3196

Editor: Amberly Peterson

DESCRIPTION AND INTERESTS
As the official publication of Key Club International, this magazine focuses on service and leadership. It provides its readers with information and tips on becoming better students and better Key Club members. Circ: 240,000.

Audience: 14–18 years
Frequency: Twice each year
Website: www.keyclub.org/magazine

FREELANCE POTENTIAL
20% written by nonstaff writers. Publishes 4 freelance submissions yearly; 5% by unpublished writers, 15% by authors who are new to the magazine. Receives 100 queries yearly.

SUBMISSIONS
Query with outline/synopsis and clips or writing samples. Accepts hard copy, email queries to magazine@kiwanis.org, and simultaneous submissions if identified. SASE. Responds in 1 month.

- Articles: 1,000–1,500 words. Informational, self-help, and service-related articles. Topics include education, teen concerns, community service, leadership, school activities, social issues, and careers.
- Depts/columns: Staff written.
- Artwork: Color prints and illustrations.
- Other: Submit seasonal material about back to school, college, and summer activities 3–7 months in advance.

SAMPLE ISSUE
24 pages (5% advertising): 4 articles; 3 depts/columns. Sample copy, free with 9x12 SASE ($.83 postage). Guidelines available.

- "Save the Earth." Article lists several fun and different ways to be eco-conscious.
- "Stop Spinning." Article provides tips from experienced Key Club leaders on keeping things together when responsibilities pile up.

RIGHTS AND PAYMENT
First North American serial rights. All material, $150–$350. Pays on acceptance. Provides 3 contributor's copies.

➡️EDITOR'S COMMENTS
We urge you to read our magazine before submitting material. We especially like articles that are the product of first-hand interviews. Keep in mind that we are read by an international audience.

Keys for Kids

P.O. Box 1001
Grand Rapids, MI 49510

Editor: Hazel Marett

DESCRIPTION AND INTERESTS
Published by CBH Ministries, *Keys for Kids* publishes daily devotionals, or "keys," for children. Each devotional is a story that helps guide children on their Christian journey. Circ: 70,000.

Audience: 6–14 years
Frequency: 6 times each year
Website: www.keysforkids.org

FREELANCE POTENTIAL
100% written by nonstaff writers. Publishes 30 freelance submissions yearly; 50% by unpublished writers, 90% by authors who are new to the magazine. Receives 120 unsolicited mss each year.

SUBMISSIONS
Send complete ms. Accepts hard copy and email submissions to hazel@cbhministries.org. SASE. Responds in 2 months.

- Articles: 400 words. Devotionals with related Scripture passages and a key thought. Topics include contemporary social issues, family life, trust, friendship, salvation, witnessing, prayer, marriage, and faith.

SAMPLE ISSUE
80 pages: 59 devotionals. Sample copy, free with 9x12 SASE. Writers' guidelines available at website.

- "Secret Friend?" Devotional tells the story of a boy who learns that he need not be afraid to let his friends know that Jesus is his best friend.
- "The Right Focus." Devotional teaches that in order to avoid temptation, we must keep our eyes focused on our master—Jesus.
- "Awesome Wisdom." Devotional relates how scientists often take their cues from nature as an illustration of the wisdom of God.

RIGHTS AND PAYMENT
First, second, and reprint rights. Written material, $25. Pays on acceptance. Provides 1 contributor's copy.

➡️EDITOR'S COMMENTS
Our basic format of a devotional is to tell a story (not a Bible story) and then give it practical application to a child's life. Please avoid using Pollyanna-type children in your devotionals. We want to reach real children, and the way to do that is by writing about real children. Don't be afraid to use some humor.

Kid Magazine Writers

The Kids' Ark

9 Arrowhead Drive
Ledyard, CT 06339

Editor: Jan Fields

DESCRIPTION AND INTERESTS
This online journal helps writers hone their skills for the children's magazine market. Hits per month: 2,000.

Audience: Children's magazine writers
Frequency: Monthly
Website: www.kidmagwriters.com

FREELANCE POTENTIAL
60% written by nonstaff writers. Publishes 50–80 freelance submissions yearly; 15% by unpublished writers, 20% by authors who are new to the magazine. Receives 12–24 queries, 120 unsolicited mss yearly.

SUBMISSIONS
Query or send complete ms. Accepts email submissions to editor@kidmagwriters.com (no attachments). Response time varies.

- Articles: 500+ words. Informational, inspirational, and how-to articles; interviews; essays; and personal experience pieces. Topics include tips for young writers; print and online markets; contests; time management; writing courses and software; nonfiction, fiction, and poetry writing techniques; and media reviews.
- Depts/columns: 500+ words. "Word Wizard," "Editors Speak," "Consider This," "In My Office," "That's a Fact," "Storytellers," "Meter Readers," and "In the Beginning."

SAMPLE ISSUE
Sample copy and writers' guidelines available at website.

- "Writing With Kids." Article discusses balancing writing with mothering young children.
- Sample dept/column: "That's a Fact" discusses how writers can use recent finding in brain research to craft articles for maximum learning potential.

RIGHTS AND PAYMENT
One-time rights. No payment.

↪EDITOR'S COMMENTS
We've added a number of regular columnists, so at this time we're mostly open to inspirational articles about fitting writing into life. Helpful articles on general writing topics—such as manuscript tracking or taxes—are also of current interest. Please note that most of the manuscripts we receive are fiction, which we do *not* publish.

P.O. Box 3160
Victoria, TX 77903

Editor: Joy Mygrants

DESCRIPTION AND INTERESTS
The articles in this Christian children's magazine are designed to offer an alternative to negative media influences and peer pressures that threaten our children. The articles in each themed issue focus on the truth about God's love. They are non-denominational and Bible-based. Circ: 8,000+.

Audience: 6–12 years
Frequency: Quarterly
Website: www.thekidsark.com

FREELANCE POTENTIAL
60% written by nonstaff writers. Publishes 12 freelance submissions yearly; 80–100% by authors who are new to the magazine. Receives 25 unsolicited mss yearly.

SUBMISSIONS
Send complete ms. Accepts email submissions to thekidsarksubmissions@yahoo.com (Microsoft Word attachments; note theme to which you are submitting in subject line). Responds in 2 months.

- Articles: To 650 words. Informational articles and personal experience pieces. Topics include religion, faith, and God's love.
- Fiction: To 650 words. Genres include contemporary, historical, and science fiction—all with Christian themes.
- Other: Puzzles, games, and comics.

SAMPLE ISSUE
32 pages: 9 articles; 3 stories; 7 activities. Sample copy, guidelines, and theme list available at website.

- "A Stubborn Heart." Story features a stubborn boy to illustrate God's warning against harboring a stubborn heart.
- "A Loving Home in Sri Lanka." Personal essay tells of a boy's experience in a dysfunctional home until God's people intervened and got help for the family.

RIGHTS AND PAYMENT
First North American serial, second, worldwide, and electronic rights. Written material, $100. Reprints, $25. Pays on publication.

↪EDITOR'S COMMENTS
Our purpose is to enlighten children with the love and power of God through Jesus, and to give children a sound biblical foundation on which to base their later decisions.

Kids Life

1426 22nd Avenue
Tuscaloosa, AL 35401

Publisher: Mary Jane Turner

DESCRIPTION AND INTERESTS
Kids Life fills its pages with articles on topics of interest to parents, as well as information on family-oriented events. All information must relate to parents living in western Alabama. Circ: 30,000.

Audience: Parents
Frequency: 6 times each year
Website: www.kidslifemagazine.com

FREELANCE POTENTIAL
75% written by nonstaff writers. Publishes 12 freelance submissions yearly; 50% by unpublished writers, 10% by authors who are new to the magazine. Receives 240 queries, 240 unsolicited mss yearly.

SUBMISSIONS
Query or send complete ms. Accepts email submissions to kidslife@comcast.net. Availability of artwork improves chance of acceptance. Responds in 2 weeks.

- Articles: 1,000 words. Informational articles and personal experience pieces. Topics include parenting, education, sports, child care, religion, cooking, crafts, health, travel, and current events.
- Depts/columns: Staff written.
- Artwork: Color prints; JPEG files. Line art.
- Other: Filler.

SAMPLE ISSUE
50 pages (60% advertising): 4 articles; 5 depts/columns. Sample copy, free with SASE.

- "Teens Today: Too Label Conscious?" Article argues that teens care more about clothing labels than nutrition labels.
- "4-H: Celebrating 100 years in Alabama." Article looks at the history and legacy of the 4-H programs in Alabama.
- "A Factory of Fun." Article profiles a Tuscaloosa couple who went into business for themselves with the Fun Factor family entertainment center.

RIGHTS AND PAYMENT
Rights vary. Written material, to $30. Pays on publication. Provides 1 contributor's copy.

➙ EDITOR'S COMMENTS
Our magazine is free to parents and distributed widely throughout our region. Parents turn to us for local information; therefore, all articles must pertain to the region.

Kids' Ministry Ideas

55 West Oak Ridge Drive
Hagerstown, MD 21740

Editor: Candy DeVore

DESCRIPTION AND INTERESTS
Kids' Ministry Ideas is a resource publication for those leading children to Jesus. It supports children's ministry leaders with informative articles, resources, and programming ideas from a Seventh-day Adventist perspective. Circ: 4,500.

Audience: Adventist youth ministry leaders
Frequency: Quarterly
Website: www.kidsministryideas.com

FREELANCE POTENTIAL
100% written by nonstaff writers. Publishes 60 freelance submissions yearly.

SUBMISSIONS
Query or send complete ms. Accepts hard copy and email to cdevore@rhpa.org. SASE. Response time varies.

- Articles: 300–800 words. Informational and how-to articles; and essays. Topics include religious education, youth ministry, family issues, working with volunteers, lesson plans and props, faith, and prayer.
- Depts/columns: Word lengths vary. Leadership training, teaching tips, and crafts.
- Other: Submit seasonal material 6–12 months in advance.

SAMPLE ISSUE
32 pages: 3 articles; 7 depts/columns. Sample copy available. Guidelines available at website.

- "The Ministry of Volunteerism." Article extols the advantages of inviting others to join in volunteer activities.
- Sample dept/column: "Capturing Curiosity" discusses discipline as an act of teaching and love, and explains that God sometimes disciplines, out of love, to teach a lesson.

RIGHTS AND PAYMENT
First North American serial rights. Written material, $20–$100. Pays 5–6 weeks after acceptance. Provides 2 contributor's copies.

➙ EDITOR'S COMMENTS
Articles on a wide range of subjects appear in our magazine, but they all offer practical ideas and easy-to-understand instruction that people can implement in their area of ministry. Use of sidebars, boxes, and lists of resources or other information is strongly encouraged, as this dilutes copy intensity and makes articles more readable.

Kids VT

P.O. Box 1089
Shelburne, VT 05482

Editor: Susan Holson

DESCRIPTION AND INTERESTS
This family magazine puts the focus on children and fun, with articles on family recreation, family travel, positive parenting, and education. Its articles are localized to Vermont. Circ: 25,000.

Audience: Parents
Frequency: 10 times each year
Website: www.kidsvt.com

FREELANCE POTENTIAL
75% written by nonstaff writers. Publishes 50–60 freelance submissions yearly; 20% by authors who are new to the magazine. Receives 480–960 unsolicited mss yearly.

SUBMISSIONS
Send complete ms. Accepts email submissions to editorial@kidsvt.com (no attachments) and simultaneous submissions if identified. Responds if interested.

- Articles: 500–1,500 words. Informational articles; profiles; interviews; and humor. Topics include the arts, education, recreation, nature, the environment, music, camps, pregnancy, infancy, and parenting.
- Depts/columns: Word lengths vary. News and media reviews.
- Other: Activities and games. Submit seasonal material 2 months in advance.

SAMPLE ISSUE
32 pages (50% advertising): 9 articles; 8 depts/columns. Guidelines and editorial calendar available at website.

- "Family Fun on the Cheap." Article outlines several ways to have fun in the summer without spending too much money.
- Sample dept/column: "First With Kids" reports on the importance of using sunscreen on children, and explains what to do should a child get too much sun.

RIGHTS AND PAYMENT
One-time and reprint rights. Written material, payment rates vary. Pays 30 days after publication. Provides 1–2 contributor's copies.

⇢EDITOR'S COMMENTS
Because of our preference for local angles on all articles, we are especially happy to hear from local writers. All articles should be of interest to parents and provide them with useful information that they didn't have before.

Kiki

214 East 8th Street, 5th Floor
Cincinnati, OH 45202

Editor-in-Chief: Jamie G. Bryant

DESCRIPTION AND INTERESTS
Kiki is a fashion magazine and a creativity journal for tween girls. It is geared toward girls who have a flair for style and fashion, but who also want to expand their horizons through articles about travel, the fashion business, crafts, and sewing. Circ: Unavailable.

Audience: Girls, 8–14 years
Frequency: Quarterly
Website: www.kikimag.com

FREELANCE POTENTIAL
50% written by nonstaff writers. Publishes 40 freelance submissions yearly; 25% by authors who are new to the magazine.

SUBMISSIONS
Query. Accepts hard copy. SASE. Responds in 3 months.

- Articles: Word lengths vary. Informational and how-to articles; profiles; interviews; and personal experience pieces. Topics include fashion, beauty, health, fitness, the arts, crafts, social issues, travel, and business.
- Depts/columns: Word lengths vary. Book reviews, new product information, craft and sewing projects, fashion.

SAMPLE ISSUE
80 pages: 17 articles; 12 depts/columns. Sample copy, $7.95 with 9x12 SASE. Guidelines available at website.

- "Two Great Ideas for Seasonal Money Makers." Article explains two ways that enterprising young people can make money during the winter holidays.
- "The Wide World of Textiles." Article explains the origins, processing, and uses of wool and cotton.
- Sample dept/column: "Kiki Book Club" offers a review of the Prague history book, *Castle*, by David Macaulay.

RIGHTS AND PAYMENT
All rights. Written material, $.50–$1 per word. Pays on publication. Provides 2 contributor's copies.

⇢EDITOR'S COMMENTS
We are always looking for great writing on interesting topics our readers will enjoy. Referrals for art and photo sources, if applicable, are appreciated. We are not interested in articles about boys, sex, or social issues.

Know
The Science Magazine for Curious Kids

Lacrosse

501-3960 Quadra Street
Victoria, British Columbia V8X 4A3
Canada

Managing Editor: Adrienne Mason

113 West University Parkway
Baltimore, MD 21210

Editor: Paul Krome

DESCRIPTION AND INTERESTS
Know seeks to encourage interest and appreciation for science in children while providing positive role models for both boys and girls. Each issue revolves around a particular theme. Circ: 13,000.

Audience: 6–9 years
Frequency: 6 times each year
Website: www.knowmag.ca

DESCRIPTION AND INTERESTS
All things lacrosse, from player profiles and training tips to youth and collegiate program previews, are featured in this magazine. Published by US Lacrosse, the sport's national governing body, the magazine's goal is to educate and entertain its readers—both players and fans. Circ: 250,000.

Audience: Youth and college lacrosse players
Frequency: Monthly
Website: www.laxmagazine.com

FREELANCE POTENTIAL
50% written by nonstaff writers. Publishes 150 freelance submissions yearly; 5% by unpublished writers, 30% by authors who are new to the magazine. Receives 300 queries, 180 unsolicited mss yearly.

FREELANCE POTENTIAL
30% written by nonstaff writers. Publishes 60 freelance submissions yearly; 5% by unpublished writers, 10% by authors who are new to the magazine. Receives 60 queries yearly.

SUBMISSIONS
Query with résumé and clips for nonfiction. Send complete ms for fiction and poetry. Accepts hard copy and email submissions to adrienne@knowmag.ca. SASE. Responds to queries in 1 month, to mss in 3 months.

- Articles: 250 words. Informational and how-to articles; science experiments; and interviews. Topics include chemistry, physics, biology, ecology, zoology, geology, technology, and mathematics.
- Fiction: To 500 words. Theme-related stories.
- Depts/columns: 200–250 words. Science news and discoveries, scientist profiles, astronomy, paleontology, and random facts.
- Other: Poetry. Puzzles, games, and activities.

SUBMISSIONS
Query with clips or résumé. Accepts email queries to pkrome@usalacrosse.org. SASE. Responds in 1 month.

- Articles: 800–1,000 words. Informational and how-to articles; profiles; and interviews. Topics include lacrosse gear, training, rules, strategies, leagues, coaching methods, competitions, and events; and sports medicine.
- Depts/columns: 300 words. Organization news and events; tips for players, coaches, and officials; and profiles of personalities.

SAMPLE ISSUE
32 pages (6% advertising): 5 articles; 8 depts/columns. Sample copy, guidelines, and theme list available at website.

- "She's A Rock Star." Article profiles a geologist who works in British Columbia.
- Sample dept/column: "Digging Dinos" takes a look at the gorgosaurus.

SAMPLE ISSUE
96 pages (35% advertising): 3 articles; 8 depts/columns. Sample copy, $5. Writers' guidelines available.

- "Recruiting U: Best Foot Forward." Article provides five tips for giving college coaches the best impression.
- "Comings and Goings." Article discusses the departures and return of players in the National Lacrosse League.
- Sample dept/column: "Classroom" gives five tips for sliding on defense.

RIGHTS AND PAYMENT
First North American serial rights. Written material, $.40–$.50 Canadian per word. Pays on publication. Provides 2 contributor's copies.

RIGHTS AND PAYMENT
Exclusive rights. Articles, $100–$300. Depts/columns, $100–$150. Pays on publication. Provides 1+ contributor's copies.

⟶EDITOR'S COMMENTS
We are currently not accepting nonfiction, but we welcome short fiction or poetry submissions that relate to one of our upcoming themes. The editorial themes can be found at our website.

⟶EDITOR'S COMMENTS
We seek articles from writers with extensive knowledge about the sport. Of special interest are articles about youth players.

Ladies' Home Journal

Meredith Corporation
375 Lexington Avenue, 9th Floor
New York, NY 10017

Deputy Editor: Margot Gilman

DESCRIPTION AND INTERESTS
For more than a century, *Ladies' Home Journal* has been a staple among women's magazines. Its editorial mix includes a large dose of family- and parenting-related articles covering topics such as child development, education, relationships, and family health. Circ: 4.1 million.

Audience: Women
Frequency: Monthly
Website: www.lhj.com

FREELANCE POTENTIAL
85% written by nonstaff writers. Publishes 25 freelance submissions yearly; 1% by unpublished writers, 5% by authors who are new to the magazine. Receives 2,400 queries yearly.

SUBMISSIONS
Query with résumé, outline, and clips or writing samples for nonfiction. Accepts fiction through literary agents only. Accepts hard copy. SASE. Responds in 1–3 months.

- Articles: 1,500–2,000 words. Informational and how-to articles; profiles; interviews; and personal experience pieces. Topics include family issues, parenting, social concerns, fashion, beauty, and women's health.
- Fiction: Word lengths vary.
- Depts/columns: Word lengths vary. Motherhood, marriage, self-help, beauty, home, health, food, news, and lifestyle features.

SAMPLE ISSUE
166 pages (15% advertising): 7 articles; 1 story; 14 depts/columns. Sample copy, $2.49 at newsstands.

- "Seven Myths About Bad Posture, Dispelled." Article discusses the many facets of posture, and addresses several myths about it.
- "When Not to Sleep With Your Husband." Article addresses the sleep problems some couples experience.

RIGHTS AND PAYMENT
All rights. All material, payment rates vary. Pays on publication. Provides 2 contributor's copies.

✒ EDITOR'S COMMENTS
Generally speaking, we should not be the place unpublished authors come to for their first break. While an exceptional piece by an unpublished writer will get our attention, we tend to work with authors who have experience writing for consumer magazines.

Ladybug
The Magazine for Young Children

70 East Lake Street, Suite 300
Chicago, IL 60601

Submissions Editor: Jenny Gillespie

DESCRIPTION AND INTERESTS
Bursting with colorful illustrations, stories, and poetry, *Ladybug* is designed to be read aloud to kids in preschool and kindergarten. It is part of the Cricket Magazine Group, which includes *Babybug, Spider,* and *Cricket.* Circ: 125,000.

Audience: 3–6 years
Frequency: 9 times each year
Website: www.ladybugmagkids.com

FREELANCE POTENTIAL
100% written by nonstaff writers. Publishes 100 freelance submissions yearly. Receives 2,400 unsolicited mss yearly.

SUBMISSIONS
Send complete ms with word count. Accepts hard copy and simultaneous submissions if identified. SASE. Responds in 6 months.

- Articles: To 400 words. Informational and how-to articles; and humor. Topics include nature, family, animals, the environment, and other age-appropriate topics.
- Fiction: To 800 words. Read-aloud, early reader, picture, and rebus stories. Genres include adventure, humor, fantasy, folktales, and contemporary and multicultural fiction.
- Other: Puzzles, learning activities, games, crafts, finger plays, action rhymes, cartoons, and songs. Poetry, to 20 lines.

SAMPLE ISSUE
36 pages (no advertising): 5 stories; 3 poems; 2 activities; 1 song; 3 cartoons. Sample copy, $5. Guidelines available at website.

- "Yoga in the Garden." Activity describes and illustrates four yoga postures for children.
- "Spider's Riddle." Story depicts a spider spinning an egg sack as other creatures try to guess what she's making.

RIGHTS AND PAYMENT
Rights vary. Stories and articles, $.25 per word; $25 minimum. Poems, $3 per line; $25 minimum. Other material, payment rates vary. Pays on publication. Provides 6 contributor's copies.

✒ EDITOR'S COMMENTS
In addition to read-aloud and early-reader stories, we seek nonfiction work centering on concepts, vocabulary, and simple explanations of things in a young child's world. Poetry should be rhythmic and rhyming, serious or humorous, and from a child's perspective.

L.A. Parent

443 East Irving Drive, Suite A
Burbank, CA 91504

Editor: Carolyn Graham

DESCRIPTION AND INTERESTS
This magazine is filled with informative articles on family issues, parenting, childhood development, relationships, and education. Serving parents in the Los Angeles region, it also features regional information on recreational and educational opportunities in the area. Circ: 120,000.

Audience: Parents
Frequency: Monthly
Website: www.laparent.com

FREELANCE POTENTIAL
70% written by nonstaff writers. Publishes 20 freelance submissions yearly; 5% by unpublished writers, 10% by authors who are new to the magazine. Receives 120 queries yearly.

SUBMISSIONS
Query with clips. Accepts hard copy. SASE. Responds in 6 months.

- Articles: 400–1,500 words. Informational, practical application, and how-to articles; profiles; and interviews. Topics include parenting and family issues, health, fitness, social issues, travel, and gifted and special education.
- Depts/columns: 1,000 words. Family life, technology, travel destinations, and crafts.
- Artwork: B/W and color prints and transparencies.

SAMPLE ISSUE
58 pages (60% advertising): 2 articles; 8 depts/columns. Sample copy, $3. Guidelines and theme list available.

- "When the Party's in the Pool." Article provides tips on keeping everyone—especially the little ones—safe around a pool.
- Sample dept/column: "Check Up" offers advice for unemployed or uninsured parents who are dealing with doctors' bills.

RIGHTS AND PAYMENT
First serial rights. Written material, payment rates vary. Pays on publication. Provides contributor's copies.

⟶EDITOR'S COMMENTS
While we are always looking for articles that will interest parents, we must insist that they have a tie-in to the Los Angeles area. We accept queries from experienced writers as well as experienced parents.

Launch Pad

Teen Missions International
885 East Hall Road
Merritt Island, FL 32953

Editor: Linda Maher

DESCRIPTION AND INTERESTS
This is the official publication of Teen Missions International, an evangelical mission organization dedicated to providing short-term mission experiences to teens. It provides news of the organization to former and current members, including debriefings from recently completed missions, as well as inspirational short stories about mission work. Circ: Unavailable.

Audience: YA–Adult
Frequency: Annually
Website: www.teenmissions.org

FREELANCE POTENTIAL
5% written by nonstaff writers. Publishes 10 freelance submissions yearly; 15% by unpublished writers, 10% by authors who are new to the magazine. Receives 12–24 queries yearly.

SUBMISSIONS
Query. Accepts hard copy. SASE. Response time varies.

- Articles: Word lengths vary. Informational and factual articles; profiles; interviews; photo-essays; and personal experience pieces. Topics include mission work and teen evangelism in various countries.
- Fiction: Word lengths vary. Inspirational and ethnic/multicultural fiction.
- Depts/columns: Word lengths vary. Alumni news and teen mission opportunities.

SAMPLE ISSUE
8 pages (5% advertising): 3 articles; 7 depts/columns. Sample copy available.

- "Nate Survived 60-Foot Fall!" Personal experience pieces tells of a family member's serious injuries while on a mission in Mozambique, and how God intervened to guide him to safety.
- "New Beginnings and Continued Blessings." Article reports on missions running for the first time in several countries, as well as missions and events that are experiencing continued success.

RIGHTS AND PAYMENT
Rights vary. No payment.

⟶EDITOR'S COMMENTS
The vast majority of our material is written by people who have worked with our missions or our organizations. An extraordinarily inspirational piece will always get our attention.

Leadership for Student Activities

1904 Association Drive
Reston, VA 20191-1537

Editor: James Paterson

DESCRIPTION AND INTERESTS
Student council members find informative and inspiring articles in this magazine, which is dedicated to preparing and encouraging student leaders. Circ: 30,000.

Audience: YA
Frequency: 9 times each year
Website: www.nasc.us or **www.nhs.us**

FREELANCE POTENTIAL
67% written by nonstaff writers. Publishes 18–25 freelance submissions yearly; 75% by unpublished writers, 50% by authors who are new to the magazine. Receives 12–24 queries, 48 unsolicited mss yearly.

SUBMISSIONS
Query with clips; or send complete ms. Accepts hard copy and email submissions to jamespaterson7@gmail.com. SASE. Responds to queries in 2 weeks, to mss in 1 month.

- Articles: 1,200–1,700 words. Informational and how-to articles; profiles; and interviews. Topics include student activities, leadership development, and careers.
- Depts/columns: Reports on special events, 100–350 words. Advice for and by activity advisors, 1,000–1,500 words. National and regional news, leadership plans, and opinion pieces, word lengths vary.
- Artwork: B/W or color prints or slides.
- Other: Submit seasonal material 4 months in advance.

SAMPLE ISSUE
44 pages (21% advertising): 10 articles; 7 depts/columns. Sample copy, free with 9x12 SASE ($1.24 postage). Guidelines and theme list available.

- "Creative Kudos." Article presents creative ways schools can recognize students for their accomplishments.
- Sample dept/column: "Project Showcase" profiles a student recognition program that accomplished much more than it set out to.

RIGHTS AND PAYMENT
All rights. Written material, payment rates vary. Payment policy varies. Provides 5 copies.

➥EDITOR'S COMMENTS
We accept material from adult writers, but we also like to hear from student leaders themselves about their programs.

Leading Edge

4087 JKB
Provo, UT 84602

Fiction or Poetry Director

DESCRIPTION AND INTERESTS
Published by students of Brigham Young University, this journal is dedicated to science fiction and fantasy writing. It publishes stories and poetry in those genres, and is especially open to the work of new writers. Each issue also includes staff-written articles on the craft of writing fantasy and science fiction. Circ: 200.

Audience: YA–Adult
Frequency: Twice each year
Website: www.leadingedgemagazine.com

FREELANCE POTENTIAL
95% written by nonstaff writers. Publishes 18 freelance submissions yearly; most by unpublished writers. Receives 300 unsolicited mss each year.

SUBMISSIONS
Send complete ms. Accepts hard copy. No simultaneous submissions. SASE. Responds in 2–4 months.

- Articles: Staff written.
- Fiction: To 15,000 words. Genres include science fiction and fantasy.
- Depts/columns: Staff written.
- Other: Poetry dealing with science fiction and fantasy themes; no line limit.

SAMPLE ISSUE
120 pages (no advertising): 3 articles; 6 stories; 4 depts/columns; 3 poems. Sample copy, $5.95. Guidelines available in each issue and at website.

- "Of Wizards, Dragons, and Lessons." Story tells of a put-upon wizard who must deal with a comrade whose bad luck follows him everywhere.
- "Love Spells." Story finds a tormented wizard fighting his impulses toward his beautiful student, and questioning the ethics of putting her under a spell to make her love him.

RIGHTS AND PAYMENT
First North American serial rights. Fiction, $.01 per word, minimum $10. Poetry, $10 for first 4 pages, $1.50 per each additional page. Pays on publication. Provides 2 contributor's copies.

➥EDITOR'S COMMENTS
Because we are interested in helping new authors improve, we critique each story and send our comments to the author. If you do not wish to be critiqued, just let us know.

Learning & Leading with Technology

180 West Eighth Avenue, Suite 300
Eugene, OR 97401-2916

Managing Editor: Paul Wurster

DESCRIPTION AND INTERESTS
As the flagship publication of the International Society for Technology in Education, this magazine publishes articles that support the increased use of technology in learning environments and provide practical ideas for doing so. Circ: 25,000.
Audience: Educators, grades K–12
Frequency: 8 times each year
Website: www.iste.org/LL

FREELANCE POTENTIAL
90% written by nonstaff writers. Publishes 100 freelance submissions yearly; 60% by unpublished writers, 75% by authors who are new to the magazine. Receives 192 queries yearly.

SUBMISSIONS
Query. Accepts email queries to submissions@iste.org and simultaneous submissions if identified. Response time varies.

- Articles: 300–2,000 words. Informational and how-to articles; and personal experience pieces. Topics include computers and computer science, software, technology, media applications, teaching methods, and telecommunications.
- Depts/columns: Word lengths vary. Research, software reviews, and curriculum ideas.
- Artwork: Color prints. Line art.

SAMPLE ISSUE
48 pages (20% advertising): 3 articles; 14 depts/columns. Sample copy, free with 9x12 SASE (3 first-class stamps). Guidelines and editorial calendar available at website.

- "Remixing Chemistry Class." Article discusses the success of two teachers who make vodcast lectures to free up class time for hands-on activities.
- Sample dept/column: "Bloggers Beat" makes an argument against schools restricting students' use of computer games and Internet social sites.

RIGHTS AND PAYMENT
All rights; returns limited rights to author upon request. No payment. Provides 3 copies.

➥EDITOR'S COMMENTS
We need more short pieces (300 to 400 words) on practical uses of technology in the classroom. We are always happy to hear about successful programs that embrace technology.

Lexington Family Magazine

138 East Reynolds Road, Suite 201
Lexington, KY 40517

Publisher: Dana Tackett

DESCRIPTION AND INTERESTS
Parents in central Kentucky turn to this family magazine for its many articles on topics relevant to their experiences, such as raising happy children, relationships, and family health. Circ: 30,000.
Audience: Parents
Frequency: Monthly
Website: www.lexingtonfamily.com

FREELANCE POTENTIAL
50% written by nonstaff writers. Publishes 36 freelance submissions yearly; 40% by authors who are new to the magazine. Receives 250 queries and unsolicited mss yearly.

SUBMISSIONS
Query or send complete ms. Accepts hard copy and email to info@lexingtonfamily.com. SASE. Response time varies.

- Articles: 500–1,500 words. Informational and how-to articles. Topics include parenting, the arts, hobbies, current events, education, health, fitness, recreation, regional history, multicultural issues, popular culture, science, technology, family travel, and women's issues.
- Depts/columns: 800 words. News briefs and family health tips.
- Artwork: B/W or color prints. Line art.
- Other: Poetry. Puzzles and activities.

SAMPLE ISSUE
32 pages (50% advertising): 5 articles; 4 depts/columns. Sample copy, free with 9x12 SASE ($1.50 postage). Guidelines and theme list available.

- "The Summer Fun Food Challenge." Article discusses the challenges of eating healthy amid summer picnics and parties, and provides tips for healthy summer eating.
- Sample dept/column: "Fit Mommy" explains a regular exercise routine that can be started two months after having a baby.

RIGHTS AND PAYMENT
All rights. Written material, payment rates vary. Pays on publication. Provides 2 copies.

➥EDITOR'S COMMENTS
We rely heavily on our readers for articles and resources. Parents—specifically, mothers—comprise a large part of our freelance staff.

LibrarySparks

401 South Wright Road
P.O. Box 5207
Janesville, WI 53547

Submissions

DESCRIPTION AND INTERESTS
LibrarySparks contains fun and engaging programming ideas for elementary-school and public librarians. It offers practical, ready-to-use lessons and activities, all centered on a theme. Circ: Unavailable.

Audience: Librarians and teachers, grades K–6
Frequency: 9 times each year
Website: www.librarysparks.com

FREELANCE POTENTIAL
100% written by nonstaff writers. Publishes 15 freelance submissions yearly; 25% by authors who are new to the magazine. Receives 20 queries yearly.

SUBMISSIONS
Query. Accepts hard copy and email queries to librarysparks@sfsdayton.com. SASE. Response time varies.

- Articles: Word lengths vary. Informational articles and profiles. Topics include connecting literature to curricula, lesson plans for librarians, teaching library skills, children's authors and illustrators, and ideas for motivating children to read.
- Depts/columns: Word lengths vary. New resources, author profiles, storytelling activities, lesson plans, and helpful hints.
- Other: Reproducible activities and crafts.

SAMPLE ISSUE
56 pages (no advertising): 1 article; 14 depts/columns. Sample copy available at website. Guidelines and editorial calendar available.

- "Travel and Transportation." Article offers cross-curricular activities and resources that touch on history and politics, science and technology, economics, civic life, and sports.
- Sample dept/column: "Keep 'em Reading" encourages librarians to write the book that's inside of them.
- Sample dept/column: "Storytime" offers a sample program for taking children on an imaginary trip through stories.

RIGHTS AND PAYMENT
Rights vary. Written material, payment rates vary. Pays on publication. Provides 1 copy.

➥EDITOR'S COMMENTS
Please be sure to include your name, school or library name and address, home mailing address, home phone, and email address.

The Lion

Lions Clubs International
300 West 22nd Street
Oak Brook, IL 60523-8842

Senior Editor: Jay Copp

DESCRIPTION AND INTERESTS
The Lion is a publication of Lions Clubs International. As such, its articles report on the projects of chapters throughout the world and the club's official international charitable projects; and it also features profiles of Lions Club members who exemplify the organization's credo of service. Circ: 600,000.

Audience: Lions Clubs members
Frequency: 10 times each year
Website: www.lionsclubs.org

FREELANCE POTENTIAL
20% written by nonstaff writers. Publishes 20 freelance submissions yearly; 30% by authors who are new to the magazine. Receives 100 queries and unsolicited mss yearly.

SUBMISSIONS
Prefers query; will accept complete ms. Accepts hard copy and email submissions to jay.copp@lionsclubs.org. SASE. Responds to queries in 10 days, to mss in 2 months.

- Articles: To 1,500 words. Informational articles; profiles; humor; and photo-essays. Topics include Lions Clubs service projects, disabilities, social issues, and special education.
- Depts/columns: Staff written.
- Artwork: 5x7 or larger color prints; digital JPEG files.

SAMPLE ISSUE
56 pages (6% advertising): 11 articles; 16 depts/columns. Sample copy, free. Writers' guidelines available.

- "It's Definitely the Shoes." Article profiles a service project by an Oregon chapter that provided free shoes to 35 school children in need.
- "Helen Keller Who?" Article examines the life of Helen Keller, who challenged Lions Clubs members to become crusaders for the blind.

RIGHTS AND PAYMENT
All rights. Written material, $100–$700. Pays on acceptance. Provides 4–10 contributor's copies.

➥EDITOR'S COMMENTS
If you are a freelancer and a member of the Lions Clubs, we'd like to hear from you. The majority of our material comes from members, reporting on projects. Please note that we do not accept jokes or travel pieces.

Listen Magazine

55 West Oak Ridge Drive
Hagerstown, MD 21740

Editor: Céleste Perrino-Walker

DESCRIPTION AND INTERESTS
Used as a classroom tool, *Listen Magazine* strives to educate teens about the dangers of drugs, alcohol, tobacco, and destructive behaviors, while encouraging good physical, social, and mental habits. Circ: 40,000.

Audience: Students, grades 7–12
Frequency: 9 times each year
Website: www.listenmagazine.org

FREELANCE POTENTIAL
70% written by nonstaff writers. Publishes 90+ freelance submissions yearly; 15% by unpublished writers, 20% by authors who are new to the magazine. Receives 800–1,000 queries, 400 unsolicited mss yearly.

SUBMISSIONS
Query or send complete ms. Accepts hard copy, email to editor@listenmagazine.org, and simultaneous submissions if identified. SASE. Response time varies.

- Articles: 350–750 words. Informational articles; profiles; and self-help pieces. Topics include peer pressure, decision making, self-esteem, self-discipline, family conflict, sports, hobbies, friendship, and healthy choices.
- Depts/columns: Word lengths vary. Opinion pieces, social issues, and trends.

SAMPLE ISSUE
32 pages (no advertising): 11 articles; 6 depts/columns. Sample copy, $2 with 9x12 SASE (2 first-class stamps). Guidelines and editorial calendar available at website.

- "Dealing with Abuse." Article describes the four main kinds of abuse and offers tips for getting help.
- Sample dept/column: "Good 4 U" looks at ways to boost energy without consuming energy drinks.

RIGHTS AND PAYMENT
All rights. Written material, $.05–$.10 per word. Pays on acceptance. Provides 3 contributor's copies.

➡EDITOR'S COMMENTS
Please study our guidelines, read some back issues, and then send us a well-polished article we can't refuse. Stick to our word counts. A surprising number of unsolicited manuscripts are not considered simply because they exceed word count limits.

Live

General Council of the Assemblies of God
1445 North Boonville Avenue
Springfield, MO 65802-1894

Editor: Richard Bennett

DESCRIPTION AND INTERESTS
A take-home paper for adult Sunday school classes, *Live* seeks to encourage Christians to live for God by presenting realistic stories that apply biblical principles to everyday problems. Circ: 45,000.

Audience: 18+ years
Frequency: Quarterly, in weekly sections

FREELANCE POTENTIAL
100% written by nonstaff writers. Publishes 110 freelance submissions yearly; 20% by unpublished writers, 20% by authors who are new to the magazine. Receives 120 queries, 1,440 unsolicited mss yearly.

SUBMISSIONS
Query or send complete ms. Accepts hard copy, email submissions to rl-live@gph.org, and simultaneous submissions if identified. SASE. Responds in 6 weeks.

- Articles: 800–1,100 words. Informational articles; humor; and personal experience pieces. Topics include family issues, parenting, and religious history.
- Fiction: 800–1,100 words. Genres include inspirational fiction, adventure, and stories about family celebrations and traditions.
- Other: Poetry, to 12–25 lines. Filler, 300–600 words. Submit seasonal material 18 months in advance.

SAMPLE ISSUE
8 pages (no advertising): 2 articles; 1 poem. Sample copy, free with #10 SASE (1 first-class stamp). Guidelines available.

- "Thanks for Having Me." Article tells the story of a preacher who searched for his birth mother.
- "Ten Ways to Get More From Your Daily Bible Reading." Article suggests various approaches to reading the Bible in order to understand it more deeply.

RIGHTS AND PAYMENT
First and second rights. Written material, $.10 per word for first rights; $.07 per word for second rights. Pays on acceptance. Provides 2 contributor's copies.

➡EDITOR'S COMMENTS
We do not accept science or Bible fiction. Stories should be encouraging, challenging, and humorous—not preachy or critical.

Living for the Whole Family

1251 Virginia Avenue
Harrisonburg, VA 22802

Editor: Melodie Davis

DESCRIPTION AND INTERESTS
Though it has a Christian mission, this regional tabloid does not assume a Christian audience. Its articles focus on general parenting topics as well as a wide variety of other issues faced in the home and workplace. Circ: 150,000.

Audience: Families
Frequency: Quarterly
Website: www.livingforthewholefamily.com

FREELANCE POTENTIAL
90% written by nonstaff writers. Publishes 50 freelance submissions yearly; 20% by unpublished writers, 40% by authors who are new to the magazine. Receives 480 unsolicited mss each year.

SUBMISSIONS
Send complete ms. Accepts hard copy and email to melodiemd@msn.com (include title in subject line and email address in body of message). SASE. Responds in 3–4 months.

- Articles: 500 words. Informational, how-to, and inspirational articles; profiles; and personal experience pieces. Topics include family, relationships, marriage, parenting, social issues, spirituality, and community service.
- Depts/columns: Staff written.
- Artwork: B/W and color prints.

SAMPLE ISSUE
32 pages (30% advertising): 14 articles; 2 depts/columns. Sample copy, free with 9x12 SASE (4 first-class stamps). Guidelines available at website.

- "If . . . Then . . ." Article recommends using cognitive behavioral therapy to discipline children and teach them about consequences.
- "Calling All Dads: Report to School Immediately." Article stresses the importance of father involvement in education.

RIGHTS AND PAYMENT
One-time and second rights. Articles, $30–$60. Artwork, $10–$15. Pays 3 months after publication. Provides 2 contributor's copies.

✒ EDITOR'S COMMENTS
While we are an evangelical Christian organization, we need to be wise in how we approach readers. We don't want to turn them off with preaching or sermonizing. We can win over readers by supplying great reading material for the family.

Living Safety

Canada Safety Council
1020 Thomas Spratt Place
Ottawa, Ontario K1G 5L5
Canada

President: Jack Smith

DESCRIPTION AND INTERESTS
Safety is the name of the game in this magazine for Canadians. Articles cover safety consciousness in the home, on the road, on the job, and at play. It is published by the Canada Safety Council. Circ: 80,000.

Audience: All ages
Frequency: Quarterly
Website: www.safety-council.org

FREELANCE POTENTIAL
75% written by nonstaff writers. Publishes 25 freelance submissions yearly; 65% by unpublished writers, 10% by authors who are new to the magazine. Receives 25 queries yearly.

SUBMISSIONS
Query with résumé and clips or writing samples. Accepts hard copy. SAE/IRC. Responds in 2 weeks.

- Articles: 1,500–2,500 words. Informational articles. Topics include recreational, home, traffic, and school safety; and health issues.
- Depts/columns: Word lengths vary. Safety news, research findings, opinions, and product recalls.
- Other: Children's activities.

SAMPLE ISSUE
30 pages (no advertising): 4 articles; 4 depts/columns; 1 kids' page. Sample copy, free with 9x12 SAE/IRC. Guidelines available.

- "Theme Park Safety." Article provides tips for staying safe at a theme park.
- "Cellphones Driving Motorists to Distraction." Article explores the effectiveness of laws that curb or prohibit cellphone use.
- Sample dept/column: "Touring Down the River" explains how to keep safe during a boat tour.

RIGHTS AND PAYMENT
All rights. Articles, to $500. Depts/columns, payment rates vary. Pays on acceptance. Provides 1–5 contributor's copies.

✒ EDITOR'S COMMENTS
We deal primarily in prevention and do not use horrifying tales as the focus of the articles. However, writers may introduce an article with a story as a means of enhancing the piece and capturing the reader's attention. Canada's provinces, regions, or cultures should be incorporated in all material.

Long Island Woman

P.O. Box 176
Malverne, NY 11565

Publisher: Arie Nadboy

DESCRIPTION AND INTERESTS
This regional magazine features entertaining and informative articles on everything from celebrities and entertainment to finance and beauty. Circ: 40,000.

Audience: Women, 35–65 years
Frequency: Monthly
Website: www.liwomanonline.com

FREELANCE POTENTIAL
50% written by nonstaff writers. Publishes 25 freelance submissions yearly. Receives 500 queries, 350 unsolicited mss yearly.

SUBMISSIONS
Query or send complete ms. Accepts email submissions to editor@liwomanonline.com. Availability of artwork improves chance of acceptance. Responds in 8–10 weeks.

- Articles: 350–2,000 words. Informational and how-to articles; profiles; and interviews. Topics include regional news, lifestyles, family, health, sports, fitness, nutrition, dining, fashion, beauty, business, finance, decorating, gardening, entertainment, media, travel, and celebrities.
- Depts/columns: 500–1,000 words. Book reviews, health advice, personal essays, and profiles.
- Artwork: Electronic B/W and color prints. Line art.
- Other: Submit seasonal material 90 days in advance.

SAMPLE ISSUE
40 pages (60% advertising): 3 articles; 5 depts/columns; 1 calendar. Sample copy, $5. Guidelines available at website.

- "Two Rivers Run Through It." Article profiles Joan and Melissa Rivers about their lives and their careers.
- Sample dept/column: "Health" explains why drinking alcohol can inhibit weight loss.

RIGHTS AND PAYMENT
One-time and electronic rights. Written material, $70–$200. Kill fee, 20%. Pays on publication. Provides 1 tearsheet.

➔ EDITOR'S COMMENTS
Please include with your submission suggested headlines, subheadlines, and a brief biography. Also, send along photographs or other artwork that may enhance your article.

The Lutheran Digest

P.O. Box 4250
Hopkins, MN 55343

Editor: David L. Tank

DESCRIPTION AND INTERESTS
This digest-sized magazine publishes a blend of secular and light theological material in a bid to be a spiritual supplement to believers, and to encourage others to embrace the Lutheran faith. Circ: 70,000.

Audience: Families
Frequency: Quarterly
Website: www.lutherandigest.com

FREELANCE POTENTIAL
100% written by nonstaff writers. Publishes 80 freelance submissions yearly; 30% by authors who are new to the magazine. Receives 300 unsolicited mss yearly.

SUBMISSIONS
Send complete ms with author biography. Prefers hard copy; will accept faxes to 952-933-5708 and email submissions to tldi@lutherandigest.com (Microsoft Word or PDF attachments). SASE. Responds in 2–3 months.

- Articles: Word lengths vary. Informational articles; personal experience pieces; and confession pieces. Topics include religion, home life, education, cooking, gardening, music, consumer interest, personal relationships, and crafts.
- Other: Poetry, 2 stanzas. Filler, recipes, jokes. Submit seasonal material 6 months in advance.

SAMPLE ISSUE
64 pages: 20 articles; 4 activities; 11 poems. Sample copy, $3.50 with 6x9 SASE. Guidelines available at website.

- "In Holy Time." Personal experience piece relates how the author found peace during a routine commute when he noticed other passengers reading their holy books.
- "Five Minutes at the Mic." Article encourages us to think how we could spread the word of the Lord if we only had five minutes to do so.

RIGHTS AND PAYMENT
One-time and second rights. Articles, $35. Poetry and filler, no payment. Pays on acceptance. Provides 1 contributor's copy.

➔ EDITOR'S COMMENTS
We look for stories that show how God intervened in someone's life, or those that reflect a Lutheran-Christian perspective. We will reject articles that we deem too preachy.

The Magazine

643 Queen Street East
Toronto, Ontario M4M 1G4
Canada

Editor: Karen Wong

DESCRIPTION AND INTERESTS
An entertainment digest for kids, *The Magazine* features contests, surveys, posters, movies, music, video games, and tips for a healthy lifestyle. Circ: 15,000.

Audience: 8–14 years
Frequency: Monthly
Website: www.themagazine.ca

FREELANCE POTENTIAL
60% written by nonstaff writers. Publishes 20 freelance submissions yearly; 60% by unpublished writers, 30% by authors who are new to the magazine. Receives 240 queries yearly.

SUBMISSIONS
Query or send complete ms. Accepts hard copy. SAE/IRC. Response time varies.

- Articles: To 1,000 words. Informational articles; profiles; interviews; and humor. Topics include popular culture, movies, music, video games, books, and lifestyle subjects.
- Depts/columns: Media reviews, to 4 sentences. News, entertainment, and health briefs, word lengths vary.
- Other: Contests, quizzes, surveys, posters, and horoscopes.

SAMPLE ISSUE
112 pages: 8 articles; 24 depts/columns; 10 contests; 3 posters; 1 quiz. Sample copy, $3.95.

- "There Will Be Blood." Article previews the movie version of *Harry Potter and the Half-Blood Prince*.
- "Happy Anniversary, SpongeBob!" Article details the editors' five favorite episodes.
- Sample dept/column: "Hear This" includes reviews of the latest albums from Billy Talent and Tiny Masters of Today.

RIGHTS AND PAYMENT
All rights. Written material, $10–$60 Canadian. Payment policy varies.

➤EDITOR'S COMMENTS
We empower youth to write for us, typically through educators. In fact, most of our editorial content comes from writers ages 12 to 25. (The peer-to-peer editorial vibe cannot really be reproduced by people over the age of 30.) We encourage kids to write about their passion, whether it be skateboarding or sci-fi, SpongeBob or the Sims. Top 5 and Top 10 lists are always popular.

Magazine of Fantasy & Science Fiction

P.O. Box 3447
Hoboken, NJ 07030

Editor: Gordon Van Gelder

DESCRIPTION AND INTERESTS
Since 1949, this award-winning magazine has been publishing science fiction and fantasy from well-known authors as well as new writers. It also publishes humor and cartoons, and reprints of classic fantasy and science fiction stories written by the masters. Circ: 45,000.

Audience: YA–Adult
Frequency: 6 times each year
Website: www.sfsite.com/fsf

FREELANCE POTENTIAL
98% written by nonstaff writers. Publishes 60–90 freelance submissions yearly; 10% by unpublished writers, 20% by authors who are new to the magazine. Receives 6,000–8,400 unsolicited mss yearly.

SUBMISSIONS
Send complete ms. Accepts hard copy. No simultaneous submissions. SASE. Responds in 2 months.

- Fiction: To 25,000 words. Short stories and novellas. Genres include science fiction, fantasy, and humor.
- Depts/columns: Staff written.

SAMPLE ISSUE
258 pages (1% advertising): 4 novellas; 3 short stories; 6 depts/columns. Sample copy, $6. Guidelines available at website.

- "The Avenger of Love." Story follows an old man who enters into a parallel world, aided by a talking dog, to revisit the days of his first love.
- "Stratosphere." Story involves an American baseball player on a Japanese team playing a game on the moon, and hitting a ball so far it becomes part of the universe.

RIGHTS AND PAYMENT
First world rights with option of anthology rights. Written material, $.06–$.09 per word. Pays on acceptance. Provides 2 copies.

➤EDITOR'S COMMENTS
Science fiction and humor will get our attention quicker than fantasy pieces (we get a lot of those). Yes, we said humor. Science fiction can be funny, too! Please note that we do not accept freelance submissions for any nonfiction articles, including book and film reviews, and genre critiques. Those are all handled in-house.

Mahoning Valley Parent

100 DeBartolo Place, Suite 210
Youngstown, OH 44512

Editor & Publisher: Amy Leigh Wilson

DESCRIPTION AND INTERESTS
Targeting parents in the Mahoning Valley region of Ohio, this magazine provides information on child development, family issues, education, and family recreation. It also includes directories of local events and services. Circ: 50,000.
Audience: Parents
Frequency: Monthly
Website: www.forparentsonline.com

FREELANCE POTENTIAL
99% written by nonstaff writers. Publishes 100 freelance submissions yearly; 5% by unpublished writers, 20% by authors who are new to the magazine. Receives 500 unsolicited mss each year.

SUBMISSIONS
Send complete ms. Accepts hard copy and email to editor@mvparentmagazine.com. Retains all material for possible use; does not respond until publication. Include SASE if retaining ms is not acceptable.

- Articles: 1,000–1,800 words. Informational and how-to articles; profiles; and reviews. Topics include regional news, current events, parenting, the environment, nature, health, crafts, travel, recreation, hobbies, and ethnic and multicultural subjects.
- Depts/columns: Word lengths vary. Parenting issues, book reviews, events for kids.
- Artwork: B/W and color prints.
- Other: Submit seasonal material 3 months in advance.

SAMPLE ISSUE
42 pages (70% advertising): 5 articles; 6 depts/columns. Sample copy, free with 9x12 SASE. Guidelines and editorial calendar available.

- "Limit Screen Time Without Creating Scream Time." Article offers techniques for reducing children's television viewing time.
- Sample dept/column: "Special Parents, Special Kids" discusses the importance of appreciating miracles, both small and large.

RIGHTS AND PAYMENT
One-time rights. Articles, $20–$50. Pays on publication. Provides tearsheets.

✒ EDITOR'S COMMENTS
We like articles to which all parents can relate. However, we love articles to which Mahoning Valley parents can specifically relate.

The Majellan
Champion of the Family

P.O. Box 43
Brighton, Victoria 3186
Australia

Editor: Father Michael Gilbert

DESCRIPTION AND INTERESTS
The Majellan offers its readers topical articles about family life from a Christian perspective. It focuses on articles that nourish faith and are spiritually uplifting. It is a digest-sized publication of the Redemptorists of the Catholic Church. Circ: 23,000.
Audience: Parents
Frequency: Quarterly
Website: www.majellan.org.au

FREELANCE POTENTIAL
40% written by nonstaff writers. Publishes 60 freelance submissions yearly; 15% by unpublished writers, 20% by authors who are new to the magazine. Receives 36 unsolicited mss each year.

SUBMISSIONS
Send complete ms. Accepts hard copy and email submissions to editor@majellan.org.au (Microsoft Word or RTF attachments). SAE/IRC. Response time varies.

- Articles: 750–1,500 words. Informational articles and personal experience pieces. Topics include marriage, parenting, and Catholic family life.
- Depts/columns: Staff written.
- Other: Filler; readers' prayers and photos.

SAMPLE ISSUE
48 pages (15% advertising): 9 articles; 3 depts/columns.

- "Adult Children . . . Still at Home." Article provides advice for managing a relationship with adult, but dependent, children.
- "What's Wrong with Abortion?" Article opines that abortion is, on several different levels, akin to stealing.
- "Anorexia Nervosa: A Silent Killer." Article examines this disease.

RIGHTS AND PAYMENT
Rights vary. Written material, $50–$80 Australian. Pays on acceptance.

✒ EDITOR'S COMMENTS
We are particularly looking for short, inspiring, biographical articles about any facet of Christian family life. We are open to new topics, as long as the articles uphold the sanctity of marriage and/or provide guidance or information on dealing with family matters from a Christian perspective.

Maryland Family

10750 Little Patuxent Parkway
Columbia, MD 21044

Editor: Betsy Stein

DESCRIPTION AND INTERESTS

This free regional magazine serves parents in the greater Baltimore area with information on local resources, events, and family recreational opportunities. Its factual articles cover issues such as education, health, and child rearing. Circ: 50,000.

Audience: Parents
Frequency: Monthly
Website: www.marylandfamilymagazine.com

FREELANCE POTENTIAL

75% written by nonstaff writers. Publishes 50 freelance submissions yearly; 10% by unpublished writers, 10% by authors who are new to the magazine. Receives 360–600 queries yearly.

SUBMISSIONS

Query describing areas of expertise. Accepts hard copy. SASE. Responds in 1 month.

- Articles: 800–1,000 words. Informational and how-to articles; profiles; and personal experience pieces. Topics include family issues, parenting, education, recreation, travel, summer camp, sports, and health.
- Depts/columns: Word lengths vary. News briefs, local events, and health tips. "Family Matters," 100–400 words.
- Artwork: Color prints or transparencies.
- Other: Submit seasonal material 2–3 months in advance.

SAMPLE ISSUE

46 pages (50% advertising): 7 articles; 2 depts/columns. Sample copy, free with 9x12 SASE.

- "*Footloose* at Drama Learning Center." Article previews upcoming local performances of the stage musical adapted from the hit 1980s film.
- "Teachers Can Go Wild at the Zoo on Saturday." Article announces a free education festival to be held at the Maryland Zoo in Baltimore that includes staff development and in-service workshops for teachers.

RIGHTS AND PAYMENT

First and electronic rights. Written material, payment rates vary. Pays on publication. Provides 1 contributor's copy.

►EDITOR'S COMMENTS

We welcome queries from local freelance writers, particularly those with expertise in a area relevant to children and families.

Massive Online Gamer

4635 McEwen Drive
Dallas, TX 75244

Editor: Douglas Kale

DESCRIPTION AND INTERESTS

Dedicated to the world of MMO (massively multiplayer online) games, this magazine covers game descriptions, strategies, and techniques. It also includes reviews of new science fiction, fantasy, adventure, pirate, automobile, and war games to hit the market. Circ: 100,000.

Audience: YA–Adult
Frequency: 6 times each year
Website: www.massiveonlinegamer.com

FREELANCE POTENTIAL

75% written by nonstaff writers. Publishes 80 freelance submissions yearly; 20% by unpublished writers, 70% by authors who are new to the magazine.

SUBMISSIONS

Query with writing sample and list of MMO experience. Prefers email queries to dkale@ beckett.com; will accept hard copy. SASE. Response time varies.

- Articles: Word lengths vary. Informational and how-to articles; personal experience pieces; and interviews. Topics include MMO game descriptions, strategies, and gaming techniques.
- Depts/columns: Word lengths vary. MMO etiquette, technology, contests, and news.

SAMPLE ISSUE

88 pages: 21 articles; 4 depts/columns. Sample copy and guidelines available upon email request to mog@beckett.com.

- "Age of Conan Leveling Guide." Article explains the beginning levels of this game and offers playing tips.
- "Star Wars Galaxies." Article celebrates the game's fifth anniversary and discusses what's to come in the near future.
- Sample dept/column: "Gaming Terms" shares the meaning of some of the most common gaming terms.

RIGHTS AND PAYMENT

All rights. Written material, $25–$150. Pays 45 days after publication.

►EDITOR'S COMMENTS

Our readers include experienced as well as first-time gamers, so your article should appeal to both. We are only interested in working with authors who have extensive MMO knowledge.

MetroFamily

306 South Bryant, Suite C-152
Edmond, OK 73034

Editor: Mari Farthing

DESCRIPTION AND INTERESTS

Geared to families living in central Oklahoma, *MetroFamily* features informative and inspirational articles that help parents be more successful and have more fun with their families. Circ: 35,000.

Audience: Parents
Frequency: Monthly
Website: www.metrofamilymagazine.com

FREELANCE POTENTIAL

60% written by nonstaff writers. Publishes 45 freelance submissions yearly; 10% by unpublished writers, 10% by authors who are new to the magazine. Receives 1,000 queries and unsolicited mss yearly.

SUBMISSIONS

Query or send complete ms. Accepts email to editor@metrofamilymagazine.com. Responds to queries in 3 weeks, to mss in 1 month.

- Articles: 300–600 words. Informational and how-to articles; profiles; and personal experience pieces. Topics include parenting, education, health and fitness, travel, and recreational activities.
- Depts/columns: Staff written.

SAMPLE ISSUE

42 pages: 3 articles; 11 depts/columns. Sample copy and writers' guidelines, free with 10x13 SASE.

- "Dancing and Cheering: A Leap of Faith." Article profiles a dance class designed specifically for children with special needs.
- "Exploring Oklahoma." Article highlights things to see and do for families on a day-trip to nearby Ponca City.
- "How to Manage Sensory Processing Disorders." Article provides insight into these disorders and offers suggestions for improving behavior at home and in school.

RIGHTS AND PAYMENT

First North American serial rights. Articles, $25–$50. Kill fee, 100%. Pays on publication. Provides 1 contributor's copy.

❧EDITOR'S COMMENTS

We assign articles to local writers only. Prospective authors must be thoroughly familiar with the region, and be able to provide accurate information about described activities and destinations.

MetroKids

1412–1414 Pine Street
Philadelphia, PA 19102

Executive Editor: Tom Livingston

DESCRIPTION AND INTERESTS

Parents living in the greater Philadelphia area read *MetroKids* for coverage of regional events, resources, and issues relating to education and parenting. Circ: 130,000.

Audience: Parents
Frequency: Monthly
Website: www.metrokids.com

FREELANCE POTENTIAL

30% written by nonstaff writers. Publishes 25 freelance submissions yearly; 10% by authors who are new to the magazine. Receives 600 unsolicited mss yearly.

SUBMISSIONS

Send complete ms. Accepts email submissions to editor@metrokids.com (Microsoft Word or text attachments). Availability of artwork improves chance of acceptance. Responds if interested.

- Articles: 550–900 words. Informational, how-to, and self-help articles. Topics include pregnancy, childbirth, parenting, pets, computers, education, health, fitness, nature, the environment, recreation, and social issues.
- Depts/columns: 550–700 words. School news, product recalls, health notes, opinions, book reviews, nature activities, special education information, and local events.
- Artwork: Color prints or transparencies.

SAMPLE ISSUE

56 pages: 4 articles; 1 special section; 13 depts/columns. Sample copy, free with 9x12 SASE. Guidelines available.

- "Breathalyzers? Drug Tests?" Article tells how area schools are reaching beyond the classroom to prevent drug and alcohol abuse.
- Sample dept/column: "Eye on Nature" recommends vegetable gardening with kids.

RIGHTS AND PAYMENT

One-time and electronic rights. Written material, $35–$50. Artwork, payment rates vary. Pays on publication. Provides 1 contributor's copy.

❧EDITOR'S COMMENTS

Our departments and features tend to be practical and information-laden. We seldom use first-person material. We prefer articles that quote experts rather than state their advice in the writer's voice. We also favor local sources.

Metro Parent Magazine

22041 Woodward Avenue
Ferndale, MI 48220

Managing Editor: Julia Elliott

DESCRIPTION AND INTERESTS
Metro Parent Magazine is distributed free throughout the Detroit area. Parents who pick it up find coverage of education; developmental, child-rearing, and behavioral issues; and family health, entertainment, and travel in the Motor City and beyond. Circ: 80,000.

Audience: Parents
Frequency: Monthly
Website: www.metroparent.com

FREELANCE POTENTIAL
75% written by nonstaff writers. Publishes 250 freelance submissions yearly; 5% by unpublished writers, 35% by authors who are new to the magazine. Receives 960+ queries and unsolicited mss yearly.

SUBMISSIONS
Query or send complete ms. Accepts email submissions to jelliott@metroparent.com. Responds in 1–2 days.

- Articles: 1,500–2,500 words. Informational, self-help, and how-to articles; interviews; and personal experience pieces. Topics include pregnancy, childbirth, parenting, family life, education, child development, social issues, travel, finance, fitness, health, recreation, entertainment, and nature.
- Depts/columns: 850–900 words. Women's health, family fun, new product information, media reviews, crafts, and computers.

SAMPLE ISSUE
68 pages (60% advertising): 6 articles; 12 depts/columns. Sample copy, free. Guidelines available at website.

- "Does Diet Affect Behavior?" Article seeks to answer this question.
- "School Supplies Lists Grow." Article tells how tighter school budgets now require parents to supply more than the basics.

RIGHTS AND PAYMENT
First rights. Articles, $150–$300. Depts/columns, $50–$100. Pays on publication. Provides 1 contributor's copy.

➤EDITOR'S COMMENTS
We welcome queries and certain submissions from qualified journalists under the specific guidelines detailed at our website. We will also review articles available for reprint, but they must be identified as such.

Midwifery Today

P.O. Box 2672
Eugene, OR 97402

Managing Editor: Cheryl K. Smith

DESCRIPTION AND INTERESTS
Read by natural childbirth practitioners and educators, *Midwifery Today* publishes articles on natural childbirth and breastfeeding, as well as softer and more philosophical material on these topics, such as poetry, personal essays, and humor. Circ: 4,000.

Audience: Childbirth practitioners
Frequency: Quarterly
Website: www.midwiferytoday.com

FREELANCE POTENTIAL
90% written by nonstaff writers. Publishes 80–100 freelance submissions yearly; 35% by unpublished writers, 50% by authors who are new to the magazine. Receives 120–144 queries, 96–108 unsolicited mss yearly.

SUBMISSIONS
Query with author background; or send complete ms. Prefers email submissions to editorial@midwiferytoday.com (Microsoft Word or RTF attachments). No simultaneous submissions. Responds in 1 month.

- Articles: 800–1,500 words. Informational and instructional articles; profiles; interviews; personal experience pieces; and media reviews. Topics include feminism, health, fitness, medical care and services, diet, nutrition, and multicultural and ethnic issues related to childbirth.
- Depts/columns: Staff written.
- Artwork: Digital images at 300 dpi.

SAMPLE ISSUE
72 pages (10% advertising): 24 articles; 7 depts/columns. Sample copy, $12.50. Guidelines and editorial calendar available at website.

- "The Rule of 10 Versus Women's Primal Wisdom." Article discusses why women have been taught to wait to push until fully dilated.
- "Midwifery in New York." Article addresses the low number of midwives in New York, and explains how to become licensed there.

RIGHTS AND PAYMENT
Joint rights. Written material, no payment. Artwork, payment rates vary. Pays on publication. Provides 2 contributor's copies and 1-year subscription for articles longer than 800 words.

➤EDITOR'S COMMENTS
We're looking for more clinical articles with an international angle.

Minnesota Conservation Volunteer

500 Lafayette Road
St. Paul, MN 55155-4046

Editor: Kathleen Weflen

DESCRIPTION AND INTERESTS
Minnesota Conservation Volunteer is a donor-supported magazine advocating conservation and careful use of Minnesota's natural resources. Targeting school-age children and their teachers primarily, it celebrates the best of the state's plants, wildlife, and natural history. Circ: 150,000.
Audience: Middle-grade students and teachers
Frequency: 6 times each year
Website: www.mndr.gov/magazine

FREELANCE POTENTIAL
60% written by nonstaff writers. Publishes 25 freelance submissions yearly. Receives hundreds of queries, 40 unsolicited mss yearly.

SUBMISSIONS
Query with synopsis for feature articles and "Field Notes." Send complete ms for essays. Accepts hard copy and email queries to kathleen.weflen@dnr.state.mn.us. SASE. Response time varies.

- Articles: 1,200–1,800 words. Informational articles and essays. Topics include the natural resources, wildlife, state parks, lakes, grasslands, groundwater, biofuels, fishing, and outdoor recreation of Minnesota.
- Depts/columns: "Field Notes," 200–500 words. "A Sense of Place," and "Close Encounters," 800–1,200 words. "Young Naturalists," conservationist Q&As, and wildlife profiles; word lengths vary.
- Other: Student activities and teacher guides.

SAMPLE ISSUE
82 pages: 5 articles; 7 depts/columns. Sample copy and guidelines available at website.

- "A Sticky Situation for Pollinators." Article discusses the problems native bees are experiencing due to habitat loss.
- "Nature's Recyclers." Article profiles the disgusting but thoroughly useful "recyclers" such as maggots, fungi, and bacteria.

RIGHTS AND PAYMENT
First North American serial rights with option to purchase electronic rights. Articles and essays, $.50 per word plus $100 for electronic rights. Payment policy varies.

➡️EDITOR'S COMMENTS
All of our readers live in Minnesota and look to us to provide information about their state.

Mission

223 Main Street
Ottawa, Ontario K1S 1C4
Canada

Editor: Peter Pandimakil

DESCRIPTION AND INTERESTS
Mission is a "journal of mission studies" that focuses on intercultural and interreligious issues that promote faith-based values. Written in both French and English, it presents thought-provoking articles on religion, history, and current events, as well as book reviews. Circ: 400.
Audience: YA–Adult
Frequency: Twice each year
Website: www.ustpaul.ca

FREELANCE POTENTIAL
95% written by nonstaff writers. Publishes 6–9 freelance submissions yearly; 5% by unpublished writers, 30% by authors who are new to the magazine. Receives 84 mss yearly.

SUBMISSIONS
Send complete ms with résumé. Accepts disk submissions (RTF files), email submissions to ppandimakil@ustpaul.ca, and simultaneous submissions if identified. SAE/IRC. Responds in 1–2 months.

- Articles: 8,000–10,000 words. Bilingual articles; reviews; and personal experience pieces. Topics include current events; history; religion; and multicultural, ethnic, and social issues.
- Fiction: Word lengths vary. Historical, multicultural, ethnic, and problem-solving stories.
- Artwork: 8x10 B/W or color prints.

SAMPLE ISSUE
348 pages (no advertising): 9 articles; 6 book reviews. Sample copy, $12 U.S. with 8x10 SAE/IRC. Guidelines available.

- "Initial Inquiries into a Missionary Spirituality: A Missionary Pilgrimage." Article examines the inner spirituality and reflection that occurs during a mission.
- "Native Theology in Latin America." Article discusses the history of religion among indigenous cultures that date back more than 500 years.

RIGHTS AND PAYMENT
Rights vary. No payment. Provides 3 copies.

➡️EDITOR'S COMMENTS
We're interested in seeing more themed articles, especially those covering praxis-oriented issues. Our writers include well-known missiologists, theologians, and scholars.

Momentum

National Catholic Educational Association
1077 30th Street NW, Suite 100
Washington, DC 20007-3852

Editor: Brian Gray

DESCRIPTION AND INTERESTS
Written for Catholic educators and administrators, *Momentum* covers school trends, methodology, and management. Circ: 23,000.
Audience: Teachers, school administrators, and parish catechists
Frequency: Quarterly
Website: www.ncea.org

FREELANCE POTENTIAL
95% written by nonstaff writers. Publishes 90 freelance submissions yearly; 20% by unpublished writers, 65% by authors who are new to the magazine. Receives 60 unsolicited mss each year.

SUBMISSIONS
Send complete ms with résumé and bibliography. Accepts hard copy, disk submissions (Microsoft Word), and email submissions to momentum@ncea.org. SASE. Responds in 1–3 months.

- Articles: 1,000–1,500 words. Informational and scholarly articles on education. Topics include teacher and in-service education, educational trends, technology, research, management, and public relations—all as they relate to Catholic schools.
- Depts/columns: Book reviews, 300 words. "Trends in Technology," 900 words. "From the Field," 700 words.

SAMPLE ISSUE
80 pages (20% advertising): 15 articles; 7 depts/columns. Sample copy, free with 9x12 SASE ($1.05 postage). Guidelines and editorial calendar available.

- "Just Feeling Bad Is Not Good Enough." Article describes a school-wide effort to embrace social justice after reading a compelling book about a Sudanese slave.
- Sample dept/column: "Catholic Educators Lose Bright Star" reflects upon the life and death of Tim Russert.

RIGHTS AND PAYMENT
First rights. Articles, $75. Depts/columns, $50. Pays on publication. Provides 2 copies.

➻EDITOR'S COMMENTS
We prefer email or phone conversations with authors before they submit their work. Shorter articles—those that cover one idea—have a greater chance of acceptance.

MOM Magazine

2532 Santiam Highway SE, #102
Albany, OR 97322

Editor: Krista Klinkhammer

DESCRIPTION AND INTERESTS
This magazine was created by moms, targets moms, and is written by moms. It publishes articles on family life, women's well-being, career life, and family time, as well as personal pieces designed to inspire and support other mothers. Circ: 60,000.
Audience: Mothers
Frequency: 6 times each year
Website: www.mommag.com

FREELANCE POTENTIAL
80% written by nonstaff writers. Publishes 25 freelance submissions yearly; 50% by unpublished writers, 50% by authors who are new to the magazine. Receives 240 queries, 120 unsolicited mss yearly.

SUBMISSIONS
Query or send complete ms. Accepts email to editor@mommag.com (Microsoft Word attachments). Availability of artwork improves chance of acceptance. Response time varies.

- Articles: 500 words. Informational articles; profiles; and personal experience pieces. Topics include parenting, pregnancy, family life, recreation and activities, pets, health, and fitness.
- Depts/columns: Word lengths vary. Family travel, fatherhood issues, book reviews.
- Artwork: 5x7 JPEG or TIFF images at 300 dpi, with photo releases.
- Other: Call-outs, 25–50 words. Statistics, resources, and recipes.

SAMPLE ISSUE
32 pages: 12 articles; 6 depts/columns. Guidelines available at website.

- "Weighing Her Options." Article profiles a mother who underwent bariatric surgery to lose weight and be healthier for her children.
- Sample dept/column: "Stress Busters" offers easy ideas for reducing one's stress level.

RIGHTS AND PAYMENT
Reprint rights. No payment.

➻EDITOR'S COMMENTS
We invite mothers to share their ideas and experiences with our readers. We are open to any topic of interest to mothers, including personal stories (of success or even failure). And because moms are not afraid to laugh at themselves, the tone can be light.

MOMSense

2370 South Trenton Way
Denver, CO 80231-3822

Editor: Mary Darr

DESCRIPTION AND INTERESTS

This magazine is designed to inform, inspire, and nurture mothers of preschoolers from a Christian perspective. Circ: 120,000.

Audience: Mothers
Frequency: 6 times each year
Website: www.momsense.com

FREELANCE POTENTIAL

70% written by nonstaff writers. Publishes 45–50 freelance submissions yearly; 20% by unpublished writers, 20% by authors who are new to the magazine. Receives 360–480 unsolicited mss yearly.

SUBMISSIONS

Send complete ms. Prefers email submissions to momsense@mops.org (Microsoft Word attachments); will accept hard copy. Availability of artwork improves chance of acceptance. SASE. Response time varies.

- Articles: 500–1,000 words. Informational articles; profiles; and personal experience pieces. Topics include parenting, religion, and humor.
- Depts/columns: Word lengths vary. Parenting and family life.
- Artwork: B/W or color prints or transparencies.
- Other: Accepts seasonal material 6–12 months in advance.

SAMPLE ISSUE

32 pages: 12 articles; 8 depts/columns. Sample copy, free. Guidelines available.

- "Looking Up When Feeling Down." Article explains the difference between having a bad day and suffering from depression, and includes a sidebar about helping a friend who is depressed.
- Sample dept/column: "My Sense" is a first-person piece about a mom getting over her fear of hiring a babysitter for the first time.

RIGHTS AND PAYMENT

First rights. Written material, $.15–$.25 per word. Payment policy varies. Provides contributor's copies.

➾EDITOR'S COMMENTS

Each issue is theme-based, so content should be appropriate to a particular theme. We like humorous and inspirational stories as well as well-researched articles of interest to moms with young children.

Mom Writer's Literary Magazine

1006 Black Oak Drive
Liberty, MO 64068

Editor-in-Chief: Samantha Gianulis

DESCRIPTION AND INTERESTS

Mom Writer's Literary Magazine features creative writing by mothers as well as profiles of "mom writers," book reviews, and poetry. It seeks writing that is "down-to-earth, thoughtful, complex, humorous, sincere, penetrating, and raw." Circ: 10,000.

Audience: Mothers
Frequency: Quarterly
Website: www.momwriterslitmag.com

FREELANCE POTENTIAL

90% written by nonstaff writers. Publishes 64 freelance submissions yearly; 90% by unpublished writers, 95% by authors who are new to the magazine. Receives 600–1,200 queries and unsolicited mss yearly.

SUBMISSIONS

Query for author profiles. Send complete ms for creative nonfiction and book reviews. Accepts email to editor@momwriterslitmag.com (no attachments). Responds in 2–4 weeks.

- Articles: Creative nonfiction essays and memoir excerpts, to 2,000 words. Profiles and Q&A interviews with mom writers, 800–2,000 words. Book reviews, 700–1,000 words. Topics include biological, adoptive, foster, and expectant mothers; stepmothers; grandmothers; and motherhood issues.
- Depts/columns: Staff written.
- Other: Poetry, line lengths vary.

SAMPLE ISSUE

52 pages: 8 essays; 5 profiles; 3 reviews; 11 depts/columns; 6 poems. Sample copy and guidelines available at website.

- "The Necklace." Essay describes how a woman comes to tell her young daughter of her bout with mental illness.
- "All in a Mom-Day's Work." Personal experience piece recounts the home renovation project undertaken by the author and her husband.

RIGHTS AND PAYMENT

One-time electronic rights. No payment.

➾EDITOR'S COMMENTS

While our writing is as inherently different as our DNA, we believe all mom writers are woven together as part of one collective strand. Never restrain the voice within you that needs to be expressed and heard.

Mothering

P.O. Box 1690
Santa Fe, NM 87504

Articles Editor: Candace Walsh

DESCRIPTION AND INTERESTS
Inspirational as well as practical articles on natural family living fill the pages of this unique parenting magazine. Circ: 100,000.

Audience: Parents
Frequency: 6 times each year
Website: www.mothering.com

FREELANCE POTENTIAL
100% written by nonstaff writers. Publishes 40 freelance submissions yearly; 20% by unpublished writers, 70% by authors who are new to the magazine. Receives hundreds of queries each year.

SUBMISSIONS
Query with outline. Prefers email queries to editorial@mothering.com; will accept hard copy. SASE. Responds in 2–4 weeks.

- Articles: 2,000 words. Informational and factual articles; profiles; and personal experience pieces. Topics include pregnancy, childbirth, midwifery, health, homeopathy, teen issues, and organic food.
- Depts/columns: Word lengths vary. Cooking, book and product reviews, health news, parenting updates, and inspirational pieces.
- Artwork: 5x7 B/W and color prints.
- Other: Children's activities and crafts. Poetry about motherhood and families. Submit seasonal material 6–8 months in advance.

SAMPLE ISSUE
104 pages (35% advertising): 3 articles; 9 depts/columns. Sample copy, $5.95 with 9x12 SASE. Guidelines available at website.

- "Off to Work We Go—Baby in Tow." Article discusses job opportunities that allow mothers to bring their children to work with them.
- Sample dept/column: "Living Treasure" profiles a man who founded an organization dedicated to helping men become the best fathers they can be.

RIGHTS AND PAYMENT
First rights. Written material, $100+. Artwork, payment rates vary. Pays on publication. Provides 2 contributor's copies and a 1-year subscription.

⏩EDITOR'S COMMENTS
Articles with a strong point of view of contemporary issues will likely get our attention, particularly those that come from the heart.

MultiCultural Review

194 Lenox Avenue
Albany, NY 12208

Editor: Lyn Miller-Lachmann

DESCRIPTION AND INTERESTS
MultiCultural Review is a trade journal and book review for educators and librarians at all levels. Its primary focus is on the United States, though articles that present comparative perspectives or focus on the roots of American ethnic, racial, or religious groups are also welcomed. Circ: 3,500+.

Audience: Teachers and librarians
Frequency: Quarterly
Website: www.mcreview.com

FREELANCE POTENTIAL
80% written by nonstaff writers. Publishes 600 freelance submissions yearly; 10% by unpublished writers, 20% by authors who are new to the magazine. Receives 120 queries yearly.

SUBMISSIONS
Query with résumé and writing samples. Accepts email queries to mcreview@aol.com. Responds in 2–3 months.

- Articles: 2,000–6,000 words. Informational and how-to articles; bibliographic essays; interviews; and opinion pieces. Topics include multiculturalism in the U.S., ethnography of specific groups, books, authors, media, education, and libraries.
- Depts/columns: Book and media reviews, 200–500 words. News, 1,500–2,000 words.
- Artwork: Line art. Prints, charts, or graphs.

SAMPLE ISSUE
98 pages (10% advertising): 5 articles; 3 depts/columns; 123 book reviews. Sample copy, $15. Writers' guidelines and editorial calendar available.

- "C Is for Culture." Article looks at multicultural alphabet books.
- Sample dept/column: "News Notes" summarizes a study by the American Library Association on services for non-English speakers.

RIGHTS AND PAYMENT
First serial rights. Articles, $50–$100. Reviews, no payment. Pays on publication. Provides 2 contributor's copies.

⏩EDITOR'S COMMENTS
We are now giving more coverage, in both our feature articles and our reviews, to children's and young adult books relative to adult titles. Reviews of multicultural poetry are also sought.

MultiMedia & Internet@Schools

14508 NE 20th Avenue, Suite 102
Vancouver, WA 98686

Editor: David Hoffman

DESCRIPTION AND INTERESTS
MultiMedia & Internet@Schools shares practical information on education technology tools and resources, and how they can be used to further teaching and learning. It is read by school library, media, and technology specialists. Circ: 12,000.

Audience: School media and technology specialists and teachers
Frequency: 6 times each year
Website: www.mmischools.com

FREELANCE POTENTIAL
90% written by nonstaff writers. Publishes 20–24 freelance submissions yearly; 20% by unpublished writers, 20% by authors who are new to the magazine. Receives 60 queries each year.

SUBMISSIONS
Query or send complete ms. Accepts email submissions to hoffmand@infotoday.com. Availability of artwork improves chance of acceptance. Responds in 6–8 weeks.

- Articles: 1,500 words. Informational and how-to articles. Topics include K–12 education, the Internet, technology, multimedia and electronic resources, and curriculum integration.
- Depts/columns: Word lengths vary. Product news, reviews, and ideas from educators.
- Artwork: TIFF images at 300 dpi.

SAMPLE ISSUE
48 pages (15% advertising): 3 articles; 8 depts/columns. Sample copy and guidelines, $7.95 with 9x12 SASE.

- "Aha! Science." Article thoroughly reviews a supplemental science program of instruction, lessons, games, simulations, journaling, activities, and quizzes for grades 3–5.
- Sample dept/column: "A Look At . . ." examines digital resources for language arts.

RIGHTS AND PAYMENT
First rights. Written material, $300–$500. Artwork, payment rates vary. Pays on publication. Provides 2 contributor's copies.

•➤EDITOR'S COMMENTS
We try to point library media specialists in the right direction with features and columns that help them identify and understand the future of educational technology.

Muse

Carus Publishing
70 East Lake Street, Suite 300
Chicago, IL 60603

Associate Editor: Elizabeth Preston

DESCRIPTION AND INTERESTS
This self-described "magazine of life, the universe, and pie-throwing" focuses on science, history, art, and discovery. It uses only writers with subject expertise, except in the case of its first-person, reader-contributed "Muserology" column. Circ: 45,000.

Audience: 10+ years
Frequency: 9 times each year
Website: www.musemagkids.com

FREELANCE POTENTIAL
100% written by nonstaff writers. Of the freelance submissions published yearly, 20% are by authors who are new to the magazine.

SUBMISSIONS
All work is assigned. Send résumé and clips. Response time varies.

- Articles: To 2,500 words. Informational articles; interviews; and photo-essays. Topics include science, nature, the environment, history, culture, anthropology, sociology, technology, and the arts.
- Depts/columns: Word lengths vary. Science news, Q&As, math problems, and personal experience pieces.
- Other: Cartoons, contests, and activities.

SAMPLE ISSUE
40 pages (no advertising): 4 articles; 7 depts/columns. Sample copy and guidelines available at website.

- "How to Win the World Memory Championship." Article examines ways in which the human memory can be enhanced.
- "Gobekli Tepe: The World's First Temple?" Article describes a recent archaeological discovery of 11,000-year-old carved stones.
- Sample dept/column: "Muserology" tells of the author's family trip to the Tibetan Children's Village.

RIGHTS AND PAYMENT
Rights vary. Written material, payment rates vary. Payment policy varies.

•➤EDITOR'S COMMENTS
Our magazine is a guidebook for intellectual exploration, not a collection of facts. It sends kids on adventures to such places as under the sea and outer space. Its kid-friendly articles are designed to get kids to ask questions and think for themselves.

Music Educators Journal

Music Educators National Conference
1806 Robert Fulton Drive
Reston, VA 20191

Submissions: Caroline Arlington

DESCRIPTION AND INTERESTS
The goal of this magazine is, to put it simply, to advance music education. It covers all aspects, including techniques, teaching philosophy, and current issues. Circ: 80,000.

Audience: Music teachers
Frequency: Quarterly
Website: www.menc.org

FREELANCE POTENTIAL
85% written by nonstaff writers. Publishes 30 freelance submissions yearly; 25% by unpublished writers. Receives 100 unsolicited mss each year.

SUBMISSIONS
Send complete ms. Accepts hard copy (send 6 copies of ms) and email to caroline@menc.org (Microsoft Word attachments). No simultaneous submissions. SASE. Responds in 3 months.

- Articles: 1,800–3,500 words. Informational and instructional articles; and historical studies of music education. Topics include teaching methods and philosophy, and current trends in music teaching and learning.
- Depts/columns: Media reviews, teaching tips, technology updates, and association news.
- Artwork: High-contrast 5x7 or 8x10 prints; TIFF images at 300 dpi.
- Other: Submit seasonal material 8–12 months in advance.

SAMPLE ISSUE
62 pages (40% advertising): 5 articles; 7 depts/columns. Sample copy, $6 with 9x12 SASE ($2 postage). Writers' guidelines available at website.

- "Student-Centered Instruction: Involving Students in Their Own Education." Article explains how educators can successfully create and teach in a student-centered classroom without losing control of the learning environment.
- Sample dept/column: "For Your Library" reviews several books that will appeal to music educators.

RIGHTS AND PAYMENT
All rights. Written material, no payment. Artwork, $10. Provides 2 contributor's copies.

➡EDITOR'S COMMENTS
We welcome original, accurate, and timely submissions from music educators.

My Light Magazine

Editor: Jennifer Gladen

DESCRIPTION AND INTERESTS
This e-zine is dedicated to helping Catholic children understand their faith and build a relationship with God. It publishes short stories, articles, poetry, Bible stories, and age-appropriate crafts. Hits per month: 1,000.

Audience: 4–12 years
Frequency: Monthly
Website: www.mylightmagazine.com

FREELANCE POTENTIAL
95% written by nonstaff writers. Publishes 180 freelance submissions yearly; 50% by unpublished writers, 75% by authors who are new to the magazine.

SUBMISSIONS
Send complete ms with bibliography and brief author bio. Accepts email submissions to submissions@mylightmagazine.com (Microsoft Word attachments). Response time varies.

- Articles: 300–800 words. Informational articles. Topics include prayer, Jesus's teachings and parables, the rosary, Mary, the saints, Holy Mass, God's creation, spiritual experiences, respect for parents and teachers, Catholic values, and living the Beatitudes.
- Fiction: 300–800 words. Stories that represent Christian lifestyles and morals.
- Depts/columns: 500 words. Activities, prayers, crafts.
- Artwork: Color line art.
- Other: Poetry, to 24 lines.

SAMPLE ISSUE
38 pages: 4 articles; 2 stories; 5 depts/columns; 4 poems. Sample copy, guidelines, and theme list available at website.

- "How the Ladybug Got Its Name." Article explains that ladybugs got their name from European farmers, who prayed to the Virgin Mary for help in ridding their crops of aphids.
- "An All Soul's Day Celebration." Story shows how two young girls help their elderly neighbor commemorate All Soul's Day.

RIGHTS AND PAYMENT
One-time electric rights. No payment.

➡EDITOR'S COMMENTS
We now accept profiles of saints. Please follow our submissions guidelines, or risk having your article rejected.

Nashville Parent

2270 Rosa L. Parks Boulevard
Nashville, TN 37228

Editor-in-Chief: Susan Day

DESCRIPTION AND INTERESTS
In this magazine, Nashville parents find a host of informative articles on topics of interest to them: parenting, child development, education, recreation, and family health. All material published is localized to the Nashville region. Circ: 85,000.

Audience: Parents
Frequency: Monthly
Website: www.parentworld.com

FREELANCE POTENTIAL
15–20% written by nonstaff writers. Publishes 400 freelance submissions yearly; 40% by authors who are new to the magazine. Receives 1,200 unsolicited mss yearly.

SUBMISSIONS
Send complete ms. Accepts hard copy, Macintosh disk submissions with hard copy, and email to npinfo@nashvilleparent.com. Availability of artwork improves chance of acceptance. SASE. Response time varies.

- Articles: 800–1,000 words. Informational and how-to articles; profiles; interviews; photo-essays; and personal experience pieces. Topics include parenting, family issues, current events, social issues, health, music, travel, recreation, religion, the arts, crafts, computers, and multicultural and ethnic issues.
- Depts/columns: Staff written.
- Artwork: B/W or color prints.
- Other: Submit Christmas, Easter, and Halloween material 2 months in advance.

SAMPLE ISSUE
108 pages (50% advertising): 6 articles; 9 depts/columns. Sample copy, free with 9x12 SASE. Guidelines available.

- "Ma-Ma! How to Soothe Separation Anxiety." Article provides tips for dealing with a baby's separation distress.
- "Mastering Morning Madness." Article offers advice for decreasing before-school chaos.

RIGHTS AND PAYMENT
One-time rights. Written material, $35. Pays on publication. Provides 3 contributor's copies.

➛ EDITOR'S COMMENTS
All articles submitted should have at least two elements: They should be informative, and they should have a Nashville angle.

National Geographic Kids

National Geographic Society
1145 17th Street NW
Washington, DC 20036-4688

Executive Editor: Julie Agnone

DESCRIPTION AND INTERESTS
This offspring of the venerable magazine of discovery grabs the attention of young, would-be explorers and introduces them to the wonders of the world. It features pictures by renowned *National Geographic* photographers as well as games, activities, and articles that present nature and geography in a child-friendly format. Circ: 1.3 million.

Audience: 6–14 years
Frequency: 10 times each year
Website: http://kids.nationalgeographic.com

FREELANCE POTENTIAL
85% written by nonstaff writers. Publishes 20–25 freelance submissions yearly; 1% by unpublished writers, 30% by authors who are new to the magazine. Receives 360 queries each year.

SUBMISSIONS
Query with clips. Accepts hard copy. Responds if interested.

- Articles: Word lengths vary. Informational articles. Topics include geography, archaeology, paleontology, history, entertainment, and the environment.
- Depts/columns: Word lengths vary. News and trends, amazing animals, and fun facts.
- Other: Puzzles, games, and jokes.

SAMPLE ISSUE
32 pages (20% advertising): 3 articles; 8 depts/columns; 4 activities. Sample copy, $3.95. Guidelines available.

- "Animal Talk." Article describes seven surprising ways in which animals and humans communicate with one another.
- "Behind the Scenes of the New Movie *Harry Potter and the Half-Blood Prince*." Article explains some of the film's special effects.
- Sample dept/column: "Amazing Animals" tells how two puppies saved the life of a 3-year-old boy lost in the frigid woods for nearly 24 hours.

RIGHTS AND PAYMENT
All rights. Written material, payment rates vary. Artwork, $100–$600. Pays on acceptance. Provides 3–5 contributor's copies.

➛ EDITOR'S COMMENTS
Our "Amazing Animals" section is the best place for authors to break in to our magazine.

National Geographic Little Kids

National Geographic Society
1145 17th Street NW
Washington, DC 20036

Executive Editor: Julie Agnone

DESCRIPTION AND INTERESTS
This award-winning magazine for preschool kids introduces young explorers to the animal kingdom and world cultures through short, simple stories and activities—all accompanied by eye-catching photos. Circ: Unavailable.

Audience: 3–6 years
Frequency: 6 times each year
Website: http://littlekids.
nationalgeographic.com

FREELANCE POTENTIAL
10% written by nonstaff writers. Publishes 5 freelance submissions yearly.

SUBMISSIONS
Query with résumé. Accepts hard copy. SASE. Responds if interested.

- Articles: Word lengths vary. Informational articles. Topics include animals, nature, the environment, science, history, and multicultural topics.
- Fiction: Word lengths vary. Rebus stories about animals and other cultures.
- Depts/columns: Basic science experiments, craft projects, and recipes.
- Other: Games, jokes, and activities.

SAMPLE ISSUE
24 pages (no advertising): 5 articles; 1 rebus; 2 depts/columns; 5 activities. Sample copy, $3.95.

- "Canada Lynxes Grow Up." Article tells how lynx kittens make their way to adulthood.
- "Explore With Toot & Puddle." Rebus tells the story of two piglets and their different approaches to traveling and discovery.
- Sample dept/column: "Science Experiment" demonstrates how the sense of smell affects the sense of taste.

RIGHTS AND PAYMENT
All rights. Written material, payment rates vary. Pays on acceptance. Provides 3–5 copies.

◆EDITOR'S COMMENTS

We provide everything parents need to help their preschool tot become a bright, curious explorer—animal stories that develop pre-reading skills; features about different cultures that inspire a sense of understanding; interactive experiments that introduce simple science; and fun puzzles and games that teach logic, counting, and other skills.

Natural Life

P.O. Box 112
Niagara Falls, NY 14304

Editor: Wendy Priesnitz

DESCRIPTION AND INTERESTS
Natural family living is the focus of this magazine, which provides progressive and useful tips on applying green living principles and practices to everyday life. Articles cover sustainable housing, organic gardening, well-being, and natural parenting. Circ: 85,000.

Audience: Parents
Frequency: 6 times each year
Website: www.naturallifemagazine.com

FREELANCE POTENTIAL
50% written by nonstaff writers. Publishes 40 freelance submissions yearly; 20% by unpublished writers, 20–30% by authors who are new to the magazine. Receives 180 queries each year.

SUBMISSIONS
Query with detailed outline and 50- to 200-word synopsis. Accepts email to editor@naturallifemagazine.com and simultaneous submissions if identified. Responds in 3–5 days.

- Articles: 2,500–3,500 words. Informational and how-to articles; profiles; interviews; and personal experience pieces. Topics include green living, eco-travel, natural parenting, unschooling, lifelong learning, self-directed learning, and social issues.
- Depts/columns: Staff written.
- Artwork: Color prints. High-resolution TIFF images at 300 dpi.

SAMPLE ISSUE
62 pages: 15 articles; 4 depts/columns. Sample copy, $6.95 with 9x12 SASE ($6 postage); also available at newsstands. Guidelines available at website.

- "A Dome for a Home." Article explains that using a dome in home construction is less expensive and more efficient.
- "Summer Sports, Self-Propelled Style." Article offers examples of fun summer sports that are easy on the planet.

RIGHTS AND PAYMENT
One-time print and non-exclusive electronic rights. No payment. Provides author's copies.

◆EDITOR'S COMMENTS

We prefer that our articles be written by people involved in what they are writing about rather than by professionals. Real-life personal experience pieces are especially welcome.

Nature Friend Magazine

4253 Woodcock Lane
Dayton, VA 22821

Editor: Kevin Shank

DESCRIPTION AND INTERESTS
This magazine celebrates and explores "the wonders of God's creation," whether they be animals, birds, fish, plants, or heavenly bodies. Circ: 15,000.
Audience: 6–12 years
Frequency: Monthly
Website: www.naturefriendmagazine.com

FREELANCE POTENTIAL
90% written by nonstaff writers. Publishes 50 freelance submissions yearly; 5% by unpublished writers, 10% by authors who are new to the magazine. Receives 480–720 unsolicited mss yearly.

SUBMISSIONS
Send complete ms. Accepts hard copy. SASE. Response time varies.

- Articles: 250–900 words. Informational and how-to articles. Topics include science, nature, wildlife, and astronomy.
- Fiction: 300–900 words. Themes include adventure, wildlife, and nature.
- Depts/columns: 100–450 words. Seasonal, nature-related stories; activities; and science experiments.
- Artwork: High-resolution digital images with accompanying contact prints.
- Other: Nature-related puzzles and games.

SAMPLE ISSUE
24 pages (no advertising): 7 articles; 6 depts/columns; 4 activities. Sample copy and writers' guidelines, $9.

- "Treasures of the Snow." Article examines the formation of snowflakes.
- "Hot Sun Makes Night Lights." Article explains the phenomena of aurora borealis and aurora australis.
- Sample dept/column: "Who Am I?" challenges children to identify a creature based only on its description.

RIGHTS AND PAYMENT
One-time rights. Written material, $.05 per word. Artwork, $25–$75 per photo. Pays on publication. Provides 1 tearsheet.

➼EDITOR'S COMMENTS
We are a conservative Christian publisher. We desire to partner with like-minded writers who help us fulfill our goal of honoring God in the process of educating and entertaining children.

The New Era

50 East North Temple Street, Room 2420
Salt Lake City, UT 84150-3220

Managing Editor: Richard M. Romney

DESCRIPTION AND INTERESTS
Targeting teen members of Latter-day Saints, as well as their parents and church leaders, this magazine features stories of faith and Gospel application. Circ: 230,000.
Audience: YA–Adults
Frequency: Monthly
Website: www.newera.lds.org

FREELANCE POTENTIAL
20–40% written by nonstaff writers. Publishes 50 freelance submissions yearly; 5% by unpublished writers, 5% by authors who are new to the magazine. Receives 1,500 queries yearly.

SUBMISSIONS
Query. Accepts hard copy and email queries to newera@ldschurch.org. SASE. Responds in 2 months.

- Articles: 200–500 words. Informational and self-help articles; profiles; and personal experience pieces. Photo features and interviews, to 1,500 words. Topics include Gospel messages, religion, social issues, missionary work, family relationships, testimonies, humor, and Scripture.
- Depts/columns: Word lengths vary. News items, events, and youth church activities.
- Artwork: Digital images at 300 dpi; color transparencies.
- Other: Poetry, to 30 lines.

SAMPLE ISSUE
50 pages (no advertising): 12 articles; 5 depts/columns; 1 poem. Sample copy, $1.50 with 9x12 SASE or at website. Guidelines available at website.

- "I Changed My Life in Just 30 Minutes a Day." Article explains how a teen found focus and meaning in his life through reading the Book of Mormon.
- Sample dept/column: "Questions and Answers" offers ideas for finding one's testimony and belief.

RIGHTS AND PAYMENT
All rights. Written material, $.03–$.12 per word. Pays on acceptance. Provides 2 contributor's copies.

➼EDITOR'S COMMENTS
We welcome stories, testimonies, and the personal experiences of young people, as well as articles by adults on faith and LDS history.

N.E.W. Kids

2920 South Webster Avenue
Green Bay, WI 54301

Editor: Jen Hogeland

DESCRIPTION AND INTERESTS
This tabloid for parents living in northeast
Wisconsin (N.E.W.) seeks to keep readers well-
informed of family-oriented activities and
issues. Circ: 40,000.

Audience: Parents
Frequency: Monthly
Website: www.newfoxkids.com

FREELANCE POTENTIAL
30% written by nonstaff writers. Publishes
10–12 freelance submissions yearly; 10% by
unpublished writers, 10% by authors who are
new to the magazine. Receives 120–240
queries yearly.

SUBMISSIONS
Query or send complete ms. Accepts email
submissions to editor@newfoxkids.com.
Response time varies.

- Articles: To 750 words. Informational and
  how-to articles; humor; and personal experience pieces. Topics include parenting, child
  development, family issues, education,
  special needs, regional and national news,
  crafts, hobbies, music, the arts, health, fitness, sports, recreation, pets, travel, popular
  culture, and multicultural and ethnic issues.
- Depts/columns: To 750 words. Women's and
  children's health, school news, and essays.
- Other: Submit seasonal material 4 months
  in advance.

SAMPLE ISSUE
12 pages (50% advertising): 7 articles; 5 depts/
columns. Sample copy, free with 9x12 SASE.
Guidelines and editorial calendar available.

- "Host a Practical But Themed Hawaiian
  Party." Article tells how to throw a birthday
  party on a budget.
- Sample dept/column: "Rookie Dad" recounts
  a daughter's foray into clarinet lessons.

RIGHTS AND PAYMENT
Rights negotiable. All material, payment rates
vary. Pays on publication. Provides 1 contributor's copy upon request.

➻EDITOR'S COMMENTS
As always, we seek family-friendly, informative articles. We are especially in need of
activities for parents and kids, and articles
about building ethics such as honesty and
integrity in children.

New Moon

P.O. Box 161287
Duluth, MN 55816

Managing Editor: Joe Kelly

DESCRIPTION AND INTERESTS
Girls from around the world create and choose
the content of *New Moon*, which was founded
to help them develop their full potential
through self-discovery, creativity, and community. Some adult-written work, including fiction, is also featured. Circ: 25,000.

Audience: 8–12 years
Frequency: 6 times each year
Website: www.newmoon.com

FREELANCE POTENTIAL
90% written by nonstaff writers. Publishes 50
freelance submissions yearly; 85% by unpublished writers, 20% by authors who are new to
the magazine. Receives 720 queries and unsolicited mss yearly.

SUBMISSIONS
Female authors only. Query or send complete
ms. Prefers email submissions to girl@
newmoongirlmedia.com; will accept hard copy
and simultaneous submissions if identified.
Does not return mss. Responds in 4–6 months.

- Articles: 300–1,200 words. Profiles and interviews. Topics include activism, school, fitness, recreation, science, technology, and
  social and multicultural issues.
- Fiction: 900–1,600 words. Empowering stories about girls ages 8–12.
- Depts/columns: Word lengths vary. "Go Girl!"
  (activism and athletics), "Global Village,"
  "Women's Work," "Herstory," "Body
  Language," and "Science Side Effects."
- Other: Poetry and artwork by girls ages 8–12.

SAMPLE ISSUE
50 pages (no advertising): 1 article; 1 story;
12 depts/columns, 2 poems. Sample copy, $7.
Guidelines and theme list available at website.

- "25 Beautiful Girls." Article features profiles
  of 25 girls nominated by friends, family, and
  mentors for their inner beauty.
- Sample dept/column: "Check It Out" is a
  book review by a 10-year-old girl.

RIGHTS AND PAYMENT
All rights. Written material, $.06–$.10 per
word. Pays on publication. Provides 3 contributor's copies.

➻EDITOR'S COMMENTS
What's on your mind? What are your dreams?
What do you worry about? We want to hear it.

New York Family

79 Madison Avenue, 16th Floor
New York, NY 10016

Editor: Eric Messinger

DESCRIPTION AND INTERESTS
This magazine for sophisticated and active parents in Manhattan offers expert advice with a lighthearted tone on a broad spectrum of topics. It also features fashion spreads, profiles of family-oriented businesses, and a full calendar of events and activities for children. Circ: 40,000.
Audience: Parents
Frequency: Monthly
Website: www.newyorkfamily.com

FREELANCE POTENTIAL
50% written by nonstaff writers. Publishes 40 freelance submissions yearly; 40% by authors who are new to the magazine. Receives 200 queries yearly.

SUBMISSIONS
Query with clips. Accepts hard copy. SASE. Response time varies.

- Articles: 800–1,200 words. Informational articles; profiles; interviews; photo-essays; and personal experience pieces. Topics include education, music, recreation, regional news, social issues, travel, and parenting advice and techniques.
- Depts/columns: 400–800 words. News and media reviews.

SAMPLE ISSUE
82 pages: 4 articles; 10 depts/columns. Sample copy, free with 9x12 SASE. Writers' guidelines available.

- "In the Name of Love." Article profiles Rufus Griscom and Alisa Volkman, founders of the parenting website Babble.com.
- "Love Connections." Article offers expert advice for couples on managing intimacy, commitment, and parenting.
- Sample dept/column: "On Second Thought" is a personal essay by a father about kissing his son goodnight.

RIGHTS AND PAYMENT
First rights. Written material, $25–$300. Pays on publication. Provides 3 contributor's copies.

⟶EDITOR'S COMMENTS
We strive to capture the challenges and joys of raising children in the most exciting city in the world. Our editorial mix—from the front cover to the endpaper humor essay—is smart, provocative, and engaging.

New York Times Upfront

Scholastic Inc.
557 Broadway
New York, NY 10012-3999

Editor: Elliott Rebhun

DESCRIPTION AND INTERESTS
This magazine, appearing both in print and online, brings the news of the New York Times to high school students. It publishes articles on national and international current events and issues, as well as profiles of young achievers and essays by teens. It also publishes teacher editions to facilitate classroom discussions. Circ: 300,000.
Audience: 14–18 years
Frequency: 14 times each year
Website: www.upfrontmagazine.com

FREELANCE POTENTIAL
10% written by nonstaff writers. Publishes 2 freelance submissions yearly; 10% by authors who are new to the magazine. Receives 144 queries yearly.

SUBMISSIONS
Query with résumé and clips. Accepts hard copy. Availability of artwork improves chance of acceptance. SASE. Responds in 2–4 weeks if interested.

- Articles: 500–1,200 words. Informational articles; profiles; and interviews. Topics include current events, politics, history, media, technology, social issues, careers, the arts, the environment, and multicultural and ethnic issues.
- Depts/columns: Word lengths vary. Essays by teens, opinions, news briefs, and trends.
- Artwork: Color prints or transparencies.
- Other: Cartoons.

SAMPLE ISSUE
Sample copy and editorial calendar available at website. Guidelines available.

- "Mission Impossible?" Article provides a report card on President Obama's first eight months in office.
- "China's Next Generation." Article reports on the teens of China, who are coming of age as China becomes the newest global power.

RIGHTS AND PAYMENT
All rights. All material, payment rates vary. Pays on publication.

⟶EDITOR'S COMMENTS
We do not use many freelancers, as the majority of our material comes from The New York Times newsroom. But we are always looking for new talent.

The Next Step Magazine

86 West Main Street
Victor, NY 14564

Editor-in-Chief: Laura Jeanne Hammond

DESCRIPTION AND INTERESTS
Subtitled "Your Life, After High School," this magazine targets high school students with articles designed to prepare them for the next stage of life. It covers educational issues, college life, money management, personal responsibility, and career planning. Circ: 800,000.

Audience: 14–21 years
Frequency: 5 times each year
Website: www.nextSTEPmag.com

FREELANCE POTENTIAL
90% written by nonstaff writers. Publishes 40 freelance submissions yearly.

SUBMISSIONS
Query. Accepts email queries to laura@nextSTEPmag.com. Response time varies.

- Articles: 700–1,000 words. Informational, self-help, and how-to articles; profiles; interviews; personal experience and opinion pieces; humor; and essays. Topics include college planning, financial aid, campus tours, choosing a career, life skills, résumé writing, public speaking, personal finances, computers, multicultural and ethnic issues, sports, and special education.
- Depts/columns: Word lengths vary. Personal experience pieces written by college students.

SAMPLE ISSUE
38 pages: 12 articles; 3 depts/columns. Sample copy available at website. Writers' guidelines available.

- "Military vs. Civilian Life." Article examines the pros and cons of a career in the military and one in civilian life.
- "Are Your Classes Too Hard or Too Easy?" Article helps sophomores and juniors plan their final years of high school.
- Sample dept/column: "Shout Out" is an essay about the lessons one girl took from her modest upbringing.

RIGHTS AND PAYMENT
All rights. Written material, payment rates vary. Pays within 1 month of acceptance.

••EDITOR'S COMMENTS
Authors can be professional educators or counselors who work with transitioning high school students; or they can be high school or college students themselves, writing from their own experience.

NJCAA Review

1755 Telstar Drive, Suite 103
Colorado Springs, CO 80920

Executive Editor: Wayne Baker

DESCRIPTION AND INTERESTS
Formerly called *JUCO Review,* this magazine provides updates on sporting events, programs, athletes, and coaches at junior colleges around the country. It is published by the National Junior College Athletic Association. Circ: 3,300.

Audience: YA–Adult
Frequency: 10 times each year
Website: www.njcaa.org

FREELANCE POTENTIAL
30–40% written by nonstaff writers. Publishes 3–5 freelance submissions yearly. Receives 12 unsolicited mss yearly.

SUBMISSIONS
Send complete ms. Accepts hard copy. Availability of artwork improves chance of acceptance. SASE. Responds in 2 months.

- Articles: 1,500–2,000 words. Informational articles. Topics include sports, college, careers, health, fitness, and NJCAA news.
- Artwork: B/W prints and transparencies.

SAMPLE ISSUE
20 pages (25% advertising): 5 articles. Sample copy, $4 for current issue; $3 for back issue with 9x12 SASE. Editorial calendar available.

- "Kaskaskia College: Your Opportunity for Success." Article profiles this Illinois junior college and its impressive athletic facilities and programs.
- "68th NJCAA Annual Meeting Recap." Article highlights the changes and improvements that came about at this four-day annual conference in Rhode Island.
- "NJCAA Lacrosse." Article profiles the five lacrosse players who will be inducted into the Hall of Fame.

RIGHTS AND PAYMENT
One-time rights. No payment. Provides 3 contributor's copies.

••EDITOR'S COMMENTS
Writers should have a strong knowledge of the junior college sports system and programs. Our main editorial focus is on the programs, players, and coaches of our member colleges; however, we sometimes publish pieces on health, fitness, and nutrition. We are always interested in hearing news from our member schools.

Northumberland Kids

39 Queen Street, Suite 203
Coburg, Ontario K9A 1M8
Canada

Editor: Susan Stanton

DESCRIPTION AND INTERESTS
In addition to listings of family resources, classes, and services in Ontario's Northumberland County, this magazine offers articles on parenting issues, academics, and child development. Circ: Unavailable.

Audience: Parents
Frequency: Monthly
Website: www.northumberlandkids.com

FREELANCE POTENTIAL
40–50% written by nonstaff writers. Publishes 25 freelance submissions yearly. Receives 240–300 queries yearly.

SUBMISSIONS
Query. Accepts email queries to sstanton@northumberlandkids.com (Microsoft Word or text file attachments). Response time varies.

- Articles: 1,200–1,400 words. Informational articles; profiles; and interviews. Topics include parenting, health and fitness, current events, nature, the environment, family recreation, social issues, and special education.
- Depts/columns: 750 words. Safety, health and nutrition, recreation, media reviews, alternative medicine, and the environment.
- Artwork: High-resolution digital images at 300 dpi.

SAMPLE ISSUE
32 pages: 3 articles; 7 depts/columns. Sample copy and guidelines available at website.

- "Eco Schools Pave the Way." Article explores the ways local schools are incorporating environmental education into the curricula.
- "Scouts and Guides: The Adventure Continues." Article profiles the Scouts Canada and Girl Guides of Canada programs as they celebrate their centennials.
- Sample dept/column: "Growing Up" explains the signs and behavior that indicate when a child is ready for potty training.

RIGHTS AND PAYMENT
First rights. Written material, payment rates vary. Pays on publication.

EDITOR'S COMMENTS
Articles should offer insight, perspective, or guidance to our readers, and they should be written in a readable, informal style. All material should relate to Northumberland County or Canada.

OC Family

1451 Quail Street, Suite 201
Newport Beach, CA 92660

Editor: Kim Porrazzo

DESCRIPTION AND INTERESTS
This regional newsmagazine for parents in Orange County, California, covers the spectrum of family life, from education to recreation. Circ: 60,000.

Audience: Parents
Frequency: Monthly
Website: www.ocfamily.com

FREELANCE POTENTIAL
82% written by nonstaff writers. Publishes 50 freelance submissions yearly; 1% by unpublished writers, 1% by authors who are new to the magazine. Receives 144 queries yearly.

SUBMISSIONS
Query. Accepts hard copy. SASE. Responds in 1 month.

- Articles: 800–2,500 words. Informational articles and profiles. Topics include education, the Internet, family activities, fine arts, regional food and dining, consumer interest, parenting, grandparenting, and child development issues.
- Depts/columns: Word lengths vary. Family life, personal finance, book and software reviews, and women's health.
- Artwork: B/W or color prints.

SAMPLE ISSUE
204 pages (60% advertising): 3 articles; 20 depts/columns; 2 directories. Sample copy, free with 9x12 SASE. Editorial calendar available.

- "50 Must-Do Summer Activities." Article recommends such fun as local water parks, lemonade stands, laser shows, and picnics.
- Sample dept/column: "Education" tells how to keep kids learning throughout the summer to avoid "brain drain."

RIGHTS AND PAYMENT
One-time rights. Written material, $100–$500. Artwork, $90. Kill fee, $50. Pays 45 days after publication. Provides 3 contributor's copies.

EDITOR'S COMMENTS
In the past, we have received far too many essay-type submissions and not enough factual articles specific to Orange County. Please keep our audience in mind as you are formulating your query. As this is California, we can never get enough coverage of fitness and nutrition—but, again, please use local resources and experts.

Odyssey

Carus Publishing
30 Grove Street, Suite C
Peterborough, NH 03458

Senior Editor: Elizabeth E. Lindstrom

DESCRIPTION AND INTERESTS

Subtitled "Adventures in Science," *Odyssey* publishes fiction and informational articles that are rich in scientific accuracy and take a kid-friendly, high-energy approach to the subject at hand to keep young minds interested in science. Circ: 25,000.

Audience: 10–16 years
Frequency: 9 times each year
Website: www.odysseymagazine.com

FREELANCE POTENTIAL

70% written by nonstaff writers. Publishes 60 freelance submissions yearly; 2% by unpublished writers, 25% by authors who are new to the magazine. Receives 300 queries yearly.

SUBMISSIONS

Query with outline, author biography, bibliography, and clips or writing samples. Accepts hard copy. Artwork improves chance of acceptance. SASE. Responds in 5 months if interested.

- Articles: 750–1,000 words. Informational articles; biographies; and interviews. Topics include math, science, and technology.
- Fiction: 1,000 words. Science fiction and science-related stories.
- Depts/columns: Word lengths vary. Astronomy, animals, profiles, and science news.
- Artwork: B/W or color prints.
- Other: Activities, to 500 words. Seasonal material about space or astronomy events.

SAMPLE ISSUE

50 pages (no advertising): 7 articles; 11 depts/columns; 3 activities. Sample copy, $4.50 with 9x12 SASE (4 first-class stamps). Guidelines and theme list available at website.

- "Cool Roofs." Article explains how "cool" roofs and rooftop gardens can save on energy usage.
- Sample dept/column: "Person to Discover" offers a profile of a modern traffic engineer, who explains his support of roundabouts.

RIGHTS AND PAYMENT

All rights. Written material, $.20–$.25 per word. Artwork, payment rates vary. Pays on publication. Provides 2 contributor's copies.

➛EDITOR'S COMMENTS

All materials must relate to the theme of a specific upcoming issue—as outlined at our website—in order to be considered.

The Old Schoolhouse

P.O. Box 8436
Gray, TN 37615

Editors: Paul & Gena Suarez

DESCRIPTION AND INTERESTS

The Old Schoolhouse is written for parents who choose to educate their children at home. Its articles offer positive, informative, and supportive looks at all facets of home-based education, family life, and parenting, often from a Christian perspective. Circ: 50,000.

Audience: Homeschool families
Frequency: Quarterly
Web: www.thehomeschoolmagazine.com

FREELANCE POTENTIAL

80% written by nonstaff writers. Publishes 160 freelance submissions yearly; 30% by unpublished writers, 50% by authors who are new to the magazine. Receives 192 queries yearly.

SUBMISSIONS

Query with outline, sample paragraphs, and brief author biography. Accepts electronic queries via website (homeschoolblogger.com users should note their user name on query). No simultaneous submissions. Responds in 4–6 weeks.

- Articles: 1,000–2,000 words. Informational and how-to articles; and personal experience pieces. Topics include homeschooling, education, family life, art, music, spirituality, literature, child development, teen issues, science, history, and mathematics.
- Depts/columns: Word lengths vary. Short news items, teaching styles, opinion pieces, teaching children with special needs, and humorous pieces.

SAMPLE ISSUE

220 pages (40% advertising): 6 articles; 21 depts/columns. Sample copy and guidelines available at website.

- "We Just Stopped By to Encourage You." Article provides words of encouragement from several homeschooling parents.
- Sample dept/column: "Natural Schoolhouse" explains how raising alpacas changed the way one mother homeschooled her kids.

RIGHTS AND PAYMENT

First rights. Written material, payment rates vary. Pays on publication. Provides 2 copies.

➛EDITOR'S COMMENTS

We like anecdotes and articles that inspire others, as well as research pieces and professional technical articles related to education.

On Course

General Council of the Assemblies of God
1445 North Boonville Avenue
Springfield, MO 65802-1894

Editor: Amber Weigand-Buckley

DESCRIPTION AND INTERESTS
This publication of the National Youth Ministry of the Assemblies of God hopes to empower teens to grow in a real-life relationship with Christ. Its articles directly address real issues teens face while emphasizing a biblical approach. Circ: 160,000.

Audience: 12–18 years
Frequency: Quarterly
Website: www.oncourse.ag.org

FREELANCE POTENTIAL
95% written by nonstaff writers. Publishes 32 freelance submissions yearly; 30% by unpublished writers, 40% by authors who are new to the magazine.

SUBMISSIONS
All work is assigned. Send audition ms with résumé. Prefers hard copy and email submissions to oncourse@ag.org; will accept Macintosh-compatible CD submissions. SASE. Response time varies.

- Articles: To 800 words. Informational and how-to articles; profiles; humor; and personal experience pieces. Topics include social issues, music, health, religion, sports, careers, college, and multicultural subjects.
- Fiction: To 800 words. Genres include contemporary, humorous, multicultural, and sports-themed fiction.
- Depts/columns: Word lengths vary. Profiles and brief news items.

SAMPLE ISSUE
32 pages (33% advertising): 6 articles; 9 depts/columns. Sample copy, free. Guidelines available at website.

- "Overflow: What Would You Give to Change Your World?" Article discusses how three boys held an outdoor "rock-a-thon" to raise money for a missions project.
- "On a Mission to Reach the World." Article interviews the rapper Lecrae on his music and his faith.

RIGHTS AND PAYMENT
First and electronic rights. Written material, payment rates vary. Payment policy varies. Provides 5 contributor's copies.

➬EDITOR'S COMMENTS
Please note we do not want unsolicited articles; we assign according to scheduled topics.

Organic Family Magazine

P.O. Box 1614
Wallingford, CT 06492-1214

Editor: Catherine Wong

DESCRIPTION AND INTERESTS
Organic Family Magazine features articles on organic eating, and then some. It also provides information on changing one's lifestyle (and that of the whole family) toward a more organic and natural foundation, including parenting attitudes, gardening, and natural wellness. Circ: 200.

Audience: Families
Frequency: Twice each year
Website: www.organicfamilymagazine.com

FREELANCE POTENTIAL
90% written by nonstaff writers. Publishes 40 freelance submissions yearly.

SUBMISSIONS
Query or send complete ms. Prefers email submissions to sciencelibrarian@hotmail.com; will accept hard copy. SASE. Response time varies.

- Articles: Word lengths vary. Informational articles; interviews; and personal experience pieces. Topics include nature, organic agriculture, conservation, parenting, natural pet care, herbs, organic gardening, nutrition, progressive politics, health, wellness, and environmental issues.
- Fiction: Word lengths vary. Stories about nature and the environment.
- Depts/columns: Word lengths vary. New product reviews, recipes, profiles of conservation organizations, and media reviews.
- Other: Poetry.

SAMPLE ISSUE
28 pages: 8 articles; 1 story; 11 depts/columns; 1 poem. Sample copy and guidelines available at website.

- "Bright, Rich, and Organic." Article explains how to redesign a room using as many organic products as possible; offers a specific design project as an example.
- "Controlling Pests Naturally." Article looks at ways to control garden insects without the use of pesticides.

RIGHTS AND PAYMENT
One-time rights. No payment. Provides 1 contributor's copy.

➬EDITOR'S COMMENTS
There's a plethora of ways to go organic, and we're interested in articles about all of them. Material must be researched and accurate.

Our Children

National PTA
541 North Fairbanks Court, Suite 1300
Chicago, IL 60611-3396

Editor: Marilyn Ferdinand

DESCRIPTION AND INTERESTS
Published by the National Parent-Teacher Association (PTA), *Our Children* focuses on the state of education in America and encourages parents to get involved with their children's schools. It also covers the operations of PTA chapters. Circ: 31,000.

Audience: Parents; teachers; administrators
Frequency: 5 times each year
Website: www.pta.org

FREELANCE POTENTIAL
50% written by nonstaff writers. Publishes 20–25 freelance submissions yearly; 75% by authors who are new to the magazine. Receives 180–240 queries and unsolicited mss yearly.

SUBMISSIONS
Query or send complete ms. Accepts email submissions to mferdinand@pta.org. No simultaneous submissions. Responds in 2 months.

- Articles: 600–1,000 words. Informational and how-to articles. Topics include running local PTA chapters, child welfare, education, schools, and family life.
- Depts/columns: Word lengths vary. Short updates on parenting and education issues, and advice from PTA members.
- Artwork: 3x5 or larger color prints or slides.
- Other: Submit seasonal material 3 months in advance.

SAMPLE ISSUE
24 pages (no advertising): 5 articles; 9 depts/columns. Sample copy, $2.50 with 9x12 SASE ($1 postage). Writers' guidelines and editorial calendar available.

- "Internet Safety." Article suggests ways parents can protect their children from harmful messages conveyed through electronic media, whether it be the Internet, television, movies, or music.
- Sample dept/column: "Nutrition" describes the reasons for and consequences of childhood obesity.

RIGHTS AND PAYMENT
First rights. No payment. Provides 3 contributor's copies.

❖EDITOR'S COMMENTS
Our motto is "Every Child. One Voice." We are always open to fresh ideas and perspectives from our members.

Our Little Friend

Pacific Press Publishing
P.O. Box 5353
Nampa, ID 83653-5353

Editor: Aileen Andres Sox

DESCRIPTION AND INTERESTS
Our Little Friend is published for preschool-age children in Seventh-day Adventist Sunday school classes. It features stories and Bible lessons meant to impart church doctrine to young minds. Circ: 35,000.

Audience: 1–6 years
Frequency: Weekly
Website: www.ourlittlefriend.com

FREELANCE POTENTIAL
20% written by nonstaff writers. Publishes 52 freelance submissions yearly; 10% by unpublished writers, 10% by authors who are new to the magazine. Receives 240 unsolicited mss each year.

SUBMISSIONS
Send complete ms. Accepts hard copy, email submissions to ailsox@pacificpress.com, and simultaneous submissions if identified. SASE. Responds in 4 months.

- Articles: 500–650 words. Devotionals, Bible lessons, and true stories that teach Christian values. Topics include school and family.
- Fiction: 500–650 words. Short stories that portray God's love for children, personal faith, and contemporary issues.
- Artwork: Color prints. Line art.
- Other: Submit seasonal material 7 months in advance.

SAMPLE ISSUE
8 pages (no advertising): 5 stories; 2 Bible lessons. Sample copy, free with 9x12 SASE (2 first-class stamps). Guidelines available.

- "Hannah Shares." Story tells of a little girl whose greediness gives way to generosity when she meets another girl who has less than she does.
- "Joash, The Boy King." Article shares the Bible story of Joash and provides related activities for parents to do with their toddlers as reinforcement.

RIGHTS AND PAYMENT
One-time rights. Written material, $25–$50. Pays on acceptance. Provides 3 contributor's copies.

❖EDITOR'S COMMENTS
Stories must be written to be read aloud to babies, toddlers, and older preschool kids in a manner they will understand.

Pack-O-Fun

2400 East Devon, Suite 292
Des Plaines, IL 60018-4618

Editor: Annie Niemiec

DESCRIPTION AND INTERESTS
Not only is this magazine a pack of fun, it's packed with fun that can be replicated again and again as crafts, games, and activities. Targeting parents, teachers, and others who work with children, *Pack-O-Fun* is filled with easy projects and games that kids of all ages can handle. Circ: 15,000.
Audience: Parents and teachers
Frequency: 6 times each year
Website: www.pack-o-fun.com

FREELANCE POTENTIAL
50% written by nonstaff writers. Receives 504 unsolicited mss yearly.

SUBMISSIONS
Send complete ms with instructions, brief materials list, and photographs of project. Accepts hard copy and email submissions to aniemiec@amoscrafts.com (attach files). SASE. Responds in 4–6 weeks.

- Articles: To 200 words. How-to articles; craft projects; and party ideas.
- Depts/columns: Word lengths vary. Art ideas, projects for children and adults to do together, Vacation Bible School projects, photos of readers' projects.
- Artwork: B/W or color prints or JPEG files. Line art.

SAMPLE ISSUE
66 pages (10% advertising): 39 crafts; 4 depts/columns. Sample copy, $4.99 with 9x12 SASE (2 first-class stamps). Writers' guidelines available at website.

- "Pretty Bird Wind Catcher." Article explains how to make wind chimes using recycled jar lids, craft foam, and spray paint.
- "Uncle Sam Hat Favors." Article provides instructions for putting a little patriotic pizzazz into a Fourth of July party with Uncle Sam-themed party favors.

RIGHTS AND PAYMENT
All rights. All material, $25–$150. Pays 30 days after signed contract. Provides 3 contributor's copies.

⚫EDITOR'S COMMENTS
Our needs are simple: We want fun, innovative projects that are easy for children to complete. The more original your idea, the better. You must include step-by step instructions.

Pageantry

P.O. Box 160307
Alamonte Springs, FL 32716

Editor: Frank Abel

DESCRIPTION AND INTERESTS
Would-be beauty queens read this "bible of the pageant industry" for expert tips on hairstyling, makeup, jewelry, fitness, modeling, etiquette, and interviewing—in other words, everything they need to know to win a beauty competition. Circ: Unavailable.
Audience: YA–Adult
Frequency: Quarterly
Website: www.pageantry-digital.com

FREELANCE POTENTIAL
10% written by nonstaff writers. Publishes 5 freelance submissions yearly.

SUBMISSIONS
Query. Accepts hard copy and email queries to editor@pageantrymagazine.com. SASE. Response time varies.

- Articles: Word lengths vary. Informational articles; profiles; interviews; and personal experience pieces. Topics include beauty pageants, celebrities, fitness, modeling, makeup tips, interviewing techniques, dance, winning psychology, judges' perspectives, etiquette, coaching, talent competitions, and fashion.
- Depts/columns: Word lengths vary. Jewelry, makeup, hairstyles, fitness, body shaping, modeling, personal advice, teen issues, winner profiles, etiquette, news, opinions, show business, and celebrities.

SAMPLE ISSUE
144 pages: 4 articles; 25 depts/columns. Sample copy, $4.95.

- "Hoosier Queen." Article profiles Katie Stam, the first Miss America to hail from Indiana.
- Sample dept/column: "Breaking Into Showbiz" encourages readers to be prepared with headshots and comp cards when their agent isn't with them.
- Sample dept/column: "Your Look: Jewelry" explains how to choose the proper accessories for an evening gown.

RIGHTS AND PAYMENT
First North American serial rights. Written material, payment rates vary. Payment policy varies. Provides 1 contributor's copy.

⚫EDITOR'S COMMENTS
We look for writers who can join us in celebrating the glamour lifestyle. Celebrity interviews are always of interest to us, as is coverage of international pageant news.

Parentguide

419 Park Avenue South, 13th Floor
New York, NY 10016

Editor: Jenna Greditor

DESCRIPTION AND INTERESTS
A regional publication for parents in the New York metropolitan area, *Parentguide* centers on raising children through elementary school. It publishes articles on general parenting issues as well as those more focused on its local readership. Circ: 280,000.

Audience: Parents
Frequency: Monthly
Website: www.parentguidenews.com

FREELANCE POTENTIAL
80% written by nonstaff writers. Publishes 100 freelance submissions yearly; 5% by unpublished writers, 50% by authors who are new to the magazine. Receives 12 queries and unsolicited mss yearly.

SUBMISSIONS
Query or send complete ms with résumé. Prefers email to jenna@parentguidenews.com (Microsoft Word attachments); will accept hard copy. SASE. Responds in 3–4 weeks.

- Articles: 750–1,500 words. Informational and self-help articles; humor; and personal experience pieces. Topics include parenting, family, education, regional and social issues, popular culture, and careers.
- Depts/columns: 500 words. Local news and events, health, travel, and reviews.

SAMPLE ISSUE
70 pages (39% advertising): 10 articles; 7 depts/columns. Sample copy, free with 10x13 SASE. Guidelines available.

- "Born Too Early." Article offers expert information about premature births.
- "Becoming Bilingual." Article shares the benefits of learning two languages as a child.
- "Game On." Article lists several physical activities to boost children's brains, health, and fitness.

RIGHTS AND PAYMENT
Rights vary. No payment. Provides 1 contributor's copy.

➥EDITOR'S COMMENTS
We cater to the needs of parents who have children under the age of 12 and live in the tri-state area of New York, New Jersey, and Connecticut. We are especially interested in articles that illuminate issues and events pertaining to New York City families.

Parenting

135 West 50th Street, 3rd Floor
New York, NY 10026

Submissions Editor

DESCRIPTION AND INTERESTS
The pages of *Parenting* are filled with "what matters to moms"—primarily, information and advice on child development, behavior, and health—but also family entertainment, crafts, and other activities. Coverage begins at the prenatal stage and extends through age 12. Circ: 2 million+.

Audience: Parents
Frequency: 11 times each year
Website: www.parenting.com

FREELANCE POTENTIAL
80% written by nonstaff writers. Publishes 10–15 freelance submissions yearly; 5% by unpublished writers, 10% by authors who are new to the magazine. Receives 1,000 queries each year.

SUBMISSIONS
Query with clips. Accepts hard copy. SASE. Responds in 1–2 months.

- Articles: 1,000–2,500 words. Informational, how-to, and self-help articles; profiles; and personal experience pieces. Topics include child development, behavior, and health; pregnancy; and family activities.
- Depts/columns: 100–1,000 words. Parenting tips, child development by age range, work and family, and health and beauty for moms.

SAMPLE ISSUE
96 pages (50% advertising): 6 articles; 18 depts/columns. Sample copy, $5.95 (mark envelope Attn: Back Issues). Guidelines available.

- "Little Ways to Let Go." Article describes ways in which kids try to gain more independence and tells how to give it to them—one step at a time.
- "Sock Away More Cash!" Article suggests several ways to save the family dollar.
- Sample dept/column: "Ages & Stages: 5 to 6" discusses making and keeping promises.

RIGHTS AND PAYMENT
First world rights with 2 months exclusivity. Written material, payment rates vary. Pays on acceptance. Provides 1 contributor's copy.

➥EDITOR'S COMMENTS
We provide mothers with the emotional support and affirmation they want and the mom-tested ideas they can really use. Many of our writers are parents themselves.

Parenting New Hampshire

150 Dow Street
Manchester, NH 03101

Editor: Melanie Hitchcock

DESCRIPTION AND INTERESTS
This magazine is a valuable source of information about parenting issues, as well as a resource for family-related businesses and services in the state. Circ: 27,500.
Audience: Parents
Frequency: Monthly
Website: www.parentingnh.com

FREELANCE POTENTIAL
85% written by nonstaff writers. Publishes 25–35 freelance submissions yearly; 20% by unpublished writers, 50% by authors who are new to the magazine. Receives 1,200 queries, 240–360 unsolicited mss yearly.

SUBMISSIONS
Query or send complete ms with writing samples. Accepts hard copy, disk submissions, and email submissions to news@parentingnh.com. SASE. Response time varies.

- Articles: Word lengths vary. Informational and how-to articles; profiles; and interviews. Topics include parenting, education, maternity, childbirth, special needs, gifted education, fathering, child development, summer fun, birthday parties, holidays, back-to-school issues, and health.
- Depts/columns: Word lengths vary. Child development, parenting issues, and health and wellness.
- Other: Submit seasonal material 3 months in advance.

SAMPLE ISSUE
54 pages (42% advertising): 5 articles; 12 depts/columns. Sample copy, free. Guidelines available at website.

- "The Changing Plate of School Lunch." Article examines the switch to healthier fare at school cafeterias across the state.
- Sample dept/column: "Dad on Board" discusses the bonding benefits of father/daughter weekends.

RIGHTS AND PAYMENT
All rights. Articles, $30. Other material, payment rates vary. Pays on acceptance. Provides 3 contributor's copies.

⟶EDITOR'S COMMENTS
We give first preference to local writers and to those writing about topics pertaining to parenting in New Hampshire.

ParentingUniverse.com

Best Parenting Resources, LLC
546 Charing Cross Drive
Marietta, GA 30066

Editor: Alicia Hagan

DESCRIPTION AND INTERESTS
Read by both expectant and experienced mothers, this online magazine hits all the highs and lows of parenthood—from challenges such as discipline, toilet training, and school issues to fun stuff such as baby's milestones, family activities, and entertainment. Hits per month: 2+ million.
Audience: Women
Frequency: Daily
Website: www.parentinguniverse.com

FREELANCE POTENTIAL
90% written by nonstaff writers. Publishes 500+ freelance submissions yearly. Receives 5,000+ queries, 144 unsolicited mss yearly.

SUBMISSIONS
Query or send complete ms. Prefers submissions through website; will accept email submissions to alicia@parentinguniverse.com. Response time varies.

- Articles: Word lengths vary. Informational, how-to, and self-help articles; profiles; interviews; reviews; and personal experience pieces. Topics include pregnancy, childbirth, newborns, parenting skills, education, health, fitness, recreation, arts and crafts, and family activities.
- Depts/columns: Word lengths vary. Parenting tips and guidelines.

SAMPLE ISSUE
Sample issue and writers' guidelines available at website.

- "Healthy Pregnancy, Healthy Baby." Article stresses the importance of exercise, nutrition, and prenatal care.
- Sample dept/column: "Homeschool" tells how one mother went from an "accidental" homeschooler to a committed one.

RIGHTS AND PAYMENT
Electronic rights. Written material, payment rates vary. Pays on publication. Provides 2 contributor's copies.

⟶EDITOR'S COMMENTS
We encourage our members to submit their own stories, whether they be original or reprints (with permission) from another newsletter or magazine. Our content covers all topics of interest to parents of young children, including pregnancy and childbirth.

ParentLife

One LifeWay Plaza
Nashville, TN 37234-0172

Content Editor: Jodi Skulley

DESCRIPTION AND INTERESTS

ParentLife offers parenting information, advice, and inspiration from a Christian perspective. Targeting expectant parents and parents of children age 12 and under, its mission is to offer biblical solutions to today's family challenges. Circ: 76,000.

Audience: Parents
Frequency: Monthly
Website: www.lifeway.com/parentlifeblog

FREELANCE POTENTIAL

90% written by nonstaff writers. Publishes 12–15 freelance submissions yearly; 5% by unpublished writers, 5% by authors who are new to the magazine. Receives 800 queries, 200 unsolicited mss yearly.

SUBMISSIONS

Query or send complete ms. Accepts hard copy and email submissions to jodi.skulley@lifeway.com. SASE. Response time varies.

- Articles: 500–1,500 words. Informational and how-to articles; and personal experience pieces. Topics include family issues, religion, education, health, and hobbies.
- Depts/columns: 500 words. Age-appropriate advice, fathers' perspectives, single parenting, working parents, expectant parents, and medical advice.
- Artwork: Color prints and transparencies.
- Other: Accepts seasonal material for Christmas and Thanksgiving.

SAMPLE ISSUE

48 pages: 8 articles; 15 depts/columns. Sample copy, $2.95 with 10x13 SASE. Writers' guidelines available.

- "Love Without Regret." Article profiles singer-songwriter Jeremy Camp, his relationship with God, and his approach to family life.
- Sample dept/column: "Single Parent Life" offers advice for helping children deal with the loss of a parent.

RIGHTS AND PAYMENT

Non-exclusive rights. Written material, $125–$350. Pays on publication. Provides 1 contributor's copy.

❖EDITOR'S COMMENTS

We need articles written by professionals—or by parents who have "been there"—that offer information and encouragement for families.

Parents & Kids

785 North President Street
Jackson, MS 39202

Editor: Gretchen Cook

DESCRIPTION AND INTERESTS

Topics of interest to parents in central Mississippi are covered in this magazine, including health and safety, cooking, entertainment, education, and local events. Circ: 35,000.

Audience: Parents
Frequency: Monthly
Website: www.parents-kids.com

FREELANCE POTENTIAL

80% written by nonstaff writers. Publishes 80 freelance submissions yearly; 50% by unpublished writers. Receives 396 unsolicited mss each year.

SUBMISSIONS

Send complete ms. Accepts email submissions to magazine@parents-kids.com (text in body of message and Microsoft Word attachments). Responds in 6 weeks.

- Articles: 700 words. Informational, self-help, and how-to articles. Topics include the arts, computers, crafts and hobbies, health and fitness, multicultural and ethnic issues, recreation, regional news, social issues, special education, sports, and family travel.
- Depts/columns: 500 words. Travel, cooking, and computers.
- Artwork: Prefers digital images; will accept B/W prints or transparencies. Line art.
- Other: Submit seasonal material 3–6 months in advance.

SAMPLE ISSUE

44 pages (54% advertising): 7 articles; 12 depts/columns. Sample copy, free with 9x12 SASE ($1.06 postage). Guidelines available at website.

- "My Deal with God." Essay recounts a mother's frightful experience when she lost her son at the beach.
- Sample dept/column: "Parent Points" includes information about SIDS.

RIGHTS AND PAYMENT

One-time rights. Written material, $25. Pays on publication. Provides 1 tearsheet.

❖EDITOR'S COMMENTS

To increase your chances of acceptance, think in terms of your topic and our readers: Which local programs/assistance can make life better? What does the average area parent need to know about this topic?

Parents' Press

1454 Sixth Street
Berkeley, CA 94710

Editor: Dixie M. Jordan

DESCRIPTION AND INTERESTS
By featuring practical and research-based articles on all aspects of parenting, this magazine hopes to provide San Francisco-area parents with information that allows them to make the best choices for their families. Coverage includes child development, education, health, and relationship topics. Circ: 75,000.
Audience: Parents
Frequency: Monthly
Website: www.parentspress.com

FREELANCE POTENTIAL
15–20% written by nonstaff writers. Publishes 25–50 freelance submissions yearly; 15% by authors who are new to the magazine. Receives hundreds of unsolicited mss yearly.

SUBMISSIONS
Send complete ms. Accepts hard copy and email submissions to parentsprs@aol.com. SASE. Responds in 2 months.

- Articles: To 1,500 words. Informational and how-to articles. Topics include child development, education, health, safety, party planning, and local family events and activities.
- Depts/columns: Staff written.
- Artwork: B/W prints and transparencies. Line art.
- Other: Submit seasonal material 2 months in advance.

SAMPLE ISSUE
32 pages (63% advertising): 7 articles; 4 depts/columns. Sample copy, $3 with 9x12 SASE ($1.93 postage). Guidelines available at website.

- "A Suitable Job for a Mother." Article features an interview with author Ayelet Waldman about balancing work and motherhood.
- "Downsized Birthday Parties Go 'Old School.'" Article discusses an informal poll that revealed parents are spending less on children's birthday parties.

RIGHTS AND PAYMENT
All or second rights. Articles, $50–$500. Pays 45 days after publication.

➔EDITOR'S COMMENTS
We prefer articles that have a strong San Francisco focus. Health, education, and child development articles are generally written by professionals in the field.

Parent:Wise Austin

5501 A Balcones Drive, Suite 102
Austin, TX 78731

Editor/Publisher: Kim Pleticha

DESCRIPTION AND INTERESTS
This regional magazine targets parents in the central Texas region, featuring articles and essays about family life. It also lists local events and resources. Circ: 32,000.
Audience: Parents
Frequency: Monthly
Website: www.parentwiseaustin.com

FREELANCE POTENTIAL
25% written by nonstaff writers. Publishes 15+ freelance submissions yearly; 33% by authors who are new to the magazine.

SUBMISSIONS
Send complete ms. Accepts email submissions to editor@parentwiseaustin.com. Response time varies.

- Articles: To 650 words. Essays and humor. Topics include parenting, family life, education, regional news, and people in the Austin community who work to make life better for other families.
- Depts/columns: To 650 words. Humor about parenting and family life, and medical advice.
- Other: Poetry about parenting, children, or families; to 24 lines.

SAMPLE ISSUE
40 pages: 3 articles; 6 depts/columns; 3 calendars. Sample copy and writers' guidelines available at website.

- "Sports Car Girl, Minivan Life." Essay chronicles the author's evolution from sports car addict to minivan-owning (and -loving) mom with two children and a 100-pound dog.
- Sample dept/column: "My Life as a Parent" offers a humorous take on a man's "new reality" after having children.

RIGHTS AND PAYMENT
First North American serial and Internet rights. Written material, payment rates vary. Payment policy varies.

➔EDITOR'S COMMENTS
We prefer to work with local authors; however, we will consider out-of-area writers if they are able to fully localize an article. All material must relate to our central Texas region. Please note that cover articles are not open to freelancers, but are assigned to established writers known to us.

Partners

Christian Light Publications
P.O. Box 1212
Harrisonburg, VA 22803-1212

Editor: Etta G. Martin

DESCRIPTION AND INTERESTS
This Mennonite publication is written for Sunday school children. Each issue, divided into four weekly parts, contains stories meant to teach youngsters the principles of the faith and an understanding of the Bible. Circ: 6,857.

Audience: 9–14 years
Frequency: Monthly
Website: www.clp.org

FREELANCE POTENTIAL
98% written by nonstaff writers. Publishes 200–500 freelance submissions yearly; 5% by unpublished writers, 5% by authors who are new to the magazine. Receives 200–300 unsolicited mss yearly.

SUBMISSIONS
Send complete ms. Prefers email submissions to partners@clp.org; will accept hard copy and simultaneous submissions if identified. SASE. Responds in 6 weeks.

- Articles: 200–800 words. Informational articles. Topics include Bible customs, nature, and church history and teachings.
- Fiction: 400–1,600 words. Features stories that emphasize Mennonite beliefs and biblical standards.
- Other: Word puzzles and activities with Christian themes. Poetry; no free verse. Submit seasonal material 6 months in advance.

SAMPLE ISSUE
16 pages (no advertising): 4 stories; 2 articles; 7 poems; 4 activities. Sample copy, free with 9x12 SASE ($1.17 postage). Guidelines and theme list available.

- "Come Back, Charley, Come Back, Joy." Story tells of a boy who learns the rewards of being a blessing to others.
- "Why Did God Make Beetles?" Article explains the role of "good" bugs.

RIGHTS AND PAYMENT
First, reprint, or multiple-use rights. Articles and stories, $.04–$.06 per word. Poetry, $.50–$.75 per line. Activities, payment rates vary. Pays on acceptance. Provides 1 author's copy.

⟶EDITOR'S COMMENTS
Stories must impart a spiritual lesson, preferably related to a theme. Please be sure to ask for our theme list.

Passport

WordAction Publishing
2923 Troost Avenue
Kansas City, MO 64109

Assistant Editor: Laura Lohberger

DESCRIPTION AND INTERESTS
Distributed to Sunday school students each week, *Passport* features stories and activities that reinforce religious education curriculum. Its themes conform to the doctrine of the Church of the Nazarene, and its mission is to provide resources that meet people's need for spiritual transformation and holy living. Circ: 55,000.

Audience: 11–12 years
Frequency: Weekly
Website: www.wordaction.com

FREELANCE POTENTIAL
90% written by nonstaff writers. Publishes 30 freelance submissions yearly; 20% by unpublished writers, 20% by authors who are new to the magazine. Receives 240 queries and unsolicited mss yearly.

SUBMISSIONS
Query with author bio; or send complete ms. Accepts hard copy and email submissions to lslohberger@wordaction.com. SASE. Responds in 4–6 weeks.

- Articles: Staff written.
- Depts/columns: "Survival Guide," 400–500 words; hot topics with spiritual applications. "Curiosity Island," 200–300 words; hobbies, activities, tips, and career ideas.
- Other: Puzzles, activities, and cartoons.

SAMPLE ISSUE
8 pages (no advertising): 1 article; 2 depts/columns; 2 activities; 1 cartoon. Sample copy, free with 5x7 SASE. Writers' guidelines and theme list available.

- Sample dept/column: "Survival Guide" says there is no such thing as a bad prayer.
- Sample dept/column: "Curiosity Island" encourages students to keep a diary.

RIGHTS AND PAYMENT
Multi-use rights. "Survival Guide," $25. "Curiosity Island," cartoons, and puzzles, $15. Pays on publication. Provides 1 contributor's copy.

⟶EDITOR'S COMMENTS
Write about hot topics with spiritual applications for 11- to 12-year-old kids. We like a casual style that holds short attention spans. Avoid extensive cultural or holiday references—remember that you are writing for an international audience.

Pediatrics for Parents

P.O. Box 219
Gloucester, MA 01931

Editor: Richard J. Sagall, M.D.

DESCRIPTION AND INTERESTS
This newsletter seeks accurate medical information for parents concerned about their children's health and development. It publishes articles on all aspects of childhood health, prevention, and treatment. Circ: 250,000.

Audience: Parents
Frequency: 6 times each year
Website: www.pedsforparents.com

FREELANCE POTENTIAL
50% written by nonstaff writers. Publishes 30 freelance submissions yearly; 50% by unpublished writers, 50% by authors who are new to the magazine. Receives 50 queries and unsolicited mss yearly.

SUBMISSIONS
Query or send complete ms. Accepts email submissions to articles@pedsforparents.com (Microsoft Word attachments). Response time varies.

- Articles: 750–1,500 words. Informational articles. Topics include prevention, fitness, medical advances, new treatment options, wellness, and pregnancy.
- Depts/columns: Word lengths vary. New product information, and article reprints.

SAMPLE ISSUE
16 pages (no advertising): 12 articles; 6 depts/columns. Sample copy, $3; also available via the website. Guidelines available at website.

- "Simple Strategies to End Those 'Can't Get to Sleep' Blues." Article presents strategies for helping children get into a healthy nighttime sleep pattern.
- "Hypertension in Children." Article reports an increase in hypertension among children and adolescents, and offers tips that could help prevent it.

RIGHTS AND PAYMENT
First rights. Written material, to $25. Pays on publication. Provides 3 contributor's copies and a 1-year subscription.

➝EDITOR'S COMMENTS
We seek articles that describe general, medical, and pediatric problems, advances, or new treatments. All information must be medically accurate, and either be written by a medical professional or contain specific reference citations.

Piedmont Parent

P.O. Box 530
King, NC 27021

Editor: Myra Wright

DESCRIPTION AND INTERESTS
Parenting issues, family relationships, education, and family recreation are thoroughly covered in this magazine serving parents in the Winston-Salem and High Point regions of North Carolina. Circ: 39,000.

Audience: Parents
Frequency: Monthly
Website: www.piedmontparent.com

FREELANCE POTENTIAL
50% written by nonstaff writers. Publishes 36–40 freelance submissions yearly; 25% by unpublished writers, 50% by authors who are new to the magazine. Receives 1,000+ queries and unsolicited mss yearly.

SUBMISSIONS
Query or send complete ms. Accepts email to editor@piedmontparent.com (Microsoft Word attachments) and simultaneous submissions if identified. Responds in 1–2 months.

- Articles: 500–1,200 words. Informational and how-to articles; interviews; and personal experience pieces. Topics include child development, day care, summer camps, gifted and special education, local and regional news, science, social issues, sports, popular culture, health, and travel.
- Depts/columns: 600–900 words. Family health and parenting news.
- Other: Family games and activities.

SAMPLE ISSUE
40 pages (47% advertising): 8 articles; 5 depts/columns. Sample copy, free with 9x12 SASE ($1.50 postage). Guidelines and theme list available.

- "Is Your Child Ready for Middle School?" Article examines the many challenges and experiences one's child will face in his new school.
- Sample dept/column: "Is My Kid OK?" offers help for telling children about a divorce.

RIGHTS AND PAYMENT
One-time rights. Written material, payment rates vary. Pays on publication. Provides 1 tearsheet.

➝EDITOR'S COMMENTS
Reliable, local sources must be present in all articles. We are open to many topics, as long as they can lend some information or encouragement to parents.

Pikes Peak Parent

30 South Prospect Street
Colorado Springs, CO 80903

Editor: George Lewis

DESCRIPTION AND INTERESTS
Distributed free throughout greater Colorado Springs, *Pikes Peak Parent* prides itself on providing relevant, reliable, and wide-ranging resources for families living in the area. Circ: 30,000.

Audience: Parents
Frequency: Monthly
Website: www.pikespeakparent.com

FREELANCE POTENTIAL
5% written by nonstaff writers. Publishes 4 freelance submissions yearly; 2% by authors who are new to the magazine. Receives 60 queries yearly.

SUBMISSIONS
Query with writing samples. Accepts hard copy and email queries to parent@gazette.com. SASE. Response time varies.

- Articles: 800–1,500 words. Informational and how-to articles. Topics include regional news and resources, parenting issues, family life, travel, health, safety, sports, social issues, and recreation.
- Depts/columns: Word lengths vary. News, opinions, grandparenting, health, family issues, profiles, and events.

SAMPLE ISSUE
20 pages (50% advertising): 8 articles; 5 depts/columns. Sample copy, free with 9x12 SASE.

- "Eight Tips to Get Kids Interested in Gardening." Article recommends teaching children how to cook what they harvest, among other suggestions for getting them involved.
- "What's For Lunch?" Article features an interview with a registered dietician, who discusses packing healthful meals for school.
- Sample dept/column: "First Person" reveals ways parents can earn extra money during tight economic times.

RIGHTS AND PAYMENT
All rights on assigned pieces; second rights on reprints and unsolicited pieces. Written material, payment rates vary. Pays on publication. Provides 1 contributor's copy.

⟿EDITOR'S COMMENTS
We tend to receive a lot of personal essays about parenting. We'd rather see locally-sourced articles on practical topics that Colorado Springs parents can use.

Pittsburgh Parent

P.O. Box 374
Bakerstown, PA 15007

Editor: Patricia Poshard

DESCRIPTION AND INTERESTS
Practical and positive parenting information fills the pages of this magazine, which targets Pittsburgh-area families. Circ: 50,000+.

Audience: Parents
Frequency: Monthly
Website: www.pittsburghparent.com

FREELANCE POTENTIAL
80% written by nonstaff writers. Publishes 120 freelance submissions yearly; 20% by authors who are new to the magazine. Receives 1,500 queries and unsolicited mss yearly.

SUBMISSIONS
Query or send complete ms. Accepts hard copy, email to editor@pittsburghparent.com, and simultaneous submissions if identified. SASE. Response time varies.

- Articles: Cover story, 2,500–2,750 words. Other material, 400–900 words. Informational articles; profiles; and interviews. Topics include family issues, parenting, education, science, fitness, health, nature, college, computers, and multicultural subjects.
- Fiction: 1,000 words. Genres include mystery, adventure, and historical and multicultural fiction.
- Depts/columns: Word lengths vary. Education, teen issues, book reviews, and humor.
- Other: Submit seasonal material 3 months in advance.

SAMPLE ISSUE
44 pages (65% advertising): 10 articles; 5 depts/columns. Sample copy, free. Guidelines and editorial calendar available.

- "Mompreneurs." Article profiles two companies that were started by mothers working out of their homes.
- "Summer Water Safety." Article discusses important things parents need to know to keep their children safe around water.
- Sample dept/column: "Pop" offers ideas for hosting a cake-decorating party.

RIGHTS AND PAYMENT
First serial rights. Written material, payment rates vary. Pays 45 days after publication. Provides 1 tearsheet.

⟿EDITOR'S COMMENTS
We'll consider only those articles that feature a Pittsburgh angle and local sources.

PKA's Advocate

1881 Little Westkill Road
Prattsville, NY 12468

Publisher: Patricia Keller

DESCRIPTION AND INTERESTS

This tabloid provides a forum for emerging writers to get their work and thoughts published. It publishes a variety of material—including short stories, essays, poetry, and opinion pieces—on a variety of topics, as long as it is not overtly religious, violent, pornographic, or anti-environmental. Circ: 10,000.

Audience: YA–Adult
Frequency: 6 times each year

FREELANCE POTENTIAL

90% written by nonstaff writers. Publishes 150 freelance submissions yearly; 65% by unpublished writers, 35% by authors who are new to the magazine. Receives 1,500 unsolicited mss each year.

SUBMISSIONS

Send complete ms. Accepts hard copy. No simultaneous submissions. SASE. Responds in 6–10 weeks.

- Articles: To 1,500 words. Informational articles; personal experience pieces; profiles; and essays. Topics include horses and other animals, the arts, humor, nature, and recreation.
- Fiction: To 1,500 words. Genres include contemporary, historical, realistic, and science fiction; adventure; fantasy; folktales; romance; mystery; suspense; and stories about animals, nature, and the environment.
- Artwork: 8x10 B/W or color prints. Line art.
- Other: Gaited Horse Association Newsletter, published within. Poetry, no line limit. Puzzles and recipes.

SAMPLE ISSUE

20 pages (50% advertising): 2 articles; 3 stories; 16 poems. Sample copy, $5. Writer's guidelines available.

- "Shack in the Woods." Personal essay waxes nostalgic about a childhood spent fearing a mysterious old woman living in a shack.
- "A Snake Called Alexander." Article shares the author's experience with a pet snake.

RIGHTS AND PAYMENT

First rights. No payment. Provides 2 copies.

➬EDITOR'S COMMENTS

We currently seek horse-related stories, poetry, photos, and cartoons. Most stories we select are nature- or animal-oriented.

Playground Magazine

360 B Street
Idaho Falls, ID 83402

Editor: Lane Lindstrom

DESCRIPTION AND INTERESTS

This "complete resource for your playground needs" covers the planning, installation, and safety of public playgrounds. Circ: 35,000.
Audience: Adults
Frequency: 7 times each year
Website: www.playgroundmag.com

FREELANCE POTENTIAL

25% written by nonstaff writers. Publishes 8 freelance submissions yearly; 30% by authors who are new to the magazine. Receives 24–48 queries and unsolicited mss yearly.

SUBMISSIONS

Query or send complete ms. Accepts hard copy and email submissions to lindstrm@harrispublishing.com. SASE. Responds in 1–2 months.

- Articles: 800–1,200 words. Informational and how-to articles. Topics include the planning, design, and installation of playgrounds; types of play structures; surfacing; safety; maintenance; skate parks; aquatic features; and fundraising.
- Depts/columns: Word lengths vary. Legal issues, news, industry updates, manufacturer profiles, landscaping, design, and the developmental value of play.

SAMPLE ISSUE

56 pages: 1 article; 9 depts/columns; 1 directory. Sample copy, $5. Guidelines and editorial calendar available.

- "Three Components of Successful Safety Programs." Article details the need for duty of care, standard of care, and best practices.
- Sample dept/column: "Dream Spaces" spotlights a new playground in Los Angeles that provides access for children of all abilities.
- Sample dept/column: "Value of Play" describes the developmental benefits of restoring risky play to playgrounds.

RIGHTS AND PAYMENT

First serial rights. Articles, $100–$300. Depts/columns, $50–$175. Payment policy varies.

➬EDITOR'S COMMENTS

The goal of this magazine is to support the manufacturers' goals of providing great play spaces for children, which includes promoting the value of play.

Plays

The Drama Magazine for Young People

P.O. Box 600160
Newton, MA 02460

Editor: Elizabeth Preston

DESCRIPTION AND INTERESTS
Quality scripts suitable for performance by middle school and high school students are published in each issue of this magazine. Various topics are acceptable, as long as they are wholesome. Circ: 5,300.

Audience: 6–17 years
Frequency: 7 times each year
Website: www.playsmag.com

FREELANCE POTENTIAL
100% written by nonstaff writers. Publishes 75 freelance submissions yearly; 25% by unpublished writers, 50% by authors who are new to the magazine. Receives 250 queries and unsolicited mss yearly.

SUBMISSIONS
Query for adaptations of classics and folktales. Send complete ms for other material. Accepts hard copy. SASE. Responds to queries in 2 weeks, to mss in 1 month.

- Fiction: One-act plays for high school, to 5,000 words; for middle school, to 3,750 words; for elementary school, to 2,500 words. Also publishes skits, monologues, puppet plays, and dramatized classics. Genres include patriotic, historical, and biographical drama; mystery; melodrama; fairy tales and folktales; comedy; and farce.
- Other: Submit seasonal material 4 months in advance.

SAMPLE ISSUE
64 pages (5% advertising): 7 plays; 1 radio play. Sample copy, free with 6x9 SASE ($.76 postage). Guidelines available.

- "Shirley Chisholm: 'Unbought and Unbossed.'" Play shows the rise of Shirley Chisholm from underprivileged girl to the first elected black congresswoman.
- "The Love Potion." Based on the opera, *L'Elisir d'Amore*, play tells how a peasant wins the heart of a wealthy village girl.

RIGHTS AND PAYMENT
All rights. Written material, payment rates vary. Pays on acceptance. Provides 1 author's copy.

☛EDITOR'S COMMENTS
We are looking for more large-cast plays as well as plays based on contemporary topics. Plays should be secular in theme and be simple to produce.

Pockets

The Upper Room
1908 Grand Avenue
P.O. Box 340004
Nashville, TN 37203-0004

Editor: Lynn W. Gilliam

DESCRIPTION AND INTERESTS
This colorful Christian magazine includes stories, articles, and activities that reinforce the truth of a loving God, and show young readers how to live their faith each day. Circ: 98,000.

Audience: 6–11 years
Frequency: 11 times each year
Website: www.pockets.org

FREELANCE POTENTIAL
97% written by nonstaff writers. Publishes 220 freelance submissions yearly; 20% by unpublished writers, 30% by authors who are new to the magazine. Receives 2,000 mss yearly.

SUBMISSIONS
Send complete ms. Accepts hard copy. SASE. Responds in 2 months.

- Articles: 400–1,000 words. Informational articles; profiles; and personal experience pieces. Topics include multicultural and community issues, and persons whose lives reflect their Christian commitment.
- Fiction: 600–1,400 words. Stories that demonstrate Christian values.
- Depts/columns: Word lengths vary. Scripture readings and lessons; recipes.
- Artwork: Color prints; digital images to 300 dpi.
- Other: Poetry. Puzzles, activities, games.

SAMPLE ISSUE
48 pages (no advertising): 1 article; 6 stories; 6 depts/columns; 10 activities; 3 poems. Sample copy, free with 9x12 SASE (4 first-class stamps). Guidelines and theme list available at website.

- "Nothing Special." Story shows how a girl learns to appreciate the many blessings in her life.
- "Boredom Busters." Story tells how a young boy changes his ungrateful attitude.

RIGHTS AND PAYMENT
First and second rights. Written material, $.14 per word. Poetry, $2 per line. Games, $25–$50. Pays on acceptance. Provides 3–5 copies.

☛EDITOR'S COMMENTS
Because each issue revolves around a theme, writers should always consult our theme list. We are always looking for 600-word stories written for children ages five to seven.

Pocono Parent Magazine

P.O. Box 291
Analomink, PA 18320

Editor: Teri O'Brien

DESCRIPTION AND INTERESTS
Delivered directly to parents in Monroe County, Pennsylvania, this magazine offers informative and reader-friendly features on raising children from birth to age 17. It focuses on ideas, activities, products, and services that help improve the quality of family life—from universal parenting concerns to specific how-to and where-to information. Circ: 10,000.

Audience: Parents
Frequency: 6 times each year
Website: www.poconoparent.com

FREELANCE POTENTIAL
25% written by nonstaff writers. Publishes 20 freelance submissions yearly.

SUBMISSIONS
Send complete ms. Accepts email submissions to editor@poconoparent.com (no attachments). Response time varies.

- Articles: 750–1,000 words. Informational and how-to articles; profiles; interviews; reviews; photo-essays; and personal experience pieces. Topics include parenting, family issues, child care, education, social issues, current events, health, fitness, nature, the environment, recreation, and regional news.
- Depts/columns: Word lengths vary. Family finances, teen and tween issues, restaurant reviews, pets, and family fitness.

SAMPLE ISSUE
40 pages: 6 articles; 13 depts/columns. Sample copy and guidelines available at website.

- "Children & Sunglasses." Article stresses the importance of protecting children's (and adults') eyes from the sun.
- "Organic Gardening, Safer Pesticides, and Organic Food." Article explains the dangers of chemical pesticides and offers recipes for six homemade bug repellents.

RIGHTS AND PAYMENT
Rights vary. Written material, payment rates vary. Payment policy varies. Provides 2 contributor's copies.

➥EDITOR'S COMMENTS
The most important piece of advice for any freelancer is this: Know your audience. Every article should answer the question, "What can parents in Monroe County do to help their children?" Please be creative yet practical.

Pointe

110 William Street, 23rd Floor
New York, NY 10038

Managing Editor: Carol Rubin

DESCRIPTION AND INTERESTS
Each issue of this respected ballet magazine revolves around a theme, ranging from summer programs for ballet students to life as a professional dancer. Circ: 40,000.

Audience: All ages
Frequency: 6 times each year
Website: www.pointemagazine.com

FREELANCE POTENTIAL
75% written by nonstaff writers. Publishes 1–2 freelance submissions yearly; 10% by unpublished writers, 25% by authors who are new to the magazine. Receives 12 queries each year.

SUBMISSIONS
Query. Accepts hard copy. SASE. Responds in 2 months.

- Articles: 1,200 words. Informational articles; profiles; interviews; personal experience pieces; and photo-essays. Topics include ballet companies, dancers, choreographers, news, trends, festivals and events, premieres, and auditions.
- Depts/columns: 800–1,000 words. Premieres, news, interviews with directors, profiles of dancers and companies, advice, and tips on technique.
- Artwork: B/W or color prints or transparencies; digital photos. Line art.

SAMPLE ISSUE
80 pages (50% advertising): 5 articles; 14 depts/columns. Sample copy, guidelines, and theme list available.

- "A Day's Work." Article follows Pittsburgh Ballet Theatre corps member Eva Trapp through a matinee of *Don Quixote*.
- Sample dept/column: "Director's Choice" offers a Q&A with the artistic director of the Scottish Ballet about what he looks for when auditioning dancers.

RIGHTS AND PAYMENT
All rights. Written material, payment rates vary. Pays on acceptance. Provides 2 author's copies.

➥EDITOR'S COMMENTS
Our mission is to provide practical and timely information, written in a clear, simple, journalistic style, that readers can easily understand and learn from. Please submit queries at least four months prior to the issue date.

Positive Parenting Newsletter

P.O. Box 1312
Ventura, CA 93002

Owner: Deborah Fox

DESCRIPTION AND INTERESTS
Positive Parenting is an online newsletter designed to give parents the information, resources, and support they need to deal with children's behavior and discipline issues. It accepts material from parents as well as child behavior experts. Hits per month: Unavailable.

Audience: Parents
Frequency: Updated regularly
Website: www.positiveparenting.com

FREELANCE POTENTIAL
30% written by nonstaff writers. Publishes 2–3 freelance submissions yearly; 10–20% by unpublished writers, 80% by authors who are new to the magazine. Receives 48–72 unsolicited mss yearly.

SUBMISSIONS
Send complete ms. Accepts email to info@positiveparenting.com. Response time varies.

- Articles: 500–1,000 words. Informational and how-to articles; and personal experience pieces. Topics include parenting.
- Depts/columns: Word lengths vary. Success stories, reviews.
- Other: Seasonal and holiday-related parenting tips.

SAMPLE ISSUE
4 articles. Guidelines available at website.

- "Understanding Forgetting Behavior." Article discusses children's forgetful behavior, and explains what parents do to enable it.
- "Baby Tantrums." Article explains why babies have tantrums and what parents can do to prevent or ease them.
- Sample dept/column: "Success Stories" shares parents' achievements in turning their children's bad behavior around.

RIGHTS AND PAYMENT
Rights vary. No payment.

➥EDITOR'S COMMENTS
Feature articles, reviews of parenting books, and our "Success Stories" department present the best opportunities for new writers. Please note that we receive many "Success Stories" submissions, but we publish only those that we feel are relevant to parents. All material must be written in a way that provides practical parenting ideas and honors the role parents play in a child's development.

Prehistoric Times

145 Bayline Circle
Folsom, CA 95630-8077

Editor: Mike Fredericks

DESCRIPTION AND INTERESTS
Prehistoric Times delves into the world of prehistoric creatures with general information as well as scientific articles on the prehistoric eras and paleontology. Collectibles and dinosaur-inspired artwork are other areas the magazine regularly covers. Circ: Unavailable.

Audience: YA–Adult
Frequency: Quarterly
Website: www.prehistorictimes.com

FREELANCE POTENTIAL
30% written by nonstaff writers. Publishes 20+ freelance submissions yearly; 75% by unpublished writers, 75% by authors who are new to the magazine. Receives 24+ unsolicited mss each year.

SUBMISSIONS
Send complete ms. Accepts email submissions to pretimes@comcast.net (attach file). Response time varies.

- Articles: 1,500–2,000 words. Informational articles. Topics include dinosaurs, paleontology, prehistoric life, drawing dinosaurs, and dinosaur-related collectibles.
- Depts/columns: Word lengths vary. Field news, dinosaur models, media reviews, interviews, and detailed descriptions of dinosaurs and other prehistoric species.

SAMPLE ISSUE
60 pages (30% advertising): 8 articles; 15 depts/columns. Sample copy, $7. Guidelines available via email request to pretimes@comcast.net.

- "Tyrannosaurus in the 'Savage Rex' Era." Article details this dinosaur's life, as well as how it has been depicted in art throughout the years.
- Sample dept/column: "Non-Extinct Dinosaur" reviews a book that introduces children to the world of dinosaurs.

RIGHTS AND PAYMENT
All rights. Written material, payment rates vary. Payment policy varies.

➥EDITOR'S COMMENTS
We divide our space fairly evenly between informational articles on the dinosaurs themselves (and the scientists who study them) and dinosaur-related hobbies, such as collecting, painting, and model building.

Preschool Playhouse

Urban Ministries
1551 Regency Court
Calumet City, IL 60409

Senior Editor: Judy Hull

DESCRIPTION AND INTERESTS
This Sunday school take-home paper "for God's little children" presents Bible lessons, stories of Christian values, and related activities with a message that children can apply to their own lives. Published by Urban Ministries, it focuses on teaching African American preschool children how to recognize and pass on God's love. Circ: 50,000.

Audience: 2–5 years
Frequency: Quarterly, with weekly take-home sections
Website: www.urbanministries.com

FREELANCE POTENTIAL
25% written by nonstaff writers. Publishes 12 freelance submissions yearly; 10% by unpublished writers, 25% by authors who are new to the magazine.

SUBMISSIONS
All material is assigned. Send résumé with clips or writing samples. Accepts hard copy. SASE. Response time varies.

- Articles: Word lengths vary. Informational articles; and Bible stories. Topics include Jesus, love, compassion, helping others, sharing, and other Christian values.
- Other: Bible-based games and activities.

SAMPLE ISSUE
4 pages (no advertising): 1 article; 1 Bible story; 2 activities. Sample copy, free. Guidelines available.

- "Showing Love to Others." Article tells how a little boy with leg braces doesn't hesitate to help others.
- "Love Everyone." Bible story recounts a verse from the book of John and encourages children to apply it to their lives.

RIGHTS AND PAYMENT
All rights. Written material, payment rates vary. Pays on publication. Provides 1 author's copy.

➥EDITOR'S COMMENTS
We are called by God to create, produce, and distribute quality Christian education products; to deliver exemplary customer service; and to provide quality Christian educational services, which will empower God's people—especially those within the black community—to evangelize, disciple, and equip others to serve Christ, His kingdom, and His Church.

PresenTense Magazine

214 Sullivan Street, Suite 2A
New York, NY 10012

Editor: Ariel Beery

DESCRIPTION AND INTERESTS
This magazine explores Jewish life in the here and now for young Jews. It seeks original, quality writing from experienced writers as well as new Jewish voices. Circ: 30,000.

Audience: YA–Adult
Frequency: 3 times each year
Website: www.presentensemagazine.org

FREELANCE POTENTIAL
80% written by nonstaff writers. Publishes 40 freelance submissions yearly; 40% by unpublished writers, 70% by new authors.

SUBMISSIONS
Query or send complete ms. Accepts email to editor@presentensemagazine.org (include submission type, title, and word count in subject line, and attach document) and simultaneous submissions if identified. Responds to queries in 2 weeks, to mss in 2 months.

- Articles: Features, 800–1,200 words. Profiles, 600–700 words. Sidebars, 50–250 words. Topics include Judaism, the Diaspora, Zionism, Israel, activism, community, education, relationships, and health.
- Fiction: 1,000–3,000 words. Genres vary.
- Depts/columns: "Paradigm Shift," 1,200–2,000 words. "Around the World," 600–800 words. News and pop-culture briefs, 400–500 words. Reviews, 300–800 words.
- Artwork: Digital photos and scans of line art, paintings, and cartoons at 300 dpi.
- Other: Photo-essays, 12 photos, 600 words. Poetry, to 300 words.

SAMPLE ISSUE
64 pages: 8 articles; 28 depts/columns. Sample copy and guidelines available at website.

- "Good Job: Growth of Service Learning for the Jews." Article explains what painting a house in 2009 can teach young people about age-old Jewish values.
- Sample dept/column: "Ideas & Innovation" tells how two young teachers are pursuing social justice through education.

RIGHTS AND PAYMENT
First rights. No payment. Provides 3 copies.

➥EDITOR'S COMMENTS
As part of our mandate to showcase new Jewish voices, we are especially interested in giving exposure to new fiction writers and poets.

Primary Street

Urban Ministries
1551 Regency Court
Calumet City, IL 60409

Editor: Janet Grier

DESCRIPTION AND INTERESTS
Primary Street is a take-home story paper designed to supplement elementary school students' religious education classes. Specifically targeting African American children, it is filled with Bible stories, Scripture lessons, and religious themed activities. Circ: 50,000.

Audience: 6–8 years
Frequency: Quarterly
Website: www.urbanministries.com

FREELANCE POTENTIAL
25% written by nonstaff writers. Publishes 15 freelance submissions yearly; 25% by unpublished writers, 25% by authors who are new to the magazine. Receives 180 queries yearly.

SUBMISSIONS
All material is assigned. Query with résumé and writing samples. Accepts hard copy. SASE. Response time varies.

- Articles: Word lengths vary. Informational and how-to articles; personal experience pieces; photo-essays; and Bible stories. Topics include religion, Christian values, nature, the environment, animals, pets, crafts, hobbies, African history, multicultural and ethnic subjects, regional news, and social issues.
- Other: Bible verses, activities, puzzles, and games.

SAMPLE ISSUE
4 pages (no advertising): 1 article; 1 Bible story; 1 memory verse; 4 activities. Sample copy, free. Guidelines available.

- "Jesus Is Wonderful: They Sing to Jesus in Heaven." Bible story tells how Jesus is worthy of opening God's scroll because He died for our sins.
- "Jeanine." Article describes Jeanine as a good girl who deserved a reward from her teacher, just as Jesus deserves our worship for all he has done.

RIGHTS AND PAYMENT
All rights. Written material, payment rates vary. Pays on publication. Provides 1 author's copy.

➔EDITOR'S COMMENTS
Please note that all material is assigned. Send us religious-themed material you've written and information about your religious education experience, and perhaps we'll add you to our list of writers.

Primary Treasure

Pacific Press Publishing
P.O. Box 5353
Nampa, ID 83653-5353

Editor: Aileen Andres Sox

DESCRIPTION AND INTERESTS
Published by the Seventh-day Adventist Church, this magazine is a take-home paper designed to augment elementary school-age Sabbath school lessons. It publishes true stories that reflect Jesus's love, Christian values, and the lessons of the church. Circ: 250,000.

Audience: 6–9 years
Frequency: Weekly
Website: www.primarytreasure.com

FREELANCE POTENTIAL
10% written by nonstaff writers. Publishes 52 freelance submissions yearly; 10% by unpublished writers, 30% by authors who are new to the magazine. Receives 240 unsolicited mss each year.

SUBMISSIONS
Query for serials. Send complete ms for other submissions. Accepts hard copy, email submissions to ailsox@pacificpress.com, and simultaneous submissions if identified. SASE. Responds in 4 months.

- Articles: 600–1,000 words. True stories about children in Christian settings; and true, problem-solving pieces that help children learn about themselves in relation to God and others. Material must be consistent with Seventh-day Adventist beliefs and practices.
- Other: Submit seasonal material 7 months in advance.

SAMPLE ISSUE
16 pages (no advertising): 4 articles; 1 Bible story; 1 puzzle. Sample copy, free with 9x12 SASE (2 first-class stamps). Writers' guidelines available.

- "Tornado!" Story relates a family's experience when a fierce tornado hit their town, and they realized that God protected them from harm.
- "A Room for Grandma." Story tells of the sacrifices a family happily makes in order for their grandmother to move in with them.

RIGHTS AND PAYMENT
One-time rights. Written material, $25–$50. Pays on acceptance. Provides 3 copies.

➔EDITOR'S COMMENTS
When writing, remember that your audience consists of very young children. All material must illustrate a Christian belief.

Principal

1615 Duke Street
Alexandria, VA 22314

Managing Editor: Vanessa St. Gerard

DESCRIPTION AND INTERESTS
A professional publication for elementary school principals, this magazine covers a range of topics related to school administration, including policy trends, legislation, educational issues, and management. Circ: 28,000.
Audience: K–8 school administrators
Frequency: 5 times each year
Website: www.naesp.org

FREELANCE POTENTIAL
90% written by nonstaff writers. Publishes 20 freelance submissions yearly; 80% by authors who are new to the magazine. Receives 150 unsolicited mss yearly.

SUBMISSIONS
Send complete ms. Accepts hard copy, PC-compatible disk submissions, and email submissions to publications@naesp.org. No simultaneous submissions. SASE. Responds in 6 weeks.

- Articles: 1,000–2,500 words. Informational and instructional articles; profiles; and opinion and personal experience pieces. Topics include elementary education, gifted and special education, parenting, mentoring, and technology.
- Depts/columns: 750–1,500 words. "Parents & Schools," "It's the Law," "Practitioner's Corner," "Tech Support," "A Touch of Humor," "Principal's Bookshelf," "Ten to Teen," "The Reflective Principal," and "Speaking Out."

SAMPLE ISSUE
72 pages (25% advertising): 9 articles; 9 depts/columns. Sample copy, $8. Guidelines and theme list available.

- "Practices for Identifying Gifted Students." Article examines the traits of gifted and talented students.
- "Where Are All the Students of Color in Gifted Education?" Article argues that there is still much to be done to ensure that all students have access to gifted and talented programs.

RIGHTS AND PAYMENT
All North American serial rights. No payment. Provides 3 contributor's copies.

❖EDITOR'S COMMENTS
All articles must be thoroughly researched and footnoted.

Queens Parent

1040 Avenue of the Americas, 4th Floor
New York, NY 10018

Editor-in-Chief: Helen Freedman

DESCRIPTION AND INTERESTS
This tabloid paper is published for parents living in New York City's borough of Queens and neighboring Nassau County. It contains articles of general interest as well as copious information of local interest—all on raising happy and healthy children. Circ: 285,000.
Audience: Parents
Frequency: Monthly
Website: www.nymetroparents.com

FREELANCE POTENTIAL
50% written by nonstaff writers. Publishes 300 freelance submissions yearly. Receives 12 queries, 72 unsolicited mss yearly.

SUBMISSIONS
Query or send complete ms. Accepts hard copy and email submissions to hfreedman@davlermedia.com. SASE. Responds in 1 week.

- Articles: 800–1,000 words. Informational articles; profiles; interviews; and personal experience pieces. Topics include family issues, education, camp, health, nutrition, fitness, current events, and regional news.
- Depts/columns: Staff written.
- Other: Submit seasonal material 4 months in advance.

SAMPLE ISSUE
78 pages: 12 articles; 9 depts/columns. Sample copy, free with 10x13 SASE.

- "The Back-to-Basics Baby." Article looks at whether early-learning products really give babies and toddlers an edge.
- "As Your Child Grows, Consider a Health Care Proxy." Article points out that once children reach age 18, parents are no longer legally able to make health-care decisions for them without filing the proper paperwork.
- "Is It a Cold? The Flu? Or Allergies?" Article tells how to recognize and prevent allergy symptoms in children.

RIGHTS AND PAYMENT
First New York area rights. No payment.

❖EDITOR'S COMMENTS
We are happy to read and consider all submissions. Keep in mind that we never publish memoirs, fiction, or poetry. We are also not reading travel pieces right now. Many of our articles are posted at our website in addition to being printed in the newspaper.

Rainbow Kids

P.O. Box 202
Harvey, LA 70059

Editor: Martha Osborne

DESCRIPTION AND INTERESTS
Rainbow Kids is an online magazine and resource center for individuals considering adoption as well as those already involved in the adoption process. It features informational articles, personal experience pieces, and resource lists. Hits per month: 1.5 million.
Audience: Adoptive families
Frequency: Monthly
Website: www.rainbowkids.com

FREELANCE POTENTIAL
10% written by nonstaff writers. Publishes 10–20 freelance submissions yearly; 50% by authors who are new to the magazine.

SUBMISSIONS
Send complete ms. Accepts email submissions to martha@rainbowkids.com (Microsoft Word attachments). Responds in 2–3 days.

- Articles: Word lengths vary. Informational articles and personal experience pieces. Topics include all matters related to adoption and adoptive families, both domestic and foreign. Also publishes adoption guidelines, adoption events, and photo listings.

SAMPLE ISSUE
Sample copy and writers' guidelines available at website.

- "Positive Outcomes: A Background on Your Child's Pre-Adoptive Life." Article explores the many situations a child may have encountered prior to adoption.
- "Korea Slowly Closes to Adoption." Article reports on the South Korean government's plans to stop international adoptions, ending the longest-running international adoption program in the world.

RIGHTS AND PAYMENT
Limited electronic rights. No payment.

➹EDITOR'S COMMENTS
We're always looking for articles on the financial aspect of adoption, parent support groups, transracial adoption, and special needs adoption. All writers must be familiar, either professionally or personally, with the adoption process. We love personal adoption stories, especially those written by adoptive teens. We regret that we cannot offer payment for submissions, as we are a volunteer-based website.

Rainbow Rumpus

P.O. Box 6881
Minneapolis, MN 55406

Editor-in-Chief: Beth Wallace

DESCRIPTION AND INTERESTS
This online magazine is written for the children of lesbian, gay, bisexual, or transgender (LGBT) parents. It looks for articles and stories that celebrate the diversity of these families, as well as the ways in which all families are alike. Hits per month: 9,000.
Audience: 4–18 years
Frequency: Monthly
Website: www.rainbowrumpus.org

FREELANCE POTENTIAL
40% written by nonstaff writers. Publishes 40 freelance submissions yearly; 10% by new authors. Receives 12 unsolicited mss yearly.

SUBMISSIONS
Send complete ms. Accepts email submissions to fictionandpoetry@rainbowrumpus.org (Microsoft Word attachments; include "Submission" in subject line). Responds in 2 weeks.

- Articles: Staff written.
- Fiction: Stories for children 4–12 years, 800–2,500 words. Stories for teens, to 5,000 words. Publishes most genres.
- Depts/columns: Staff written.
- Other: Poetry, no line limit.

SAMPLE ISSUE
Sample copy and writers' guidelines available at website.

- "What Is Grandma Blogging?" Article explains what blogs are, shares their benefits, and warns of their dangers.
- "The Greenest Green I've Ever Seen." Story tells of a boy who, while visiting his two uncles in Chicago, discovers that the river has been dyed green for St. Patrick's Day.

RIGHTS AND PAYMENT
First North American electronic and anthology rights. Fiction, $75. Poetry, payment rates vary. Pays on publication.

➹EDITOR'S COMMENTS
We would like to receive more work from new authors, so we're glad you're thinking of writing for *Rainbow Rumpus*! While stories should celebrate the diversity of LGBT-headed families and their communities, they should *not* center on family structure or on children being teased about their families. Stories should be written from a child's point of view.

Raising Arizona Kids

7000 East Shea Boulevard, Suite 1470
Scottsdale, AZ 85254-5257

Assistant Editor: Mary Holden

DESCRIPTION AND INTERESTS
The goal of this magazine is to enlighten, inform, challenge, support, and amuse Arizona parents with articles on childcare, health, nutrition, and family lifestyles. Circ: Unavailable.

Audience: Parents
Frequency: Monthly
Website: www.raisingarizonakids.com

FREELANCE POTENTIAL
65% written by nonstaff writers. Publishes 12 freelance submissions yearly; 1% by unpublished writers, 1% by authors who are new to the magazine. Receives 44 queries yearly.

SUBMISSIONS
Query with clips. Accepts hard copy and email queries to maryh@raisingarizonakids.com. SASE. Response time varies.

- Articles: 1,000–2,000 words. Informational and how-to articles; profiles; interviews; personal experience pieces; and photo-essays. Topics include parenting issues, children, health and fitness, college and careers, current events, education, social issues, travel, and recreation.
- Depts/columns: Word lengths vary. News, parenting issues, family matters, profiles.
- Other: Journal articles, 500 words.

SAMPLE ISSUE
46 pages: 2 articles; 6 depts/columns; 1 journal article. Sample copy and guidelines available at website.

- "Focus on Fathers." Article profiles three local men, who discuss their experiences with fatherhood.
- "Breaking Up Is Hard to Do." Article explains the benefits of a divorce support group for children.
- Sample dept/column: "Ages & Stages" offers suggestions for dealing with children's questions about death.

RIGHTS AND PAYMENT
Rights vary. Articles, $125. Journal articles, $100. Depts/columns, payment rates vary. Pays 30 days after publication.

➥EDITOR'S COMMENTS
Our core readers are caring, open-minded, and intellectually curious parents of children from birth through high school. All articles should feature local resources.

The Reading Teacher

International Reading Association
800 Barksdale Road
P.O. Box 8139
Newark, DE 19714-8139

Managing Editor: James Henderson

DESCRIPTION AND INTERESTS
The Reading Teacher serves as an open forum for teachers and administrators to discuss practices, issues, and trends in children's literacy learning. Research-based articles and reports, as well as essays, are featured in each issue. Circ: 57,500.

Audience: Literacy educators
Frequency: 8 times each year
Website: www.reading.org

FREELANCE POTENTIAL
95% written by nonstaff writers. Publishes 50 freelance submissions yearly; 20% by unpublished writers, 30% by authors who are new to the magazine. Receives 300 unsolicited mss each year.

SUBMISSIONS
Send complete ms. Accepts electronic submissions via http://mc.manuscriptcentral.com/rt. Responds in 1–2 months.

- Articles: To 6,000 words. Informational and how-to articles; profiles; and personal experience pieces. Topics include literacy, reading education, instructional techniques, classroom strategies, reading research, and educational technology.
- Depts/columns: 1,500–2,500 words. Reviews of children's books, teaching tips, and material on cultural diversity.

SAMPLE ISSUE
84 pages (17% advertising): 5 articles; 5 depts/columns. Sample copy, $10. Writers' guidelines available.

- "Reader Response Meets New Literacies: Empowering Readers in Online Learning Communities." Article studies the benefits of computer-based reading material and electronic journals.
- Sample dept/column: "Urban Literacy" discusses effective classroom strategies for learning English as a second language.

RIGHTS AND PAYMENT
All rights. No payment. Provides 5 contributor's copies for articles, 2 copies for depts/columns.

➥EDITOR'S COMMENTS
We welcome submissions from a broad range of literacy professionals covering a variety of topics that deal with literacy among children in the preschool through teen years.

Reading Today

International Reading Association
800 Barksdale Road
P.O. Box 8139
Newark, DE 19714-8139

Editor-in-Chief: John Micklos Jr.

DESCRIPTION AND INTERESTS
This trade publication for reading teachers publishes articles on a wide range of topics, from interviews with children's book authors to descriptions of innovative reading programs. It is mailed to members of the International Reading Association (IRA). Circ: 82,000.

Audience: IRA members
Frequency: 6 times each year
Website: www.reading.org

FREELANCE POTENTIAL
30% written by nonstaff writers. Publishes 30 freelance submissions yearly; 10% by unpublished writers, 40% by authors who are new to the magazine. Receives 300 queries, 240 unsolicited mss yearly.

SUBMISSIONS
Prefers query; will accept complete ms. Prefers email submissions to readingtoday@ reading.org; will accept hard copy and simultaneous submissions if identified. SASE. Responds in 1 month.

- Articles: 500–1,000 words. Informational articles and interviews. Topics include reading, reading education, community programs, staffing, assessment, funding, children's books, and censorship.
- Depts/columns: To 750 words. News; education policy updates; and ideas for administrators, teachers, and parents.
- Artwork: Digital images.

SAMPLE ISSUE
44 pages (30% advertising): 2 articles; 9 depts/columns; 1 special section. Sample copy, $6. Guidelines available.

- "Easy as A-B-C." Article describes a reading program titled "About the Beautiful Communities of Illinois."
- Sample dept/column: "Parents and Reading" tells how caregivers can encourage a lifelong love of reading in young children.

RIGHTS AND PAYMENT
All rights. Written material, $.20–$.30 per word. Pays on acceptance. Provides 3 contributor's copies.

➡️EDITOR'S COMMENTS
Unfortunately, we offer fewer freelance opportunities this year due to reduced page counts. We want ideas for motivating kids to read.

Red River Family Magazine

P.O. Box 7654
Lawton, OK 73506

Executive Editor: Laura Clevenger

DESCRIPTION AND INTERESTS
This magazine targets parents in general—but mothers ages 25–54 specifically—with information on parenting, family issues, children's health, and education. Articles are specifically tailored for parents in southwest Oklahoma and north Texas. Circ: 20,000.

Audience: Parents
Frequency: Monthly
Website: www.redriverfamily.com

FREELANCE POTENTIAL
34% written by nonstaff writers. Publishes 100 freelance submissions yearly; 10% by unpublished writers, 80% by authors who are new to the magazine.

SUBMISSIONS
Query with clips or writing samples. Accepts email queries to publisher@redriverfamily.com. Response time varies.

- Articles: Word length varies. Informational and how-to articles; profiles; interviews; and personal experience pieces. Topics include parenting, family life, social issues, education, special education, health and fitness, college and careers, technology, nature, the environment, and recreation.
- Depts/columns: Word lengths vary. Military life, education, green living, media reviews, fitness, safety, regional news.

SAMPLE ISSUE
34 pages: 3 articles; 11 depts/columns. Guidelines available via email request to publisher@redriverfamily.com.

- "Scouting Builds Leadership, Citizenship, Success . . . and It's Fun!" Article explains how children can grow and thrive in the healthy, rewarding environment of Scouting.
- Sample dept/column: "Green Living" offers tips for implementing "green" elements into one's lifestyle.

RIGHTS AND PAYMENT
One-time print and 2-year electronic rights. Articles, $20–$50. Payment policy varies.

➡️EDITOR'S COMMENTS
Our editorial tone is patriotic and pro-military, but we do not have any political or religious agenda. Short articles and briefs are always welcome, as are articles for website publication only.

Relate

1601 Parkway Drive
Findlay, OH 45840

Submissions: Mary Bowman

DESCRIPTION AND INTERESTS
This lifestyle magazine with a subtle Christian tone encourages girls to be themselves, and to set an example in speech, in life, in love, in faith, and in purity. Circ: 10,000.

Audience: Girls, 15–19 years
Frequency: Quarterly
Website: www.relatemag.com

FREELANCE POTENTIAL
80% written by nonstaff writers. Publishes 40 freelance submissions yearly; 40% by unpublished writers, 50% by authors who are new to the magazine. Receives 240 queries yearly.

SUBMISSIONS
Query with writing samples. Accepts email queries to mary@relatemag.com. Response time varies.

- Articles: 650–1,600+ words. Informational articles; profiles; interviews; and personal experience pieces. Topics include design, beauty, health, entertainment, college, careers, faith, and relationships.
- Depts/columns: 200–800 words. Crafts, beauty and fashion tips, media reviews, celebrity interviews, teen entrepreneurs, relationships, Q&As, and reader profiles.
- Other: Quizzes and contests.

SAMPLE ISSUE
48 pages: 10 articles; 15 depts/columns; 1 quiz; 1 contest. Sample copy and guidelines available at website.

- "A Fashionista's Dream Come True." Article features an interview with Tanya Lund, an up-and-coming designer whose career was launched by a contest.
- Sample dept/column: "Career Call" details the steps to becoming a makeup artist.

RIGHTS AND PAYMENT
First North American serial and electronic rights. Written material, $50–$350. Pays on publication.

☛EDITOR'S COMMENTS
We would love to see more profiles of teen designers, volunteers, and entrepreneurs. The easiest way to begin writing for *Relate* is to contribute to our website, which publishes several additional articles each month (300 to 450 words each). Query Web editor Katie Hinderer at katie@relatemag.com.

Research in Middle Level Education Online

Portland State University
Graduate School of Education
615 SW Harrison
Portland, OR 97201

Editor: Micki M. Caskey

DESCRIPTION AND INTERESTS
This e-zine is a publication of the National Middle School Association. It is concerned with up-to-date, scholarly studies on the best practices and approaches to middle-grade education. Hits per month: 30,000.

Audience: Educators and administrators
Frequency: 10 times each year
Website: www.nmsa.org

FREELANCE POTENTIAL
100% written by nonstaff writers. Publishes 10 freelance submissions yearly; 20% by unpublished authors, 50% by authors who are new to the publication. Receives 40+ unsolicited mss yearly.

SUBMISSIONS
Send complete ms with 150- to 200-word abstract. Accepts email submissions to caskeym@pdx.edu (Microsoft Word attachments). Responds in 1 week.

- Articles: 7,000–12,000 words. Informational articles; quantitative and qualitative studies; case studies; action research studies; research syntheses; integrative reviews; and interpretations of research literature—all pertaining to middle-grade education.

SAMPLE ISSUE
Sample articles and writers' guidelines available at website.

- "Teaching and Teaming More Responsively: Case Studies in Professional Growth at the Middle Level." Article provides an analysis of observations from two teachers who worked collaboratively with other professionals over three years.
- "Origami Instruction in the Middle School Mathematics Classroom." Article explores how the use of origami in the classroom expanded students' understanding of spatial visualization.

RIGHTS AND PAYMENT
All rights. No payment.

☛EDITOR'S COMMENTS
We continue to solicit high-quality research manuscripts from those who have conducted scholarly studies in middle-grade education. Aside from the title page, manuscripts should have no reference to the author(s) to ensure a blind review.

Reunions Magazine

P.O. Box 11727
Milwaukee, WI 53211-0727

Editor: Edith Wagner

DESCRIPTION AND INTERESTS
Practical information, useful tips, and interesting stories make up the content of this magazine, which is geared toward readers involved in organizing family, school, or military reunions. Circ: 20,000.

Audience: Adults
Frequency: Quarterly
Website: www.reunionsmag.com

FREELANCE POTENTIAL
75% written by nonstaff writers. Publishes 100 freelance submissions yearly; 60% by unpublished writers, 80% by authors who are new to the magazine.

SUBMISSIONS
Send complete ms. Prefers email submissions to editor@reunionsmag.com (Microsoft Word attachments); will accept hard copy. SASE. Responds in 12–18 months.

- Articles: Word lengths vary. Informational, factual, and how-to articles; profiles; and personal experience pieces. Topics include organizing reunions; choosing reunion locations, entertainment, and activities; and genealogy.
- Depts/columns: 250–1,000 words. Opinion and personal experience pieces; and resource information.
- Artwork: Color digital images at 300 dpi or higher.
- Other: Recipes, games, cartoons, and filler.

SAMPLE ISSUE
44 pages (45% advertising): 3 articles; 6 depts/columns. Sample copy, $3. Guidelines and editorial calendar available.

- "Passing the Torch." Article outlines several steps to follow to ensure a smooth transition to a new reunion organizer.
- Sample dept/column: "Branch Office" highlights a recent family reunion that uncovered the historical ties of family members.

RIGHTS AND PAYMENT
One-time and electronic rights. Written material, payment rates vary. Payment policy varies. Provides 2 contributor's copies.

❖EDITOR'S COMMENTS
The best submissions are written with humor, expertise, passion, creativity, and a fresh approach. Reunion reports and photos are our lifeblood.

Richmond Parents Monthly

1506 Staples Mill Road, Suite 102
Richmond, VA 23230

Editor: Lee Barnes

DESCRIPTION AND INTERESTS
Richmond Parents Monthly aims to be an avenue of support and a forum for dialogue for readers in this Virginia region. Its coverage includes health, education, parenting, and entertainment. Circ: 30,000.

Audience: Parents
Frequency: Monthly
Website: www.richmondparents.com

FREELANCE POTENTIAL
75% written by nonstaff writers. Publishes 50–60 freelance submissions yearly; 5% by authors who are new to the magazine. Receives 600 queries and mss yearly.

SUBMISSIONS
Query with 3–5 clips; or send complete ms. Accepts email submissions to mail@ richmondpublishing.com. No simultaneous submissions. Availability of artwork improves chance of acceptance. Responds in 1–3 weeks.

- Articles: 400–2,200 words. Informational and self-help articles. Topics include the arts, camps, pets, home and garden, parties, education, health, and holidays.
- Depts/columns: "Your Turn" essays, 400–900 words. Family-related news, media reviews, and technology; word lengths vary.
- Artwork: Color prints or transparencies.

SAMPLE ISSUE
30 pages (15% advertising): 4 articles; 8 depts/columns; 1 calendar; 1 contest. Sample copy, free. Guidelines and editorial calendar available at website.

- "A Guide to Richmond's Public Parks." Article describes the activities and amenities available at the city's parks.
- "Making the Most of the End of Stay-at-Home Days." Article offers ideas for enjoying time with kids before going back to work.
- Sample dept/column: "The Frumpy Zone" takes a humorous look at the sleep-deprived life of a mom of three.

RIGHTS AND PAYMENT
One-time rights. Written material, $52–$295. Pays on publication.

❖EDITOR'S COMMENTS
We accept submissions from local writers only. Writers new to us are more likely to be accepted if they submit short pieces.

Sacramento Parent

457 Grass Valley Highway, Suite 5
Auburn, CA 95603

Editor-in-Chief: Shelly Bokman

DESCRIPTION AND INTERESTS
Sacramento Parent publishes articles of interest to families with children and grandchildren with a variety of lifestyles and beliefs. It features parenting and education information, and outlines events and resources related to the Sacramento region. Circ: 50,000.
Audience: Parents
Frequency: Monthly
Website: www.sacramentoparent.com

FREELANCE POTENTIAL
75% written by nonstaff writers. Publishes 50 freelance submissions yearly; 10% by unpublished writers, 25% by authors who are new to the magazine. Receives 780 queries yearly.

SUBMISSIONS
Query with writing samples. Accepts email queries to shelly@sacramentoparent.com. Response time varies.

- Articles: 700–1,000 words. Informational and how-to articles; personal experience pieces; and humor. Topics include parenting, health, fitness, finance, family travel, education, grandparenting, adoption, sports, recreation, learning disabilities, and regional news.
- Depts/columns: 300–500 words. Child development, opinions, and hometown highlights.
- Other: Submit seasonal or themed material 3 months in advance.

SAMPLE ISSUE
50 pages (50% advertising): 4 articles; 6 depts/columns. Sample copy, free with 9x12 SASE ($1.29 postage). Guidelines and theme list available at website.

- "Sister Act." Article profiles two grammar-school sisters who formed their own rock band and perform original songs.
- "Prepare to Be (Un)Schooled." Article explains the concept of letting children learn through activities that don't need lesson plans and textbooks.

RIGHTS AND PAYMENT
Second rights. Articles, $50. Depts/columns, $25–$40. Pays on publication. Provides contributor's copies.

➥EDITOR'S COMMENTS
We are especially interested in articles that promote a developmentally appropriate, healthy, and peaceful environment for kids.

San Diego Family Magazine

P.O. Box 23960
San Diego, CA 92193

Editor: Kirsten Flournoy

DESCRIPTION AND INTERESTS
This parenting magazine features authoritative articles about all aspects of parenting, education, and family issues. All information must have relevance to the Greater San Diego region. Circ: 120,000.
Audience: Parents
Frequency: Monthly
Website: www.sandiegofamily.com

FREELANCE POTENTIAL
90% written by nonstaff writers. Publishes 120–200 freelance submissions yearly; 5% by unpublished writers, 10% by authors who are new to the magazine. Receives 120 queries, 120 unsolicited mss yearly.

SUBMISSIONS
Query or send complete ms. Accepts email to kirsten@sandiegofamily.com. SASE. Responds in 1 month.

- Articles: 800–1,200 words. Informational, self-help, and how-to articles. Topics include parenting, pregnancy, childbirth, child care, education, summer camp, health, safety, nutrition, gardening, dining out, recreation, travel, sports, family finance, local events, and multicultural issues.
- Depts/columns: Word lengths vary. News briefs, tips, trends, restaurant reviews, book reviews, cooking, and gardening.
- Artwork: 3x5 or 5x7 four-color glossy prints.

SAMPLE ISSUE
154 pages (60% advertising): 12 articles; 13 depts/columns. Sample copy, $4.50 with 9x12 SASE ($1 postage). Guidelines and editorial calendar available at website.

- "Breathing Life Into Your Spring Break." Article provides ideas for turning a mundane spring break into a "staycation" that will be remembered.
- Sample dept/column: "Schools of Thought" discusses a city plan to combine small elementary schools into larger ones.

RIGHTS AND PAYMENT
First or second, and all regional rights. Written material, $1.25 per column inch. Pays on publication. Provides 1 contributor's copy.

➥EDITOR'S COMMENTS
We would love to see more articles on choosing and attending summer camps.

Santa Barbara Family Life

P.O. Box 4867
Santa Barbara, CA 93140

Editor: Nansie Chapman

DESCRIPTION AND INTERESTS
The mission of this family magazine is to educate and entertain its readers while connecting families to other members, events, activities, and businesses within the Santa Barbara community. Circ: 60,000.
Audience: Parents
Frequency: Monthly
Website: www.sbfamilylife.com

FREELANCE POTENTIAL
30% written by nonstaff writers. Publishes 5–15 freelance submissions yearly; 5% by unpublished writers, 10% by authors who are new to the magazine. Receives 240 queries each year.

SUBMISSIONS
Query or send complete ms. Accepts email to nansie@sbfamilylife.com. Responds only if interested.

- Articles: 500–1,200 words. Informational articles; profiles; photo-essays; and personal experience pieces. Topics include regional events and activities, parenting, family life, education, recreation, crafts, hobbies, and current events.
- Depts/columns: Word lengths vary. Love and relationships, arts and entertainment, and health issues.
- Other: Puzzles and activities.

SAMPLE ISSUE
32 pages: 4 articles; 7 depts/columns; 3 activities. Sample copy available at website.

- "It's Summer, It's Hot . . . It's Salsa." Article explains the history of salsa dancing and how it gained popularity in the U.S.
- Sample dept/column: "Arts & Entertainment" offers details on an outdoor summer concert series and an upcoming flute recital that features young artists.

RIGHTS AND PAYMENT
Rights vary. Written material, $25–$35. Payment policy varies.

➥EDITOR'S COMMENTS
We believe educational information that can assist family members in creating healthy, happy relationships benefits us all. To that end, we are always interested in hearing about new information that our readers will find relevant. A local angle is preferred.

Scholastic Choices

Scholastic Inc.
557 Broadway
New York, NY 10012-3999

Editor: Bob Hugel

DESCRIPTION AND INTERESTS
This magazine speaks to readers in middle school and high school about making the best choices as they grow up. It publishes articles on social issues, life skills, finances, relationships, personal responsibility, and consumer awareness. It is distributed through the school systems. Circ: 200,000.
Audience: 12–18 years
Frequency: 6 times each year
Website: www.scholastic.com

FREELANCE POTENTIAL
90% written by nonstaff writers. Publishes 30–40 freelance submissions yearly; 10% by unpublished writers. Receives 60 queries, 60 unsolicited mss yearly.

SUBMISSIONS
Query or send complete ms. Accepts hard copy and email to choicesmag@scholastic.com. SASE. Responds to queries in 2 months, to mss in 3 months.

- Articles: 500–1,000 words. Informational and self-help articles; profiles; and personal experience pieces. Topics include health, nutrition, fitness, sports, personal development, personal responsibility, family issues, relationships, safety, social issues, conservation, the environment, popular culture, careers, and substance abuse prevention.
- Depts/columns: Staff written.
- Other: Quizzes, word games, and recipes.

SAMPLE ISSUE
24 pages (20% advertising): 5 articles; 5 depts/columns. Sample copy, free with 9x12 SASE. Guidelines and editorial calendar available.

- "If Love Hurts, It Isn't Love." Article uses the incident between Rihanna and Chris Brown to discuss the issue of dating abuse.
- "So Long, Stress!" Article outlines some simple stress-reducing techniques.

RIGHTS AND PAYMENT
All rights. Written material, payment rates vary. Pays on publication. Provides 10 copies.

➥EDITOR'S COMMENTS
We look for articles that speak to teenagers in a way that is neither preachy nor condescending. All articles should focus on topics or challenges that teenagers deal with as they mature, and offer positive information.

Scholastic DynaMath

Scholastic Inc.
557 Broadway, Room 4052
New York, NY 10012-3999

Editor: Matt Friedman

DESCRIPTION AND INTERESTS
Informative articles that demonstrate real-world and exciting applications of curricular mathematics are found in this magazine, which targets students in grades three through six. Circ: 200,000.

Audience: 8–11 years
Frequency: 8 times each year
Website: www.scholastic.com

FREELANCE POTENTIAL
28% written by nonstaff writers. Publishes 16 freelance submissions yearly; 20% by unpublished writers, 20% by authors who are new to the magazine. Receives 24 queries, 48 unsolicited mss yearly.

SUBMISSIONS
Query with outline; or send complete ms. Accepts hard copy and simultaneous submissions if identified. SASE. Responds in 2–4 months.

- Articles: To 600 words. Informational articles about math skills. Topics include critical thinking; chart and graph reading; measurement; addition; subtraction; fractions; decimals; problem solving; and interdisciplinary issues, popular culture, sports, and consumer awareness—all as related to math.
- Other: Filler, puzzles, games, and jokes. Submit holiday material 4–6 months in advance.

SAMPLE ISSUE
16 pages: 5 articles; 4 activities. Sample copy, $4 with 9x12 SASE. Guidelines and editorial calendar available at website.

- "Sew Much Fun." Article explains how a costume designer for *High School Musical on Ice* measures carefully to ensure a good fit.
- "Phelps's Golden Decimals." Article focuses on using order decimals to compare racers' swim times.

RIGHTS AND PAYMENT
All rights. Articles, $250–$450. Puzzles, $25–$50. Pays on acceptance. Provides 3 copies.

☞EDITOR'S COMMENTS
We are always in need of kid-friendly applications of math that are fun and easy to grasp. Our upcoming editorial calendar covers topics such as telling time, reading bar graphs, prime numbers, and volume.

Scholastic Math Magazine

Scholastic Inc.
557 Broadway
New York, NY 10012-3999

Editor: Jack Silbert

DESCRIPTION AND INTERESTS
This classroom supplement uses pop-culture references to make learning math fun. It features exercises that not only entertain and engage middle school and high school students, but also show them how math is applied in daily life. Circ: 200,000.

Audience: 11–15 years
Frequency: Monthly
Website: www.scholastic.com/math

FREELANCE POTENTIAL
30% written by nonstaff writers. Publishes 10 freelance submissions yearly; 10% by unpublished writers. Receives 24 queries yearly.

SUBMISSIONS
Query. Accepts hard copy. SASE. Responds in 2–3 months.

- Articles: 600 words. Informational articles. Topics include real-world math, math-related news, teen issues, sports, celebrities, TV, music, movies, and current events.
- Depts/columns: 140 words. Skill-building exercises, quizzes, practice tests, and Q&As.
- Other: Puzzles, games, activities, comic strips, and mystery photos.

SAMPLE ISSUE
16 pages (no advertising): 4 articles; 1 dept/column; 1 comic strip. Sample copy, free with 9x12 SASE (3 first-class stamps). Guidelines and editorial calendar available.

- "Wizard in Training." Article features an interview with actor Tom Felton, who plays Draco Malfoy in the *Harry Potter* films, and presents math problems based on reading a London train schedule.
- Sample dept/column: "Fast Math" features short math problems plucked from daily life.

RIGHTS AND PAYMENT
All rights. Articles, $300+. Depts/columns, $35. Pays on publication.

☞EDITOR'S COMMENTS
From the 2010 U.S. Census to the Winter Olympics, we show students that math is everywhere. We strive to bring real-life math, literacy, and fun into the classroom. Please be aware that all articles must contain at least one significant math problem (with a solution for the teacher's guide) that relates to the topic being discussed.

Scholastic Parent & Child

Scholastic, Inc.
557 Broadway
New York, NY 10012-3999

Associate Editor: Samantha Brody

DESCRIPTION AND INTERESTS
Delivering focused content for parents of children from birth to age 12, *Scholastic Parent & Child* delves into topics that are important to every parent, including child development, family well-being, health, food, activities, travel, community, and kid-related products. Circ: 7.8 million.

Audience: Parents
Frequency: 8 times each year
Website: www.parentandchildonline.com

FREELANCE POTENTIAL
50% written by nonstaff writers. Publishes 20 freelance submissions yearly; 15% by authors who are new to the magazine. Receives 1,200 queries, 600 unsolicited mss yearly.

SUBMISSIONS
Query or send complete ms. Accepts hard copy. SASE. Responds to queries in 3 months, to mss in 2 months.

- Articles: 500–1,000 words. Informational articles and interviews. Topics include child development, education, and parenting.
- Depts/columns: Word lengths vary. Literacy, health, parent/teacher relationships, arts and crafts, child development, product reviews, travel, cooking, and family issues.

SAMPLE ISSUE
88 pages (33% advertising): 5 articles; 11 depts/columns. Sample copy, $2.95. Guidelines available.

- "Making a World of Difference." Article suggests ways for families to "go green," while teaching kids to be more aware of their environment.
- Sample dept/column: "Take Your Time" explains how upgrading a mom's technical gear can help her save time, be more informed, and manage her family schedule.

RIGHTS AND PAYMENT
All rights. Written material, payment rates vary. Pays on publication. Provides author's copies.

➥EDITOR'S COMMENTS
While we are happy to receive articles on just about any parent-, child-, or family-related topic, we are particularly interested in receiving articles about beauty and those written from a dad's point of view. We'd also be open to considering fiction.

Scholastic Scope

Scholastic Inc.
557 Broadway
New York, NY 10012-3999

Executive Editor: Lucy Lehrer

DESCRIPTION AND INTERESTS
This magazine from Scholastic features articles and fiction on topics that interest teens. What's more, all material is geared toward strengthening reading, comprehension, and writing skills. It is meant to be used as a teen magazine as well as a teaching tool, with corresponding reproducibles and teaching guides available. Circ: 550,000.

Audience: 12–18 years
Frequency: 17 times each year
Website: www.scholastic.com/scope

FREELANCE POTENTIAL
10% written by nonstaff writers. Of the freelance submissions published yearly, 2% are by unpublished writers, 10% are by new authors. Receives 200–300 queries yearly.

SUBMISSIONS
Query with résumé, outline/synopsis, and clips. Accepts hard copy. SASE. Response time varies.

- Articles: 1,000 words. News and features that appeal to teens; and profiles of young adults who have overcome obstacles, performed heroic acts, or have had interesting experiences.
- Fiction: 1,500 words. Contemporary, realistic stories about relationships and family problems, school issues, and other teen concerns; and science fiction.
- Depts/columns: Staff written.
- Other: Puzzles and activities. Submit seasonal material 4 months in advance.

SAMPLE ISSUE
22 pages (8% advertising): 4 articles; 1 play; 3 depts/columns; 1 puzzle. Sample copy, $1.75 with 9x12 SASE (2 first-class stamps); also available at website.

- "Night at the Museum: Battle of the Smithsonian." Article presents a play based on the popular movie.
- "Swimming With Sharks." Article profiles an underwater explorer.

RIGHTS AND PAYMENT
Rights vary. Written material, $100+. Pays on acceptance. Provides 2 contributor's copies.

➥EDITOR'S COMMENTS
We look for high-interest material that will build reading and language skills.

School Arts

Davis Publications
2223 Parkside Drive
Denton, TX 76201

Editor: Nancy Walkup

DESCRIPTION AND INTERESTS
This magazine provides school art teachers with inspiration and project ideas suitable for specific grade levels. Circ: 20,000.
Audience: Art teachers, grades K–12
Frequency: 9 times each year
Website: www.schoolartsonline.com

FREELANCE POTENTIAL
75% written by nonstaff writers. Publishes 200 freelance submissions yearly; 60% by unpublished writers, 60% by authors who are new to the magazine. Receives 300 unsolicited mss each year.

SUBMISSIONS
Send complete ms with artwork. Prefers disk submissions with images; will accept email submissions to nwalkup@verizon.net (attach files). Responds in 1–2 months.

- Articles: 300–800 words. Informational, how-to, and self-help articles. Topics include teaching art, artistic techniques, art history, classroom projects and activities, curriculum development, and art programs for gifted and disabled students.
- Depts/columns: 500–1,200 words. Crafts, new product reviews, and opinions.
- Artwork: B/W and color prints and slides; high-resolution digital images. Line art.

SAMPLE ISSUE
68 pages (40% advertising): 9 articles; 12 depts/columns. Sample copy, $5. Guidelines and editorial calendar available at website.

- "The Japanese Art of Kyoketsu-zome." Article gives step-by-step instructions for creating dyed-paper art.
- Sample dept/column: "Museum Musings" describes an exhibit of folk art "critters."

RIGHTS AND PAYMENT
First serial rights. Written material, $25–$150. Artwork, payment rates vary. Pays on publication. Provides 6 contributor's copies.

➟EDITOR'S COMMENTS
Our articles are written by art teachers themselves, whose ideas and advice are valuable to their peers throughout the world. We love when teachers share with us their successful lessons, areas of concern, and approaches to teaching art.

The School Librarian's Workshop

1 Deerfield Court
Basking Ridge, NJ 07920

Editor: Ruth Toor

DESCRIPTION AND INTERESTS
This trade magazine serves library science professionals working in school settings. It publishes articles on professional development, literacy programs, working in schools, technology trends, leadership skills, and current books. Circ: 7,000.
Audience: School librarians
Frequency: 6 times each year
Website:
    www.school-librarians-workshop.com

FREELANCE POTENTIAL
28% written by nonstaff writers. Publishes 20 freelance submissions yearly; 10% by unpublished writers, 10% by authors who are new to the magazine. Receives 24 unsolicited mss each year.

SUBMISSIONS
Send 2 copies of complete ms. Prefers disk submissions (Microsoft Word); will accept hard copy. SASE. Responds in 3 weeks.

- Articles: To 1,000 words. Informational, how-to, and practical application articles; profiles; and interviews. Topics include librarianship, literature, special education, ethnic studies, computers, technology, social and multicultural issues, and the environment.
- Artwork: Line art.
- Other: Submit seasonal material 8 months in advance.

SAMPLE ISSUE
24 pages (no advertising): 13 articles. Sample copy, free with 9x12 SASE. Guidelines and theme list available at website.

- "The Evolution of Evolution." Article explains how to create a research project to help students study Charles Darwin, evolution, and even Creationism.
- "Got Game?" Article argues that allowing board gaming in the library can provide students with an unexpected learning resource.

RIGHTS AND PAYMENT
First rights. No payment. Provides 3 contributor's copies.

➟EDITOR'S COMMENTS
We seek practical articles dealing with all aspects of library media programs and/or current trends that will affect them. We always want to hear from librarians with new ideas.

School Library Journal

360 Park Avenue South
New York, NY 10010

Executive Editor: Rick Margolis

DESCRIPTION AND INTERESTS
School Library Journal serves school and public librarians who work with young people. In addition to the many book reviews in each issue, it features informative articles on library management, programs, integrating libraries into the school curriculum, technology, and information literacy. Circ: 34,500.

Audience: Children's and YA librarians
Frequency: Monthly
Website: www.slj.com

FREELANCE POTENTIAL
80% written by nonstaff writers. Publishes 25 freelance submissions yearly; 60% by unpublished writers, 60% by authors who are new to the magazine. Receives 48–72 unsolicited mss each year.

SUBMISSIONS
Query or send complete ms. Accepts disk submissions (ASCII or Microsoft Word) and email to rmargolis@reedbusiness.com. SASE. Responds to queries in 1 month, to mss in 3 months.

- Articles: 1,500–2,500 words. Informational articles and interviews. Topics include children's and young adult literature, school library management, and library careers.
- Depts/columns: 1,500–2,500 words. Book and media reviews, descriptions of successful library programs, and opinion pieces.
- Artwork: Color prints. Color tables and charts. Cartoons.

SAMPLE ISSUE
116 pages (25% advertising): 5 articles; 9 depts/columns; 3 review sections. Sample copy, $6.75 with 9x12 SASE. Guidelines available at website.

- "KT the Magnificent." Article looks at the accomplishments and contributions of a popular school librarian.
- Sample dept/column: "First Steps" explains how and why parents and librarians should "model" reading behavior for children.

RIGHTS AND PAYMENT
First rights. Articles, $400. Depts/columns, $100–$200. Pays on publication. Provides 4 contributor's copies.

➝EDITOR'S COMMENTS
We want articles that provide librarians with the resources they need to be true innovators.

School Library Media Activities Monthly

3520 South 35th Street
Lincoln, NE 68506

Managing Editor: Deborah Levitov

DESCRIPTION AND INTERESTS
This professional magazine supports school library media specialists as they plan collaborative lessons and units with teachers. Its articles focus on strengthening literacy skills and teaching the research process. Circ: 12,000.

Audience: School library and media specialists, grades K–12
Frequency: 10 times each year
Website: www.schoollibrarymedia.com

FREELANCE POTENTIAL
90% written by nonstaff writers. Publishes 30 freelance submissions yearly; 20% by unpublished writers, 30% by authors who are new to the magazine. Receives 36 queries, 36 unsolicited mss yearly.

SUBMISSIONS
Query or send complete ms with bibliographic citations and brief author vita. Accepts email submissions to dlevitov@abc-clio.com (Microsoft Word attachments). Responds in 2 months.

- Articles: 1,000–1,500 words. Informational and factual articles. Topics include media education and promotion, information technology, integration of curriculum materials, and library management.
- Depts/columns: Word lengths vary. Activities, lesson plans, tips for professional growth.
- Artwork: B/W prints. Line art.

SAMPLE ISSUE
58 pages: 3 articles; 12 depts/columns. Sample copy and guidelines available at website.

- "Library Media Specialists and Assisted Technology." Article discusses the many new technologies that exist to help students with physical as well as cognitive disabilities.
- "Instructional Trends from AASL Journals: 1972–2007." Article analyzes the evolution in professional thinking over the past three decades.
- Sample dept/column: "Skill of the Month" offers examples of online education options.

RIGHTS AND PAYMENT
All rights. Written material, payment rates vary. Pays on publication. Provides 3+ copies.

➝EDITOR'S COMMENTS
Please include a short vita that will be used to explain your credentials in the byline of the article.

The School Magazine

Private Bag 3
Ryde, New South Wales 2112
Australia

Editor: Suzanne Eggins

DESCRIPTION AND INTERESTS
The School Magazine offers a diverse mix of quality short stories, poems, plays, and nonfiction for school-age children. Each of its four editions, targeted to different age and ability levels, also includes puzzles, cartoons, and activities. Circ: 150,000.

Audience: 8–12 years
Frequency: 10 times each year
Web: www.curriculumsupport.education.nsw.gov.au/services/schoolmagazine

FREELANCE POTENTIAL
70% written by nonstaff writers. Publishes 100 freelance submissions yearly; 10% by unpublished writers, 10% by authors who are new to the magazine. Receives 96 queries, 360 unsolicited mss yearly.

SUBMISSIONS
Query for nonfiction. Send complete ms for fiction. Accepts hard copy. Material is not returned. Responds via email in 6–8 weeks.

- Articles: 800–2,000 words. Informational articles. Topics include nature, pets, the environment, history, biography, science, technology, and multicultural and ethnic issues.
- Fiction: 800–2,000 words. Genres include adventure; humor; fantasy; science fiction; horror; mystery; folktales; and contemporary, multicultural, and historical fiction.
- Depts/columns: Staff written.

SAMPLE ISSUE
34 pages (no advertising): 1 article; 5 stories; 3 depts/columns; 3 poems. Guidelines and sample issue available at website.

- "If The Shoe Fits . . ." Article explores the history of shoes and the types of shoes worn in different countries.
- "Irritating Irma." Story is a humorous tale about a girl's encounter with a dragon.

RIGHTS AND PAYMENT
One-time serial rights. Written material, $270 Australian per 1,000 words. Poetry, payment rates vary. Pays on acceptance. Provides 2 contributor's copies.

➹EDITOR'S COMMENTS
Since our readers are primarily Australian children, manuscripts should address the interests and points of view of this audience.

Science Activities

Heldref Publications
1319 18th Street NW
Washington, DC 20036-1802

Managing Editor: Miriam Aronin

DESCRIPTION AND INTERESTS
One of Heldref Publications' many magazines devoted to research and practice in kindergarten through twelfth grade education, *Science Activities* publishes hands-on projects and curriculum ideas for teachers. Circ: 1,286.

Audience: Teachers, grades K–12
Frequency: Quarterly
Website: www.heldref.org

FREELANCE POTENTIAL
95% written by nonstaff writers. Publishes 25 freelance submissions yearly; 25% by unpublished writers, 50% by authors who are new to the magazine. Receives 36–48 unsolicited mss each year.

SUBMISSIONS
Send complete ms through http://mc.manuscriptcentral.com/sa only. Responds in 3 months.

- Articles: Word lengths vary. Informational and how-to articles; profiles; and personal experience pieces. Topics include hands-on projects in behavioral, biological, chemical, Earth, environmental, physical, and technological science.
- Depts/columns: Staff written.
- Artwork: B/W prints and slides. Line art.

SAMPLE ISSUE
40 pages (1% advertising): 5 articles; 2 depts/columns. Sample copy available via email request to SA@heldref.org. Guidelines available at website.

- "Exploring Predation and Animal Coloration Through Outdoor Activity." Article describes two activities to help children understand the reasons behind animals' coloring.
- "Seasonal Change Investigations." Article describes how to use technological tools to explore and report the causes and effects of seasonal changes in a pond.

RIGHTS AND PAYMENT
All rights. No payment. Provides contributors with free access to articles online.

➹EDITOR'S COMMENTS
We are interested in classroom-tested projects, experiments, and curriculum ideas. For the best chance of acceptance, please follow the detailed submissions guidelines found at our website.

Science and Children

National Science Teachers Association
1840 Wilson Boulevard
Arlington, VA 22201-3000

Managing Editor: Valyach Mayes

DESCRIPTION AND INTERESTS
Elementary school science teachers read this magazine for articles on trends, science and education news, and new program ideas for creative teaching. Circ: 18,000.
Audience: Science teachers, preK–grade 8
Frequency: 9 times each year
Website: www.nsta.org/elementaryschool

FREELANCE POTENTIAL
99% written by nonstaff writers. Publishes 25 freelance submissions yearly; 95% by unpublished writers, 50% by authors who are new to the magazine. Receives 360 unsolicited mss each year.

SUBMISSIONS
Practicing educators only. Send complete ms. Accepts email submissions to msrs@nsta.org. Responds in 6 months.

- Articles: To 1,500 words. Informational and how-to articles; profiles; interviews; reviews; and personal experience pieces. Topics include science education, teacher training and techniques, staff development, classroom activities, astronomy, biology, chemistry, physics, and Earth science.
- Depts/columns: To 1,500 words. "Helpful Hints," and "In the Schools," to 500 words.
- Other: Submit seasonal material 1 year in advance.

SAMPLE ISSUE
76 pages (2% advertising): 7 articles; 8 depts/columns; 2 calendars. Sample copy, free. Guidelines available at website.

- "Breezy Power: From Wind to Energy." Article outlines a lesson that combines the science concepts of renewable energy and producing electricity with the technology concepts of design and the environment.
- "YouTube in the Classroom." Article offers ideas for capitalizing on students' appetite for YouTube to stimulate learning.

RIGHTS AND PAYMENT
All rights. No payment. Provides 2 contributor's copies.

⇨EDITOR'S COMMENTS
We want to hear what's working well in your classroom. Writers should be aware that all submissions go through a peer review process to validate their accuracy.

The Science Teacher

National Science Teachers Association
1840 Wilson Boulevard
Arlington, VA 22201-3000

Managing Editor: Stephanie Liberatore

DESCRIPTION AND INTERESTS
This publication of the National Science Teachers Association is filled with information and resources that help high school science teachers do their jobs better. Circ: 29,000.
Audience: Science teachers, grades 7–12
Frequency: 9 times each year
Website: www.nsta.org/highschool

FREELANCE POTENTIAL
100% written by nonstaff writers. Of the freelance submissions published yearly, 70% are by unpublished writers, 50% are by authors who are new to the magazine. Receives 360 unsolicited mss yearly.

SUBMISSIONS
Send complete ms. Accepts electronic submissions via http://mc.manuscriptcentral.com/nsta. Responds in 1 month.

- Articles: 2,000 words. Informational articles; classroom projects; and experiments. Topics include science education, biology, Earth science, computers, social issues, space technology, and sports medicine.
- Depts/columns: 500 words. Science updates, association news, science careers.
- Artwork: 5x7 or larger B/W prints. Line art, tables, and diagrams.

SAMPLE ISSUE
84 pages (40% advertising): 6 articles; 6 depts/columns. Sample copy, $4.25 with 9x12 SASE ($.77 postage). Guidelines available in each issue and at website.

- "Mentoring New Science Teachers." Article addresses the importance of mentoring, and provides a checklist to help assess the skills of new teachers.
- Sample dept/column: "Idea Bank" offers tips and techniques for creative teaching.

RIGHTS AND PAYMENT
First rights. No payment. Provides contributor's copies.

⇨EDITOR'S COMMENTS
We accept material from experienced science teachers or professionals only. Publishing in our journal is your opportunity to make a significant contribution to science programs at your level of practice. Your article should share the complete experience, including what you did, what worked, and ways to improve.

Science Weekly

P.O. Box 70638
Chevy Chase, MD 20813

Publisher: Dr. Claude Mayberry

DESCRIPTION AND INTERESTS
Science Weekly is an interactive instructional tool for parents and teachers that helps children grow in their love and knowledge of science. Its six editions are geared to different reading and ability levels up to grade six, and focus on biology, life and physical sciences, and technology. Circ: 200,000.
Audience: Grades K–6
Frequency: 14 times each year
Website: www.scienceweekly.com

FREELANCE POTENTIAL
100% written by nonstaff writers. Publishes 15 freelance submissions yearly; 5% by authors who are new to the magazine. Receives 3,000–5,000 queries yearly.

SUBMISSIONS
Send résumé only. All work is assigned to writers living in the District of Columbia, Maryland, or Virginia. Accepts hard copy. SASE. Response time varies.

- Articles: Word lengths vary. Informational articles. Topics include space exploration, ecology, the environment, nature, biology, the human body, meteorology, oceanography, navigation, nutrition, photography, physical science, and secret codes.
- Other: Theme-related puzzles, games, and activities.

SAMPLE ISSUE
4 pages (no advertising): 1 article; 6 activities. Sample copy, theme list, and writers' guidelines available.

- "Marsupials." Article describes the different animals that belong to this group and how they live, eat, and raise their young.
- "Coral Reefs." Article details how coral reefs are made and which animals make their homes in them.

RIGHTS AND PAYMENT
All rights. All material, payment rates vary. Pays on publication.

➥EDITOR'S COMMENTS
We are committed to publishing a quality, research-based magazine that covers vibrant topics to engage our young readers. Since we work on assignment only, please send us your résumé if you live in Washington, D.C., Maryland, or Virginia.

Scouting

Boy Scouts of America
1325 West Walnut Hill Lane
P.O. Box 152079
Irving, TX 75015-2079

Managing Editor: Scott Daniels

DESCRIPTION AND INTERESTS
Scouting is read by Scout leaders, volunteers, and others involved with Boy Scouts of America. It provides information on the organization, ideas for leadership training, and keys to successful programs. Circ: 1 million.
Audience: Scout leaders and parents
Frequency: 5 times each year
Website: www.scoutingmagazine.org

FREELANCE POTENTIAL
80% written by nonstaff writers. Publishes 4–6 freelance submissions yearly; 5–10% by authors who are new to the magazine. Receives 150 queries yearly.

SUBMISSIONS
Query with outline. Accepts hard copy. SASE. Responds in 3 weeks.

- Articles: 500–1,200 words. Informational and how-to articles; profiles; humor; and personal experience pieces. Topics include Scout programs, leadership, volunteering, nature, social issues and trends, and history.
- Depts/columns: 500–700 words. Family activities, outdoor activities, short profiles, scouting news.
- Other: Quizzes, puzzles, and games.

SAMPLE ISSUE
48 pages (33% advertising): 4 articles; 6 depts/columns. Sample copy, $2.50 with 9x12 SASE. Guidelines available at website.

- "As Good as It Gets." Article reports on a gathering of elite Scouts in Wyoming to take part in the largest service project in U.S. Forest Service history.
- "Show of Faith." Article explains the religious emblems that are available for Scouts to earn, and explains how to start a discussion of religion in one's own Scouting group.
- Sample dept/column: "Outdoor Smarts" offers instruction in five basic canoeing maneuvers.

RIGHTS AND PAYMENT
First North American serial rights. Written material, $300–$800. Pays on acceptance. Provides 2 contributor's copies.

➥EDITOR'S COMMENTS
Most of our freelance articles come from volunteer and professional Scouters. We are read by adult leaders, not the Scouts themselves.

Seattle's Child

4303 198th Street NW
Lynnwood, WA 98036

Managing Editor: Liz Gillespie

DESCRIPTION AND INTERESTS
Seattle's Child is a family-friendly magazine covering issues and topics of interest to parents living in the Seattle region. It publishes articles on parenting, family health, child development, social issues, and recreational opportunities in the area. Circ: 80,000.

Audience: Parents
Frequency: Monthly
Website: www.seattleschild.com

FREELANCE POTENTIAL
80% written by nonstaff writers. Publishes 30 freelance submissions yearly; 10% by unpublished writers, 25% by authors who are new to the magazine. Receives 120+ queries yearly.

SUBMISSIONS
Query with outline. Accepts hard copy, email queries to editor@seattleschild.com, and simultaneous submissions if identified. SASE. Responds in 1 month.

- Articles: Word lengths vary. Informational and how-to articles; and personal experience pieces. Topics include family, parenting, social issues, health, fitness, nutrition, regional news, family travel, and recreation.
- Depts/columns: Word lengths vary. Profiles, cooking, and media reviews.

SAMPLE ISSUE
46 pages (30% advertising): 6 articles; 4 depts/columns. Sample copy, $3 with 9x12 SASE. Guidelines and theme list available.

- "The Circumcision Question." Article examines the factors to consider when deciding whether to circumcise a baby boy.
- Sample dept/column: "Educating Mom" explains why parents should encourage kids to get involved in sports.

RIGHTS AND PAYMENT
Rights vary. Written material, $100–$450. Pays 30 days after publication. Provides 2 contributor's copies.

➥EDITOR'S COMMENTS
We are open to articles on a variety of topics, as long as they are of interest to and informative for parents in our area. We insist that all articles focus on local issues and use local sources. If you are not based in the Seattle region, you must still be able to do this in order to be considered.

Seek

Standard Publishing Company
8805 Governor's Hill Drive, Suite 400
Cincinnati, OH 45249

Editor: Margaret K. Williams

DESCRIPTION AND INTERESTS
Inspirational stories and Bible lessons make up the content of these pamphlets that are geared to young adults. Written from a Christian perspective, *Seek* is used in Sunday school lessons. Circ: 27,000.

Audience: YA–Adult
Frequency: Weekly
Website: www.standardpub.com

FREELANCE POTENTIAL
80% written by nonstaff writers. Publishes 150 freelance submissions yearly; 50% by authors who are new to the magazine. Receives 50 unsolicited mss yearly.

SUBMISSIONS
Send complete ms. Prefers email to seek@standardpub.com; will accept hard copy. No simultaneous submissions. SASE. Responds in 3–6 months.

- Articles: 600–1,200 words. Inspirational, devotional, and personal experience pieces. Topics include religious and contemporary issues, Christian living, coping with moral and ethical dilemmas, and controversial subjects.
- Fiction: 600–1,200 words. Stories about Christian living, moral and ethical problems, controversial topics, and dealing with contemporary life challenges.
- Other: Submit seasonal material 1 year in advance.

SAMPLE ISSUE
8 pages (no advertising): 2 articles; 1 Bible lesson. Sample copy, free with 6x9 SASE. Guidelines and theme list available.

- "Are You Running Low on Hope Today?" Article explains the need to turn to God when faced with life's trials and tribulations.
- "A Mother's Love." Article discusses the strength of Mary's love for her son and what one can learn from her experiences.

RIGHTS AND PAYMENT
First and second rights. Written material, $.05–$.07 per word. Pays on acceptance. Provides 5 contributor's copies.

➥EDITOR'S COMMENTS
We are interested in inspirational fiction and nonfiction submissions that correspond to our themed issues.

Seventeen

300 West 57th Street, 17th Floor
New York, NY 10019

Editor

DESCRIPTION AND INTERESTS
Targeting teenage girls, *Seventeen* gives its readers information on fashion, health, beauty, relationships, and boys. It also publishes interviews with fashion leaders and celebrities, and articles on pop culture. Circ: 2 million.

Audience: Girls, 13–21 years
Frequency: Monthly
Website: www.seventeen.com

FREELANCE POTENTIAL
20% written by nonstaff writers. Publishes 20 freelance submissions yearly; 5% by unpublished writers, 40% by authors who are new to the magazine. Receives 46 queries, 200 unsolicited mss yearly.

SUBMISSIONS
Query with outline and clips or writing samples for nonfiction. Send complete ms for fiction. Accepts hard copy and simultaneous submissions if identified. SASE. Response time varies.

- Articles: 650–3,000 words. Informational and self-help articles; profiles; and personal experience pieces. Topics include relationships, dating, family issues, current events, social concerns, friendship, pop culture, fashion, health and fitness, and beauty.
- Fiction: 1,000–3,000 words. Stories that feature female teenage experiences.
- Depts/columns: 500–1,000 words. Fashion, beauty, health, and fitness.
- Other: Submit seasonal material 6 months in advance.

SAMPLE ISSUE
166 pages (50% advertising): 7 articles; 24 depts/columns. Sample copy, $2.99 at newsstands. Guidelines available.

- "Total Betrayal." Article reports on a coach who secretly took photos of one of his female players.
- Sample dept/column: "Dating" offers ideas on meeting new boys.

RIGHTS AND PAYMENT
First rights. Written material, $1–$1.50 per word. Pays on acceptance.

➛EDITOR'S COMMENTS
We pride ourselves on being current with everything—from fashion trends to dating advice to the hottest celebrities in our interviews. We expect our writers to be, too.

Sharing the Victory

Fellowship of Christian Athletes
8701 Leeds Road
Kansas City, MO 64129

Editorial Assistant: Ashley Burns

DESCRIPTION AND INTERESTS
Published by the Fellowship of Christian Athletes (FCA), *Sharing the Victory* seeks to inform, inspire, and involve coaches and athletes so that "they may make an impact for Jesus Christ." Circ: 80,000.

Audience: Athletes & coaches, grades 7 and up
Frequency: 9 times each year
Website: www.sharingthevictory.com

FREELANCE POTENTIAL
40% written by nonstaff writers. Publishes 20 freelance submissions yearly; 25% by unpublished writers, 10% by authors who are new to the magazine. Receives 48 queries and unsolicited mss yearly.

SUBMISSIONS
Query with outline and writing samples; or send complete ms. Accepts hard copy. Availability of artwork improves chance of acceptance. SASE. Response time varies.

- Articles: To 1,200 words. Informational articles; profiles; interviews; and personal experience pieces. Topics include sports, athletes, coaches, competition, training, focus, faith, missions, and Christian education.
- Depts/columns: Staff written.
- Artwork: Color prints.
- Other: Submit seasonal material 3–4 months in advance.

SAMPLE ISSUE
38 pages (30% advertising): 5 articles; 11 depts/columns. Sample copy, $1 with 9x12 SASE (3 first-class stamps). Guidelines available.

- "On a Mission." Q&A with Major League Baseball pitcher Albert Pujols discusses his charity work and his faith.
- "Pure & Simple." Article takes a realistic look at male sexual purity.
- "The Master." Article reveals how a late-life encounter with Christ transformed legendary sports broadcaster Pat Summerall.

RIGHTS AND PAYMENT
First serial rights. Articles, $150–$400. Pays on publication.

➛EDITOR'S COMMENTS
All story submissions should have an FCA connection. We are always seeking profiles of female Christian athletes and coaches (who are members of the FCA, of course).

Shine Brightly

P.O. Box 87334
Canton, MI 48187

Editor: Sara Lynne Hilton

DESCRIPTION AND INTERESTS
Published by the GEM Girls' Clubs program, *Shine Brightly* publishes articles that empower young girls and help them accept and lead a Christian life of serving God. Circ: 15,500.

Audience: Girls, 9–14 years
Frequency: 9 times each year
Website: www.gemsgc.org

FREELANCE POTENTIAL
30% written by nonstaff writers. Publishes 20 freelance submissions yearly; 15% by unpublished writers, 90% by new authors. Receives 500 unsolicited mss yearly.

SUBMISSIONS
Send complete ms. Accepts hard copy and simultaneous submissions if identified. SASE. Responds in 1 month.

- Articles: 50–500 words. Informational and how-to articles; profiles; humor; and personal experience pieces. Topics include community service, stewardship, contemporary social issues, family and friend relationships, and peer pressure.
- Fiction: 400–900 words. Genres include contemporary and science fiction; romance, mystery, and adventure. Also publishes stories about nature, animals, and sports.
- Depts/columns: Staff written.
- Artwork: 5x7 or larger B/W or color prints.
- Other: Puzzles, activities, and cartoons.

SAMPLE ISSUE
24 pages (no advertising): 4 articles; 1 story; 3 depts/columns; 2 activities. Sample copy, $1 with 9x12 SASE ($.75 postage). Writers' guidelines available.

- "Green Team." Article shows how people can make a significant change in the world by altering their buying habits.
- "Out Came the Sun." Story finds a young girl, dealing with the death of her grandfather, finding solace in the lessons he taught her.

RIGHTS AND PAYMENT
First, second, and simultaneous rights. Articles and fiction, $.02–$.05 per word. Other material, payment rates vary. Pays on publication. Provides 2 contributor's copies.

✎EDITOR'S COMMENTS
Articles should be fun but informative. Stories should be inspiring and empowering.

Single Mother

National Organization of Single Mothers
P.O. Box 68
Midland, NC 28107-0068

Editor: Andrea Engber

DESCRIPTION AND INTERESTS
This online magazine is dedicated to the challenges and joys of being a single mother. It features informative articles, resources, personal essays, and lots of support for women raising children without a partner. Hits per month: 3,000–5,000.

Audience: Single mothers
Frequency: Monthly
Website: www.singlemothers.org

FREELANCE POTENTIAL
10% written by nonstaff writers. Publishes 6 freelance submissions yearly. Receives 12–24 queries and unsolicited mss yearly.

SUBMISSIONS
Query or send complete ms. Accepts hard copy. SASE. Response time varies.

- Articles: Word lengths vary. Informational articles; essays; and opinion and personal experience pieces. Topics include parenting, money and time management, absent dads, dating, handling ex-families, death, pregnancy and childbirth, paternity, custody, and visitation rights.
- Depts/columns: Word lengths vary. News, book reviews, advice.

SAMPLE ISSUE
Sample issues available at website.

- "Single Moms by Choice or Circumstance—Required Reading." Essay presents "inescapable truths," both good and bad, about being a single mother.
- "So Overwhelmed You Can't See Straight?" Essay outlines the importance of recognizing that sometimes one person can't do it all, and that it's OK to ask for help.

RIGHTS AND PAYMENT
Rights vary. Written material, payment rates vary. Payment policy varies.

✎EDITOR'S COMMENTS
We are a magazine (and resource website) dedicated to the subject of single motherhood and supporting single mothers with information, empathy, and advice. Each of our contributors are single mothers, either through divorce, separation, or death; or because of a decision to have a child without a partner. We care less about how well you write than what it is you have to offer.

Sisterhood Agenda

524 Ridge Street
Newark, NJ 07104

Editor: Angela D. Coleman

DESCRIPTION AND INTERESTS

Targeting women and girls of African descent, *Sisterhood Agenda* is committed to uplifting and aiding the self-development of its readers. It appears in both online and print versions. Circ: 500,000.

Audience: 13–32 years
Frequency: Quarterly
Website: www.sisterhoodagenda.com

FREELANCE POTENTIAL

75% written by nonstaff writers. Publishes 80 freelance submissions yearly; 75% by unpublished writers, 90% by authors who are new to the magazine. Receives 1,000 unsolicited mss each year.

SUBMISSIONS

Send complete ms. Accepts email submissions to acoleman@sisterhoodagenda.com (Microsoft Word attachments). Availability of artwork improves chance of acceptance. Response time varies.

- Articles: To 500 words. Informational articles; profiles; and photo-essays. Topics include Africa, ancestry, heritage, history, current events, health, nutrition, music, fashion, beauty, self-esteem, fitness, technology, life skills, celebrities, and community service.
- Fiction: Word lengths vary. Genres include multicultural, ethnic, and inspirational fiction.
- Depts/columns: First-person essays; to 300 words. News briefs, book reviews, hair tips, and affirmations; word lengths vary.
- Artwork: Digital images at 300 dpi.
- Other: Poetry, to 15 lines.

SAMPLE ISSUE

50 pages: 6 articles; 23 depts/columns. Sample copy, guidelines, and editorial calendar available at website.

- "The Hidden Buying Power of African American Women." Article profiles black women and their purchasing power.
- "Shaping Up With Your Sisters." Article extols the benefits of working out with others.

RIGHTS AND PAYMENT

One-time rights. No payment.

➡EDITOR'S COMMENTS

We accept a variety of material on a wide range of topics, as long as the information benefits black girls and young women.

Six78th

P.O. Box 450
Newark, CA 94560

Editorial Director: Carol S. Rothchild

DESCRIPTION AND INTERESTS

Six78th, a lifestyle magazine for girls in middle school (its title refers to sixth, seventh, and eighth grades), strives to be a representational voice of tween culture. It presents articles on topics that are not only of interest to its readership, but also encourage parents and teachers to help girls navigate personal and school success. Circ: Unavailable.

Audience: Girls, 10–14 years
Frequency: 6 times each year
Website: www.six78th.com

FREELANCE POTENTIAL

12% written by nonstaff writers. Publishes 5–10 freelance submissions yearly; 5% by unpublished writers, 5% by authors who are new to the magazine. Receives 60–120 queries each year.

SUBMISSIONS

Query. Accepts email queries to carol@six78th.com. Responds in 2 months.

- Articles: Word lengths vary. Informational and self-help articles; profiles; interviews; and personal experience pieces. Topics include school, current events, health and fitness, sports, music, entertainment, popular culture, celebrities, and social issues.
- Depts/columns: Word lengths vary. Reviews, nutrition, fashion, friendship.

SAMPLE ISSUE

58 pages: 6 articles; 13 depts/columns. Sample copy, $4.50 with 9x12 SASE. Writers' guidelines available.

- "Abigail Breslin." Interview with the 12-year-old actress discusses her latest film and her favorite things.
- Sample dept/column: "Oops & Ohs" contains anecdotes about readers' most embarrassing moments.

RIGHTS AND PAYMENT

Rights vary. Written material, payment rates vary. Pays on publication. Provides 5 contributor's copies.

➡EDITOR'S COMMENTS

Our entire staff genuinely believes in protecting girls from growing up sooner than they are ready. Therefore, we offer age-appropriate content with a stylish design that makes readers feel like a part of something big.

Skating

United States Figure Skating Association
20 First Street
Colorado Springs, CO 80906

Director of Publications: Troy Schwindt

DESCRIPTION AND INTERESTS
Figure skaters and members of the U.S. Figure Skating Association read this magazine for news from the skating world, profiles of professional and amateur skaters, and articles on techniques, training, and coaching. Circ: 45,000.

Audience: 5 years–Adult
Frequency: 11 times each year
Website: www.usfigureskating.org

FREELANCE POTENTIAL
70% written by nonstaff writers. Publishes 15 freelance submissions yearly; 10% by unpublished writers, 20% by authors who are new to the magazine. Receives 72 queries and unsolicited mss yearly.

SUBMISSIONS
Query with résumé, clips or writing samples, and photo ideas; or send complete ms. Accepts hard copy, MacIntosh zip disk submissions, and email to skatingmagazine@usfigureskating.org. SASE. Responds in 1 month.

- Articles: 750–2,000 words. Informational articles; profiles; and interviews. Topics include association news, competitions, techniques, personalities, and training.
- Depts/columns: 600–800 words. Competition results, profiles of skaters and coaches, sports medicine, fitness, and technique tips.
- Artwork: B/W and color prints, slides, or transparencies; digital images at 300 dpi.

SAMPLE ISSUE
56 pages: 5 articles; 11 depts/columns. Sample copy, $3 with 9x12 SASE. Writers' guidelines available.

- "Fundamental Difference." Article discusses the 2009 World Championships and how Evan Lysacek's focus on the fundamentals earned him the championship.
- Sample dept/column: "Ask Mr. Edge" looks at technical issues related to boots and blades.

RIGHTS AND PAYMENT
First serial rights. Articles, $75–$150. Depts/columns, $75. Artwork, payment rates vary. Pays on publication. Provides 5–10 copies.

➡ EDITOR'S COMMENTS
All writers must be well-versed in figure skating and/or the association.

Skipping Stones
A Multicultural Magazine

P.O. Box 3939
Eugene, OR 97403-0939

Editor: Arun N. Toké

DESCRIPTION AND INTERESTS
The articles in *Skipping Stones* facilitate an exchange of ideas and experiences among children and adults from diverse cultural and socioeconomic backgrounds. Circ: 2,500.

Audience: 7–17 years
Frequency: 5 times each year
Website: www.skippingstones.org

FREELANCE POTENTIAL
90% written by nonstaff writers. Publishes 175–200 freelance submissions yearly; 60% by unpublished writers, 75% by new authors. Receives 3,600 unsolicited mss yearly.

SUBMISSIONS
Send complete ms with author information. Accepts hard copy, Macintosh disk submissions, and email to editor@skippingstones.org (Microsoft Word attachments). SASE. Responds in 4–6 months.

- Articles: 750–1,000 words. Informational articles; photo-essays; profiles; interviews; humor; and personal experience pieces. Topics include cultural and religious celebrations, architecture, living abroad, family, careers, disabilities, sustainable living, nature, technology, parenting, and activism.
- Fiction: To 1,000 words. Genres include multicultural fiction and folktales.
- Depts/columns: 100–200 words. Health issues, book reviews, school topics, Q&As.
- Other: Puzzles and games. Poetry by children, to 30 lines. Submit seasonal material 3–4 months in advance.

SAMPLE ISSUE
36 pages (no advertising): 17 articles; 1 story; 7 depts/columns; 12 poems. Sample copy, $6 with 9x12 SASE (4 first-class stamps). Guidelines available at website.

- "Train Trip to Mississippi." Article tells of the author's experience with segregation in 1955.
- "Reflections from Costa Rica." Article looks at a girl's missionary trip to Costa Rica.

RIGHTS AND PAYMENT
First and non-exclusive reprint rights. No payment. Provides author's copies and discounts.

➡ EDITOR'S COMMENTS
Although we do accept short stories, we encourage creative, informational stories rather than true fiction.

SLAP

High Speed Productions
1303 Underwood Avenue
San Francisco, CA 94124

Editor: Mark Whiteley

DESCRIPTION AND INTERESTS
Now offered exclusively online, *SLAP* serves a readership of die-hard skateboarders with information they need, including techniques, gear, and profiles of skaters. It also includes articles on the music, art, and lifestyle popular with this demographic. Hits per month: 200,000.
Audience: YA
Frequency: Updated daily
Website: www.slapmagazine.com

FREELANCE POTENTIAL
40% written by nonstaff writers. Publishes 24 freelance submissions yearly; 20% by unpublished writers.

SUBMISSIONS
Send complete ms. Accepts hard copy, disk submissions, and simultaneous submissions if identified. Availability of artwork improves chance of acceptance. SASE. Responds in 2 months.

- Articles: Word lengths vary. Informational and how-to articles; profiles; interviews; and personal experience pieces. Topics include skateboarding techniques, equipment, and competition; music; art; and pop culture.
- Depts/columns: Word lengths vary. Media reviews, interviews, gear, gossip, and skateboard tricks.
- Artwork: 35mm B/W negatives; color prints and transparencies. Line art.
- Other: Photo-essays, cartoons, and contests.

SAMPLE ISSUE
Sample copy available at website. Guidelines and editorial calendar available.

- "Snowblind in South America with 5boro and Friends." Article recounts the author's trip to Bogota, Columbia, to check out the culture, food, drink, and of course, skateboarding.
- Sample dept/column: "Behind the Lens" offers the inside dish on what happened when the authors attempted to film some skateboarding video and encountered a construction worker on meth.

RIGHTS AND PAYMENT
First rights. All material, payment rates vary. Pays on publication. Provides 1 copy.

◆EDITOR'S COMMENTS
Since we're online exclusively now, we want more photos and video with your article.

South Florida Parenting

1701 Green Road, Suite B
Deerfield Beach, FL 33064

Editor: Kyara Lomer

DESCRIPTION AND INTERESTS
Covering everything from parenting issues and family travel to education and regional events, this magazine offers comprehensive information of interest to parents in southern Florida. Circ: 110,000.
Audience: Parents
Frequency: Monthly
Website: www.sfparenting.com

FREELANCE POTENTIAL
85% written by nonstaff writers. Publishes 90 freelance submissions yearly; 10% by authors who are new to the magazine. Receives 996 unsolicited mss yearly.

SUBMISSIONS
Prefers complete ms; will accept query. Accepts hard copy and email submissions to krlomer@tribune.com. SASE. Responds in 2–3 months.

- Articles: 800–1,500 words. Informational and how-to articles; profiles; interviews; and personal experience pieces. Topics include family life, travel, parenting, education, leisure, music, health, and regional events and activities.
- Depts/columns: To 750 words. Family finances, health, nutrition, infant care, and pre-teen issues.

SAMPLE ISSUE
122 pages (60% advertising): 6 articles; 6 depts/columns. Guidelines available.

- "No Strings Attached." Article discusses how parents can take a step back so children can learn their independence.
- Sample dept/column: "Family Travel" spotlights Branson, Missouri, as a great place for a family vacation.

RIGHTS AND PAYMENT
One-time regional rights. Written material, $50–$300. Pays on publication. Provides contributor's copies upon request.

◆EDITOR'S COMMENTS
We prefer features that use sources and settings in South Florida. We rarely work with writers outside the region; however, we may consider insightful, captivating essays and features, particularly if they deal with universal themes or topics.

South Jersey Mom

P.O. Box 2413
Vineland, NJ 08362-2413

Editor: Adrienne Richardson

DESCRIPTION AND INTERESTS

"Sharing real stories from moms who have been there and done that," *South Jersey Mom* sets itself apart from other parenting magazines by featuring inspiring stories, debates over hot parenting issues, and local opinions about national issues. Circ: 38,000.

Audience: Parents
Frequency: Monthly
Website: www.southjerseymom.com

FREELANCE POTENTIAL

98% written by nonstaff writers. Publishes 50–75 freelance submissions yearly; 40% by unpublished writers, 10% by authors who are new to the magazine. Receives 180 queries each year.

SUBMISSIONS

Query with 2 writing samples. Accepts email queries to adrienne@southjerseymom.com. Response time varies.

- Articles: Word lengths vary. Informational articles; profiles; and personal experience pieces. Topics include parenting, trends, family issues, pregnancy, technology, education, exercise, safety, sports, and recreation.
- Depts/columns: Word lengths vary. Health topics, gear, technology.

SAMPLE ISSUE

32 pages: 7 articles; 12 depts/columns. Sample copy available at website. Writers' guidelines and editorial calendar available.

- "Is Cleaning Your Home Making Your Family Sick?" Article reviews the most hazardous household chemicals and their dangers and offers examples of safer alternatives.
- "Black History Month." Article recognizes area mothers and children doing great deeds in honor of Black History Month.
- Sample dept/column: "Penny-Pinching Pointers" suggests websites that allow bartering and swapping of unwanted products.

RIGHTS AND PAYMENT

Rights vary. No payment.

➫EDITOR'S COMMENTS

Our stories are about regional children and families as well as family-friendly businesses. Articles are written by local writers using sources and settings in South Jersey.

Southwest Florida Parent & Child

2442 Dr. Martin Luther King Jr. Boulevard
Fort Myers, FL 33901

Editor: Pamela Smith Hayford

DESCRIPTION AND INTERESTS

Parents in the southwestern region of Florida turn to this magazine for information on parenting and family issues and child development. Fun topics such as children's fashion, crafts, local family activities, and recreational opportunities are also covered. Circ: 23,000.

Audience: Parents
Frequency: Monthly
Website: www.gulfcoast.momslikeme.com

FREELANCE POTENTIAL

75% written by nonstaff writers. Publishes 160 freelance submissions yearly; 5% by unpublished writers, 25% by authors who are new to the magazine. Receives 275 queries and unsolicited mss yearly.

SUBMISSIONS

Query or send complete ms. Accepts email submissions to pamela@swflparentchild.com. Response time varies.

- Articles: To 500 words. Informational articles; profiles; and personal experience pieces. Topics include family issues, parenting, education, travel, sports, health, fitness, computers, and social and regional issues.
- Depts/columns: To 500 words. Dining, travel, parenting, education, and nutrition.

SAMPLE ISSUE

90 pages (15% advertising): 3 articles; 17 depts/columns. Guidelines available.

- "Even a Toddler Can Volunteer." Article outlines the many ways that kids can volunteer with charitable organizations.
- "Hybrid Schools." Article profiles two Florida schools that are combining homeschooling with brick-and-mortar class time.
- Sample dept/column: "Kids Cooking" offers ideas for putting something a little different in kids' lunchboxes.

RIGHTS AND PAYMENT

All rights. Written material, $25–$200. Pays on publication.

➫EDITOR'S COMMENTS

We look for articles that will interest as well as inform parents. Please note that all submissions must relate or be localized to the southwestern Florida region. We are open to submissions from new writers, as long as others can learn from what you have to say.

Spaceports & Spidersilk

Editor: Marcie Lynn Tentchoff

DESCRIPTION AND INTERESTS
Like its print cousin, *Beyond Centauri,* this online magazine focuses on science fiction (and fact), fantasy, and "Ewwww, gross!" stories. Hits per month: Unavailable.

Audience: 8–17 years
Frequency: Continually updated
Website: www.samsdotpublishing.com/spacesilk/main.htm

FREELANCE POTENTIAL
100% written by nonstaff writers. Publishes 60 freelance submissions yearly; 25% by unpublished writers, 25% by authors who are new to the magazine. Receives 360–480 unsolicited mss yearly.

SUBMISSIONS
Send complete ms. Accepts email submissions to spacesilk@yahoo.com (fiction and nonfiction as RTF attachments, poetry in body of email; include "Submission: Title" in subject line). Response time varies.

- Articles: To 800 words. Interviews and essays. Topics include science and the environment.
- Fiction: To 2,000 words. Genres include fantasy, science fiction, and mild horror.
- Artwork: B/W and color line art.
- Other: Quizzes. Poetry, to 25 lines.

SAMPLE ISSUE
5 stories; 1 article; 6 poems; 1 serial. Sample copy and guidelines available at website.

- "Round the Bend." Story tells of a young man who helps an old witch get home, and is blissfully rewarded.
- "Frosty Man." Story tells how a magical snowman brings peace to a boy and his dad, if only for a night.

RIGHTS AND PAYMENT
First or reprint and electronic rights. Written material, $2 for original, $1 for reprints. Cover artwork, $10. Pays on acceptance.

➡️EDITOR'S COMMENTS
We want spooky, not terrifying. Or, to put it another way, we want campfire stories that will allow you to sleep in the tent afterwards. As always, we need more stories about outer space adventures, especially those centering on problems faced by adolescents living in space colonies.

Sparkle

P.O. Box 7259
Grand Rapids, MI 49510

Senior Editor: Sara Lynne Hilton

DESCRIPTION AND INTERESTS
Geared to girls in first through third grades, this Christian magazine strives to encourage its readers to live life like Christ and serve the needs of others at home, in school, and in their communities. Circ: 7,000.

Audience: Girls, 6–9 years
Frequency: 6 times each year
Website: www.gemsgc.org

FREELANCE POTENTIAL
80% written by nonstaff writers. Publishes 20 freelance submissions yearly; 80% by unpublished writers, 90% by authors who are new to the magazine. Receives 100 unsolicited mss each year.

SUBMISSIONS
Send complete ms. Accepts hard copy. SASE. Responds in 4–6 weeks.

- Articles: 100–400 words. Informational articles. Topics include animals, sports, music, musicians, famous people, interaction with family and friends, service projects, and dealing with school work.
- Fiction: 100–400 words. Genres include adventure, mystery, and contemporary fiction.
- Other: Puzzles, games, recipes, party ideas, short humorous pieces, cartoons, and inexpensive craft projects.

SAMPLE ISSUE
16 pages (no advertising): 2 articles; 1 story; 5 activities; 1 Bible lesson; 1 poem. Sample copy, $1 with 9x12 SASE. Guidelines and theme list available.

- "They Did What?" Article highlights some of the craziest world records and suggests small things readers can do to make a big difference.
- "The Cupcake Problem." Story tells of a girl who asks God for help in dealing with a classmate who isn't always nice.

RIGHTS AND PAYMENT
Rights vary. Articles, $20. Other material, payment rates vary. Pays on publication. Provides 2 contributor's copies.

➡️EDITOR'S COMMENTS
We like to see articles that connect with our audience and build Christian character. Stories should be realistic and delightful to read, yet educational and inspirational.

Spider
The Magazine for Children

Cricket Magazine Group
70 East Lake Street, Suite 300
Chicago, IL 60601

Submissions Editor

DESCRIPTION AND INTERESTS
Established in 1994, this member of the Cricket Magazine Group publishes short stories, poetry, folktales, and nonfiction articles for young children. Circ: 60,000.

Audience: 6–9 years
Frequency: 9 times each year
Website: www.cricketmag.com
   www.spidermagkids.com

FREELANCE POTENTIAL
85% written by nonstaff writers. Publishes 60 freelance submissions yearly; 35% by unpublished writers, 35% by authors who are new to the magazine. Receives 1,800 unsolicited mss each year.

SUBMISSIONS
Send complete ms; include bibliography for nonfiction. Accepts hard copy and simultaneous submissions if identified. SASE. Responds in 6 months.

- Articles: 300–800 words. Informational and how-to articles; profiles; and interviews. Topics include nature, animals, science, technology, history, multicultural issues, foreign cultures, and the environment.
- Fiction: 300–1,000 words. Easy-to-read stories. Genres include humor; fantasy; fairy tales; folktales; and realistic, historical, and science fiction.
- Other: Recipes, crafts, puzzles, games, and math and word activities. Poetry, to 20 lines.

SAMPLE ISSUE
34 pages (no advertising): 1 article; 4 stories; 3 activities; 3 poems. Sample copy, $5 with 9x12 SASE. Guidelines available at website.

- "Boogers at Work." Article uses humor to explain the reason we have mucus in our noses and how "boogers" are formed.
- "King for a Day." Story relates a King's Day celebration that goes sour for a young boy who tries to cheat.

RIGHTS AND PAYMENT
All rights. Articles and fiction, to $.25 per word. Poetry, to $3 per line. Pays on publication. Provides 2 contributor's copies.

➡ EDITOR'S COMMENTS
We would like to see more submissions of science fiction stories, as well as original fairy tales.

SportingKid

2050 Vista Parkway
West Palm Beach, FL 33411

Managing Editor: Greg Bach

DESCRIPTION AND INTERESTS
Written for parents, coaches, and others who work with children in organized sports, this magazine focuses on "building the value of sports" while ensuring kids have fun and rewarding experiences. Circ: 300,000.

Audience: Parents, coaches, and officials
Frequency: Quarterly
Website: www.nays.org/sportingkid

FREELANCE POTENTIAL
15% written by nonstaff writers. Publishes 10 freelance submissions yearly; 5% by unpublished writers, 15% by authors who are new to the magazine. Receives 180 queries, 60 unsolicited mss yearly.

SUBMISSIONS
Query or send complete ms. Accepts email submissions to sportingkid@nays.org. Responds in 1 month.

- Articles: To 1,000 words. Informational and how-to articles; and profiles. Topics include youth sports, coaching, parenting, officiating, health, and safety.
- Depts/columns: 750 words. New product information, the culture of youth sports, and coaching and parenting tips.

SAMPLE ISSUE
32 pages: 7 articles; 4 depts/columns.

- "Wood vs. Metal Bats." Article takes a look at the heated debate over which type of bat is safest for children.
- "Big Things Come In Small Packages." Article profiles a 14-year-old basketball player who is among her league's leading scorers.
- Sample dept/column: "Perspective" shares the valuable lessons that Hank Paulson, the CEO of Goldman Sachs, learned on the football field.

RIGHTS AND PAYMENT
First and electronic rights. Written material, payment rates vary. Pays on publication.

➡ EDITOR'S COMMENTS
Tip-oriented articles are a continual need, specifically those that help coaches plan practices and manage their game day responsibilities. Articles explaining how officials can perform their jobs more effectively are always welcome.

Sports Illustrated Kids

Time & Life Building
1271 Avenue of the Americas, 32nd Floor
New York, NY 10020

Managing Editor: Bob Der

DESCRIPTION AND INTERESTS
This sports magazine caters to the younger sports fan. It provides information on professional sports and athletes, to be sure, but it also puts an emphasis on young athletes and teen sports. Circ: 1.1 million.

Audience: 8–14 years
Frequency: Monthly
Website: www.sikids.com

FREELANCE POTENTIAL
3–5% written by nonstaff writers. Publishes 1–2 freelance submissions yearly. Receives 40–50 queries and unsolicited mss yearly.

SUBMISSIONS
Query or send complete ms. Accepts hard copy. SASE. Responds in 2 months.

- Articles: Lead articles and profiles, 500–700 words. Short features, 500–600 words. Informational articles; profiles; and interviews. Topics include professional and aspiring athletes, various sports, fitness, health, safety, hobbies, and technology.
- Depts/columns: Word lengths vary. Events coverage, team and player profiles, news, pro tips, humor, and video-game reviews.
- Other: Puzzles, games, trivia, comics, and sports cards. Poetry and artwork by children.

SAMPLE ISSUE
56 pages (24% advertising): 5 articles; 7 depts/columns; 1 comic; 1 puzzle; 1 quiz. Sample copy and editorial calendar available at website. Guidelines available.

- "Speed Racer." Article profiles sprinter Allyson Felix as part of a preview of the Summer Olympics in Beijing.
- Sample dept/column: "Warmup" provides tips from the Baltimore Orioles' second baseman about how to field a ground ball.

RIGHTS AND PAYMENT
All rights. Articles, $100–$1,500. Depts/columns, payment rates vary. Pays on acceptance. Provides contributor's copies.

◆❖EDITOR'S COMMENTS
We do not limit ourselves to mainstream sports. We'd like to hear from you if you can write about any sport that kids are involved with. Writers should note, however, that we use freelancers sparingly. Shorter items and departments present the best chance.

Start

EduGuide: Partnership for Learning
321 North Pine
Lansing, MI 48933

Editor: Rebecca Kavanaugh

DESCRIPTION AND INTERESTS
This digest-sized publication from the EduGuide Partnership is written for parents to give them a "roadmap to super kids." It contains articles on all aspects of raising kids from their earliest months through the preschool years, including early literacy, child development, and family issues. Circ: 90,000.

Audience: Parents
Frequency: 6 times each year
Website: www.eduguide.org

FREELANCE POTENTIAL
100% written by nonstaff writers. Publishes 60 freelance submissions yearly.

SUBMISSIONS
Query. Accepts hard copy and email queries to info@partnershipforlearning.org. SASE. Response time varies.

- Articles: 150–800 words. Informational and how-to articles; and personal experience pieces. Topics include parenting, health and safety, literacy, and child development.

SAMPLE ISSUE
8 pages: 3 articles. Sample copy, free with 9x12 SASE. Guidelines available.

- "A Different Story." Article discusses how children approach the concept of reading differently, learn through varying methods, and set their own pace.
- "Our Kids Won't Slow Down for Storytime." Article provides strategies for parents who are seeking to foster a love of reading in their kids.
- "Read All About It." Article provides—for each stage in a child's first years—activities for introducing books and reading into children's daily lives.

RIGHTS AND PAYMENT
Rights vary. Articles, $75–$150. Pays on publication.

◆❖EDITOR'S COMMENTS
Please note that most of the articles we publish are written by professionals in the education, early literacy, or child development professions. That said, we also value the input of real parents with real experience and real lessons learned that, if shared with others, can offer support, encouragement, and information.

Stone Soup
The Magazine by Young Writers and Artists

P.O. Box 83
Santa Cruz, CA 95063

Editor: Gerry Mandel

DESCRIPTION AND INTERESTS
Stone Soup, a literary magazine, consists of stories, poems, book reviews, and art by young people under 14 years of age from around the world. Circ: 20,000.

Audience: 8–14 years
Frequency: 6 times each year
Website: www.stonesoup.com

FREELANCE POTENTIAL
100% written by nonstaff writers. Publishes 72 freelance submissions yearly; 90% by authors who are new to the magazine. Receives 12,000 unsolicited mss yearly.

SUBMISSIONS
Send complete ms. Accepts submissions from writers under 14 years of age only. Accepts hard copy. No simultaneous submissions. SASE. Responds in 6 weeks if interested.

- Fiction: To 2,500 words. Genres include multicultural, ethnic, historical, and science fiction; adventure; mystery; and suspense.
- Depts/columns: Word lengths vary. Book reviews.
- Artwork: B/W and color line art.
- Other: Poetry, line lengths vary.

SAMPLE ISSUE
48 pages (no advertising): 8 stories; 3 poems; 2 book reviews. Sample copy and guidelines available at website.

- "Mirror, Mirror." Story tells how a girl learns that being in the popular crowd isn't always as important as it seems.
- "Where My Family Is." Story follows a girl's journey from Ireland to America during the potato famine.
- Sample dept/column: "Book Review" discusses *The Joys of Love,* a book about love, self-image, and coming of age.

RIGHTS AND PAYMENT
All rights. Written material, $40. Artwork, $25. Pays on publication. Provides 2 contributor's copies.

➥EDITOR'S COMMENTS
We would like to see stories about the topics you feel most strongly about. Whether your writing is about imaginary situations or real ones, use your own experiences and observations to give your work a sense of authenticity, depth, and reality.

Stories for Children Magazine

54 East 490 South
Ivins, UT 84738

Fiction/Poetry: Sandie Lee
Nonfiction: Angelika Lochner

DESCRIPTION AND INTERESTS
Available to readers online only, *Stories for Children* publishes short stories, articles, poems, coloring pages, and word puzzles for children, as well as reviews and interviews with children's book authors. Hits per month: 5,000+.

Audience: 3–12 years
Frequency: Monthly
Web: http://storiesforchildrenmagazine.org

FREELANCE POTENTIAL
90% written by nonstaff writers. Publishes 356 freelance submissions yearly; 7% by unpublished writers, 23% by authors who are new to the magazine. Receives 120 queries, 840 unsolicited mss yearly.

SUBMISSIONS
Prefers complete ms for fiction and nonfiction; will accept query for nonfiction. Accepts email submissions of fiction and poetry to sandielee@storiesforchildrenmagazine.org; nonfiction to angelikalochner@storiesforchildrenmagazine.org (Microsoft Word attachments). Response time varies.

- Articles: 150–1,200 words. Informational and how-to articles; and personal experience pieces. Topics include animals, history, nature, the environment, science, technology, and multicultural and ethnic issues.
- Fiction: 150–1,200 words. Genres include fantasy, light horror, humor, mystery, suspense, and science fiction.
- Other: Poetry, to 16 lines. Puzzles, games, crafts, recipes.

SAMPLE ISSUE
9 articles; 12 stories; 4 poems; 4 activities. Guidelines available at website.

- "Little Known Facts About Groundhogs." Article offers information about these animals.
- "What's in the Barn?" Story tells of two curious children and a mysterious sound.

RIGHTS AND PAYMENT
One-time non-exclusive rights. No payment (except for anthology inclusion).

➥EDITOR'S COMMENTS
We'd like to see more nonfiction for ages three to six and seven to nine, as well as craft projects and word puzzles for our age demographic. Everything in our e-zine should be fun for readers.

Story Mates

Christian Light Publications
P.O. Box 1212
Harrisonburg, VA 22803-1212

Editor: Crystal Shank

DESCRIPTION AND INTERESTS
Story Mates features short stories, poems, and activities that follow the biblical principles of conservative Mennonites. It is used and distributed in Sunday school classrooms. Circ: 6,340.

Audience: 4–8 years
Frequency: Monthly
Website: www.clp.org

FREELANCE POTENTIAL
90% written by nonstaff writers. Publishes 200 freelance submissions yearly. Receives 600 unsolicited mss yearly.

SUBMISSIONS
Send complete ms. Accepts hard copy and email submissions to storymates@clp.org. SASE. Responds in 6 weeks.

- Fiction: Stories related to Sunday school lessons and true-to-life stories, to 800 words. Picture stories, 120–150 words.
- Other: Bible puzzles, crafts, and activities. Poetry, word lengths vary. Submit seasonal material 6 months in advance.

SAMPLE ISSUE
20 pages (no advertising): 4 articles; 4 poems; 8 puzzles. Sample copy, free with 9x12 SASE ($1.20 postage). Writers' guidelines and theme list available.

- "A Blind Man and a Bouquet." Story revolves around a boy with an injury who learns an important lesson from a blind man.
- "Benny the Helper." Story features a boy who learns that even though he is little, there are ways he can help people.
- "Quite a Variety." Story tells of a girl who learns to appreciate the variety of people that God has created.

RIGHTS AND PAYMENT
First, reprint, or multiple-use rights. Fiction, $.04–$.06 per word. Poetry, $.50–$.75 per line. Puzzles, $10. Other material, payment rates vary. Pays on acceptance. Provides 1 contributor's copy.

⚫EDITOR'S COMMENTS
Stories should build conviction and Christian character while teaching a lesson. They should feel true to life while being readable and age appropriate. Please familiarize yourself with our guidelines and theme list to understand the stories we publish.

Student Assistance Journal

1270 Rankin Drive, Suite F
Troy, MI 48083

Editor: Julie Flaming

DESCRIPTION AND INTERESTS
This "Voice of Student Assistance Programs" serves professionals who work with at-risk and troubled children. It features articles on programs and initiatives that help students struggling with substance abuse, violence, and behavioral and emotional issues. Circ: 5,000.

Audience: Student assistance professionals
Frequency: Quarterly
Website: www.prponline.net

FREELANCE POTENTIAL
90% written by nonstaff writers. Publishes 12 freelance submissions yearly; 50% by unpublished writers. Receives 36 queries yearly.

SUBMISSIONS
Industry professionals should send complete ms. Accepts hard copy, IBM disk submissions, and simultaneous submissions if identified. SASE. Accepts email queries from those outside the field to editorial@prponline.net. Responds only if interested.

- Articles: 1,500 words. Informational and how-to articles; and personal experience pieces. Topics include high-risk students, special education, drug testing, substance abuse prevention, school violence, legal issues, federal funding, and staff development.
- Depts/columns: 750–800 words. Book reviews, events, commentaries, news briefs, legal issues, media resources, and research.

SAMPLE ISSUE
34 pages (20% advertising): 4 articles; 2 depts/columns. Sample copy, free. Writers' guidelines available.

- "Vicarious Terror: The New Face of Compassion Fatigue." Article presents the symptoms of vicarious terror, and advises professionals how to be spot it in themselves and the children with whom they work.
- "Sharing the Disease of Addiction." Article raises the question of whether family members' confusion and fear about a loved one's addiction treatment would be mitigated through treatment directed at them?

RIGHTS AND PAYMENT
First rights. No payment. Provides 5 copies.

⚫EDITOR'S COMMENTS
All material must address the professionals who work with high-risk children.

SuperScience

Scholastic Inc.
557 Broadway
New York, NY 10012-3999

Editor: Elizabeth Carney

DESCRIPTION AND INTERESTS
SuperScience hopes to inspire students to make scientific discoveries as they read fascinating news stories, engage in hands-on activities, and learn about current science topics. It is distributed through the classroom. Circ: 200,000.

Audience: Grades 3–6
Frequency: 8 times each year
Website: www.scholastic.com/superscience

FREELANCE POTENTIAL
80% written by nonstaff writers. Publishes 50 freelance submissions yearly; 15% by authors who are new to the magazine. Receives 60–120 queries yearly.

SUBMISSIONS
Query with résumé and clips. Accepts hard copy. SASE. Response time varies.

- Articles: 100–600 words. Informational and how-to articles; profiles; interviews; and personal experience pieces. Topics include Earth, physical, and life sciences; health; technology; chemistry; nature; and the environment.
- Depts/columns: Word lengths vary. Science news, mysteries, and experiments.
- Artwork: 8x10 B/W and color prints. Line art.
- Other: Puzzles and activities.

SAMPLE ISSUE
16 pages (no advertising): 3 articles; 5 depts/columns. Sample copy, free with 9x12 SASE. Guidelines available. Editorial calendar available at website.

- "Building in Space." Article explains how astronauts work to piece together the International Space Station.
- "Beating the Heat." Article discusses the interesting ways in which several desert animals stay cool.
- Sample dept/column: "Science Mystery" teaches kids about vascular flowers as they perform an experiment to solve a mystery.

RIGHTS AND PAYMENT
First rights. Articles, $75–$650. Other material, payment rates vary. Pays on acceptance. Provides 2 contributor's copies.

☞EDITOR'S COMMENTS
Please keep in mind that each issue of our magazine comes with a teacher's edition that includes at least 20 extra teaching strategies and ways to support the curriculum.

Swimming World and Junior Swimmer

90 Bell Rock Plaza, Suite 200
Sedona, AZ 86351

Editor: Jayson Marsteller

DESCRIPTION AND INTERESTS
Self-described as the foremost authority on all aspects of competitive swimming, this magazine features training tips, inspirational stories, new products, and meet results. Its *Junior Swimmer* section includes articles written by and for children. Circ: 50,000.

Audience: All ages
Frequency: Monthly
Web: www.swimmingworldmagazine.com

FREELANCE POTENTIAL
60% written by nonstaff writers. Publishes 100 freelance submissions yearly; 5% by unpublished writers. Receives 192+ queries yearly.

SUBMISSIONS
Query. Accepts hard copy and email queries to jaysonm@swimmingworldmagazine.com. SASE. Responds in 1 month.

- Articles: 500–3,500 words. Informational and how-to articles; profiles; and personal experience pieces. Topics include swimming, training, competition, medical advice, swim drills, nutrition, dry land exercise, exercise physiology, and fitness.
- Depts/columns: 500–750 words. Swimming news, new product reviews, and nutrition advice.
- Artwork: Color prints and transparencies. Line art.
- Other: Activities, games, and jokes. Submit seasonal material 1–2 months in advance.

SAMPLE ISSUE
62 pages (30% advertising): 13 articles; 6 depts/columns. Sample copy, $4.50 with 9x12 SASE ($1.80 postage). Guidelines available.

- "Then & Now." Article takes a look at two record-holding distance swimmers, one from the 1970s and the other from today.
- Sample dept/column: "How They Train" profiles a high school swimmer and details his workout schedule.

RIGHTS AND PAYMENT
All rights. Written material, $.12 per word. Artwork, payment rates vary. Pays on publication. Provides 2–5 contributor's copies.

☞EDITOR'S COMMENTS
Your article should appeal to one of our reader segments—adult or teen competitive swimmers, coaches, or technical directors.

Syracuse Parent

5910 Firestone Drive
Syracuse, NY 13206

Editor: Jennifer Wing

DESCRIPTION AND INTERESTS
Syracuse Parent is a family-friendly magazine packed with articles on topics of interest to parents in the central New York region. In addition, it features the educational resources, recreational opportunities, and events available to families in the region. Circ: 26,500.

Audience: Parents
Frequency: Monthly
Website: www.syracuseparent.com

FREELANCE POTENTIAL
40% written by nonstaff writers. Publishes 15 freelance submissions yearly; 25% by unpublished writers, 10% by authors who are new to the magazine. Receives 95 queries yearly.

SUBMISSIONS
Query. Accepts hard copy. SASE. Responds in 4–6 weeks.

- Articles: 800–1,000 words. Informational and how-to articles; profiles; interviews; personal experience and practical application pieces; and humor. Topics include parenting, family issues, pets, education, health, current events, regional news, social issues, nature, the environment, technology, music, travel, recreation, and sports.
- Depts/columns: Staff written.
- Other: Submit seasonal material 3–4 months in advance.

SAMPLE ISSUE
24 pages (50% advertising): 6 articles; 7 depts/columns. Sample copy, $1 with 9x12 SASE. Guidelines and editorial calendar available.

- "Is Your Child Getting Enough Daily Exercise?" Article explains how parents can determine if their children are getting the proper amount of exercise.
- "Head Lice: Myths, Facts, and How to Get Rid of Them." Article offers facts and advice for dealing with an issue that makes parents' skin crawl.

RIGHTS AND PAYMENT
First North American rights. Articles, $25–$30. Pays on publication.

➥ EDITOR'S COMMENTS
Articles should be tailored to readers in our region; that is, they should have local subjects, sources, and resources. If they are not, we will likely disregard them.

Take Five Plus

General Council of the Assemblies of God
1445 North Boonville Avenue
Springfield, MO 65802-1894

Director of Editorial Services: Paul Smith

DESCRIPTION AND INTERESTS
This pocket-sized devotional guide is for teens only. It features age-appropriate Bible lessons and devotionals featuring situations to which teens can relate—each offering Scriptural support and advice in making Christian decisions. Circ: 20,000.

Audience: 12–19 years
Frequency: Quarterly
Website: www.gospelpublishing.com

FREELANCE POTENTIAL
98% written by nonstaff writers. Of the freelance submissions published yearly, 10% are by authors who are new to the magazine.

SUBMISSIONS
All material is assigned. Send letter of introduction with résumé, church background, and clips or writing samples. Accepts hard copy. SASE. Responds in 3 months.

- Articles: 200–235 words. Daily devotionals based on Scripture readings.
- Artwork: Accepts material from teens only. 8x10 B/W prints and 35mm color slides. 8x10 or smaller line art.
- Other: Poetry written by teens, to 20 lines.

SAMPLE ISSUE
104 pages (no advertising): 90 devotionals; 4 poems. Sample copy and guidelines available.

- "Saying No to Grabbing." Devotional uses the story of people grabbing money from an overturned armored truck as an example of giving in to temptation and sin.
- "No More Delay." Devotional teaches that God's kingdom is eagerly awaiting Jesus' return to earth.
- "Gifted to Serve." Devotional explains that we are each gifted by God to serve others, and we fulfill that service in many ways.

RIGHTS AND PAYMENT
First rights. Written material, $.05 per word. Artwork, payment rates vary. Pays on publication. Provides 2 contributor's copies.

➥ EDITOR'S COMMENTS
We're looking for writers who can take a Bible verse or Scripture reading and relate it to teens' interests and experiences. We do not accept unsolicited devotionals, but are always looking to welcome freelance writers who understand our structure.

TAP: The Autism Perspective

10153½ Riverside Drive, Suite 243
Toluca Lake, CA 91602

Publisher: Nicki Fischer

DESCRIPTION AND INTERESTS
The Autism Perspective (TAP) offers inspirational stories, articles about new therapies and treatments, personal accounts, and advocacy advice for those living with autism spectrum disorders. It is read by autistic people and their caregivers in 15 countries worldwide. Circ: Unavailable.
Audience: Adults
Frequency: Quarterly
Website: www.theautismperspective.org

FREELANCE POTENTIAL
100% written by nonstaff writers. Publishes 120–140 freelance submissions yearly. Receives 360 queries yearly.

SUBMISSIONS
Query. Accepts hard copy and email queries to submissions@theautismperspective.org. SASE. Response time varies.

- Articles: 800–2,000 words. Informational articles and personal experience pieces. Topics include autism spectrum disorders and related developmental disabilities, treatments, therapies, intervention, and research.
- Depts/columns: "Understanding Autism," personal accounts of living with ASD, 800–1,200 words. Grandparent and sibling perspectives, to 550 words.
- Artwork: B/W or color prints. Line art.

SAMPLE ISSUE
100 pages: 16 articles; 12 depts/columns. Sample copy and guidelines available at website.

- "Rainy Days and Wednesdays." Personal essay by an autistic man talks about the weather, and how it relates to his feelings.
- "It Takes a Village." Article addresses the high expense of raising a special needs child, and presses for the passage of autism-specific "parity laws" in each state.

RIGHTS AND PAYMENT
All rights. All material, payment rates vary. Payment policy varies. Provides 1 copy.

✒ EDITOR'S COMMENTS
Our goal is to enrich and enhance the lives of those living with autism and offer new sources of hope. We present the full perspective of options available to make every person feel a little less alone in his or her struggles, hopes, and dreams.

Tar Heel Junior Historian

North Carolina Museum of History
4650 Mail Service Center
Raleigh, NC 27699-4650

Editor: Lisa Coston Hall

DESCRIPTION AND INTERESTS
This publication of the North Carolina Museum of History contains articles about the state's rich history presented in a way that attracts young history buffs. Circ: 9,000.
Audience: 9–18 years
Frequency: Twice each year
Website: http://ncmuseumofhistory.org

FREELANCE POTENTIAL
50% written by nonstaff writers. Publishes 12 freelance submissions yearly; 20% by unpublished writers, 50% by authors who are new to the magazine.

SUBMISSIONS
Query. Accepts hard copy and email queries to lisa.hall@ncdcr.gov. SASE. Response time varies.

- Articles: 700–1,000 words. Informational articles; profiles; interviews; and personal experience pieces. Topics include regional history; geography; government; and social, multicultural, and ethnic issues pertaining to North Carolina history.
- Artwork: B/W and spot color prints or transparencies. Line art.
- Other: Puzzles, activities, and word games.

SAMPLE ISSUE
38 pages (no advertising): 29 articles. Sample copy, $5 with 9x12 SASE ($2 postage). Guidelines and theme list available.

- "Hanged for Murder, But Was She Guilty?" Article retells the case of Frankie Silver, who was the first woman hanged for murder in North Carolina.
- "The Wild Horses of Currituck." Article examines the theories about how the wild horses of the Outer Banks arrived there, and how they are endangered.
- "Surry County's Original Siamese Twins." Article profiles Chang and Eng Bunker, famous conjoined twins, and their thousands of descendants who continue to live in North Carolina.

RIGHTS AND PAYMENT
All rights. No payment. Provides 10 contributor's copies.

✒ EDITOR'S COMMENTS
We seek articles with historical relevance and a topic that will interest youngsters.

TC Magazine

915 East Market, Box 10750
Searcy, AR 72149

Managing Editor: Laura Edwards

DESCRIPTION AND INTERESTS
TC Magazine is a Christian lifestyle magazine for teenagers. Its articles tackle the issues with which contemporary teenagers are faced, but with a positive, faith-based perspective. It also covers all the topics near and dear to a teen's heart: pop culture, sports, and relationships. Circ: 7,000+.
Audience: 13–19 years
Frequency: Quarterly
Website: www.tcmagazine.org

FREELANCE POTENTIAL
35% written by nonstaff writers. Publishes 5–10 freelance submissions yearly; 20% by unpublished writers, 30% by authors who are new to the magazine. Receives 60 queries and unsolicited mss yearly.

SUBMISSIONS
Query or send complete ms. Prefers email to editor@tcmagazine.org (Microsoft Word attachments); will accept hard copy. SASE. Response time varies.

- Articles: 450–700 words. Informational articles; profiles; interviews; and personal experience pieces. Topics include faith, youth groups, sports, health, humor, music, film, fashion, art, and relationships.
- Depts/columns: Word lengths vary. College, style, entertainment, media reviews, humor, personal essays, and Q&A interviews.

SAMPLE ISSUE
48 pages: 5 articles; 9 depts/columns. Sample copy, $3.95. Guidelines available at website.

- "Josh Hamilton." Personal experience piece reveals the author's feelings about meeting the baseball player who overcame addiction through his faith.
- "Scribblenauts." Interview with a video game creator reveals what it's like to work in a teen's dream job.

RIGHTS AND PAYMENT
All rights. Written material, payment rates vary. Payment policy varies.

⇢EDITOR'S COMMENTS
Many of our articles are assigned or written by staff. But we are always interested in unique subjects (as long as they are a fit with us) and interviews/first person stories. We always welcome teenage writers.

Teacher Librarian

4501 Forbes Boulevard, Suite 200
Lanham, MD 20706

Managing Editor: Corinne O. Burton

DESCRIPTION AND INTERESTS
Teacher Librarian is designed specifically for library professionals working with children and young adults. It features relevant articles exploring current issues of the profession, such as collaboration, leadership, technology, advocacy, information literacy, and management. Circ: 10,000.
Audience: Library professionals
Frequency: 5 times each year
Website: www.teacherlibrarian.com

FREELANCE POTENTIAL
60% written by nonstaff writers. Publishes 10 freelance submissions yearly; 25% by unpublished writers, 5% by new authors. Receives 6 queries and unsolicited mss yearly.

SUBMISSIONS
Query or send complete ms with résumé and abstract or bibliography. Accepts hard copy, disk submissions, and email submissions to editor@teacherlibrarian.com. SASE. Responds in 2 months.

- Articles: 2,000+ words. Informational and analytical articles; and profiles. Topics include library funding, technology, leadership, library management, audio/visual material, cooperative teaching, and young adult library services.
- Depts/columns: Staff written.
- Artwork: B/W or color prints. Cartoons and line art.

SAMPLE ISSUE
86 pages (20% advertising): 9 articles; 13 depts/columns; 17 review sections. Guidelines and editorial calendar available.

- "From *Mad* Magazine to Facebook: What Have We Learned?" Article makes the argument that schools should allow students access to all forms of technology and its educationally beneficial applications.
- Sample dept/column: "Primary Voices" maintains that it is important for librarians to mentor other school professionals and volunteers.

RIGHTS AND PAYMENT
All rights. Written material, $100. Pays on publication. Provides 2 contributor's copies.

⇢EDITOR'S COMMENTS
We welcome articles on any aspect of library services for children and young adults.

Teachers of Vision

227 North Magnolia Avenue, Suite 2
Anaheim, CA 92801

Submissions: Judy Turpen

DESCRIPTION AND INTERESTS
Teachers of Vision serves as a source of information for Christian educators working in public or private schools. A publication of the Christian Educators Association International, it publishes articles designed to empower teachers to draw on their faith to better fulfill their mission as educators. Circ: 8,000.

Audience: Educators
Frequency: Quarterly
Website: www.ceai.org

FREELANCE POTENTIAL
78% written by nonstaff writers. Publishes 70–75 freelance submissions yearly; 5% by unpublished writers, 15% by authors who are new to the magazine. Receives 36–60 unsolicited mss yearly.

SUBMISSIONS
Send complete ms with brief biography. Prefers email submissions to tov@ceai.org; will accept hard copy. SASE. Responds in 2–3 months.

- Articles: How-to articles, personal experience pieces, and documented reports; 800–1,000 words. Topics include education issues, educational philosophy, and methodology. Interviews with noted Christian educators; 500–800 words. Teaching techniques, news, and special event reports; 400–500 words.
- Depts/columns: 100–200 words. Reviews of books, videos, curricula, games, and other resources for K–12 teachers.
- Other: Submit seasonal material 4 months in advance.

SAMPLE ISSUE
24 pages (1% advertising): 13 articles; 9 depts/columns. Sample copy, free with 9x12 SASE (5 first-class stamps). Guidelines available at website.

- "The Power of Encouragement." Article provides nine guidelines for igniting students' desire to learn.
- Sample dept/column: "Teaching Christianly" evaluates teaching tips on Christian merit.

RIGHTS AND PAYMENT
First and electronic rights. Articles, $20–$40. Pays on publication. Provides 3 copies.

➦EDITOR'S COMMENTS
We need articles on teaching math, science, and history in public schools.

Teaching Theatre

2343 Auburn Avenue
Cincinnati, OH 45219

Editor: James Palmarini

DESCRIPTION AND INTERESTS
With a focus on the middle school and high school levels, this magazine targets theatre teachers with articles on teaching strategies and student assessment, and innovative program ideas. Circ: 5,000.

Audience: Theatre teachers
Frequency: Quarterly
Website: www.edta.org

FREELANCE POTENTIAL
70% written by nonstaff writers. Publishes 15 freelance submissions yearly; 30% by unpublished writers, 50% by authors who are new to the magazine. Receives 75 queries yearly.

SUBMISSIONS
Query with outline. Accepts hard copy. SASE. Responds in 1 month.

- Articles: 1,000–3,000 words. Informational articles and personal experience pieces. Topics include theatre education, the arts, and curricula.
- Depts/columns: Word lengths vary. Classroom exercises, ideas, technical advice, and textbook or play suggestions.

SAMPLE ISSUE
36 pages (3–5% advertising): 4 articles; 2 depts/columns. Sample copy, $2 with 9x12 SASE ($2 postage). Guidelines available.

- "Directing the Design: Creating the Visual World of the Play." Article discusses the important role of the stage designer in setting the tone of a production.
- "Making the Grade: The Role of Assessment in the Theatre Classroom." Article discusses new modes of assessment that will meet the needs of the school district and be helpful to students.
- Sample dept/column: "Promptbook" tells of the author's experience in trying to integrate drama into a K–8 school for the first time.

RIGHTS AND PAYMENT
One-time rights. Written material, payment rates vary. Pays on publication. Provides 3 contributor's copies.

➦EDITOR'S COMMENTS
Most of our articles are written by theatre teachers themselves and offer information, advice, support, and—most importantly—new ideas for teachers in the field.

Teach Kids! Essentials

P.O. Box 348
Warrenton, MO 63383-0348

Senior Editor: Yolanda Derstine

DESCRIPTION AND INTERESTS

Geared to and written by Christian educators of children ages four to eleven, this newsletter features short articles and teaching tips that provide insight and ideas for use in the classroom. Circ: Unavailable.

Audience: Christian educators
Frequency: Monthly
Website: www.cefonline.com

FREELANCE POTENTIAL

90% written by nonstaff writers. Publishes 120 freelance submissions yearly; 20% by unpublished writers, 90% by authors who are new to the magazine. Receives 24–36 unsolicited mss each year.

SUBMISSIONS

Send complete ms. Accepts email submissions to yolanda.derstine@cefonline.com. Responds if interested.

- Articles: To 250 words. Informational and how-to articles; profiles; and personal experience pieces. Topics include religion, education, teaching techniques, classroom management, discipleship, curriculum, and programming and activity ideas.

SAMPLE ISSUE

8 pages: 8 articles. Sample copy available.

- "Help Children Learn About Confession of Sin." Article suggests a lesson that teaches about sin and forgiveness.
- "Understand the ADHD Brain." Article explains how an ADHD brain works and discusses what teachers can do to help an ADHD child learn.
- "Kids Can Help Provide Bibles." Article reports on ways to get involved in sending new and used Bibles to less fortunate children around the world.

RIGHTS AND PAYMENT

All rights. No payment. Provides 2 contributor's copies and a 1-year subscription.

⟶ EDITOR'S COMMENTS

Please keep your submissions brief. Word count must be under 250 words. We are particularly interested in material that relates to classroom discipline, games for review, and working with at-risk children. We welcome submissions from unpublished writers who work in Christian education.

Tech Directions

Prakken Publications
832 Phoenix Drive
P.O. Box 8623
Ann Arbor, MI 48107

Managing Editor: Susanne Peckham

DESCRIPTION AND INTERESTS

Technical and vocational educators find the latest information on teaching techniques and new projects in this magazine. Circ: 43,000.

Audience: Teachers and administrators
Frequency: 10 times each year
Website: www.techdirections.com

FREELANCE POTENTIAL

80% written by nonstaff writers. Publishes 50 freelance submissions yearly; 50% by unpublished writers, 50% by new authors. Receives 150 queries, 80 unsolicited mss yearly.

SUBMISSIONS

Query or send complete ms. Accepts hard copy and email submissions to susanne@ techdirections.com. SASE. Availability of artwork improves chance of acceptance. Responds to queries in 1 week, to mss in 1 month.

- Articles: To 3,000 words. Informational and how-to articles. Topics include teaching techniques and unusual projects in the fields of automotive, building trades, computers, drafting, electronics, graphics, hydraulics, industrial arts, lasers, manufacturing, radio and TV, robotics, software, welding, woodworking, and other vocational education.
- Depts/columns: Word lengths vary. Legislation updates; technology news and history; media reviews; and new product information.
- Artwork: Color prints, slides, and transparencies; B/W prints. B/W line art. CAD plots.
- Other: Puzzles, games, and quizzes.

SAMPLE ISSUE

32 pages (40% advertising): 6 articles; 7 depts/columns. Sample copy, $5 with 9x12 SASE (2 first-class stamps). Guidelines available.

- "Digital Camera Project Fosters Communication Skills." Article describes how to create a photo-illustrated document.
- Sample dept/column: "Mastering Computers" covers the latest in e-book readers and online bookstores.

RIGHTS AND PAYMENT

All rights. Articles, $50+. Depts/columns, to $25. Pays on publication. Provides 3 copies.

⟶ EDITOR'S COMMENTS

We also publish cartoons, anecdotes, brain teasers, and puzzles related to our field.

Techniques

ACTE
1410 King Street
Alexandria, VA 22314

Managing Editor: Susan Emeagwali

DESCRIPTION AND INTERESTS
With the tagline "Connecting Education and Careers," *Techniques* is a magazine about career and technical education and those professionals who provide it. It includes articles on trends, professionals, research, and preparing youth and adults for careers. It is published by the Association for Career and Technical Education. Circ: 30,000.

Audience: Educators
Frequency: 8 times each year
Website: www.acteonline.org

FREELANCE POTENTIAL
60% written by nonstaff writers. Publishes 10–20 freelance submissions yearly; 15% by unpublished writers, 30% by authors who are new to the magazine. Receives 96 queries and unsolicited mss yearly.

SUBMISSIONS
Query or send complete ms. Accepts email submissions to semeagwali@acteonline.org (Microsoft Word attachments). Availability of artwork improves chance of acceptance. Responds in 4 months.

- Articles: 1,000–2,500 words. Informational and how-to articles; case studies; and profiles. Topics include career and technical education programming, practices, and policy; integrating career education and academics; technology; and environmental issues.
- Depts/columns: "Research Report," to 2,500 words. Academic articles.
- Artwork: Digital images at 300 dpi. Charts and graphs.

SAMPLE ISSUE
62 pages (30% advertising): 10 articles; 11 depts/columns. Sample copy, guidelines, and editorial calendar available at website.

- "Moving Into the Future with MUVEs." Article reports on the rising use of multi-user virtual environments in education.
- "Gazing Into the Future." Article examines the sweeping changes that have taken place in career and technical education.

RIGHTS AND PAYMENT
All rights. No payment.

☛EDITOR'S COMMENTS
We are looking for profiles of interesting people in the field as well as journalistic articles.

Teen Graffiti

P.O. Box 452721
Garland, TX 75045-2721

Publisher: Sharon Jones-Scaife

DESCRIPTION AND INTERESTS
The title of this magazine is a metaphor for writing on the imaginary walls that block communication between teens and their peers, teachers, and parents. Here young people can express their concerns and creativity. Circ: 10,000.

Audience: 12–19 years
Frequency: 6 times each year
Website: www.teengraffiti.com

FREELANCE POTENTIAL
70% written by nonstaff writers. Publishes 30–40 freelance submissions yearly. Receives many queries and unsolicited mss yearly.

SUBMISSIONS
Teen writers only. Query or send complete ms. Prefers email to editor@teengraffiti.com; will accept hard copy. SASE. Response time varies.

- Articles: 250–500 words. Informational articles; personal experience and opinion pieces; and essays. Topics include college, careers, current events, popular culture, sex, health, and social issues.
- Depts/columns: 100–200 words. Advice and resources from teachers, teen-to-teen advice, and media reviews.
- Artwork: B/W and color prints from teens.
- Other: Poetry written by teens.

SAMPLE ISSUE
32 pages (3% advertising): 4 articles; 4 depts/columns; 6 poems. Sample copy, $2.75 with 9x12 SASE. Guidelines available.

- "A Future with Hope." Article profiles a teenage mother who is attending college, working, and raising a three-year-old.
- Sample dept/column: "High School & Beyond" offers tips for overcoming a fear of public speaking.

RIGHTS AND PAYMENT
One-time rights. No payment.

☛EDITOR'S COMMENTS
You must be 12 to 19 years old to be published in our magazine. Include your name, year of birth, home address, telephone number, email address, and the name of your school and English teacher on each submission. If due to the very personal nature of a piece you don't want your name published, we will respect your request, but you still must include your name and contact information.

Teen Tribute

71 Barber Greene Road
Toronto, Ontario M3C 2A2
Canada

Editor: Toni-Marie Ippolito

DESCRIPTION AND INTERESTS

From movies to music to celebrities, *Teen Tribute* covers it all for its teen readers. It features reviews of films and music, as well as profiles of celebrities and coverage of teen social issues. Circ: 300,000.

Audience: 14–18 years
Frequency: Quarterly
Website: www.tribute.ca

FREELANCE POTENTIAL

10% written by nonstaff writers. Publishes 5–10 freelance submissions yearly; 1% by authors who are new to the magazine. Receives 24 queries yearly.

SUBMISSIONS

Query with clips or writing samples. Accepts hard copy and email queries to tippolito@ tribute.ca. Availability of artwork improves chance of acceptance. SAE/IRC. Responds in 1–2 months.

- Articles: 400–500 words. Informational articles; profiles; interviews; and personal experience pieces. Topics include movies, the film industry, music, the arts, entertainment, popular culture, and social issues.
- Depts/columns: Word lengths vary. Media reviews, fashion and beauty tips, new product reviews, relationship advice, gear and gadgets, and horoscopes.
- Artwork: Color prints or transparencies.

SAMPLE ISSUE

38 pages (50% advertising): 9 articles; 10 depts/columns. Sample copy, $1.95 Canadian with 9x12 SAE/IRC ($.86 Canadian postage).

- "Two Men. One Dream. Blades of Glory." Article reviews the movie *Blades of Glory*.
- Sample dept/column: "Interview" provides an interview with actress and singer Ashley Tisdale about her new CD.

RIGHTS AND PAYMENT

First serial rights. Written material, $100–$400 Canadian. Artwork, payment rates vary. Pays on publication. Provides 1 contributor's copy.

✒️EDITOR'S COMMENTS

If teenagers are talking about it, we cover it. We are open to submissions on any topic that would interest teenagers, but be aware that our focus is on popular culture, movies, and celebrities.

Teen Voices

P.O. Box 120-027
Boston, MA 02112-0027

Managing Editor: Rebecca Steinitz

DESCRIPTION AND INTERESTS

With the tagline "Because You're More Than a Pretty Face," *Teen Voices* reaches out to teen girls and young women with articles that address the serious topics and challenges in their lives. It is not a beauty magazine, nor is it filled with articles about boys. *Teen Voices* appears both online and in print. Circ: 55,000.

Audience: Teen girls
Frequency: Monthly (website); Twice each year (print)
Website: www.teenvoices.com

FREELANCE POTENTIAL

95% written by nonstaff writers. Publishes 100 freelance submissions yearly; 95% by unpublished writers, 95% by new authors. Receives 2,000 unsolicited mss each year.

SUBMISSIONS

Accepts mss written by girls ages 13–19 only. Send complete ms. SASE. Response time varies.

- Articles: Word lengths vary. Informational and self-help articles; interviews; and profiles. Topics include ethnic and religious traditions, the Internet, multicultural issues, surviving sexual assault, family relationships, teen motherhood, international life, disability, health, nutrition, cooking, the arts, the media, and activism.
- Fiction: Word lengths vary. Humorous, inspirational, contemporary, ethnic, and multicultural fiction.
- Depts/columns: Word lengths vary. Media reviews, arts and culture, international issues, food, and opinion pieces.
- Other: Poetry; comic strips.

SAMPLE ISSUE

56 pages (8% advertising): 3 articles; 10 depts/columns; 5 poems. Guidelines and editorial calendar available.

- "Teen Voices on TV." Article examines how teens have been portrayed on television.
- Sample dept/column: "Small World" offers insight into an Afghan girl's world.

RIGHTS AND PAYMENT

First or one-time rights. No payment. Provides 5 contributor's copies.

✒️EDITOR'S COMMENTS

We like articles that inspire girls to change the world.

Texas Child Care Quarterly

P.O. Box 162881
Austin, TX 78716-2881

Editor: Louise Parks

DESCRIPTION AND INTERESTS
Published by the Texas Workforce Commission, *Texas Child Care Quarterly* serves as a training journal for caregivers working with children. It publishes articles on child development theory as well as "child-building" articles that describe hands-on activities. Circ: 32,000.

Audience: Teachers and child-care workers
Frequency: Quarterly
Website: www.childcarequarterly.com

FREELANCE POTENTIAL
50% written by nonstaff writers. Publishes 12–15 freelance submissions yearly; 10% by unpublished writers, 50% by authors who are new to the magazine. Receives 24–36 unsolicited mss yearly.

SUBMISSIONS
Query with outline; or send complete ms. Accepts hard copy with disk and email to editor@childcarequarterly.com. No simultaneous submissions. SASE. Responds in 3 weeks.

- Articles: 2,500 words. Informational, theoretical, and how-to articles. Topics include child growth and development, school-family communication, health and safety, program administration, professional development, and hands-on activities.
- Depts/columns: Staff written.

SAMPLE ISSUE
44 pages (no advertising): 6 articles; 5 depts/columns. Sample copy, $6.25; also available at website. Guidelines available at website.

- "Block Play: Classroom Essentials." Article offers guidelines for appropriate block play at different age levels, and describes its educational and developmental benefits.
- "Enliven Summer with Science." Article suggests science activities that can emerge from children's play and exploration outdoors during summer break.

RIGHTS AND PAYMENT
All rights. No payment. Provides 3 contributor's copies and a 1-year subscription.

➻EDITOR'S COMMENTS
Submissions are reviewed by our editorial staff with the support of the Editorial Review Committee. Those selected for publication may be returned to the author for revision to meet the magazine's writing criteria.

Thrasher

1303 Underwood Avenue
San Francisco, CA 94121

Managing Editor: Ryan Henry

DESCRIPTION AND INTERESTS
Teen boys and young men who are thoroughly into skateboarding and snowboarding find the kind of articles they crave in this magazine, which is written in the sports language that only fans understand. Circ: 200,000.

Audience: Boys, 12–20 years
Frequency: 13 times each year
Website: www.thrashermagazine.com

FREELANCE POTENTIAL
20% written by nonstaff writers. Publishes 20 freelance submissions yearly; 100% by unpublished writers. Receives 72–120 unsolicited mss yearly.

SUBMISSIONS
Send complete ms. Prefers email submissions to info@thrashermagazine.com (Microsoft Word attachments); will accept Macintosh disk submissions, hard copy, and simultaneous submissions if identified. Artwork improves chance of acceptance. SASE. Responds in 1 month.

- Articles: To 1,500 words. Informational articles; profiles; and interviews. Topics include skateboarding, snowboarding, and music.
- Fiction: To 2,500 words. Stories with skateboarding and snowboarding themes.
- Depts/columns: 750–1,000 words. News, tips, art, 'zines, and profiles.
- Artwork: Color prints or transparencies; 35mm B/W negatives. Line art.

SAMPLE ISSUE
220 pages (45% advertising): 12 articles; 10 depts/columns. Sample copy, $3.99. Guidelines available.

- "Tommy Guerrero." Article features an interview with the unique skateboard pioneer and Latin musician.
- Sample dept/column: "'Zine Thing" offers a review of the alternative music magazine *Razorcake.*

RIGHTS AND PAYMENT
First North American serial rights. Written material, $.15 per word. Artwork, payment rates vary. Pays on publication. Provides 2 copies.

➻EDITOR'S COMMENTS
We accept material only from writers who are also into skateboarding and snowboarding; you must be able to walk the walk and talk the talk.

Time For Kids

Time-Life Building
1271 Avenue of the Americas, 25th Floor
New York, NY 10020

Editor: Martha Pickerill

DESCRIPTION AND INTERESTS
This classroom version of *Time* magazine boils down world news for students in elementary and middle grades. Each weekly issue is published in three age-appropriate editions: Big Picture, News Scoop, and World Report, with editorial content that spans the curricula of kindergarten through seventh grade. Circ: 4.1 million.

Audience: 5–12 years
Frequency: Weekly
Website: www.timeforkids.com

FREELANCE POTENTIAL
4% written by nonstaff writers. Publishes 4 freelance submissions yearly.

SUBMISSIONS
All work is assigned. Send résumé only. Accepts hard copy. Responds if interested.

- Articles: Word lengths vary. Informational and biographical articles. Topics include world news, current events, animals, education, health, fitness, science, technology, math, social studies, geography, multicultural and ethnic issues, music, popular culture, recreation, regional news, sports, travel, and social issues.
- Depts/columns: Word lengths vary. Profiles and short news items.
- Artwork: Color prints or transparencies.
- Other: Theme-related activities.

SAMPLE ISSUE
8 pages (no advertising): 1 article; 8 depts/columns. Sample copy, $3.95.

- "Man on the Moon." Article reviews the U.S. space program 40 years after the first lunar landing, and offers a look at some of NASA's future plans.
- Sample dept/column: "More News" includes a piece that discusses why summer homework should be banned.

RIGHTS AND PAYMENT
All rights. Written material, payment rates vary. Pays on publication.

⟶EDITOR'S COMMENTS
We bring real news and enlightening information to young people so that they can develop a lifelong interest in, and a connection to, world events. Our magazine enables our readers to become literate, critical thinkers, and informed, responsible citizens.

Today's Catholic Teacher

2621 Dryden Road, Suite 300
Dayton, OH 45439

Editor-in-Chief: Mary Noschang

DESCRIPTION AND INTERESTS
Catholic Teacher, written for educators in Catholic schools, is filled with information designed to help teachers succeed in the classroom. In addition to articles on technology, professional development, networking, and prayer education, it also publishes news of Catholic education around the country. Circ: 50,000.

Audience: Teachers, grades K–12
Frequency: 6 times each year
Website: www.catholicteacher.com

FREELANCE POTENTIAL
95% written by nonstaff writers. Publishes 20 freelance submissions yearly; 50% by authors who are new to the magazine. Receives 190+ queries and unsolicited mss yearly.

SUBMISSIONS
Query or send complete ms. Accepts hard copy, disk submissions with hard copy, email to mnoschang@peterli.com, and simultaneous submissions if identified. SASE. Responds to queries in 1 month, to mss in 3 months.

- Articles: 600–1,500 words. Informational, self-help, and how-to articles. Topics include technology, fundraising, classroom management, curriculum development, administration, and educational issues and trends.
- Depts/columns: Word lengths vary. Opinion, news, software, character development, curricula, teaching tools, and school profiles.
- Artwork: 8x10 color prints, slides, or transparencies.
- Other: Reproducible activity pages.

SAMPLE ISSUE
70 pages (45% advertising): 7 articles; 9 depts/columns. Sample copy, $3. Writers' guidelines available.

- "Emotions, Memory, and Reading." Article discusses the connection between emotions and memory in the development of literacy.
- Sample dept/column: "School of the Month" profiles the successful programs of a Catholic school in Georgia.

RIGHTS AND PAYMENT
All rights. Written material, $100–$250. Pays on publication. Provides contributor's copies.

⟶EDITOR'S COMMENTS
We look for articles that provide insight to the field that can't be found elsewhere.

Today's Christian Woman

465 Gundersen Drive
Carol Stream, IL 60188

Assistant Editor: Andrea Bianchi

DESCRIPTION AND INTERESTS
Today's Christian Woman tackles topics from a woman-first perspective, without shying away from the tough issues. It covers spiritual, physical, and intellectual concerns. Circ: 210,000.

Audience: Women
Frequency: 6 times each year
Website: www.todayschristianwoman.com

FREELANCE POTENTIAL
85% written by nonstaff writers. Publishes 65 freelance submissions yearly; 5% by unpublished writers. Receives 1,200 queries yearly.

SUBMISSIONS
Query with résumé; length, summary, and purpose of article; and author credentials. Accepts hard copy. No simultaneous submissions. Availability of artwork improves chance of acceptance. SASE. Responds in 2–3 months.

- Articles: 1,000–2,000 words. Informational and self-help articles; personal experience pieces; and humor. Topics include parenting, family life, relationships, spiritual living, contemporary women's concerns, and turning points in life.
- Depts/columns: 100–300 words. First-person narratives, reviews, and pieces on parenting and faith.

SAMPLE ISSUE
56 pages (25% advertising): 12 articles; 6 depts/columns. Sample copy, $5 with 9x12 SASE ($3.19 postage). Guidelines available.

- "The Gift of Gratitude." Interview with television news anchor Deborah Norville discusses her book *Thank You Power*.
- "Life After Chocolate." Personal experience piece shares what the author has learned from living with diabetes.
- Sample dept/column: "Women in the Word" looks at the biblical prostitute Rahab.

RIGHTS AND PAYMENT
First rights. Written material, $.20 per word. Pays on acceptance. Provides 2 author's copies.

➻EDITOR'S COMMENTS
We wrap our editorial around these four scriptural "pillars"—heart, soul, strength, and mind. Articles should be personal in tone, use real-life anecdotes from a variety of women, and contain a distinctive evangelical Christian perspective.

Today's Parent

1 Mount Pleasant Road, 8th Floor
Toronto, Ontario M4Y 2Y5
Canada

Managing Editor

DESCRIPTION AND INTERESTS
Today's Parent reaches families across Canada with articles designed to help them navigate the waters from preschool through high school. Topics covered range from early childhood development to teen dating, with information on pediatric health, education, and discipline in between. Circ: 215,000.

Audience: Parents
Frequency: Monthly
Website: www.todaysparent.com

FREELANCE POTENTIAL
Of the freelance submissions published yearly, many are by unpublished writers and authors who are new to the magazine. Receives many queries yearly.

SUBMISSIONS
Query with clips and projected word count. Accepts hard copy, faxes to 416-764-2801, and email queries to editors@todaysparent.com. SAE/IRC. Responds in 6 weeks if interested.

- Articles: 1,500–2,500 words. Informational, how-to, and self-help articles. Topics include parenting, discipline, child development, health, nutrition, pregnancy, and childbirth.
- Depts/columns: "Your Turn," 650 words. "Mom Time," "Education," "Health," and "Behaviour," 1,200 words.

SAMPLE ISSUE
146 pages (15% advertising): 6 articles; 13 depts/columns. Sample copy and guidelines available at website.

- "High School Confidential." Article features advice from today's teens on how parents can help their kids adjust to high school.
- Sample dept/column: "Tween & Teen" examines what happens when daughters begin wearing makeup.

RIGHTS AND PAYMENT
All North American serial rights. Articles, $1,500–$2,500. "Your Turn," $200. Other depts/columns, $1,200. Pays 30 days after acceptance. Provides 2 contributor's copies.

➻EDITOR'S COMMENTS
Our goal is to support our readers in making good parenting choices. To that end, we look for editorial content that strikes a balance between the lighthearted and the investigative, with an overall emphasis on the positive.

Toledo Area Parent News

1120 Adams Street
Toledo, OH 43624

Managing Editor: Gina Sares

DESCRIPTION AND INTERESTS

Parents in the greater Toledo, Ohio, area read this magazine for up-to-date information on parenting issues, children's health information, and education and recreation opportunities in the area. Circ: 81,000.

Audience: Parents
Frequency: Monthly
Website: www.toledoparent.com

FREELANCE POTENTIAL

75% written by nonstaff writers. Publishes 12 freelance submissions yearly; 10% by unpublished writers, 20% by authors who are new to the magazine. Receives 48 queries and unsolicited mss yearly.

SUBMISSIONS

Query with clips; or send complete ms. Prefers email to gsares@toledoparent.com; will accept hard copy. SASE. Responds in 1 month.

- Articles. 700–2,000 words. Informational articles; profiles; and interviews. Topics include family issues, parenting, teen issues, education, social issues, health, and fitness.
- Depts/columns: Word lengths vary. Restaurant reviews, brief news items related to family issues.

SAMPLE ISSUE

48 pages (60% advertising): 2 articles; 9 depts/columns. Sample copy available via email request to kdevol@toledocitypaper.com. Guidelines and editorial calendar available.

- "School's Back!" Article provides tips for helping kids make the back-to-school transition.
- "Claiming a Piece of Summer for Myself." Personal essay describes how a mom created a special, private space for herself.
- Sample dept/column: "Food Fight" offers a review of a waterfront pizza restaurant.

RIGHTS AND PAYMENT

All North American serial rights. Written material, $30–$200. Pays on publication.

☛ EDITOR'S COMMENTS

If you want to get our attention with your article, make sure it has these three elements: a relevance to the Toledo area; practical information that parents can use in their daily lives with their children; and a conversational tone that invites readers into the subject without preaching to them.

Treasure Valley Family

13191 West Scotfield Street
Boise, ID 83713-0899

Publisher: Liz Buckingham

DESCRIPTION AND INTERESTS

Parenting, education, and child development issues are all covered in this regional magazine for parents and families. It also provides information on recreation and other family resources in the region. Circ: 20,000.

Audience: Parents
Frequency: Monthly
Website: www.treasurevalleyfamily.com

FREELANCE POTENTIAL

50% written by nonstaff writers. Publishes 10–15 freelance submissions yearly; 1–2% by authors who are new to the magazine. Receives 1,800 queries and unsolicited mss yearly.

SUBMISSIONS

Prefers query with clips; will accept complete ms with 1-sentence author bio. Accepts hard copy and email submissions to magazine@treasurevalleyfamily.com (Microsoft Word attachments). SASE. Responds in 2–3 months.

- Articles: 1,000–1,300 words. Informational and how-to articles. Topics include health, preschool, child care, education, summer camp, sports, travel, recreation, teen issues, college, party planning, crafts, hobbies, and the arts.
- Depts/columns: 700–900 words. Events, activities, advice, news, product reviews, age-specific issues, book reviews, women's health, profiles of local agencies, and interviews with area families.

SAMPLE ISSUE

48 pages (45% advertising): 4 articles; 3 depts/columns. Sample copy, free with 9x12 SASE ($1.50 postage). Guidelines and theme list/editorial calendar available at website.

- "Stately Idaho." Article provides several family- and budget-friendly destinations within Idaho, as well as fun state facts.
- Sample dept/column: "Body Shop" offers information on the dangers of indoor tanning.

RIGHTS AND PAYMENT

First North American serial rights. All material, payment rates vary. Pays 10% more for Web rights. Pays on publication. Provides 2 copies.

☛ EDITOR'S COMMENTS

We look for pieces that offer informational reporting and that use sources from our publishing region.

Tulsa Kids Magazine

1820 South Boulder Avenue, Suite 400
Tulsa, OK 74119-4409

Editor: Betty Casey

DESCRIPTION AND INTERESTS
Serving parents in the greater Tulsa region of
Oklahoma, this magazine publishes articles on
a variety of parenting topics, family issues,
education, and recreational opportunities in
the area. Circ: 20,000.
Audience: Parents
Frequency: Monthly
Website: www.tulsakids.com

FREELANCE POTENTIAL
99% written by nonstaff writers. Publishes
100+ freelance submissions yearly; 5% by
unpublished writers, 1% by authors who are
new to the magazine. Receives 1,200 unsolicited mss yearly.

SUBMISSIONS
Send complete ms. Accepts hard copy, disk
submissions, and simultaneous submissions if
identified. SASE. Responds in 2–3 months.

- Articles: 500–800 words. Informational articles; profiles; interviews; humor; and personal
  experience pieces. Topics include family life,
  education, parenting, recreation, entertainment, college, health, fitness, careers, crafts,
  and social issues.
- Depts/columns: 100–300 words. News, book
  reviews, safety, and family cooking.

SAMPLE ISSUE
64 pages (50% advertising): 5 articles; 11
depts/columns. Sample copy, free with 10x13
SASE ($.75 postage). Guidelines available.

- "Mompreneurs." Article profiles several
  women who run their own businesses while
  raising their families.
- "I Hate You! When Your Child Lashes Out."
  Article explains why young children lash out
  in anger, and provides tips for helping them
  deal with their new emotions.
- Sample dept/column: "Mom's Journal"
  relates the author's feelings and fears about
  becoming a stay-at-home mom.

RIGHTS AND PAYMENT
One-time rights. Written material, $25–$100.
Payment policy varies. Provides 1 author's copy.

➡EDITOR'S COMMENTS
If you think parents would find information,
support, or humor through your article, we'd
be interested in it. We prefer pieces that
relate to the Tulsa region.

Turtle

Children's Better Health Institute
1100 Waterway Boulevard
P.O. Box 567
Indianapolis, IN 46206-0567

Editor: Terry Harshman

DESCRIPTION AND INTERESTS
This magazine for preschool children offers
wholesome and positive stories, articles,
and activities that educate and entertain its
readers while promoting healthy living and
good values. Circ: 382,000.
Audience: 2–5 years
Frequency: 6 times each year
Website: www.turtlemag.org

FREELANCE POTENTIAL
50% written by nonstaff writers. Publishes 45
freelance submissions yearly.

SUBMISSIONS
Send complete ms. Accepts hard copy. SASE.
Responds in 3 months.

- Articles: To 500 words. Informational articles
  and book reviews. Topics include health,
  fitness, nutrition, nature, the environment,
  science, hobbies, and crafts.
- Fiction: 100–150 words for rebus stories.
  Genres include mystery; adventure; fantasy;
  humor; problem-solving stories; and contemporary, ethnic, and multicultural fiction.
- Depts/columns: To 500 words. Crafts, health
  tips, and recipes.
- Other: Puzzles, activities, and games. Poetry,
  4–8 lines. Submit seasonal material 8
  months in advance.

SAMPLE ISSUE
36 pages (6% advertising): 2 articles; 2 stories;
15 activities. Sample copy, $1.75 with 9x12
SASE. Guidelines available at website.

- "Turtle's Favorite Books." Article offers a
  description of a children's book called
  Little Chick.
- "Oliver's Twist." Story tells of an octopus
  who learns that being different from the
  other fish in the sea is good when he saves
  his friend from a great white shark.

RIGHTS AND PAYMENT
All rights. Articles and fiction, to $.32 per
word. Other material, payment rates vary.
Pays on publication. Provides up to 10 contributor's copies.

➡EDITOR'S COMMENTS
Our hope is to promote healthy physical,
educational, creative, social, and emotional
growth through our content. Please check our
website for current editorial needs.

Twins

5748 South College Avenue, Unit D
Fort Collins, CO 80525

Editor-in-Chief: Christa D. Reed

DESCRIPTION AND INTERESTS
The joys and challenges of raising twins, triplets, and higher-order multiples are covered in this magazine through positive and educational articles. Each issue includes practical information on child development, parenting, family travel, and new products, as well as personal essays. Circ: 40,000.

Audience: Parents
Frequency: Quarterly
Website: www.twinsmagazine.com

FREELANCE POTENTIAL
50% written by nonstaff writers. Publishes 10–12 freelance submissions yearly. Receives 252 queries yearly.

SUBMISSIONS
Query. Accepts email queries to editor@businessworld.com. Responds in 3 months.

- Articles: 800–1,300 words. Informational and how-to articles; profiles; and personal experience pieces. Topics include parenting, family life, health, fitness, education, music, the arts, house and home, nutrition, diet, sports, social issues, crafts, and hobbies.
- Depts/columns: To 800 words. News, new product information, opinion pieces, and short items on child development.

SAMPLE ISSUE
56 pages (30% advertising): 9 articles; 15 depts/columns. Sample copy, $5.50. Guidelines available at website.

- "I Am a Mom of Twins." Essay recounts how the author's experience of losing one of her twins in utero led to her work with the Fetal Hope Foundation.
- "When Twins Differ in Abilities." Article explains how to handle academic or athletic differences in twins.
- Sample dept/column: "Life Coach" offers tips for smooth traveling with kids.

RIGHTS AND PAYMENT
All rights. Written material, $50–$100. Pays on publication. Provides 2 contributor's copies.

➥EDITOR'S COMMENTS
We are looking for articles that are friendly and conversational in tone as they offer parenting guidance and helpful ideas for raising twins and higher-order multiples. If you have a great story idea, email your query to us.

The Universe in the Classroom

Astronomical Society of the Pacific
390 Ashton Avenue
San Francisco, CA 94112

Editor

DESCRIPTION AND INTERESTS
This e-zine is dedicated to helping educators teach students about astronomy and the universe. It provides information on astronomical topics, classroom activities, and other resources to help teachers bring those topics to the classroom. Hits per month: 10,000.

Audience: Teachers
Frequency: Quarterly
Website: www.astrosociety.org/uitc

FREELANCE POTENTIAL
75% written by nonstaff writers. Publishes 8 freelance submissions yearly; 10% by unpublished writers, 75% by authors who are new to the magazine. Receives 12 queries yearly.

SUBMISSIONS
Query. Accepts email queries to astroed@astrosociety.org. Availability of artwork improves chance of acceptance. Responds in 1 month.

- Articles: 3,000 words. Informational and factual articles; and classroom activities. Topics include astronomy and astrobiology.
- Artwork: Color prints and transparencies.
- Other: Hands-on activities.

SAMPLE ISSUE
Sample copy available at website.

- "A Silent Cry for Dark Skies." Article explains the negative impact a decreasing night sky—due to increased light emission from cities—has on astronomical research, human health, and the planet's ecosystems.
- "How Fast Are You Moving When You Are Sitting Still?" Article explains our movement through the galaxy, and features a classroom activity that illustrates our place in the vast universe.

RIGHTS AND PAYMENT
One-time rights. No payment.

➥EDITOR'S COMMENTS
Due to the educational and highly scientific nature of our topics, we must insist that writers be professors, researchers, or otherwise well-credentialed in astronomy. All articles must include a resource list for teachers, as well as detailed classroom activities based on the article's topic. If we accept your query idea, you will be given specific guidelines regarding the crafting of your article.

U-Turn Magazine

United Services Automotive Association
9800 Fredericksburg Road
San Antonio, TX 78288-0264

Editor: Roger Slavens

DESCRIPTION AND INTERESTS
This magazine strives to educate its teen readers about relevant topics and help them become responsible adults. Read by the children of current and former military personnel, it features articles on preparing for college, careers, personal finance, and relationships. Circ: 500,000.
Audience: 13–17 years
Frequency: Quarterly
Website: www.usaa.com/uturn

FREELANCE POTENTIAL
80% written by nonstaff writers. Publishes 10 freelance submissions yearly; 5% by unpublished writers, 10% by authors who are new to the magazine. Receives 20 queries yearly.

SUBMISSIONS
Query with clips. Accepts hard copy and email queries to uturn@usaa.com. SASE. Responds in 6–8 weeks if interested.

- Articles: Word lengths vary. Informational articles; profiles; and personal experience pieces. Topics include the arts, college, careers, hobbies, current events, history, music, popular culture, recreation, science, technology, social issues, sports, travel, teen driving, money, safety, and relationships.
- Other: Puzzles, games, activities, jokes, and quizzes.

SAMPLE ISSUE
32 pages (no advertising): 3 articles; 4 depts/columns. Sample copy, free with 9x12 SASE ($2 postage). Writers' guidelines and theme list available.

- "Passions That Pay." Article profiles four teens who have turned their hobbies, such as tennis and crafts, into part-time jobs.
- "Amazing (But True!) Driving Tales." Article shares funny anecdotes from teens trying to get their driver's license.
- "Extra Credit." Article explains six ways to earn college credits while still in high school.

RIGHTS AND PAYMENT
All rights. Written material, payment rates vary. Pays on acceptance. Provides 3–5 contributor's copies.

⏺EDITOR'S COMMENTS
While most topics are developed in-house, we welcome and encourage your ideas.

Vancouver Family Magazine

P.O. Box 820264
Vancouver, WA 98682

Editor: Nikki Klock

DESCRIPTION AND INTERESTS
Parenting and childcare issues, relationships, health and fitness, and education are some of the topics covered in this magazine for families living in the Clark County region of Washington. Rounding out the editorial mix are reports on local events and recreational news. Circ: 7,000.
Audience: Families
Frequency: Monthly
Web: www.vancouverfamilymagazine.com

FREELANCE POTENTIAL
90% written by nonstaff writers. Publishes 25–30 freelance submissions yearly; 30% by unpublished writers, 40% by authors who are new to the magazine. Receives 400+ queries each year.

SUBMISSIONS
Query. Accepts hard copy. SASE. Response time varies.

- Articles: Word lengths vary. Informational articles. Topics include parenting, family-related issues, health and fitness, relationships, and recreation.
- Depts/columns: Word lengths vary. Parenting and family issues, local family-related businesses, local news.

SAMPLE ISSUE
32 pages (50% advertising): 5 articles; 7 depts/columns. Editorial calendar available.

- "Maximum Impact Coaching: For the Love of Kids." Article suggests strategies for coaches to stretch their influence off the field and into everyday lives.
- "Born to Be a Star." Article interviews a mother on her new blog about the birth of her fourth child.
- Sample dept/column: "Feeding Our Families" offers recipes for Father's Day barbeques and picnics in the park.

RIGHTS AND PAYMENT
Rights vary. Assigned articles, $.15 per word. Payment policy varies.

⏺EDITOR'S COMMENTS
We prefer to work with writers who live in and have firsthand knowledge of our region. Information on new or interesting area events, businesses, and services is always of interest to us.

VegFamily

4920 Silk Oak Drive
Sarasota, FL 34232

Editor: Cynthia Mosher

DESCRIPTION AND INTERESTS
VegFamily is an online magazine and resource center dedicated to vegan family living. It offers recipes as well as informational articles related to a health-conscious, organic family lifestyle. Hits per month: 10,000.
Audience: YA–Adult
Frequency: Monthly
Website: www.vegfamily.com

FREELANCE POTENTIAL
50% written by nonstaff writers. Publishes 150+ freelance submissions yearly; 90% by unpublished writers, 50% by authors who are new to the magazine. Receives 60 queries each year.

SUBMISSIONS
Query. Accepts email queries to cynthia@vegfamily.com. Responds in 2 weeks.

- Articles: 700+ words. Informational, self-help, and how-to articles; profiles; and personal experience pieces. Topics include vegan pregnancy and health, vegan cooking, natural parenting, animal rights, the environment, and green living.
- Depts/columns: 700+ words. Nutrition advice, recipes, cooking tips, health issues, vegan news, opinions, family profiles, and parenting issues by age group.
- Artwork: JPEG and GIF files.
- Other: Activities. Submit seasonal material 2 months in advance.

SAMPLE ISSUE
Sample copy available at website.

- "10 Great Green Opportunities." Article examines 10 job markets that are showing an interest in—and providing opportunities for—"green" workers.
- Sample dept/column: "Vegan Teens" takes a look at the challenges of maintaining a vegan lifestyle in college.

RIGHTS AND PAYMENT
First and electronic rights. Articles, $10–$30. Pays on publication.

◆EDITOR'S COMMENTS
We clearly seek articles about enjoying a vegan diet and lifestyle, but we are also a family magazine. We welcome articles on pregnancy, parenting, and family issues (although a vegan angle is always appreciated!).

VerveGirl

401 Richmond Street West, Suite 245
Toronto, Ontario M5V 1X3
Canada

Editor-in-Chief: Xania Khan

DESCRIPTION AND INTERESTS
VerveGirl is a lifestyle publication for Canadian teenage girls. As such, it covers all the topics of interest to these readers, including fashion, pop culture, school, careers, and contemporary social issues. It produces separate editions in French and in English. Circ: 150,000 English; 30,000 French.
Audience: Girls, 13–24 years
Frequency: 8 times each year
Website: www.vervegirl.com

FREELANCE POTENTIAL
50% written by nonstaff writers. Publishes 10–20 freelance submissions yearly. Receives 200 queries yearly.

SUBMISSIONS
Query. Accepts hard copy. SAE/IRC. Response time varies.

- Articles: Word lengths vary. Informational and self-help articles; profiles; interviews; and personal experience pieces. Topics include health, nutrition, fitness, fashion, beauty, social issues, current events, the environment, education, careers, and music.
- Depts/columns: Word lengths vary. Entertainment, fashion and beauty, and health and wellness.
- Other: Quizzes.

SAMPLE ISSUE
50 pages: 5 articles; 5 depts/columns. Sample copy available at website.

- "Free the Children's Commitment to Change." Article profiles Free the Children, an organization dedicated to building schools, small businesses, and clean water reservoirs in developing countries.
- "Life After Retail." Article explains creative ways girls can parlay their retail job skills into a future career.
- Sample dept/columns: "Fashion and Beauty" presents a primer on the many uses of the essential oil Vitamin E.

RIGHTS AND PAYMENT
Rights vary. Written material, payment rates vary. Pays on publication.

◆EDITOR'S COMMENTS
While many topics, especially fashion and beauty, know no geographic bounds, other subjects should relate to Canada.

Vibrant Life

55 West Oak Ridge Drive
Hagerstown, MD 21740

Editor: Heather Quintana

DESCRIPTION AND INTERESTS
Vibrant Life provides practical information to promote better health and happier families. The country's oldest health publication, it was launched in 1885 under the name *Pacific Health Journal Temperance Advocate*. Circ: 21,711.

Audience: Families
Frequency: 6 times each year
Website: www.vibrantlife.com

FREELANCE POTENTIAL
95% written by nonstaff writers. Publishes 25 freelance submissions yearly; 30% by unpublished writers, 60% by authors who are new to the magazine. Receives 300 queries, 144 unsolicited mss yearly.

SUBMISSIONS
Prefers complete ms; will accept query. Accepts hard copy and email to vibrantlife@rhpa.org (Microsoft Word attachments). SASE. Responds in 1 month.

- Articles: 450–1,500 words. Informational, how-to, and self-help articles; profiles; and interviews. Topics include health, fitness, nutrition, family, spiritual balance, challenges and triumphs, safety, and environmental stewardship.
- Depts/columns: Word lengths vary. Health news, medical advice, green living, spiritual guidance, family life, and recipes.

SAMPLE ISSUE
32 pages: 3 articles; 9 depts/columns. Sample copy and guidelines, $1 with 9x12 SASE (3 first-class stamps).

- "Look on the Bright Side." Article describes five strategies to help readers develop a new outlook on life.
- Sample dept/column: "Going Green" offers tips for environmentally friendly shopping.

RIGHTS AND PAYMENT
Full, nonexclusive rights. Written material, $100–$300. Pays on publication. Provides 3 contributor's copies.

☛ EDITOR'S COMMENTS
We seek more first-person accounts and information for young families, as well as articles that incorporate a holistic view of health: mind, body, and spirit. Articles representing a happy, healthy outlook are welcome.

The Village Family

501 40th Street SW, Suite 201
Fargo, ND 58103

Editor: Laurie Neill

DESCRIPTION AND INTERESTS
A publication of the Village Family Service Center, this magazine features articles designed to educate and encourage families to develop positive relationships. Most of its material is directly related to the Fargo region. Circ: 25,000.

Audience: Families
Frequency: 6 times each year
Website: www.thevillagefamily.org

FREELANCE POTENTIAL
90% written by nonstaff writers. Publishes 18 freelance submissions yearly; 5–10% by authors who are new to the magazine. Receives 720 queries, 24 unsolicited mss yearly.

SUBMISSIONS
Query or send complete ms with brief author biography. Accepts email submissions to magazine@thevillagefamily.org. Response time varies.

- Articles: 1,500–2,500 words. Informational, self-help, and how-to articles; profiles; interviews; and personal experience pieces. Topics include current events, social issues, relationships, parenting, and health and fitness.
- Depts/columns: Word lengths vary. Crafts, health tips, recipes, relationships, opinion.

SAMPLE ISSUE
46 pages (15% advertising): 7 articles; 6 depts/columns. Writers' guidelines available at website.

- "Talking to Your Children About Racism." Article provides tips for helping children understand racism, fairness, and equality.
- "Making a Close Knit Community." Article explains how to get involved with knitting for charity.
- Sample dept/column: "Dad's View." offers a humorous essay on getting ready, however inefficiently, for Christmas.

RIGHTS AND PAYMENT
First and electronic rights. Written material, $.07 per word. Reprints, $30–$50. Pays on publication.

☛ EDITOR'S COMMENTS
Articles featuring information for the elderly, and articles that tackle tough social or family issues are welcome here. Please note that we no longer accept hard copy.

VOYA Magazine

4501 Forbes Boulevard, Suite 200
Lanham, MD 20706

Editor-in-Chief: RoseMary Honnold

DESCRIPTION AND INTERESTS

Formerly titled *Voice of Youth Advocates*, this magazine is written for librarians and other professionals who work with young adults. It features reviews of young adult literature and articles on issues relating to the teen experience. Circ: 7,000.

Audience: Librarians
Frequency: 6 times each year
Website: www.voya.com

FREELANCE POTENTIAL

95% written by nonstaff writers. Publishes 100 freelance submissions yearly; 5% by unpublished writers, 60% by authors who are new to the magazine. Receives 60 queries yearly.

SUBMISSIONS

Query with résumé, synopsis, and market analysis. Accepts hard copy and email queries to editors@voya.com. Availability of artwork improves chance of acceptance. SASE. Responds in 2–4 months.

- Articles: 750–3,500 words. Informational and how-to articles; book reviews; and book lists. Topics include young adult literature, contemporary authors, and library programs.
- Depts/columns: Staff written.
- Artwork: B/W and color prints.
- Other: Submit seasonal material 1 year in advance.

SAMPLE ISSUE

174 pages (20% advertising): 6 articles; 9 depts/columns; 176 reviews. Sample copy, free with 9x12 SASE. Writers' guidelines available at website.

- "Crossing the Lines." Article offers a conversation with author Paul Volponi, who writes books for teens that feature people of color.
- "The New Literacy Equation: Books + Computers = Multiplatform." Article discusses the new media technology that is changing the way young adults do their reading.

RIGHTS AND PAYMENT

All rights. Written material, $50–$125. Pays on publication. Provides 3 contributor's copies.

◆ EDITOR'S COMMENTS

We are looking for cutting-edge topics of interest to those who serve young adults in library settings. We look for authors who have hands-on experience in the field.

Washington Family Magazine

485 Spring Park Place, Suite 500
Herndon, VA 20170

Managing Editor: Marae Leggs

DESCRIPTION AND INTERESTS

This magazine serves parents in Washington, D.C. with information about topics of interest to them, including parenting issues, children's health and development, education, and family fun to be had in the region. Circ: 100,000.

Audience: Parents
Frequency: Monthly
Website: www.thefamilymagazine.com

FREELANCE POTENTIAL

75% written by nonstaff writers. Publishes 90 freelance submissions yearly; 50% by unpublished writers, 50% by authors who are new to the magazine. Receives 1,200 queries yearly.

SUBMISSIONS

Query with outline. Accepts email queries to editor@thefamilymagazine.com (Microsoft Word attachments). No simultaneous submissions. Response time varies.

- Articles: 800–900 words. Informational, how-to, and self-help articles; and personal experience pieces. Topics include parenting, family life, relationships, fitness, crafts, hobbies, the arts, education, music, multicultural and ethnic issues, social issues, and travel.
- Depts/columns: Word lengths vary.
- Artwork: B/W prints and transparencies. Line art.
- Other: Submit seasonal material at least 3 months in advance.

SAMPLE ISSUE

126 pages (50% advertising): 14 articles; 9 depts/columns. Sample copy, $4. Guidelines and editorial calendar available at website.

- "What's for Lunch?" Article reports how parents can raise the nutritional level of bag lunches without sacrificing the yum factor.
- Sample dept/column: "Hands-on Kids Activities" offers activity ideas that explain some of the wonders of science.

RIGHTS AND PAYMENT

Exclusive regional and Web rights. Articles, $50. Depts/columns and artwork, payment rates vary. Pays on publication. Provides 1 tearsheet for contributors.

◆ EDITOR'S COMMENTS

We prefer to work with local authors. If you are not working locally, you must still be able to localize your material to our region.

Washington Parent

4701 Sangamore Road, Suite 270
Bethesda, MD 20186

Editor: Margaret Hut

DESCRIPTION AND INTERESTS
Washington Parent hopes to educate and support families living in and around the U.S. capital with articles on child development, education, travel, and entertainment. Circ: 75,000.
Audience: Families
Frequency: Monthly
Website: www.washingtonparent.com

FREELANCE POTENTIAL
90% written by nonstaff writers. Publishes 20 freelance submissions yearly. Receives 1,000 queries yearly.

SUBMISSIONS
Query. Accepts email queries to contactus@washingtonparent.net (Microsoft Word or WordPerfect attachments). Response time varies.

- Articles: 1,000–1,200 words. Informational and how-to articles. Topics include regional news and events, parenting and family issues, entertainment, gifted and special education, child development, health, fitness, the environment, and multicultural and ethnic issues.
- Depts/columns: Word lengths vary. Family travel, book and media reviews, education, topics relating to children with special needs, and short news items.

SAMPLE ISSUE
98 pages (63% advertising): 7 articles; 8 depts/columns; 3 special resource sections. Sample copy, writers' guidelines, and editorial calendar available.

- "Redefining the Work-Family Balance." Article profiles a local woman who has managed a successful career while raising two young children.
- Sample dept/column: "Goodstuff" includes travel tips and deals.

RIGHTS AND PAYMENT
First rights. Written material, payment rates vary. Provides 3 contributor's copies.

➥EDITOR'S COMMENTS
We are proud to be recognized as the trusted resource for parents in the region. We welcome all useful and interesting ideas that deal with raising children. Preference is given to local writers; however, we sometimes publish articles from authors outside the area.

Weatherwise

1319 Eighteenth Street NW
Washington, DC 20036

Managing Editor: Margaret Benner

DESCRIPTION AND INTERESTS
Weatherwise shares the wondrous forces of nature with a general readership, examining the science behind various phenomena while emphasizing the human element. Circ: 5,800.
Audience: YA–Adult
Frequency: 6 times each year
Website: www.weatherwise.org

FREELANCE POTENTIAL
50% written by nonstaff writers. Publishes 36 freelance submissions yearly; 30% by authors who are new to the magazine. Receives 100 queries yearly.

SUBMISSIONS
Query with outline, résumé, and clips. Accepts email queries to ww@heldref.org. No simultaneous submissions. Availability of artwork improves chance of acceptance. Responds in 2 months.

- Articles: 1,500–2,000 words. Informational articles; photo-essays; and reviews. Topics include meteorology, climate change, storms, safety, and other topics related to weather—all with a scientific basis.
- Depts/columns: 800–1,500 words. Weather Q&As, book and software reviews, weather highlights, forecasts, and historical pieces.
- Artwork: Color prints or transparencies; digital files.

SAMPLE ISSUE
82 pages: 6 articles; 9 depts/columns. Guidelines available at website.

- "The Climate and Weather of Delaware, Maryland, and Washington, D.C." Article examines the diverse weather patterns of this area.
- "Harnessing the Sun." Article relates the promises of solar energy.

RIGHTS AND PAYMENT
All rights. All material, payment rates vary. Pays on publication.

➥EDITOR'S COMMENTS
We begin planning an issue at least six months before the cover date. In other words, think hurricanes in January and blizzards in July. Published articles are often chosen as much for the quality and impact of the photographs as for editorial excellence. Authors must at least provide sources, leads, or ideas for illustrating an article.

Westchester Family

7 Purdy Street, Suite 201
Harrison, NY 10528

Editor: Jean Sheff

DESCRIPTION AND INTERESTS
Westchester Family serves as a resourceful guide for parents living in this New York county. Included in its pages are informative and insightful articles on parenting, health and safety, and education. Each issue also includes comprehensive events and activities calendars. Circ: 59,000.
Audience: Parents
Frequency: Monthly
Website: www.westchesterfamily.com

FREELANCE POTENTIAL
80% written by nonstaff writers. Publishes 40 freelance submissions yearly; 10% by unpublished writers, 30% by authors who are new to the magazine. Receives 800 queries yearly.

SUBMISSIONS
Query with clips. Accepts hard copy. SASE. Response time varies.

- Articles: 800–1,200 words. Informational articles; profiles; interviews; photo-essays; and personal experience pieces. Topics include education, music, recreation, regional news, social issues, special and gifted education, travel, and women's issues.
- Depts/columns: 400–800 words. News and media reviews.

SAMPLE ISSUE
90 pages (52% advertising): 3 articles; 11 depts/columns; 5 calendars. Sample copy, free with 9x12 SASE. Guidelines available.

- "What's Up with Boys." Article presents the viewpoints of three experts on what boys need to thrive in today's world.
- "23 Gold-Winning Parenting Products." Article reports on the winners of the National Parenting Publications Awards.
- Sample dept/column: "Learn by Doing" offers tips from a local chef on getting kids to help in the kitchen.

RIGHTS AND PAYMENT
First rights. Written material, $25–$200. Pays on publication. Provides 1 contributor's copy.

➛EDITOR'S COMMENTS
We like to see in-depth reporting that is written in an easy-to-read style. But don't send us something that has been overdone. We want fresh and new topics that are of interest to parents in our region.

Westchester Parent

1040 Avenue of the Americas, 4th Floor
New York, NY 10018

Editor-in-Chief: Helen Freedman

DESCRIPTION AND INTERESTS
Westchester Parent reaches families living just north of New York City in the primarily affluent communities of Westchester County in New York, and Greenwich and Stamford in Connecticut. Like the other regional publications in its group, the tabloid covers issues and events of local interest, as well as articles on more general parenting topics. Circ: 285,000.
Audience: Parents
Frequency: Monthly
Website: www.nymetroparents.com

FREELANCE POTENTIAL
50% written by nonstaff writers. Publishes 300 freelance submissions yearly. Receives 12 queries, 72 unsolicited mss yearly.

SUBMISSIONS
Query or send complete ms. Accepts hard copy and email submissions to hfreedman@ davlermedia.com. SASE. Responds in 1 week.

- Articles: 800–1,000 words. Informational articles; profiles; interviews; and personal experience pieces. Topics include family issues, education, camp, health, nutrition, fitness, current events, and regional news.
- Depts/columns: Staff written.
- Other: Submit seasonal material 4 months in advance.

SAMPLE ISSUE
96 pages: 12 articles; 9 depts/columns. Sample copy, free with 10x13 SASE.

- "Game Time: Boys vs. Girls." Article details the detrimental effects of violent video games on children, and tells parents how to limit and monitor them.
- "A Bridge to Family." Article profiles a program that helps teenagers living in foster care transition to being part of a family.
- "Are You At Risk for a Pre-Term Birth?" Article describes a new, FDA-approved test that helps doctors manage high-risk pregnancies.

RIGHTS AND PAYMENT
First New York area rights. No payment.

➛EDITOR'S COMMENTS
Writers must be familiar with our coverage area and readership demographics. Please note that we do not publish memoirs, fiction, or poetry. In some cases, we will pay a modest fee for assigned pieces.

West Coast Families

13988 Maycrest Way, Unit 140
Richmond, British Columbia V6V 3C3
Canada

Submissions Editor

DESCRIPTION AND INTERESTS
Serving families in Canada's British Columbia province, *West Coast Families* offers articles on parenting issues, child development, family fun, and health and fitness. Circ: 50,000.

Audience: Parents
Frequency: 8 times each year
Website: www.westcoastfamilies.com

FREELANCE POTENTIAL
75% written by nonstaff writers. Publishes 40 freelance submissions yearly; 25% by authors who are new to the magazine. Receives 300 queries yearly.

SUBMISSIONS
Query. Accepts hard copy and email queries to editor@westcoastfamilies.com. SAE/IRC. Response time varies.

- Articles: 600–800 words. Informational, self-help, and how-to articles; profiles; interviews, and personal experience pieces. Topics include family life, parenting, recreation, travel, religion, current events, health, fitness, finance, education, sports, hobbies, science, technology, nature, and pets.
- Depts/columns: Staff written.
- Other: Puzzles, activities, and jokes. Submit seasonal material 3 months in advance.

SAMPLE ISSUE
40 pages (8% advertising): 6 articles; 5 depts/columns. Sample copy, free with 9x12 SAE/IRC ($1.45 postage); also available for download at website. Guidelines and editorial calendar available.

- "Go Green and Save on Back to School." Article outlines ways to save money on school supplies.
- "Are Your Kids Stressed?" Article shares professional advice on how to minimize anxiety factors for kids.

RIGHTS AND PAYMENT
One-time and electronic rights. Written material, payment rates vary. Pays on publication. Provides contributor's copies upon request.

⚫EDITOR'S COMMENTS
When crafting your article, remember that we serve readers in British Columbia, and that all material must have a Canadian angle. We want to hear from parents about what they have learned from their children.

Western New York Family Magazine

3147 Delaware Avenue, Suite B
Buffalo, NY 14217

Editor: Michele Miller

DESCRIPTION AND INTERESTS
Parents living in New York's Erie and Niagara counties turn to this magazine for articles on child-rearing, family bonding, education, and children's health. It also publishes information on regional family-oriented events. Circ: 25,000.

Audience: Parents
Frequency: Monthly
Website: www.wnyfamilymagazine.com

FREELANCE POTENTIAL
90% written by nonstaff writers. Publishes 125–150 freelance submissions yearly; 30% by unpublished writers, 30% by authors who are new to the magazine. Receives 1,200 unsolicited mss yearly.

SUBMISSIONS
Send complete ms with 2-sentence bio. Accepts email submissions to michele@ wnyfamilymagazine.com (text in body of email along with Microsoft Word attachment) and simultaneous submissions if identified. Response time varies.

- Articles: "UpFront" articles, 2,000–2,500 words. Other features, 750–1,500 words. Informational, how-to, and self-help articles; creative nonfiction; humor; and personal experience pieces. Topics include parenting, education, and special needs children.
- Depts/columns: Word lengths vary. News briefs, reviews, family travel, recipes, fatherhood, and single parenting.
- Other: Submit seasonal material 3 months in advance.

SAMPLE ISSUE
64 pages (40% advertising): 11 articles; 12 depts/columns. Sample copy, $2.50 with 9x12 SASE ($1.79 postage). Guidelines and editorial calendar available at website.

- "Are You a Helicopter Parent?" Article discusses the trend of over-involved parenting.
- Sample dept/column: "The Newbie Dad" offers insight into fathers' conversations.

RIGHTS AND PAYMENT
First or reprint and electronic rights. Written material, $35–$200. Pays on publication.

⚫EDITOR'S COMMENTS
Local writers will always receive preferential treatment from us. We have just gone digital, so online rights are assumed with purchase.

West Virginia Family Magazine

P.O. Box 107
Buckhannon, WV 26201

Editor: Carla Cosner

DESCRIPTION AND INTERESTS
The message of this award-winning regional magazine is "family first." It features informative and practical articles on health, safety, education, family travel, and entertainment. A comprehensive calendar is included in each issue. Circ: 17,000.

Audience: Parents
Frequency: 6 times each year
Website: www.wvfamilymagazine.com

FREELANCE POTENTIAL
85% written by nonstaff writers. Publishes 25–40 freelance submissions yearly; 10% by unpublished writers, 25–30% by authors who are new to the magazine.

SUBMISSIONS
Send complete ms. Accepts email submissions to editor@wvfamilymagazine.com. Responds in 6 weeks.

- Articles: 500–850 words. Informational and how-to articles; profiles; interviews; and personal experience pieces. Topics include careers, gifted and special education, current events, health and fitness, recreation, and social issues.
- Depts/columns: Word lengths vary. Child development, safety, parenting issues, finance, and regional news.

SAMPLE ISSUE
26 pages: 3 articles; 6 depts/columns; 1 guide; 1 calendar. Sample copy, free. Guidelines and editorial calendar available.

- "2009 Safe Teen Driving Series." Article offers tips for keeping teen drivers safe.
- "Volunteer: It's Good for Your Health." Article discusses research on the health benefits of volunteering and tells how to get started.
- Sample dept/column: "Ages & Stages" provides ideas for keeping children of all ages entertained while in the car.

RIGHTS AND PAYMENT
One-time print and electronic rights. Articles, $25. Filler, payment rates vary. Pays on publication. Provides 1 contributor's copy.

☛EDITOR'S COMMENTS
We're looking for health, safety, and education articles that include a local source. Your article should quickly and directly get to the point and offer solutions.

What If?

19 Lynwood Place
Guelph, Ontario N1G 2V9
Canada

Managing Editor: Mike Leslie

DESCRIPTION AND INTERESTS
What If? offers Canadian teens a venue to express their opinions, publish their writing, and display their artistic talents for other teens to enjoy. It seeks poetry, fiction, editorials, reviews, and artwork. Circ: 3,000.

Audience: 12–19 years
Frequency: Quarterly
Website: www.whatifmagazine.com

FREELANCE POTENTIAL
95% written by nonstaff writers. Publishes 100 freelance submissions yearly; 95% by unpublished writers, 90% by authors who are new to the magazine. Receives 3,000 unsolicited mss each year.

SUBMISSIONS
Canadian authors only. Send complete ms. Accepts hard copy, email submissions to editor@whatifmagazine.com (Microsoft Word attachments), and simultaneous submissions if identified. Availability of artwork improves chance of acceptance. SASE. Responds in 3 months.

- Articles: To 1,500 words. Opinion pieces and personal essays. Topics vary.
- Fiction: To 3,000 words. Genres include contemporary, realistic, inspirational, and science fiction; mystery; suspense; fantasy; and humor.
- Depts/columns: Word lengths vary. Reviews and interviews.
- Artwork: Color prints. Line art.
- Other: Poetry, to 20 lines.

SAMPLE ISSUE
48 pages (3% advertising): 2 essays; 8 stories; 8 poems; 4 depts/columns. Sample copy, $8 with 9x12 SAE. Guidelines available.

- "Global Warming." Humorous essay presents the economic upside of global warming.
- Sample dept/column: *"What If?* Interviews" offers an interview with author Arthur Slade.

RIGHTS AND PAYMENT
First rights. No payment. Provides 2 contributor's copies.

☛EDITOR'S COMMENTS
We never see enough editorials or opinion pieces. Please note that we offer many contests that provide even more opportunities for young authors to become published.

What's Up?

Canada's Family Magazine

496 Metler Road
Ridgeville, Ontario L0S 1M0
Canada

Editor-in-Chief: Paul Baswick

DESCRIPTION AND INTERESTS

This photo-filled publication provides articles on all aspects of parenting and family life. Topics covered include education, child development, health and nutrition, social issues, entertainment, safety, and family recreational opportunities. Circ: 100,000.
Audience: Families
Frequency: 6 times each year
Website: www.whatsupfamilies.com

FREELANCE POTENTIAL

80% written by nonstaff writers. Publishes 30 freelance submissions yearly; 60% by authors who are new to the magazine. Receives 348 queries yearly.

SUBMISSIONS

Canadian authors only. Query. Accepts email queries to paul@whatsupfamily.ca. Response time varies.

- Articles: Word lengths vary. Informational articles; profiles; and interviews. Topics include education, family issues, travel, fitness, nutrition, health, the arts, and entertainment.
- Depts/columns: Word lengths vary. "Mom Time," "Health Matters," "Finances," "Baby Steps," "From the Kitchen," "Learning Curves," "Family Travel," "What's Up with Dad?" "Kids' Space," "Cool Careers," "Kid Craft," and other children's activities.

SAMPLE ISSUE

82 pages (15% advertising): 3 articles; 17 depts/columns.

- "Safe or Sheltered?" Article examines whether it is healthy for parents to monitor their child's every move.
- Sample dept/column: "Health Matters" discusses the potential risks of a human bite and explains how to treat it.

RIGHTS AND PAYMENT

All rights. Written material, payment rates vary. Payment policy varies. Provides copies.

EDITOR'S COMMENTS

Because we serve the needs of Canadian readers, we must insist on working only with Canadian writers. All material must have relevance to Canadian families. Keep in mind that our audience consists primarily of families with young children.

Wire Tap Magazine

Independent Media Institute
77 Federal Road
San Francisco, CA 94107

Associate Editor

DESCRIPTION AND INTERESTS

Wire Tap Magazine provides young progressives with a forum for their activism and opinions. It seeks to promote social justice through its news coverage, features, and personal essays. Hits per month: 60,000.
Audience: 18–30 years
Frequency: Updated daily
Website: www.wiretapmag.org

FREELANCE POTENTIAL

95% written by nonstaff writers. Publishes 120 freelance submissions yearly. Receives 300 queries yearly.

SUBMISSIONS

Query. Accepts email queries to submissions@ wiretapmag.org (no attachments). Response time varies.

- Articles: Word lengths vary. Informational articles; profiles; interviews; and personal experience pieces. Topics include social issues, politics, culture, current events, the environment, immigration, relationships, peace, education, and youth activism.
- Depts/columns: Word lengths vary. Reviews, politics, and news.
- Other: Poetry.

SAMPLE ISSUE

Sample copy and writers' guidelines available at website.

- "Racial Profiling in a Post-Racial America." Article looks at several recent arrests of black men, including the author.
- "Homeless Not Helpless: Reaching My Goals." Personal essay tells how the author overcame adversity.

RIGHTS AND PAYMENT

Electronic rights. Written material, $50–$400 for assigned pieces. No payment for unsolicited submissions. Payment policy varies.

EDITOR'S COMMENTS

We are always looking for new writers, activists, and artists to add to the site. We are happy to review all submissions from young people, but we are most likely to publish writing that is generally respectful and socially responsible, written in a personal voice, well-researched, has a call to action, and seeks to include those who have not traditionally had a voice.

Writers' Journal

Val-Tech Media
P.O. Box 394
Perham, MN 56573-0394

Editor: Leon Ogroske

DESCRIPTION AND INTERESTS

This magazine for writers of all specialties is chock full of information about the skills and techniques needed for successful fiction and nonfiction writing. The business side of writing and publishing is also covered. Circ: 23,000.

Audience: YA–Adult
Frequency: 6 times each year
Website: www.writersjournal.com

FREELANCE POTENTIAL

50% written by nonstaff writers. Publishes 40 freelance submissions yearly; 20% by unpublished writers, 80% by authors who are new to the magazine. Receives 200 queries and unsolicited mss yearly.

SUBMISSIONS

Query with clips; or send complete ms. Accepts hard copy and email submissions to writersjournal@writersjournal.com (text only). SASE. Responds in 2–6 months.

- Articles: 1,200–2,200 words. Informational and how-to articles; profiles; and interviews. Topics include fiction writing, travel writing, technical writing, business writing, screenwriting, journalism, poetry, writing skills and styles, punctuation, interviewing techniques, research, record-keeping, income venues, finance, and self-publishing.
- Depts/columns: Staff written.
- Other: Poetry, to 15 lines.

SAMPLE ISSUE

64 pages (10% advertising): 7 articles; 6 stories; 11 depts/columns. Sample copy, $6 with 9x12 SASE. Guidelines available at website.

- "Snazzy First Lines." Article offers several approaches to writing opening sentences that will catch an editor's eye.
- "A Few Kind Words About Passive Voice." Article discusses how best to use the passive voice in writing.

RIGHTS AND PAYMENT

First North American serial rights. Articles, $30. Poetry, $5 per poem. Pays on publication. Provides 2 contributor's copies upon request and a 1-year subscription.

⇨EDITOR'S COMMENTS

We look for highly informative articles that feature a positive and practical approach, particularly those written with a narrow focus.

Yes Mag

501-3960 Quadra Street
Victoria, British Columbia V8X 4A3
Canada

Managing Editor: Jude Isabella

DESCRIPTION AND INTERESTS

This "science magazine for adventurous minds" targets middle-grade readers with engaging articles on everything from astronomy to zoology. Circ: 23,000.

Audience: 9–14 years
Frequency: 6 times each year
Website: www.yesmag.ca

FREELANCE POTENTIAL

70% written by nonstaff writers. Publishes 30 freelance submissions yearly; 5% by unpublished writers, 15% by authors who are new to the magazine. Receives 300 queries yearly.

SUBMISSIONS

Query. Accepts email queries to editor@yesmag.ca. Response time varies.

- Articles: Features, 300–800 words. Short, theme-related articles, 300–600 words. Informational articles, 250 words. Topics include astronomy, biology, chemistry, ecology, engineering, math, science, technology, nature, and the environment.
- Depts/columns: 250 words. Science and technology news, entomology, world records, environmental updates, book and product reviews, and experiments.

SAMPLE ISSUE

32 pages (no advertising): 5 articles; 6 depts/columns. Sample copy, $4.50 Canadian with SAE/IRC. Guidelines and theme list available.

- "Panning for Pigments." Article describes the work of an artist who creates his own colors from plants and other materials found within 100 miles of the Cambridge Center for the Arts in Ontario.
- "Fishing for the Future." Article explains the snowball effect of overfishing.
- Sample dept/column: "Hot or Not" features kids' reviews of science kits and books.

RIGHTS AND PAYMENT

First and one-time Korean rights. "Sci & Tech Watch," $100. Articles, $145 per page. Pays on publication. Provides 1 contributor's copy.

⇨EDITOR'S COMMENTS

Our magazine is published in partnership with Actua, a Canadian not-for-profit organization that supports the development and delivery of hands-on science, engineering, and technology programs for youth.

Young Adult Today

1551 Regency Court
Calumet City, IL 60409

Editor: Aja Carr

DESCRIPTION AND INTERESTS
Young Adult Today, published by Urban Ministries, is a study guide for young, urban, Christian adults. It features articles and Bible lessons designed to help them make Christian decisions in today's sometimes challenging world. Circ: 25,000.
Audience: 18–24 years
Frequency: Quarterly
Website: www.youngadulttoday.net

FREELANCE POTENTIAL
90% written by nonstaff writers. Publishes 52 freelance submissions yearly; 50% by unpublished writers, 50% by authors who are new to the magazine. Receives 240 queries yearly.

SUBMISSIONS
All material is assigned. Query with résumé. No unsolicited mss. Accepts hard copy. SASE. Responds in 2 months.

- Articles: To 400 words. Informational and inspirational articles; Bible lessons; devotional readings; and Bible study guides that explain how Scripture lessons can be applied to modern life.

SAMPLE ISSUE
80 pages (4% advertising): 1 article; 13 teaching plans; 13 corresponding Bible study guides. Sample copy, $2.25 with 9x12 SASE ($.87 postage). Guidelines available.

- "Five Ways to Look Like Jesus." Article outlines five elements to living a life modeled after Jesus' teachings.
- "Jesus as God's Son." Bible study examines the many ways the Bible establishes Jesus as God's son.
- "Help From Higher Up." Teaching plan illustrates our need to sometimes ask for help or mercy from someone.

RIGHTS AND PAYMENT
Rights negotiable. Written material, $150 per lesson. Pays on publication.

➻EDITOR'S COMMENTS
Please note that all of our material is assigned. We seek submissions of feature articles and educational pieces that will empower God's people, particularly within the black community. We'd like to hear from writers who understand our magazine and the message we are relaying to our readers.

Young Adult Today Leader

1551 Regency Court
Calumet City, IL 60409

Editor: Aja Carr

DESCRIPTION AND INTERESTS
Young Adult Today Leader is the companion magazine to *Young Adult Today*. While the latter targets young adults with Christian messages, the former targets leaders of youth education ministries with weekly lesson plans, Bible lessons, and articles to inspire their ministry. Circ: 15,000.
Audience: Religious educators
Frequency: Quarterly
Website: www.youngadulttoday.net

FREELANCE POTENTIAL
90% written by nonstaff writers. Publishes 52 freelance submissions yearly; 50% by unpublished writers, 50% by authors who are new to the magazine. Receives 240 queries yearly.

SUBMISSIONS
All work is assigned. Query with résumé. No unsolicited mss. Accepts hard copy. SASE. Responds in 2 months.

- Articles: Informational and inspirational articles, word lengths vary. Devotionals, 400 words. Topics include current events and social issues as they relate to Christianity and the Bible.

SAMPLE ISSUE
96 pages (no advertising): 1 article; 13 lesson plans; 13 Bible study guides. Sample copy, $2.25 with 9x12 SASE ($.87 postage). Guidelines available.

- "Five Ways to Look Like Jesus." Article offers five simple ways that we can emulate Jesus in our lives and in our actions.
- "Forgiving Sins." Lesson plan outlines techniques for getting a class to talk about sinning and forgiving.
- "Christ as Teacher." Bible study guide outlines Scripture verses that describe Christ's powerful and dependable teachings, and discusses the role of the modern Bible teacher.

RIGHTS AND PAYMENT
Rights negotiable. Written material, $150. Pays on publication.

➻EDITOR'S COMMENTS
Although we assign all work, we are interested in hearing from Christian teachers who can add to our formula of inspiring teachers and providing them with practical, reproducible Bible teaching plans.

Young Rider

P.O. Box 8237
Lexington, KY 40533

Editor: Lesley Ward

DESCRIPTION AND INTERESTS
As the name indicates, this magazine is written for young horse riders and lovers. Each issue includes a mix of profiles, entertaining stories, and practical information on riding techniques and horse care. Circ: 92,000.

Audience: 6–14 years
Frequency: 6 times each year
Website: www.youngrider.com

FREELANCE POTENTIAL
20% written by nonstaff writers. Publishes 20 freelance submissions yearly; 5% by unpublished writers, 5% by authors who are new to the magazine. Receives 96 queries yearly.

SUBMISSIONS
Query. Accepts email queries to yreditor@bowtieinc.com (Microsoft Word attachments). Responds in 2 weeks.

- Articles: Word lengths vary. Informational and how-to articles; and profiles. Topics include horseback riding, training, careers, English and Western riding techniques, and general horse care.
- Fiction: 1,200 words. Stories that feature horses, ponies, and youth themes.
- Artwork: Color prints, transparencies, and high-resolution digital images.

SAMPLE ISSUE
64 pages (28% advertising): 6 articles; 9 depts/columns. Sample copy, $3.99 with 9x12 SASE ($1 postage). Guidelines and editorial calendar available.

- "Galloping Along with Gina Miles." Article interviews the 2008 Olympic Silver Medalist.
- "Helping Horses in Need." Article profiles a rider who gave up shows to volunteer her time with a horse rescue.
- Sample dept/column: "Bookbag" shares new releases that will appeal to horse lovers.

RIGHTS AND PAYMENT
First serial rights. Written material, $.10 per word. Artwork, payment rates vary. Pays on publication. Provides 2 contributor's copies.

➡EDITOR'S COMMENTS
Currently we are looking for more celebrity features that focus on famous horses, riders, and young celebrities who ride. Also of interest are well-written fictional short stories.

Young Salvationist

The Salvation Army
615 Slaters Lane
Alexandria, VA 22314

Editor: Captain Amy Reardon

DESCRIPTION AND INTERESTS
The articles in this magazine address the contemporary social issues and life experiences affecting young adult Christians. Practical, inspirational, and humorous stories are featured. Circ: 48,000.

Audience: 13–21 years
Frequency: 10 times each year
Website: www.salpubs.com

FREELANCE POTENTIAL
80% written by nonstaff writers. Publishes 40 freelance submissions yearly; 20% by unpublished writers, 30% by authors who are new to the magazine. Receives 36 queries, 120 unsolicited mss yearly.

SUBMISSIONS
Prefers complete ms; will accept query. Accepts hard copy, email submissions to ys@usn.salvationarmy.org, and simultaneous submissions. SASE. Responds in 4–6 weeks.

- Articles: To 1,000 words. How-to, inspirational, and personal experience articles; profiles; interviews; and humor. Topics include religion and issues of relevance to teens.
- Depts/columns: Word lengths vary. "Blog of the Month," "On Olivia's Mind," social justice, and music reviews.
- Other: Submit seasonal material 6 months in advance.

SAMPLE ISSUE
24 pages (no advertising): 5 articles; 6 depts/columns. Sample copy and guidelines available at website.

- "Slave-Free Chocolate." Article tells how much of the cocoa used in chocolate is farmed by child laborers and includes information on fair-trade certified chocolate.
- Sample dept/column: "Blog of the Month" recounts an inspirational story from a Young Salvationist student.

RIGHTS AND PAYMENT
First and second rights. Written material, $.15 per word for first rights; $.10 per word for reprints. Pays on acceptance. Provides 4 contributor's copies.

➡EDITOR'S COMMENTS
Our need for outside freelancers is decreasing; however, we are currently looking for articles that address gender specific issues.

Youth & Christian Education Leadership

1080 Montgomery Avenue
Cleveland, TN 37311

Editorial Assistant: Tammy Hatfield

DESCRIPTION AND INTERESTS
A product of the Church of God Publishing House, this magazine is directed toward the people who work within Christian education—Sunday school teachers, youth pastors, Christian education directors, and outreach workers. Circ: 10,000.
Audience: Adults
Frequency: Quarterly
Website: www.pathwaypress.org

FREELANCE POTENTIAL
10% written by nonstaff writers. Publishes 10 freelance submissions yearly; 90% by unpublished writers, 10% by authors who are new to the magazine. Receives 30–35 queries, 20–25 unsolicited mss yearly.

SUBMISSIONS
Prefers complete ms with author biography; will accept queries. Accepts disk submissions (Microsoft Word files) and email to tammy_hatfield@pathwaypress.org. SASE. Responds in 3 weeks.

- Articles: 500–1,000 words. Informational and how-to articles; profiles; interviews; humor; and personal experience pieces. Topics include current events, music, religion, social issues, psychology, parenting, and multicultural and ethnic subjects.
- Depts/columns: Staff written.

SAMPLE ISSUE
30 pages (2% advertising): 10 articles; 6 depts/columns. Sample copy, $1.25 with 9x12 SASE (2 first-class stamps). Guidelines available at website.

- "Discipleship and Early Childhood." Article explains that good discipleship is essential for a start in a child's life, and provides tips on getting children started.
- "Parental Discipleship." Article makes the argument that parents are the primary disciplers of their own children, and gives readers the tools to get parents involved.

RIGHTS AND PAYMENT
First rights. Written material, $25–$50. Kill fee, 50%. Pays on publication. Provides 1–10 contributor's copies.

➡️EDITOR'S COMMENTS
All articles should be as inspiring to readers as they are informational.

Youth Today

1331 H Street NW
Washington, DC 20005

Editor: Nancy Lewis

DESCRIPTION AND INTERESTS
Youth Today is written for professionals who work with children and youth, in any capacity. It covers government programs, youth development, legislation, trends in juvenile justice, job training, mentoring, foster parenting, and fundraising. Circ: 12,000.
Audience: Youth workers
Frequency: 10 times each year
Website: www.youthtoday.org

FREELANCE POTENTIAL
50% written by nonstaff writers. Publishes 25 freelance submissions yearly; 10% by authors who are new to the magazine. Receives 36 queries yearly.

SUBMISSIONS
Query with résumé and clips. Accepts hard copy and email queries to nlewis@ youthtoday.org. SASE. Responds in 3 months.

- Articles: 1,000–2,500 words. Informational articles; news and research reports; profiles of youth workers and youth programs; and business features. Topics include foster care, child abuse, program management, violence, adolescent health, juvenile justice, job training, school-to-work programs, after-school programs, mentoring, and other social issues related to youth development.
- Depts/columns: Word lengths vary. Book and video reviews, news briefs, opinion pieces, and people in the news.

SAMPLE ISSUE
36 pages (50% advertising): 42 articles; 5 depts/columns. Sample copy, $5. Writers' guidelines available.

- "Life After Debt?" Article provides a news analysis that shows borrowing private money to attend for-profit colleges is risky.
- "National Service Agency Firing Draws Heat." Article reports on the firing of a national service officer.

RIGHTS AND PAYMENT
First and Internet rights. Written material, $.50–$.75 per word. Pays on acceptance. Provides 2 contributor's copies.

➡️EDITOR'S COMMENTS
We are more newspaper than trade magazine. As such, we prefer freelancers who cut their teeth in journalism.

YouthWorker Journal

750 Old Hickory Boulevard, Suite 1-150
Brentwood, TN 37027

Editor: Steve Rabey

DESCRIPTION AND INTERESTS
Practical and inspirational articles designed to help Christian youth workers fulfill their calling are found in this magazine. Each themed issue covers successful programs and activities as well as mission news from around the world. Circ: 10,000.
Audience: Adults who work with youth
Frequency: 6 times each year
Website: www.youthworker.com

FREELANCE POTENTIAL
95% written by nonstaff writers. Publishes 50+ freelance submissions yearly; 15% by unpublished writers, 25% by authors who are new to the magazine. Receives 720 queries yearly.

SUBMISSIONS
Query with short biography. Prefers email queries to steve@youthworker.com (include "Query" in subject line); will accept hard copy and faxes to 615-305-4412. SASE. Responds in 6–8 weeks.

- Articles: Word lengths vary. Informational and practical application articles; personal experience pieces; and reviews. Topics include youth ministry, theology, spreading Christ's word, student worship, family ministry, education, family issues, popular culture, the media, and volunteering.
- Depts/columns: Word lengths vary. National and regional trends; youth workers' quotes.

SAMPLE ISSUE
64 pages (30% advertising): 12 articles; 11 depts/columns. Sample copy, $8. Guidelines and theme list available at website.

- "Be a Blessing to Your School." Article explains how youth workers can partner with schools to help students.
- Sample dept/column: "Worldview" profiles Urbana, the triennial student missions conference held in St. Louis.

RIGHTS AND PAYMENT
All rights. Written material, $15–$300. Pays on publication. Provides 1 contributor's copy.

➡️EDITOR'S COMMENTS
If you have an article that our readers need to read and you can write it for us in a clear and compelling style, we want to hear from you. Please also check out our themes. Many of our articles are centered around them.

Zamoof!

644 Spruceview Place South
Kelowna, British Columbia V1V 2P7
Canada

Editor/Publisher: TeLeni Koochin

DESCRIPTION AND INTERESTS
Zamoof! is a magazine filled with fun for children—games, stories, activities, comics, and jokes. It also features articles, interviews, and stories designed to give them direction and guidance as they go about making choices in their lives. Circ: 5,000–7,000.
Audience: 7–12 years
Frequency: 6 times each year
Website: www.zamoofmag.com

FREELANCE POTENTIAL
7% written by nonstaff writers. Publishes 9 freelance submissions yearly; 50% by unpublished writers, 100% by authors who are new to the magazine. Receives 60 queries, 36 unsolicited mss yearly.

SUBMISSIONS
Canadian authors only. Query or send complete ms. Prefers email submissions to mail@zamoofmag.com; will accept hard copy. SASE. Responds in 2–4 weeks.

- Articles: Staff written.
- Fiction: Currently closed to submissions.
- Depts/columns: "Feet Up," 375 words; humorous, serious, or thought-provoking essays written for parents about parenting and family life. "Pet Horoscopes," 25 words per sign; humorous horoscopes written for pets.

SAMPLE ISSUE
82 pages: 11 articles; 3 stories; 6 depts/columns; 4 comics. Sample copy, $3.99 with 6x9 SASE ($2.01 postage). Guidelines available at website.

- "Green Grabber Strikes Again!" Story tells of a mysterious "green grabber" who steals children's things when they forget to clean up their rooms.
- Sample dept/column: "Pet Horoscopes" features humorous predictions for a variety of household pets.

RIGHTS AND PAYMENT
Writer retains rights. Written material, $.20 per word. Pays on publication. Provides 3 copies.

➡️EDITOR'S COMMENTS
Most material is written by staff writers or our readers, but freelancers can submit short stories (although we're currently closed to submissions), "Feet Up," and "Pet Horoscopes."

Additional Listings

We have selected the following magazines to offer you additional publishing opportunities. Many of these magazines range from general interest publications to women's magazines to craft and hobby magazines. While children, young adults, parents, or teachers are not their primary target audience, these publications do publish a limited amount of material related to or of interest to children.

As you review the listings that follow, use the Description and Interests section as your guide to the particular needs of each magazine. This section offers general information about the magazine and its readers' interests, as well as the type of material it usually publishes. The Freelance Potential section will provide information about the publication's receptivity to freelance manuscripts.

After you survey the listings to determine if your work meets the magazine's specifications, be sure to read a recent sample copy and the current writers' guidelines before submitting your material.

Action Pursuit Games

2400 East Katella Avenue
Anaheim, CA 92806

Editor: Liisa Sullivan

DESCRIPTION AND INTERESTS: Paintball techniques and strategies are the mainstay of *Action Pursuit Games*. Published monthly, it also features in-depth product reviews and recreational league information. Circ: 80,000.
Website: www.actionpursuitgames.com

FREELANCE POTENTIAL: 60% written by non-staff writers. Publishes 150+ freelance submissions yearly; 20% by unpublished writers, 30% by authors who are new to the magazine. Receives 480 unsolicited mss yearly.

SUBMISSIONS AND PAYMENT: Sample copy, $4.99 with 9x12 SASE (15 first-class stamps). Send complete ms with artwork. Accepts hard copy and email submissions to liisa.sullivan@verizon.net. SASE. Responds in 1 month. All rights. Articles, 300–2,000 words. Depts/columns, 300–500 words. Digital images. All material, payment rates vary. Pays on publication. Provides 1 contributor's copy.

African American Family

22041 Woodward Avenue
Ferndale, MI 48220

Editor: Lori Robinson

DESCRIPTION AND INTERESTS: Targeting families in the Detroit area, this monthly publication features articles on parenting, education, social issues, current events, entertainment, and travel. Profiles of local personalities and business leaders and local activity listings are a staple of each issue. Most of its material cites local sources. Circ: Unavailable.
Website: www.africanamericanfamily-magazine.com

FREELANCE POTENTIAL: 80% written by non-staff writers. Publishes 20 freelance submissions each year.

SUBMISSIONS AND PAYMENT: Guidelines available at website. Query. Accepts email queries to lrobinson@metroparent.com. Response time varies. Rights vary. Articles and depts/columns, word lengths and payment rates vary. Pays on publication.

AKC Family Dog

American Kennel Club
260 Madison Avenue
New York, NY 10016

Features Editor: Mara Bovsun

DESCRIPTION AND INTERESTS: Dog owners turn to this magazine for the latest news on training, grooming, health care, behavior, and nutrition, and for breed-specific information. Its material seeks to not only educate, but also to entertain and inspire. *AKC Family Dog* is published six times each year. Knowledgeable freelancers who can write for an audience of sophisticated dog owners are welcome. Circ: 180,000.
Website: www.akc.org

FREELANCE POTENTIAL: 70% written by non-staff writers. Publishes 24–30 freelance submissions yearly; 15% by authors who are new to the magazine. Receives 60–120 queries yearly.

SUBMISSIONS AND PAYMENT: Sample copy, $3.95 with 9x12 SASE. Guidelines available. Query with outline. Accepts email queries to mbb@akc.org. Responds immediately. First North American serial rights. Articles, 1,000–2,000 words; $125–$500. Pays on publication.

Akron Family

TNT Publications
11630 Chillicothe Road
Chesterland, OH 44026

Editor: Terri Nighswonger

DESCRIPTION AND INTERESTS: This monthly is one of several parenting magazines serving an eight-county area in northeastern Ohio. It offers parents of children from tots to teens local information on education, child care, summer camp, party planning, and family travel. Circ: 75,000.
Website: www.neohiofamily.com

FREELANCE POTENTIAL: 50% written by non-staff writers. Publishes 40–50 freelance submissions yearly; 33% by authors who are new to the magazine. Receives 500 queries yearly.

SUBMISSIONS AND PAYMENT: Guidelines available. Sample copy and theme list available at website. Query with clips. Accepts email queries to editor@tntpublications.com. Responds if interested. Exclusive rights. Articles, 500+ words. Depts/columns, word lengths vary. High-resolution JPEG and TIFF images. All material, payment rates vary. Pays on publication. Provides 1 contributor's copy.

The ALAN Review

Louisiana State University
11M Peabody Hall
Baton Rouge, LA 70803

Editor: Dr. Steven T. Bickmore

DESCRIPTION AND INTERESTS: Published three times each year by the Assembly of Literature for Adolescents, this magazine keeps English teachers abreast of trends in young adult literature. Please consult the guidelines for specific submission requirements. Circ: 2,500.
Website: www.alan-ya.org

FREELANCE POTENTIAL: 84% written by non-staff writers. Publishes 38 freelance submissions yearly; 5% by unpublished writers, 65% by new authors. Receives 90 unsolicited mss yearly.

SUBMISSIONS AND PAYMENT: Sample copy, free. Guidelines available in each issue. Send complete ms. Accepts email submissions to alanreview@lsu.edu (Microsoft Word attachments; include "ALAN manuscript submission" in subject line). No simultaneous submissions. Responds in 2 months. All rights. Articles, to 3,000 words. Depts/columns, word lengths vary. No payment. Provides 2 contributor's copies.

Amazing Kids!

5267 Warner Avenue, Suite 235
Huntington Beach, CA 92649

Editor: Alyse Rome

DESCRIPTION AND INTERESTS: As a project of the nonprofit group Community Partners, *Amazing Kids!* is dedicated to inspiring excellence in children. Much of its online content is contributed by children and young adults, although mature writers are welcome to submit profiles for the "Kids of the Month" section. Hits per month: 640,000.
Website: www.amazing-kids.org

FREELANCE POTENTIAL: 40% written by non-staff writers. Publishes 70 freelance submissions yearly; 90% by unpublished writers, 70% by authors who are new to the magazine. Receives 3,000 queries and unsolicited mss yearly.

SUBMISSIONS AND PAYMENT: Sample copy available at website. Query or send complete ms. Accepts email submissions to info@ amazing-kids.org. Response time varies. All rights. Articles, word lengths vary. No payment.

American History

Weider History Magazine Group
19300 Promenade Drive
Leesburg, VA 20176-6500

Editorial Director: Roger Vance

DESCRIPTION AND INTERESTS: History enthusiasts read this magazine for well-researched articles on the people and events that have shaped the United States. *American History* is published every other month and looks for articles that present historical facts combined with lively, entertaining writing. Circ: 100,000.
Website: www.thehistorynet.com/ahi

FREELANCE POTENTIAL: 80% written by non-staff writers. Publishes 30 freelance submissions yearly; 50% by authors who are new to the magazine. Receives 1,200 queries yearly.

SUBMISSIONS AND PAYMENT: Sample copy and guidelines, $6 with return label. Query with 1- to 2-page proposal. Accepts hard copy. SASE. Responds in 10 weeks. All rights. Articles, 2,000–4,000 words; $.20 per word. Depts/columns, word lengths vary; $75. Pays on acceptance. Provides 5 contributor's copies.

American School Board Journal

1680 Duke Street
Alexandria, VA 22314

Editor-in-Chief: Glenn Cook

DESCRIPTION AND INTERESTS: The National School Boards Association publishes this professional journal for educators, administrators, and members of school boards nationwide. Each monthly issue offers its readers articles on topics such as leadership, management, and policy. It serves as an open forum of opinions on the issues affecting education. Circ: 50,200.
Website: www.asbj.com

FREELANCE POTENTIAL: 50% written by non-staff writers. Publishes 35 freelance submissions yearly. Receives 360 queries yearly.

SUBMISSIONS AND PAYMENT: Sample copy, $5. Prefers query with clips; will accept complete ms. Accepts hard copy. SASE. Responds in 2 months. All rights. Articles, 2,200–2,500 words. Depts/columns, 1,000–1,200 words. Solicited articles, $800. Unsolicited articles and depts/columns, no payment. Pays on publication. Provides 3 contributor's copies.

AMomsLove.com

1308 Midland Beaver Road
Industry, PA 15052

Editor: Caroline G. Shaw

DESCRIPTION AND INTERESTS: This online magazine is "chock-full of insightful articles for busy mothers." Appearing monthly, it is read by stay-at-home moms as well as those working outside of the home. Topics run the gamut from baby care to parenting teenagers, and everything in between. Book reviews, kid-friendly recipes, and birthday party ideas are other regular features. Hits per month: 30,000.
Website: www.amomslove.com

FREELANCE POTENTIAL: 75% written by nonstaff writers. Publishes 60 freelance submissions yearly; 20% by authors new to the magazine.

SUBMISSIONS AND PAYMENT: Sample copy and guidelines available at website. Send complete ms with short bio. Accepts email submissions to mom@amomslove.com (HTML or Microsoft Word attachments). Response time varies. First rights. Articles, 700–1,100 words. No payment.

Art Jewelry

21027 Crossroads Circle
Waukesha, WI 53187

Editor: Hazel Wheaton

DESCRIPTION AND INTERESTS: This magazine provides step-by-step instructions for creating handcrafted jewelry. It seeks coverage of wireworking and beginner-level projects. Circ: 40,000.
Website: www.artjewelry.com

FREELANCE POTENTIAL: 60% written by nonstaff writers. Publishes 50 freelance submissions yearly; 30% by unpublished writers, 50% by authors who are new to the magazine. Receives 240–360 queries yearly.

SUBMISSIONS AND PAYMENT: Sample copy and guidelines, $6.95. Query with jewelry samples, prints, or JPEG images. Accepts hard copy, email to editor@artjewelrymag.com, and submissions via www.contribute.kalmbach.com. SASE. Responds in 1 month. All rights. Articles, 500–700 words for beginner projects; 1,000–2,000 words for intermediate projects; 2,000–3,000 words for advanced projects. Pays on acceptance. Provides 2 contributor's copies.

The Apprentice Writer

Writers Institute
Susquehanna University, Box GG
Selinsgrove, PA 17870-1001

Director: Gary Fincke

DESCRIPTION AND INTERESTS: Edited and produced by Susquehanna University writing students, *The Apprentice Writer* publishes poems, stories, and personal essays by high school students. It is published each September. Circ: 10,500.
Website: www.susqu.edu/writers/
highschoolstudents.htm

FREELANCE POTENTIAL: 100% written by nonstaff writers. Publishes 80 freelance submissions yearly; 95% by unpublished writers, 95% by authors who are new to the magazine. Receives 4,000 unsolicited mss yearly.

SUBMISSIONS AND PAYMENT: Sample copy, $3 with 9x12 SASE ($1.17 postage). Guidelines available at website. Send complete ms by March 1. Accepts hard copy and simultaneous submissions if identified. SASE. Responds in May. First rights. Articles and fiction, 7,000 words. Poetry, no line limits. No payment. Provides 2 contributor's copies.

Athens Parent

P.O. Box 1251
Athens, GA 30603

Editor-in-Chief: Shannon Walsh Howell

DESCRIPTION AND INTERESTS: Appearing eight times each year, this regional magazine focuses on the well-being of children. It is read by parents, grandparents, educators, child care providers, and others who care for children. Topics covered include health and safety, education, recreation, adoption, foster care, family life, financial planning, and local news and events. Circ: Unavailable.
Website: www.athensparent.com

FREELANCE POTENTIAL: 85% written by nonstaff writers. Publishes 40 freelance submissions yearly. Receives 500 queries yearly.

SUBMISSIONS AND PAYMENT: Guidelines and theme list available at website. Query. Accepts hard copy and and email queries to mail@metromags.com. SASE. Response time varies. First rights. Articles and depts/columns, word lengths and payment rates vary. Payment policy varies.

Austin Family

P.O. Box 7559
Round Rock, TX 78683-7559

Editor: Melanie Dunham

DESCRIPTION AND INTERESTS: Formerly published monthly, this free regional magazine now appears three to five times per month. It publishes material that promotes "smart parenting" and "healthy homes." Circ: 35,000.
Website: www.austinfamily.com

FREELANCE POTENTIAL: 85% written by non-staff writers. Publishes 18 freelance submissions yearly; 10% by unpublished writers, 50% by authors who are new to the magazine. Receives 1,200 queries and unsolicited mss yearly.

SUBMISSIONS AND PAYMENT: Sample copy, free. Query or send complete ms. Accepts email submissions to editor2003@austinfamily.com and simultaneous submissions if identified. Availability of artwork improves chance of acceptance. Responds in 3–6 months. First and second serial rights. Articles, 800–1,200 words. Depts/columns, 800 words. B/W prints. All material, payment rates vary. Pays on publication.

Baton Rouge Parents

11831 Wentling Avenue
Baton Rouge, LA 70816-6055

Editor: Amy Foreman-Plaisance

DESCRIPTION AND INTERESTS: Residents of Baton Rouge seeking to provide their kids with healthy, stimulating, caring environments pick up this magazine each month for locally-oriented advice and information. Circ: 55,000.
Website: www.brparents.com

FREELANCE POTENTIAL: 95% written by non-staff writers. Publishes 50+ freelance submissions yearly; 15% by unpublished writers, 30% by authors who are new to the magazine.

SUBMISSIONS AND PAYMENT: Guidelines available via email request to brpm@brparents.com. Query with outline, source list, brief author biography, and 2 writing samples. Accepts hard copy and email queries to brpm@brparents.com (include "Article Query" in subject line). SASE. Response time varies. First North American serial rights. Written material, word lengths vary; $25–$70. Kill fee, $10. Pays on publication. Provides 2 contributor's copies.

BabagaNewz

11141 Georgia Avenue, Suite 406
Silver Spring, MD 20902

Editor: Mark Levine

DESCRIPTION AND INTERESTS: This innovative magazine and website target Jewish middle school students and their teachers. It encourages young people to explore Jewish values, traditions, and holidays. *BabagaNewz* is published eight times each year and seeks exciting, thought-provoking articles. Circ: 41,029.
Website: www.babaganewz.com

FREELANCE POTENTIAL: 30% written by nonstaff writers. Publishes 20 freelance submissions yearly; 10% by authors who are new to the magazine.

SUBMISSIONS AND PAYMENT: Sample copy and guidelines available by email request to aviva@babaganewz.com. All material is written on assignment. Query with résumé. Accepts hard copy. SASE. Response time varies. All rights. Articles and depts/columns, word lengths and payment rates vary. Pays on acceptance. Provides contributor's copies upon request.

Bay Area Parent

1660 South Amphlett Boulevard, Suite 335
San Mateo, CA 94402

Editor: Peggy Spear

DESCRIPTION AND INTERESTS: This regional parenting magazine is published monthly in three editions: East Bay; San Francisco and Peninsula; and Silicon Valley. In addition to articles on issues and resources specific to parents in the San Francisco Bay area, it offers authoritative features with national scope and local relevance. Circ: 80,000.
Website: www.bayareaparent.com

FREELANCE POTENTIAL: 50% written by non-staff writers. Publishes 15–20 freelance submissions yearly. Receives 100+ queries yearly.

SUBMISSIONS AND PAYMENT: Prefers submissions from local authors. Sample copy and guidelines available at website. Query. Accepts hard copy. SASE. Responds in 2 months. One-time rights. Articles, 1,200–1,400 words. Depts/columns, word lengths vary. Written material, $.06 per word. Pays on publication. Provides 1 contributor's copy.

Beckett Plushie Pals

4635 McEwen Road
Dallas, TX 75244

Editor: Doug Kale

DESCRIPTION AND INTERESTS: This magazine explores the virtual worlds of plush toys through entertaining and informative articles, interviews with toymakers, and new product reviews. It is read by children ages seven and up who collect and enjoy products such as Webkinz, Club Penguin, and Beanie Babies. It appears monthly. Circ: 100,000.
Website: www.beckettplushiepals.com

FREELANCE POTENTIAL: 50% written by non-staff writers. Publishes 20 freelance submissions yearly; 50% by authors who are new to the magazine. Receives 50–100 queries yearly.

SUBMISSIONS AND PAYMENT: Sample copy and guidelines available. Query with 3–5 article ideas. Accepts email queries to plushiepals@beckett.com. Responds in 1–2 months. First rights. Written material, word lengths vary; $25–$100. Pays on publication. Provides 2 contributor's copies.

Biography Today

Omnigraphics Inc.
P.O. Box 625
Holmes, PA 19043

Managing Editor

DESCRIPTION AND INTERESTS: Appearing six times each year, *Biography Today* offers profiles of artists, authors, business leaders, actors, musicians, artists, scientists and inventors, sports figures, and world leaders. It looks for thoroughly-researched profiles that delve into the life of the individual without skirting the controversial aspects. Its material targets children ages nine and up. Circ: 9,000.
Website: www.biographytoday.com

FREELANCE POTENTIAL: 50% written by non-staff writers. Publishes several freelance submissions yearly. Receives 12 queries yearly.

SUBMISSIONS AND PAYMENT: Sample copy and guidelines available with 9x12 SASE. Query with résumé. Accepts hard copy. SASE. Responds in 2 months. All rights. Articles, 2,000–5,000 words; payment rates vary. Pays on publication. Provides 2 contributor's copies.

Birmingham Parent

115-C Hilltop Business Drive
Pelham, AL 35124

Editor: Carol Evans

DESCRIPTION AND INTERESTS: Parents in central Alabama read this monthly for information on raising happy, healthy children. It prefers to work with local writers. Circ: 35,000.
Website: www.birminghamparent.com

FREELANCE POTENTIAL: 50% written by nonstaff writers. Publishes 30+ freelance submissions yearly; 5% by authors who are new to the magazine.

SUBMISSIONS AND PAYMENT: Sample copy and guidelines available at website. Query with résumé, clips, and availability of artwork; or send complete ms. Accepts email submissions to editor@birminghamparent.com (include "Query" in subject line). Responds in 1 month. First North American serial and electronic rights. Articles, 700–1,500 words; payment rates vary. JPEG files at 300 dpi; no payment. Pays within 30 days of publication. Provides 2 contributor's copies.

Bop

330 North Brand, Ste. 1150
Glendale, CA 91203

Editor-in-Chief: Leesa Coble

DESCRIPTION AND INTERESTS: The latest celebrity news for teens and tweens is covered in this monthly publication. It offers celebrity interviews and behind the scenes reports on the movie, television, and movie industries. Each issue is also filled with color photos of today's hottest teen and tween stars, quizzes, contests, and games. At this time, *Bop* is not accepting submissions. Check the website for updates to this policy. Circ: 200,000+.
Website: www.bopmag.com

FREELANCE POTENTIAL: 100% staff-written.

SUBMISSIONS AND PAYMENT: Sample copy, $3.99 at newsstands. Not accepting queries or unsolicited mss at this time.

Brain, Child

P.O. Box 714
Lexington, VA 24450

Editors: Jennifer Niesslein & Stephanie Wilkinson

DESCRIPTION AND INTERESTS: Subtitled "The Magazine for Thinking Mothers," this quarterly offers a thoughtful look at raising children. Insightful articles, personal essays, and fiction combine to provide a wide range of perspectives on diverse topics, from prenatal learning to raising teens to grandparenting. Circ: 30,000.
Website: www.brainchildmag.com

FREELANCE POTENTIAL: 90% written by nonstaff writers. Publishes 40 freelance submissions yearly; 15% by unpublished writers, 60% by authors who are new to the magazine. Receives 300 queries, 2,400 unsolicited mss yearly.

SUBMISSIONS AND PAYMENT: Sample copy and guidelines, $5. Query or send ms. Accepts email to editor@brainchildmag.com. Responds in 2 months. Electronic rights. Articles, 3,000 words. Personal essays, 800–4,500 words. Fiction, 1,500–4,500 words. Written material, payment rates vary. Pays on publication.

Calgary's Child

#723, 105-150 Crowfoot Crescent NW
Calgary, Alberta T3G 3T2
Canada

Editor: Ellen Percival

DESCRIPTION AND INTERESTS: Published six times each year, *Calgary's Child* seeks to empower parents in the city through comprehensive coverage of the issues that concern them. These include education, child care, health, recreation, entertainment, family travel, housing, and community development. All submissions must have a distinct Calgary angle; therefore, local authors are favored. Circ: 60,000.
Website: www.calgaryschild.com

FREELANCE POTENTIAL: 90% written by nonstaff writers. Publishes 210 freelance submissions yearly; 20% by authors who are new to the magazine.

SUBMISSIONS AND PAYMENT: Sample copy available at website. Query with outline. Accepts email queries to calgaryschild@shaw.ca. No simultaneous submissions. Response time varies. Exclusive Calgary rights. Articles, 400–500 words; to $50 Canadian. Payment policy varies.

Camping Today

126 Hermitage Road
Butler, PA 16001

Editor: DeWayne Johnston

DESCRIPTION AND INTERESTS: This newsletter for members of Family Campers and RVers is issued 10 times each year. It covers camping destinations, new RV models and conveniences, wildlife and conservation, and vehicle maintenance and safety. It is *not* interested in personal experience pieces about the writer's first or worst camping experience. Circ: 10,000.
Website: www.fcrv.org

FREELANCE POTENTIAL: 40% written by nonstaff writers. Publishes 15–20 freelance submissions yearly; 10% by unpublished writers. Receives 240 unsolicited mss yearly.

SUBMISSIONS AND PAYMENT: Guidelines and theme list available. Send complete ms with artwork. Accepts hard copy. SASE. Responds in 2 months. One-time rights. Articles, 1,000–3,000 words. Depts/columns, word lengths vary. JPEG files. Written material, $35–$150. Pays on publication. Provides 1+ contributor's copies.

Canoe & Kayak Magazine

33046 Calle Aviador
San Juan Capistrano, CA 92675

Managing Editor: Jeff Moag

DESCRIPTION AND INTERESTS: Published seven times each year, this photo-filled magazine takes the reader to flatwater and whitewater paddling destinations around the world. It also features new product reviews, how-to articles, and profiles. Circ: 63,000.
Website: www.canoekayak.com

FREELANCE POTENTIAL: 90% written by nonstaff writers. Publishes 25 freelance submissions yearly; 5% by unpublished writers, 25% by authors who are new to the magazine. Receives 100 queries and unsolicited mss yearly.

SUBMISSIONS AND PAYMENT: Sample copy, free with 9x12 SASE (7 first-class stamps). Query or send complete ms. Accepts email submissions to editor@canoekayak.com. Responds in 6–8 weeks. All rights. Articles, 400–2,000 words. Depts/columns, 150–750 words. Written material, $.15–$.50 per word. Pays within 30 days of publication. Provides 1 contributor's copy.

Catalyst Chicago

Independent Reporting on Urban Schools

332 South Michigan Avenue, Suite 500
Chicago, IL 60604

Editor-in-Chief: Veronica Anderson

DESCRIPTION AND INTERESTS: *Catalyst Chicago* calls itself "an editorially independent news service" that covers politics, policies, and problems related to school reform. The magazine seeks to stimulate constructive dialogue about improving public schools. It is published five times each year by the Community Renewal Society. Circ: 9,000.
Website: www.catalyst-chicago.org

FREELANCE POTENTIAL: 15% written by non-staff writers. Publishes 6 freelance submissions yearly; 25% by authors who are new to the magazine. Receives 45 queries yearly.

SUBMISSIONS AND PAYMENT: Sample copy and guidelines, $2. Query or send letter of introduction. Accepts hard copy and email queries to editorial@catalyst-chicago.org. SASE. Response time varies. All rights. Articles, to 2,300 words; $1,700. Pays on acceptance. Provides 1 contributor's copy.

Chickadee

Bayard Press Canada
10 Lower Spadina Avenue, Suite 400
Toronto, Ontario M4V 2V2
Canada

Submissions Editor

DESCRIPTION AND INTERESTS: Each issue of this "discovery magazine" for children ages six to nine is centered on a theme meant to instantly draw in beginning readers. It features word and math puzzles, science experiments, crafts, and stories to help children hone their problem-solving skills, both in the classroom and at home. Like its sister publications *Chirp* and *Owl*, *Chickadee* does not accept unsolicited manuscripts or queries. Circ: 85,000.
Website: www.owlkids.com

FREELANCE POTENTIAL: 5% written by non-staff writers. Publishes 1 freelance submission each year.

SUBMISSIONS AND PAYMENT: Sample copy, $4. Guidelines and theme list available. All work is assigned. Send résumé only. Accepts hard copy. No SASE. All rights. Fiction, 650–700 words; $250. Pays on acceptance. Provides 2 contributor's copies.

Cat Fancy

3 Burroughs
Irvine, CA 92618

Editor: Susan Logan

DESCRIPTION AND INTERESTS: This monthly magazine for cat lovers accepts contributions of feline news and trends all year long; however, feature queries must be submitted between January and May. Circ: 290,000.
Website: www.catchannel.com

FREELANCE POTENTIAL: 95% written by non-staff writers. Publishes 150 freelance submissions yearly; 10% by unpublished writers, 70% by authors who are new to the magazine. Receives 500+ queries yearly.

SUBMISSIONS AND PAYMENT: Guidelines available. Query with clips. Accepts email to query@catfancy.com. Availability of artwork improves chance of acceptance. Response time varies. First rights. Articles, 600–1,000 words. Depts/columns, 600 words. 35mm slides; high-resolution digital images with contact sheets. All material, payment rates vary. Pays on publication. Provides 2 contributor's copies.

Children's Advocate

Action Alliance for Children
The Hunt Home
1201 Martin Luther King Jr. Way
Oakland, CA 94612-1217

Editor: Jeanne Tepperman

DESCRIPTION AND INTERESTS: *Children's Advocate* is published six times each year, in English and Spanish, by the nonprofit Action Alliance for Children. It is distributed free to those in California who work with children, whether they be subsidized childcare providers, children's librarians, teachers, or parents. Each issue examines trends and public policy pertaining to children's welfare. Circ: 15,000.
Website: www.4children.org

FREELANCE POTENTIAL: 60% written by non-staff writers. Publishes 24 freelance submissions each year.

SUBMISSIONS AND PAYMENT: Sample copy and guidelines available. All work is assigned. Send résumé and writing samples. Accepts hard copy. SASE. Response time varies. First North American serial rights. Articles, 500 or 1,000 words; $.25 per word. Pays on acceptance. Provides 3 contributor's copies.

Chirp

Bayard Press Canada
10 Lower Spadina Avenue, Suite 400
Toronto, Ontario M4V 2V2
Canada

Submissions Editor

DESCRIPTION AND INTERESTS: This little sister of *Chickadee* and *Owl* targets children ages two through six with games, puzzles, rhymes, and stories meant to stimulate little minds. Published nine times each year, it does not accept unsolicited manuscripts or queries; all content is assigned. Writers may introduce themselves by sending a brief résumé and a list of publishing credits. Circ: 60,000.
Website: www.owlkids.com

FREELANCE POTENTIAL: 10% written by non-staff writers. Publishes 1–3 freelance submissions yearly; 1% by unpublished writers.

SUBMISSIONS AND PAYMENT: Sample copy, $3.50. Guidelines available. All work is assigned. Send résumé only. Accepts hard copy. No SASE. All rights. Written material, 300–400 words; payment rates vary. Pays on acceptance. Provides 2 contributor's copies.

Cincinnati Parent

1901 Broad Ripple Avenue
Indianapolis, IN 46220

Executive Editor: Lynette Rowland

DESCRIPTION AND INTERESTS: Parents in the greater Cincinnati area read this monthly tabloid for a local perspective on raising a family. Its content includes articles on education, health, and child development, along with guides to finding family-oriented events, goods, and services in the region. Circ: 120,000.
Website: www.cincinnatiparent.com

FREELANCE POTENTIAL: 25–40% written by nonstaff writers. Publishes 30 freelance submissions yearly.

SUBMISSIONS AND PAYMENT: Guidelines available at website. Query with writing sample; state areas of interest. Accepts email queries to editor@cincinnatiparent.com. Responds if interested. First rights. Articles, 1,500–2,000 words. Depts/columns, 800–1,000 words. First rights. Written material, $.10–$.15 per word. Reprints, $40–$75. Pays on publication. Provides 1 contributor's copy.

Cincinnati Family Magazine

10945 Reed Hartman Highway, Suite 221
Cincinnati, OH 45242

Editor: Sherry Hang

DESCRIPTION AND INTERESTS: Distributed free of charge each month, *Cincinnati Family Magazine* keeps parents in this greater metropolitan area up to date on education issues, entertainment options, and health news. Circ: 55,000.
Website: www.cincinnatifamilymagazine.com

FREELANCE POTENTIAL: 25% written by non-staff writers. Publishes 20–24 freelance submissions yearly; 5% by unpublished writers, 5% by authors who are new to the magazine. Receives 200 queries, 300 unsolicited mss yearly.

SUBMISSIONS AND PAYMENT: Guidelines and editorial calendar available. Query or send complete ms. Accepts hard copy and email submissions to sherryh@daycommail.com. SASE. Response time varies. First rights. Articles, word lengths vary; $75–$125. Depts/columns, word lengths and payment rates vary. Pays 1 month after publication.

Classic Toy Trains

21027 Crossroads Circle
Waukesha, WI 53187

Editor: Carl Swanson

DESCRIPTION AND INTERESTS: Each month, *Classic Toy Trains* publishes articles for model train enthusiasts demonstrating intricate track layouts, repairs, and other projects. It also provides news for collectors. Circ: 55,000.
Website: www.classictoytrains.com

FREELANCE POTENTIAL: 60% written by non-staff writers. Publishes 40–50 freelance submissions yearly; 20% by unpublished writers, 20% by authors who are new to the magazine. Receives 96 queries, 60 unsolicited mss yearly.

SUBMISSIONS AND PAYMENT: Sample copy, $4.95 with 9x12 SASE ($3 postage). Prefers query; will accept complete ms. Accepts hard copy, disk submissions (Microsoft Word), and email submissions to editor@classictoytrains.com. SASE. Responds in 3 months. All rights. Articles, 500–5,000 words; $75 per page. Depts/columns, word lengths and payment rates vary. Pays on acceptance. Provides 1 contributor's copy.

Clubhouse

P.O. Box 15
Berrien Springs, MI 49103

Editor: Elaine Trumbo

DESCRIPTION AND INTERESTS: *Clubhouse* began life in 1951 as a monthly print publication with a distinctively Christian perspective. Today it is exclusively available online, publishing stories, puzzles, games, and other activities for children ages 9 through 12. It is currently using only previously published material, and therefore is not accepting queries or unsolicited manuscripts. Please check the website for updates to this policy. Hits per month: Unavailable.
Website: www.yourstoryhour.org/clubhouse

FREELANCE POTENTIAL: 85% written by non-staff writers. Publishes several freelance submissions yearly; 75% by unpublished writers, 95% by authors who are new to the magazine.

SUBMISSIONS AND PAYMENT: Sample copy available at website. Send complete ms. Accepts hard copy. SASE. Response time varies. All rights. Articles and fiction, 1,500 words. B/W line art. All material, payment rates vary.

Coins

F & W Publications
700 East State Street
Iola, WI 54990

Editor: Robert Van Ryzin

DESCRIPTION AND INTERESTS: If you bandy about terms like "commem" and "mintage," then you could write for *Coins*, a magazine that covers the extensive world of coins, medals, and tokens for avid collectors. It seeks insightful information about coins and compelling personal essays on coin collecting for its knowledgeable readership. The magazine is published monthly. Circ: 60,000.
Website: www.coinsmagazine.net

FREELANCE POTENTIAL: 40% written by non-staff writers. Publishes 70 freelance submissions yearly; 5% by authors who are new to the magazine. Receives 36–60 queries yearly.

SUBMISSIONS AND PAYMENT: Sample copy and guidelines, free. Query. Accepts hard copy. SASE. Responds in 1–2 months. All rights. Articles, 1,500–2,500 words; $.04 per word. Work for hire. Pays on publication. Provides contributor's copies upon request.

Coastal Family Magazine

340 Eisenhower Drive, Suite 240
Savannah, GA 31406

Managing Editor: Laura Gray

DESCRIPTION AND INTERESTS: This tabloid, published monthly, is distributed free of charge throughout Savannah and South Carolina's Lowcountry. It is read by parents who are looking for things to do with their children, as well as for the latest information on parenting, child development, education, health, and other pertinent topics. While in the past *Coastal Family Magazine* has been a good market for freelance writers, it is currently not accepting unsolicited submissions. Circ: 18,000.
Website: www.coastalfamily.com

FREELANCE POTENTIAL: Currently not accepting freelance submissions. Please check website for updates to this policy.

College News

39 South LaSalle, Unit 420
Chicago, IL 60603

Copy Editor: Marina Ricci

DESCRIPTION AND INTERESTS: This quarterly magazine for college students covers fun stuff like entertainment and spring break alongside more serious pursuits like careers and finance. Whatever the topic, however, the tone is light and energetic, as is the layout. Most content is written by journalism students interning with the magazine. It would like to see more articles on careers and studying abroad. Circ: Unavailable.
Website: www.collegenews.com

FREELANCE POTENTIAL: 30% written by non-staff writers. Publishes 20 freelance submissions yearly; 70% by unpublished writers, 20% by authors who are new to the magazine. Receives 600 queries yearly.

SUBMISSIONS AND PAYMENT: Sample copy available at website. Guidelines available. Query. Accepts email to marinar@bostonhannah.com. Responds immediately. All rights. Articles, 400 words. No payment. Provides 1 contributor's copy.

ColumbiaKids

Washington State Historical Society
1911 Pacific Avenue
Tacoma, WA 98402

Managing Editor: Stephanie Lile

DESCRIPTION AND INTERESTS: Twice each year, *ColumbiaKids* is updated with informative articles and stories based on Pacific Northwest history. It targets children ages 4 to 14 who live in the states of Washington, Oregon, Idaho, and Alaska. Only well-researched, regional subjects will be considered. Hits per month: 5,000+.
http://columbia.washingtonhistory.org/kids

FREELANCE POTENTIAL: 80% written by non-staff writers. Publishes several freelance submissions yearly.

SUBMISSIONS AND PAYMENT: Sample copy and guidelines available at website. Query or send complete ms. Accepts hard copy and email submissions to columbiakids@wshs.wa.gov (no attachments). SASE. Response time varies. First world electronic and archival rights. Articles, 800–1,200 words; $200. Depts/columns, 200–800 words; $100–$500. Poetry, word games, jokes, and rebuses, $25–$50. Pays on publication.

Complex Child E-Magazine

Editor: Susan Agrawal

DESCRIPTION AND INTERESTS: *Complex Child E-Magazine* is a monthly online publication primarily written by parents of children with special healthcare needs and/or disabilities. It offers informational articles on medical conditions, treatments, insurance, and special education. Profiles of families are also a part of its editorial mix. Hits per month: Unavailable.
Website: www.complexchild.com

FREELANCE POTENTIAL: 25% written by nonstaff writers. Publishes 15–20 freelance submissions yearly; 15% by authors who are new to the magazine.

SUBMISSIONS AND PAYMENT: Sample copy and writers' guidelines available at website. Query. Accepts email queries to submit@complexchild.com (Microsoft Word or text file attachments). Responds in 1–2 months. Limited-time electronic rights. Articles, word lengths vary. No payment.

Community College Week

P.O. Box 1305
Fairfax, VA 22038

Editor: Paul Bradley

DESCRIPTION AND INTERESTS: Faculty and administrators at community, technical, and junior colleges turn to this magazine for the latest information on academic issues, technology, and employment opportunities. *Community College Week* is published twice each month. Circ: 18,000.
Website: www.ccweek.com

FREELANCE POTENTIAL: 75% written by non-staff writers. Publishes 75 freelance submissions yearly; 40% by authors who are new to the magazine. Receives 60 queries yearly.

SUBMISSIONS AND PAYMENT: Guidelines available. Query with clips, résumé, and source list. Prefers email to editor@ccweek.com; will accept hard copy. SASE. Responds in 1 month. First serial rights. Articles, 600–1,200 words. Depts/columns, word lengths vary. Written material, $.35 per word. Kill fee, $.15 per word. Pays on publication. Provides 6 contributor's copies.

Cookie

4 Times Square
New York, NY 10036

Acquisitions: Mireille Hyde

DESCRIPTION AND INTERESTS: Targeting busy, sophisticated parents who demand more from a parenting magazine, *Cookie* covers topics such as family travel, pregnancy, kids' fashion, health and fitness, nutrition, and home decorating. Each issue also features movie, book, and product reviews. It is published 10 times each year. Circ: 400,000.
Website: www.cookiemag.com

FREELANCE POTENTIAL: 50% written by non-staff writers. Publishes 10 freelance submissions yearly. Receives 600–1,200 queries yearly.

SUBMISSIONS AND PAYMENT: Sample copy available at newsstands. Query. Accepts hard copy and email queries to editor@cookiemag.com (include "Freelance Pitch" in the subject line). SASE. Response time varies. Rights vary. Articles, word lengths and payment rates vary. Pays on publication.

Co-Op Thymes

1007 SE Third Street
Corvallis, OR 97333

Marketing Coordinator: Emily Hagen

DESCRIPTION AND INTERESTS: This newspaper is published monthly by Oregon's First Alternative Co-Op, a community-owned natural foods store. Its readers are interested in healthy, organic, local products, and sustainable living. In addition to feature articles on such topics, *The Co-Op Thymes* offers recipes, tips, and news from the local organic community. It welcomes submissions, especially those offering information on the health benefits of natural products. Circ: 5,000.
Website: www.firstalt.coop

FREELANCE POTENTIAL: 10% written by nonstaff writers. Publishes 24 freelance submissions yearly; 50% by unpublished writers, 50% by authors who are new to the magazine. Receives 36 queries yearly.

SUBMISSIONS AND PAYMENT: Sample copy, free. Query. Accepts email queries to thymes@firstalt.coop. Responds in 1–3 days. No payment.

Creative Child Magazine

2505 Anthem Village Drive, Suite E619
Henderson, NV 89052

Editor: Scott Reichert

DESCRIPTION AND INTERESTS: Published six times each year, *Creative Child Magazine* seeks to bring out the artist in every child. It offers arts and crafts ideas; tips for stimulating young imaginations; profiles of creative kids; and articles on nurturing musical talent, creative toys, family travel, and health and safety concerns. Circ: 50,000.
Website: www.creativechild.com

FREELANCE POTENTIAL: 25% written by nonstaff writers. Publishes 20 freelance submissions each year.

SUBMISSIONS AND PAYMENT: Sample copy, free with 9x12 SASE (4 first-class stamps). Query. Accepts hard copy and email queries to creativechild@earthlink.net. SASE. Responds in 1–3 months. First print and electronic rights. Articles and depts/columns, word lengths vary; payment rates vary. Pays on publication. Provides contributor's copies.

Craft Bits

P.O. Box 3106
Birkdale, Queensland 4159
Australia

Editor: Shellie Wilson

DESCRIPTION AND INTERESTS: This online crafts magazine seeks to promote awareness of the benefits of creativity for all people, young children through seniors. To that end, it offers projects the whole family can enjoy. Scrapbooking, candlemaking, recycled crafts, seasonal crafts, and beading are among the projects presented. Queries for complicated craft ideas should include step-by-step instructions accompanied by photos. Hits per month: 60,000.
Website: www.craftbits.com

FREELANCE POTENTIAL: 5% written by nonstaff writers. Publishes many freelance submissions yearly.

SUBMISSIONS AND PAYMENT: Sample copy available at website. Query with JPEG images. Accepts email queries to staff@craftbits.com. Responds in 1–2 months. All rights. Articles and depts/columns, word lengths vary; $45 (USD). Kill fee, $10 (USD). Pays on publication.

Crow Toes Quarterly

186-8120 No. 2 Road, Suite 361
Richmond, British Columbia V7C 4C1
Canada

Managing Editor: Christopher Millin

DESCRIPTION AND INTERESTS: *Crow Toes Quarterly* has been restructured into an online-only publication. Targeting children ages eight to thirteen, it offers a mix of "playfully dark" fiction, entertaining articles, and vibrant artwork. Hits per month: Unavailable.
Website: www.crowtoesquarterly.com

FREELANCE POTENTIAL: 90% written by nonstaff writers. Publishes 24 freelance submissions yearly; 90% by unpublished writers, 100% by authors who are new to the magazine. Receives 180 unsolicited mss yearly.

SUBMISSIONS AND PAYMENT: Guidelines available at website. Send complete ms. Accepts hard copy and email submissions to info@crowtoesquarterly.com. SASE. Responds in 4 months. First Canadian serial rights. Articles, word lengths vary. Fiction, to 3,000 words. B/W or color JPEG images at 300 dpi; line art. No payment.

Curriculum Review

Paperclip Communications
125 Paterson Avenue, Suite 4
Little Falls, NJ 07424

Editor: Laura Betti

DESCRIPTION AND INTERESTS: Published nine times during each school year, *Curriculum Review* provides teachers and administrators working at all grade levels with information about what really works in school. Classroom-tested lesson plans, teaching tips, reviews of programs and resources, essays, and coverage of legislative news affecting education are offered. Circ: 5,000.
Website: www.curriculumreview.com

FREELANCE POTENTIAL: 2% written by non-staff writers. Publishes 10 freelance submissions yearly. Receives 24 queries yearly.

SUBMISSIONS AND PAYMENT: Sample copy, free with 9x12 SASE (2 first-class stamps). Query. Accepts hard copy. SASE. Responds in 1 month. One-time rights. Articles, to 4,000 words. Depts/columns, word lengths vary. Written material, payment rates vary. Payment policy varies. Provides contributor's copies.

Dog Fancy

BowTie Inc.
P.O. Box 6050
Mission Viejo, CA 92690-6050

Managing Editor: Annamaria Barajas

DESCRIPTION AND INTERESTS: Dog lovers fancy this monthly magazine, which celebrates canine companions of all breeds and backgrounds. Its editorial goal is to help readers be responsible dog owners. To that end, it seeks well-researched articles on canine health, nutrition, grooming, and training. Circ: 270,000.
Website: www.dogfancy.com

FREELANCE POTENTIAL: 80% written by non-staff writers. Publishes 20–25 freelance submissions yearly; 25% by authors who are new to the magazine. Receives 1,200 queries yearly.

SUBMISSIONS AND PAYMENT: Guidelines available. Sample copy, $4.50 at newsstands. Query with résumé, outline, and clips. Accepts hard copy. SASE. Responds in 2–3 months. First North American serial rights. Articles, 1,200–1,800 words. Depts/columns, 650 words. All material, payment rates vary. Pays on publication. Provides 2 contributor's copies.

Dirt Rider Magazine

2570 East Cerritos Avenue
Anaheim, CA 92806

Editor

DESCRIPTION AND INTERESTS: This monthly magazine for dirt bike riders of all ages offers riding tips, technical information, product reviews, and competition news, as well as profiles of racers. With its photo-heavy layout, it strongly encourages the inclusion of photographs with editorial submissions. Circ: 131,000.
Website: www.dirtrider.com

FREELANCE POTENTIAL: 10% written by non-staff writers. Publishes 20 freelance submissions each year.

SUBMISSIONS AND PAYMENT: Query. Accepts hard copy. Availability of artwork improves chance of acceptance. SASE. Response time varies. Rights vary. Articles and depts/columns, word lengths vary. 5x5 JPEG images at 300 dpi; include captions and signed model releases for all persons depicted. All material, payment rates vary. Pays on publication. Provides 1 contributor's copy.

Dollhouse Miniatures

68132 250th Avenue
Kasson, MN 55944

Editor-in-Chief: Kelly Rud

DESCRIPTION AND INTERESTS: In print for more than 36 years, *Dollhouse Miniatures* is now published six times each year. It features in-depth interviews with top "mini" manufacturers, how-to articles on projects, and photo-essays of dollhouses. Circ: 25,000.
Website: www.dhminiatures.com

FREELANCE POTENTIAL: 30% written by non-staff writers. Publishes 8–10 freelance submissions yearly; 10% by unpublished writers, 30% by authors who are new to the magazine. Receives 60 queries yearly.

SUBMISSIONS AND PAYMENT: Sample copy, $6.95 with 9x12 SASE ($1.95 postage). Query with outline. Accepts hard copy and email queries to kelly@dhminiatures.com. SASE. Responds in 2 months. All rights. Articles and depts/columns, word lengths vary; $75 per published page. Pays on publication. Provides 1 contributor's copy.

Dolls

P.O. Box 5000
Iola, WI 54945

Editor: Carie Ferg

DESCRIPTION AND INTERESTS: Readers of this monthly magazine know that dolls are not just child's play. Each issue of *Dolls* features comprehensive coverage of doll collecting, including profiles of artists and manufacturers, show and other event information, and articles about the history of dolls. It does not publish nostalgia pieces. Circ: 20,000.
Website: www.dollsmagazine.com

FREELANCE POTENTIAL: 85% written by non-staff writers. Publishes 50 freelance submissions yearly; 10% by authors who are new to the magazine. Receives 40 unsolicited mss yearly.

SUBMISSIONS AND PAYMENT: Send complete ms. Accepts email submissions to carief@jonespublishing.com. Availability of artwork improves chance of acceptance. Response time varies. One-time rights. Articles, 1,000–2,000 words; $200. Color prints, slides, or transparencies; JPG images at 300 dpi. Pays on publication.

Dyslexia Online Magazine

Submissions: Teresa Burns

DESCRIPTION AND INTERESTS: *Dyslexia Online Magazine* offers a wealth of both fresh and archived articles aimed at helping dyslexic children to learn, educators to teach, and parents to cope. It features personal stories of raising a child with dyslexia as well as informational articles on topics such as handling stress and learning to read. Hits per month: 150,000.
Website: www.dyslexia-parent.com/magazine

FREELANCE POTENTIAL: 50% written by non-staff writers. Publishes several freelance submissions yearly; 10% by unpublished writers, 10% by authors who are new to the magazine. Receives 24 unsolicited mss yearly.

SUBMISSIONS AND PAYMENT: Sample copy and guidelines available at website. Send complete ms. Accepts email submissions to dyslextest@aol.com (no attachments). Responds in 2 weeks. All rights. Articles, word lengths vary. No payment.

Early Years

128 North Rail Avenue
Front Royal, VA 22603

Editor: Tia Gibbo

DESCRIPTION AND INTERESTS: Parents of preschool and kindergarten youngsters read this newsletter for its brief yet informative articles on preparing their children for school. It appears nine times each year. Many of its regular features also include sound advice for parents who want to be more involved in the educational process. Circ: 60,000.
Website: www.rfeonline.com

FREELANCE POTENTIAL: 100% written by nonstaff writers. Publishes 80 freelance submissions yearly; 28% by unpublished writers. Receives 36 queries yearly.

SUBMISSIONS AND PAYMENT: Sample copy, free with 9x12 SASE (2 first-class stamps). Query with résumé and clips. Accepts hard copy. SASE. Responds in 1 month. All rights. Articles, 225–300 words. Depts/columns, 175–200 words. Written material, $.60 per word. Pays on acceptance. Provides 5 contributor's copies.

East Texas Teen

10278 CR 2167
Whitehouse, TX 75791

Editor: Heather Nielson

DESCRIPTION AND INTERESTS: Tweens and teens in the East Texas region read this magazine for the latest fashion advice, beauty tips, and articles on social issues, recreation, popular culture, and health. Each issue also features an essay from a local teen. All material is written from a conservative perspective. *East Texas Teen* is published six times each year. Circ: Unavailable.
Website: www.easttexasteen.com

FREELANCE POTENTIAL: 15–20% written by nonstaff writers. Publishes 10 freelance submissions yearly. Receives 180 queries yearly.

SUBMISSIONS AND PAYMENT: Sample copy available. Query with brief author bio and clips. Accepts hard copy and email submissions to info@easttexasteen.com. SASE. Responds in 4–6 weeks. First rights. Written material, word lengths vary. No payment. Provides 2 contributor's copies.

Eco-Kids Magazine

P.O. Box 3306 Hermit Park
Townsville, Queensland
Australia 4812

Editor: Lynette Stein

DESCRIPTION AND INTERESTS: *Eco-Kids Magazine* targets children interested in living eco-conscious and greener lives. It offers recipes, crafts, and articles on topics such as growing your own garden, eco-shopping, and recycling. Profiles of young people who are making a difference in their communities also appear regularly. The magazine is published monthly; its website is updated daily. Circ: 30,000.
Website: www.ecobites.com

FREELANCE POTENTIAL: 30% written by non-staff writers. Publishes 15 freelance submissions yearly; 25% by unpublished writers, 50% by authors who are new to the magazine.

SUBMISSIONS AND PAYMENT: Query or send complete ms. Accepts hard copy and electronic submissions through the website. SAE/IRC. Response time varies. Rights vary. Articles, word lengths and payment rates vary. Pays on publication. Provides 2 contributor's copies.

EFCA Today

418 Fourth Street NE
Charlottesville, VA 22902

Editor: Diane McDougall

DESCRIPTION AND INTERESTS: This quarterly publication of the Evangelical Free Church of America (EFCA) is distributed to its pastors, elders, deacons, religious education teachers, and other members. Each themed issue deals with some aspect of spirituality and evangelism and how it relates to today's society. *EFCA Today* strongly prefers queries from members of EFCA. Circ: 40,000.
Website: www.efcatoday.org

FREELANCE POTENTIAL: 80% written by non-staff writers. Publishes several freelance submissions yearly.

SUBMISSIONS AND PAYMENT: Sample copy and guidelines, $1 with 9x12 SASE (5 first-class stamps). Query. Accepts email queries to dianemc@journeygroup.com. Response time varies. First rights. Articles, 200–700 words. Cover theme articles, 300–1,000 words. Written material, $.23 per word. Pays on acceptance.

The Education Revolution

417 Roslyn Road
Roslyn Heights, NY 11577

Executive Editor: Jerry Mintz

DESCRIPTION AND INTERESTS: Published by the Alternative Education Resource Organization (AERO), this quarterly magazine seeks to provide resources "that support self-determination in learning and the natural genius in everyone." Its content, aimed at both teachers and parents, covers such topics as homeschooling, public and private alternative schools, charter schools, and learner-centered approaches to education. It seeks queries from experienced educators, including homeschooling parents. Circ: 5,000.
Website: www.educationrevolution.org

FREELANCE POTENTIAL: 20% written by non-staff writers. Publishes 10 freelance submissions yearly; 40% by authors who are new to the magazine. Receives 180 queries yearly.

SUBMISSIONS AND PAYMENT: Query. Accepts hard copy. SASE. Responds in 1 month. Rights vary. Articles and depts/columns, word lengths vary. No payment.

The Elementary School Journal

University of Missouri, College of Education
202 London Hall
Columbia, MO 65211-1150

Managing Editor: Gail M. Hinkel

DESCRIPTION AND INTERESTS: This peer-reviewed, academic journal publishes articles on both education theory and research and their implications for teaching practice. Published five times each year, *The Elementary School Journal* also occasionally publishes integrative research reviews and in-depth conceptual analyses of schooling. Circ: 2,200.
Website: www.journals.uchicago.edu/ESJ

FREELANCE POTENTIAL: 100% written by nonstaff writers. Publishes several freelance submissions yearly.

SUBMISSIONS AND PAYMENT: Sample copy, $13.50. Guidelines available at website. Send 4 copies of complete ms with an abstract of 100–150 words. Accepts hard copy. SASE. Response time varies. Rights vary. Articles, 1,200–2,000 words. Depts/columns, 600–800 words. Written material, word lengths vary. No payment.

Encyclopedia of Youth Studies

130 Essex Street
South Hamilton, MA 01982

Editor: Dean Borgman

DESCRIPTION AND INTERESTS: This online encyclopedia, updated regularly, targets those who work with children and young adults, including educators, social workers, teen center directors, and youth ministers. Its content covers more than 200 issues vital to youth. Articles are carefully researched and offer practical applications. Hits per month: Unavailable.
Website: www.centerforyouth.org

FREELANCE POTENTIAL: 20% written by non-staff writers. Publishes 5–10 freelance submissions yearly; 85% by unpublished writers, 85% by authors who are new to the magazine. Receives 48 queries, 12 unsolicited mss yearly.

SUBMISSIONS AND PAYMENT: Sample copy and guidelines available at website. Query or send complete ms. Accepts email submissions to cys@centerforyouth.org. Responds to queries in 1 week, to mss in 1 month. All rights. Articles, 600 words. No payment.

Entertainment Magazine

P.O. Box 3355
Tucson, AZ 85722

Publisher: Robert Zucker

DESCRIPTION AND INTERESTS: Founded as an Arizona regional magazine in 1977, this monthly publication went entirely online in 1995. Today it provides entertainment news, interviews, profiles, and informational articles on the music and film industries to website visitors from around the world. Hits per month: 500,000+.
Website: www.emol.org

FREELANCE POTENTIAL: 60% written by non-staff writers. Publishes dozens of freelance submissions yearly; 75% by unpublished writers, 25% by authors who are new to the magazine. Receives hundreds of queries yearly.

SUBMISSIONS AND PAYMENT: Sample copy and guidelines available at website. Query. Accepts email queries to emol@emol.org. Responds in 1–2 days. Author retains rights. Articles, to 1,000 words. B/W digital images. No payment.

Equestrian

4047 Iron Works Parkway
Lexington, KY 40511

Editor: Brian Sosby

DESCRIPTION AND INTERESTS: Since 1932, *Equestrian* has provided national coverage of equestrian sports for American readers. It is published 10 times each year by the United States Equestrian Federation (USEF), with articles on horse breeds, equine health, USEF competitions, and distinguished riders. Circ: 90,000.
Website: www.usef.org

FREELANCE POTENTIAL: 50% written by non-staff writers. Publishes 50 freelance submissions yearly; 10% by authors who are new to the magazine. Receives 200 queries yearly.

SUBMISSIONS AND PAYMENT: Sample copy and guidelines available. Query with résumé and writing samples. Accepts email queries to bsosby@usef.org. Responds in 1 week. First rights. Articles, 2,000–3,000 words. Depts/columns, 500–1,000 words. Written material, payment rates vary. Kill fee, 50%. Pays on publication. Provides 1 contributor's copy.

eSchoolNews

7920 Norfolk Avenue, Suite 900
Bethesda, MD 20814

Editor: Greg Downey

DESCRIPTION AND INTERESTS: This online magazine, which also appears in print each month, stays on the cutting edge of technology news as it relates to education. Read by school administrators and teachers at all grade levels, it covers such topics as software, computer systems, websites, and new products, and offers resources for professional development and the classroom. Hits per month: 100,000.
Website: www.eschoolnews.com

FREELANCE POTENTIAL: 20% written by non-staff writers. Publishes 6–8 freelance submissions yearly. Receives 100 unsolicited mss yearly.

SUBMISSIONS AND PAYMENT: Sample copy available at website. Prefers query; will accept complete ms. Accepts hard copy and email submissions to gdowney@eschoolnews.com. SASE. Response time varies. Rights vary. Articles and depts/columns, word lengths and payment rates vary. Pays on acceptance.

Family-Life Magazine

100 Professional Center Drive, Suite 104
Rohnert Park, CA 94928

Publisher/Editor: Sharon Gowan

DESCRIPTION AND INTERESTS: Providing information on education, health, parenting, and local issues of importance to families in Sonoma, Mendocino, and Lake counties, *Family-Life* is published monthly. It prefers articles with a local angle, but will consider anything that will "wow" its readers. Circ: 40,000.
Website: www.family-life.us

FREELANCE POTENTIAL: 40% written by non-staff writers. Publishes 24–36 freelance submissions yearly; 10% by unpublished writers. Receives 120+ unsolicited mss yearly.

SUBMISSIONS AND PAYMENT: Guidelines and editorial calendar available. Send complete ms. Accepts hard copy and email submissions to sharon@family-life.us (in body of email or as Microsoft Word attachment). Response time varies. All rights. Written material, 650–1,150 words; $.08 per word. Reprints, $35–$50. Pays on publication. Provides 1 contributor's copy.

Family Motor Coaching

8291 Clough Pike
Cincinnati, OH 45244

Editor: Robbin Gould

DESCRIPTION AND INTERESTS: Families that enjoy motor home traveling are the target audience of this monthly magazine. It offers travel tips, destination reviews, and recreation ideas. Circ: 110,000.
Website: www.fmca.com

FREELANCE POTENTIAL: 75% written by non-staff writers. Publishes 50 freelance submissions yearly; 10% by unpublished writers, 10% by authors who are new to the magazine. Receives 600 queries, 300 unsolicited mss yearly.

SUBMISSIONS AND PAYMENT: Sample copy and guidelines, $3.99. Prefers query with résumé, outline, and clips; will accept complete ms with résumé. Accepts hard copy and email submissions to magazine@fmca.com. SASE. Response time varies. First North American serial and electronic rights. Articles, 1,200–2,000 words. Depts/columns, 1,000 words. Written material, $50–$500. Pays on acceptance. Provides 1 contributor's copy.

Family Safety & Health

1121 Spring Lake Drive
Itasca, IL 60143

Editor: Tim Hodson

DESCRIPTION AND INTERESTS: Appearing quarterly, this publication strives to promote safety in the home, workplace, and recreational areas. It offers informational articles with facts and statistics that are written in an easy-to-understand style. All of its articles are written on a work-for-hire basis. Circ: 225,000.
Website: www.nsc.org

FREELANCE POTENTIAL: 1% written by nonstaff writers. Publishes 5 freelance submissions yearly; 20% by authors who are new to the magazine.

SUBMISSIONS AND PAYMENT: Sample copy, $4 with 9x12 SASE ($.77 postage). No queries or unsolicited mss; send résumé and clips only. All work is done on a work-for-hire basis. Accepts hard copy. All rights. Articles, 1,200 words; payment rate varies. Pays on acceptance. Provides 2 contributor's copies.

Family Tree Magazine

4700 East Galbraith Road
Cincinnati, OH 45236

Editor: Allison Stacy

DESCRIPTION AND INTERESTS: Celebrating and preserving family histories is the focus of this magazine that is published six times each year. It offers articles on genealogy research, ethnic heritage, and photo preservation. Circ: 60,000.
Website: www.familytreemagazine.com

FREELANCE POTENTIAL: 80% written by non-staff writers. Publishes several freelance submissions yearly; 5% by unpublished writers, 10% by authors who are new to the magazine. Receives 480 queries yearly.

SUBMISSIONS AND PAYMENT: Sample copy, $6 at www.fwmagazines.com. Guidelines available at website. Query with clips. Accepts hard copy and email queries to ftmedit@fwmedia.com. SASE. Responds in 3 months. All rights. Articles, 2,000–3,500 words. Depts/columns, 300–1,000 words. Written material, payment rates vary. Kill fee, 25%. Pays on publication. Provides 2 contributor's copies.

Farm & Ranch Living

5925 Country Lane
Greendale, WI 53129

Editor

DESCRIPTION AND INTERESTS: Focusing on the people side of the farm and ranch lifestyle, this magazine is published every other month. It features profiles of present day farmers and ranchers. Circ: 350,000.
Website: www.farmandranchliving.com

FREELANCE POTENTIAL: 90% written by non-staff writers. Publishes 36 freelance submissions yearly; 50% by unpublished writers, 50% by authors who are new to the magazine. Receives 120 queries and unsolicited mss yearly.

SUBMISSIONS AND PAYMENT: Sample copy, $2. Query or send complete ms. Accepts hard copy and email submissions to editors@farmandranchliving.com. Availability of artwork improves chance of acceptance. SASE. Responds in 6 weeks. One-time rights. Articles, 1,200 words. Depts/columns, 350 words. Color prints. Written material, $10–$150. Pays on publication. Provides 1 contributor's copy.

FatherMag.com

P.O. Box 231891
Houston, TX 77223

Managing Editor: John Gill

DESCRIPTION AND INTERESTS: Available in two editions—"Family Life" and "Family Strife"—this online magazine tackles the issues surrounding fatherhood with humor and earnestness alike. Topics include new fatherhood, stay-at-home fathers, single-parent adoption, role models, the joys of fatherhood, and—on the "strife" side—parental alienation and custody issues. *FatherMag.com* also publishes book reviews, fiction, and poetry by, for, and about dads. Hits per month: 1 million.
Website: www.fathermag.com

FREELANCE POTENTIAL: 95% written by non-staff writers. Publishes 50 freelance submissions yearly; 50% by authors new to the magazine.

SUBMISSIONS AND PAYMENT: Sample copy and guidelines available at website. Query. Accepts email queries to jgill@fathermag.com. Response time varies. One-time rights. Articles and fiction, word lengths vary. No payment.

Fido Friendly

P.O. Box 160
Marsing, ID 83639

Editor: Nicholas Sveslosky

DESCRIPTION AND INTERESTS: A travel magazine for dog owners, *Fido Friendly* shares information about pet-friendly hotels, parks, and other destinations throughout the U.S. and Canada. It is published six times each year. Circ: 44,000.
Website: www.fidofriendly.com

FREELANCE POTENTIAL: 90% written by non-staff writers. Publishes 25 freelance submissions yearly; 10% by unpublished writers, 10% by authors who are new to the magazine. Receives 100 queries yearly.

SUBMISSIONS AND PAYMENT: Sample copy, $5 with 9x12 SASE (4 first-class stamps). Query with sample paragraph. Accepts email queries to fieldeditor@fidofriendly.com. Responds in 1 month. First rights. Articles, 800–1,200 words; $.10 per word. Pays on publication. Provides 1 contributor's copy.

FineScale Modeler

21027 Crossroads Circle
P.O. Box 1612
Waukesha, WI 53187

Editor: Matthew Usher

DESCRIPTION AND INTERESTS: This "essential tool for model builders" is published 10 times each year. New writers have the best chance of breaking into print with a short article focusing on a single technique. Circ: 60,000.
Website: www.finescale.com

FREELANCE POTENTIAL: 85% written by non-staff writers. Publishes 40 freelance submissions yearly; 20% by authors who are new to the magazine. Receives 200 queries yearly.

SUBMISSIONS AND PAYMENT: Sample copy and guidelines available at website. Prefers query; will accept complete ms with bio. Accepts hard copy and disk submissions with hard copy. No simultaneous submissions. Availability of artwork improves chance of acceptance. SASE. Responds in 1–4 months. All rights. Articles, 750–3,000 words. Digital photos, slides, prints, and scale drawings. All material, payment rates vary. Pays on acceptance. Provides 1 copy.

Fort Lauderdale Family Magazine

7045 SW 69th Avenue
South Miami, FL 33143

Publisher: Janet Jupiter

DESCRIPTION AND INTERESTS: This regional monthly for parents in the Fort Lauderdale area of Florida covers it all; from child care to camp, education to entertainment, finance to fitness. Each issue also includes a guide to local family-friendly events. Contributing writers must be intimately familiar with the Fort Lauderdale community, just as articles must have a local hook. Circ: Unavailable.
Website: www.familymagazine.biz

FREELANCE POTENTIAL: 30% written by non-staff writers. Publishes 15–20 freelance submissions yearly.

SUBMISSIONS AND PAYMENT: Sample copy available at website. Query. Accepts hard copy and email queries to familymag@bellsouth.net. SASE. Response time varies. One-time rights. Articles and depts/columns, word lengths vary; payment rates vary. Pays on publication. Provides contributor's copies.

Gay Parent Magazine

P.O. Box 750852
Forest Hills, NY 11375-0852

Editor: Angeline Acain

DESCRIPTION AND INTERESTS: This magazine, published six times each year, identifies issues unique to homosexual parents and offers insight into them. It also covers topics affecting all parents, such as choosing a school or summer camp, but from a gay perspective. Circ: 10,000.
Website: www.gayparentmag.com

FREELANCE POTENTIAL: 3% written by non-staff writers. Publishes 6 freelance submissions yearly; 1% by authors who are new to the magazine. Receives 75 unsolicited mss yearly.

SUBMISSIONS AND PAYMENT: Sample copy and guidelines, $3.50. Send complete ms. Accepts email submissions to gayparentmag@gmail.com. Availability of artwork improves chance of acceptance. Response time varies. One-time rights. Articles, 500–1,000 words; $.10 per word. Color prints or digital images; payment rates vary. Pays on publication. Provides contributor's copies upon request.

GirlMogul Magazine

309 Main Street
Lebanon, NJ 08833

Editor: Andrea Stein

DESCRIPTION AND INTERESTS: Not your typical girls' magazine, *GirlMogul* focuses on enhancing the self-confidence and worldly knowledge of today's tween girl. Targeting girls ages seven to thirteen, it looks for well-researched submissions with sidebars. It is interested in eco-friendly topics and profiles of tween girls making a difference. Circ: Unavailable.
Website: www.girlmogul.com

FREELANCE POTENTIAL: 15–20% written by nonstaff writers. Plans to publish several freelance submissions yearly.

SUBMISSIONS AND PAYMENT: Sample copy available. Query with author bio; or send complete ms. Accepts hard copy and email submissions to andrea@girlmogul.com. No simultaneous submissions. SASE. Response time varies. First rights. Written material, word lengths vary. No payment. Provides 2 contributor's copies.

Go! Magazine

2711 South Loop Drive, Suite 4700
Ames, IA 50010

Editor: Rebekah Bovenmyer

DESCRIPTION AND INTERESTS: *Go! Magazine* is an online publication, updated six times each year, for teens and young adults who want to explore career opportunities in transportation. It offers informative articles as well as personal experience pieces. Freelance writers are welcome to make submissions for contests only. Hits per month: Unavailable.
Website: www.go-explore-trans.org

FREELANCE POTENTIAL: 50–75% written by nonstaff writers. Publishes 2 freelance submissions yearly.

SUBMISSIONS AND PAYMENT: Sample copy, guidelines, and theme list available at website. Query. Accepts email queries to editor@go-explore-trans.com. Response time varies. First world electronic and archival rights. Articles, 1,000–1,500 words. Depts/columns, 750–1,250 words. JPEGs. Written material, $.25 per word. Artwork, $25 per photo. Payment policy varies.

Good Housekeeping

Hearst Corporation
300 West 57th Street
New York, NY 10019-5288

Executive Editor: Judith Coyne

DESCRIPTION AND INTERESTS: Read mainly by working mothers, this monthly magazine offers content that reflects the balance between career and family. Other topics include health, beauty, and fashion. Circ: 25 million.
Website: www.goodhousekeeping.com

FREELANCE POTENTIAL: 80% written by non-staff writers. Publishes 50+ freelance submissions yearly. Receives 18,000–24,000 queries yearly.

SUBMISSIONS AND PAYMENT: Guidelines available at website. Sample copy, $2.50 at newsstands. Query with résumé and clips for nonfiction; SASE. Send complete ms for fiction; mss not returned. Accepts hard copy. Responds in 4–6 weeks. All rights for nonfiction; first North American serial rights for fiction. Articles, 750–2,500 words; to $2,000. Essays, to 1,000 words; to $750. Fiction, to 3,000 words; payment rates vary. Pays on acceptance. Provides 1 contributor's copy.

Grandparents.com

281 Rosedale Avenue
Wayne, PA 19087

Editor

DESCRIPTION AND INTERESTS: This e-zine is considered by many to be the go-to destination for grandparents on the World Wide Web. It serves as a valuable resource for information on activities and events for grandparents and their grandchildren; and its new product reviews of toys, books, games, gear, movies, and other media are the result of hands-on experience. The balance of its content consists of personal experience pieces, essays, profiles, and interviews. Hits per month: Unavailable.
Website: www.grandparents.com

FREELANCE POTENTIAL: Publishes several freelance submissions yearly.

SUBMISSIONS AND PAYMENT: Sample copy and writer's guidelines available at website. Query. Accepts email queries to stories@ grandparents.com. Response time varies. Electronic rights. Articles, word lengths vary. No payment.

Grand Rapids Family

549 Ottawa Avenue NW, Suite 201
Grand Rapids, MI 49503

Editor: Carole Valade

DESCRIPTION AND INTERESTS: This regional monthly, published for families living in western Michigan, offers feature stories on local people, places, and events. Informative articles cover travel and recreation, health and safety, education, finances, and other issues of interest to families. Media and product reviews, interviews and profiles, and news items are also included in each issue. Circ: 30,000.
Website: www.grfamily.com

FREELANCE POTENTIAL: 20% written by non-staff writers. Publishes 15 freelance submissions each year.

SUBMISSIONS AND PAYMENT: Guidelines available with #10 SASE. Query or send complete ms. Accepts hard copy. SASE. Responds to queries in 2 months, to mss in 6 months. All rights. Articles and depts/columns, word lengths and payment rates vary. B/W or color prints, $25. Kill fee, $25. Pays on publication.

Harford County Kids

P.O. Box 1666
Bel Air, MD 21014

Publisher: Joan Fernandez

DESCRIPTION AND INTERESTS: This publication is read by parents living in Harford County, Maryland, and its environs for local news and event coverage, profiles, interviews, and personal essays. Published monthly, it also features informative articles on family issues such as childbirth, child care, child development, health, safety, education, finances, dining and entertainment, and the arts. Circ: 22,000.
Website: www.countyparents.com

FREELANCE POTENTIAL: 75% written by non-staff writers. Publishes 20 freelance submissions each year.

SUBMISSIONS AND PAYMENT: Guidelines available. Query. Accepts hard copy and email queries to joanf@aboutdelta.com. SASE. Response time varies. First print and electronic rights. Articles and depts/columns, word lengths and payment rates vary. Pays on publication. Provides 1 contributor's copy.

Henry Parents Magazine

3651 Peachtree Parkway, Suite 325
Suwanee, GA 30024

Editor: Terrie Carter

DESCRIPTION AND INTERESTS: Appearing monthly for residents of Henry County, Georgia, this magazine seeks profiles of local families and informational articles on such topics as finance, health, and child rearing. The publication also spotlights local resources, services, and goods of particular interest to families. Local writers are preferred. Circ: Unavailable.
Website: www.henryparents.com

FREELANCE POTENTIAL: 75% written by non-staff writers. Publishes several freelance submissions yearly.

SUBMISSIONS AND PAYMENT: Sample copy available at website. Query or send complete ms. Accepts email submissions to editor@ henryparents.com. Responds in 1 month. First and nonexclusive online archival rights. Articles, 500–1,000 words. Depts/columns, word lengths vary. Written material, payment rates vary. Pays on publication. Provides 2 contributor's copies.

The High School Journal

Editorial Office, School of Education
University of North Carolina, CB#3500
Chapel Hill, NC 27599

Managing Editor: Meredith Sinclair

DESCRIPTION AND INTERESTS: *The High School Journal* is read by high school administrators and educators for its articles covering topics related to adolescent growth and development and secondary school education. Research reports and informed opinion are also included in each quarterly issue. Circ: 800.
Website: www.uncpress.unc.edu

FREELANCE POTENTIAL: 100% written by nonstaff writers. Publishes 20–30 freelance submissions yearly; 25% by unpublished writers, 85% by authors who are new to the magazine. Receives 324 unsolicited mss yearly.

SUBMISSIONS AND PAYMENT: Sample copy, $7.50 with 9x12 SASE. Send 3 copies of complete ms. Accepts email submissions to gwn@ unc.edu. Responds in 3–4 months. All rights. Articles, 1,500–2,500 words. Depts/columns, 300–400 words. No payment. Provides 3 contributor's copies.

Highlights High Five

807 Church Street
Honesdale, PA 18431-1895

Editor: Kathleen Hayes

DESCRIPTION AND INTERESTS: Launched in 2007 by the folks at *Highlights for Children*, this monthly publication targets children ages two through six and their caregivers. It was created to help parents encourage their young child's development while having fun together. Each issue contains a mix of read-aloud stories and age-appropriate puzzles and activities, all based on educational principles and widely accepted child-development theories. At press time, *High Five* was accepting very few freelance manuscripts. Most of its read-aloud stories and poems are commissioned, while the regular features are produced in-house. Please check the website for changes to this policy. Circ: Unavailable.
Website: www.highlights.com

FREELANCE POTENTIAL: Publishes few freelance submissions yearly.

SUBMISSIONS AND PAYMENT: Not accepting freelance submissions at this time.

High School Years

128 North Royal
Front Royal, VA 22630

Submissions Editor: Jennifer Hutchinson

DESCRIPTION AND INTERESTS: Appearing monthly during the school year, this publication shows parents how to help their high school students succeed academically. It also offers parenting advice on other issues related to success in school and beyond. It is not accepting submissions at this time. Circ: 300,000.
Website: www.rfeonline.com

FREELANCE POTENTIAL: 100% written by nonstaff writers. Publishes 80 freelance submissions yearly; 25% by unpublished writers. Receives 36 unsolicited mss yearly.

SUBMISSIONS AND PAYMENT: Sample copy, guidelines, and editorial calendar, free with 9x12 SASE. Query with résumé and clips when submissions reopen. SASE. Responds in 1 month. All rights. Articles, 225–300 words. Depts/columns, 175–200 words. Written material, $.60 per word. Pays on acceptance. Provides 5 contributor's copies.

Hip Mama

P.O. Box 12525
Portland, OR 97212

Editor: Kerlin Richter

DESCRIPTION AND INTERESTS: This "reader-written zine for progressive families" targets parents outside the mainstream culture: young parents, gay parents, and homeschooling parents, for instance. It looks for honest and daring first-person essays on motherhood, families of color, and teen issues; it is not interested in expert advice or academic treatises. *Hip Mama* is "published when it's published," typically four times each year. Circ: 5,000.
Website: www.hipmamazine.com

FREELANCE POTENTIAL: 95% written by non-staff writers.

SUBMISSIONS AND PAYMENT: Sample copy, $5.95. Guidelines and theme list available at website. Send complete ms. Accepts email submissions to hipmamazine@gmail.com (Microsoft Word attachments). Responds in 1 month. Rights vary. Articles, 250–1,500 words. B/W prints, digital images in JPG format; line art. No payment.

Home Times Family Newspaper

P.O. Box 22547
West Palm Beach, FL 33416

Editor: Dennis Lombard

DESCRIPTION AND INTERESTS: This "good little newspaper for God and country" is published monthly. It presents a non-denominational, biblical perspective on world and national news, entertainment, sports, and science, and seeks profiles of people who model biblical values. Circ: 4,000.
Website: www.hometimesnewspaper.org

FREELANCE POTENTIAL: 67% written by non-staff writers. Publishes 25 freelance submissions yearly; 10% by unpublished writers, 10% by authors who are new to the magazine. Receives 360 unsolicited mss yearly.

SUBMISSIONS AND PAYMENT: Sample copy and guidelines, $3. Send complete ms. Accepts hard copy and simultaneous submissions if identified. SASE. Responds in 1 month. One-time print and electronic rights. Articles, to 1,000 words; $5–$25. Depts/columns, word lengths and payment rates vary. Pays on publication. Provides contributor's copies upon request.

Home & School Connection

128 North Royal Avenue
Front Royal, VA 22630

Submissions: Matt McGraff

DESCRIPTION AND INTERESTS: "Working together for school success" is the idea behind this newsletter, distributed monthly to parents of elementary school students. Through short, upbeat articles on everything from reading to testing to bullying, *Home & School Connection* seeks to provide busy parents with practical ideas that promote academic success for their children, and more effective parenting for themselves. It is not reviewing manuscripts or queries, but interested writers may send a letter of introduction and a résumé. Circ: Unavailable.
Website: www.rfeonline.com

FREELANCE POTENTIAL: 100% written by nonstaff writers. Publishes 80 freelance submissions yearly; 28% by unpublished writers, 14% by authors who are new to the magazine.

SUBMISSIONS AND PAYMENT: Sample copy, free with 9x12 SASE (2 first-class stamps). All work is assigned. Send résumé.

Horse & Rider

2000 South Stemmons Freeway, Suite 101
Lake Dallas, TX 75065

Editor: Juli Thurson

DESCRIPTION AND INTERESTS: Competitive and recreational horseback riders read this monthly magazine for articles covering all aspects of Western horseback riding, grooming and training; breed information; and coverage of major equine events. Circ: 165,000.
Website: www.horseandrider.com

FREELANCE POTENTIAL: 15% written by non-staff writers. Publishes 20–30 freelance submissions yearly; 3% by unpublished writers, 1% by authors who are new to the magazine. Receives 120 queries yearly.

SUBMISSIONS AND PAYMENT: Sample copy and guidelines, $3.50. Query. Accepts hard copy and email queries to horseandrider@equinenetwork.com. SASE. Responds in 3 months. All rights. Articles, 600–1,200 words. Depts/columns, to 900 words. Written material, $25–$400. Pays on acceptance. Provides 1 contributor's copy.

Horse Illustrated

P.O. Box 8237
Lexington, KY 40533

Editor: Elizabeth Moyer

DESCRIPTION AND INTERESTS: This monthly magazine for horse lovers is always looking to expand its "stable" of talented freelance equestrian journalists. Circ: 200,000.
Website: www.horseillustrated.com

FREELANCE POTENTIAL: 80% written by nonstaff writers. Publishes 10–20 freelance submissions yearly. Receives 480 queries, 240 unsolicited mss yearly.

SUBMISSIONS AND PAYMENT: Guidelines available. Prefers complete ms; will accept query with detailed outline, resources, and clips. Accepts hard copy. No simultaneous submissions. Availability of artwork improves chance of acceptance. SASE. Responds in 2–3 months. First North American serial rights. Articles, 1,500–2,000 words; $300–$425. Depts/columns, 1,000–1,400 words; $50–$100. Color transparencies or 35mm prints; payment rates vary. Pays on publication. Provides 2 contributor's copies.

Hot Rod

6420 Wilshire Boulevard
Los Angeles, CA 90048

Editor: David Freiburger

DESCRIPTION AND INTERESTS: Each month, this magazine fills its pages with hot rods in both words and images. From races to repairs to reviews, fans get bumper-to-bumper coverage of the hot rod world. Also featured are profiles of drivers, track tests, and how-to articles. New writers are encouraged to submit material on car news items and car features. Circ: 680,000.
Website: www.hotrod.com

FREELANCE POTENTIAL: 15% written by non-staff writers. Publishes 24 freelance submissions yearly. Receives 288 queries yearly.

SUBMISSIONS AND PAYMENT: Sample copy, $3.50 at newsstands. Guidelines available. Query. Accepts hard copy. SASE. Response time varies. All rights. Articles, 3,000 characters per page; $250–$300 per page. Depts/columns, word lengths vary; $100 per page. B/W and color prints and 35mm color transparencies; payment rates vary. Pays on publication.

Houston Family Magazine

233 West 21st Street
Houston, TX 77708

Editor: Dana Donovan

DESCRIPTION AND INTERESTS: This monthly publication targets parents living in Harris, Fort Bend, Brazoria, Galveston, and Montgomery counties in Texas. It offers informational articles on education, child care, recreation, and regional events. Profiles of local families are also a part of each issue. Circ: 60,000.
Website: www.houstonfamilymagazine.com

FREELANCE POTENTIAL: 20% written by non-staff writers. Publishes 20 freelance submissions yearly; 25% by authors new to the magazine.

SUBMISSIONS AND PAYMENT: Sample copy and guidelines available at website. Query or send complete ms. Accepts email submissions to editor@houstonfamilymagazine.com. Response time varies. First and limited-time electronic rights. Articles and depts/columns, word lengths and payment rates vary. Pays on publication. Provides 2 contributor's copies.

I.D.

Cook Communications Ministries
4050 Lee Vance View
Colorado Springs, CO 80918

Editor: Doug Mauss

DESCRIPTION AND INTERESTS: *I.D.* is a weekly Sunday school take-home journal for high school students. It features Bible stories accompanied by relevant lessons and activities, with advice on contemporary topics such as school, community service, careers, and relationships woven in. Writers should regularly check the website for changes to this magazine's submissions policy. Circ: 50,000.
Website: www.davidccook.com

FREELANCE POTENTIAL: 20% written by non-staff writers.

SUBMISSIONS AND PAYMENT: Guidelines available. Send résumé only; no queries or unsolicited mss. All work is assigned. Accepts hard copy. SASE. Responds in 6 months. Rights vary. Articles, 600–1,200 words; $50–$300. B/W and color prints; payment rates vary. Pays on acceptance. Provides 1 contributor's copy.

I Love Cats

1040 First Avenue, Suite 323
New York, NY 10022

Editor: Lisa Allmendinger

DESCRIPTION AND INTERESTS: Stories and photos depicting the joys of feline companionship grace the pages of *I Love Cats*, which is published six times each year. Though it offers fiction as well as articles, it is not interested in reviewing stories that feature personified cats. Circ: 25,000.
Website: www.iluvcats.com

FREELANCE POTENTIAL: 90% written by non-staff writers. Publishes 100+ freelance submissions yearly; 60% by unpublished writers, 70% by authors who are new to the magazine. Receives 6,000 unsolicited mss yearly.

SUBMISSIONS AND PAYMENT: Sample copy and guidelines, $5.95 with 9x12 SASE. Send complete ms. Accepts email to ilovecatseditorial@sbcglobal.net. Responds in 1–2 months. All rights. Articles and fiction, 500–1,000 words; $50–$100. JPEG images; payment rates vary. Pays on publication. Provides 1 contributor's copy.

Indian Life Newspaper

P.O. Box 3765
Redwood Post Office
Winnipeg, Manitoba R2W 3R6
Canada

Editor: Jim Uttley

DESCRIPTION AND INTERESTS: *Indian Life Newspaper* covers the social, cultural, and spiritual issues of the North American Indian Church, whose members live in the U.S. and Canada. Consistent with its readership, most of the paper's contributing writers are of Native American or First Nations ancestry. Circ: 20,000.
Website: www.indianlife.org

FREELANCE POTENTIAL: 80% written by non-staff writers. Publishes 20 freelance submissions yearly; 10% by unpublished writers, 40% by authors who are new to the magazine. Receives 300 unsolicited mss yearly.

SUBMISSIONS AND PAYMENT: Sample copy, $3 with #9 SAE. Prefers query; will accept complete ms. Accepts hard copy and disk submissions. SAE (no IRC). Responds in 1 month. First rights. Articles, 250–2,000 words; $.15 per word, to $150. Pays on publication. Provides 3 contributor's copies.

Inside Kung-Fu

Action Pursuit Group
2400 East Katella Avenue #300
Anaheim, CA 92806

Editor: Dave Cater

DESCRIPTION AND INTERESTS: Beginning students and kung-fu experts alike enjoy this monthly magazine that covers this Chinese-style martial art. Articles on traditional forms of fighting, weaponry, and kung-fu history, and profiles of master martial arts figures are featured in each issue. Circ: 65,000.
Website: www.insidekung-fu.com

FREELANCE POTENTIAL: 80% written by non-staff writers. Publishes 80–100 freelance submissions yearly; 50% by unpublished writers, 50% by authors who are new to the magazine. Receives 504 queries yearly.

SUBMISSIONS AND PAYMENT: Sample copy and guidelines, $2.95 with 9x12 SASE. Query. Accepts hard copy and email queries to dcater@beckett.com. SASE. Responds in 4–6 weeks. First rights. Articles, 1,500 words. Depts/columns, 750 words. Written material, payment rates vary. Pays on publication.

Inspired Mother

The Design Center
10816 Millington Ct., Suite 110
Cincinnati, OH 45242

Editor: Jennifer Hogan Redmond

DESCRIPTION AND INTERESTS: This online publication targets mothers striving to raise children who will make a positive difference in this world. It is published online each month and features profiles of inspirational mothers who have achieved success in their personal and/or professional lives. Hits per month: Unavailable.
Website: www.inspiredmother.com

FREELANCE POTENTIAL: 40% written by non-staff writers. Publishes 15–20 freelance submissions yearly; 50% by authors who are new to the magazine.

SUBMISSIONS AND PAYMENT: Sample copy and writers' guidelines available at website. Send complete ms. Accepts hard copy and email submissions to editor@inspiredmother.com. SASE. Response time varies. Limited-time electronic rights. Feature articles, to 1,500 words. Short stories and narratives, to 750 words. No payment.

James Hubbard's My Family Doctor

P.O. Box 38790
Colorado Springs, CO 80906

Managing Editor: Leigh Ann Hubbard

DESCRIPTION AND INTERESTS: This consumer magazine, published quarterly, offers reliable and timely health information written by licensed health-care professionals. Geared toward the general public, articles are free of overly technical language. Circ: 60,000.
Website: www.myfamilydoctormag.com

FREELANCE POTENTIAL: 90% written by non-staff writers. Publishes 114 freelance submissions yearly; 8% by unpublished writers, 11% by authors who are new to the magazine.

SUBMISSIONS AND PAYMENT: Sample copy, $4.95 at newsstands. Guidelines available. Query with writing samples. Accepts email to managingeditor@familydoctormag.com. Response time varies. First North American serial, exclusive syndication, and electronic rights. Articles, 400–1,200 words. Depts/columns and filler, 200–400 words. Written material, to $.30 per word. Pays on publication.

Junior Storyteller

P.O. Box 205
Masonville, CO 80541

Editor: Vivian Dubrovin

DESCRIPTION AND INTERESTS: This quarterly is written for children ages 9 to 14 who wish to carry on the tradition of oral storytelling. It is now published online as well as in print. Circ: 500.
Website: www.storycraft.com

FREELANCE POTENTIAL: 50% written by non-staff writers. Publishes several freelance submissions yearly; 25% by unpublished writers, 25% by authors who are new to the magazine. Receives numerous queries yearly.

SUBMISSIONS AND PAYMENT: Sample copy, $4. Guidelines available at website. Query. Accepts hard copy and email to jrstoryteller@storycraft.com. No simultaneous submissions. Availability of artwork improves chance of acceptance. SASE. Response time varies. First North American serial rights. Articles and fiction, 350–1,000 words; $50–$125. B/W or color prints or digital photos; payment rates vary. Pays on acceptance. Provides 10 contributor's copies.

Just 4 Kids Magazine

11201 Terrace Meadow Way
Manor, TX 78653

Editor: Mauri Gandy

DESCRIPTION AND INTERESTS: Each month, *Just 4 Kids Magazine* offers wholesome readings for children ages 7 to 12 that teach about God's love. Its content comprises puzzles, games, stories, poems, recipes, Scripture, and family devotions—all on a specific theme. Submissions should help children experience a Christian lifestyle, but should also reflect the diversity of the journal's readership. Circ: Unavailable.
Website: www.just4kidsmagazine.com

FREELANCE POTENTIAL: Publishes several freelance submissions yearly.

SUBMISSIONS AND PAYMENT: Sample copy, guidelines, and theme list available at website. Query or send complete ms. Accepts hard copy. SASE. Response time varies. First and electronic rights. Articles, 300–1,000 words; $.10 per word. Fiction and Bible stories, 400–1,400 words; $.10 per word. Depts/columns, word lengths vary; $5–$10. Payment policy varies.

Kahani

P.O. Box 590155
Newton Centre, MA 02459

Editor: Monika Jain

DESCRIPTION AND INTERESTS: *Kahani*, a literary magazine geared specifically to South Asian children, publishes both fiction and non-fiction. Each quarterly issue revolves around a theme, always celebrating South Asian culture and people, and never advocating a religious or political agenda. Circ: Unavailable.
Website: www.kahani.com

FREELANCE POTENTIAL: 50% written by non-staff writers. Publishes several freelance submissions yearly.

SUBMISSIONS AND PAYMENT: Guidelines and editorial calendar available at website. Query with clips for articles; send complete ms for fiction. Accepts email to writers@kahani.com (include "Feature Query" or "Fiction Submission" in the subject line). Responds if interested for articles; in 1 month for fiction. Rights vary. Articles, 400–600 words. Fiction, to 950 words. No payment. Provides contributor's copies.

Kansas 4-H Journal

116 Umberger Hall
Kansas State University
Manhattan, KS 66506-3714

Editor: Rhonda Atkinson

DESCRIPTION AND INTERESTS: Published six times each year for 4-H club members in Kansas, this journal features news, photo-essays, how-to articles, and personal experience pieces relating to club activities and programs. Due to the specific focus of the magazine, writers must have firsthand knowledge of 4-H programs—particularly those in Kansas—to be considered for publication. Circ: Unavailable.

FREELANCE POTENTIAL: 60% written by non-staff writers. Publishes 100 freelance submissions yearly; 10% by unpublished writers, 20% by authors who are new to the magazine. Receives 696 queries and unsolicited mss yearly.

SUBMISSIONS AND PAYMENT: Sample copy and editorial calendar, $5. Query or send complete ms. Accepts hard copy. SASE. Response time varies. Rights vary. Articles, 500 words; payment rates vary. Payment policy varies.

Kansas School Naturalist

Emporia State University
Department of Environmental Sciences
P.O. Box 4050
Emporia, KS 66801-5087

Editor: John Richard Schrock

DESCRIPTION AND INTERESTS: This journal is sent free of charge to Kansas teachers, school administrators, and school librarians, and to others upon request. Its editorial goal is to educate young people about natural history and conservation. Each issue spotlights a particular aspect of the state's ecology. It appears on an irregular basis. Circ: 10,000.
Website: www.emporia.edu/ksn

FREELANCE POTENTIAL: 50% written by non-staff writers. Of the freelance submissions published yearly, 20% are by unpublished writers, 75% are by authors who are new to the magazine.

SUBMISSIONS AND PAYMENT: Sample copy, free. Query or send complete ms. Accepts hard copy and email submissions to ksnaturl@emporia.edu. SASE. Response time varies. All rights. Articles, word lengths vary. B/W or color prints or transparencies. No payment. Provides contributor's copies.

Keeping Family First Online

P.O. Box 36594
Detroit, MI 48236

Executive Editor: Anita S. Lane

DESCRIPTION AND INTERESTS: *Keeping Family First* offers practical solutions and advice for time-stretched, busy moms and dads. Articles contributed by experts address such topics as parenting challenges, education, health, and family-building activities. Each quarterly issue also features inspirational articles, personal experience pieces, and profiles of families. Hits per month: 40,000.
Website: www.keepingfamilyfirst.org

FREELANCE POTENTIAL: 100% written by nonstaff writers. Publishes 70 freelance submissions yearly; 56% by unpublished writers, 10% by authors who are new to the magazine.

SUBMISSIONS AND PAYMENT: Sample copy and guidelines available at website. Query. Accepts email queries through the website only. Response time varies. Rights vary. Articles and depts/columns, word lengths vary. No payment.

Keyboard

1111 Bay Hill Drive, Suite 125
San Bruno, CA 94066

Managing Editor: Debbie Greenberg

DESCRIPTION AND INTERESTS: Amateur and professional keyboardists read this monthly magazine for its artist profiles, product reviews and guides, and instructional information. Circ: 61,000.
Website: www.keyboardmag.com

FREELANCE POTENTIAL: 25–35% written by nonstaff writers. Publishes 120 freelance submissions yearly; 35% by unpublished writers, 55% by authors who are new to the magazine. Receives 60–120 unsolicited mss yearly.

SUBMISSIONS AND PAYMENT: Sample copy and guidelines available via email request. Send complete ms with résumé. Accepts hard copy and email submissions to keyboard@musicplayer.com. SASE. Responds in 3 months. All rights. Articles, 500–3,000 words. Depts/columns, 400–600 words. Written material, payment rates vary. Pays on publication. Provides 5 contributor's copies.

Kids

341 East Lancaster Avenue
Downington, PA 19335

Editor: Bob Ludwick

DESCRIPTION AND INTERESTS: This monthly tabloid shares news of the public elementary and intermediate schools in Chester County, Pennsylvania, with its constituents. Articles include profiles of teachers and students; informational pieces on school programs; and general education and health news with local relevance. For obvious reasons, contributors must be familiar with Chester County to be considered for publication. Circ: 42,000.

FREELANCE POTENTIAL: 90% written by nonstaff writers. Publishes 120 freelance submissions yearly; 20% by unpublished writers. Receives several queries yearly.

SUBMISSIONS AND PAYMENT: Sample copy and editorial calendar, free with 9x12 SASE. Query with résumé. Accepts hard copy. SASE. Responds in 1 week. All rights. Articles and depts/columns, to 500 words. No payment. Provides 2 contributor's copies.

Kids Discover

192 Lexington Avenue, Room 1003
New York, NY 10016-6913

Editor: Stella Sands

DESCRIPTION AND INTERESTS: This award-winning magazine for children ages seven to twelve features a single nonfiction topic dealing with natural or social sciences in each issue. All of its articles feature vivid photographs and follow-up activities, promoting a hands-on approach to learning. Recent themes include the Constitution, ancient Greece, the Great Depression, and money. *Kids Discover* is published monthly. Circ: 400,000.
Website: www.kidsdiscover.com

FREELANCE POTENTIAL: 100% written by staff writers.

SUBMISSIONS AND PAYMENT: Sample copy available upon email request to editor@kidsdiscover.com. Not accepting queries or unsolicited mss at this time.

KidSpirit Magazine

77 State Street
Brooklyn, NY 11201

Editor: Elizabeth Dabney Hochman

DESCRIPTION AND INTERESTS: Written by and for youth ages 11 to 15, *KidSpirit Magazine* publishes short fiction, poetry, reviews, and themed features on a quarterly basis. It looks for works that tackle such "big questions" as ethics, morals, science, and spirituality. Circ: 5,000.
Website: www.kidspiritmagazine.com

FREELANCE POTENTIAL: 100% written by nonstaff writers. Publishes 40 freelance submissions yearly; 100% by unpublished writers. Receives 30 queries, 20 unsolicited mss yearly.

SUBMISSIONS AND PAYMENT: Guidelines and theme list available at website. Accepts submissions from children ages 11–15 only. Query with author bio for features; send complete ms for other works. Accepts hard copy and email to info@kidspiritmagazine.com. SASE. Responds in 1 month. Rights vary. Written material, word lengths vary. No payment. Provides 2 contributor's copies.

The Kids' Storytelling Club

P.O. Box 205
Masonville, CO 80541

Editor: Vivian Dubrovin

DESCRIPTION AND INTERESTS: *The Kids' Storytelling Club* is an online magazine for beginning storytellers, whether they be kids themselves or those who teach them. It features information on oral storytelling techniques for children ages 9 to 12, including how to make and use props. Articles also guide novices in creating their own stories, and finding venues in which to tell them. Hits per month: 4,000+.
Website: www.storycraft.com

FREELANCE POTENTIAL: 70% written by nonstaff writers. Publishes many freelance submissions yearly; many by unpublished writers, most by authors who are new to the magazine.

SUBMISSIONS AND PAYMENT: Guidelines available at website. Query. Accepts hard copy and email queries to jrstoryteller@storycraft.com. SASE. Response time varies. First rights. Articles, 500 words. Fiction, 250–500 words. Written material, $25. Pays on acceptance.

Kid Zone

WordAction Publishing Company
2923 Troost Avenue
Kansas City, MO 64109

Assistant Editor: Laura S. Lohberger

DESCRIPTION AND INTERESTS: This successor to WordAction's *Discoveries* is a weekly take-home paper that correlates with the publisher's third- to fourth-grade Sunday school curriculum. It features stories, crafts, and family service projects alongside daily devotionals, puzzles, cartoons, and trivia. Stories must be contemporary and portray believable, true-to-life experiences of 8- to 10-year-old kids. They should not preach or moralize, but teach. Circ: 35,000.
Website: www.wordaction.com

FREELANCE POTENTIAL: 75% written by non-staff writers.

SUBMISSIONS AND PAYMENT: Guidelines available. Theme list available at website. Query or send complete ms. Accepts hard copy. SASE. Responds in 6–8 weeks. Multiple-use rights. Stories, to 500 words; $25. Trivia, 200–250 words; $10–$15. Cartoons and puzzles, $15. Pays on acceptance. Provides 1 contributor's copy.

KIND News

Humane Society Youth
67 Norwich Essex Turnpike
East Haddam, CT 06423

Manager: Catherine Vincent

DESCRIPTION AND INTERESTS: Published nine times each year in three leveled classroom editions, *KIND News* encourages good character in children with an emphasis on kindness to animals, respect for natural habitats, good citizenship, and peaceful conflict resolution. Every issue contains fascinating facts about animals, tricky brainteasers, KIND Club projects, celebrity profiles, and short stories and opinion pieces contributed by children. Circ: 1 million.
Website: www.kindnews.org

FREELANCE POTENTIAL: 5% written by non-staff writers. Publishes few freelance submissions yearly.

SUBMISSIONS AND PAYMENT: Sample copy available at website. All material is assigned. Send résumé and clips only. Accepts hard copy. Responds if interested. Exclusive rights. Articles and depts/columns, word lengths and payment rates vary. Pays on acceptance.

Kindred

P.O. Box 971
Mullumbimby, New South Wales 2482
Australia

Editor: Kali Wendorf
U.S. Editorial Contact: Lisa Reagan

DESCRIPTION AND INTERESTS: Addressing family life from a sustainability and natural living perspective, *Kindred* is published quarterly. It focuses on personal growth, natural parenting, and environmental concerns. Its material supports healthy parental bonding and attachment. Circ: Unavailable.
Website: www.kindredmagazine.com.au

FREELANCE POTENTIAL: 80% written by nonstaff writers. Publishes 12–16 freelance submissions yearly; 70% by unpublished writers, 70% by authors who are new to the magazine. Receives 120 queries, 120 unsolicited mss yearly.

SUBMISSIONS AND PAYMENT: Sample copy and guidelines available. Query or send complete ms with list of sources. Accepts email submissions to kali@kindredmagazine.com.au (Microsoft Word attachments). Response time varies. First rights. Articles, word lengths vary. No payment.

Kittens USA

3 Burroughs
Irvine, CA 92618

Managing Editor: Lisa King

DESCRIPTION AND INTERESTS: This annual publication from the editors of *Cat Fancy* is chock-full of information for people interested in adopting kittens. It includes basic care and nutrition information, reviews of toys and products, and listings of kitten adoptions. Circ: 78,350.
Website: www.catchannel.com

FREELANCE POTENTIAL: 80% written by nonstaff writers. Publishes 10–12 freelance submissions yearly; 10–20% by authors who are new to the magazine.

SUBMISSIONS AND PAYMENT: Sample copy and guidelines available at website. Send complete ms. Accepts email submissions to kittensusa@bowtieinc.com. Response time varies. Exclusive North American serial rights. Articles and depts/columns, word lengths and payment rates vary. Payment policy varies. Provides 2 contributor's copies.

Kiwibox.com

330 West 38th Street, Suite 1602
New York, NY 10018

Submissions Editor: Bianca Mbraum

DESCRIPTION AND INTERESTS: Written, edited, and designed exclusively by teens, this online zine features the musings and imaginings of America's youth. It is updated weekly with a variety of fiction and articles on everything from science to sports to shopping to serious social issues. As *Kiwibox.com* was built with the hope of creating an Internet community driven by teens, only submissions from young adults will be considered. Hits per month: 10 million.
Website: www.kiwibox.com

FREELANCE POTENTIAL: 90% written by non-staff writers. Publishes numerous freelance submissions yearly.

SUBMISSIONS AND PAYMENT: Teen authors only. Sample copy available at website. Send complete ms. Accepts email submissions to bianca@kiwibox.com. Responds in 2 weeks. All rights. Articles, 350 words. Fiction, word lengths vary. No payment.

KnoWonder!

869 E. 4500 S., #500
Salt Lake City, UT 84107

Editor: Phillip Chipping

DESCRIPTION AND INTERESTS: Families with children ages three to ten enjoy this new magazine that offers approximately 30 stories each month. Each issue also features three articles for parents on topics that help parents connect with their children. It is also currently interested in crafts and activities. Circ: Unavailable.
Website: www.knowonder.com

FREELANCE POTENTIAL: 75% written by non-staff writers. Publishes 350–400 freelance submissions yearly; 50% by authors who are new to the magazine.

SUBMISSIONS AND PAYMENT: Sample copy, free with 9x12 SASE. Send complete ms. Accepts submissions through the website only. Response time varies. First and limited electronic rights. Articles, 700–1,700 words; $150. Fiction, 450–1,600 words; top 3 stories from each issue (as voted on by readers) receive $300, $200, and $100, respectively. Pays on publication.

Lake/Geauga Family

TNT Publications
11630 Chillicothe Road
Chesterland, OH 44026

Editor: Terri Nighswonger

DESCRIPTION AND INTERESTS: This publication appears each month with regionally focused articles on parenting at all stages. It covers such topics as education, child care, summer camp, party planning, family health, fitness, and travel. Circ: 75,000.
Website: www.neohiofamily.com

FREELANCE POTENTIAL: 50% written by non-staff writers. Publishes 40–50 freelance submissions yearly; 33% by authors who are new to the magazine. Receives 6,000 queries yearly.

SUBMISSIONS AND PAYMENT: Guidelines available. Sample copy and theme list available at website. Query with clips. Accepts email queries to editor@tntpublications.com. Responds if interested. Exclusive rights. Articles, 500+ words. Depts/columns, word lengths vary. High-resolution JPEG and TIF images. All material, payment rates vary. Pays on publication. Provides 1 contributor's copy.

Language Arts Journal

Ohio State University
333 Arps Hall
1945 North High Street
Columbus, OH 43210

Language Arts Editorial Team

DESCRIPTION AND INTERESTS: Literacy and language arts teachers read this magazine, published six times each year, for professional information related to teaching at every level from preschool through eighth grade. Circ: 12,000.
Website: www.ncte.org

FREELANCE POTENTIAL: 90% written by non-staff writers. Publishes 60 freelance submissions yearly; 15% by unpublished writers, 30% by authors who are new to the magazine. Receives 200 unsolicited mss yearly.

SUBMISSIONS AND PAYMENT: Sample copy, $12.50 from NCTE, 1111 W. Kenyon Road, Urbana, IL 61801-1096. Guidelines and theme list available by email to langarts@osu.edu. Send 6 copies of ms; include Microsoft Word file on disk. Accepts hard copy and disk submissions. SASE. Responds in 3–12 months. All rights. Articles, 2,500–6,500 words. Depts/columns, word lengths vary. No payment. Provides 2 contributor's copies.

The Learning Edge

Clonlara School
1289 Jewett
Ann Arbor, MI 48104

Editor: Judy Geiner

DESCRIPTION AND INTERESTS: Students and families enrolled in the Clonlara School Home Based Education Program read this newsletter that covers topics specifically related to home education. It features profiles of Clonlara students and offers strategies to get the most out of the home education experience. Circ: 1,000.
Website: www.clonlara.org

FREELANCE POTENTIAL: 25% written by non-staff writers. Of the freelance submissions published yearly, 10% are by unpublished writers, 1% are by authors who are new to the magazine. Receives 12 queries yearly.

SUBMISSIONS AND PAYMENT: Sample copy available on request. Accepts submissions from Clonlara students and families only. Send complete ms. Accepts hard copy. SASE. Responds in 1 month. Rights vary. Written material, word lengths vary. No payment. Provides 1 contributor's copy.

Literary Mama

1416 11th Avenue
San Francisco, CA 94122

Editor-in-Chief: Caroline Grant

DESCRIPTION AND INTERESTS: Devoted to motherhood and all its complexities, this monthly e-zine features poetry, fiction, and nonfiction. It seeks submissions about parenting older children or being a young mother. Hits per month: 55,000.
Website: www.literarymama.com

FREELANCE POTENTIAL: 88% written by non-staff writers. Publishes 120 freelance submissions yearly; 15% by unpublished writers, 50% by authors who are new to the magazine. Receives 120 queries, 3,000 unsolicited mss yearly.

SUBMISSIONS AND PAYMENT: Sample copy and guidelines available at website. Query for profiles, reviews, and columns. Send complete ms for all other work. Accepts email submissions; see website for appropriate editor and email address. Responds in 1–4 months. Non-exclusive rights. Articles and fiction, to 6,000 words. Depts/columns, 1,000–1,600 words. Poetry, no line limit. No payment.

Library Media Connection

130 Cremona Drive
Santa Barbara, CA 93117

Editor: Marlene Woo-Lun

DESCRIPTION AND INTERESTS: School librarians and media specialists at all grade levels through high school read this magazine for articles on the latest research in the field, as well as for book and media reviews. The magazine appears seven times each year. Circ: 14,000.
Website: www.linworth.com

FREELANCE POTENTIAL: 90% written by non-staff writers. Publishes 215 freelance submissions yearly; 50% by unpublished writers, 50% by authors who are new to the magazine. Receives 144 queries, 144 unsolicited mss yearly.

SUBMISSIONS AND PAYMENT: Sample copy, $11 with 9x12 SASE. Query or send complete ms with résumé. Accepts hard copy, disk submissions (Microsoft Word or ASCII), and email submissions to linworth@linworthpublishing.com. SASE. Responds in 2 weeks. All rights. Written material, payment rates vary. Pays on publication. Provides 4 contributor's copies.

Little Rock Family

122 East Second Street
Little Rock, AR 72201

Submissions Editor

DESCRIPTION AND INTERESTS: As its name suggests, *Little Rock Family* is written for parents living in the capital region of Arkansas. Its content focuses on family-friendly entertainment, recreation, events, and dining; pediatric health; education issues; and, of course, parenting and child care concerns—all from a local perspective. As this magazine has recently reduced its use of freelance writers, a close familiarity with Little Rock is an absolute necessity for those wishing to contribute. Circ: 20,000.
Website: www.littlerockfamily.com

FREELANCE POTENTIAL: 1% written by non-staff writers. Publishes few freelance submissions each year.

SUBMISSIONS AND PAYMENT: Query. Accepts hard copy. SASE. Response time varies. First rights. Articles and depts/columns, word lengths and payment rates vary. Payment policy varies.

Living with Teenagers

One LifeWay Plaza
Nashville, TN 37234-0174

Editor: Bob Bunn

DESCRIPTION AND INTERESTS: Christian parents raising teenagers are the target audience of this monthly magazine. It looks to support and strengthen the bonds of family through its biblically-based articles and discussions of the challenges of raising a teen in today's society. Circ: 35,000.
Website: www.lifeway.com/people

FREELANCE POTENTIAL: 90% written by non-staff writers. Publishes several freelance submissions yearly.

SUBMISSIONS AND PAYMENT: Sample copy, free. All material is written on assignment. Send résumé and writing samples to be considered for an assignment. Accepts hard copy. SASE. Responds if interested. All rights with non-exclusive license to the writer. Articles, 600–1,200 words; $100–$300. Pays on acceptance. Provides 3 contributor's copies.

Long Island Parent

152 West 19th Street
Huntington Station, NY 11746

Editor: Lisa Burby

DESCRIPTION AND INTERESTS: Distributed free in Suffolk and Nassau counties, this magazine targets local parents of children up to the age of 16. It offers coverage of regional events and articles on family health, travel, recreation, and education. *Long Island Parent* is published six times each year. Circ: 55,000.
Website: www.liparentonline.com

FREELANCE POTENTIAL: 25–30% written by nonstaff writers. Publishes 20 freelance submissions yearly; 30% by authors who are new to the magazine.

SUBMISSIONS AND PAYMENT: Sample copy and guidelines available. Query or send complete ms. Accepts hard copy and email submissions to editor@liparentonline.com. SASE. Responds in 2–4 months. First rights. Written material, word lengths and payment rates vary. Pays on publication. Provides 2 contributor's copies.

Lowcountry Parent

134 Columbus Street
Charleston, SC 29403

Submissions Editor: Shannon Brigham

DESCRIPTION AND INTERESTS: *Lowcountry Parent* is a regional publication of interest to families residing in Charleston, South Carolina, and its environs. Each monthly issue offers informative articles on a wide range of topics, such as parenting, education, child development, health and safety, finances, and travel. It also provides up-to-date event and activities listings, party planning ideas, and profiles of local personalities. Circ: 41,000.
Website: www.lowcountry.com

FREELANCE POTENTIAL: Publishes few freelance submissions yearly; 10% by authors who are new to the magazine.

SUBMISSIONS AND PAYMENT: Sample copy, free. Local writers only. Send résumé. Responds if interested. One-time rights. Articles and depts/columns, word lengths vary. Written material, $15–$100. Pays on publication. Provides 3 contributor's copies.

MAD Magazine

1700 Broadway
New York, NY 10019

Submissions Editor

DESCRIPTION AND INTERESTS: *Mad Magazine* gives its young adult and adult readers hard-hitting satire, edgy humor, and utter silliness in every monthly issue. It does not publish short stories; rather it looks for funny, quick takes on cultural themes and fads. Many pieces are accompanied by comic-strip illustrations. Circ: 250,000.
Website: www.madmag.com

FREELANCE POTENTIAL: 90% written by nonstaff writers. Publishes 25 freelance submissions each year.

SUBMISSIONS AND PAYMENT: Sample copy, $4.99 at newsstands. Guidelines available at website. Query or send complete ms. Prefers email to submissions@madmagazine.com; will accept hard copy if submission includes artwork. SASE. Responds if interested. All rights. Written material, word lengths vary; $500 per printed page. Graphic artwork, payment rates vary. Pays on acceptance. Provides 1 contributor's copy.

Metro Parent

P.O. Box 13660
Portland, OR 97213

Editor: Marie Sherlock

DESCRIPTION AND INTERESTS: Parents and families in the Portland area read this monthly publication for articles on child care and development, education, and regional news. A calendar of local events and activities is also included in each issue. *Metro Parent* is distributed free of charge and prefers to work with writers who live in the region. Circ: 45,000.
Website: www.metro-parent.com

FREELANCE POTENTIAL: 75% written by non-staff writers. Publishes 50 freelance submissions yearly; 20% by unpublished writers. Receives 240 queries yearly.

SUBMISSIONS AND PAYMENT: Sample copy and theme list, $2. Query with outline. Accepts hard copy, email to editor@metro-parent.com, and simultaneous submissions if identified. SASE. Responds in 1 month. Rights vary. Written material, word lengths and payment rates vary. Pays on publication.

Miami Family Magazine

7045 SW 69th Avenue
South Miami, FL 33143

Publisher: Janet Jupiter

DESCRIPTION AND INTERESTS: Families living in and around Miami read this magazine for coverage of local activities, personalities, and news. Its articles discuss topics from cooking to careers, sports to social issues, and education to entertainment, all penned by writers who know the city and its culture. Published monthly, it also offers pet care advice, media reviews, and regional event coverage. Circ: Unavailable.
Website: www.familymagazine.biz

FREELANCE POTENTIAL: 30% written by non-staff writers. Publishes 15–20 freelance submissions yearly.

SUBMISSIONS AND PAYMENT: Sample copy available at website. Query. Accepts hard copy and email queries to familymag@bellsouth.net. SASE. Response time varies. One-time rights. Articles and depts/columns, word lengths and payment rates vary. Pays on publication. Provides contributor's copies.

Metro Spirit

700 Broad Street
Augusta, GA 30901

Editor: Tom Grant

DESCRIPTION AND INTERESTS: Formerly titled *Metro Augusta Parent*, this monthly targets Georgia families with its articles on parenting, child care, education, and regional events and activities. It also offers profiles of local families and businesses, and reviews of movies, television programs, and area restaurants. Circ: Unavailable.
Website: www.metrospirit.com

FREELANCE POTENTIAL: 80% written by non-staff writers. Publishes 50 freelance submissions yearly; 5% by unpublished writers, 5% by authors who are new to the magazine. Receives 240 queries yearly.

SUBMISSIONS AND PAYMENT: Sample copy, free with SASE. Guidelines available. Query. Accepts hard copy and email queries to editor@metrospirit.com. SASE. Response time varies. First rights. Written material, word lengths and payment rates vary. Payment policy varies. Provides 1 contributor's copy.

Michigan History For Kids

702 West Kalamazoo
Lansing, MI 48909

Assistant Editor: Christine Schwerin

DESCRIPTION AND INTERESTS: Published by the staff of *Michigan History* magazine (which in turn is published by the Michigan Historical Center), this quarterly is designed to make history fun for young readers. Each issue features articles, travel suggestions, and activities centered around a particular theme. Topics covered are aligned with the fifth-grade Michigan Educational Assessment Program. Circ: Unavailable.
Website: www.michiganhistorymagazine.com

FREELANCE POTENTIAL: 90% written by non-staff writers. Publishes several freelance submissions yearly; 100% by authors who are new to the magazine.

SUBMISSIONS AND PAYMENT: Sample copy, $4.95. Guidelines available. Query with résumé. Accepts hard copy. SASE. Response time varies. Rights vary. Articles and depts/columns, word lengths and payment rates vary. Pays on publication. Provides 2 contributor's copies.

Minnesota Parent

1115 Hennepin Avenue South
Minneapolis, MN 55403

Editor: Tricia Cornell

DESCRIPTION AND INTERESTS: Read by parents residing in Minnesota, this monthly magazine covers a variety of topics. Parents of newborns through teens find articles on growth and development, education, behavior, and health and safety. Also provided is information on regional events, news, and issues; new product and media reviews; arts and crafts; and humorous pieces. Circ: 70,000.
Website: www.mnparent.com

FREELANCE POTENTIAL: 50% written by nonstaff writers. Publishes 24 freelance submissions each year.

SUBMISSIONS AND PAYMENT: Query. Accepts hard copy and email queries to tcornell@mnpubs.com. SASE. Response time varies. First serial and electronic rights. Articles and depts/columns, word lengths vary; $50–$350. Pays on publication. Provides 2 contributor's copies.

Montessori Life

281 Park Avenue South
New York, NY 10010

Co-Editors: Kathy Carey and Carey Jones

DESCRIPTION AND INTERESTS: Research, curricula, and educational issues are covered in this quarterly magazine for Montessori families and educators. Its editorial mix includes academic and informational articles, profiles, and media reviews. Circ: 10,500.
Website: www.amshq.org

FREELANCE POTENTIAL: 90% written by nonstaff writers. Publishes 40 freelance submissions yearly; 30% by unpublished writers, 30% by authors who are new to the magazine. Receives 120–240 unsolicited mss yearly.

SUBMISSIONS AND PAYMENT: Sample copy, $5 with 9x12 SASE. Guidelines and editorial calendar available at website. Send complete ms. Accepts email to edmontessorilife@aol.com. Responds in 3 months. All rights. Articles, 1,000–4,000 words. Depts/columns, 500–1,000 words. Written material, payment rates vary. Pays on publication. Provides 1–5 author's copies.

Model Airplane News

Air Age Publishing
20 Westport Road
Wilton, CT 06897

Executive Editor: Debra Cleghorn

DESCRIPTION AND INTERESTS: Written by and for airplane modeling enthusiasts, this magazine provides how-to articles on all aspects of the hobby. Each monthly issue also offers new product reviews and plenty of instructive and inspiring illustrations. Circ: 95,000.
Website: www.modelairplanenews.com

FREELANCE POTENTIAL: 80% written by nonstaff writers. Publishes 100+ freelance submissions yearly; 33% by authors who are new to the magazine. Receives 144–288 queries yearly.

SUBMISSIONS AND PAYMENT: Sample copy and guidelines, $3.50 with 9x12 SASE. Query with outline and biography describing model experience. Accepts hard copy. Availability of artwork improves chance of acceptance. SASE. Responds in 6 weeks. North American serial rights. Articles, 1,700–2,000 words; $175–$600. 35mm color slides. Pays on publication. Provides up to 6 contributor's copies.

Motivos Bilingual Magazine

P.O. Box 34391
Philadelphia, PA 19101

Publisher: Jenee Chiznick

DESCRIPTION AND INTERESTS: Published quarterly in a bilingual format, *Motivos* features socially and culturally relevant content aimed at Latino youth. Each of its four departments (culture, life, college, and careers) showcases student voices; it prefers to receive pre-edited work through a liaison teacher at the writer's school. Circ: 75,000.
Website: www.motivosmag.com

FREELANCE POTENTIAL: 50% written by nonstaff writers. Publishes 30 freelance submissions yearly; 40% by unpublished writers, 50% by authors who are new to the magazine.

SUBMISSIONS AND PAYMENT: Guidelines available at website. Send complete ms. Accepts hard copy and email submissions to editor@motivosmag.com. SASE. Response time varies. First North American serial rights. Articles, 400–800 words; payment rates vary. Payment policy varies. Provides 2 contributor's copies.

Mysteries Magazine

P.O. Box 131
Waynesville, NC 28786

Editor: Jeremiah Greer

DESCRIPTION AND INTERESTS: This magazine "explores mysteries from modern times to yesteryear" in carefully researched, factual articles. Science-related items are especially sought. Quarterly issues also include book, movie, music, and game reviews. Circ: 15,000.
Website: www.mysteriesmagazine.com

FREELANCE POTENTIAL: 30% written by nonstaff writers. Publishes 12 freelance submissions yearly; 20% by authors who are new to the magazine. Receives 240 queries yearly.

SUBMISSIONS AND PAYMENT: Sample copy, $8. Guidelines available at website. Query. Accepts email queries to editor@mysteriesmagazine.com. Responds in 1 month. First North American serial rights. Articles, 3,000–5,000 words. Depts/columns, 1,200–1,500 words. Book reviews, 200–500 words. Written material, $.05 per word. Pays on publication. Provides 2 contributor's copies.

National Geographic Explorer

1145 17th Street NW
Washington, DC 20036

Editor-in-Chief: Jacalyn Mahler

DESCRIPTION AND INTERESTS: *National Geographic Explorer* is designed for students in grades two through six as a passport to destinations around the world. Each issue brings its young readers informative and entertaining articles about science and social studies topics, following their classroom curricula. Published seven times each year, it is accompanied by a teacher's guide. Circ: Unavailable.
Website:
  http://magma.nationalgeographic.com/ngexplorer

FREELANCE POTENTIAL: 5% written by nonstaff writers. Publishes few freelance submissions yearly.

SUBMISSIONS AND PAYMENT: Send résumé only. All material is assigned. Accepts hard copy. SASE. Responds if interested. All rights. Articles and fiction, word lengths and payment rates vary. Pays on acceptance.

NASSP Bulletin

Sage Publications
2455 Teller Road
Thousand Oaks, CA 91320

Editor

DESCRIPTION AND INTERESTS: The National Association of Secondary School Principals offers this quarterly professional journal as a forum for the latest research and news in the field. Peer-reviewed articles provide information that promotes learning and achievement. Please note that all manuscripts submitted must conform to American Psychological Association (APA) style. Circ: 2,000.
Website: http://bulletin.sagepub.com

FREELANCE POTENTIAL: 100% written by nonstaff writers. Publishes 20–25 freelance submissions yearly; 15% by unpublished writers, 30% by authors who are new to the magazine. Receives 150 unsolicited mss yearly.

SUBMISSIONS AND PAYMENT: Sample copy, free with 9x12 SASE. Guidelines available at website. Send complete ms. Accepts hard copy with CD. SASE. Responds in 4–6 weeks. All rights. No payment. Provides 2 author's copies.

Natural Solutions

2995 Wilderness Place, Suite 205
Boulder, CO 80301

Editor: Lauren Piscopo

DESCRIPTION AND INTERESTS: Ten times each year, *Natural Solutions* spotlights the latest news and breakthroughs in the field of alternative medicine. Its articles focus on nutrition and spiritual and mental health. Many of its articles target parents of young children who have questions about picky eaters, vaccinations, and child development. Circ: 225,000.
Website: www.naturalsolutionsmag.com

FREELANCE POTENTIAL: 95% written by nonstaff writers. Publishes 40–50 freelance submissions yearly; 25% by authors who are new to the magazine. Receives 30 queries yearly.

SUBMISSIONS AND PAYMENT: Sample copy, $4.95 at newsstands. Guidelines available. Query with clips. Accepts email to editor@naturalsolutionsmag.com. Response time varies. All rights. Articles and depts/columns, word lengths and payment rates vary. Pays within 45 days of acceptance. Provides 2 author's copies.

Neapolitan Family Magazine

P.O. Box 110656
Naples, FL 34108

Editor: Andrea Breznay

DESCRIPTION AND INTERESTS: *Neapolitan Family Magazine*, distributed monthly throughout Collier County, Florida, offers its readers "everything the Naples family wants to know." This includes news of local events and issues, features on family travel and entertainment, and coverage of area schools. Circ: 11,000.
Website: www.neafamily.com

FREELANCE POTENTIAL: 90% written by nonstaff writers. Publishes 40 freelance submissions yearly; 20% by authors who are new to the magazine. Receives 500 unsolicited mss yearly.

SUBMISSIONS AND PAYMENT: Guidelines and editorial calendar available at website. Sample copy, free with 9x12 SASE. Send complete ms. Prefers email submissions to andrea@neafamily.com; will accept hard copy. SASE. Responds in 1 month. Rights vary. Articles and depts/columns, word lengths and payment rates vary. Pays on publication.

New Jersey Suburban Parent

Middlesex Publications
850 Route 1
North Brunswick, NJ 08902

Editor: Melodie Dhondt

DESCRIPTION AND INTERESTS: Each month, this tabloid helps its readers decide where to go, what to do, and how to do it. It is published in three geographical editions that provide parents with the resources they need to care for, educate, and entertain their kids. Circ: 77,000.
Website: www.njparentweb.com

FREELANCE POTENTIAL: 80% written by nonstaff writers. Publishes 12 freelance submissions yearly; 20% by unpublished writers, 40% by authors who are new to the magazine. Receives 12 queries yearly.

SUBMISSIONS AND PAYMENT: Sample copy, guidelines, and editorial calendar, free with 9x12 SASE. Query with writing samples. Accepts hard copy and simultaneous submissions if identified. SASE. Responds in 1–2 months. Rights vary. Articles, 700–1,000 words; $30. B/W and color prints; payment rates vary. Pays on acceptance. Provides 1+ contributor's copies.

New Jersey Family

1122 Route 22 West
Mountainside, NJ 07092

Editor: Farn Dupre

DESCRIPTION AND INTERESTS: This magazine, distributed monthly throughout northern and central New Jersey, provides coverage of family-related issues and events. Article topics range from parenting advice and child development information to summer camps and entertainment options. Circ: 126,000.
Website: www.njfamily.com

FREELANCE POTENTIAL: 60% written by nonstaff writers. Publishes 150 freelance submissions yearly; 33% by unpublished writers, 33% by authors who are new to the magazine. Receives 240 queries yearly.

SUBMISSIONS AND PAYMENT: Guidelines available at website. Query with writing samples. Accepts email to editor@njcountyfamily.com (no attachments). Response time varies. First rights. Articles, 750–1,000 words. Depts/columns, word lengths vary. Written material, payment rates vary. Payment policy varies.

The Northland

P.O. Box 841
Schumacher, Ontario P0N 1G0
Canada

Submissions Editor

DESCRIPTION AND INTERESTS: This quarterly publication has a very narrow focus: news pertaining to the Anglican Church of Canada's Diocese of Moosonee. Its articles cover service projects, retreats, conferences, and other church news, as well as transcriptions of sermons, prayers, and essays on spirituality. Only contributions from church members or other writers personally familiar with the diocese are considered for publication. Circ: 300.

FREELANCE POTENTIAL: 100% written by nonstaff writers. Publishes several freelance submissions yearly. Receives few unsolicited mss each year.

SUBMISSIONS AND PAYMENT: Sample copy available. Send complete ms. Accepts hard copy. SASE. Response time varies. Rights vary. Articles and depts/columns, word lengths vary. No payment.

North Star Family Matters

689 East Promontory Road
Shelton, WA 98584

Editor-in-Chief

DESCRIPTION AND INTERESTS: Parents of children up to the age of 15 living in the Puget Sound region read this monthly magazine for information on all aspects of child rearing and family life. It also offers kid-friendly features and activities designed to help children reach their full potential. Circ: 32,000.
Website: www.northstarfamilymatters-magazine.com

FREELANCE POTENTIAL: 60% written by non-staff writers. Publishes 50 freelance submissions yearly; 60% by unpublished writers, 80% by authors who are new to the magazine.

SUBMISSIONS AND PAYMENT: Guidelines available. Query. Accepts email queries to submit@northstarfamilymattersmagazine.com. Response time varies. First and electronic rights. Articles, 300–1,500 words; payment rates vary. Payment policy varies. Provides 1 contributor's copy.

North State Parent

P.O. Box 1602
Mount Shasta, CA 96067

Submissions: Lisa Shara

DESCRIPTION AND INTERESTS: The mission of this monthly magazine is to nurture and encourage the powerful bond of family by covering topics of interest to parents, grandparents, and guardians of children. It is distributed free to parents in Butte, Shasta, Southern Siskiyou, and Tehama counties. Most of its material features a local slant. Circ: 18,000+.
Website: www.northstateparent.com

FREELANCE POTENTIAL: 90% written by non-staff writers. Publishes 20 freelance submissions each year.

SUBMISSIONS AND PAYMENT: Guidelines available at website. Send complete ms. Accepts hard copy and email submissions to lisa@northstateparent.com. SASE. Response time varies. First rights. Articles, 700–1,000 words. Depts/columns, 300–500 words. Written material, $35–$75. Pays on publication. Provides 2 contributor's copies.

The Numismatist

American Numismatic Association
818 North Cascade Avenue
Colorado Springs, CO 80903-3279

Editor-in-Chief: Barbara J. Gregory

DESCRIPTION AND INTERESTS: Coin collectors who are members of the American Numismatic Association read this monthly magazine, which also covers the collecting of medals, tokens, and paper money. Circ: 30,500.
Website: www.money.org

FREELANCE POTENTIAL: 60% written by non-staff writers. Publishes 36 freelance submissions yearly; 20% by unpublished writers, 10% by authors who are new to the magazine. Receives 48 unsolicited mss yearly.

SUBMISSIONS AND PAYMENT: Sample copy and guidelines, free with 9x12 SASE ($2.50 postage). Send complete ms with biography. Prefers email submissions to editor@money.org; will accept hard copy and disk submissions. SASE. Responds in 8–10 weeks. Perpetual non-exclusive rights. Articles, to 3,500 words; $.12 per word. Pays on publication. Provides 5 contributor's copies.

The Olive Branch
The Youth Magazine of Seeds of Peace

P.O. Box 25045
Jerusalem, Israel

Editor: Eric Kapenga

DESCRIPTION AND INTERESTS: Published quarterly, *The Olive Branch* seeks to sow "Seeds of Peace" through the written contributions of that organization's young membership. Its factual articles, profiles, and personal experience pieces on such topics as war and reconciliation are written by youth from regions of conflict worldwide. Circ: 16,000.
Website: www.seedsofpeace.org

FREELANCE POTENTIAL: 100% written by nonstaff writers. Publishes 200 freelance submissions yearly; 95% by unpublished writers, 90% by authors who are new to the magazine.

SUBMISSIONS AND PAYMENT: Sample copy available at website. Accepts submissions from Seeds of Peace members only. Query or send complete ms. Accepts hard copy and email submissions to eric@seedsofpeace.org. SASE. Response time varies. Rights vary. Written material, word lengths vary. No payment.

Owl

Bayard Press Canada
10 Lower Spadina Avenue, Suite 400
Toronto, Ontario M4V 2V2
Canada

Submissions Editor

DESCRIPTION AND INTERESTS: Through entertaining articles and activities, *Owl* helps children ages 8 through 12 discover and appreciate the natural world around them. The magazine is issued nine times each year. While all content is assigned, writers may send a résumé and a letter of introduction listing their publishing credits. Circ: 104,000.
Website: www.owlkids.com

FREELANCE POTENTIAL: 60% written by non-staff writers. Publishes 1–3 freelance submissions yearly; 5% by unpublished writers, 10% by authors who are new to the magazine.

SUBMISSIONS AND PAYMENT: Sample copy, $4.28 Canadian. Guidelines available. All work is assigned. Send résumé only. Accepts hard copy. No SASE. All rights. Articles, 500–1,000 words; $200–$500 Canadian. Pays on acceptance. Provides 1 contributor's copy.

Parenting for High Potential

P.O. Box 21351
Baton Rouge, LA 70894

Editor: Dr. Jennifer Jolly

DESCRIPTION AND INTERESTS: Published quarterly by the National Association for Gifted Children, *Parenting for High Potential* provides guidance on raising—and nurturing—exceptional children. Its articles are geared not only toward enhancing the academic performance of gifted students, but also toward equipping parents to deal with the psychological challenges faced by their children. Circ: 4,000.
Website: www.nagc.org

FREELANCE POTENTIAL: 100% written by nonstaff writers. Publishes 10–12 freelance submissions yearly; 50% by authors who are new to the magazine. Receives 20–30 unsolicited mss each year.

SUBMISSIONS AND PAYMENT: Guidelines available. Send complete ms. Accepts email submissions to jjolly@lsu.edu. Responds in 6–8 weeks. First rights. Articles and depts/columns, word lengths vary. No payment.

ParentingHumor.com

P.O. Box 2128
Weaverville, NC 28787

Editor-in-Chief: Sharon Byrer

DESCRIPTION AND INTERESTS: This electronic magazine is enjoyed by parents, grandparents, and child-care providers looking to find the humor in pregnancy, new parent experiences, the terrible twos, and beyond. It is updated weekly with material from writers who have "been there, done that." New and veteran authors are welcome to submit their queries. Hits per month: Unavailable.
Website: www.parentinghumor.com

FREELANCE POTENTIAL: 98% written by non-staff writers. Publishes 350 freelance submissions yearly. Receives 300 queries yearly.

SUBMISSIONS AND PAYMENT: Sample copy, guidelines, and submission form available at website. Query. Accepts email queries to staff@parentinghumor.com. Response time varies. One-time electronic rights. Offers publication of the author's biography and a link to the author's website.

Parents' Choice

Parents' Choice Foundation
201 West Padonia Road, Suite 303
Timonium, MD 21093

Editor: Claire Green

DESCRIPTION AND INTERESTS: This consumer-oriented publication is updated on the Web once each month, and appears in newsletter form twice each year. Produced by the Parents' Choice Foundation, this e-zine promotes awareness of toys and other entertainment for children, recommending age-appropriate, educational, and socially sound products. Hits per month: 1 million.
Website: www.parents-choice.org

FREELANCE POTENTIAL: 80% written by non-staff writers. Publishes numerous freelance submissions yearly.

SUBMISSIONS AND PAYMENT: Sample copy available at website. Query or send complete ms. Accepts hard copy, email to submissions@parents-choice.org, and simultaneous submissions if identified. SASE. Response time varies. All rights. Articles, to 1,500 words; payment rates vary. Pays on acceptance.

Parents Express

290 Commerce Drive
Fort Washington, PA 19034

Editor: Daniel Sean Kaye

DESCRIPTION AND INTERESTS: Each issue of this monthly regional magazine provides parents in the Philadelphia area and southern New Jersey with timely coverage of local events and informative articles on topics of interest to families. Circ: 49,000.
Website: www.parents-express.net

FREELANCE POTENTIAL: 30% written by non-staff writers. Publishes 25–30 freelance submissions yearly; 25% by unpublished writers, 75% by authors who are new to the magazine. Receives several queries yearly.

SUBMISSIONS AND PAYMENT: Sample copy, free with 9x12 SASE ($2.14 postage). Query with clips or writing samples. Accepts hard copy and email to dkaye@montgomerynews.com. SASE. Responds in 1 month. One-time rights. Articles, 300–1,000 words; $35–$200. Depts/columns, 600–800 words; payment rates vary. Pays on publication. Provides contributor's copies.

Parents Magazine

375 Lexington Avenue
New York, NY 10017

Editor

DESCRIPTION AND INTERESTS: *Parents Magazine* offers information and inspiration to new, adoptive, and expectant parents alike. Each monthly issue blends well-researched articles on health and safety, relationships, and education from experts in the forefront of their fields, along with personal experience pieces from the front lines of parenting. It also publishes recipes and product reviews. Circ: Unavailable.
Website: www.parents.com

FREELANCE POTENTIAL: 50% written by non-staff writers. Publishes 50 freelance submissions yearly. Receives 1,200 queries yearly.

SUBMISSIONS AND PAYMENT: Sample copy, $3.50 with 9x12 SASE (4 first-class stamps). Query with clips. Accepts hard copy. SASE. Responds in 6 weeks. Rights vary. Articles and depts/columns, word lengths and payment rates vary. Pays on publication. Provides 2 contributor's copies.

Pathways to Family Wellness

327 North Middletown Road
Media, PA 19063

Editor

DESCRIPTION AND INTERESTS: The goal of this quarterly publication is to empower parents and family health professionals with inspiration and information. It focuses on parenting issues, mind and body, personal growth, health awareness, and informed choices. Potential writers should familiarize themselves with the publication and writing style prior to submitting their material. Circ: 12,000.
Website: www.pathwaystofamilywellness.com

FREELANCE POTENTIAL: 20% written by non-staff writers. Publishes 10 freelance submissions each year.

SUBMISSIONS AND PAYMENT: Guidelines available. Send complete ms with 50-word author bio. Accepts email submissions to editor@icpa4kids.com and simultaneous submissions if identified. Responds in 3 weeks. First or reprint rights. Articles, 900–2,000 words. No payment. Provides 2 contributor's copies.

The Pink Chameleon

Editor: Dorothy P. Freda

DESCRIPTION AND INTERESTS: A family-oriented e-zine, *The Pink Chameleon* seeks humorous and inspirational stories that offer hope, even in sadness. It also publishes short anecdotes and poetry. Hits per month: 100.
Website: www.geocities.com/ thepinkchameleon/index.html

FREELANCE POTENTIAL: 95% written by non-staff writers. Publishes 50–100 freelance submissions yearly; 40% by unpublished writers, 60% by authors who are new to the magazine. Receives 144–180 unsolicited mss yearly.

SUBMISSIONS AND PAYMENT: Sample copy and guidelines available at website. Send complete ms with author bio. Accepts email submissions to dpfreda@juno.com (no attachments). No simultaneous submissions. Responds in 4–6 weeks. Electronic rights for 1 year. Articles and fiction, to 2,500 words. Poetry, to 36 lines. No payment.

Popcorn Magazine For Children

8320 Brookfield Road
Richmond, VA 23227

Editor: Charlene Warner Coleman

DESCRIPTION AND INTERESTS: Now available primarily online and updated monthly, *Popcorn Magazine* aims to teach children ages 7 to 14 "without seeming to." It does so through engaging articles, stories, and activities, and encourages submissions that feature world cultures, the arts, sports, adventure, mystery, and traditional tales. Circ: 250,000.
Website: www.popcornmagazine.net

FREELANCE POTENTIAL: 75% written by non-staff writers. Publishes 1,000 freelance submissions yearly. Receives numerous unsolicited mss each year.

SUBMISSIONS AND PAYMENT: Sample copy, $3.95 at website. Guidelines available at website. Send complete ms. Accepts hard copy. SASE. Response time varies. Rights vary. Articles, word lengths vary; $75. Fiction, to 800 words; $75. Craft projects; $25+. Payment policy varies.

Prairie Messenger

Box 190, 100 College Drive
Muenster, Saskatchewan S0K 2Y0
Canada

Associate Editor: Maureen Weber

DESCRIPTION AND INTERESTS: Catholics living in the prairie lands of Saskatchewan and Manitoba read this weekly newspaper for a religious perspective on world events. Submissions of human-interest stories no longer than 800 words are welcome. Circ: 6,800.
Website: www.prairiemessenger.ca

FREELANCE POTENTIAL: 60% written by non-staff writers. Publishes 10 freelance submissions yearly. Receives 30 queries and mss yearly.

SUBMISSIONS AND PAYMENT: Sample copy, $1 with 9x12 SAE/IRC. Guidelines available at website. Query or send complete ms. Accepts email to pm.canadian@stpeterspress.ca. Responds in 1 month if interested. First rights. Articles and opinion essays, 800–2,500 words; $55–$75 Canadian. Depts/columns, word lengths vary; $3 Canadian per column inch. B/W prints, $20 Canadian. Pays at the end of each month. Provides 1 contributor's copy.

Premier Baby and Child

5100 Windance Place
Holly Springs, NC 27540

Editor & Publisher: Robyn Mangrum

DESCRIPTION AND INTERESTS: This annual publication is packed with tips for parents of children from birth to age six. Targeting families living in the Triangle region of North Carolina, it features profiles of local families and businesses. Product reviews and decorating ideas for nurseries and children's rooms are also a part of each issue. Circ: 35,000.
Website: www.premierbaby.com

FREELANCE POTENTIAL: 100% written by nonstaff writers. Publishes several freelance submissions yearly; 50% by unpublished writers.

SUBMISSIONS AND PAYMENT: Sample copy and guidelines available. Query with résumé and clips. Accepts hard copy and email queries to publisher@premierbaby.com. SASE. Response time varies. All rights. Articles, 250–500 words. Depts/columns, word lengths vary. Written material, $50–$100. Pays on publication. Provides 2 contributor's copies.

PTO Today

100 Stonewall Boulevard, Suite 3
Wrentham, MA 02093

Editor-in-Chief: Craig Bystrynski

DESCRIPTION AND INTERESTS: *PTO Today* aims to provide ideas, insight, and inspiration to parent-teacher organizations at elementary and middle schools across the U.S. It is read primarily by group leaders for its how-to articles on fundraising, parent recruitment, organization, management, projects, and working with school staff. Circ: 80,000.
Website: www.ptotoday.com

FREELANCE POTENTIAL: 65% written by nonstaff writers. Publishes 35 freelance submissions yearly; 5% by unpublished writers, 15% by authors who are new to the magazine. Receives 120–180 queries yearly.

SUBMISSIONS AND PAYMENT: Guidelines available. Query. Accepts email queries to editor@ptotoday.com. Responds in 2 months. First and electronic rights. Articles, 1,200–1,500 words; payment rates vary. Pays on acceptance. Provides 1 contributor's copy.

Purple Circle Magazine

14200 FM 1062
Canyon, TX 79015

Editor: Melita Cramblet

DESCRIPTION AND INTERESTS: "America's youth livestock magazine" is written for the adults involved in the junior livestock show circuit, whether they be parents or producers. Featuring coverage of 4-H and FFA events and exhibitors, *Purple Circle* focuses on those who raise and show championship cattle, hogs, sheep, and goats—hence the "purple" in its title. It is published 10 times each year. Circ: 3,300.
Website: www.purplecircle.com

FREELANCE POTENTIAL: 50% written by non-staff writers. Publishes 40 freelance submissions yearly; 99% by unpublished writers.

SUBMISSIONS AND PAYMENT: Sample copy available. Query or send complete ms. Accepts hard copy. SASE. Response time varies. Exclusive rights. Articles and depts/columns, word lengths vary. No payment. Provides 2 contributor's copies.

Racquetball

1685 West Uintah
Colorado Springs, CO 80904

Editor: Jim Hiser

DESCRIPTION AND INTERESTS: Published six times each year by the United States Racquetball Association, this magazine covers all aspects of its eponymous sport, from tips on technique to player profiles to the tournament circuit. It is read by association members and recreational players. Circ: 40,000.
Website: www.usaracquetball.com

FREELANCE POTENTIAL: 50% written by non-staff writers. Publishes 24–30 freelance submissions yearly; 80% by unpublished writers, 20% by authors who are new to the magazine. Receives 100 queries yearly.

SUBMISSIONS AND PAYMENT: Sample copy and guidelines, $4. Prefers query; will accept complete ms. Prefers email to jhiser@usra.org; will accept hard copy. SASE. Responds in 9 weeks. One-time rights. Articles, 1,500–2,000 words. Depts/columns, 500–1,000 words. Written material, $.03–$.07 per word. Pays on publication,

Ranger Rick

National Wildlife Federation
11100 Wildlife Center Drive
Reston, VA 20190-5362

Editor: Mary Dalheim

DESCRIPTION AND INTERESTS: This classic monthly magazine for "nature kids" ages 7 to 12 is written primarily by staffers and contracted freelancers, but it will review résumés and clips. It prides itself on providing exciting articles that motivate even reluctant readers, while simultaneously sharing with children the joys of the outdoors and the benefits of wildlife conservation. Circ: 560,000.
Website: www.nwf.org/rangerrick

FREELANCE POTENTIAL: 10% written by non-staff writers. Publishes few freelance submissions yearly. Receives 1,200 queries yearly.

SUBMISSIONS AND PAYMENT: Sample copy and guidelines available at website. All work is assigned. Send résumé and clips only. Accepts hard copy. SASE. Responds if interested. Rights vary. Articles and fiction, 900 words; payment rates vary. Pays on acceptance. Provides 2 contributor's copies.

Rangers Now

General Council of the Assemblies of God
1445 North Boonville Avenue
Springfield, MO 65802-1894

Editor: John Hicks

DESCRIPTION AND INTERESTS: This new annual magazine replaces *High Adventure* as the official publication of the National Royal Rangers. It is produced in six editions, one for each age group, and looks to help readers foster a relationship with Jesus Christ. It targets boys in kindergarten through high school. Circ: 87,000.
Website: www.royalrangers.ag.org

FREELANCE POTENTIAL: 40% written by nonstaff writers. Publishes 6–10 freelance submissions yearly. Receives 150–200 unsolicited mss yearly.

SUBMISSIONS AND PAYMENT: Sample copy, free with 9x12 SASE. Guidelines available. Query. Accepts hard copy. SASE. Responds in 1–2 weeks. First or all rights. Articles, 1,000 words. Depts/columns, word lengths vary. Written material, payment rates vary. Pays on publication. Provides 2 contributor's copies.

Read

Weekly Reader
1 Reader's Digest Road
Pleasantville, NY 10570

Editor: Bryon Cahill

DESCRIPTION AND INTERESTS: Read by middle school and high school students ages 12 through 14, this magazine offers classic works of fiction, nonfiction, poetry, and drama in a way that facilitates good classroom discussion. New, original works of the highest caliber may be considered, depending on editorial needs and editorial calendar. *Read* is published 16 times during the school year by Weekly Reader Corporation. Circ: 160,000.
Website: www.weeklyreader.com

FREELANCE POTENTIAL: 60% written by non-staff writers. Receives 900 queries yearly.

SUBMISSIONS AND PAYMENT: No queries or unsolicited mss. Send résumé only. All work is assigned. Responds if interested. First North American serial and electronic one-time use rights. Articles, 1,000–2,000 words. Written material, payment rates vary. Pays on acceptance. Provides 5 contributor's copies.

Read, America!

3900 Glenwood Avenue
Golden Valley, MN 55422

Editor & Publisher: Roger Hammer

DESCRIPTION AND INTERESTS: A quarterly newsletter for literacy professionals, *Read, America!* features articles on literacy programs and related issues, as well as fun yet motivational poetry and stories for children. The latter offer the best opportunities for writers to become published by the newsletter, which is always interested in finding and recognizing new talent. It is not, however, interested in introspective or complicated writing. Circ: 10,000.

FREELANCE POTENTIAL: 50% written by non-staff writers. Publishes 50 freelance submissions yearly; 100% by authors who are new to the magazine. Receives 1,500 unsolicited mss yearly.

SUBMISSIONS AND PAYMENT: Sample copy and guidelines, $7.50. Send complete ms. Accepts hard copy. No simultaneous submissions. SASE. Responds in 2–3 months. All rights. Articles and fiction, to 1,000 words; $50. Pays on acceptance.

Redbook

Hearst Corporation
300 West 57th Street, 22nd Floor
New York, NY 10019

Articles Department

DESCRIPTION AND INTERESTS: *Redbook* is read by women ages 25 to 44 for its timely articles on health, fashion and decorating trends, and social issues. Also offered are beauty tips, relationship advice, and celebrity profiles and interviews. Essays and personal experience pieces are balanced by expert-written articles. The magazine appears monthly. Circ: 2.3 million.
Website: www.redbookmag.com

FREELANCE POTENTIAL: 5% written by non-staff writers. Publishes 10 freelance submissions yearly; 2% by unpublished writers. Receives 9,960+ queries yearly.

SUBMISSIONS AND PAYMENT: Sample copy, $2.99 at newsstands. Guidelines available at website. Query with clips and source list. Accepts hard copy. SASE. Responds in 3–4 months. All rights. Articles, 1,000–3,000 words; $.75–$1 per word. Depts/columns, 1,000–5,000 words; payment rates vary. Pays on acceptance.

Reptiles

P.O. Box 6050
Mission Viejo, CA 92690

Editor: Russ Case

DESCRIPTION AND INTERESTS: This magazine caters to reptile and amphibian hobbyists. Published monthly, it covers a variety of related topics, including captive care, field herping, and herpetocultural trends. It seeks articles on husbandry, field herping, and trends. Circ: 40,000.
Website: www.reptilechannel.com

FREELANCE POTENTIAL: 60% written by non-staff writers. Publishes 55 freelance submissions yearly; 50% by unpublished writers, 40% by authors who are new to the magazine. Receives 120 queries yearly.

SUBMISSIONS AND PAYMENT: Sample copy, $4.99 at newsstands. Query with description of herp background. Accepts email queries to reptiles@bowtieinc.com. Responds in 2–3 months. First North American serial rights. Articles and depts/columns, word lengths and payment rates vary. Payment policy varies. Provides 2 contributor's copies.

The Rock

Cook Communications Ministries
4050 Lee Vance View
Colorado Springs, CO 80918

Editor: Doug Mauss

DESCRIPTION AND INTERESTS: This weekly Sunday school publication for middle school students presents Bible lessons and contemporary stories of morality in an upbeat and artistically current format. It also features puzzles, games, and personal experience pieces with a strong Christian message. Though primarily staff written, it will review résumés and writing samples of interested freelancers. Circ: 35,000.
Website: www.davidccook.com

FREELANCE POTENTIAL: 10% written by non-staff writers. Publishes 2–3 freelance submissions yearly; 20% by unpublished writers.

SUBMISSIONS AND PAYMENT: Guidelines available at website. All work is assigned. Send résumé or writing samples only. Accepts hard copy. SASE. Response time varies. Rights negotiable. Written material, word lengths and payment rates vary. Pays on acceptance. Provides 1 contributor's copy.

Rugby

33 Kings Highway
Orangeburg, NY 10962

Editor: Ed Hagerty

DESCRIPTION AND INTERESTS: Rugby is alive and well in the United States, as this monthly magazine devoted to the sport demonstrates. A relatively small but dedicated group of fans read Rugby for coverage of matches, teams, leagues, players, and "all the news that's fit." Circ: 10,500.
Website: www.rugbymag.com

FREELANCE POTENTIAL: 50% written by non-staff writers. Publishes 400 freelance submissions yearly; 50% by unpublished writers, 50% by authors who are new to the magazine. Receives 600 queries and unsolicited mss yearly.

SUBMISSIONS AND PAYMENT: Sample copy and guidelines, $4 with 9x12 SASE ($1.70 postage). Query or send complete ms. Accepts hard copy and disk submissions. SASE. Responds in 2 weeks. All rights. Written material, word lengths and payment rates vary. Pays on publication. Provides 3 contributor's copies.

Scholastic News

557 Broadway
New York, NY 10012

Submissions Editor. Editions 4–6: Lee Baier

DESCRIPTION AND INTERESTS: Scholastic News is a weekly paper distributed to elementary school students by their classroom teachers. Six editions correspond to the respective grades targeted. Its contents reflect current events, and it includes other articles on topics of interest to the elementary grade student, written in age-appropriate language. At this time, it is not open to freelance submissions. Circ: 1 million+.
Website: www.scholastic.com

FREELANCE POTENTIAL: 5% written by non-staff writers.

SUBMISSIONS AND PAYMENT: Not accepting queries or manuscripts at this time.

Scholastic News English/Español

557 Broadway
New York, NY 10012

Editor

DESCRIPTION AND INTERESTS: This monthly bilingual magazine is aimed at Spanish-speaking students in grades one through three. Its content is designed to help ELL readers develop the skills needed to make a smooth transition to English proficiency. Many articles cover topics related to Latino cultures. Circ: 125,000.
Website: www.scholastic.com

FREELANCE POTENTIAL: 10% written by non-staff writers. Publishes several freelance submissions yearly. Receives many unsolicited mss each year.

SUBMISSIONS AND PAYMENT: Sample copy and editorial calendar available at website. Query or send complete ms with résumé. Accepts hard copy and simultaneous submissions if identified. SASE. Responds in 1–3 months. All rights. Articles, to 500 words; $75–$500. Pays on publication. Provides 3+ contributor's copies.

Science World

Scholastic Inc.
557 Broadway
New York, NY 10012-3999

Editor: Patricia Janes

DESCRIPTION AND INTERESTS: This Scholastic classroom publication for grades six to ten features articles, hands-on experiments, and activities that cover all areas of the science curriculum: physical science, life science, Earth and space science, environmental science, and technology. Circ: 40,000.
Website: www.scholastic.com/scienceworld

FREELANCE POTENTIAL: 50% written by non-staff writers. Receives 120 queries yearly.

SUBMISSIONS AND PAYMENT: Sample copy, editorial calendar, and guidelines, free with 9x12 SASE. All articles are assigned. Query with list of publishing credits and clips or writing samples. Accepts hard copy. SASE. Responds in 2 months if interested. All rights. Articles, to 750 words; $200–$650. Depts/columns, 200 words; $100–$125. Written material, $.10 per word. Kill fee, 50%. Pays on publication. Provides 2 contributor's copies.

Scuola Calcio Coaching Magazine

P.O. Box 15669
Wilmington, NC 28408

Submissions: Antonio Saviano

DESCRIPTION AND INTERESTS: *Scuola Calcio Coaching Magazine* shares the Italian principles of soccer coaching with those in other countries who wish to guide players toward excellence from a very young age. Published nine times each year, it details drills and goals for children as young as five. Circ: 350+.
Website: www.soccercoachingmagazine.com

FREELANCE POTENTIAL: 20% written by non-staff writers. Publishes 120 freelance submissions yearly; 5% by unpublished writers, 10% by authors who are new to the magazine. Receives 1,000–1,200 queries yearly.

SUBMISSIONS AND PAYMENT: Guidelines available. Query. Accepts hard copy and email to magazine@soccercoachingmagazine.com (Microsoft Word attachments). SASE. Response time varies. Worldwide rights. Articles and depts/columns, word lengths and payment rates vary. Payment policy varies.

Scott Stamp Monthly

Scott Publishing Company
P.O. Box 828
Sidney, OH 45365

Editor: Donna Houseman

DESCRIPTION AND INTERESTS: Stamp collectors read this monthly magazine to keep on top of the latest stamp releases. Feature articles cover building and protecting a stamp collection, among related topics. Circ: 35,000.
Website: www.scottstampmonthly.com

FREELANCE POTENTIAL: 70% written by non-staff writers. Publishes 100 freelance submissions yearly; 15% by unpublished writers, 15% by authors who are new to the magazine. Receives 180 queries and unsolicited mss yearly.

SUBMISSIONS AND PAYMENT: Sample copy and guidelines, $3.50 with 9x12 SASE ($2.07 postage). Prefers query; will accept complete ms. Accepts hard copy and disk submissions (Microsoft Word). SASE. Responds in 1 month. First rights. Articles, 1,000–2,000 words; $75–$150. Depts/columns, word lengths and payment rates vary. Pays on publication. Provides 1 contributor's copy.

Sesame Street Magazine

One Lincoln Plaza
New York, NY 10023

Editor: Rebecca Herman

DESCRIPTION AND INTERESTS: Published 11 times each year, *Sesame Street Magazine* features the well-known characters of the venerable public television show in short stories, poetry, activities, and finger plays. Each issue includes opportunities for children ages two through five to learn math concepts and the alphabet, as well as good manners, safety, and healthy choices, all while having fun. Although freelance work is not accepted, prospective authors may send résumés and clips of their published writing. Circ: 650,000.
Website: www.sesamestreet.com

FREELANCE POTENTIAL: 100% staff written.

SUBMISSIONS AND PAYMENT: All material is written in-house. Writers interested in working for this magazine should submit a résumé and clips of their published work.

Shameless

360A Bloor Street W
P.O. Box 68548
Toronto, Ontario M5S 1X1
Canada

Editor: Megan Griffith-Greene

DESCRIPTION AND INTERESTS: Three times each year, this magazine provides thought-provoking and creative articles designed to encourage Canadian girls to achieve their goals and make a difference in the world. It covers a wide range of topics including politics, current events, sexuality, health, and the arts. Each issue also includes profiles of successful female role models. Circ: 3,000.
Website: www.shamelessmag.com

FREELANCE POTENTIAL: 30% written by non-staff writers. Publishes 25 freelance submissions each year.

SUBMISSIONS AND PAYMENT: Guidelines available at website. Query with clips. Prefers email queries to submit@shamelessmag.com; will accept hard copy. SAE/IRC. Response time varies. First and electronic rights. Articles, 600–2,200 words. Profiles, 300–500 words. No payment.

Sierra

85 Second Street, 2nd Floor
San Francisco, CA 94105

Managing Editor

DESCRIPTION AND INTERESTS: The environment and conservation efforts to protect it are the focus of the carefully researched articles appearing in this magazine. It is published six times each year for a readership that is knowledgeable and active in the cause. Circ: 620,000.
Website: www.sierraclub.org/sierra

FREELANCE POTENTIAL: 45% written by non-staff writers. Publishes 50 freelance submissions yearly; 10% by authors who are new to the magazine. Receives 480–720 queries yearly.

SUBMISSIONS AND PAYMENT: Sample copy, $3 with 9x12 SASE ($1.99 postage). Guidelines available at website. Query. Accepts hard copy. SASE. Responds in 6–8 weeks. First North American serial, reproduction, and archival rights. Articles, 1,000–3,000 words. Depts/columns, to 1,500 words. Written material, $100–$3,000. Pays on acceptance. Provides 2 contributor's copies.

Sharing Space

Creative Response to Conflict
521 North Broadway
P.O. Box 271
Nyack, NY 10960

Executive Director: Priscilla Prutzman

DESCRIPTION AND INTERESTS: Published by the nonprofit Creative Response to Conflict (CRC), *Sharing Space* helps teachers motivate young people to resolve their conflicts peacefully and positively. Its articles and curriculum address the general themes of cooperation, communication, affirmation, mediation, conflict resolution, problem-solving, bias awareness, diversity, and responses to and the prevention of bullying. The newsletter also shares organizational and international news pertinent to CRC's mission of building a just and peaceful world. Circ: Unavailable.
Website: www.crc-global.org

FREELANCE POTENTIAL: 10% written by non-staff writers. Receives 600–1,200 queries yearly.

SUBMISSIONS AND PAYMENT: Query. Accepts hard copy. SASE. Responds in 1–2 weeks. No payment. Written material, word lengths vary. Line art. Provides contributor's copies.

Simply You Magazine

P.O. Box 284
Phillips, WI 54555-0284

Editor

DESCRIPTION AND INTERESTS: This e-zine offers advice and true-life stories meant to help teens find their dreams and turn them into reality. Its content focuses on being true to oneself, and includes articles on relationships and other coming-of-age issues; entertainment updates; product reviews; and message boards, where teens can share insights with each other. Hits per month: 10,000.
Website: www.simplyyoumagazine.com

FREELANCE POTENTIAL: 25% written by non-staff writers. Publishes 20–40 freelance submissions yearly; 25% by unpublished writers, 50% by authors who are new to the magazine. Receives 12–36 unsolicited mss yearly.

SUBMISSIONS AND PAYMENT: Sample copy available at website. Send complete ms. Accepts email to lynne@simplyyoumagazine.com. Responds in 1–2 months. All rights. Written material, word lengths vary. No payment.

Skiing

5720 Flatiron Parkway
Boulder, CO 80301

Editor: Jake Bogoch

DESCRIPTION AND INTERESTS: Six times each year, this magazine shows up on newsstands and in mailboxes, bursting with action photos of extreme skiers and jargon-laden articles, profiles, and gear reviews. Circ: 300,000.
Website: www.skiingmag.com

FREELANCE POTENTIAL: 60% written by non-staff writers. Publishes 50 freelance submissions yearly; 2% by unpublished writers, 5% by authors who are new to the magazine. Receives 180 queries yearly.

SUBMISSIONS AND PAYMENT: Sample copy and guidelines, $2.50 with 9x12 SASE ($1 postage). Query with clips or writing samples. No simultaneous submissions. Prefers email to editor@skiingmag.com; will accept hard copy. SASE. Responds in 2–4 months. First universal and all media rights. Articles and depts/columns, word lengths vary; $1 per word. Pays on acceptance. Provides contributor's copies.

Smithsonian Zoogoer

Friends of the National Zoo
National Zoological Park
3001 Connecticut Avenue NW
Washington, DC 20008

Editor: Cindy Han

DESCRIPTION AND INTERESTS: *Smithsonian Zoogoer* aims to enlighten and entertain readers with feature stories about the National Zoo's animals, staff, and research; natural history; wildlife biology; and conservation. All submissions must be reviewed by experts in the field. The magazine is published six times each year. Circ: 40,000.
Website: www.fonz.org/zoogoer.htm

FREELANCE POTENTIAL: 15% written by non-staff writers. Publishes 8–10 freelance submissions yearly; 5% by authors who are new to the magazine. Receives 60 queries yearly.

SUBMISSIONS AND PAYMENT: Guidelines available. Query with sources, bio, and clips. Accepts hard copy and email queries to hanc@si.edu (Microsoft Word or text attachments). SASE. Responds in 1–2 months. First rights. Articles, 2,000 words. Depts/columns, 800–1,500 words. Written material, $.80 per word. Pays on acceptance. Provides 5 author's copies.

Small Town Life

1046 Barnett Hill Road
Punxsutawney, PA 15767

Editor: Jennifer Forrest

DESCRIPTION AND INTERESTS: From the home of groundhog Punxsutawney Phil comes this quaint and quintessential magazine about, well, small town life. Published six times each year, it features feel-good stories and personal experience pieces to delight readers of all ages. Circ: 5,000.
Website: www.smalltownlifemagazine.com

FREELANCE POTENTIAL: 80% written by non-staff writers. Publishes 60 freelance submissions yearly; 10% by unpublished writers, 25% by authors who are new to the magazine.

SUBMISSIONS AND PAYMENT: Sample copy, $5. Guidelines available at website. Query with clips; or send complete ms. Accepts disk submissions and email submissions to editor@smalltownlifemagazine.com. SASE. Response time varies. First rights. Articles, 3–4 pages. Depts/columns, 500–700 words. No payment. Provides 2 contributor's copies.

Soccer Youth

P.O. Box 983
Morehead, KY 40351

Editor: Nathan Clinkenbeard

DESCRIPTION AND INTERESTS: *Soccer Youth* targets coaches and children ages seven to fourteen who play or have an interest in the sport of soccer. It features profiles of both professional and school-age players and presents articles on everything from techniques and drills to fundraising. It is published every other month and also features comics, puzzles, and quizzes as part of its editorial mix. Circ: 50,000.
Website: www.socceryouth.com

FREELANCE POTENTIAL: 50% written by non-staff writers. Publishes 10–20 freelance submissions yearly.

SUBMISSIONS AND PAYMENT: Query with word count and availability of artwork. Prefers email submissions to info@socceryouth.com; will accept hard copy. SASE. Response time varies. All rights. Articles and depts/columns, word lengths and payment rates vary. Pays on publication.

Socialist Appeal

P.O. Box 4244
St. Paul, MN 55104

Editor: John Peterson

DESCRIPTION AND INTERESTS: This "Marxist voice of workers and youth" is published eight times each year by the Workers International League. It publishes articles and analysis from a working-class perspective, which are meant to provide an alternative to America's capitalist system and its two dominant political parties. The bulk of its content is contributed by freelance writers. Circ: 700.
Website: www.socialistappeal.org

FREELANCE POTENTIAL: 90% written by nonstaff writers. Publishes 80–100 freelance submissions yearly; 25% by authors who are new to the magazine.

SUBMISSIONS AND PAYMENT: Sample copy available at website. Query or send complete ms. Accepts hard copy. SASE. Response time varies. Rights vary. Articles, word lengths vary. No payment.

Spigot Science Magazine

P.O. Box 103
Blawenburg, NJ 08504

Editor-in-Chief: Valeria Girandola

DESCRIPTION AND INTERESTS: This interdisciplinary e-zine for upper-elementary and middle school students is updated six times each year with fresh articles built on a common theme. While such themes are typically scientific on the surface—telescopes, cells, insects, or electricity, for example—articles are designed to be applied to other subjects as well. All submissions should reflect familiarity with national science standards. Hits per month: Unavailable.
Website: www.spigotsciencemag.com

FREELANCE POTENTIAL: 10% written by nonstaff writers. Publishes 10 freelance submissions each year.

SUBMISSIONS AND PAYMENT: Sample copy, guidelines, and editorial calendar available at website. Query. Accepts email queries to vgirandola@spigotsciencemag.com Response time varies. Limited-time electronic rights. Articles, 300–400 words. No payment.

Spirit

Sisters of St. Joseph of Carondelet
1884 Randolph Avenue
St. Paul, MN 55105-1700

Editor: Joan Mitchell

DESCRIPTION AND INTERESTS: Catholic teens in religious education classes receive this take-home paper. Published 28 times each year, it provides readers with inspirational, Gospel-based messages to help them navigate along the path of their spiritual journey. Its mission is "bringing teens to the Gospel and the Gospel into teens' lives." Most of the content is produced in-house, and although the magazine is not accepting unsolicited material at this time, writers interested in this publication should check the website for any changes to this current "no submissions" policy. Circ: 25,000.
Website: www.goodgroundpress.com

FREELANCE POTENTIAL: 25% written by nonstaff writers. Publishes 1–2 freelance submissions each year.

SUBMISSIONS AND PAYMENT: Sample copy, free. Not accepting queries or unsolicited material at this time.

Spirit! Magazine

48 Scotland Hill Road
Chestnut Ridge, NY 10977

Editor-in-Chief: Gershon Sabol

DESCRIPTION AND INTERESTS: *Spirit! Magazine* is an informative, yet culturally sensitive, publication for parents and families of children with disabilities whose exposure to mainstream media is limited. Published quarterly, its articles target a child's total support network, including parents, grandparents, siblings, babysitters, and medical professionals. Circ: 1,000.
Website: www.spiritmag.org

FREELANCE POTENTIAL: 90% written by nonstaff writers. Publishes 20–30 freelance submissions yearly; 50% by unpublished writers, 30% by authors who are new to the magazine.

SUBMISSIONS AND PAYMENT: Sample copy available. Query or send complete ms. Accepts hard copy and email submissions to gershon@spiritmag.org. SASE. Response time varies. All rights. Articles and depts/columns, word lengths vary. No payment. Provides a 1-year subscription for contributors.

Sporting Youth

P.O. Box 1137
Watkinsville, GA 30677

Editor: Rebecca Mobley

DESCRIPTION AND INTERESTS: This publication, read by families living in northeast Georgia, covers the region's youth sports scene. Children, teens, and their parents find lively articles on local athletes and programs, tips from coaches, and event and competition coverage. Appearing six times each year, *Sporting Youth* also keeps readers updated on all school sporting news. Circ: 5,000.
Website: www.sportingyouthga.com

FREELANCE POTENTIAL: 50% written by non-staff writers. Publishes 25 freelance submissions each year.

SUBMISSIONS AND PAYMENT: Sample copy available at website. Query or send complete ms. Accepts email submissions to mail@sportingyouthga.com. Responds in 1 month. One-time rights. Articles and depts/columns, word lengths vary. No payment. Provides contributor's copies.

Story Station

Viatouch
P.O. Box 22624
Houston, TX 77227

Editor

DESCRIPTION AND INTERESTS: Fun stories for children and adults appear in this monthly webzine. It accepts fiction in any genre, but prefers stories with upbeat endings that have at least one protagonist in the 6 to 12 age range. *Story Station* also includes a Teacher Article section featuring material for classroom use. Hits per month: Unavailable.
Website: www.viatouch.com

FREELANCE POTENTIAL: 100% written by nonstaff writers. Publishes 50–100 freelance submissions yearly.

SUBMISSIONS AND PAYMENT: Sample copy and guidelines available at website. Send complete ms with brief author bio. Accepts email submissions to storystation@viatouch.com (Microsoft Word, WordPerfect, or RTF files). Responds in 1–2 months. Electronic rights for 120 days. Fiction, 1,500–3,000 words; $.01 per word. Pays on publication.

The Storyteller

2441 Washington Road
Maynard, AR 72444

Editor: Regina Williams

DESCRIPTION AND INTERESTS: This quarterly magazine publishes short stories, articles, essays, and poetry with the goal of inspiring creativity and helping writers to polish their craft. Circ: 700.
Website: www.thestorytellermagazine.com

FREELANCE POTENTIAL: 99% written by nonstaff writers. Publishes 300 freelance submissions yearly; 50% by unpublished writers, 40% by authors who are new to the magazine. Receives 7,200 unsolicited mss yearly.

SUBMISSIONS AND PAYMENT: Sample copy, $6 with 9x12 SASE ($1.54 postage). Guidelines available. Send complete ms. Accepts hard copy and simultaneous submissions if identified. SASE. Responds in 1–2 weeks. First North American serial rights. Articles and fiction, to 2,500 words; $.025 per word. Poetry, to 40 lines; $1 per poem. Payment policy varies.

Storytelling Magazine

National Storytelling Network
P.O. Box 795
Jonesborough, TN 37659

Submissions: Kit Rogers

DESCRIPTION AND INTERESTS: *Storytelling Magazine* is published five times each year for professional storytellers and others who are interested in learning and preserving the oral tradition. Produced by the National Storytelling Network, it features real-aloud stories (especially useful for children's librarians), ideas and inspiration, and articles on oral storytelling techniques. Queries from experienced storytellers are welcome. Circ: 2,000.
Website: www.storynet.org

FREELANCE POTENTIAL: 100% written by nonstaff writers. Publishes 100 freelance submissions yearly. Receives 48 unsolicited mss yearly.

SUBMISSIONS AND PAYMENT: Sample copy, $6. Query. Accepts email queries to kit@storynet.org. Response time varies. First North American serial rights. Articles, 1,000–2,000 words. Depts/columns, 500 words. No payment. Provides 2 contributor's copies.

Street Brand

Editor: Kofo Baptist

DESCRIPTION AND INTERESTS: Appearing three times each year, *Street Brand* is a faith-based, youth culture magazine. It looks to encourage teens to become more aware of the world around them with thought-provoking articles on topics including conservation, social action, politics, and religion. It also features profiles of teens making a difference. Circ: 3,000. Website: www.streetbrand.com

FREELANCE POTENTIAL: 100% written by nonstaff writers. Publishes 30 freelance submissions yearly; 50% by unpublished writers, 40% by authors who are new to the magazine.

SUBMISSIONS AND PAYMENT: Sample copy and guidelines available. Query or send complete ms. Accepts email submissions to mailbag@streetbrand.com. Responds in 2 months. First and limited-time electronic rights. Written material, word lengths vary. No payment. Provides 2 contributor's copies.

Surfing

950 Calle Amanecer, Suite C
San Clemente, CA 92673

Editor: Travis Ferre

DESCRIPTION AND INTERESTS: Surfer dudes ages 13 to 30 read this monthly magazine for articles on living the surf life. It covers such topics as technique, gear, fashion, and—of course—where to catch the biggest waves. Circ: 105,000. Website: www.surfingmagazine.com

FREELANCE POTENTIAL: 20% written by nonstaff writers. Publishes 15 freelance submissions yearly; 50% by unpublished writers. Receives 72 queries and unsolicited mss yearly.

SUBMISSIONS AND PAYMENT: Sample copy, $3.99 at newsstands. Guidelines available. Query or send complete ms. Accepts hard copy, disk submissions (QuarkXPress or Microsoft Word), and simultaneous submissions if identified. SASE. Responds in 1 month. One-time rights. Articles, 2,000–3,000 words. Depts/columns, 35–500 words. Written material, $.10–$.25 per word. Pays on publication. Provides 2 contributor's copies.

Supertwins

P.O. Box 306
East Islip, NY 11730

Editor: Maureen Boyle

DESCRIPTION AND INTERESTS: Published quarterly by MOST (Mothers of Supertwins), this magazine targets families with multiples — whether they are expecting twins or already the parents of grade-school children. It features both humorous and informative articles written by parents and professionals on such topics as pregnancy and child-rearing. Circ: Unavailable. Website: www.mostonline.org

FREELANCE POTENTIAL: 90% written by nonstaff writers. Publishes 80 freelance submissions yearly. Receives 100 queries, 10 unsolicited mss each year.

SUBMISSIONS AND PAYMENT: Sample copy, $5 with 9x12 SASE. Query or send complete ms. Accepts hard copy and email submissions to info@mostonline.org. SASE. Response time varies. Rights vary. Articles and depts/columns, word lengths and payment rates vary. Pays on publication. Provides 2 contributor's copies.

Susie

3741 Bloomington Street, #4
Colorado Springs, CO 80922

Editor: Susie Shellenberger

DESCRIPTION AND INTERESTS: This new magazine for Christian girls ages 13 through 19 is named for the former creator and editor of *Brio*. It includes a mix of fiction and nonfiction on topics of interest to today's teens. Published monthly, *Susie* debuted in May 2009 and although it does not currently pay for written material, this policy may change as the publication grows. Circ: 60,000. Website: www.susiemag.com

FREELANCE POTENTIAL: 50% written by nonstaff writers. Publishes 20 freelance submissions each year.

SUBMISSIONS AND PAYMENT: Guidelines available. Send complete ms. Accepts email submissions to susieshell@comcast.net (include "Freelance" in the subject field). Response time varies. First rights. Written material, word lengths vary. No payment. Provides 2 contributor's copies.

Synchro Swimming USA

132 East Washington, Suite 820
Indianapolis, IN 46204

Editor: Taylor Payne

DESCRIPTION AND INTERESTS: Published by the United States Synchronized Swimming organization for its members, this online magazine covers all aspects of the Olympic sport, from coaching and choreography to costuming and judging. It welcomes contributions from its young members about the joys and challenges of synchronized swimming, as well as team profiles. Its content is updated quarterly. Hits per month: 7,000.
Website: www.usasynchro.org

FREELANCE POTENTIAL: 50% written by non-staff writers. Publishes 12 freelance submissions yearly; 50% by unpublished writers, 50% by authors who are new to the magazine.

SUBMISSIONS AND PAYMENT: Sample copy available at website. Query or send complete ms. Accepts hard copy. SASE. Response time varies. All rights. Written material, word lengths vary. No payment.

Teen Times

1910 Association Drive
Reston, VA 20191

Communications Coordinator: Leslie Shields

DESCRIPTION AND INTERESTS: Published quarterly by Family, Career, and Community Leaders of America (FCCLA), *Teen Times* is written by its student members. Articles cover such topics as family issues, career planning, community service, and leadership skills. Circ: 219,000.
Website: www.fcclainc.org

FREELANCE POTENTIAL: 50% written by non-staff writers. Publishes 12–16 freelance submissions yearly; 80% by unpublished writers, 20% by authors who are new to the magazine. Receives 5 queries yearly.

SUBMISSIONS AND PAYMENT: Sample copy, free with 9x12 SASE. Accepts submissions from FCCLA student members only. Query or send complete ms. Accepts hard copy. Availability of artwork improves chance of acceptance. SASE. Response time varies. All rights. Articles and depts/columns, word lengths vary. No payment. Provides contributor's copies upon request.

Teachers & Writers

520 Eighth Avenue, Suite 2020
New York, NY 10018

Editor: Susan Karwoska

DESCRIPTION AND INTERESTS: *Teachers & Writers* is a quarterly magazine for those who teach creative writing to children at all grade levels. It seeks inventive ideas and exercises to help teachers (and writers) hone their craft. Circ: 3,000.
Website: www.twc.org

FREELANCE POTENTIAL: 60% written by non-staff writers. Publishes 8 freelance submissions yearly; 5% by unpublished writers, 50% by authors who are new to the magazine. Receives 50 unsolicited mss yearly.

SUBMISSIONS AND PAYMENT: Guidelines available. Send complete ms. Accepts hard copy and simultaneous submissions if identified. SASE. Response time varies. First serial rights. Articles, 700–5,000 words. Depts/columns, word lengths vary. Written material, $20 per printed column. Pays on publication. Provides 10 contributor's copies.

ThisWeek Community Newspapers

7801 North Central Drive
Lewis Center, OH 43035

Editor: Ben Cason

DESCRIPTION AND INTERESTS: The communities in central Ohio are covered by this network of 22 regional publications, known as *ThisWeek Community Newspapers*. Readers find local news, announcements, and event coverage, as well as articles about family life, parenting, education, and child care. Writers with a regional connection are preferred. Issues appear monthly. Circ: 200,000+.
Website: www.thisweeknews.com

FREELANCE POTENTIAL: 100% written by nonstaff writers. Publishes 100 freelance submissions yearly.

SUBMISSIONS AND PAYMENT: Sample copy, free with 9x12 SASE. Query. Accepts email queries to editorial@thisweeknews.com (no attachments). Responds in 1 month. First or reprint rights. Written material, word lengths vary; $.10–$.20 per word. Pays on publication. Provides 2 contributor's copies.

Tidewater Parent

258 Granby Street
Norfolk, VA 23510

Editor: Jennifer O'Donnell

DESCRIPTION AND INTERESTS: This free, comprehensive magazine targets today's active parents and families. In conjunction with its new website, it provides Virginia parents with information on child care, health, nutrition, and travel. Each monthly issue also covers local events and activities. *Tidewater Parent* prefers to work with local writers. Circ: 48,000.
Website: www.mytidewatermoms.com

FREELANCE POTENTIAL: 90% written by non-staff writers. Publishes 40 freelance submissions yearly; 10% by unpublished writers, 50% by authors who are new to the magazine. Receives 72 unsolicited mss yearly.

SUBMISSIONS AND PAYMENT: Send complete ms. Will accept previously published material that can be reprinted. Accepts hard copy. SASE. Response time varies. Rights vary. Articles, 800–1,200 words; $25. Kill fee, 50%. Pays on publication. Provides 1 contributor's copy.

Tiger Beat

330 North Brand, Ste. 1150
Glendale, CA 91203

Editor-in-Chief: Leesa Coble

DESCRIPTION AND INTERESTS: The teen media world is the focus of this monthly magazine for young adults, primarily girls, ages 10 to 16. It features profiles and pictorials about the latest movie, television, and music sensations appealing to this age group. It features coverage of Hollywood events, interviews, quizzes, and reviews. Each issue is packed with color photos. *Tiger Beat* is not accepting submissions at this time. Check its website for updates to this policy. Circ: 200,000.
Website: www.tigerbeatmag.com

FREELANCE POTENTIAL: 100% staff-written.

SUBMISSIONS AND PAYMENT: Sample copy, $3.99 at newsstands. Not accepting queries or unsolicited mss at this time.

Toy Farmer

7496 106th Avenue SE
LaMoure, ND 58458-9404

Editorial Assistant: Cheryl Hegvik

DESCRIPTION AND INTERESTS: Collectors of toy tractors and other farm-themed toys read *Toy Farmer* for manufacturer profiles, coverage of collector events and auctions, farm toy histories, and information about trends related to the hobby. It is published monthly. Circ: 27,000.
Website: www.toyfarmer.com

FREELANCE POTENTIAL: 100% written by nonstaff writers. Publishes 50 freelance submissions yearly; 20% by unpublished writers, 20% by authors who are new to the magazine. Receives several queries yearly.

SUBMISSIONS AND PAYMENT: Sample copy, guidelines, and editorial calendar, $5 with 9x12 SASE. Query with writing samples. Accepts hard copy. SASE. Responds in 1 month. First rights. Articles, 1,500 words. Depts/columns, 800 words. Written material, $.10 per word. Pays on publication. Provides 2 contributor's copies.

Toy Trucker & Contractor

7496 106th Avenue SE
LaMoure, ND 58458-9404

Editorial Assistant: Cheryl Hegvik

DESCRIPTION AND INTERESTS: Model truck and equipment collectors read this monthly magazine for how-to and informational articles on all aspects of the hobby. Each issue features profiles of collectors and unique collections, and information on toy shows. Circ: 8,000.
Website: www.toytrucker.com

FREELANCE POTENTIAL: 100% written by nonstaff writers. Publishes 60 freelance submissions yearly; 10% by unpublished writers, 20% by authors who are new to the magazine. Receives 12 queries yearly.

SUBMISSIONS AND PAYMENT: Guidelines and editorial calendar available. Query with writing samples. Accepts hard copy. SASE. Responds in 1 month. First North American serial rights. Articles, 1,000–5,000 words. Depts/columns, word lengths vary. Written material, $.10 per word. Pays on publication. Provides 2 contributor's copies.

Trains

21027 Crossroads Circle
P.O. Box 1612
Waukesha, WI 53187-1612

Editor: Jim Wrinn

DESCRIPTION AND INTERESTS: Train enthusiasts of all ages read this monthly publication for informative and entertaining articles on steam, diesel, and electric locomotives of the past and present. Railroad news, train preservation, and technology are covered in each issue. Circ: 95,000.
Website: www.trainsmag.com

FREELANCE POTENTIAL: 95% written by non-staff writers. Publishes 300–400 freelance submissions yearly; 25% by unpublished writers, 50% by authors who are new to the magazine. Receives 120 queries and unsolicited mss yearly.

SUBMISSIONS AND PAYMENT: Sample copy, $5.95. Guidelines available at website. Prefers query; will accept complete ms. Accepts email submissions to editor@trainsmag.com. Responds in 6 months. All rights. Articles and depts/columns, word lengths vary; $.10–$.15 per word. Pays on acceptance. Provides 2 author's copies.

Trumbull County Parent

100 DeBartolo Place, Suite 210
Youngstown, OH 44512

Editor & Publisher: Amy Leigh Wilson

DESCRIPTION AND INTERESTS: Families living in Trumbull county, Ohio, turn to this monthly magazine for kid-friendly activities, parenting articles, and regional news. Potential writers should have a familiarity with the area. Circ: 50,000.
Website: www.forparentsonline.com

FREELANCE POTENTIAL: 99% written by non-staff writers. Publishes 100 freelance submissions yearly; 5% by unpublished writers, 20% by authors who are new to the magazine. Receives 500 unsolicited mss yearly.

SUBMISSIONS AND PAYMENT: Sample copy, free with 9x12 SASE. Send complete ms. Accepts hard copy and email submissions to editor@myparentmagazine.com. SASE. Response time varies. One-time rights. Articles, 1,000–1,800 words. Depts/columns, word lengths vary. Written material, $20–$50. Pays on publication. Provides 1 contributor's copy.

Transworld Snowboarding

2052 Corte del Nogal, Suite B
Carlsbad, CA 92011

Managing Editor: Annie Fast

DESCRIPTION AND INTERESTS: Packed with photos of snowboarding stunts, this hefty journal covers all aspects of the sport—including techniques, professional snowboarders, reviews of new gear, and destinations. Read primarily by young adults, it seeks more travel pieces written from a snowboarder's point of view. It is published eight times each year. Circ: 1.4 million.
Website: www.twsnow.com

FREELANCE POTENTIAL: 10% written by non-staff writers. Publishes 10 freelance submissions yearly; 5% by authors who are new to the magazine. Receives 120 queries yearly.

SUBMISSIONS AND PAYMENT: Sample copy, $3.99 at newsstands. Guidelines and theme list available. Query. Accepts email queries to annie.fast@transworld.net. Responds in 1 month. Rights vary. Articles, to 1,600 words. Depts/columns, 300 words. Written material, $.35 per word. Pays on publication.

Turtle Trails & Tales

P.O. Box 19623
Reno, NV 89511

Editor: Virginia Castleman

DESCRIPTION AND INTERESTS: Now available exclusively online, *Turtle Trails & Tales* continues to publish multicultural stories and articles aimed at helping children understand other cultures. Committed to publishing new writers, it seeks pieces that reflect the similarities and differences of the world's children. Hits per month: Unavailable.
Website: www.publisher-match.com

FREELANCE POTENTIAL: 80% written by non-staff writers. Of the freelance submissions published yearly, 40% are by unpublished writers, 50% are by authors who are new to the magazine. Receives 120 unsolicited mss yearly.

SUBMISSIONS AND PAYMENT: Sample copy, guidelines, and theme list available at website. Send complete ms. Accepts hard copy and email submissions to vcastleman@sbcglobal.net. SASE. Responds in 3 months. Electronic rights. Articles, 750 words. Fiction, 500–800 words. No payment.

Twist

270 Sylvan Avenue
Englewood Cliffs, NJ 07632

Associate Editor: Tina Donvito

DESCRIPTION AND INTERESTS: Published 10 times each year, *Twist* offers upbeat articles and celebrity news from the entertainment and fashion world. It features interviews with today's hottest tween and teen stars, as well as profiles of today's teens facing real-life issues. Circ: 230,000.
Website: www.twistmagazine.com

FREELANCE POTENTIAL: 5% written by non-staff writers. Publishes 10 freelance submissions yearly; 5% by unpublished writers, 5% by authors who are new to the magazine. Receives 240 queries yearly.

SUBMISSIONS AND PAYMENT: Sample copy, $3.99 with 9x12 SASE. Guidelines available. Query. Accepts hard copy. SASE. Responds in 2–3 weeks. First North American serial rights. Written material, word lengths and payment rates vary. Pays on acceptance. Provides 2 contributor's copies.

Unique Magazine

Editor & Publisher: Kristine Rademacher

DESCRIPTION AND INTERESTS: This monthly online publication is dedicated to addressing the challenges faced by families with children who have special needs. *Unique* is a faith-based magazine that welcomes informational articles, personal experience pieces, family activities, and profiles. It prefers submissions that focus on the family, rather than a child's specific condition. Hits per month: Unavailable.
Website: www.myuniquekid.com

FREELANCE POTENTIAL: 20% written by non-staff writers. Publishes 5–10 freelance submissions yearly.

SUBMISSIONS AND PAYMENT: Sample copy and guidelines available at website. Send complete ms with author bio. Accepts email submissions to editor@myuniquekid.com. Responds if interested. Limited-time electronic rights. Articles, 500–1,250 words. Poetry, to 15 lines. No payment.

Vegetarian Journal

P.O. Box 1463
Baltimore, MD 21203

Managing Editor: Debra Wasserman

DESCRIPTION AND INTERESTS: Published quarterly by the nonprofit Vegetarian Resource Group, *Vegetarian Journal* covers vegetarianism and the interrelated issues of health, nutrition, ecology, ethics, and world hunger. In addition to recipes and cooking tips, it offers parents advice on instilling in their children a lifelong understanding of and appreciation for vegetarianism. It also encourages social action to promote public health and vegetarian choices in schools. Circ: 20,000.
Website: www.vrg.org

FREELANCE POTENTIAL: 50% written by non-staff writers. Publishes 10 freelance submissions yearly; 5% by authors new to the magazine.

SUBMISSIONS AND PAYMENT: Sample copy, $4. Query with author bio. Accepts hard copy. Submit seasonal material 1 year in advance. SASE. Responds in 1 week. One-time rights. Written material, word lengths vary; $200. Pays on acceptance. Provides 3+ contributor's copies.

Voices from the Middle

University of Texas at San Antonio
Dept. of Interdisciplinary Learning & Teaching
One UTSA Circle
San Antonio, TX 78249

Editor: Roxanne Henkin

DESCRIPTION AND INTERESTS: This quarterly magazine is read by middle school teachers. It features articles on literacy education, learning, and teaching, as well as personal experience pieces, literature reviews, and information on professional resources. Circ: 9,000.
Website: www.ncte.org/pubs/journals/vm

FREELANCE POTENTIAL: 70% written by non-staff writers. Publishes 12 freelance submissions yearly; 60% by unpublished writers, 85% by authors who are new to the magazine. Receives 150 unsolicited mss yearly.

SUBMISSIONS AND PAYMENT: Sample copy, $6. Guidelines and theme list available at website. Send 3 copies of ms. Accepts hard copy and email to voices@utsa.edu (Microsoft Word attachments; note issue for which you are submitting in subject line). SASE. Responds in 3–5 months. First and second rights. Articles, 2,500–4,000 words. No payment. Provides 2 copies.

Volta Voices

Alexander Graham Bell Association
for the Deaf and Hard of Hearing
3417 Volta Place NW
Washington, DC 20007-2778

Editor: Melody Felzin

DESCRIPTION AND INTERESTS: Timely articles on hearing loss and spoken language education, as well as other topics of interest to the deaf community, comprise the contents of this publication. Topics range from new technologies to social aspects of hearing loss. Published six times each year, it is read by the deaf and hearing impaired, their families, educators, researchers, and other professionals. Circ: 5,500.
Website: www.agbell.org

FREELANCE POTENTIAL: 90% written by non-staff writers. Publishes 6–8 freelance submissions yearly; 50% by unpublished writers. Receives 24 unsolicited mss yearly.

SUBMISSIONS AND PAYMENT: Sample copy available at website. Send complete ms. Accepts email to editor@agbell.org (Microsoft Word attachments). Responds in 1–3 months. All rights. Articles, 500–2,000 words. No payment. Provides 3 contributor's copies.

The Water Skier

USA Water Ski
1251 Holy Cow Road
Polk City, FL 33868-8200

Editor: Scott Atkinson

DESCRIPTION AND INTERESTS: Issued nine times each year, *The Water Skier* offers informative, how-to articles on technique and training, along with profiles of champion water-skiers, exhaustive competition coverage, gear information, and lots of action photography. It is published by USA Water Ski, the sport's official association in America and a member of the United States Olympic Committee. Circ: 20,000.
Website: www.usawaterski.org

FREELANCE POTENTIAL: 20% written by non-staff writers. Publishes 10–12 freelance submissions yearly; 10% by authors who are new to the magazine. Receives 20–30 queries yearly.

SUBMISSIONS AND PAYMENT: Sample copy, $1.25 with 9x12 SASE. Query. Accepts hard copy. SASE. Responds in 1 month. All rights. Articles, 1,000 words. Fiction, 500–1,000 words. Written material, payment rates vary. Pays on publication. Provides 1 contributor's copy.

Wanna Bet?

North American Training Institute
314 West Superior Street, Suite 508
Duluth, MN 55802

Submissions Editor

DESCRIPTION AND INTERESTS: This online magazine for middle school students is an extension of the *Kids Don't Gamble . . . Wanna Bet?* curriculum developed by the North American Training Institute. It features age-appropriate articles on the dangers of gambling addiction for both adults and children; how and where to get help; and healthy, alternative activities. Guided in part by a student editor, the e-zine is updated monthly. Hits per month: 60,000.
Website: www.wannabet.org

FREELANCE POTENTIAL: 25% written by non-staff writers. Publishes numerous freelance submissions yearly.

SUBMISSIONS AND PAYMENT: Sample copy available at website. Query or send complete ms. Accepts email submissions to wannabet@wannabet.org. Response time varies. Electronic rights. Written material, word lengths vary. No payment.

Wild West

Weider History Group
19300 Promenade Drive
Lansdown Town Center, VA 20176

Editor: Greg Lalire

DESCRIPTION AND INTERESTS: Historical accuracy is imperative in this chronicle of the American frontier, which covers all eras of the region's expansion. *Wild West* also looks for articles that use action and quotes to heighten reader interest. It is published six times each year. Circ: 50,000.
Website: www.thehistorynet.com

FREELANCE POTENTIAL: 80% written by non-staff writers. Publishes 60 freelance submissions yearly; 10% by unpublished writers, 20% by authors who are new to the magazine. Receives 250 queries yearly.

SUBMISSIONS AND PAYMENT: Sample copy and guidelines, $6. Query with résumé, outline, illustration ideas, source lists, and clips or writing samples. Accepts hard copy. SASE. Responds in 4–6 months. All rights. Articles, to 3,500 words; $300. Depts/columns, to 1,200 words; $150. Pays on publication.

Women Today Magazine

Box 300 STN "A"
Vancouver, British Columbia V6C 2X3
Canada

Senior Editor: Claire Colvin

DESCRIPTION AND INTERESTS: A monthly online magazine, *Women Today* offers its female readers information about the issues that affect them everyday: relationships, marriage, parenting, career, health, beauty, fitness, spirituality, and finances—all from a Christian perspective. Hits per month: Unavailable.
Website: www.womentodaymagazine.com

FREELANCE POTENTIAL: 30–50% written by nonstaff writers. Publishes 20–30 freelance submissions yearly; 15% by unpublished writers, 25% by authors who are new to the magazine. Receives 450 unsolicited mss yearly.

SUBMISSIONS AND PAYMENT: Sample copy, guidelines, and editorial calendar available at website. Send complete ms. Accepts submissions through online submission system only. Responds in 4–6 weeks. One-time rights. Articles, 1,000–1,200 words. Depts/columns, 600–1,000 words. No payment.

Woodall's CamperWays

P.O. Box 8686
Ventura, CA 93002

Managing Editor: Maryanne Sullivan

DESCRIPTION AND INTERESTS: This monthly tabloid for RV enthusiasts celebrates the joys of RV travel and addresses its challenges. Features on mid-Atlantic and New England destinations are needed. Writers must provide photos to accompany their articles. Circ: Unavailable.
Website: www.woodalls.com

FREELANCE POTENTIAL: 90% written by nonstaff writers. Publishes several freelance submissions yearly; 10% by authors who are new to the magazine. Receives 300 queries yearly.

SUBMISSIONS AND PAYMENT: Guidelines available. Query. Accepts email queries to editor@ woodallpub.com (Microsoft Word attachments). Availability of artwork required for acceptance. Responds in 2 months. First North American serial and electronic rights. Articles, 1,000–1,400 words; $50–$200. Depts/columns, by assignment only. High-resolution digital images. Pays on acceptance. Provides 2 contributor's copies.

World Around You

Laurent Clerc National Deaf Education Center
KDES, Suite 3600
800 Florida Avenue NE
Washington, DC 20002

Submissions

DESCRIPTION AND INTERESTS: Updated five times each year, *World Around You* is an e-zine for the hearing impaired, with a particular focus on students and young adults. It features essays, personal experience pieces, and profiles of deaf individuals. Articles cover the careers and accomplishments of the hearing impaired. *World Around You* is published by Gallaudet University, the only college in the world exclusively for deaf students.
Website: http://clerccenter.gallaudet.edu/ worldaroundyou/

FREELANCE POTENTIAL: 10% written by nonstaff writers. Publishes 3–5 freelance submissions yearly. Receives 48 queries yearly.

SUBMISSIONS AND PAYMENT: Sample copy available at website. Query. Accepts hard copy. SASE. Responds in 1 month. Rights negotiable. Articles, word lengths and payment rates vary. Pays on publication.

Youngbucks-outdoors.com

10350 Highway 80 East
Montgomery, AL 36117

Online Editor: Daniel Dye

DESCRIPTION AND INTERESTS: Published for readers ages seven through thirteen, this online magazine offers articles about the great outdoors. It focuses on exploring America's natural destinations, as well as developing outdoor skills such as hunting, camping, and hiking. Age-appropriate articles on health are also included. Hits per month: 200,000.
Website: www.youngbucksoutdoors.com

FREELANCE POTENTIAL: 60% written by nonstaff writers. Publishes 15–20 freelance submissions yearly.

SUBMISSIONS AND PAYMENT: Guidelines available. Query with detailed photo information. Availability of artwork improves chance of acceptance. Accepts hard copy and email to ddye@ buckmasters.com. SASE. Responds in 1 week. First rights. Articles, 400 words. Fiction, to 500 words. Color prints and transparencies. All material, payment rates vary. Pays on publication.

Your Big Backyard

National Wildlife Federation
11100 Wildlife Center Drive
Reston, VA 20190-5362

Editorial Department

DESCRIPTION AND INTERESTS: This little brother to *Ranger Rick* shares its sibling's commitment to wildlife conservation education, though for a younger set: children ages three to seven. It also shares a restrictive submissions policy, accepting only résumés and clips from unfamiliar writers. Each monthly issue contains articles and activities about nature and animals that appeal to young children. Circ: 400,000.
Website: www.nwf.org/yourbigbackyard

FREELANCE POTENTIAL: 10% written by non-staff writers. Publishes 3 freelance submissions yearly. Receives 1,200 queries yearly.

SUBMISSIONS AND PAYMENT: Sample copy and guidelines available at website. All work is assigned. Send résumé and clips only. Accepts hard copy. SASE. Response time varies. Rights vary. Written material, word lengths and payment rates vary. Pays on acceptance. Provides 2 contributor's copies.

Your Child

820 Second Avenue
New York, NY 10017

Editor: Kay E. Pomerantz

DESCRIPTION AND INTERESTS: Published by the United Synagogue of Conservative Judaism, this online newsletter is written for parents of young Jewish children. It addresses relevant social issues, offers parenting strategies, reviews books and movies, discusses holiday observances, and suggests projects that families can do together. All articles must be written from a conservative Jewish perspective. The newsletter is issued three times each year. Hits per month: 3,000.
Website: www.uscj.org

FREELANCE POTENTIAL: Of the freelance submissions published yearly, 50% are by unpublished writers.

SUBMISSIONS AND PAYMENT: Sample copy available at website. Query or send complete ms. Accepts hard copy and email submissions to kaykp@aol.com. SASE. Response time varies. All rights. Articles, word lengths vary. No payment.

Youth Runner Magazine

P.O. Box 1156
Lake Oswego, OR 97035

Editor: Dan Kesterson

DESCRIPTION AND INTERESTS: Published 10 times each year, *Youth Runner Magazine* covers track and field and cross-country running for student athletes in middle school and high school. It seeks "fresh talent" and new ideas, and welcomes submissions from professional writers as well as from students and coaches. Circ: Unavailable.
Website: www.youthrunner.com

FREELANCE POTENTIAL: 30% written by non-staff writers. Publishes 10 freelance submissions yearly; 50% by unpublished writers, 30% by authors who are new to the magazine. Receives 60 unsolicited mss yearly.

SUBMISSIONS AND PAYMENT: Sample copy available. Send complete ms. Accepts email submissions to dank@youthrunner.com. Response time varies. First rights. Articles and depts/columns, word lengths and payment rates vary. Payment policy varies.

Yummy Mummy

13988 Maycrest Way, Unit 140
Richmond, British Columbia V6V 3C3
Canada

Managing Editor: Anya Leugkh

DESCRIPTION AND INTERESTS: All aspects of motherhood are covered in this regional magazine that targets parents living in British Columbia. It is published eight times each year, with two issues devoted exclusively to dads. It looks for quick tips as well as informative articles geared toward enhancing a mom's quality of life. Circ: 10,000.
Website: www.yummymummymag.com

FREELANCE POTENTIAL: 75% written by non-staff writers. Publishes 40 freelance submissions yearly; 35% by authors who are new to the magazine. Receives 300 queries yearly.

SUBMISSIONS AND PAYMENT: Sample copy available at website. Query. Accepts email queries to editor@yummymummymag.com. Response time varies. One-time print and electronic rights. Articles, 600–800 words; payment rates vary. Pays on publication. Provides contributor's copies upon request.

Contests and Awards

Selected Contests and Awards

Entering a writing contest will provide you with a chance to have your work read by established writers and qualified editors. Winning or placing in a contest or an award program can open the door to publication and recognition of your writing. If you don't win, try to read the winning entry if it is published; doing so will give you some insight into how your work compares with its competition.

For both editors and writers, contests generate excitement. For editors, contests are a source to discover new writers. Entries are more focused because of the contest guidelines, and therefore more closely target an editor's current needs.

For writers, every contest entry is read, often by more than one editor, as opposed to unsolicited submissions that are often relegated to a slush pile.

And you don't have to be the grand-prize winner to benefit—non-winning manuscripts are often purchased by the publication for future issues.

To be considered for the contests and awards that follow, your entry must fulfill all of the requirements mentioned. Most are looking for unpublished article or story manuscripts, while a few require published works. Note special entry requirements, such as whether or not you can submit the material yourself, need to be a member of an organization, or are limited in the number of entries you can send. Also, be sure to submit your article or story in the standard manuscript submission format.

For each listing, we've included the address, the contact, a description, the entry requirements, the deadline, and the prize. In some cases, the 2010 deadlines were not available at press time. We recommend that you write to the addresses provided or visit the websites to request an entry form and the contest guidelines, which usually specify the current deadline.

Arizona Literary Contest

Contest Coordinator
6145 W. Echo Lane
Glendale, AZ 85302

DESCRIPTION: The Arizona Authors Association sponsors this annual contest, which is open to members and non-members alike. Unpublished work in the categories of short story, essay, article, poetry, and novel is eligible.
Website: www.azauthors.com/contest.html

REQUIREMENTS: Entry fees range from $10 to $30 depending on category. Check website for fees and word length requirements. Accepts hard copy. Manuscripts are not returned. Visit the website or send an SASE for complete guidelines.

PRIZES: First-prize winners in each category receive $100. Second- and third-prize winners receive $50 and $25, respectively. Winning entries are published or featured in *Arizona Literary Magazine*.

DEADLINE: Entries are accepted between January 1 and July 1.

Waldo M. and Grace C. Bonderman Youth Theatre Playwriting Competition

Indiana Repertory Theatre
140 West Washington Street
Indianapolis, IN 46204

DESCRIPTION: The Indiana Repertory Theatre sponsors this annual competition to encourage the creation of artistic theatrical scripts for young people. Open to adult writers, it accepts original scripts or adaptations with proper proof that the work is in the public domain, or that permission has been granted by the copyright holder.
Website: www.indianarep.com/Bonderman

REQUIREMENTS: No entry fee. Plays for grades one to three should have a running time of about 30 minutes; those for grades three and above should run approximately 45 minutes. Complete guidelines are posted at the website.

PRIZES: Awards are presented to the top 10 finalists. Four cash awards of $1,000 are also awarded to the playwrights whose entries are selected for development.

DEADLINE: April 15.

Baker's Plays High School Playwriting Contest

Attn: High School Playwriting Contest
45 W. 25th Street
New York, NY 10010

DESCRIPTION: Baker's Plays sponsors this annual contest to encourage aspiring high school authors to consider the creative possibilities of writing for the stage.
Website: www.bakersplays.com

REQUIREMENTS: Open to high school students only. No entry fee or length limitations. Plays must be accompanied by the signature of a sponsoring high school English teacher. Manuscripts must be firmly bound and typed. Include an SASE for return of manuscript. Visit the website for contest rules and entry form.

PRIZES: First-place winner receives a cash award of $500; second-place winner receives $250; and third-place winner receives $100. Each winning play is published in a collection by Baker's Plays with a royalty-earning contract.

DEADLINE: Entries are accepted between November 1 and January 30.

Canadian Writer's Journal Short Fiction Contest

Box 1178
New Liskeard, Ontario P0J 1P0
Canada

DESCRIPTION: Canadian citizens or landed immigrants may participate in this contest sponsored by *Canadian Writer's Journal*.
Website: www.cwj.ca

REQUIREMENTS: Entry fee, $5. Maximum length, 1,500 words. Multiple entries accepted. Accepts hard copy. Author's name must not appear on manuscript. Include a cover sheet with author's name, address, and short biography. Manuscripts are not returned. Visit the website for complete information.

PRIZES: First-place winner receives a cash prize of $150. Second- and third-place winners receive cash prizes of $100 and $50, respectively. Winning entries are published in *Canadian Writer's Journal*.

DEADLINE: April 30.

CAPA Competition

c/o Dan Uitti
Connecticut Authors and Publishers Association
P.O. Box 715
Avon, CT 06001

DESCRIPTION: Sponsored by the Connecticut Authors and Publishers Association and open to residents of Connecticut, this competition is held annually. It accepts original, unpublished entries in the categories of children's story, short story, personal essay, and poetry.
Website: http://aboutcapa.com

REQUIREMENTS: Entry fee, $10 for one story or essay or up to 3 poems. Children's stories, to 2,000 words. Personal essays, to 1,500 words. Poetry, to 30 lines. Multiple entries are accepted. Accepts hard copy. Submit 4 copies of each entry. Manuscripts are not returned.

PRIZES: First-place winners in each category receive $100. Second-place winners receive $50 each.

DEADLINE: May 31.

Children's Writer Contests

Children's Writer
95 Long Ridge Rd
West Redding, CT 06896

DESCRIPTION: *Children's Writer* newsletter sponsors two contests every year, each with specific requirements. Contests for 2010 call for an article on a science topic geared to 11-year-old readers, and historical fiction for young teens. Original, unpublished work is eligible.
Website: www.childrenswriter.com

REQUIREMENTS: No entry fee for subscribers. For non-subscribers, a $10 entry fee includes a 6-month subscription to the newsletter. Word lengths vary according to individual contest requirements. Multiple entries are accepted; each must be accompanied by its own entry form. Accepts hard copy. Manuscripts are not returned. Visit the website for entry form and complete contest rules.

PRIZES: Cash prizes vary for each contest. Winning entries are published in *Children's Writer.*

DEADLINE: February 28 and October 31.

Delacorte Press Contest

Random House, Inc.
1745 Broadway, 9th Floor
New York, NY 10019

DESCRIPTION: The Delacorte Press Contest for a First Young Adult Novel is held annually to encourage the creation of high-quality young adult fiction. All entries should feature contemporary settings and plots appropriate for readers ages 12 to 18. Manuscripts submitted to a previous Delacorte Press contest are ineligible.
Website: www.randomhouse.com

REQUIREMENTS: No entry fee required. Length, 100–224 pages. Limit 2 entries per competition. Accepts hard copy. Include a cover letter with brief plot summary. Visit the website for complete submission information.

PRIZES: Winner receives a publishing contract from Delacorte Press Books for Young Readers, a $7,500 advance against royalties, and a cash prize of $1,500.

DEADLINE: Entries are accepted between October 1 and December 31.

Delacorte Yearling Contest

Random House, Inc.
1745 Broadway, 9th Floor
New York, NY 10019

DESCRIPTION: Formerly known as the Marguerite de Angeli Contest, the Delacorte Yearling Contest for a First Middle-Grade Novel is held each year to encourage the writing of contemporary or historical fiction set in North America for readers ages 9 to 12. U.S. and Canadian authors are eligible to participate.
Website: www.randomhouse.com

REQUIREMENTS: No entry fee required. Length, 96–160 pages. Limit 2 entries per competition. Accepts hard copy. Include a cover letter with brief plot summary. Visit the website for complete submission information.

PRIZES: Winner receives a publishing contract from Delacorte Press Books for Young Readers, a $7,500 advance against royalties, and a cash prize of $1,500.

DEADLINE: Entries are accepted between April 1 and June 30.

Shubert Fendrich Memorial Playwriting Contest

Pioneer Drama Service, Inc.
P.O. Box 4267
Englewood, CO 80155-4267

DESCRIPTION: Established in memory of the founder of Pioneer Drama Service, this contest is held annually to encourage the development of quality material for school and community theatrical groups.
Website: www.pioneerdrama.com

REQUIREMENTS: No entry fee. Plays should run between 20 and 90 minutes. Accepts hard copy. All entries must include the completed application form (available at website), musical score if applicable, and proof of production. Writers who have been published by Pioneer Drama Service are not eligible.

PRIZES: Winning entry is published by Pioneer Drama Service; winner receives a $1,000 advance on royalties.

DEADLINE: Ongoing; winner announced each June 1 from plays submitted during the previous calendar year.

H. E. Francis Award

Department of English
University of Alabama at Huntsville
Huntsville, AL 35899

DESCRIPTION: The Ruth Hindman Foundation and the UAH English Department sponsor this contest, which is held annually. Only original, previously unpublished short stories are eligible to compete.
Website: www.uah.edu/hefranciscontest

REQUIREMENTS: Entry fee, $15. Length, to 5,000 words. Accepts hard copy. Send 3 copies of manuscript. No identifying information should appear on the manuscript itself. Enclose a cover sheet with story title, word count, and author name and address. Manuscripts are not returned; send SASE for announcement of winner. Visit the website for more information.

PRIZES: First-place winner receives a cash prize of $1,000.

DEADLINE: December 31. Winner is announced in March.

Foster City International Writing Contest

c/o Foster City Parks & Recreation Dept.
650 Shell Boulevard
Foster City, CA 94404

DESCRIPTION: Held annually, this contest accepts entries in the categories of children's story, fiction, humor, poetry, and personal essay. The competition is open to original, unpublished work only.
Website: www.geocities.com/
fostercity_writers

REQUIREMENTS: Entry fee, $20. Multiple entries are accepted. Children's stories, fiction, humor, and personal experience pieces, to 3,000 words. Poetry, to 500 words. Accepts hard copy and email submissions to fostercity_writers@ yahoo.com (RTF or Microsoft Word attachments). Visit the website for complete information.

PRIZES: First place winners in each category receive a cash prize of $150.

DEADLINE: June 1.

Friends of the Library Contest

Decatur Public Library
130 N. Franklin Street
Decatur, IL 62523

DESCRIPTION: Open to writers everywhere, this contest accepts entries in the categories of essay, fiction, juvenile fiction, and poetry (rhymed or unrhymed). Previously published work is welcome.
Website: www.decatur.lib.il.us

REQUIREMENTS: Entry fee, $3; limit 5 entries per person. Accepts hard copy. Essay, to 2,000 words. Fiction and juvenile fiction, to 3,000 words. Poetry, to 40 lines. Author's name should not appear on manuscript. All submissions must be accompanied by an entry form. Complete contest rules and entry form available at the website or with SASE.

PRIZES: First-place winner receives a cash award of $50. Second- and third-place winners receive $30 and $20, respectively.

DEADLINE: September 25.

John Gardner Memorial Prize for Fiction

Harpur Palate
English Department, Binghamton University
Box 6000
Binghamton, NY 13902-6000

DESCRIPTION: Honoring John Gardner for his dedication to the creative writing program at Binghamton University, this contest is open to submissions of previously unpublished short stories.
Website: http://harpurpalate.binghamton.edu

REQUIREMENTS: Entry fee, $15; includes a 1-year subscription to *Harpur Palate*. Length, to 8,000 words. Multiple entries are accepted under separate cover. Accepts hard copy. Include a cover sheet with author's name, address, phone number, email address, and title of story. Author's name should not appear on entry. Manuscripts are not returned; enclose SASE for contest results.

PRIZES: Winner receives a cash award of $500 and publication in the summer issue of *Harpur Palate*.

DEADLINE: Entries are accepted between January 1 and March 31.

Paul Gillette Memorial Writing Contest

Pikes Peak Writers
4164 Austin Bluffs Parkway, #246
Colorado Springs, CO 80918

DESCRIPTION: For almost 20 years, Pikes Peak Writers has been sponsoring this annual contest for unpublished writers. Categories include short stories as well as book-length science fiction; fantasy; mystery/suspense; horror; romance; and mainstream, historical, young adult, and children's fiction.
Website: www.ppwc.net

REQUIREMENTS: Entry fee, $30 for members; $40 for non-members. Word lengths vary for each category. Accepts hard copy and email submissions to pgcontest@gmail.com. All entries must be accompanied by an official entry form. Visit the website or send an SASE for entry form and complete list of requirements.

PRIZES: First-place winners in each category receive $100. Second-place winners each receive $50.

DEADLINE: November 1.

Ghost Story Contest

c/o Friends of the Library
P.O. Box 821
Lockhart, TX 78644

DESCRIPTION: The "Scare the Dickens Out of Us" Ghost Story Contest, sponsored by the Friends of the Dr. Eugene Clark Library, is held annually in conjunction with the Dickens Christmas in Lockhart festival. Stories submitted must revolve around a character from a Charles Dickens novel. In addition, they must be set in the month of December and feature any one of the December holidays. Entries must be original and unpublished.
Website: www.clarklibraryfriends.com

REQUIREMENTS: Entry fee, $20. Length, to 4,000 words. Limit one entry per writer. Accepts hard copy accompanied by entry form. Visit the website for full contest rules and required form.

PRIZES: First-place winner receives $500 and a trophy. Second- and third-place winners receive $250 and $150, respectively.

DEADLINE: October 1.

Highlights for Children Fiction Contest

Fiction Contest
803 Church Street
Honesdale, PA 18431

DESCRIPTION: Sponsored by the popular children's magazine, this annual contest is open to all writers and looks for well-written short stories for ages 2 through 12. Entries should not contain violence, crime, or derogatory humor.
Website: www.highlights.com

REQUIREMENTS: No entry fee. Length, to 500 words. Multiple entries are accepted. Accepts hard copy. Include an SASE for return of manuscript. Send an SASE or visit the website for complete competition guidelines.

PRIZES: Winner receives a cash award of $1,000 and publication in *Highlights for Children* (requires all rights).

DEADLINE: Entries must be postmarked between January 1 and January 31.

Insight Writing Contest

Insight
55 West Oak Ridge Drive
Hagerstown, MD 21740-7390

DESCRIPTION: *Insight* magazine sponsors this annual contest for student writers (up to age 22) as well as adults. Entries that are true, unpublished, and feature a strong spiritual message are eligible.
Website: www.insightmagazine.org

REQUIREMENTS: No entry fee. Length, 1,500–2,000 words (no more than 7 pages). Accepts hard copy and email submissions to insight@rhpa.org. Multiple entries are accepted; each must be accompanied by a cover sheet (available at the website or with SASE). Author's name must not appear on manuscript. Enclose an SASE for return of manuscript.

PRIZES: Winners receive cash awards ranging from $50 to $250. Winning entries are published in *Insight*.

DEADLINE: June 2.

Memoirs Ink Writing Contest

10866 Washington Blvd., Suite 518
Culver City, CA 90232

DESCRIPTION: Original personal essays, memoirs, or stories based on autobiographical experiences are eligible to compete in this contest, which is held twice each year. Entries must be written in the first person. Submissions from international authors are welcome, as long as they are written in the English language.
Website: www.memoirsink.com

REQUIREMENTS: Entry fee, $17. Length, to 1,500 words for February contest; to 3,000 words for August contest. Multiple submissions are accepted. Accepts hard copy with contest submission form and electronic submissions through the website. Author name should appear on submission form only. Visit the website for full contest rules and submission form.

PRIZES: First prize, $1,000; second prize, $500; third prize, $250.

DEADLINE: August 15 and February 15.

Milkweed Prize for Children's Literature

Milkweed Editions
1011 Washington Avenue South, Suite 300
Minneapolis, MN 55415

DESCRIPTION: Milkweed Editions presents this annual prize to the best fiction manuscript for 8- to 13-year-old readers that it receives during the calendar year. Picture books, folktales, retellings of legends, and collections of short stories are not eligible to compete. Manuscripts previously submitted to Milkweed should not be resubmitted. The purpose of the Milkweed Prize is to encourage authors to create novels for this important group of discriminating readers. It looks for work of high literary quality that embodies humane values and contributes to cultural understanding.
Website: www.milkweed.org

REQUIREMENTS: No entry fee. Visit the website for complete guidelines.

PRIZES: Winner receives a $10,000 advance against royalties.

DEADLINE: Ongoing.

National Children's Theatre Competition

Actors' Playhouse/Miracle Theatre
280 Miracle Mile
Coral Gables, FL 33134

DESCRIPTION: Original, unpublished musicals for children ages 5 to 12 may compete for this annual prize. New adaptations of public-domain titles are also eligible. Musicals that both children and adults can enjoy are preferred, as are those that lend themselves to simplified settings.
Website: www.actorsplayhouse.org

REQUIREMENTS: Entry fee, $10. Multiple entries are accepted; each must be accompanied by entry fee and official entry form. Plays should have a running time of 45–60 minutes and require no more than 8 adult actors to play any number of roles. Accepts hard copy. Detailed guidelines and entry form are available at the website.

PRIZES: Winner receives a cash prize of $500; winning musical will be a featured production of the National Children's Theatre Festival.

DEADLINE: April 1.

New Millennium Writings Awards

Room M2
P.O. Box 2463
Knoxville, TN 37901

DESCRIPTION: This competition, sponsored by *New Millennium Writings* literary journal, accepts submissions in the categories of fiction, nonfiction, short-short fiction, and poetry. It places no restrictions on style, content, or number of entries submitted. Previously published material is eligible if it appeared online or in a print publication with a circulation below 5,000.
Website: www.newmillenniumwritings.com

REQUIREMENTS: Entry fee, $17. Fiction and nonfiction, to 6,000 words. Short-short fiction, to 1,000 words. Poetry, to 3 poems; limit 5 pages total. Accepts hard copy and submissions through the website. Author name and contact information should appear on cover page only. Visit the website for details.

PRIZES: First-place winners in each category receive a cash prize of $1,000.

DEADLINE: November 17.

New Voices Award

Lee & Low Books
95 Madison Avenue
New York, NY 10016

DESCRIPTION: Writers of color who are U.S. residents and who have not previously published a picture book are encouraged to enter this contest. It is open to picture books only, which may be fiction, nonfiction, or poetry for children ages 5 to 12. Folklore and animal stories are not considered. Manuscripts previously submitted for this award or to Lee & Low Books are not eligible.
Website: www.leeandlow.com

REQUIREMENTS: No entry fee. Length, to 1,500 words. Limit 2 submissions per entrant. Include cover letter with author name, contact information, and brief biographical note, including cultural and ethnic background. Accepts hard copy. Guidelines available at the website.

PRIZES: Winner receives $1,000 and a publishing contract from Lee & Low Books.

DEADLINE: Entries are accepted between May 1 and September 30.

Pacific Northwest Writers Association Literary Contest

PMB 2717
1420 NW Gilman Boulevard, Suite 2
Issaquah, WA 98027

DESCRIPTION: The Pacific Northwest Writers Association sponsors this annual contest that offers awards in 11 categories, including juvenile short story or picture book, nonfiction, memoir, young adult novel, and screenwriting.
Website: www.pnwa.org

REQUIREMENTS: Entry fee $35 for members; $50 for non-members. Limit one entry per category. Word lengths vary for each category; visit the website for complete requirements. Send 2 hard copies of manuscript; include a 3x5 card with author's name, address, and title of entry. Visit the website for more information.

PRIZES: Winners in each category receive prizes ranging from $150 to $600.

DEADLINE: February 20.

Pockets Annual Fiction Contest

Box 340004
1908 Grand Avenue
Nashville, TN 37203-0004

DESCRIPTION: *Pockets*, a magazine for children ages 6 to 12, sponsors this annual contest. Most types of fiction are eligible, with the exception of historical and biblical fiction.
Website: www.pockets.org

REQUIREMENTS: No entry fee. Length, 1,000–1,600 words. Multiple entries are accepted. Accepts hard copy. Manuscript must list accurate word count on cover sheet. Entries not adhering to the word-length requirement will be disqualified. Send an SASE for return of manuscript. Because of a magazine redesign, the contest was not held in 2009. Visit the website to check for any changes that may take effect with the 2010 contest.

PRIZES: Winner receives a cash award of $1,000 and publication in *Pockets*.

DEADLINE: Submissions must be postmarked between March 1 and August 15.

San Antonio Writers Guild Writing Contests

P.O. Box 34775
San Antonio, TX 78265

DESCRIPTION: Each year, the San Antonio Writers Guild awards prizes in the following categories: novel, short story, essay, memoir, and poetry. All work submitted must be unpublished.
Website: www.sawritersguild.org

REQUIREMENTS: Entry fee, $10 for members; $20 for non-members. Word limits vary according to category. Limit two entries per category. Submit two hard copies with entry form. Author's identifying information should appear on the entry form only, not on the entry itself. Visit the website or send an SASE for complete guidelines and entry form.

PRIZES: First-place winners receive a cash prize of $100. Second- and third-place winners receive cash prizes of $50 and $25, respectively.

DEADLINE: October 1.

Seven Hills Literary Contest

Tallahassee Writers Association
P.O. Box 3428
Tallahassee, FL 32315

DESCRIPTION: This contest offers awards in the categories of short story, flash fiction, and creative nonfiction. The fourth category alternates between children's picture book and children's chapter book, depending on the year.
Website: www.twaonline.org

REQUIREMENTS: Entry fee, $10 for members, $15 for non-members. Length, to 2,500 words; to 500 words for flash fiction. Submit 3 hard copies. Include cover sheet with category and title of entry, author name, contact information, and brief biography. Name should not appear on the entry itself. Visit the website for detailed contest guidelines.

PRIZES: First-place winners in each category receive $100. Second- and third-place winners receive $75 and $50, respectively. All winning entries are published in *Seven Hills Review*.

DEADLINE: September 30.

Seventeen's Fiction Contest

Hearst Communications, Inc.
300 W. 57th St, 17th Floor
New York, NY 10019

DESCRIPTION: Sponsored by Hearst Communications, this annual fiction contest is open to female writers between the ages of 13 and 21 who are residents of the U.S. or Canada. It accepts original, previously unpublished short stories, which are judged according to three criteria: creativity, originality, and writing ability.
Website: www.seventeen.com

REQUIREMENTS: No entry fee. Length, to 500 words. Multiple entries are accepted. Accepts electronic submissions through the website only; each submission must be accompanied by the entry form posted at the website.

PRIZES: Grand-prize winner receives a cash prize of $5,000 and publication in *Seventeen*. Cash prizes and possible publication are awarded to second- and third-place winners.

DEADLINE: December 31.

Skipping Stones Awards

Skipping Stones
P.O. Box 3939
Eugene, OR 97403

DESCRIPTION: *Skipping Stones*, a multicultural magazine for children, offers prizes to books, magazines, and electronic or print teaching resources that deal with the themes of multicultural, international, and social consciousness, or environmental awareness.
Website: www.skippingstones.org

REQUIREMENTS: Entry fee, $50. Send 4 copies of each print entry; 2 copies of video or DVD entry. Material published between January 2008 and February 2010 is eligible. Entries must be accompanied by an entry form/guideline sheet, available at the website or with SASE.

PRIZES: Cash prizes are awarded to the first- through fourth-place winners.

DEADLINE: February 1.

Kay Snow Writing Contest

Willamette Writers
9045 SW Barbur Boulevard, Suite 5A
Portland, OR 97219-4027

DESCRIPTION: This annual contest, named for the founder of Willamette Writers, is open to original, unpublished submissions only. It awards prizes in six categories, including three juvenile subcategories: short story, novel excerpt, and article.
Website: www.willamettewriters.com

REQUIREMENTS: Entry fee, $10 for members; $15 for non-members. Word limits vary according to category. Send 3 hard copies with entry form and 3x5 card with author name, contact information, and title of entry. Author's name should not appear on the entry itself. Manuscripts are not returned. Visit the website or send an SASE for detailed guidelines and entry forms.

PRIZES: First-place winners receive a cash prize of $300. Second- and third-place winners receive cash prizes of $150 and $50, respectively.

DEADLINE: April 23.

SouthWest Writers Contest

SouthWest Writers Workshop
3721 Morris NE
Albuquerque, NM 87110

DESCRIPTION: To encourage and honor excellence in writing, SouthWest Writers offers prizes in 16 categories, including the juvenile categories of middle-grade or young adult short story; fiction or nonfiction picture book; and middle-grade or young adult novel.
Website: www.southwestwriters.org

REQUIREMENTS: Entry fees, word lengths, and other requirements vary for each category; check website for specific information. Send 2 hard copies of submission with entry form. Author's name and contact information should not appear on the entry itself. Send 3 hard copies with SASE and additional fee if you wish to purchase an optional critique.

PRIZES: First-place winners receive $150; second- and third-place winners in each category receive $100 and $50, respectively.

DEADLINE: May 1.

Sydney Taylor Manuscript Competition

Aileen Grossberg
204 Park Street
Montclair, NJ 07042

DESCRIPTION: The Association of Jewish Libraries sponsors this annual award. Entries must be book-length works of fiction for 8- to 11-year-old readers. Writers who have not previously published book-length fiction are eligible. Entries should reveal the positive aspects of Jewish life and deepen the understanding of Judaism for all children, Jewish and non-Jewish.
Website: www.jewishlibraries.org

REQUIREMENTS: No entry fee. Length, 64–200 pages. Limit one entry per competition. Submit 6 hard copies, disk, or electronic PDF; cover letter with personal statement and manuscript summary; curriculum vitae; application; and release form. Contest rules and required forms available at website or with SASE.

PRIZES: Winner receives a cash prize of $1,000.

DEADLINE: December 15.

Tennessee Williams Fiction Contest

Tennessee Williams/New Orleans Literary Festival
938 Lafayette Street, Suite 514
New Orleans, LA 70113

DESCRIPTION: Writers who have not yet published a book of fiction may submit unpublished short stories to this annual competition.
Website: www.tennesseewilliams.net

REQUIREMENTS: Entry fee, $25. Length, to 7,000 words. Multiple entries and simultaneous submissions accepted. Accepts hard copy and electronic submissions through the website. Author's name should not appear on manuscript; include a separate page with story title, name, and full contact information. Full guidelines available at the website or with SASE.

PRIZES: Winner receives a cash prize of $1,500; winning story is published in the *New Orleans Review.*

DEADLINE: November 15.

Tennessee Williams One-Act Play Competition

Tennessee Williams/New Orleans Literary Festival
938 Lafayette Street, Suite 514
New Orleans, LA 70113

DESCRIPTION: One-act plays that have not previously been produced, published, or performed are eligible to compete in this annual contest.
Website: www.tennesseewilliams.net

REQUIREMENTS: Entry fee, $25. Plays should be one act only and should not exceed one hour in running time. Playwright's name should not appear on the script. Include two title pages; one affixed to the script with title only, and an unattached page with title and author contact information. Accepts hard copy and electronic submissions through the website. Visit the website for more information.

PRIZES: Winner receives a cash prize of $1,500, and both a staged reading and a full production of the winning play.

DEADLINE: November 15.

Paul A. Witty Short Story Award

International Reading Association
P.O. Box 8139
Newark, DE 19714-8139

DESCRIPTION: The International Reading Association presents this annual award to a short story published in a magazine for children during the previous calendar year. It looks for short stories that could serve as a literary standard for young people.
Website: www.reading.org

REQUIREMENTS: No entry fee. No word length limitations. Accepts hard copy accompanied by a copy of the periodical. Limit 3 entries per magazine. Author or publishers may nominate pieces for this award. For additional information, visit the website or send an SASE.

PRIZES: A cash award of $1,000 is presented to the winner.

DEADLINE: December 1.

Utah Original Writing Competition

617 E South Temple
Salt Lake City, UT 84102

DESCRIPTION: Writers who reside in Utah are eligible to enter this competition, which has been held for more than 50 years. Categories of competition include novel, autobiography or biography, book-length story collection, young adult book, poetry, short story, and personal essay. This is now a "first book" contest, meaning that writers submitting to one of the book categories must be unpublished in that category.
Website: http://arts.utah.gov

REQUIREMENTS: No entry fee. Word lengths vary for each category; check website for specific information. Limit one entry per category. Accepts hard copy. Entries must be accompanied by submission card, available at website. Manuscripts are not returned.

PRIZES: Winners receive cash prizes ranging from $750 to $1,000.

DEADLINE: June 25.

WOW! Women on Writing Flash Fiction Contests

Contest Coordinator

DESCRIPTION: The WOW! Women on Writing e-zine holds these contests quarterly to inspire creativity, communication, and recognition of contestants. All styles of writing are welcome; however, writers are advised to consider the sensibilities of the guest judge if they are serious about winning.
Website: www.wow-womenonwriting.com

REQUIREMENTS: Entry fee, $10. Length, 250–300 words. Multiple entries are accepted. Accepts electronic submissions through the website. Contest closes when 300 stories have been submitted.

PRIZES: First prize, $200. Second and third prizes, $150 and $100, respectively. All winning stories are published at the website.

DEADLINE: February 28; May 31; August 31; and November 30.

Writers-Editors Network Annual Competition

CNW/FFWA
P.O. Box A
North Stratford, NH 03590

DESCRIPTION: Formerly known as the CNW/FFWA Florida State Writing Competition, this contest is open to non-members as well as members of Cassel Network of Writers (CNW). Entries are accepted in four divisions: nonfiction, fiction, children's literature, and poetry. See website for breakdown of categories within those divisions.
Website: www.writers-editors.com

REQUIREMENTS: Entry fees and word lengths vary. Multiple entries accepted. Accepts hard copy. No stapled entries. Manuscripts are not returned. Visit the website for official entry form, list of categories, category guidelines, and judging criteria.

PRIZES: Each first-place winner receives $100; second-place winners, $75; third-place winners, $50. All winners also receive certificates.

DEADLINE: March 15.

The Writing Conference, Inc., Writing Contests

P.O. Box 664
Ottawa, KS 66067-0664

DESCRIPTION: The Writing Conference awards prizes for original, unpublished poetry, narratives, and essays written by students in elementary school, middle school, and high school. All entries must relate to the contest topic, which changes every year. The Writing Conference, a nonprofit organization, sponsors a variety of services and activities designed to improve the writing and reading skills of young people.
Website: www.writingconference.com

REQUIREMENTS: No entry fee. Limit one entry per student. Accepts hard copy. Visit the website or send an SASE for contest topic, complete guidelines, and required forms.

PRIZES: Winners in each category receive a plaque and publication in *The Writer's Slate*, an online magazine read by students and teachers.

DEADLINE: January 8.

Writers' Journal Writing Contests

P.O. Box 394
Perham, MN 56573-0374

DESCRIPTION: *Writers' Journal* sponsors a number of contests annually. Open to all writers, the contests include the categories of horror/ghost stories, romance, science fiction/fantasy, and poetry.
Website: www.writersjournal.com

REQUIREMENTS: Entry fees range from $3 to $15. Word lengths and guidelines vary for each contest. Accepts hard copy. Visit the website or send an SASE for complete contest information.

PRIZES: Winners of these contests receive cash prizes and publication in *Writers' Journal*.

DEADLINE: Varies for each category.

Writing for Children Competition

Writers' Union of Canada
90 Richmond Street, Suite 200
Toronto, Ontario M5E 1C7
Canada

DESCRIPTION: The Writers' Union of Canada sponsors this annual contest, which is open to Canadian citizens and landed immigrants only. Writers who have not yet published a book and who are not under contract with a book publisher are eligible to compete.
Website: www.writersunion.ca

REQUIREMENTS: Entry fee, $15. Length, to 1,500 words. Multiple entries are accepted. Accepts hard copy. Entries are not returned. Author name and title of entry must appear on every page. Include a cover sheet with author name and contact information. Send an SASE or visit the website for complete guidelines.

PRIZES: Winner receives a cash prize of $1,500. The Writers' Union of Canada will submit the winning entry and the finalists to three children's book publishers.

DEADLINE: April 23.

Indexes

2010 Market News

New Listings

AKC Family Dog
Akron Family
Bay Area Parent
Birmingham Parent
Child Care Information
    Exchange
CKI Magazine
College News
Community College Week
Complex Child E-Magazine
Co-Op Thymes
Delacorte Press Contest
Delacorte Yearling Contest
East Texas Teen
Eco-Kids Magazine
Equine Journal
Family Motor Coaching
Family Tree
The Forensic Teacher
For Every Woman
Ghost Story Contest
GirlMogul Magazine
Hip Mama
Horse & Rider
Houston Family Magazine
Inspired Mother

Jeunesse: Young People,
    Texts, Cultures
Just 4 Kids
Kid Zone (MO)
KIND News
Kittens USA
KnoWonder!
Lake/Geauga Family
Long Island Parent
Memoirs Ink Writing
    Contest
Metro Spirit
Michigan History for Kids
New Voices Award
NJCAA Review
Northumberland Kids
Pathways to Family
    Wellness
Positive Parenting
    Newsletter
Rangers Now
Red River Family Magazine
Seven Hills Literary Contest
Sharing Space
Kay Snow Writing Contest
Spigot Science Magazine
Spirit! Magazine

Street Brand
Susie
Tennessee Williams Fiction
    Contest
Trains
Trumbull County Parent
Unique Magazine
VOYA Magazine
West Virginia Family
Woodall's CamperWays
Writers-Editors Network
    Annual Competition

2010 Market News (cont.)

Deletions and Name Changes

AIM Magazine: Ceased publication

Atlanta Baby: Ceased publication

Baby Dallas: Merged with **Dallas Child**

Bay Area Baby: Unable to contact

Beta Journal: Ceased publication

Bird Times Many: Removed at editor's request

Black Woman and Child: Suspended publication

Breakaway: Ceased publication

Brio: Ceased publication

Brio & Beyond: Ceased publication

ByLine: Ceased publication

Caledonia Times: Ceased publication

Characters: Ceased publication

Charlotte Baby & Child: Ceased publication

Childbirth Magazine: Unable to contact

Children's Digest: Ceased publication

Children's Playmate: Ceased publication

Civilized Revolt: Ceased publication

Connecticut's County Kids: Ceased publication

Cousteau Kids: Ceased publication

Dogs for Kids: Ceased publication

Dovetail: Ceased publication

Earthwatch Institute Journal: Ceased publication

Fuel: Magazine undergoing major changes

Golfer Girl Magazine: Phasing out of publication

Gumbo Teen Magazine: Ceased publication

High School Writer (Junior High Edition): Ceased publication

High School Writer (Senior): Ceased publication

Hit Parader: Ceased publication

Ignite Your Faith: Ceased publication

Inside Out: Ceased publication

KidsandKaboodle.com: Ceased publication

Kid Zone (MI): Ceased publication

The Lamp-Post: Ceased publication

Learning Through History: Ceased publication

Lifted Magazine: Ceased publication

Look-Look Magazine: Ceased publication

MAD Kids: Ceased publication

Moo-Cow Fan Club: Ceased publication

Mother Verse Magazine: On hiatus

M: The Magazine for Montessori Families: Unable to contact

Muslim Girl: On indefinite hiatus

New Expression: Ceased publication

Northwest Baby & Child: Ceased publication

Once Upon a Time . . .: Ceased publication

Parent and Preschooler Newsletter: Ceased publication

Plum Magazine: On hiatus

Prep Traveler: Ceased publication

Radio Control Boat Modeler: Ceased publication

Radio Control Car Action: Ceased publication

Softball Youth: Ceased publication

t&T News: Unable to contact

Teachers Interaction: 100% staff written

Teen: Ceased publication

Teen Strings: Ceased publication

Teenwire.com: Ceased publication

Today's Christian: Ceased publication

Transitions Abroad: Ceased publication

U Mag: Ceased publication

USA Gymnastics: 100% staff written

U.25 Magazine: Ceased publication

Winner: Ceased publication

Young People's Press: 100% staff written

Fifty+ Freelance

You can improve your chances of selling by submitting to magazines that fill their pages with freelance material. Of the 656 markets listed in this directory, we have listed 78 markets that buy at least 50% of their freelance material from writers who are new to the magazine. Of course, there are no guarantees; but if you approach these magazines with well-written manuscripts targeted to their subject, age range, and word-limit requirements, you can increase your publication odds.

The ALAN Review
Alateen Talk
Amazing Kids!
American Secondary
   Education
The Apprentice Writer
Autism Asperger's Digest
bNetS@vvy
Brain, Child
Bread For God's Children
Brilliant Star
Calliope
Capper's
Cat Fancy
Child Care Information
   Exchange
Childhood Education
Children and Families
Children's Ministry
The Claremont Review
The Clearing House
Clubhouse
Creative Connections
Creative Kids
Dig
Dimensions
Educational Horizons
Education Forum
Education Week
Elementary School Writer
Encyclopedia of Youth
   Studies
Fort Myers & Southwest
   Florida
Group
Highlights for Children

The High School Journal
I Love Cats
Indy's Child
Insight
Jack And Jill
Journal of School Health
Justine
Kansas School Naturalist
Keyboard
Keys for Kids
The Kids' Ark
Kindred
Learning & Leading with
   Technology
Massive Online Gamer
Momentum
Mom Writer's Literary
   Magazine
Mothering
My Light Magazine
North Star Family Matters
The Olive Branch
Our Children
Parents Express
The Pink Chameleon
Positive Parenting
   Newsletter
Prehistoric Times
PresenTense Magazine
Principal
Read, America!
Red River Family Magazine
Reunions Magazine
SchoolArts
School Library Journal
Shine Brightly

Sisterhood Agenda
Skipping Stones
Sparkle
Stone Soup
Teach Kids Essentials
Teen Voices
The Universe in the
   Classroom
Voices from the Middle
VOYA Magazine
What If?
What's Up? Canada's
   Family Magazine
Writers' Journal
Zamoof! Magazine

Category Index

To help you find the appropriate market for your manuscript or query letter, we have compiled a category and subject index listing magazines according to their primary editorial interests. Pay close attention to the markets that overlap. For example, when searching for a market for your rock-climbing adventure story for 8- to 12-year-old readers, you might look under the categories "Adventure Stories" and "Middle-grade (Fiction)." If you have an idea for an article about blue herons for early readers, look under the categories "Animals/Pets" and "Early Reader (Nonfiction)" to find possible markets. Always check the magazine's listing for explanations of specific needs.

For your convenience, we have listed below all of the categories that are included in this index. If you don't find a category that exactly fits your material, try to find a broader term that covers your topic.

Adventure Stories
Animals (Fiction)
Animals/Pets (Nonfiction)
Audio/Video
Bilingual (Nonfiction)
Biography
Boys' Magazines
Canadian Magazines
Career/College
Child Care
Computers
Contemporary Fiction
Crafts/Hobbies
Current Events
Drama
Early Reader (Fiction)
Early Reader (Nonfiction)
Education/Classroom
Factual/Informational
Fairy Tales
Family/Parenting
Fantasy
Folktales/Folklore
Games/Puzzles/Activities
Geography
Gifted Education
Girls' Magazines
Health/Fitness

Historical Fiction
History
Horror
How-to
Humor (Fiction)
Humor (Nonfiction)
Inspirational Fiction
Language Arts
Mathematics
Middle-grade (Fiction)
Middle-grade (Nonfiction)
Multicultural/Ethnic
 (Fiction)
Multicultural/Ethnic
 (Nonfiction)
Music
Mystery/Suspense
Nature/Environment
 (Fiction)
Nature/Environment
 (Nonfiction)
Personal Experience
Photo-Essays
Popular Culture
Preschool (Fiction)
Preschool (Nonfiction)
Profile/Interview
Read-aloud Stories

Real life/Problem-
 solving
Rebus
Recreation/Entertainment
Regional (Fiction)
Regional (Nonfiction)
Religious (Fiction)
Religious (Nonfiction)
Reviews
Romance
Science Fiction
Science/Technology
Self-help
Services/Clubs
Social Issues
Special Education
Sports (Fiction)
Sports (Nonfiction)
Travel
Western
Writing
Young Adult (Fiction)
Young Adult (Nonfiction)
Young Author (Fiction)
Young Author
 (Nonfiction)

Fantasy

Historical Fiction

History

Music

Personal Experience

Photo-Essays

Popular Culture

Preschool (Fiction)

Read–aloud Stories

Real life/
Problem–solving

Rebus

Recreation/
Entertainment

Reviews

Self–help

Services/Clubs

Sports (Nonfiction)

Young Author (Fiction)

Young Author (Nonfiction)

Magazine and Contest Index

The following codes have been used to indicate each publication's readership: **YA**=Young adults, **A**=Adults, **E**=Educators (including librarians, teachers, administrators, student group leaders, and child-care professionals), **F**=Family (general interest), **P**=Parents. We have listed age ranges when specified by the editor.

If you do not find a particular magazine, turn to Market News on page 322.

★ indicates a newly listed magazine